THE ACCOUNTING PROBLEM SOLVER®

REGISTERED TRADEMARK

A Complete Solution Guide to Any Textbook

William D. Keller, Ed.D.
Professor of Accounting
Ferris State University
Big Rapids, Michigan

Research and Education Association
61 Ethel Road West
Piscataway, New Jersey 08854

THE ACCOUNTING PROBLEM SOLVER ®

Printed in the United States of America

Library of Congress Catalog Card Number 95-67787

International Standard Book Number 0-87891-973-2

PROBLEM SOLVER is a registered trademark of Research and Education Association, Piscataway, New Jersey 08854

WHAT THIS BOOK IS FOR

Students have generally found accounting a difficult subject to understand and learn. Despite the publication of hundreds of textbooks in this field, each one intended to provide an improvement over previous textbooks, students continue to remain perplexed as a result of the numerous conditions that must often be remembered and correlated in solving a problem. Various possible interpretations of terms used in accounting also contributed to much of the difficulties experienced by students.

In a study of the problem, REA found the following basic reasons underlying students' difficulties with accounting taught in schools:

(a) No systematic rules of analysis have been developed which students may follow in a step-by-step manner to solve the usual problems encountered. This results from the fact that the numerous different conditions and principles which may be involved in a problem, lead to many possible different methods of solution. To prescribe a set of rules to be followed for each of the possible variations, would involve an enormous number of rules and steps to be searched through by students, and this task would perhaps be more burdensome than solving the problem directly with some accompanying trial and error to find the correct solution route.

(b) Textbooks currently available will usually explain a given principle in a few pages written by a professional who has an insight in the subject matter that is not shared by students. The explanations are often written in an abstract manner which leaves the students confused as to the application of the principle. The explanations given are not sufficiently detailed and extensive to make the student aware of the wide range of applications and different aspects of the principle being studied. The numerous possible variations of principles and their applications are usually not discussed, and it is left for the students to discover these for themselves while doing exercises. Accordingly, the average student is expected to rediscover that which has been long known and practiced, but not published or explained extensively.

(c) The examples usually following the explanation of a topic are too few in number and too simple to enable the student to obtain a thorough grasp of the principles involved. The explanations do not provide sufficient basis to enable a student to solve problems that may be subsequently assigned for homework or given on examinations.

The examples are presented in abbreviated form which leaves out much material between steps, and requires that students derive the omitted material themselves. As a result, students find the examples difficult to understand— contrary to the purpose of the examples.

Examples are, furthermore, often worded in a confusing manner. They do not state the problem and then present the solution. Instead, they pass through a general discussion, never revealing what is to be solved for.

Examples, also, do not always include diagrams/graphs, wherever appropriate, and students do not obtain the training to draw diagrams or graphs to simplify and organize their thinking.

(d) Students can learn the subject only by doing the exercises themselves and reviewing them in class, to obtain experience in applying the principles with their different ramifications.

In doing the exercises by themselves, students find that they are required to devote considerably more time to accounting than to other subjects of comparable credits, because they are uncertain with regard to the selection and application of the theorems and principles involved. It is also often necessary for students to discover those "tricks" not revealed in their texts (or review books), that make it possible to solve problems easily. Students must usually resort to methods of trial-and-error to discover these "tricks," and as a result they find that they may sometimes spend several hours to solve a single problem.

(e) When reviewing the exercises in classrooms, instructors usually request students to take turns in writing solutions on the boards and explaining them to the class. Students often find it difficult to explain in a manner that holds the interest of the class, and enables the remaining students to follow the material written on the boards. The remaining students seated in the class are, furthermore, too occupied with copying the material from the boards, to listen to the oral explanations and concentrate on the methods of solution.

This book is intended to aid students in accounting overcoming the difficulties described, by supplying detailed illustrations of the solution methods which are usually not apparent to students. The solution methods are illustrated by problems selected from those that are most often assigned for class work and given on examinations. The problems are arranged in order of complexity to enable students to learn and understand a particular topic by reviewing the problems in sequence. The problems are illustrated with detailed step-by-step explanations, to save the students the large amount of time that is often needed to fill in the gaps that are usually found between steps of illustrations in textbooks or review/outline books.

The staff of REA considers accounting a subject that is best learned by allowing students to view the methods of analysis and solution techniques themselves. This approach to learning the subject matter is similar to that practiced in various scientific laboratories, particularly in the medical fields.

In using this book, students may review and study the illustrated problems at their own pace; they are not limited to the time allowed for explaining problems on the board in class.

When students want to look up a particular type of problem and solution, they can readily locate it in the book by referring to the index which has been extensively prepared. It is also possible to locate a particular type of problem by glancing at just the material within the boxed portions. To facilitate rapid scanning of the problems, each problem has a heavy border around it. Furthermore, each problem is identified with a number immediately above the problem at the right-hand margin.

To obtain maximum benefit from the book, students should familiarize themselves with the section, "How To Use This Book," located in the front pages.

MAX FOGIEL, PH.D.
Program Director

HOW TO USE THIS BOOK

This book can be an invaluable aid to students in accounting as a supplement to their textbooks. The book is subdivided into 22 chapters, each dealing with a separate topic. The subject matter is developed beginning with income statements of corporations, stocks, retained earnings, extends through the balance sheet, cash and receivables, inventories, income tax accounting leases, changes in accounting systems and analysis of errors, and analysis of financial statements.

TO LEARN AND UNDERSTAND
A TOPIC THOROUGHLY

1. Refer to your class text and read the section pertaining to the topic. You should become acquainted with the principles discussed there. These principles, however, may not be clear to you at that time.

2. Then locate the topic you are looking for by referring to the "Table of Contents" in front of this book, "The Accounting Problem Solver."

3. Turn to the page where the topic begins and review the problems under each topic, in the order given. For each topic, the problems are arranged in order of complexity, from the simplest to the more difficult. Some problems may appear similar to others, but each problem has been selected to illustrate a different point or solution method.

To learn and understand a topic thoroughly and retain its contents, it will be generally necessary for students to review the problems several times. Repeated review is essential in order to gain experience in recognizing the principles that should be applied, and in selecting the best solution technique.

TO FIND A PARTICULAR PROBLEM

To locate one or more problems related to a particular subject matter, refer to either the index, located at the back of the book or the indexes found at the beginning of each chapter. In using the indexes, be certain to note that the numbers given refer to problem numbers, not page numbers. This arrangement of the indexes is intended to facilitate finding a problem more rapidly, since two or more problems may appear on a page.

If a particular type of problem cannot be found readily, it is recommended that the student refer to the "Table of Contents" in the front pages, and then turn to the chapter which is applicable to the problem being sought. By scanning or glancing at the material that is boxed, it will generally be possible to find problems related to the one being sought, without consuming considerable time. After the problems have been located, the solutions can be reviewed and studied in detail. For this purpose of locating problems rapidly, students should acquaint themselves with the organization of the book as found in the "Table of Contents."

In preparing for an exam, locate the topics to be covered on the exam in the "Table of Contents," and then review the problems under those topics several times. This should equip the student with what might be needed for the exam.

CONTENTS

CHAPTER 1

EARNINGS PER SHARE OF THE CORPORTION

> **Basic Attacks and Strategies for Solving Problems in this Chapter. See pages 3 to 18 for step-by-step solutions to problems.**

The most important statement in accounting is probably the **Income Statement**, because this tells the monthly Net Income or Net Loss of the business. By reading this statement carefully, the owner of a business can determine not only whether his business is doing better than it was last month, but also the reasons for its progress or regress.

An accountant needs to know how to set up an Income Statement properly so that it will mean the most to its readers. The accountant must also be able to decide what is an **Ordinary Item** and what is an **Extraordinary Item**. Extraordinary Items are those that are both Unusual and Infrequent. These must be placed in a separate section of the Income Statement toward the end of the statement. **Discontinued Operations** may be considered to be Extraordinary, but they would have to be both Infrequent and Unusual. Often they are Infrequent, perhaps, but they may not be Unusual. These could be listed as a separate section in the Income Statement, but they should not be listed under Extraordinary Items unless they are both Infrequent *and* Unusual.

Accountants must know the difference between the **Current Operating Performance Income Statement** and the **All-Inclusive Income Statement**. Accountants cannot agree on which type of statement is better, so both methods are presented. The Current Operating Performance Income Statement gives only the revenues, expenses, gains, and losses for the month thus giving a Net Income solely from the month's operations;

on the other hand, the All-Inclusive Income Statement has Extraordinary Items as well as nonrecurring items. In the Current Operating Performance Income Statement, the Extraordinary Items and nonrecurring items are relegated to the Retained Earnings Statement.

Another important point is the difference between the **Transactions Approach** and the **Capital Maintenance Approach** in making up Income Statements. Often Income Tax agents, when trying to determine a taxpayer's income for the year, are stymied because the client claims he or she has not kept records of income or expenses. Without these records, the Transactions Approach to determining Net Income cannot be followed. The tax agents must then use the more roundabout method called the Capital Maintenance Approach. This is the approach whereby the beginning capital is subtracted from the ending capital to determine the increase or decrease in capital. This figure is then adjusted for any investments or withdrawals during the year, in order to compute Net Income.

An accountant must also know the difference between **Income** and **Earnings**; Earnings are derived from the events occurring in the current period, while Income includes events occurring in the current period, as well as prior period adjustments such as a change in depreciation methods.

The computation of Net Income is not always easy, especially when the accountant does not have access to all the needed facts. In cases of this kind, it is often necessary to use the facts at hand and to interpolate in order to come up with the correct Net Income. At times, the accountant merely has increases and decreases in various items without having the totals of balances in the various accounts; this makes preparing Financial Statements more difficult.

Accounting statements are presented in different ways. The two most common types of Income Statements are the **Single-Step Income Statement** and the **Multiple-Step Income Statement**, both of which end with the same total—Net Income. The advantage of the Multiple-Step Income Statement is that it shows exactly how the Net Income is computed. The disadvantage is that the statement is often lengthy. This long type of statement is beneficial to administrators who need to know all the details.

On the other hand, the Single-Step Income Statement first lists the items of Income, followed by the items of Expense. It does not show how these items were derived. The advantage is that it is short and understandable; the disadvantage is that details of the computation are not given and must be accepted on faith by the reader. This type of statement is probably enough for stockholders, the public, and perhaps for government reports.

Since accountants do not agree on which items should be placed in the Retained Earnings Statement and which items should be placed in the Income Statement, it is often the custom of many businesses to place these two statements together so that the reader can understand the finances of the business more readily.

Step-by-Step Solutions to Problems in this Chapter, "Earnings Per Share of the Corporation"

• PROBLEM 1–1

The Brown Company wishes to borrow money from the First National Bank and plans to submit the following Income Statement to the bank. Look it over and tell how it can be improved.

Income Statement

Sales		700,000
Dividends		32,000
Gain on Recovery of Insurance from Fire Loss		40,000
Total Income		772,000
Less:		
Advertising Expense	20,000	
Cost of Goods Sold	400,000	
Salaries Expense	10,000	
Loss on Old Inventories	20,000	
Total		450,000
Income before Income Tax		322,000
Income Tax		15,000
Net Income after Tax		307,000

SOLUTION:

Suggestions for revision of this Income Statement:

1. The Income Statement needs a full heading, including the name of the company and the period of time that the statement includes.

2. The Gain on Recovery of Insurance from Fire Loss should be classified as an Extraordinary Item in a separate section of the Income Statement.

3. Cost of Goods Sold should be listed first.

4. Loss on Old Inventory might be classified at the bottom of the Income Statement as an Unusual Item.

• PROBLEM 1–2

A revised Income Statement appears as follows:

Brown Bakery
Income Statement
For Year Ended December 31, 1994

Income:		
Sales		700,000
Expenses:		
Cost of Goods Sold	400,000	
Advertising Expense	20,000	
Selling Expense	10,000	
Total Operating Expense		430,000
Net Operating Income		270,000
Other Income:		
Dividend Income		32,000
Income before Extraordinary Income		302,000
Extraordinary Income:		
Gain on Recovery of Insurance from Fire Loss	40,000	
Loss on Old Inventories	20,000	
Total Extraordinary Income		20,000
Net Income before Income Tax		322,000
Less Income Tax		15,000
Net Income after Income Tax		307,000

Should the following items be placed under Extraordinary Items at the end of the Income Statement, or should they be placed elsewhere?

1. A rare earthquake destroyed a company factory.

2. The company incurred a large loss because of an unsuccessful registration of a stock issue.

3. A large corporate farm loses a great portion of its corn crop because of a hailstorm. Hailstorms are rare in this section of the country.

4. During the year the corporation sold much of its stock which had previously been held for investment.

5. The corporation relocates its plant and has high relocation costs.

6. The company incurred a large loss on repurchasing its large bond issue. These bonds have been outstanding for five years. The company regularly repurchases its bonds.

7. A railroad company lost a large sum because of flooded-out tracks. Flood losses usually occur every three or four years.

SOLUTION:

In order to be placed in the Extraordinary Items section of the Income Statement, an occurrence must be both Unusual *and* Infrequent. The answers to the above losses are as follows:

1. The earthquake is rare, so it is Unusual and and Infrequent. The loss of the company's factory would be considered an Extraordinary Item.

2. Registration of stock issues with the Securities and Exchange Commission is not Unusual, so this would not be an Extraordinary Item.

3. Since hailstorms are rare in the section of the country in which the corporate farm is located, this would be an Unusual and Infrequent occurrence and would be listed in the Income Statement as an Extraordinary Item.

4. It is not unusual for a corporation to sell its stock held for investment. This would be listed in the Income Statement as either a gain or a loss, but not as an Extraordinary Item.

5. Relocation is a customary and continuing business activity, so the high relocation costs would not be listed under Extraordinary Items.

6. Yes, the loss on repurchasing its bonds is an Extraordinary Item, according to Financial Accounting Standards Board Statement No. 4.

7. The loss from damaged tracks by the railroad company should be put down on its Income Statement as a loss, but not as an Extraordinary Item, since the loss occurs fairly regularly.

• PROBLEM 1-3

What is the difference between a Current Operating Performance Income Statement, an All-Inclusive Income Statement, and a Statement of Income and Retained Earnings?

SOLUTION:

Current Operating Performance Income Statement shows Net Income as a the best possible indication of the earning power of a business. Only items of Revenue and Expense applicable to the regular operations of the current period should be used in determining Net Income for the period.

An All-Inclusive Income Statement has all Extraordinary and Nonrecurring items included in the Income Statement in the determination of Net Income. This is also called the Clean Surplus Method, since it cleans all Extraordinary and Nonrecurring items from the Earned Surplus Statement and puts these in the Income Statement.

The Statement of Income and Retained Earnings is a paper combining the two statements, with the Income Statement first, then the Retained Earnings Statement. By placing these on the same paper, the reader can see how these two statements mesh.

In the Current Operating Performance Income Statement, the current Income and expenses are listed first in order to get Net Income. Material nonrecurring items are not included in the Income Statement but are placed in the Retained Earnings Statement.

On the other hand, in the All-Inclusive Income Statement, the Non-operating and Nonrecurring items and corrections of the prior periods' profits would be added or deducted toward the bottom of the Income Statement. Extraordinary charges and credits should be segregated on the same Income Statement in a separate section.

• PROBLEM 1-4

The Smith Construction Company was formed five years ago. Nine thousand shares of Common Stock were originally sold at $15 per share. Later, 2,000 more common shares were sold at $20 per share. At the time of liquidation, corporate assets were sold for $1,000,000, and $50,000—the total liabilities—were paid off. The remaining cash was distributed to stockholders. During the entire five years that the corporation was in business, it paid total dividends of $50,000. Compute the corporate income during its five years of life.

SOLUTION:

There are two ways to figure the Net Income of a firm: the Transactions Approach and the Capital Maintenance Approach. The most common is the Transactions Approach, using an Income Statement and deducting expenses from Income. On the other hand, the Capital Maintenance (change in equity) Approach measures Income based on Capital Values at two points in time. Of course, the change in capital is adjusted for investments and withdrawals in order to compute Income.

In this case, the Transactions Approach cannot be used because we have no information regarding expenses and Income and gains and losses. Therefore, the Capital Maintenance Approach must be used, as follows:

The Smith Construction Company, formed five years ago, sold 9,000 shares of Common Stock @ $15. (9,000 × $15 = $135,000—the beginning capital) Later they sold 2,000 more shares of Common Stock @ $20. (2,000 × $20 = $40,000)

At liquidation, they sold assets for cash of $1,000,000 and paid off $50,000—their total liabilities.

($1,000,000 – $50,000 = $950,000 ending capital)

Ending Capital	$950,000	Dividends	$50,000
Less Beginning Capital	135,000	Less Additional Investment	40,000
Change in Capital	$815,000	Net Withdrawal by Owners	$10,000

Chance in Capital	$815,000
Less Net Withdrawal by Owners	10,000
Net Income over the Life of the Corporation	$805,000

• PROBLEM 1–5

There are really two definitions of Income: that of economists and that of accountants. The interpretation of the word Income by economists is that it is a measurement not only of money coming in, but also of such factors as increase in knowledge. This is difficult to measure in terms of dollars. On the other hand, accountants do not try to measure Quality, but only Quantity—that is, Dollars of Income.

There are various ideas as to the meaning of Income. For instance, the Statement of Financial Accounting Concepts No. 5, entitled "Recognition and Measurement in Financial Statements of Business Enterprises," defines Income somewhat differently from Earnings. What is the difference? Also, what is the difference between Earnings and Comprehensive Income?

SOLUTION:

1. Earnings refers only to events that occur in the current period (such as Income less expenses). On the other hand, Non-Income also includes the cumulative effect on prior periods of a change in accounting principle. For instance, if in a prior period the firm changed from Double-Declining-Balance Depreciation to Straight-Line Depreciation, this change would affect the Net Income of the present period also.

2. The difference between Earnings and Comprehensive Income includes the effects of certain accounting adjustments of earlier periods that are recognized in the present period (as mentioned above), and also certain other changes in Net Assets—principally certain holding Gains and Losses, such as changes in Market Values of investments in marketable equity securities classified as Noncurrent Assets, and Foreign Currency

translation adjustments. These items are included in comprehensive Income but not in Earnings.

• PROBLEM 1–6

Our auditing firm is auditing the books of a clothing manufacturing company with annual sales of $100 million. The company primarily sells clothing to civilian clothing stores, but it has one division that sells military uniforms to the U.S. Army. This division has $10 million in sales.

While working in the client's office, we overhear the Vice President, the Treasurer, and the Controller discussing the sale of the Military Clothing Division, expected to take place in July of this year, and the related reporting problems.

The Vice President thinks that this sale of the Military Clothing Division should not be segregated in the Income Statement, since it confuses the stockholders. On the other hand, the Treasurer disagrees. He feels that if an item is either Unusual or Infrequent, it should be classified as an Extraordinary Item. On the other hand, the Controller feels that if an item is both Infrequent *and* Unusual, then and only then should it be classified as an Extraordinary Item. The Controller feels that the sale of the Military Clothing Division should be shown separately, but not as an Extraordinary Item. The projected sale was mentioned in the minutes of the board meeting.

1. Does the Military Clothing Division qualify as a segment of the business in more than one way? If so, why?

2. Does the Military Clothing Division qualify as a Discontinued Operation? Why?

3. Do the minutes indicate that a formal plan has been established? If not, why?

4. When should the Gain be recognized? What if there is a Loss?

5. Who is correct about reporting the sale? (The Vice President, the Treasurer, or the Controller?) What would the Income Statement presentation be for the next fiscal year?

SOLUTION:

1. The Military Clothing Division qualifies as a segment of the business for two reasons: (1) line of business and (2) class of customer. The military clothing is a completely separate line of business, and it sells to a completely separate class of customer (the U.S. Army).

2. The Military Clothing Division DOES QUALIFY as a discontinued operation because the management has formally discussed this in the Board of Directors meeting.

3. Yes, the minutes of the Board of Directors meeting indicate that a formal plan has been established to dispose of the Military Clothing Division of the company. They have set the time for sale and have set up an active program to find a buyer and have estimated the amount of Gain that might accrue.

4. The Gain should be recognized when realized. That is, the amount of Gain on the sale of the Military Clothing Division should be put down on the books when the sale is consummated. This will probably be on the date of the actual sale. On the other hand, an expected loss would be put on the books at the measurement date, that is, at the time the loss is known.

5. The Controller is correct in the manner of reporting the sale. While the disposal of the Military Clothing Division should be reported separately from the results of continuing operations, it does not meet the criteria of an Extraordinary Item, since such a sale is not Unusual—and in order to be an Extraordinary Item, the sale must be both Unusual and Infrequent.

• PROBLEM 1-7

Below are changes in all the account balances of the Bilton Furniture Company during the current year, except for Retained Earnings.

	Increase (Decrease)		Increase (Decrease)
Cash	80,000	Accounts Payable	(30,000)
Accounts Receivable (net)	40,000	Bonds Payable	80,000
Inventory	130,000	Common Stock	100,000
Investments	(50,000)	Additional Paid-In Capital	30,000

What is the Net Income for the current year? There were no entries in the Retained Earnings account except for Net Income and a Dividend Declaration of $10,000 which was paid in the current year.

SOLUTION:

Computation of Net Income:

Change in assets:

80,000 + 40,000 + 130,000 – 50,000 = $200,000 increase in assets

Change in liabilities:

80,000 – 30,000 = –50,000 increase in liabilities

150,000 increase in Owners' Equity

Change in Owners' Equity is accounted for as follows:

Net increase		150,000
Increase in Common Stock and Additional		
Paid-In Capital (100,000 + 30,000)	130,000	
Decrease in Retained Earnings Due		
to Dividend Declaration	10,000	
Net Increase Accounted for		120,000
Increase Due to Net Income		30,000

• PROBLEM 1–8

The Financial Statements of Bill Smith, Inc., were destroyed by fire at year's end. However, the Treasurer had kept certain statistical data related to the Income Statement as follows:

1. The beginning merchandise inventory was $90,000 and decreased 20% during the current year.

2. Sales Discounts amount to $16,000.

3. 25,000 shares of Common Stock were outstanding for the entire year.

4. Interest Expense was $20,000.

5. The Income Tax Rate is 25%.

6. Cost of Goods Sold amounts to $400,000.

7. Administrative Expenses are 20% of Cost of Goods Sold but only 9% of Gross Sales.

8. Four-fifths of the operating expenses relate to sales activities.

INSTRUCTIONS: From this information prepare an Income Statement for the year 1994 first in full form, then in single-step form.

SOLUTION:

Bill Smith, Incorporated
Income Statement
For Year Ended December 31, 1994

Gross Sales	888,889	
Sales Discounts	16,000	
Net Sales		872,889
Cost of Goods Sold:		
Beginning Inventory	90,000	
Purchases	382,000	
Merchandise Available for Sale	472,000	
Ending Inventory	72,000	
Cost of Goods Sold	400,000	400,000
Gross Profit		472,889

Operating Expenses:

Administrative Expenses	80,000	
Sales Expenses	320,000	
Total Operating Expenses		400,000
Operating Income		72,889
Interest Expense		20,000
Net Income before Income Tax		52,889
Income Tax		13,222
Net Income after Income Tax		39,667

Earnings Per Share ($39,667 divided by 20,000 shares outstanding) $1.98

Bill Smith, Incorporated
Single-Step Income Statement
For Year Ended December 31, 1994

Net Sales		872,889
Expenses:		
Cost of Goods Sold	400,000	
Administrative Expenses	80,000	
Sales Expenses	320,000	
Interest Expense	20,000	
Income Tax Expense	13,222	
Total Expenses		833,222
Net Income		39,667

Explanation of Income Statement computations:

1. The beginning merchandise inventory was $90,000 and decreased 20% during the current year. 20% × $90,000 = $18,000 decrease in inventory. $90,000 − $18,000 = $72,000 ending inventory.

2. Sales Discounts amount to $16,000.

3. Cost of Goods Sold is given as $400,000. Administrative Expenses are 20% of Cost of Goods Sold. $400,000 × 20% = $80,000 Administrative Expenses.

4. Administrative Expenses are 9% of Gross Sales. Divide Administrative Expenses of $80,000 by 9% to get Gross Sales of $888,889.

5. Subtract Sales Discounts (given) of $16,000 from Gross Sales of $888,889, to get Net Sales of $872,889.

6. Add Cost of Goods Sold (given) of $400,000 and ending inventory (computed above) of $72,000 to get Merchandise Available for Sale of $472,000. Subtract Beginning Inventory of 90,000 (given) from Merchandise Available for Sale of 472,000 to get Purchases of $382,000.

7. Four-fifths of Operating Expenses relate to sales activities. Operating expenses consist of Sales Expenses and Administrative Expenses. Since four-fifths of Operating Expenses relate to sales activities, the other one-fifth of Operating Expenses relate to Administrative Expenses. Administrative Expenses have been computed above as $80,000. So $80,000 is one-fifth of Operating Expenses. Divide $80,000 by 1/5 and get Total Operating Expenses of $400,000. Multiply $400,000 by 4/5 and get $320,000 Sales Expenses.

8. Deduct Interest Expense of $20,000 from Operating Income of $72,000 to get Net Income before Income Tax of $52,889.

9. Since the Income Tax Rate is 25%, multiply 25% by the Net Income before Income Tax of $52,889 to get tax of $13,222. Subtract tax of $13,222 from $52,889 to get Net Income after Tax of $39,667.

10. For the Single-Step Income Statement, take the Net Sales of $872,889 from the longer Income Statement and deduct Cost of Goods Sold, Administrative Expenses, Sales Expenses, Interest Expense, and Income Tax Expense to get Total Expenses of $833,222. Then deduct these Total Expenses of $833,222 from the Net Sales of $872,889 to get Net Income of $39,667.

• PROBLEM 1-9

Prepare a Multiple-Step Income Statement for the Michael Seed Company for the year of 1994 from the following information:

1.	Interest Expense on Bonds Payable	1,800
2.	Income Taxes	12,000
3.	Transportation In	2,700
4.	Sales	100,000
5.	Merchandise Inventory—Ending	16,000
6.	Merchandise Inventory—Beginning	15,000
7.	Depreciation of Sales Equipment	6,400
8.	Sales Commissions	7,000
9.	Transportation Out	2,700
10.	Rental Revenue	17,000
11.	Purchases	60,000
12.	Purchases Returns	5,800
13.	Depreciation of Office Equipment	3,900
14.	Officers' Salaries	4,000

SOLUTION:

MICHAEL SEED COMPANY
Income Statement
For Year Ending December 31, 1994

Sales			100,000
Cost of Goods Sold Section:			
Beginning Inventory		15,000	
Purchases	60,000		
Purchases Returns	5,800		
Net Purchases		54,200	
Transportation In		2,700	
Merchandise Available for Sale		71,900	
Ending Inventory		16,000	
Cost of Goods Sold			55,900
Gross Profit on Sales			44,100

Operating Expense Section:

Selling Expenses:

Transportation Out	2,700		
Sales Commissions	7,000		
Depreciation on Sales Equipment	6,400		
Total Selling Expense		16,100	

Administration Expenses:

Officers' Salaries	4,000		
Depreciation Office Equipment	3,900		
Total Admin. Expense		7,900	
Total Operating Expense		24,000	24,000
Operating Income			20,100

Other Income:

Rent Revenue	17,000	

Other Expense:

Interest Expense on Bonds Payable	1,800	15,200
Net Income before Income Tax		35,300
Income Tax		12,000
Net Income after Income Tax		23,300

• PROBLEM 1–10

Given below is information relating to the Ward Corporation for the year 1994. Prepare a Multiple-Step Income Statement for the year 1994. Assume that 70,000 shares of Common Stock are outstanding. Also prepare a separate Statement of Retained Earnings for 1994. Federal tax is at the 30% rate.

Retained Earnings Dec. 31, 1993	2,000,000
Dividends declared	100,000
Casualty loss (Extraordinary Item) before taxes	60,000
Depreciation expenses omitted by accident in 1992	30,000
Writeoff of inventory due to obsolescence	15,000
Interest Revenue	10,000
Dividend Revenue	20,000

Administrative Expenses	40,000
Selling Expenses	60,000
Cost of Goods Sold	800,000
Net Sales	1,000,000

SOLUTION:

Ward Corporation
Income Statement
For Year Ended December 31, 1994

Net Sales		1,000,000
Cost of Goods Sold		800,000
Gross Profit on Sales		200,000
Operating Expenses:		
Administrative Expenses	40,000	
Selling Expenses	60,000	
Total Operating Expenses		100,000
Operating Income		100,000
Other Revenue:		
Dividend Revenue	20,000	
Interest Revenue	10,000	
Total Other Revenue		30,000
Subtotal		130,000
Other Expenses:		
Writeoff of Obsolescent Inventory		15,000
Net Income before Tax and Extraordinary Item		115,000
Less Income Tax (30%)		34,500
Net Income before Extraordinary Item		80,500
Extraordinary Item:		
Casualty Loss	60,000	
Less applicable tax reduction (30%)	18,000	42,000
Net Income		38,500

Per Share of Common Stock:

   (70,000 shares of Common Stock are outstanding)

Income before Extraordinary Item $1.15 per share

   ($80,500 divided by 70,000 shares)

Less Extraordinary Item (net of tax)

   ($42,000 divided by 70,000 shares)   .60 per share

Net Income

   ($38,500 divided by 70,000 shares) $ .55 per share

Ward Corporation
Retained Earnings Statement
For Year Ended December 31, 1994

Retained Earnings, January 1, 1994	2,000,000
Depreciation Expense net of tax	
($30,000 less 30% or $9,000)	21,000
Adjusted Balance	1,979,000
Net Income (from Income Statement)	38,500
Subtotal	2,017,500
Dividend Declared	100,000
Retained Earnings, December 31, 1994	1,917,500

CHAPTER 2

STOCKS

> **Basic Attacks and Strategies for Solving Problems in this Chapter. See pages 21 to 36 for step-by-step solutions to problems.**

Stocks are the backbone of a corporation. One of the first things a corporation does after receiving its charter is to issue stocks, the two types being **Common** or **Preferred**. If Common Stock has a Par Value, the Common Stock account must be kept at Par Value; if stock is No-Par but has a Stated Value, the Common Stock account must be kept at Stated Value. Only when there is neither Par Value nor Stated Value can the Common Stock account be kept at Market Value. The difference between the Par Value (or the Stated Value) and the Market Value is the figure in the **Paid-In Capital** account. The Preferred Stock account is treated in the same manner as the Common Stock account.

Some corporations deal in **Stock Subscriptions**. A company sells Stock Subscriptions when potential stockholders pay for their original shares in installments. Therefore, two extra accounts have to be set up: **Subscriptions Receivable** (an asset account somewhat akin to Accounts Receivable) and **Common Stock Subscribed** (an Owners' Equity account). When subscriptions are first sold to potential stockholders, the corporate books are debited for Subscriptions Receivable and Common Stock Subscribed is credited for the Par or Stated Value, with the difference being credited to the Paid-In Capital account. When the corporation receives payments from the subscribers, Cash is debited and Subscriptions Receivable is credited. When the full amount of the subscription price has been received from the subscribers by the corporation, the corporation issues the stock and debits Common Stock Subscribed to close out this temporary Owners' Equity account. Common Stock is credited for the total Par Value of the issue to show that the Common Stock has been mailed out to the stockholders.

When a corporation purchases back its outstanding stock, this is called **Treasury Stock**. Usually the state or national law prevents the corporation from buying back more than a certain percentage of its own stock, to prevent fraud. Treasury Stock has a debit balance on the books of the corporation and is considered to be a **Contra-Owners' Equity** account; therefore, it is deducted from the Owners' Equity in the Capital Section of the Balance Sheet. There are two methods of handling Treasury Stock: the Par Value Method and the Cost Method. Since the Par Value Method is complicated, and the Par Value means little, most accountants now use the Cost Method.

When Treasury Stock is resold to the public, Cash is debited for the actual amount of cash coming in to the corporation. Treasury Stock is credited for an amount determined by multiplying the number of shares resold by the Treasury Stock purchase price per share. Any difference between the two figures is then placed in the Paid-In Capital account, or, in case of a large loss, in the Retained Earnings account.

Sometimes other assets, such as Land, are received by the corporation in exchange for Treasury Stock. In this case, Land would be debited on the books of the corporation and Treasury Stock would be credited.

At times a lump sum of cash is received by the corporation from stockholders, and both Preferred Stock and Common Stock are issued by the corporation. The number of shares of each type of stock to be issued must be known, the Par Value of each type of stock must be known, and the Market Value of each type of stock must be known at the time of issue. The costs then are divided mathematically between the two types of stocks.

The Stockholders' Equity Section of the Balance Sheet needs to be computed at the end of the fiscal period. The easiest way to do this is for the accountant to make journal entries of the various transactions throughout the year, then post these journal entries to the ledger. Finally, the balances of the Owner's Equity accounts (such as Common Stock, Preferred Stock, Paid-In Capital, and Treasury Stock) are set up or listed in the Capital Section of the Balance Sheet. On the other hand, Asset Accounts, such as Cash, Land, and Subscriptions Receivable, are not considered in this computation, since the desire here is only to determine the Owners' Equity Section of the Balance Sheet.

Step-by-Step Solutions to Problems in this Chapter, "Stocks"

• PROBLEM 2-1

During its first year of operations the Jones Company had several transactions involving its Common Stock. (a) Prepare the journal entries assuming that the Common Stock has a Par Value of $10 per share. (b) Prepare the journal entries assuming that the Common Stock is No Pat with a stated value of $1 per share.

January 20 — Issued 10,000 shares for cash at $10 per share.

March 5 — Issued 1,000 shares to attorneys in payment for their services. The bill was $30,000.

July 1 — Issued 30,000 shares for cash at $12 per share.

September 1 — Issued 60,000 shares for cash at $15 per share.

SOLUTION:

Part (a) $ (in dollars)

Date	Account	Debit	Credit
January 20	Cash (10,000 shares @ $10)	100,000	
	Common Stock (10,000 shares @ $10)		100,000
March 5	Organization Costs	30,000	
	Common Stock (1,000 shares @ $10)		10,000
	Paid-In Capital		20,000
July 1	Cash (30,000 shares @ $12)	360,000	
	Common Stock (30,000 shares @ $10)		300,000
	Paid-In Capital		60,000
September 1	Cash (60,000 shares @ $15)	900,000	
	Common Stock (60,000 shares @ $10)		600,000
	Paid-In Capital		300,000

Part (b) $ (in dollars)

Date	Account	Debit	Credit
January 20	Cash (10,000 shares @ $10)	100,000	
	Common Stock (10,000 shares @ $1)		10,000
	Paid-In Capital		90,000

March 5	Organization Costs	30,000	
	Common Stock (1,000 shares @ $1)		1,000
	Paid-In Capital		29,000
July 1	Cash (30,000 shares @ $12)	360,000	
	Common Stock (30,000 shares @ $1)		30,000
	Paid-In Capital		330,000
September 1	Cash (60,000 shares @ $15)	900,000	
	Common Stock (60,000 shares @ $1)		60,000
	Paid-In Capital		840,000

• PROBLEM 2–2

Jonesville Corporation was organized early in 1993. It is authorized to issue 20,000 shares of 8%, $100 Par Preferred Stock, and 500,000 shares of No-Par Common Stock with a stated value of $1 per share. It has already issued all its authorized Common Stock.

March 10, 1993   Issued 10,000 shares of Preferred Stock for cash at $104.

April 10, 1993   Issued 200 shares of Preferred Stock for land. The land is worth $80,000.

May 1, 1993   Issued 8,000 shares of Preferred Stock for cash at $115.

Nov. 10, 1993   Issued 1,000 shares of Preferred Stock for cash at $105.

INSTRUCTIONS: Record the journal entries.

SOLUTION:

1993			$ (in dollars)
March 10	Cash (10,000 shares @ $104)	1,040,000	
	Preferred Stock (10,000 shares @ $100)		1,000,000
	Paid-In Capital		40,000
April 10	Land (Fair Market Value)	80,000	
	Preferred Stock (200 shares @ $100)		20,000
	Paid-In Capital		60,000

May 1	Cash (8,000 shares @ $115)	920,000
	Preferred Stock (8,000 shares @ $100)	800,000
	Paid-In Capital	120,000
November 10	Cash (1,000 shares @ $105)	105,000
	Preferred Stock (1,000 shares @ $100)	100,000
	Paid-In Capital	5,000

• PROBLEM 2–3

Terrance Corporation needs additional funds for building a new warehouse. They decide to sell stock on a subscription basis to set up a new asset account entitled Subscriptions Receivable and a new capital account entitled Common Stock Subscribed. The stock certificates are printed showing a $5 Par Value, and 20,000 shares are offered at $25 per share. The subscribers are to pay 20% down and the balance a year later. All the subscriptions are sold almost immediately.

Give the entry to record the original subscription, the entry to record the first down payment, the final payment, and then the entry to show the issuing of the Common Stock.

SOLUTION:

	$ (in dollars)	
Subscriptions Receivable (20,000 shares @ $25)	500,000	
Common Stock Subscribed (20,000 shares @ $5)		100,000
Paid-In Capital in Excess of Par		400,000
Cash ($500,000 × 20%)	100,000	
Subscriptions Receivable		100,000
Cash ($500,000 – $100,000)	400,000	
Subscriptions Receivable		400,000
Common Stock Subscribed	100,000	
Common Stock (20,000 shares @ $5)		100,000

• PROBLEM 2–4

James Company originally sold its Common Stock at $35 per share. Later they repurchased 50,000 shares at the regular market price of $40 per share. The Par Value is $2 per share. Give the general journal entry to record the purchase of this Treasury Stock by the Par Value Method.

SOLUTION:

	$ (in dollars)
Treasury Stock (50,000 shares @ $5)	250,000
Paid-In Capital ($35 − $2 × 50,000 shares)	1,650,000
Retained Earnings	100,000
Cash 2,000,000	

• PROBLEM 2–5

James Company originally sold its Common Stock at $35 per share. Later they repurchased 50,000 shares at the regular market price of $40 per share. The Par Value is $2 per share. Give the general journal entry to record the purchase of this Treasury Stock by the Cost Method.

SOLUTION:

	$ (in dollars)
Treasury Stock	2,000,000
Cash	2,000,000

• PROBLEM 2-6

(Continuing with the previous problem)—Several years after James Company had purchased the 50,000 shares of its own Treasury Stock at $40 per share, they sold 20,000 shares of this Treasury Stock for the present market price of $51 per share.

INSTRUCTIONS: Give the general journal entry for this transaction according to the Cost Method.

SOLUTION:

	$ (in dollars)
Cash (20,000 shares @ $51)	1,020,000
Treasury Stock (20,000 shares @ $40)	800,000
Retained Earnings ($1,020,000 – $800,000)	220,000

• PROBLEM 2-7

Fifteen thousand shares of Treasury Stock were exchanged by the James Company for undeveloped land. Since the land had not been bought or sold for a number of years prior to that time, it was difficult to determine its value. At the time of the exchange, the Common Stock of the James Company was trading on the market at $50 per share. Record the journal entry using the Cost Method. The Treasury Stock had been purchased by the company at $45 per share.

SOLUTION:

	$ (in dollars)
Land (15,000 shares @ $50)	750,000
Treasury Stock (15,000 shares @ $45)	675,000
Paid-In Capital ($750,000 – $675,000)	75,000

• PROBLEM 2-8

Crimson Company issues 400 shares of $10 Par Common Stock and 50 shares of $100 Par Preferred Stock for a lump sum of $110,000. Prepare the journal entry for issuance when the Market Value of the Common Shares is $180 each and the Market Value of the Preferred Stock is $200 each.

SOLUTION:

Par Value Computations:

Common Stock   400 shares @ $10 Par = $4,000

Preferred Stock   50 shares @ $100 Par = $5,000

Market Value Computations:

Common Stock   400 shares @ $180 market = $72,000

Preferred Stock   50 shares @ $200 market = $10,000

    Total $82,000

$$\frac{72,000}{82,000} \times \$110,000 = \$96,585.37$$

$$\frac{10,000}{82,000} \times \$110,000 = \frac{\$13,414.63}{\$110,000.00}$$

Using the above computations, we can make the following entry:

	$ (in dollars)	
Cash (Given)	110,000.00	
Common Stock (400 shares @ $10 Par)		4,000.00
Paid-In Capital, Common ($96,585.37 – $4,000)		92,585.37
Preferred Stock (50 shares @ $100)		5,000.00
Paid-In Capital, Preferred ($13,414.63 – $5,000)		8,414.63

• PROBLEM 2-9

Harrison Company is authorized to issue 200,000 shares of $10 Par Value Common Stock and 100,000 shares of 10% cumulative Preferred Stock, Par Value $100 per share. The corporation engaged in the following stock transactions through December 31, 1993: 30,000 shares of Common Stock were issued for $500,000 and 10,000 shares of Preferred Stock were issued for land valued at $1,500,000. Subscriptions for 4,500 shares of Common Stock have been taken, and 40% of the subscription price of $17 per share has been collected. Treasury Stock of 1,500 shares of Common has been purchased for $17 via the Cost Method. The Retained Earnings balance is $200,000. Prepare the Stockholders' Equity Section of the Balance Sheet.

SOLUTION:

		$ (in dollars)
Cash		500,000
Common Stock (30,000 shares @ $10 Par)		300,000
Paid-In Capital on Common Stock		200,000
Land		1,500,000
Preferred Stock (10,000 shares @ $100 Par)		1,000,000
Paid-In Capital on Preferred		500,000
Subscriptions Receivable (4,500 shares @ $17)	76,500	
Common Stock Subscribed (4,500 shares @ $10 Par)		45,000
Paid-In Capital on Common Stock		31,500
Cash ($76,500 ¥ 40%)	30,600	
Subscriptions Receivable		30,600
Treasury Stock (1,500 shares @ $17)	25,500	
Cash		25,500

The following is the ledger after the above journal entries have been posted:

Common Stock		Preferred Stock		Treasury Stock	
	300,000		1,000,000	25,500	

Paid-In Capital—Common	Pd.-In Cap.—Preferred	Com. Stock Subscribed
200,000	500,000	45,000
31,500		
231,500		

Retained Earnings
200,000

Hint: Subscriptions Receivable is an Asset account and therefore should not be included in the Capital Section of the Balance Sheet.

From the ledger above, we now fill out the Capital Section of the Balance Sheet:

Harrison Company
Capital Section of Balance Sheet
December 31, 1993

Common Stock	300,000
Paid-In Capital on Common Stock	231,500
Preferred Stock	1,000,000
Paid-In Capital on Preferred Stock	500,000
Common Stock Subscribed	45,000
Total Paid-In Capital	2,076,500
Less Treasury Stock	25,500
Subtotal	2,051,000
Plus Retained Earnings	200,000
Total Owners' Equity	2,251,000

• PROBLEM 2–10

The Brown Manufacturing Company has 100,000 shares authorized in their corporate charter but so far has issued only 40,000 shares of their own stock. Company officers have voted to build an additional factory at an estimated cost of $100,000. Financial advisors have suggested that this money be raised by selling 2,040 additional shares of their own stock which now has a market price of $50 per share. The company's business is increasing, and the new factory building is deemed necessary for the business. What entry will be made on the books of the firm when this stock is sold if brokers' fees are $2,000? Par Value is $50 per share.

SOLUTION:

	$ (in dollars)	
Cash	100,000	
Brokerage Expense	2,000	
Common Stock (2,040 shares @ $50)		102,000

• PROBLEM 2–11

James Smith has saved $5,000 and consults his broker as to an investment in line with his investment desires. The broker tells Smith of the new issue of stock by the Brown Manufacturing Company which appears to be a growing firm with possibly a rosy future. Smith places an order to buy 100 shares of the Brown Manufacturing Company stock at the present market price of $50 per share, and the brokerage fee is $100. What entry should James Smith make on his books?

SOLUTION:

	$ (in dollars)	
Investment in Common Stock of Brown Manufacturing Company	5,100	
Cash		5,100
Bought 100 shares of Common Stock of Brown Manufacturing Company @ $50 plus $100 brokerage fee		

• PROBLEM 2–12

Later, the business of the Brown Manufacturing Company continues to increase, and the board of directors decides to purchase $50,000 worth of factory equipment to use in the newly constructed factory building. The stock is still selling on the market for $50 per share, and the brokerage fee will be $1,000. The board of directors decides to sell 1,020 shares of its authorized stock in order to raise the needed cash. What entry will be made on the books of the Brown Manufacturing Company to raise the money, and what entry will be made to buy the machinery? Par Value is also $50.

SOLUTION:

	$ (in dollars)	
Cash	50,000	
Brokerage Expense	1,000	
Common Stock (1,020 shares @ $50)		51,000
Factory Equipment	50,000	
Cash		50,000

• PROBLEM 2-13

The board of directors of the Brown Manufacturing Company wants the present stockholders to maintain their Pro Rata Interest in the corporation after the new stock offerings have been sold. In order to encourage present stockholders to buy some of these new stock offerings, the board decides to issue stock rights. After consulting with the company's lawyers and brokers, they decide to issue one right for each share of stock outstanding. One day James Smith receives a letter from the Brown Manufacturing Company informing him that since he holds 100 shares of Brown Manufacturing Company Common Stock, he will receive a certificate showing he also has 100 rights, and each right allows him to buy one more share in the corporation at the price of only $40 per share. What entry does James Smith make on his books on the day he receives these 100 rights? Smith looks in the newspaper and learns that these new rights are selling on the market for $3 per share. Market Value of the stock has now risen to $60 per share.

SOLUTION:

The formula for finding the Total Cost of Rights is as follows:

$$\frac{\text{Fair Market Value of Rights}}{(\text{Fair Market Value of Rights}) + (\text{Fair Market Value of Stock})}$$

× Total Cost of Investment

or

Fair Market Value of Rights = ($3 per right × 100 rights) = $300

Fair Market Value of Stock = ($60 per share × 100 shares) = $6,000

Total Cost of Investment = $5,100 (100 shares @ $50 = $5,000 plus $100 broker's fee)

or

$$\frac{(100 \times 3)}{(100 \times 3) + (100 \times 60)} \times 5,100 = \frac{300}{300 + 6,000} \times 5,100$$

$$= \frac{300}{6,300} \times 5,100$$

$$= .0476 \times 5,100$$

$$= \$242.76$$

Thus, the Total Cost of the Stock Rights is $242.76.

Prior to the receipt of the stock rights, James Smith's account appears as follows:

Investment in Brown Manufacturing Company Common Stock

5,100	

Smith's entry on receipt of the 100 stock rights is as follows:

	$ (in dollars)
Investment in Brown Stock Rights	242.76
Investment in Brown Common Stock	242.76

After the receipt of the Stock Rights, James Smith's accounts appear as follows:

Investment in Brown Manufacturing Company Common Stock

5,100.00	242.76
4,857.24	

Investment in Brown Company Stock Rights

242.76	

As can be seen from the above accounts, the $5,100 investment of James Smith has been cut down to $4,857.24, and the $242.76 has been set up as a separate Asset titled Investment in Brown Co. Stock Rights. This is a Current Asset account. The value per right is $2.4276, computed as follows: Total value of all the 100 rights was previously found to be $242.76.

$242.76 divided by 100 shares = $2.4276

• PROBLEM 2-14

The cash value of the rights has now dropped from $3 per share to only $2.50 per share. Investor James Smith decides to sell 25 of his 100 rights on the stock market. What entry does he make?

SOLUTION:

	$ (in dollars)	
Cash	62.50	
Investment in Brown Company Stock Rights		60.69
Gain		1.81

James Smith receives cash of $62.50 as a result of selling 25 rights on the market at the present market price of $2.50 (25 × $2.50 = $62.50). The account Investment in Brown Company Stock Rights is credited for $60.69. When purchased, the rights were worth $2.4276 apiece (see above), and 25 rights were sold (25 rights @ $2.4276 = $60.69). The gain is, of course, the difference between these two figures ($62.50 − $60.69 = $1.81).

• PROBLEM 2-15

James Smith decides to exercise 50 of his 100 rights by sending them in with cash to buy 50 more shares of Brown Company Common Stock. What will be his entry for this?

SOLUTION:

	$ (in dollars)	
Investment in Brown Company Common Stock	3,000.00	
Cash		2,000.00
Investment in Brown Company Stock Rights		121.38
Gain		878.62

The fine print in the rights certificate mentions that the Common Stock can be purchased for only $40 per share if accompanied by a right. Smith has decided to buy 50 shares, so he sends in $2,000 along with his

50 rights (50 shares @ $40 per share = $2,000). Smith credits his account, Investment in Brown Company Stock Rights for $121.38 ($2.4276 value of one right, times 50 rights = $121.38). The difference of $878.62 ($3,000.00 – $2,000.00 – $121.38 = $878.62) is a gain which will need to be reported as Income on the Income Tax of James Smith.

• PROBLEM 2–16

As can be seen from the problems above, James Smith was sent 100 rights. He sold 25 rights and exercised 50 rights. He did nothing with the remaining 25 rights. After a certain period of time, as mentioned in the Rights Certificate, if the rights are not exercised or sold, they expire. This is what happened to Smith's 25 remaining rights. What entry does Smith make in his journal when his rights expire?

SOLUTION:

	$ (in dollars)	
Loss	60.69	
Investment in Brown Company Rights		60.69

The value of the expired rights is $60.69, computed as follows:

$2.4276 value of each right @ 25 rights expired = $60.69

The Investment in Brown Company Stock Rights account will look as follows:

Investment in Brown Co. Stock Rights

242.76	60.69
	121.38
	60.69
	242.76

Thus, the Current Asset account Investment in Brown Co. Stock Rights is finally cancelled out after the rights have expired.

How does the account Investment in Brown Manufacturing Company Common Stock now appear?

Investment in Brown Manufacturing Company Common Stock

5,100.00	242.76
4,857.24	
3,000.00	
7,857.24	

• PROBLEM 2-17

Some corporations fear untimely deaths of their officers. Such events can prove disastrous not only for the family, but for the corporation. Therefore, corporations are allowed to buy insurance policies on their officers with the corporation listed as beneficiary. If the corporation buys a term insurance policy on its presiding officer with a yearly premium of $1,000 and a death benefit of $25,000, what would be the entry for the premium, and what would be the entry for the death benefit?

SOLUTION:

(Entry for premium payment)	$ (in dollars)
Insurance Expense	1,000
Cash	1,000

(Entry for receipt of death benefit)	
Cash	25,000
Gain from Life Insurance Settlement	25,000

A term policy builds up no asset called Cash Surrender Value, because the policy is all protection and no savings. So when a death does occur, the entire cash settlement is a Gain from Life Insurance Settlement. This gain, however, is not taxable.

• PROBLEM 2–18

A company buys a $100,000 whole life insurance policy on one of its officers, with a yearly premium of $1,700, and with a cash surrender value as follows: Year 1—0; Year 2—$200; Year 3—$400. What entry is made on the corporate books the first year, the second year, and in the event of cash settlement at death?

SOLUTION:

(First year entry)	$ (in dollars)	
Insurance Expense	1,700	
Cash		1,700

There is no amount that goes to Cash Surrender Value the first year, so the entire $1,700 premium is debited to Insurance Expense.

(Second year entry)		
Insurance Expense	1,500	
Cash Surrender Value of Life Insurance	200	
Cash		1,700

Of the $1,700 insurance premium payment the second year of the policy, $200 is debited to the Asset account—Cash Surrender Value of Life Insurance. The remaining $1,500 is debited to Insurance Expense.

(Cash settlement entry after second year)		
Cash	100,000	
Cash Surrender Value of Life Insurance		200
Gain from Life Insurance Settlement		99,800

The full $100,000 life insurance settlement is paid on the death of the officer, so Cash is debited for $100,000. The Asset account Cash Surrender Value of Life Insurance has a debit value of $200, so this account is closed out by crediting it for $200. The remainder ($99,800) is Gain from Life Insurance Settlement. Although it is Income for the corporation, it is not taxable.

CHAPTER 3

RETAINED EARNINGS

> **Basic Attacks and Strategies for Solving Problems in this Chapter. See pages 39 to 49 for step-by-step solutions to problems.**

The **Retained Earnings** account of corporations is probably one of the least understood accounts, at least from the point of view of the general public. Some people think of it as a catch-all account, but it is not. On the contrary, it shows the general health of the corporation, to some extent. If the Retained Earnings account has a large credit balance, stockholders want their dividends increased. On the other hand, if the Retained Earnings account has a debit balance (deficit), it is an immediate sign of an unhealthy corporation.

All dividend declarations except Liquidating Dividends are deductions from Retained Earnings, since this type of dividend comes from past earnings of the corporation. On the other hand, a Liquidating Dividend, paid from stockholders' original investments, debits Paid-In Capital, Common Stock, or Preferred Stock rather than Retained Earnings.

When Retained Earnings are appropriated (set aside) for some contingency, like future planned plant expansion, the Retained Earnings account is debited, and an account like Appropriation for Plant Expansion is credited for the same amount. This cuts the balance of the Retained Earnings account so the stockholders will not so readily clamor for higher dividends.

Stock or Cash Dividends are declared by the corporate board of directors, and, unlike stock splits, the Retained Earnings account is debited, therefore reducing the amount in the Retained Earnings account. On the other hand, reported Net Income at year's end is credited to the Retained Earnings account.

Many states do not allow corporations therein to pay dividends if they have a debit balance (deficit) in their Retained Earnings account. For instance, let us say that Company X has had several years of losses, thus building up its deficit. Let us also say that in the last few months the company has been making small profits and wishes to be able to pay dividends to encourage their stockholders and also to raise the price of their stock on the market. This can be done through **Quasi-Reorganization**.

There are two methods of Quasi-Reorganization: **Deficit Reclassification** and **Deficit Reorganization**. The simpler method, Deficit Reclassification, can be accomplished by one journal entry. This entry debits Paid-In Capital and credits Retained Earnings for the amount of the deficit, thus wiping out the deficit in completely. The second method, Deficit Reorganization, is more complicated and involves writing up assets to their Fair Market Value, writing down liabilities to their true values, writing down Common Stock to its Market Value, and then writing off the rest of the deficit through Paid-In Capital.

Some corporations send assets other than cash to their stockholders. This is termed a **Property Dividend**. Property Dividends, though rarely used, are legal. The inventory is kept at cost, so this must be written off by crediting that account at cost price. The Retained Earnings account is debited for the Fair Market Value of the inventory. Any difference between these two figures will be either credited to the Gain account or debited to the Loss account. If the Fair Market Value of the inventory is not readily determinable, then the Retained Earnings account will be debited for the cost price of the inventory.

Step-by-Step Solutions to Problems in this Chapter, "Retained Earnings"

• PROBLEM 3-1

The Swift Eagle Corporation has 1,000,000 shares of Common Stock outstanding. On December 25, 1995, the board voted a $1 per share Cash Dividend to stockholders of record on January 10, 1996, and payable on January 20, 1996. (a) What are the entries if the dividend represents a distribution of earnings? (b) What are the entries if the dividend represents a distribution of Treasury Stock? (c) What are the entries if the distribution is a Liquidating Dividend?

SOLUTION:

Part (a)

1995		$ (in dollars)	
December 25	Retained Earnings	1,000,000	
	Dividends Payable		1,000,000
1996			
January 10	(No entry)		
20	Dividends Payable	1,000,000	
	Cash		1,000,000

On the date of declaration the Retained Earnings account is debited because dividends are taken out of Retained Earnings. The Retained Earnings account usually has a credit balance, so a debit to Retained Earnings cuts down the value of this account, in this case by the amount of the dividend. As soon as the dividend is declared by the board, the corporation owes the $1,000,000 to the stockholders; so the current liability account Dividends Payable is credited for the $1,000,000. On January 20, the dividend is mailed to the stockholders, so Cash is credited for $1,000,000. Dividends Payable is debited for $1,000,000 to close out this temporary account.

Part (b)

1995		$ (in dollars)	
December 25	Retained Earnings	1,000,000	
	Stock Dividends Distributable		1,000,000
1996			
January 10	(No entry)		
20	Stock Dividends Distributable	1,000,000	
	Treasury Stock		1,000,000

On the Date of Declaration the Retained Earnings account is debited because dividends are taken out of Retained Earnings. Since this is a Stock Dividend (rather than a Cash Dividend), the account Stock Dividends Distributable is credited. Stock Dividends Distributable is an Owners' Equity account, and this account will appear on the Balance Sheet at the end of the year, 1995. Let us assume that when the Treasury Stock was originally purchased by the corporation, it was purchased for $1 per share. Since the board has voted a dividend of $1 per share, on the date of the stock distribution (in this case January 20) Treasury Stock will be credited for $1,000,000 (1,000,000 shares @ $1 per share). At the same time, the account Stock Dividends Distributable will be debited for $1,000,000 to close out the account.

Part (c)

1995		$ (in dollars)	
December 25	Paid-In Capital	1,000,000	
	Dividends Payable		1,000,000
1996			
January 10	(No entry)		
20	Dividends Payable	1,000,000	
	Cash		1,000,000

Liquidating Dividends are not taken out of Retained Earnings, since these dividends come from Paid-In Capital, not from past profits. These dividends come from money previously paid in by the stockholders themselves; so Paid-In Capital is debited on the Date of Declaration. Since Liquidating Dividend is a Cash Dividend, and the money is owed by the corporation to the stockholders on the date of declaration, the current liability account Dividends Payable is credited.

On January 10, the Date of Record, the computer prints out the names, addresses, and number of shares owned by all the stockholders of record on that date, so that this information can be used to determine the amount of Cash Dividend to send to each individual shareholder. However, these are changes in subsidiary records, so no entry is made in the general journal on this date.

On January 20, the date that the dividend checks are sent out to the stockholders, Cash is credited for $1,000,000 to show the dividend checks being sent out. Dividends Payable is debited to cancel this current liability account, since the debt to the stockholders is canceled by the dividend payment.

• PROBLEM 3-2

The Smith Corporation has 3,000 shares of $100 Par Value 7% cumulative Preferred Stock and 6,000 shares of $10 Par Value Common Stock outstanding. Retained Earnings of the corporation are $100,000, and the board has authorized the company to pay out $75,000 of this amount. Cumulative Preferred Dividends are one year in arrears. (a) How much money should be paid to each class of stock if Preferred Stock is cumulative but nonparticipating? (b) How much per share to each class of stock?

SOLUTION:

Part (a)

$42,000 goes to Preferred Stock as dividends.

$33,000 goes to Common Stock as dividends.

3,000 shares of Preferred Stock outstanding times $100 Par Value per share = $300,000 total Par Value of Preferred Stock. $300,000 times .07 = $21,000 yearly Preferred Dividends. One year in arrears plus the present year equal two years of dividends to be paid. $21,000 yearly Preferred Dividends times 2 years = $42,000 Preferred Dividends to be paid. Subtract $42,000 from the $75,000 dividends authorized by the board, and the remainder is $33,000 going to the Common stockholders.

Part (b)

$14 per share for Preferred stockholders.

$5.50 per share for Common stockholders.

$42,000 Preferred Dividends divided by 3,000 shares of Preferred Stock outstanding results in $14 per share of Preferred. $33,000 Common Dividends divided by 6,000 shares of Common Stock outstanding results in $5.50 per share of Common.

• PROBLEM 3-3

Same as previous problem except that Preferred Stock is Noncumulative. Again, the Smith Corporation has 3,000 shares of $100 Par Value 7% Noncumulative Preferred Stock and 6,000 shares of $10 Par Value Common Stock. Retained Earnings of the corporation are $100,000, and the board has authorized the company to pay out $75,000 of this amount. Noncumulative Preferred Dividends were not paid last year. (a) How much money should be paid to each class of stock? (b) How much per share should be paid to each class of stock?

SOLUTION:

Part (a)

$21,000 goes to Preferred Stock as dividends.

$54,000 goes to Common Stock as dividends.

3,000 shares of Preferred Stock outstanding times $100 Par Value per share = $300,000 total Par Value of Preferred. $300,000 times .07 = $21,000 yearly Preferred Dividends. The number of years that dividends have been in arrears has no importance in Noncumulative Preferred Stock. Subtract $21,000 from $75,000 dividends authorized by the board, and the remainder of $54,000 goes to the Common stockholders.

Part (b)

$7 per share for Preferred stockholders.

$9 per share for Common stockholders.

$21,000 Preferred Dividends divided by 3,000 shares of Preferred Stock outstanding results in $7 per share Preferred. $54,000 Common Dividends divided by 6,000 shares of Common stock outstanding results in $9 per share Common.

• PROBLEM 3-4

The Jones Company has 50,000 shares of its Common Stock outstanding with a Par Value of $1 per share (50,000 @ $1 = $50,000 total Par Value of the Common Stock). Because the corporation has been doing well financially, its stock has risen to heights previously undreamed by the owners. As a result of this, however, very few shares are now being bought or sold. The board of Ddirectors believes that this is true because the price of the stock is high. In order to lower the price of the stock, the board has voted a 2-for-1 stock split, effective December 31, 1996. What entry should be made on the corporate books as of that date?

SOLUTION:

1996

December 31 (Two-for-one stock split of Common Stock of the Jones Company. Prior to the stock split, there were 50,000 shares of stock outstanding at $1 Par, for a total of $50,000 Par Value of Common Stock. Following the 2-for-1 stock split, there are now 100,000 shares of stock outstanding at $.50 Par, for a total of $50,000 Par Value of Common Stock.)

It will be noted that the only entry made for a stock split is merely an explanation in parentheses. There is no formal entry made, because nothing is to be posted from the journal to the ledger. The accounts in the ledger remain with the same dollar values as previous. The only change due to the stock split is in the number of shares outstanding and in the Par Value per share.

• PROBLEM 3-5

The Jordan Company is making good profits and recording these in its Retained Earnings account. However, it is a growing company and uses most of its extra cash for expansion. The board of directors wishes to show the stockholders how well the company is doing, but it does not have the extra cash to pay a Cash Dividend. Therefore, it decides to issue a Stock Dividend. The Par Value of the outstanding stock is $5 per share, and the Market Value of the stock is $10 per share. There are at present 100,000 shares of stock outstanding, so the board declares a 5% Stock Dividend. How will this be recorded on the books (a) at the Date of Declaration, (b) at the Date of Record, and (c) at the Date of Payment?

SOLUTION:

1996		$ (in dollars)	
January 5	Retained Earnings	50,000	
	Stock Dividends Distributable		25,000
	Paid-In Capital		25,000
18	(No entry on date of declaration)		
25	Stock Dividends Distributable	25,000	
	Common Stock		25,000

On the Date of Declaration, January 5, Retained Earnings is debited for $50,000. (There are 100,000 shares of Common Stock outstanding times a 5% Stock Dividend declared or 5,000 shares to be issued as a Stock Dividend.) The market price of the stock at the time is $10 per share (5,000 shares @ $10 = $50,000). Stock Dividends Distributable is credited for $25,000. This is an Owners' Equity account and is credited for the Par Value of the stock (5,000 shares to be issued as a Stock Dividend times $5 Par Value per share). The remaining $25,000 is credited to Paid-In Capital, which can only be paid to stockholders eventually if a Liquidating Dividend is declared.

On January 18, the Date of Declaration, no entries are made in the general journal, because no accounts in the ledger change value at this time.

On January 25, the date the stock certificates are mailed out to the stockholders, Stock Dividends Distributable is debited for $25,000 to close out this account, showing the stock has been distributed. Common Stock is credited for $25,000, the Total Par Value of the stock being mailed out, to show the stock certificates have left the company and are being sent to the stockholders.

• PROBLEM 3-6

The books of the Harrison Company have been examined, and the following information has been found: Treasury Stock has been purchased for $10,000; Common Stock with a Par Value of $50,000 has been sold; all the Net Incomes over the years that the corporation has been in existence amount to $130,000; the Appropriation for Contingencies is $5,000; the Stock Dividends distributed amount to $20,000; and the Cash Dividends distributed amount to $18,000. Treasury Stock has been sold at a gain of $3,000. What is the balance of the Retained Earnings account?

SOLUTION:

Retained Earnings

(Appropriation for			
Contingencies)	5,000	(Net incomes)	130,000
(Stock Dividends declared)	20,000		
(Cash Dividends declared)	18 000		
	43,000		
		(Balance)	87,000

The purchase of Treasury Stock does not involve the Retained Earnings account. The sale of Common Stock also does not involve the Retained Earnings account. An Appropriation takes money out of Retained Earnings and puts it in an Appropriations Account. Declarations of Cash Dividends and Stock Dividends also take money out of the Retained Earnings account. The sale of Treasury Stock at a gain does not involve Retained Earnings.

• PROBLEM 3–7

The James Lumber Company has found its fire insurance premiums rising each year. Lately these payments to the insurance company have become so high that they are prohibitive. What are three methods an accountant can use to have self-insurance for the lumber company?

SOLUTION:

METHOD ONE

At the end of each year, *make no entry on the books*. When a fire loss actually occurs, let us say, in the amount of $10,000, debit Fire Loss Expense for the period in which the loss occurs, as follows:

	$ (in dollars)	
Fire Loss Expense	10,000	
Cash		10,000

METHOD TWO

At the end of each year, make an Appropriation entry for the amount of premium that would have been paid had the company kept its insurance policy:

Retained Earnings	1,000	
Appropriation for Self-Insurance		1,000

In the event of an actual loss, debit an eExpense account for the period in which the loss occurs, and remove the Appropriation:

Fire Loss Expense	10,000	
Cash		10,000
Appropriation for Self-Insurance	10,000	
Retained Earnings		10,000

METHOD THREE

At the end of each year, accrue the Expense for the amount of premium that would have been paid had the company kept its insurance policy:

Insurance Expense	1,000	
Liability for Uninsured Losses		1,000

In the event of an actual loss, debit the Liability account and credit Cash for the actual amount of the loss:

Liability for Uninsured Losses	10,000	
Cash		10,000

• PROBLEM 3-8

The Hanson Company has had several years of losses, so now the Retained Earnings account has a deficit of $10,000 which is shown as a debit balance in the Retained Earnings account. What are two ways that the company can legally do away with this deficit through Quasi-Reorganization?

SOLUTION:

METHOD ONE—Deficit Reclassification

	$ (in dollars)	
Paid-In Capital	10,000	
Retained Earnings		10,000

METHOD TWO—Deficit Reorganization

First, write up the assets to their true value, then write up the liabilities to their true value. Next, write off the Common Stock to its true value by crediting the Paid-In Capital account. Finally credit the Retained Earnings enough to bring its debit balance up to zero by debiting Paid-In Capital.

Assets	3,000	
Liabilities	2,000	
Retained Earnings		5,000
Common Stock	3,000	
Paid-In Capital		3,000
Paid-In Capital	5,000	
Retained Earnings		5,000

The deficit in Retained Earnings would be written off as follows:

Retained Earnings

Deficit Balance	10,000	
		5,000
		5,000

• PROBLEM 3-9

In order to get rid of some of its extra inventory, and in order to interest its stockholders in its merchandise, the Hassan Furniture Company Board of Directors voted a Property Dividend under which it would give furniture to its various stockholders. The property to be given out had been purchased wholesale for $15,000 and now has a Fair Market Value of $17,000. What entry should be made on the books of the corporation on the date that the board declares this dividend?

SOLUTION:

	$ (in dollars)
Retained Earnings	17,000
Inventory	15,000
Gain	2,000

• PROBLEM 3-10

The Hassan Furniture Company board of directors voted a Property Dividend under which it would give antique furniture to its various stockholders. The property had been purchased years ago for $15,000, but the Fair Market Value now is not easily determinable. What entry should be made on the books of the corporation on the date that the board declares this dividend?

SOLUTION:

	$ (in dollars)
Retained Earnings	15,000
Inventory	15,000

Since the Fair Market Value is difficult to determine, the original cost value is used in the entry.

CHAPTER 4

EARNINGS PER SHARE OF THE CORPORTION

Basic Attacks and Strategies for Solving Problems in this Chapter. See pages 52 to 77 for step-by-step solutions to problems.

One of the most important figures that potential stockholders and actual stockholders of a corporation wish to know is the Earnings per Share of the corporation each year. Potential stockholders need to know this figure in order to compare it with Earnings per Share of other corporations to see whether the corporation in which the stockholder is interested is doing better or worse than competing corporations. Potential stockholders also need to know the Earnings per Share over several years to see if the corporation has done better or worse financially over a long period of time.

Generally, the Earnings per Share can be computed by dividing the corporation's Net Income by the number of Common Shares Outstanding. However, the computation is not as simple as this; it is compounded in complexity if the corporation has Preferred Stock Outstanding, or if it has Convertible Preferred Stock or perhaps Convertible Bonds Outstanding. It is also complicated if the number of shares of stock outstanding changes during the year.

Sometimes a corporation wishes to persuade bondholders to turn in their Convertible Bonds for Common Stock in the corporation. This is termed **Induced Conversion**. This is often done when the corporation no longer wishes to pay High Interest Eates on their outstanding bonds.

When a corporation has Convertible Preferred Stock Outstanding, its Balance Sheet should show both Primary (actual) Earnings per Share and

Fully Diluted Earnings per Share (the Earnings per Share if all the Convertible Preferred Stock were converted to Common Stock).

Annual reports and quarterly reports of most corporations show Earnings per Share, because most stockholders want and need this information; but because of the complex capital structure of many corporations, the computation of Earnings per Share can often be quite complicated.

Step-by-Step Solutions to Problems in this Chapter, "Earnings Per Share of the Corporation"

• PROBLEM 4–1

On June 1, Livingston Company issued 50 ten-year, 12% $5,000 Convertible Bonds. The fine print on the bonds mentioned that each $5,000 bond was convertible into 500 shares of Common Stock of the Livingston Company. The Bond Interest is payable June 1 and December 1. These bonds were sold at a premium of $25,000. Give the entry for this bond sale. Ignore brokerage fees.

SOLUTION:

1995		$ (in dollars)	
June 1	Cash	275,000	
	Premium on Bonds		25,000
	Bonds		250,000

• PROBLEM 4–2

In Problem 4–1, just above, what was the premium price on each individual bond?

SOLUTION:

The total premium price was given as $25,000. Since there were 50 bonds issued, we divide $25,000 by 50 bonds, getting a premium of $500 per bond.

• PROBLEM 4–3

Continuing with Problems 4–1 and 4–2 above, six months after the June 1 sale of the bonds is the first Interest Payment date—December 1. Give the entry to record the premium Amortization and the Interest Payment on that date.

SOLUTION:

1995		$ (in dollars)	
December 1	Premium on Bonds	1,250	
	Bond Interest Expense		1,250
	To record a half-year's premium Amortization		
December 1	Bond Interest Expense	15,000	
	Cash		15,000
	To record a half-year's Interest Payment		

The premium of $25,000 is to be written off over a ten-year period. But since interest is paid every half-year, the Amortization is to be written off partially on each half-year Interest Payment date. There are 20 half-years in the 10-year life of the bonds. The amount of the half-year premium Amortization is computed by dividing the $25,000 premium by the 20 half-years, giving an Amortization each half-year of $1,250. The Premium Account has a credit balance, so every half-year the Amortization entry Debits the Premium Account for the amount of the amortization, which in this case is $1,250.

The interest rate printed on the face of the bond is 12% per year, which is 6% per half-year. (12% divided by 2 = 6%.) The face value of the bonds is $250,000 (50 bonds @ $5,000 = $250,000). So multiply the

$250,000 by 6% (one half-year's interest) to get $15,000, the semi-annual Interest Payment. Bond Interest Expense is debited for $15,000 because the Livingston Company is getting the use of the money borrowed; and Cash is credited for $15,000, because the dividend checks for this amount are being mailed out to the bondholders on December 1.

• PROBLEM 4-4

Using information from Problems 4-1, 4-2, and 4-3, plus the additional information that the Par Value of the Livingston Company stock is $10 per share, let us assume that on December 1, 1995, the date of the first Interest Payment and first Amortization entry, that one bondholder mailed in his or her $5,000 bond, wishing to convert it to 500 shares of Common Stock of the Livingston Company, according to the fine print on the face of the bond, called the Bond Indenture. Also, let us assume that the Common Stock of the company is now selling on the market for $12 per share. What would be the entry on the company books to record this conversion?

SOLUTION:

1995		$ (in dollars)	
December 1	Bonds Payable	5,000	
	Premium on bonds	475	
	Loss on Conversion of Bonds	525	
	Common Stock		5,000
	Paid-In Capital in Excess of Par		1,000

One bond is being returned to the company, the face value of which is $5,000, so the Bonds Payable account is debited for $5,000. The total premium on date of bond issue was $25,000 (given). Since there were 50 bonds sold, the bond premium for each bond is $500 ($25,000 premium divided by 50 bonds sold = $500 premium). On December 1, $1,250 of the premium was amortized ($25,000 divided by 20 half-years = $1,250). This Amortization amounts to $25 Amortization per bond outstanding ($1,250 divided by 50 bonds outstanding = $25). Thus, for the one bondholder converting the one bond, the amount of premium to be written off is $475 ($500 less $25 already amortized = $475).

The Livingston Company mails the previous bondholder 500 shares of Livingston Company Common Stock, the Par Value of which is $10 per share and the Market Value of which has now increased to $12 per share. So the Common Stock account is credited for $5,000 (500 shares × $10 per share = $5,000). However, the Market Value of the stock is now $6,000 (500 shares × $12 per share = $6,000). The difference of $1,000 ($6,000 less $5,000) is credited to the Paid-In Capital in Excess of Par account, which is an Owners' Equity account.

The difference between the debits and credits is $525, which is debited as Loss on Conversion of Bonds, an Expense Account. The reason for the loss was the increase in the value of Livingston Company Common Stock, resulting in the fact that Livingston Company is sending its new stockholder Common Stock worth more than what the bondholder paid originally for the bond.

• PROBLEM 4–5

This is a continuation of Problem 4–4, except that the market price of the stock is unknown because the stock changes hands so seldom in this small, closely-held company. However, the price of the bond on the bond market has risen to $5,550. What would be the entry on the books of the Livingston Company to record the conversion of this bond, using the Market Value Approach?

SOLUTION:

1995		$ (in dollars)	
December 1	Bonds Payable	5,000	
	Premium on Bonds	475	
	Loss on Conversion of Bonds	75	
	Common Stock		5,000
	Paid-In Capital in Excess of Par		550

The corporation is receiving one bond, the face value of which is $5,000, so Bonds Payable is debited for $5,000. Premium on Bonds is credited for $475, as explained in the Solution for Problem 4-4. Common Stock is credited for $5,000, the Par Value of the stock being mailed out to the new stockholder. The market price of the bond being received is now $5,550. Although the market price of the stock being mailed out is unknown, it is assumed that it is the same price as the bond, $5,550; so the Paid-In Capital in Excess of Par account is credited for $550, the difference between the assumed Market Value of the stock and the par value of the stock ($5,550 − $5,000 = $550).

The Loss on Conversion of Bonds of $75 is merely a plug figure, the difference between the debits and credits, and used to make the debits and credits equal. The reason the Livingston Company suffers a loss on this transaction is because of the recent price increase in the value of the bond. (If the price had recently decreased, there would have been a gain shown.)

• PROBLEM 4–6

This is similar to Problem 4–5, except it is the Book Value Approach. The market price of the stock is unknown because the stock changes hands so seldom in this small, closely-held company. However, the price of the bond on the bond market has risen to $5,550. What would be the entry on the books of the Livingston Company to record the conversion of this bond, using the Book Value Approach?

SOLUTION:

1995		$ (in dollars)	
December 1	Bonds Payable	5,000	
	Premium on Bonds	475	
	Common Stock		5,000
	Paid-In Capital in Excess of Par		475

One bond is being received by the corporation from the bondholder who wishes to convert his/her bond into stock. The face value of this bond is $5,000, so the account Bonds Payable is debited. The bond was sold originally at a premium of $500, and one six-month period has elapsed so $25 of the premium has been amortized, bringing the premium to $475. Thus, Premium on Bonds account is debited for the remaining $475 to write this off.

The market price of the Common Stock is unknown but assumed to be the same price as the bond ($5,000), so the Common Stock is credited for the $5,000 and is mailed out to the new stockholder who has just converted. In this Book Value Approach, no gain or loss is recognized, and the account Paid-In Capital in Excess of Par is credited for the amount to make the debits equal the credits—in this case $475.

• PROBLEM 4-7

The Lynch Company has outstanding $400,000 Par Value Convertible Bonds, convertible into 50,000 shares of Lynch Company Common Stock at $5 Par. The bonds pay 12% interest, which seems high to the directors of the company, since Interest Rates have recently dropped. How can the Lynch Company sweeten the pie and induce its bondholders to convert to stock? What entries would be made on corporate books?

SOLUTION:

The Directors decided to pay the bondholders a total of $50,000 cash if they would agree to convert their bonds to stock. Let us say that this induces the bondholders to do so, and they mail in their bonds.

1996			$ (in dollars)
February 1	Bonds Payable	400,000	
	Common Stock		250,000
	Paid-In Capital		150,000
February 1	Debt Conversion Expense	50,000	
	Cash		50,000

Let us say the Lynch Company has received all the bonds, face value of which is $400,000. They then debit Bonds Payable for the $400,000. According to the Bond Indenture, these bonds are convertible into 50,000 shares of Lynch Company $5 Par Common Stock (50,000 shares @ $5 = $250,000). Thus, Common Stock is credited for $250,000, the Total Par Value of the stock being mailed out to the new stockholders who have just converted their bonds. The difference, $150,000, is credited to Paid-In

Capital, and is the difference between the face value of the bonds and the Par Value of the stock.

In order to get the bondholders to convert, the company sweetened the deal by mailing out $50,000 cash; so in a second entry, Debt Conversion Expense is debited for $50,000 and Cash is credited for $50,000. This $50,000 is an expense for the period in which the cash was mailed out.

• PROBLEM 4–8

Solon Corporation's preferred stockholders converted their 5,000 shares of $2 Par Value Preferred Stock, which was originally issued at a $500 premium, into 8,000 shares of Solon Common Stock, Par Value $1 per share. What entry would be made on the Solon Corporation's books?

SOLUTION:

1995		$ (in dollars)	
February 1	Preferred Stock	10,000	
	Premium on Preferred Stock	500	
	Common Stock		8,000
	Paid-In Capital		2,500

Total Par Value of the Preferred Stock converted was $10,000 (5,000 shares @ $2 Par = $10,000). So Preferred Stock was debited for $10,000 to close out this account. Since the stock was originally issued at a $500 premium, the account Premium on Preferred Stock is debited for $500 to close out this account. 8,000 shares of Solon Corporation Common Stock, Par Value of which is $1 per share, are issued, so the Common Stock Account is credited for $8,000. Paid-In Capital is credited for $2,500, which is a plug figure to make the debits and credits in the entry equal. This, of course, is done, because the Par Value of the Common Stock is less than the Par Value of the Preferred Stock.

• PROBLEM 4-9

Let us assume that the Par Value of the Solon Corporation Common Stock is $5 instead of $1. Solon Corporation's Preferred stockholders converted their 5,000 shares of $2 Par Value Preferred Stock, which was originally issued at a $500 premium, into 8,000 shares of Solon Common Stock, Par Value of $5 per share. What entry would be made on the Solon Corporation books?

SOLUTION:

1995		$ (in dollars)	
December 1	Preferred Stock	10,000	
	Premium on Preferred Stock	500	
	Retained Earnings	29,500	
	Common Stock		40,000

Total Par Value of the Preferred Stock converted was $10,000 (5,000 shares @ $2 Par = $10,000). So Preferred Stock was debited for $10,000 to close out this account. Since the stock was originally issued at a $500 premium, the account Premium on Preferred Stock is debited for $500 to close out this account. 8,000 shares of Solon Corporation Common Stock, Par Value of which is $5 per share, are issued, so the Common Stock account is credited for $40,000 (8,000 shares @ $5 = $40,000).

The plug figure to make the entry balance is to debit Retained Earnings for $29,500. The Retained Earnings account is debited or reduced to encourage the Preferred Stockholders to convert to Common Stock, the Par Value of which is greater than the Par Value of the Preferred Stock, in this instance.

Another possible entry would be as follows:

1995		$ (in dollars)	
December 1	Preferred Stock	10,000	
	Premium on Preferred Stock	500	
	Paid-In Capital	29,500	
	Common Stock		40,000

In the above entry, Paid-In Capital is debited for the $29,500, rather than debiting Retained Earnings for the $29,500. Either way is acceptable.

In the latter case, if Paid-In Capital is debited rather than debiting Retained Earnings, a greater balance will be left in the Retained Earnings account to pay out later in dividends, either Cash or Stock Dividends.

• PROBLEM 4–10

> James Brown buys 100 warrants in Lewis Company for $500 cash, or $5 per warrant ($500 divided by 100 warrants = $5 per warrant). How would this be recorded on Brown's books?

SOLUTION:

1996		$ (in dollars)
March 10	Investment in Lewis Company Warrants	500
	Cash	500

Warrants are permits to buy a certain stock at a predetermined price. Warrants are similar to rights but usually of longer duration. Some warrants are perpetual. The debit to the account Investment in Lewis Company Warrants shows that James Brown owns these warrants, and that this is an Asset Account. Cash is credited as it is used to buy these warrants.

• PROBLEM 4–11

> James Brown had purchased 100 warrants in Lewis Company for $500 cash. The fine print in the warrant certificate mentions that each warrant is exchangeable along with $10 cash for one share of Lewis Company Common Stock. This means that Brown could purchase a share of stock for $15 ($10 cash and 1 warrant costing $5 each = $15). The stock has risen to $20 on the market, and Brown decides to exercise all his warrants. What entry would be made by James Brown on his books at this time?

SOLUTION:

1996		$ (in dollars)
April 1	Investment in Lewis Company Common Stock 1,500	
	Cash ($10 x 100 warrants = $1,000)	1,000
	Investment in Lewis Company Warrants	500

Brown sends in his 100 warrants plus $10 for each warrant. The $10 times 100 warrants equals $1,000. Thus, the account Cash is credited for $1,000. The 100 warrants each originally cost Brown $5 each, or a total of $500. Brown credits Investment in Lewis Company Warrants for the $500, thus closing that account. The account Investment in Lewis Company Common Stock is debited for $1,500, the total of the cash plus the value of the warrants.

• PROBLEM 4-12

James Brown had purchased 100 warrants in Lewis Company for $500 cash. Brown's purpose in purchasing the warrants was so he would be able to exchange these in the future for Lewis Company Common Stock along with $10 cash. This means that Brown could purchase a share of stock for $15 ($10 cash and 1 warrant costing $5 each = $15). However, the market price of the stock has dropped below $15, which has discouraged Brown. The warrants on the market have also dropped, from $5 to $4. Brown decides to sell the warrants at $4 and take his loss. What entry will Brown make on his books?

SOLUTION:

1996		$ (in dollars)
April 1	Cash	400
	Loss on Sale of Warrants	100
	Investment in Lewis Company Warrants	500

James Brown sells his 100 warrants for $4 each or a total of $400 (100 warrants @ $4 = $400), so Cash is debited for the $400. The warrants had originally been purchased for $5 each for a total of $500 (100 warrants @ $5 = $500). So the account Investment in Lewis Company Warrants is credited for $500 to close out this account. The difference is debited to the Expense account Loss on Sale of Warrants for $100 ($500 − $400 = $100).

• PROBLEM 4–13

James Brown had purchased 100 warrants in Lewis Company for $500 cash. Brown's purpose in purchasing the warrants was so he would be able to exchange these in the future for Lewis Company Common Stock along with $10 cash with each warrant. This means that Brown could purchase a share of stock for $15 ($10 cash and 1 warrant costing $5 each = $15). However, the market price of the stock had dropped below $15, and this discouraged Brown. Warrants last longer than rights, but many of them eventually expire. Some warrants are perpetual and never expire, so expiration of warrants is rather rare, but it does happen. Let us say that after three years, Brown's 100 warrants expire. What entry will he make on his books?

SOLUTION:

1997		$ (in dollars)
May 1	Loss	500
	Investment in Lewis Company Warrants	500

Brown had a $500 investment in the warrants which had been allowed to expire. This is a complete loss. It is shown by a debit to the Loss account of $500. The account Investment in Lewis Company Warrants is credited for $500 to close out this account. The loss can be deducted from Brown's income for tax purposes.

• PROBLEM 4–14

Henry Jacobs purchased a $1,000 bond issued by the Hassan Corporation. This bond had five detachable warrants attached. These warrants allowed the holder to purchase the Common Stock of the Hassan Corporation at a specified price with a specified time period. The fine print on the warrants mentioned that each warrant could be used to purchase one share of Hassan $5 Par Common Stock for $10 per share. Jacobs purchased the $1,000 bond with the 5 warrants attached for a price of $1,000. What entry should Jacobs make on his books? Warrants sell on the market at $2 each.

SOLUTION:

1999		$ (in dollars)	
January 2	Investment in Warrants (5 x $2 = $10)	10	
	Investment in Hassan Bond	1,000	
	Cash		1,000
	Gain		10

Each warrant sells for $2 on the stock market, and there are 5 warrants attached to the bond. Thus, the Asset Account Investment in Warrants is debited for $10. The bond itself cost $1,000, so the asset account Investment in Hassan Bond was debited for $1,000. Cash sent to the company was $1,000, so Cash was credited for this amount. To make the entry balance, the account Gain was credited for $10.

• PROBLEM 4–15

Henry Jacobs purchased a $1,000 bond issued by the Hassan Corporation. This bond had five detachable warrants attached. These warrants allowed the holder to purchase the Common Stock of the Hassan Corporation at a specified price with a specified time period. The fine print on the warrants mentioned that each warrant could be used to purchase one share of Hassan $5 Par Common Stock for $10 per share. Jacobs decided to exercise these warrants. He tore them off the bond and mailed them in with the proper cash. What entry should Jacobs make on his books at this time?

SOLUTION:

1999		$ (in dollars)	
January 18	Investment in Hassan Common Stock	60	
	Investment in Warrants		10
	Cash ($10 x 5 shares)		50

Jacobs mailed in his 5 warrants, which he had previously listed in his Investment in Warrants account at $10 (5 warrants @ $2 per share market price = $10). In order to cancel this account and get it off the books, he now credits this account for the $10. The fine print on the warrants mentions that if he sends $10 with each warrant, this will purchase a share of Hassan Common Stock. So he sends in $50 cash ($10 x 5 shares = $50). He receives from the Hassan Company 5 shares of their Common Stock, and he debits this for $60 ($10 in warrants plus $50 in cash). He does not use the $5 Par Value in this computation.

• PROBLEM 4–16

What is a Stock Option, and why do corporations issue them?

SOLUTION:

A Stock Option is the right to buy a limited number of shares of stock at a specific price. Corporations usually issue options to their executives so that they can eventually receive additional compensation. This encourages better people to become executives of the company.

• PROBLEM 4–17

How does the Incentive Stock Option Plan differ from the Non-Qualified Stock Option Plan as far as the executives are concerned?

SOLUTION:

In the Incentive Plan, the market price and the option price are equal on the date of the grant. The executive pays no Income Tax on this date. The executive pays tax on the difference between the market price of the stock and the option price of the stock on the date when he or she exercises the option.

In the Non-Qualified Plan, the market price usually exceeds the option price on the date of the grant. The executive pays Income Tax on the date of the grant on the difference between the market price of the stock and the option price of the stock at this time.

• PROBLEM 4–18

How does the Incentive Stock Option Plan differ from the Non-Qualified Stock Option Plan as far as the corporation is concerned?

SOLUTION:

The corporation receives no tax deduction in an Incentive Stock Option Plan. In a Non-Qualified Stock Option Plan, the corporation receives a tax deduction of the difference between the market price of the stock and the option price of the stock on the date that the stock is purchased by the employee.

• PROBLEM 4–19

If the corporation receives no tax deduction in an Incentive Stock Option Plan, why does the corporation give such stock options?

SOLUTION:

The corporations often give Incentive Stock Option Plans to their executives to encourage executives to remain with the company or to recruit extremely talented people to become executives of the company.

• PROBLEM 4-20

Assume that on December 1, 1996, Lassen Corporation grants the company's Chief Executive an option to purchase 1,000 shares of the company's $10 Par Value Common Stock. The options are granted on that date and may be exercised at any time within the next five years according to the fine print in the option certificate. The option price per share is $30, and the market price of the stock at that date is $50 per share. What is the Total Compensation Expense that the corporation can deduct as Salary Expense on its Income Statement because of this option?

SOLUTION:

Market Value of 1,000 shares @ $50 per share =	$50,000
Option price of 1,000 shares @ $30 per share =	$30,000
Total Compensation Expense	$20,000

• PROBLEM 4-21

On December 1, 1996, Lassen Corporation grants the company's Chief Executive an option to purchase 1,000 shares of the company's $10 Par Value Common Stock. The options are granted on that date and may be exercised at any time within the next five years, but documents associated with the option state that the benefit period is 2 years from the starting date, December 1, 1996. What entry does the corporation make on its books as of this date?

SOLUTION:

1996		$ (in dollars)	
December 1	Deferred Compensation	20,000	
	Paid-In Capital—Stock Options		20,000

The account Deferred Compensation is a contra Owners' Equity Account, and Paid-In Capital—Stock Options is an Owners' Equity Account.

• PROBLEM 4–22

Let us say that the Lassen Corporation fiscal year ends on November 30. What entry would be made on November 30, 1997 to amortize the Deferred Compensation account?

SOLUTION:

1997		$ (in dollars)	
November 30	Compensation Expense	10,000	
	Deferred Compensation		10,000

The Deferred Compensation account is to be amortized or written off over the two-year benefit period from the starting date. So after one year, one-half of the Deferred Compensation of $20,000, or $10,000, is written off. The Compensation Expense account is debited for $10,000 and Deferred Compensation is credited for $10,000. This cuts down the balance of the Deferred Compensation account to $10,000 as follows:

Deferred Compensation			
12/1/96	20,000	11/30/97	10,000
Balance	10,000		

• PROBLEM 4–23

On December 1, 1996, the day the stock option was granted, the Lassen contra Owners' Equity Account Deferred Compensation was debited for $20,000. One year later, on November 30, 1997, an Amortization entry credited the Deferred Compensation Account for $10,000. How will this account appear on the Owners' Equity section of the Balance Sheet dated November 30, 1997? Let us assume that $500,000 of Common Stock is outstanding and that the Retained Earnings account has a credit balance of $300,000.

SOLUTION:

Lassen Corporation
Partial Balance Sheet
November 30, 1997

Stockholders' Equity Section:

Common Stock	500,000
Paid-In Capital—Stock Options	20,000
Retained Earnings	300,000
	820,000
Less Deferred Compensation	–10,000
Total Stockholders' Equity	810,000

The Paid-In Capital—Stock Options account is an Owners' Equity Account with a credit balance of $20,000, so this account is added into the Stockholders' Equity Section of the Balance Sheet. On the other hand, the Deferred Compensation Account is a contra Owners' Equity Account and the $10,000 balance at this time is subtracted from the other stockholders' equity accounts in determining Total Stockholders' Equity.

• PROBLEM 4-24

On December 1, 1996, the day the stock option was granted, the Lassen contra Owners' Equity Account Deferred Compensation was debited for $20,000. One year later, on November 30, 1997, an Amortization entry credited the Deferred Compensation account for $10,000. What will be the Amortization entry on November 30, 1998? After this entry, what will be the balance of the Deferred Compensation account?

SOLUTION:

1998		$ (in dollars)	
November 30	Compensation Expense	10,000	
	Deferred Compensation		10,000

After this entry the balance of the Deferred Compensation account will be zero, because the adjusting entries at the end of the two fiscal years have closed out this account.

• PROBLEM 4–25

On December 1, 1996, Lassen Corporation granted the company's Chief Executive an option to purchase 1,000 shares of the company's $10 Par Value Common Stock. The option price per share is $30 and the market price of the stock at that date is $50 per share. The total Compensation Expense was $20,000 ($50,000 – $30,000). On December 1, 1999, the Chief Executive exercised his option. What entry will be made on the books of the corporation at this time?

SOLUTION:

1999		$ (in dollars)	
December 1	Cash	30,000	
	Paid-In Capital—Stock Options	20,000	
	Common Stock		10,000
	Paid-In Capital in Excess of Par		40,000

When the Chief Executive exercised his option on December 1, 1999, he was allowed to buy the stock at the option price of $30 per share. He bought the entire 1,000 shares (1,000 shares @ $30 = $30,000). So the corporation received $30,000 from the Chief Executive and debited Cash $30,000.

On December 1, 1996, the date that the corporation granted the Chief Executive this option, the account Paid-In Capital—Stock Options was credited for $20,000. The debit to this account for $20,000 effectively closes out this account.

The Par Value of the Common Stock is $10 per share. The corporation is sending the Chief Executive 1,000 shares (1,000 shares @ $10 = $10,000). So the Common Stock account is credited for the Total Par Value of the stock issued—in this case, $10,000.

The Paid-In Capital in Excess of Par account is credited for $40,000 to make the debits and credits in the entry equal. There are two reasons this figure is so high: (1) The Chief Executive earned $20,000 by buying the stock so cheaply with the option, and (2) the Par Value of the stock is so much less than the option price of the stock.

• PROBLEM 4-26

The Jordan Company at year's end wishes to compute the Earnings per Share. In order to do this, it needs to know the weighted average number of shares. During the year there were 200,000 shares of Common Stock outstanding. No stock was purchased or sold. There were neither Stock Dividends nor stock splits. The 200,000 shares were outstanding during the entire year. What was the weighted average number of shares outstanding?

SOLUTION:

In this case the weighted average number of shares outstanding is the same as the actual number of shares outstanding (200,000 shares), since the number of shares outstanding did not change during the year.

• PROBLEM 4-27

The Swisher Corporation at year's end wishes to compute the Earnings per Share. In order to do this, it needs to know the weighted average number of shares. On January 1, 100,000 shares of its Common Stock were outstanding. On March 1, the corporation issued 20,000 shares for cash. On June 1, the corporation purchased 28,000 of its outstanding Common Shares which then became Treasury Stock. On October 1 the corporation issued 40,000 more Common Shares for cash. What was the weighted average number of shares outstanding?

SOLUTION:

Share Changes

January 1		No. of shares outstanding	100,000
March 1	Issued 20,000 shares for cash		+ 20,000
		No. of shares outstanding	120,000
June 1	Purchased 28,000 of its own shares to become		
	Treasury Stock		– 28,000
	No. of shares outstanding	92,000	
October 1	Issued 40,000 shares for cash		+ 40,000
	No. of shares outstanding	132,000	

Computation of Weighted Average Number of Shares Outstanding

Dates Outstanding	Number of Shares Outstanding		Fraction of Year		Weighted Shares
Jan. 1–March 1	100,000	x	2/12	=	16,666.67
March 1–June 1	120,000	x	3/12	=	30,000.00
June 1–October 1	92,000	x	4/12	=	30,666.67
October 1–Dec. 31	132,000	x	3/12	=	33,000.00
TOTAL WEIGHTED AVERAGE NUMBER OF SHARES:					110,333.34

• PROBLEM 4–28

The Swisher Corporation earned $500,000 Net Income during this past year. Of this amount, they declared dividends of $300,000. What were their Earnings per Share?

SOLUTION:

$500,000 Net Income divided by $110,333.34 total weighted average number of shares outstanding during the year = $4.53 Earnings per Share.

• PROBLEM 4-29

The Richard Corporation decided to sell Convertible Bonds in order to gain enough money to build a new factory building. A financial advisor told the corporation it would be better to sell Convertible Bonds than Non-Convertible Bonds because this would allow the bonds to be sold at cheaper rates than otherwise. It would give the new bondholders the opportunity to convert their bonds into Common Stock of the Richard Corporation a few at a time if the market price of the stock should rise. It was thought that the conversion provision in the Bond Indenture would entice the investor to buy the bonds issued at lower Interest Rates than would otherwise be obtainable.

Thus, the Richard Corporation issues 100 bonds, face value of which are $1,000 each. These are Convertible Bonds, and in this case they are issued at Par (face value). The fine print on the bond certificate states that each bond can be converted into 10 shares of $100 Par Common Stock of the Richard Corporation at the option of the bondholders. During the present year, the corporation has a weighted average of 10,000 shares of $100 Par Common Stock outstanding (10,000 shares @ $100 = $1,000,000 Par Value) .

During the present year the corporation earned $85,000 Net Income. What are the primary Earnings per Share?

SOLUTION:

$85,000 Net Income divided by 10,000 weighted average shares outstanding = $8.50 Primary Earnings per Share.

• PROBLEM 4-30

The Richard Corporation issues 100 bonds, face value of which are $1,000 each, at face value or Par. The fine print on the bond certificate states that each bond can be converted into 10 shares of $100 Par Common Stock of the Richard Corporation at the option of the bondholders. During the present year, the corporation has a weighted average of 10,000 shares of $100 Par Common Stock outstanding. What are the Fully Dilutive Earnings per Share? Net Income this past year was $85,000.

SOLUTION:

Fully Dilutive Earnings per Share assume that all the bondholders turn in their bonds for Common Stock of the Richard Corporation. All the 100 bonds would be returned to the corporation; and since each bond can be converted into 10 shares of Richard Corporation Common Stock, 1,000 more shares would be mailed out to the former bondholders (100 bonds time 10 shares per bond = 1,000 more shares).

Formerly, there were 10,000 Common Shares outstanding. Now with 1,000 more shares being mailed out, there are 11,000 shares outstanding. Since the Net Income this past year was $85,000, we divide the $85,000 by the fully dilutive 11,000 shares outstanding to get $7.727 Fully Dilutive Earnings per Share. ($85,000 Net Income divided by 11,000 outstanding shares = $7.727 Fully Dilutive Earnings per Share.)

These are called "dilutive" because they cut down the Earnings per Share. In this case if all the Convertible Bondholders turned in their bonds for the stock, the Earnings per Share would drop from $8.50 to $7.727 per share.

• PROBLEM 4–31

The Rawlings Corporation needs $50,000 to buy machinery for its factory. Financial advisors suggest that it sell 5,000 shares of Convertible Preferred Stock at $10 Par (5,000 shares @ $10 = $50,000). This is done when the market price of the Preferred Stock is somewhat higher than the Par Value, so the intake is $52,000 instead of $50,000. What entry will be made on the books of the Rawlings Corporation at this time?

SOLUTION:

1996		$ (in dollars)
March 1	Cash	52,000
	Convertible Preferred Stock (5,000 shares @ $10 par)	50,000
	Paid-In Capital	2,000

The corporation received $52,000 cash, so Cash is debited for that amount. It is giving Convertible Preferred Stock, the Par Value of which is $50,000, so it credits Convertible Preferred Stock for that amount. The difference of $2,000 is credited to Paid-In Capital.

• PROBLEM 4–32

Let us say that the Market Value of the Rawlings Corporation Common Stock rises considerably, making it financially advisable for all holders of Convertible Preferred Stock to turn in their shares for Common Stock of the Rawlings Corporation, and let us assume that all the Convertible Preferred Stockholders do this. (Note: Common Stock has a Par Value of $5 per share.) What entry would be made on the books of the Rawlings Corporation?

SOLUTION:

1997			$ (in dollars)
February 1	Convertible Preferred Stock (5,000 shares @ $10 Par)	50,000	
	Paid-In Capital	2,000	
	Common Stock (10,000 shares @ $5 Par)		50,000
	Additional Paid-In Capital		2,000

The fine print on the Convertible Preferred Stock certificates mentions that upon conversion, each share of $10 Par Preferred Stock can be converted to 2 shares of $5 Par Common Stock.

The corporation receives all 5,000 shares of Convertible Preferred Stock at $10 Par so debits this account for the Total Par Value of $50,000. Since the Paid-In Capital account had a credit balance of $2,000 when the stock was originally sold, this Paid-In Capital account is debited for $2,000 to close it out.

10,000 shares of Common Stock are given out, and each of these shares has a $5 Par Value (10,000 shares @ $5 = $50,000.) So the account Common Stock is credited for $50,000. The account Additional Paid-In Capital is credited for the difference.

• PROBLEM 4-33

In this case, let us say again that the Market Value of the Rawlings Corporation Common Stock rises considerably, making it financially advisable for all holders of Convertible Preferred Stock to turn in their shares for Common Stock of the Rawlings Corporation, and let us assume that all the Convertible Preferred Stockholders do this. Again, the fine print on the Convertible Preferred Stock certificates mentions that upon conversion, each share of $10 Par Preferred Stock can be converted into 2 shares of Common Stock. The only difference is that in this case the Par Value of the Common Stock is $20 rather than $5. What will the entry be on the corporation's books?

SOLUTION:

1997		$ (in dollars)	
February 1	Convertible Preferred Stock		
	(5,000 shares @ $10 Par)	50,000	
	Paid-In Capital	2,000	
	Retained Earnings	148,000	
	Common Stock		
	(10,000 shares @ $20 Par)		200,000

The corporation receives all 5,000 shares of Convertible Preferred Stock at $10 Par so debits this account for the Total Par Value of $50,000. Since the Paid-In Capital account had a credit balance of $2,000 when the stock was originally sold, this Paid-In Capital account is debited for $2,000 to close it out.

According to the fine print in the Preferred Stock certificates, the corporation must give two shares of Common Stock for every share of Preferred Stock converted. So the corporation mails out 10,000 shares of its Common Stock which has a Par Value of $20 per share (10,000 shares @ $20 par = $200,000). So the Common Stock account is credited for $200,000.

The plug figure to make this entry balance is a debit of $148,000, and this is usually debited to Retained Earnings because the corporation has lost out on this conversion deal, having to give Common Stock with a much higher value than the Preferred Stock received. However, this large debit of $148,000 to Retained Earnings could cut down on future dividends, since dividends are debited to the Retained Earnings account. Therefore, another choice would be to debit the Paid-In Capital account as follows:

1997		$ (in dollars)
February 1	Convertible Preferred Stock	50,000
	Paid-In Capital	2,000
	Additional Paid-In Capital	148,000
	Common Stock	200,000

• PROBLEM 4–34

The Tikhon Corporation reported a Net Income of $30,000 at the end of the year. All during the year it had 5,000 shares of 5% Non-Cumulative Convertible Preferred Stock outstanding. This Preferred Stock had a $10 Par Value, and the fine print on the Cumulative Preferred Stock certificates stated that the stockholders at any time could convert each Preferred share into 2 shares of Common Stock of the corporation. The Tikhon Corporation also had outstanding 10,000 shares of $5 Par Common Stock. What are the Primary Earnings per Share and the Fully Dilutive Earnings per Share this year, and how are these computed?

SOLUTION:

Primary Earnings per Share:	$2.75 per share
Fully Dilutive Earnings per Share:	$1.50 per share

Since the number of shares outstanding on both Common and Preferred Stock remained the same during the year (5,000 shares of Preferred Stock outstanding and 10,000 shares of Common Stock outstanding), the weighted average shares outstanding are the same figures.

The formula for computing the Primary Earnings per Share is as follows:

$$\frac{\text{Income} - \text{Dividend Claim of Preferred Stock}}{\text{Weighted Average of Common Shares Outstanding}}$$

The Dividend Claim of Preferred Stock is computed as follows:

| 5,000 | shares of Cumulative Preferred Stock outstanding during the year |
| x $10 | Par Value per share |

| $50,000 | Total Par Value of Preferred Stock |
| x .05 | 5% Preferred Stock |

| $2,500 | annual Preferred dividends |

Using the formula to compute Primary Earnings Per Share:

$$\frac{\$30,000 \text{ Net Income less } \$2,500 \text{ Dividend Claim of Preferred Stock}}{10,000 \text{ shares weighted average of Common Stock outstanding}}$$

or

$$\frac{\$27,500}{10,000} \text{ shares} = \$2.75 \text{ per share Primary Earnings.}$$

Computation of Fully Dilutive Earnings per Share:

Let us now assume that the Market Value of the Common Stock rose considerably, making it profitable to the Preferred Stockholders to convert their Preferred Stock into Common Stock of the Tikhon Corporation. Let us also assume that all the Preferred Stockholders did convert their Preferred Stock into Common Stock. The fine print on the Convertible Preferred Stock certificates mentions that each share of Preferred Stock can be converted into two shares of Common Stock. Since there are 5,000 shares of Preferred Stock outstanding, these will be exchanged for 10,000 extra shares of Common Stock. Since there were already 10,000 shares of Common Stock outstanding, the 10,000 extra shares of Common Stock would make a total of 20,000 shares of Common Stock outstanding after all the Preferred Stock was exchanged.

| 10,000 | shares of Common Stock originally outstanding |
| + 10,000 | shares of new Common Stock after the exchange |

| 20,000 | shares of Common Stock in total outstanding after the exchange |

The formula for determining Earnings per Share when there is no Preferred Stock outstanding is:

$$\frac{\text{Net Income of the Corporation}}{\text{Weighted average number of Common Shares outstanding}}$$

$$\frac{\$30,000}{20,000} \text{ shares} = \$1.50 \text{ Earnings per Share Fully Dilutive}$$

CHAPTER 5

INVESTMENTS IN STOCKS AND BONDS

> **Basic Attacks and Strategies for Solving Problems in this Chapter. See pages 80 to 142 for step-by-step solutions to problems.**

Both corporations and individuals with extra money should make this money work for them. One way to do this is to invest in stocks and bonds of other corporations.

Marketable Equity Securities are stocks we own in other corporations; **Marketable Debt Securities** are bonds we own in other corporations; these are current assets if we expect to sell within a year. If the holder plans to keep the stock in his/her possession for a year or more, it is termed **Investment in Stock** or **Investment in Bonds** and is listed in the Investment section of the Balance Sheet.

Many **Bond Indentures** (agreements) provide for the accumulation of Sinking Funds from corporate payments into this fund. Sinking Funds are a build-up of cash during bonds' lifetimes to be used to pay off the bonds at maturity. Bond Indentures requiring Sinking Funds are safer from an investor's point of view and thus can be sold at lower Interest Rates than those without Sinking Funds. Often the bank which administers the bonds for the corporation has a Trust Department, which invests the Sinking Fund Cash in stocks and bonds of other corporations.

At the bonds' maturity date, entries are made on the books of the borrowing corporation to cancel the Sinking Fund, to call in the bonds, and to repay the bondholders of the corporation.

Step-by-Step Solutions to Problems in this Chapter, "Investments in Stocks and Bonds"

• PROBLEM 5–1

What is a Marketable Equity Security?

SOLUTION:

A Marketable Equity Security is a current asset which is easily salable and which the owner expects to hold for a year or less.

• PROBLEM 5–2

Harry Smith bought 100 shares of General Motors stock @ $51 per share plus $80 brokerage fee. What entry would Harry Smith make on his books?

SOLUTION:

1996		$ (in dollars)	
June 1	Marketable Equity Securities	5,180	
	Cash		5,180

Marketable Equity Securities is a current Asset Account. It shows that the owner has purchased stock in a corporation, and that this stock is readily salable. The stock does not necessarily have to be listed on a stock exchange, but if it is sold "over the counter" instead of through a stock exchange, brokers have to be acquainted with it well enough so they can find a current price for it.

The brokerage fee of $80 is added to the cost price of the stock when recording this on the books of the corporation, because the government does not allow taxpayers to debit the broker's fee as an expense. The government does allow the $80 broker's fee to be added to the cost of the investment.

• PROBLEM 5-3

On December 31, the market price for General Motors stock is $55. Harry Smith keeps his investments at Lower of Cost or Market. What adjusting entry should Smith make at this time? Smith bought his stock at $51. He bought 100 shares.

SOLUTION:

No entry.

On December 31, the market price of the stock is $5,500 ($55 × 100 shares = $5,500). The cost price is $5,180 ($51 × 100 shares = $5,100 plus $80 broker's fee = $5,180). Since the cost of $5,100 is lower than the market price of $5,500, and since the Marketable Equity Securities account lists the asset at $5,180, we just leave that entry and make no book entry at year's end.

• PROBLEM 5-4

On December 31, the market price for General Motors stock is $30. Smith originally bought 100 shares at $51 plus $80 broker's fee. What entry should Smith make at year's end?

SOLUTION:

1996		$ (in dollars)
December 31 Unrealized Loss on Valuation of Marketable Equity Security	2,180	
Allowance for Excess of Cost of Marketable Equity Securities over Market Value		2,180

Unrealized Loss on Valuation of Marketable Equity Security is an Expense Account and will be one of the expenses in Smith's Income Statement at year's end. However, this expense is not allowed for Income Tax purposes, because it is merely a "paper loss" and not an actual loss. Only actual losses at the time of sale are allowed for Income Tax purposes.

Allowance for Excess of Cost of Marketable Equity Securities over

Market Value is a valuation account or "contra asset" account and will be found in the Balance Sheet of Smith as a subtraction from the Marketable Equity Securities account in the Current Asset section, as follows:

Harry Smith
Balance Sheet
December 31, 1996

ASSETS

Current Assets:

Cash		50,000
Marketable Equity Securities	5,180	
Less: Allowance for Excess of Cost of Marketable Equity Securities over Market Value	2,180	
		3,000 (market)

• PROBLEM 5-5

On June 1, 1996, Harry Smith bought 100 shares of General Motors stock @ $51 per share plus $80 brokerage fee. On December 31, 1996, the stock had fallen to $30 per share and an adjusting entry was made (see solution to Problem 5–4). By December 31, 1997, the stock was selling for $35 per share. Give the adjusting entry, if any, that is needed at this time.

SOLUTION:

1997		$ (in dollars)
December 31 Allowance for Excess of Cost of Marketable Equity Securities over Market Value	500	
Recovery of Unrealized Loss on Valuation of Marketable Equity Securities		500

The Balance Sheet at December 31, 1996, showed the Asset Account Marketable Equity Securities at the market price of $3,000 (100 shares @ $30 = $3,000). Since, during the year 1997, the stock has risen to $3,500 (100 shares @ $35 = $3,500), there was a "paper gain" of $500 ($3,500 – $3,000 = $500). Thus, the Allowance for Excess of Cost of Marketable

Equity Securities over Market Value account is debited for $500, bringing its balance to $1,680, as follows:

Allowance for Excess of Cost of Marketable
Equity Securities over Market Value

500	2,180
	1,680

The account Recovery of Unrealized Loss on Valuation of Marketable Equity Securities is a Revenue account, and it is credited for $500 increase in value during the year, 1997. Since the stock was not sold during the year 1997, this $500 gain is only a "paper gain" and not to be reported for Income Tax purposes.

The Recovery of Unrealized Loss on Valuation of Marketable Equity Securities account will appear as follows:

Recovery of Unrealized Loss on Valuation
of Marketable Equity Securities

	500

• PROBLEM 5–6

On June 1, 1996, Harry Smith bought 100 shares of General Motors stock @ $51 per share plus $80 brokerage fee. On December 31, 1996, the stock had fallen to $30 per share and an adjusting entry was made (see solution to Problem 5–4). By December 31, 1997, the stock had risen to $35 per share (see solution to Problem 5–5). Another adjusting entry was made.

During 1998 the stock rose more, until by December 31, 1998 the stock was selling on the market for $60 per share. Since Smith had 100 shares of this stock, it was now worth $6,000 (100 shares @ $60 = $6,000). This was a paper gain of $2,500 during the year ($6,000 – $3,500 = $2,500). What adjusting entry is made on the books of Harry Smith at the end of 1998 if he continues to keep books on the Lower of Cost or Market method?

SOLUTION:

1998	$ (in dollars)	
December 31 Allowance for Excess of Cost of Marketable Equity Securities over Market Value	1,680	
Recovery of Unrealized Loss on Valuation of Marketable Equity Securities		1,680

Since in 1998 the Market Value of the stock rises higher than the original purchase price, the Allowance for Excess of Cost of Marketable Equity Securities over Market Value account is closed out by debiting it for $1,680. The previous balance was a credit of $1,680, so the debit for the like amount closes out this account.

The account Recovery of Unrealized Loss on Valuation of Marketable Equity Securities had a previous credit balance of $500. This credit of $1,680 brings the balance up to $2,180 ($500 + $1,680 = $2,180). So the debit balance of $2,180 in the account Unrealized Loss on Valuation of Marketable Equity Security is cancelled by the credit balance of $2,180 in the account Recovery of Unrealized Loss on Valuation of Marketable Equity Securities.

Since the books are being kept at Lower of Cost or Market, the increase in value of the stock above the original purchase price is not recorded in the adjusting entries.

These are Unrealized Gains, since the stock has not been sold, and therefore they are not reportable as Income for Income Tax purposes.

• PROBLEM 5-7

On June 1, 1996, Harry Smith bought 100 shares of General Motors stock @ $51 per share plus $80 brokerage fee. At this time, the current Asset Account Marketable Equity Securities was debited for $5,180, the total of the $5,100 purchase price of the stock and the $80 brokerage fee.

On June 1, 1999, the market price of the stock rises to $65 per share, and Harry Smith sells his entire 100 shares at that price (100 shares @ $65 = $6,500). The brokerage fee of $90 is subtracted from the sales price, and the remainder, $6,410, is remitted by the broker to Harry Smith. What entry does Harry Smith make on his books at this time?

SOLUTION:

1999		$ (in dollars)	
June 1	Cash	6,410	
	Marketable Equity Securities		5,180
	Gain on Sale of Marketable Equity Securities		1,230

Harry Smith received a check from his broker for $6,410, which is the difference between the selling price of the stock, $6,500, and the broker's fee, $90 ($6,500 – $90 = $6,410). So, on his books he debits Cash for that amount—$6,410. His current Asset Account Marketable Equity Securities has a debit balance of $5,180, so Smith credits Marketable Equity Securities for $5,180 to close out that account. The difference between these two figures, $1,230, is credited to a Revenue account entitled Gain on Sale of Marketable Equity Securities. To Smith, this is Income from an actual sale, so it is reportable as Income for Income Tax purposes. It is called a Realized Gain.

• PROBLEM 5–8

Let us assume that during 1999, instead of increasing in price, the General Motors stock drops to $49 per share. This scares Harry Smith into thinking the stock may drop further, so he hurriedly sells all 100 shares of his stock before the loss gets worse. The stock sells for $4,900 (100 shares × $49 = $4,900). From this, the broker subtracts his $90 fee, leaving a balance of $4,810 which the broker remits to Smith in the form of a check. What is Smith's entry on his books on the date of sale, June 1, 1999?

SOLUTION:

1999		$ (in dollars)	
June 1	Cash	4,810	
	Loss on Sale of Marketable Equity Securities	370	
	Marketable Equity Securities		5,180

Harry Smith received cash of $4,810 after the broker sold his stock and deducted the brokerage fee, so Smith debits Cash on his books for this amount—$4,810. His current Asset Account Marketable Equity Securities has a debit balance of $5,180, so Smith credits Marketable Equity Securities for $5,180 to close out this account. The difference between these two figures, $370 ($5,180 − $4,810 = $370), is debited to an account entitled Loss on Sale of Marketable Equity Securities. To Smith, this is loss on an actual sale, so it is reportable as an Expense for Income Tax purposes. It is called a Realized Loss.

• PROBLEM 5–9

Harry Smith has sold his General Motors stock and wishes to invest this money in a safe place that will bring him decent returns. He turns to the Corporate Bond Market. His broker suggests Ford Motor Company bonds that pay 9% and are selling at a small discount. On July 1, 1999, the date of purchase, the bonds are quoted on the market at 98% ($5,000 × .98 = $4,900). This means that a $5,000 bond can now be purchased for only $4,900. However, the broker's commission of $80 is added to this, making a total payment of $4,980. What entry does Harry Smith make on his books on the date he purchases this $5,000 bond?

SOLUTION:

1999		$ (in dollars)	
July 1	Marketable Debt Securities	4,980	
	Cash		4,980

The current Asset Account Marketable Debt Securities is debited for $4,980, the amount Smith remits to his broker. This is considered the purchase price of the bond. The Financial Accounting Standards Board recommends that bonds be kept at cost, and this is being done here. Some purchasers of bonds keep their records at Lower of Cost or Market. In this case the entry would be the same, since at this time the cost price is the same as the market price.

• PROBLEM 5–10

Let us say that Interest payment dates on the bond that Harry Smith has purchased are July 1 and January 1. Smith purchased the bond on an Interest payment date. Six months later, on January 1, 2000, Smith receives a check for $225 to cover the Interest for a half a year ($5,000 × 9% × 1/2 year = $225). What entry does Smith make on his books on January 1, 2000?

SOLUTION:

2000		$ (in dollars)
January 1	Cash	225
	Bond Interest Revenue	225

Smith debits Cash for $225 because he receives a check for that amount. He credits the Revenue account entitled Bond Interest Revenue for $225 because he has been giving the Ford Motor Company the use of his money. This Revenue must be reported as Income for Income Tax purposes.

• PROBLEM 5–11

Let us say that the $5,000 bond that Harry Smith purchased was a 10-year bond with a maturity date of July 1, 2009. Smith bought the bond for only $4,900, so he bought it at a $100 discount ($5,000 – $4,900 = $100). This discount should be amortized (written off) over the life of the bond. Since it is a 10-year bond, it will be amortized over a period of 20 half-years (10 years times 2 half-years per year = 20 half-years). The Amortization period is 20 half-years because the Amortization entry is usually made at the same time as the Interest entry, and the Interest is received every half-year. What entry will be made on January 1, 2000, to amortize the discount at the end of the first half-year of the life of the bond?

SOLUTION:

2000		$ (in dollars)
January 1	Marketable Debt Securities	5
	Bond Interest Expense	5

The current Asset Account Marketable Debt Securities is debited for $5 ($100 discount divided by 20 half-years = $5). This will be done every half-year for 20 half-years, thus bringing the Marketable Debt Securities account up to $5,000 from $4,900 by the maturity date of July 1, 2009. The $80 additional brokerage fee will still be part of this account.

Bond Interest Expense is credited for $5 because the process of accruing discount deducts from this Expense account. As a rule, both Amortization of premium and Amortization of discount are carried on through the Bond Interest Expense account.

• PROBLEM 5-12

How will the Marketable Debt Securities current Asset Account appear on the books of Harry Smith after the first Amortization entry on January 1, 2000?

SOLUTION:

Marketable Debt Securities

4,980	
5	
4,985	

On July 1, 1999, the Marketable Debt Securities current Asset Account was debited for $4,980, which includes the $4,900 paid for the bond plus the $80 brokerage fee. On January 1, 1990, after Harry Smith had held the bond for 6 months, the Amortization entry debited the account for another $5, bringing it up to a balance of $4,985.

• PROBLEM 5-13

Let us say that on January 2, 2000, the first business day of the new year and of the new century, Harry Smith decides to sell the bond. At that time the market price of the bond had risen to $5,100, and the broker's fee was another $80. What entry will Harry Smith make on his books to record the sale of the bond on January 2?

SOLUTION:

2000		$ (in dollars)
January 2	Cash	5,020
	Marketable Debt Securities	4,985
	Gain on Sale of Bond	35

The bond was sold for $5,100, but the broker deducted his brokerage fee of $80, remitting the remainder of $5,020 to Harry Smith. So Harry Smith debits Cash for the $5,020. At that time on Harry Smith's books, the Marketable Debt Securities account has a debit balance of $4,985. Since Smith is mailing in his bond to his broker and giving up the legal possession of this bond, he credits Marketable Debt Securities for this amount, $4,985, to close out the account.

Smith also credits the Revenue account Gain on Sale of Bond for $35 to balance the books ($5,020 − $4,985 = $35). This Gain account is a Revenue and must be reported as Income for Income Tax purposes.

• PROBLEM 5-14

Let us say that by January 2, 2000, the first business day of the new year and of the new century, Harry Smith decides to sell the bond. However, in this case, let us say that the market price of the bond had dropped to $4,800, and still the broker's fee was another $80. What entry will Harry Smith make on his books to record the sale of the bond on January 2?

SOLUTION:

2000		$ (in dollars)
January 2	Cash	4,720
	Loss on Sale of Bond	265
	Marketable Debt Securities	4,985

The bond was sold for $4,800, but the broker deducted his brokerage fee of $80, remitting the remainder of $4,720 to Harry Smith. So Harry Smith debits cash for $4,720. At that time on Harry Smith's books, the

Marketable Debt Securities account has a debit balance of $4,985. Since Smith is mailing in his bond to his broker and giving up the legal possession of this bond, he credits Marketable Debt Securities for this amount, $4,985, to close out the account.

Smith also debits an Expense account, Loss on Sale of Bond, for $265, the difference between the $4,985 and the $4,720 ($4,985 − $4,720 = $265). This Loss account is an Expense and can be deducted from Income for Income Tax purposes.

• PROBLEM 5-15

Harry Smith decides on a long-term investment and buys a $1,000 American Telephone and Telegraph bond and another $1,000 Ameritech bond. This is done on June 1, 2001, at which time the American Telephone and Telegraph bond is selling at Par, or $1,000, and the Ameritech bond is selling at a $200 premium, or $1,200. What entry will he make on his books? Let us say the broker charges $150 for the purchase of these two bonds.

SOLUTION:

2001		$ (in dollars)	
June 1	Investment in Bonds	2,350	
	Cash		2,350

Since Harry Smith decides this is a long-term investment and that he will hold the bonds for a longer period than a year, he debits the long-term Asset Account Investment in Bonds. This is recorded under Investments under Assets in the Balance Sheet and not as a Current Asset.

The $2,350 debit to Investment in Bonds account is computed as follows: $1,000 paid for the American Telephone and Telegraph bond, $1,200 paid for the Ameritech bond, and $150 brokerage fee ($1,000 + $1,200 + $150 = $2,350). The broker has added his commission to the purchase price of the two bonds, and this commission cannot legally be deducted as an Expense but must be added to the cost of the bond.

• PROBLEM 5–16

The fine print on the Bond Indenture states that both bonds pay Interest on July 1 and January 1, and that both are 20-year bonds. How much interest will these bonds pay 1/2 year later, on January 1, 2002, if the American Telephone and Telegraph bond has an Interest Rate of 12% and the Ameritech bond has an interest rate (coupon rate) of 10%?

SOLUTION:

$60 semi-annual interest on the 12% American Telephone and Telegraph bond

$50 semi-annual interest on the 10% Ameritech bond

The face value of the American Telephone and Telegraph bond is $1,000 and it pays 12% per year or 6% per half-year (1/2 of 12% = 6%). The $60 semi-annual interest is figured as follows: $1,000 × 12% × 1/2 = $60.

Even though the Ameritech was purchased for $1,200, the face value of the bond is only $1,000, and the interest is figured on the face value of the bond. The $50 semi-annual interest on the Ameritech bond is figured as follows: $1,000 × 10% × 1/2 = $50.

• PROBLEM 5–17

What entry will be made on Harry Smith's books on January 1, 2002, the date he receives his first interest payment on the American Telephone and Telegraph bond?

SOLUTION:

2002		$ (in dollars)	
January 1	Cash	60	
	Bond Interest Revenue		60

• PROBLEM 5-18

What entry will be made on Harry Smith's books on January 1, 2002, the date he receives his first Interest Payment on the Ameritech bond?

SOLUTION:

2002		$ (in dollars)
January 1	Cash	50
	Bond Interest Revenue	50

The Bond Interest Revenue account is a Gain and reportable as Income for Income Tax purposes.

• PROBLEM 5-19

On March 1, 2002, Harry Smith buys a $1,000 Smith-Corona bond at par (for $1,000). This bond pays 10% interest annually and the Interest Payment dates are January 1 and July 1. What entry will Harry Smith make on his books on March 1, 2002?

SOLUTION:

2002		$ (in dollars)
March 1	Marketable Debt Securities	1,000.00
	Bond Interest Receivable	16.66
	Cash	1,016.66

In this case, let us assume that it is a new bond issue and therefore there is no broker's fee. Marketable Debt Securities, a Current Asset Account, is debited if Harry Smith plans to hold the bond for less than a year.

Since the Smith-Corona bond is being purchased at par ($1,000), the account Marketable Debt Securities is debited for that amount. However, the bond is being purchased two months after the last Interest Payment date. (The last interest payment date was January 1, 2002, and the bond is being purchased on March 1, 2002.) Thus, Harry Smith, the purchaser, is being charged for two months' accrued (built up) interest for the months of January and February, 2002. This interest, which amounts to $16.66, must be paid to the seller of the bond, in addition to the $1,000 Par Value. Therefore, Harry Smith writes a check for the entire $1,016.66 and credits Cash on his books for this amount. The difference of $16.66 is debited to a Current Asset Account entitled Bond Interest Receivable. ($1,000 × 10% = $100 yearly interest. $100 divided by 2/12 or two months = $16.66, which is interest for 60 days.)

• PROBLEM 5–20

On March 1, 2002, Harry Smith buys a $1,000 Smith-Corona bond at Par (for $1,000). This bond pays 10% interest annually and the Interest Payment dates are January 1 and July 1. Four months after purchasing the bond is July 1, the Interest Payment date mentioned in the fine print on the face of the bond. What entry will Harry Smith make on his books when he receives the interest check?

SOLUTION:

2002		$ (in dollars)	
July 1	Cash	50.00	
	Bond Interest Receivable		16.66
	Bond Interest Revenue		33.34

Every January 1 and July 1, for the lifetime of the bond, the holder of one $1,000 bond paying interest at 10% will receive $50 as follows: $1,000 × 10% × 1/2 = $50. Since Harry Smith receives a check for $50, he debits Cash for $50. When he previously purchased the bond on March 1 four months ago, he debited a Current Asset Account entitled Bond Interest Receivable for $16.66 for the accrued interest for the months of January and February, 2002. In order to close this account out, on July 1 he credits the Bond Interest Receivable account for $16.66 He also credits Bond Interest Revenue for $33.34, which is interest for the four months of March, April, May, and June of the year 2002. This $33.34 is Taxable Revenue to Harry Smith.

• PROBLEM 5-21

On November 1, 2005, Harry Smith decides to sell the $1,000 Smith-Corona bond, and can sell it at Par for $1,000. The brokerage fee is $50. What entry does Harry make on the date of sale?

SOLUTION:

2005		$ (in dollars)	
November 1	Cash	950.00	
	Loss on Sale of Bond	83.32	
	Bond Interest Revenue		33.32
	Marketable Debt Securities		1,000.00

Since the bond is being sold at Par, $1,000 is paid to Smith's broker, who takes his $50 brokerage fee and remits the remaining $950 to Harry Smith. Thus, Smith debits the Cash account for the $950.00. The last Interest Payment date on the bond was July 1, 2005, so between that date and the date of sale, November 1, 2005, the four months of July, August, September, and October have elapsed. The interest on the bond is $100 per year ($1,000 × 10% = $100). The interest per month is $8.33 ($100 divided by 12 months = $8.33). Since interest has accrued for four months since the last interest payment date, four months' interest is $33.32 ($8.33 × 4 = $33.32). So Harry Smith credits the account Bond Interest Revenue for $33.32.

When Smith originally bought the bond on March 1, 2002, he debited Marketable Debt Securities for $1,000. Now that he is selling the bond, he must get rid of this account: so he credits Marketable Debt Securities for $1,000. The plug figure to make the debits equal the credits in this entry is to debit the Expense account Loss on Sale of Bond for $83.32. The reasons for the loss were, first, because of the broker's fee of $50 and second because of the Bond Interest Revenue. If we subtract the Bond Interest Revenue of $33.32 from the Loss on Sale of Bond of $83.32, we get the $50 broker's fee ($83.32 − $33.32 = $50). In this case, then, the $50 broker's fee can be deducted from Income for Income Tax purposes, as a Business Expense.

• PROBLEM 5-22

On August 1, 1998, Mary Henshaw purchases a $1,000 American Telephone and Telegraph Corporation bond for $1,200, since the bond is selling at a $200 premium. The reason for this is not only because American Telephone and Telegraph is a safe investment, but also that the bond is paying 16% interest, which is higher than what most other bonds happen to be paying at this time. The fine print on the Bond Indenture mentions that Interest Payment dates are March 1 and September 1. What entry will Mary Henshaw make on her books when she purchases this bond? Let us say that Mary's future plans at this time are to hold the bond for more than a year. Let us also assume that this is a new bond issue and there are no brokerage fees at this time.

SOLUTION:

1998		$ (in dollars)
August 1	Investment in American Telephone and Telegraph 16% Bonds	1,200.00
	Bond Interest Receivable	66.67
	Cash	1,266.67

Since Mary Henshaw plans to hold the bonds for more than a year, she debits the long-term Asset Account Investment in American Telephone and Telegraph 16% Bonds. She debits this account for $1,200, which is the total of the $1,000 face value of the bond and the $200 premium.

The last Interest Payment date was March 1, 1998, and she purchases the bond on August 1, 1998, five months later. Therefore, she debits the Current Asset Account Bond Interest Receivable for $66.67, five months' accrued interest ($1,000 × 16% × 5/12 = $66.67). This is a Current Asset Account, because on the next Interest Payment date, in this case, September 1, 1998, after holding the bond only one month, she will be paid six months' interest. She credits Cash for $1,266.67 which includes the $1,000 face value of the bond plus $200 premium, plus $66.67 accrued interest.

• PROBLEM 5-23

On September 1, 1998, Mary Henshaw receives a check for 6 months' interest on the American Telephone and Telegraph Corporation bond, which she bought on August 1, 1998 for $1,000 at $200 premium. This bond pays 16% interest on March 1 and September 1 for each year and runs until March 1, 2008, the maturity date. What entry does she make on her books on September 1, 1998?

SOLUTION:

1998		$ (in dollars)	
September 1	Cash	80.00	
	Bond Interest Receivable		66.67
	Bond Interest Revenue		13.33

Because the Bond Indenture mentions that the holders of the bond on March 1 and September 1 of each year receive six months' interest, Mary Henshaw receives a check for 6 months' interest even though she has held the check only one month. So she debits Cash for $80 ($1,000 × 16% × 1/2 = $80).

On August 1, 1998, when she bought the bond, she debited the Current Asset Account Bond Interest Receivable for $66.67, which represented five months' accrued interest. Now she must cancel out this account, so she credits Bond Interest Receivable for that amount. She also credits Bond Interest Revenue for $13.33, the interest she has earned for the month of August 1998. This $13.33 is Taxable Interest Income.

• PROBLEM 5-24

On August 1, 1998, Mary Henshaw bought a $1,000 AT&T 16% bond at a $200 premium. She has decided to amortize this premium over the life of the bond and to make this Amortization entry each December 31, the last day of her calendar year. What entry will Mary Henshaw make on December 31, 1998?

SOLUTION:

1998	$ (in dollars)
December 31 Bond Interest Expense	8.70
Investment in AT&T 16% Bonds	8.70

This is a 10-year bond, and 10 years is 120 months (10 × 12 months in a year = 120 months). The bond was originally ready to sell on March 1, 1998, but Mary Henshaw didn't buy the bond until 5 months later, on August 1, 1998. Therefore, her bond runs only 115 months (120 months – 5 months = 115 months). The premium was $200 so this is divided by 115 months running to discover the monthly Amortization ($200 premium divided by 115 months running = $1.74 monthly Amortization). Since the bond was purchased on August 1, 1998 and it is now December 31, 1998, five months have elapsed since the bond was purchased. The Amortization for 5 months is therefore $8.70 ($1.74 monthly Amortization times 5 months = $8.70).

• PROBLEM 5-25

On March 1, 1999, Mary Henshaw receives an Interest Income check from AT&T Corporation. She had purchased this $1,000 bond for $1,200, since the bond was selling at a $200 premium. It pays 16% interest. The fine print on the Bond Indenture mentions that Interest Payment dates are March 1 and September 1. What entry will Mary Henshaw make on her books to record this interest?

SOLUTION:

1999	$ (in dollars)
March 1 Cash	80
Bond Interest Revenue	80

Mary Henshaw receives a check for $80 interest on her $1,000 bond at 16, ($1,000 × 16% × 1/2 = $80). She debits Cash for $80. She credits Bond Interest Revenue for $80 since she is giving the AT&T Corporation the use of her money. This is fully Taxable Interest Income.

• PROBLEM 5–26

On December 31, 1999, Mary Henshaw sells her $1,000 AT&T 16% bond for $1,300, which includes the $1,000 face value plus $300 premium on that date. She had originally purchased this bond on August 1, 1998 for $1,200, which included the $1,000 face value of the bond plus $200 premium. It is a 10-year bond with a maturity date of March 1, 2008. What entry will she make on her books when she sells this bond? (The broker charged a $50 brokerage fee also.)

SOLUTION:

It will take two entries: The first is an Amortization entry to bring the Amortization up to date, as follows:

1999	$ (in dollars)	
December 31 Bond Interest Expense	20.88	
Investment in AT&T 16% bonds		20.88

Mary Henshaw had chosen to amortize the bond premium on December 31 of each year. Her last Amortization entry was on December 31, 1998, so this Amortization will be for the entire year of 1999. The bond was purchased originally for a $200 premium to be written off over 115 months ($200 divided by 115 months = $1.74 per month). This Amortization entry is for all 12 months of 1999. So we multiply the monthly Amortization amount of $1.74 by 12 months to get the whole year's Amortization figure of $20.88 ($1.74 × 12 = $20.88).

Bond Interest Expense is debited, because Amortization is written off through that account. Investment in AT&T 16% bonds is credited to help eventually bring this account down by maturity date to the face value of the bond: $1,000.

Let us now take a look at the Investment in AT&T 16% Bonds account:

Investment in AT&T 16% Bonds

1,200.00	8.70
	20.88
	29.58
1,170.42	

As can be seen, the value of the Investment in AT&T 16% Bonds account has dropped from $1,200 to $1,170.42 during the period in which Mary Henshaw owned the bond.

The next step is to record Mary Henshaw's sale of the bond:

1999		$ (in dollars)
December 31 Cash	1,250.00	
Investment in AT&T 16% Bonds		1,170.42
Gain on Sale of Bonds		79.58

Cash was debited for $1,250, which was the $1,300 price for the sale of the bond, after subtracting the broker's $50 fee ($1,300 – $50 = $1,250). The account Investment in AT&T 16% Bonds was credited for $1,170.42 to close that long-term Asset Account. The difference of $79.58 was credited to a Revenue Account entitled Gain on Sale of Bonds. This gain is fully taxable for Income Tax purposes, due to the rise in the price of the bonds during the period in which Mary Henshaw held her bond.

• PROBLEM 5–27

Stanford Corporation has been doing well. Its sales and profits have increased over the last few years. As a result, its average price for its stock has gone up from $10 per share a few years ago to $150 per share today. However, the board of directors is concerned that there is not as much trading in the stock today as there was a few years ago. They have hired consultants to come up with answers. These consultants have determined, or at least surmised, that the reason for the decrease in the number of shares traded each day is because the stock is too high. In fact, they deem that $150 per share is too steep for the average investor.

The consultants suggest that the board authorize a stock split. Many stock splits are 2-for-1. However, a split can be in any factional amount that the board decides upon. After much discussion, the board votes on a 3-for-1 split. The corporation has 1,000,000 shares authorized by the charter, and there are at present 200,000 shares of common stock outstanding. What entry would the board of directors of the Stanford Corporation make on their books on the day they vote the 3-for-1 stock split? At present the Par Value of the stock is $60 per share.

SOLUTION:

1999		
March 1	(Three-for-one stock split in the Common Stock of Stanford Corporation.	

Prior to stock split:		
	200,000 shares outstanding @ $60 Par	$12,000,000

After stock split:		
	600,000 shares outstanding @ $20 Par	$12,000,000)

Note that there is no real general journal entry that would have to be posted to the ledger. It is merely a notation in parentheses. In reality, the present stockholders keep the stock they have and the company merely mails them more shares. In other words, the stockholders keep the 200,000 shares already outstanding, and the corporation mails them 400,000 more shares. Each stockholder's proportional share of the company remains the same as it was prior to the stock split. Because of the stock split, the number of shares outstanding is 3 times what it was before—600,000 shares outstanding instead of 200,000 shares. Also, the Par Value of the stock per share has dropped by 2/3. It is now only $20 per share instead of $60 per share. But the Total Par Value of all the shares, $12,000,000, remains the same.

• PROBLEM 5–28

Helen Tabor has some extra money which she doesn't immediately need. It was given to her by a wealthy uncle. After discussing her financial plans with her broker, she decides to buy 150 shares of Ameritech Stock which is at present selling at $45 per share. The brokerage fees are $80. What entry will she make on her books?

SOLUTION:

1999		$ (in dollars)
April 1	Investment in Ameritech Stock	6,830
	Cash	6,830

The $6,830 cost of buying stock is computed as follows: Tabor purchased 150 shares at $45 per share (150 × $45 = $6,750). To this must be added the broker's fee of $80 ($6,750 + $80 = $6,830). Therefore, on her books Helen Tabor debits her long-term Asset Account Investment in Ameritech Stock. She mails a check to her broker for $6,830 and credits the Cash account for that amount.

• PROBLEM 5-29

Several weeks after the purchase of the stock (150 shares @ $45), Helen Tabor receives the stock certificate from the corporation via her broker. She places this certificate in her safety deposit box, noting that the Par Value per share printed on the face of the certificate is $10 per share.

On June 1, Helen Tabor receives a letter from the Ameritech Corporation that the Board of Directors has declared a 5-for-1 stock split. It mentions that she does not need to send in any of her stock, but that within the next few weeks she will receive more shares of stock from the corporation. On July 1, Helen Tabor receives a certificate on which it states "600 shares." She places this certificate in her safety deposit box. What entry should Helen Tabor make on her books?

SOLUTION:

1999

July 1	(Ameritech stock split of 5-for-1.	
Prior to stock split:		
	Owned 150 shares @ $10 Par	$1,500
After stock split:		
	Owned 750 shares @ $ 2 Par	$1,500)

Note that Helen Tabor needs to make no real general journal entry because nothing needs to be posted to a ledger account. She makes only a memorandum entry on her books, and this is in parentheses. It will also be noted that she puts the stock down at Par Value rather than at Market Value.

She notes correctly that she had 150 shares of Ameritech stock at $10 Par prior to the stock split. After the stock split, since it was a 5-to-1 split, she now has five times as much stock, or 750 shares. However, on a 5-to-1 split, the Par Value after the split is only 1/5 as much as it was before the split, so the Par Value has now dropped to $2 per share. Notice that the Total Par Value of all the stock she owns ($1,500) is the same as the Total Par Value of her stock before the split. Also, the total of her account on her books, Investment in Ameritech Stock, is still $6,830, the same as it was before the stock split.

Some people argue that the market price of the stock will change on the stock exchange. This is probably true. One would think that since it is a 5-for-1 stock split, that the market price after the split would be only 1/5 of the market price prior to the stock split. But the market price is set by investors and potential investors. And often a stock split interests investors in a stock that they think is doing well. For this reason, the market price doesn't always decrease as much as a mathematician would think.

Because Tabor keeps books on the cost basis, she does not let the market price of the stock affect her accounts.

• PROBLEM 5–30

Nettie Corporation wishes to build a new warehouse. Experts figure that it will cost $50,000 to build, and this will include the cost of the building and the land, adjacent to the present factory building. The board of directors of the corporation has determined to raise this $50,000 with a Bond Issue and call on experts from a large bank in Chicago for consultation. These experts determine that under present market conditions, 10-year bonds without a Sinking Fund could be sold for 8% interest, but 10-year bonds with a Sinking Fund could be sold for 7% interest. The board decides to set up a Sinking Fund with the bank and have them go ahead and sell the 7% bonds. The agreement with the bank is that at the end of each year for ten years, the Nettie Corporation will pay the bank $4,000, which the bank is to invest as a Bond Sinking Fund for the corporation. What entries will be made when the bonds are sold?

SOLUTION:

1999		$ (in dollars)	
March 1	Cash	50,000	
	Bonds Payable		50,000

The bank in Chicago sells the Nettie Corporation bonds to investors all over the world through brokers all over the world. It remits the $50,000 to the Nettie Corporation, which uses this money to buy land and construct the warehouse. The warehouse is used to store raw materials and finished goods from the factory nearby.

• PROBLEM 5–31

Nettie Corporation, with the help of the Broad Street National Bank in Chicago, sold $50,000 worth of bonds, raising $50,000, on March 1, 1999. Interest of 7% is to be paid to the bank once a year, along with $4,000 payments to the bank for the Sinking Fund. What entries are to be made on the Nettie Corporation books at the end of the first year?

SOLUTION:

2000		$ (in dollars)	
March 1	Bond Interest Expense	3,500	
	Cash		3,500
1	Sinking Fund Cash	4,000	
	Cash		4,000
1	Service Charge Expense	1,000	
	Cash		1,000

The Broad Street National Bank in Chicago has been hired by the Nettie Corporation not only to handle the Bond Sinking Fund, but also to pay the bondholders their regular Annual Interest through the issuance of checks to each bondholder who is registered. There are 50 $1,000 bonds outstanding to cover the $50,000 issue.

Nettie Corporation sends $3,500 to the Broad Street National Bank to cover interest for the first year on the bonds outstanding ($50,000 × 7% = $3,500). Bond Interest Expense is debited because the Nettie Corporation is getting the use of the $50,000.

In the second entry, the Nettie Corporation is sending the Broad Street National Bank a check for $4,000 as agreed to in the Bond Sinking Fund agreement, which was that the Nettie Corporation was to have the bank set up a Bond Sinking Fund by sending the bank $4,000 at the end of each year that the bonds were outstanding. The Nettie Corporation debits the long-term Asset Account Bond Sinking Fund Cash for the $4,000 and credits Cash for $4,000 since the Nettie Corporation is mailing out the check.

In the third entry, the Nettie Corporation is paying the Broad Street National Bank a service charge for selling the bonds, for paying the bond-holders their interest, and for taking care of any problems of the bondhold-ers.

• PROBLEM 5–32

Shortly after receiving the $4,000 Sinking Fund money from the Nettie Corporation, the Trust Department of the Broad Street National Bank notifies the Nattie Corporation that they have invested the $4,000 in stocks and bonds of other corporations. What entry will be made on the books of the Nettie Corporation?

SOLUTION:

2000		$ (in dollars)	
April 1	Sinking Fund Investments	4,000	
	Sinking Fund Cash		4,000

Nettie Corporation debits its long-term Asset Account Bond Sinking Fund Investments for $4,000 to show that its fund is now invested in the stocks and bonds of other corporations and is not in the form of cash. Nettie Corporation credits Sinking Fund Cash to show that the cash has been invested.

• PROBLEM 5–33

The board of directors of the Nettie Corporation, through the Trust Department of the Broad Street National Bank, Chicago, sold $50,000 bonds on March 1, 1999, at 7%, for 10 years. These bonds, in their fine print, mention that a Bond Sinking Fund is being set up to pay off these bonds at the end of 10 years. On March 1, 2000, the first year's interest on the bonds is paid, and a Bond Sinking Fund is set up and run by the Trust Department of the Broad Street National Bank, Chicago. Within a month, the Trust Department has invested this money in stocks and bonds of other corporations. What entry is made on the books of the Nettie Corporation a year later to record the necessary procedures?

SOLUTION:

2001		$ (in dollars)	
March 1	Bond Sinking Fund Cash	340	
	Bond Sinking Fund Income		340
1	Bond Interest Expense	3,500	
	Cash		3,500
1	Sinking Fund Cash	4,000	
	Cash		4,000
1	Service Charge Expense	300	
	Cash		300

The Trust Department of the Broad Street National Bank, Chicago, notifies the Nettie Corporation that the Bond Sinking Fund investments in stocks and bonds of other corporations have brought in $200 in Dividend Income and $140 in Interest Income, or a total of $340 Sinking Fund Cash. Thus, the Nettie Corporation debits the long-term Asset Account Bond Sinking Fund Cash for $340 to show that the Trust Department of the Broad Street National Bank has this money in the Sinking Fund. This is a long-term Asset because, even though it is Cash, it is not in the hands of the Nettie Corporation, but is in the hands of the Trust Department of the Broad Street National Bank. It is managed by them and will be invested when a good investment opportunity comes along. The account Bond Sinking Fund Income is credited to show Revenue. This Revenue

Account is taxable by the Nettie Corporation and must be reported on its Federal Income tax.

Each year the Nettie Corporation must remit to the Broad Street National Bank the interest on the bonds for the year just ended. In this case it is an annual payment of $3,500 ($50,000 × 7%). The Trust Department of the Broad Street National Bank then mails this money to the various outstanding bondholders. So, on the Nettie Corporation books, the account Bond Interest Expense is debited for $3,500 to show that the corporation is getting the use of the money. Cash is credited for $3,500 because a check is being mailed to the bank.

The Nettie Corporation also sends the Broad Street National Bank its second $4,000 payment to the Bond Sinking Fund, so the long-term Asset Account, Sinking Fund Cash, is debited because this money is added to the Sinking Fund and is still owned by the Nettie Corporation, even though it is managed by the Broad Street National Bank. Cash is credited because a check is mailed to the bank.

Finally, the Broad Street National Bank sends a bill to the Nettie Corporation for managing the dealing with the bondholders over the past year, and this bill amounts to $300. So the Nettie Corporation debits Service Charge Expense for $300, since it is getting the bank's services, and credits Cash, since it is sending the bank a check for this amount.

• PROBLEM 5–34

The board of directors of the Nettie Corporation, through the Trust Department of the Broad Street National Bank, Chicago, sold $50,000, bonds on March 1, 1999, at 7% for 10 years. These bonds, in their fine print, mention that a Bond Sinking Fund is being set up to pay off these bonds at the end of ten years. On March 1, 2000, the first year's interest on the bonds is paid, and a Bond Sinking Fund is set up and run by the Trust Department of the Broad Street National Bank, Chicago. Within a month the Trust Department has invested this money in stocks and bonds of other corporations. How do the accounts for the Nettie Corporation look on the books of the Trust Department of the Broad Street National Bank at the end of the second year, or on March 1, 2001?

SOLUTION:

Bonds Payable

	50,000

Bond Sinking Fund Cash

4,000	4,000
340	
4,000	

Bond Sinking Fund Investments

4,000	

The $50,000 credit to Bonds Payable was made on March 1, 1999, when the bonds were sold. The first $4,000 entry to Sinking Fund Cash was made on March 1, 2000, when the Nettie Corporation deposited its first payment into the Bond Sinking Fund. A month later, on April 1, 2000, the Trust Department of the Broad Street National Bank took out $4,000 from the Bond Sinking Fund and invested it in stocks and bonds of other corporations. This accounts for the credit of $4,000 in the Sinking Fund Cash account and the debit of $4,000 in the Sinking Fund Investments account.

The $340 debit to Sinking Fund Cash was made on March 1, 2001 when the Trust Department of the Broad Street National Bank announced that the Sinking Fund investments during the previous 12 months had earned $340 in Income. The second $4,000 debit entry in the Sinking Fund Cash account was made on March 1, 2001 when the Nettie Corporation made its second $4,000 payment to the Sinking Fund.

• PROBLEM 5-35

On March 1, 1999, the Nettie Corporation, through the Trust Department of the Broad Street National Bank, Chicago, sold $50,000 of 10-year, 7% bonds with a Sinking Fund provision. On March 1, 2000, the first year's interest on the bonds is paid, and in accordance with the Bond Indenture; a Bond Sinking Fund was set up and run by the Trust Department of the Broad Street National Bank. Within a month thereafter, the Trust Department has invested the $4,000 in stocks and bonds of other corporations.

On March 1, 2001, the Trust Deptartment announced that the stocks and bonds of these corporations had earned $340 Income for the Sinking Fund. Also on this date, the Nettie Corporation made a second $4,000 payment to the Bond Sinking Fund. On April 1, the Trust Department of the Broad Street National Bank notified the Nettie Corporation that all the money in the Sinking Fund Cash had been invested in stocks and bonds of other corporations. What entry will the Nettie Corporation put on their books at this time?

SOLUTION:

2001		$ (in dollars)	
April 1	Bond Sinking Fund Investments	4,340	
	Bond Sinking Fund Cash		4,340

Prior to this entry the Sinking Fund Cash account had a balance of $4,340, of which $340 was Income earned by the Sinking Fund investments over the past year. The $4,000 in the Bond Sinking Fund was the second contribution of the Nettie Company to the sinking fund. The fine print in the Bond Indenture requires that every March 1, during the lifetime of the bonds, the Nettie Corporation makes a $4,000 contribution to Sinking Fund Cash. Since the Trust Department of the bank has invested the entire balance of Sinking Fund Cash, the Sinking Fund Investments account is debited for $4,340 and the Sinking Fund Cash account is credited for $4,340, leaving a zero balance in the Sinking Fund Cash account. Since the Sinking Fund Investment account has a previous balance of $4,000, this investment will now give it a balance of $8,340, shown in the account as follows:

Sinking Fund Investments

4,000	
4,340	

• PROBLEM 5–36

On March 1, 1999, the Nettie Corporation, through the Trust Department of the Broad Street National Bank, Chicago, sold $50,000 of 10-year 7% bonds with a Sinking Fund provision. On March 1, 2000, the first year's interest on the bonds was paid, and in accordance with the Bond Indenture, a Bond Sinking Fund was set up and run by the Trust Department of the Broad Street National Bank. Within a month thereafter, the Trust Department had invested the $4,000 in stocks and bonds of other corporations.

On March 1, 2001, the Trust Department announced that the stocks and bonds of these corporations had earned $340 income for the Sinking Fund. Also on this date the Nettie Corporation made a second $4,000 payment to the Bond Sinking Fund. On April 1, 2001, the Trust Department of the Broad Street National Bank notified the Nettie Corporation that all the money in the Sinking Fund Cash account had been invested in stocks and bonds of other corporations.

On March 1, 2002, the Trust Department of the Broad Street National Bank announced that the Sinking Fund investments had earned $700 Income for the previous 12 months. Also on this date, the Nettie Corporation made a third $4,000 payment to the Bond Sinking Fund. What entries will the Nettie Corporation make on their books on March 1, 2002?

SOLUTION:

2002			$ (in dollars)
March 1	Bond Sinking Fund Cash	700	
	Bond Sinking Fund Income		700
1	Bond Interest Expense	3,500	
	Cash		3,500
1	Bond Sinking Fund Cash	4,000	
	Cash		4,000

1	Service Charge Expense	350	
	Cash		350

On March 1, 2002, the Trust Department of the Broad Street National Bankhas notified the Nettie Corporation that the Sinking Fund investments in stocks and bonds of other corporations have brought in $700 during the past 12 months. So Nettie Corporation in the first entry debits Bond Sinking Fund Cash for this $700. This is a long-term Asset because, even though it is Cash, it is not in the hands of the Nettie Corporation. It is in the hands of the Trust Department of the Broad Street National Bank and managed by them; it is to be invested when a good investment opportunity comes along. The account Bond Sinking Fund Income is credited to show Revenue. This Revenue account is taxable to the Nettie Corporation and must be reported on its Federal Income Tax.

Each year the Nettie Corporation must remit to the Broad Street National Bank the Interest on the bonds for the year just ended. In this case it is an annual payment of $3,500 ($50,000 × 7%). The Trust Department of the Broad Street National Bank then mails this money to the various outstanding bondholders. So, on the Nettie Corporation books, the account Bond Interest Expense is debited for $3,500 to show that the corporation is getting the use of the money. Cash is credited for $3,500 because a check is being mailed to the bank.

The Nettie Corporation also sends the Broad Street National Bank its third $4,000 payment to the Bond Sinking Fund, so the long-term Asset Account, Bond Sinking Fund Cash, is debited because this money is added to the Sinking Fund and is still owned by the Nettie Corporation even though it is managed by the Broad Street National Bank. Cash is credited because a check is mailed to the bank.

Next, the Broad Street National Bank sends a bill to the Nettie Corporation for managing the dealings with the bondholders over the past year, and this bill amounts to $350. So the Nettie Corporation debits Service Charge Expense for $350, since it is getting the bank's services, and credits Cash, since it is sending the bank a check for this amount.

• PROBLEM 5-37

The Nettie Corporation, through the Trust Department of the Broad Street National Bank, Chicago, sold $50,000 of bonds on March 1, 1999, at 7% for 10 years. The fine print on these bonds mentioned that a Bond Sinking fund is being set up to pay off these bonds at the end of ten years. On March 1, 2000, the first year's Interest on the bonds is paid, and a Bond Sinking Fund is set up and run by the Trust Department of the Broad Street National Bank, Chicago. Within a month the Trust Department has invested this money in stocks and bonds of other corporations.

On March 1, 2001, the Trust Department announced that the stocks and bonds of these corporations had earned $340 Income for the Sinking Fund. Also on that date, the Nettie Corporation made a second $4,000 payment to the Bond Sinking Fund. On April 1, 2001, the Trust Department of the Broad Street National Bank notified the Nettie Corporation that all the money in the Sinking Fund Cash had been invested in stocks and bonds of other corporations.

On March 1, 2002, the Trust Department of the Broad Street National Bank announced that the Sinking Fund investments had earned $700 Income for the previous 12 months. Also on this date, the Nettie Corporation made a third $4,000 payment to the Bond Sinking Fund. What is the status of the accounts on the Nettie Corporation's books at this time?

SOLUTION:

Bonds Payable

		3/1/99	50,000

Bond Sinking Fund Cash

3/1/2000	4,000	4/1/2000	4,000
3/1/2001	340		
3/1/2001	4,000	4/1/2001	4,340
3/1/2002	700		
3/1/2002	4,000		

Bond Sinking Fund Investments

4/1/2000	4,000
4/1/2001	4,340

The Bonds Payable account has a credit balance of $50,000, showing the amount that the Nettie Corporation has borrowed from the bondholders and still owes them. The Sinking Fund Cash account has a debit balance of $4,700, of which $700 is earnings on Sinking Fund investments for the past 12 months and $4,000 is the payment to the Bond Sinking Fund by the Nettie Corporation on March 1, 2002. The Sinking Fund Investments account has a balance of $8,340, invested in stocks and bonds of other corporations.

• PROBLEM 5–38

On March 1, 1999, the Nettie Corporation, through the Trust Department of the Broad Street National Bank, Chicago, sold $50,000 of 10-year, 7% bonds with a Sinking Fund provision. On March 1, 2000, the first year's interest on the bonds is paid, and in accordance with the Bond Indenture, a Bond Sinking Fund was set up and run by the Trust Department of the Broad Street National Bank. Within a month thereafter, the Trust Department had invested the $4,000 in stocks and bonds of other corporations.

On March 1, 2001, the Trust Department announced that the stocks and bonds of these corporations had earned $340 Income for the Sinking Fund. Also on that date, the Nettie Corporation made a second $4,000 payment to the Bond Sinking Fund. On April 1, 2001 the Trust Department of the Broad Street National Bank notified the Nettie Corporation that all the money in the Bond Sinking Fund Cash account had been invested in stocks and bonds of other corporations.

On March 1, 2002, the Trust Department of the Broad Street National Bank announced that the Bond Sinking Fund investments had earned $700 Income for the previous 12 months. Also on that date, the Nettie Corporation made a third $4,000 payment to the Bond Sinking Fund.

On April 1, 2002, the Trust Department of the Broad Street National Bank announced that $2,000 of the $4,700 balance in the Bond Sinking Fund Cash account had been invested in stocks and bonds of other corporations. What journal entry will be made on the books of the Nettie Company to register this fact?

SOLUTION:

2002		$ (in dollars)	
April 1	Bond Sinking Fund Investments	2,000	
	Bond Sinking Fund Cash		2,000

The account Bond Sinking Fund Investments is debited for $2,000 because the trustees at the Broad Street National Bank have found desirable places to invest that amount of money. This brings the Bond Sinking Fund Investment account up to $6,340. The Sinking Fund Cash account is credited for $2,000, since the trustees have used this amount of money to invest and have taken it out of the Sinking Fund Cash account which they control.

• PROBLEM 5–39

On March 1, 1999, the Nettie Corporation, through the Trust Department of the Broad Street National Bank, Chicago, sold $50,000 of 10-year, 7% bonds with a Bond Sinking Fund provision. On March 1, 2000, the first year's Interest on bonds is paid, and in accordance with the Bond Indenture, a Bond Sinking Fund was set up and run by the Trust Department of the Broad Street National Bank. Each year, beginning March 1, 2000, the Nettie Corporation made a $4,000 payment to the Trust Department to be deposited in Bond Sinking Fund Cash, and shortly thereafter the Trust Department used this money to invest in stocks and bonds of other corporations.

On March 1, 2002, the Trust Department of the Broad Street National Bank announced that the Bond Sinking Fund investments had earned $700 Income for the previous 12 months. Also on that date, the Nettie Corporation made a third $4,000 payment to the Bond Sinking Fund. On April 1, 2002, the Trust Department of the Broad

Street National Bank announced that $2,000 of the $4,700 balance in the Sinking Fund Cash account had been invested in stocks and bonds of other corporations.

On March 1, 2003, the Trust Department of the Broad Street National Bank announced that the Bond Sinking Fund investments had earned $950 Income for the previous 12 months. Also, on that date the Nettie Corporation made a fourth $4,000 payment to the Bond Sinking Fund. What entries will the Nettie Corporation make on their books on March 1, 2003?

SOLUTION:

2003		$ (in dollars)	
March 1	Bond Sinking Fund Cash	950	
	Bond Sinking Fund Income		950
1	Bond Interest Expense	3,500	
	Cash		3,500
1	Bond Sinking Fund Cash	4,000	
	Cash		4,000
1	Service Charge Expense	370	
	Cash		370

On March 1, 2003 the Trust Department of the Broad Street National Bank has notified the Nettie Corporation that the Bond Sinking Fund investments in stocks and bonds of other corporations have brought in $950 during the past 12 months. So Nettie Corporation in the first entry debits Bond Sinking Fund Cash for this $950. This is a long-term Asset because even though it is Cash, it is not in the hands of the Nettie Corporation, but is in the hands of the Trust Department of the Broad Street National Bank. It is managed by them and is to be invested when a good investment opportunity comes along. The account Bond Sinking Fund Income is credited to show Revenue. This Revenue Account is taxable to the Nettie Corporation and must be reported on its Federal Income Tax return.

Each year the Nettie Corporation must remit to the Broad Street National Bank the Interest on the bonds for the year just ended. In this case it is an annual payment of $3,500 ($50,000 × 7%). The Trust Department of the Broad Street National Bank then mails this money to the various outstanding bondholders. So, on the Nettie Corporation books the account Bond Interest Expense is debited for $3,500 to show that the corporation is getting the use of the money. Cash is credited for $3,500 because a check is being mailed to the bank.

The Nettie Corporation also sends the Broad Street National Bank its fourth $4,000 payment to the Bond Sinking Fund, so the long-term Asset account Sinking Fund Cash is debited because this money is added to the Sinking Fund and is still owned by the Nettie Corporation even though it is managed by the Broad Street National Bank. Cash is credited because a check is mailed to the bank.

Next, the Broad Street National Bank sent a bill to the Nettie Corporation for managing the dealings with the bondholders over the past year, and this bill amounts to $370. So the Nettie Corporation debits Service Charge Expense for $370, since it is getting the bank's services, and credits Cash, since it is sending the bank a check for this amount.

• PROBLEM 5–40

On March 1, 1999, the Nettie Corporation, through the Trust Department of the Broad Street National Bank, Chicago, sold $50,000 of 10-year, 7% bonds with a Sinking Fund provision. On March 1, 2000, the first year's Interest on the bonds was paid, and in accordance with the Bond Indenture, a Bond Sinking Fund was set up and run by the Trust Department of the Broad Street National Bank. Within a month thereafter, the Trust Department had invested the $4,000 in stocks and bonds of other corporations.

On March 1, 2001, the Trust Department announced that the stocks and bonds of these corporations had earned $340 Income for the Sinking Fund. Also on that date, the Nettie Corporation made a second $4,000 payment to the Bond Sinking Fund. On April 1, 2001, the Trust Department of the Broad Street National Bank notified the Nettie Corporation that all the money in the Sinking Fund Cash account had been invested in stocks and bonds of other corporations.

On March 1, 2002, the Trust Department of the Broad Street National Bank announced that the Bond Sinking Fund investments had earned $700 Income for the previous 12 months. Also on that date, the Nettie Corporation made a third $4,000 payment to the Bond

Sinking Fund. On April 1, 2002, the Trust Department of the Broad Street National Bank announced that $2,000 of the $4,700 balance in the Sinking Fund Cash account had been invested in stocks and bonds of other corporations.

On March 1, 2003, the Trust Department of the Broad Street National Bank announced that the Bond Sinking Fund investments had earned $950 Income for the previous 12 months. Also on that date, the Nettie Corporation made a fourth $4,000 payment to the Bond Sinking Fund. On April 1, 2003, the Trust Department announced that $5,000 from Bond Sinking Fund Cash account was being invested in stocks and bonds of other corporations. Show the book entry for this. Also, what is the status of the accounts on the Nettie Corporation's books as of April 1, 2003?

SOLUTION:

2003			$ (in dollars)
April 1	Bond Sinking Fund Investments		5,000
	Bond Sinking Fund Cash		5,000

Bonds Payable

	3/1/99	50,000

Bond Sinking Fund Cash

3/1/2000	4,000	4/1/2000	4,000
3/1/2001	340		
3/1/2001	4,000	4/1/2001	4,340
3/1/2002	700	4/1/2002	2,000
3/1/2002	4,000	4/1/2003	5,000
3/1/2003	950		
3/1/2003	4,000		

Bond Sinking Fund Investments	
4/1/2000	4,000
4/1/2001	4,340
4/1/2002	2,000
4/1/2003	5,000

• PROBLEM 5-41

On March 1, 1999, the Nettie Corporation, through the Trust Department of the Broad Street National Bank, Chicago, sold $50,000 of 10-year, 7% bonds with a Sinking Fund provision. On March 1, 2000, the first year's Interest on the bonds was paid, and in accordance with the Bond Indenture, a Bond Sinking Fund was set up and run by the Trust Department of the Broad Street National Bank. Within a month thereafter, the Trust Department had invested the $4,000 in stocks and bonds of other corporations.

On March 1, 2001, the Trust Department announced that the stocks and bonds of these corporations had earned $340 Income for the Sinking Fund. Also on that date, the Nettie Corporation made a second $4,000 payment to the Bond Sinking Fund. On April 1, 2001, the Trust Department of the Broad Street National Bank notified the Nettie Corporation that all the money in the Sinking Fund Cash account had been invested in stocks and bonds of other corporations.

On March 1, 2002, the Trust Department of the Broad Street National Bank announced that the Sinking Fund investments had earned $700 Income for the previous 12 months. Also on that date, the Nettie Corporation made a third $4,000 payment to the Bond Sinking Fund. On April 1, 2002, the Trust Department of the Broad Street National Bank announced that $2,000 of the $4,700 balance in the Sinking Fund Cash account had been invested in stocks and bonds of other corporations.

On March 1, 2003, the Trust Department of the Broad Street National Bank announced that the Bond Sinking Fund investments had earned $950 Income for the previous 12 months. Also on that date, the Nettie Corporation made a fourth $4,000 payment to the Bond Sinking Fund. On April 1, 2003, the Trust Department announced that $5,000 from the Bond Sinking Fund Cash account was being invested in stocks and bonds of other corporations.

On March 1, 2004, the Trust Department of the Broad Street National Bank announced that the Bond Sinking Fund investments had earned $1,380 Income for the previous 12 months. Also on that date, the Nettie Corporation made a fifth $4,000 payment to the Bond Sinking Fund. On April 1, 2004, the Trust Department announced that $6,650 from the Bond Sinking Fund Cash account was being invested in stocks and bonds of other corporations. What entries will be made on the books of the Nettie Corporation on March 1 and April 1, 2004, and how will the accounts appear in the ledger after these entries have been made?

SOLUTION:

2004		$ (in dollars)	
March 1	Bond Sinking Fund Cash	1,380	
	Bond Sinking Fund Income		1,380
1	Bond Interest Expense	3,500	
	Cash		3,500
1	Bond Sinking Fund Cash	4,000	
	Cash		4,000
1	Service Charge Expense	400	
	Cash		400

The Trust Department of the Broad Street National Bank, on March 1, 2004, has notified the Nettie Corporation that the Bond Sinking Fund investments in stocks and bonds of other corporations have brought in $1,380 during the past 12 months. So, Nettie Corporation in the first entry debits Bond Sinking Fund Cash for this $1,380. This is a long-term Asset because even though it is Cash, it is not in the hands of the Nettie Corporation, but is in the hands of the Trust Department of the Broad Street National Bank. It is managed by them and is to be invested when a good investment opportunity comes along. The account Bond Sinking Fund Income is credited for $1,380 to show Revenue. This Revenue account is taxable to the Nettie Corporation and must be reported on its Federal Income Tax return.

Each year the Nettie Corporation must remit to the Broad Street

National Bank the Interest on the bonds for the year just ended. In this case it is an annual payment of $3,500 ($50,000 × 7%). The Trust Department of the Broad Street National Bank then mails this money to the various outstanding bondholders. So, on the Nettie Corporation books the account Bond Interest Expense is debited for $3,500 to show that the corporation is getting the use of the money. Cash is credited for $3,500 because a check is being mailed to the bank.

The Nettie Corporation also sends the Broad Street National Bank its fifth $4,000 payment to the Bond Sinking Fund, so the long-term Asset Account Bond Sinking Fund Cash is debited because this money is added to the Bond Sinking Fund and is still owned by the Nettie Corporation even though it is managed by the Broad Street National Bank. Cash is credited because a check for $4,000 is being mailed to the bank.

Next, the Broad Street National Bank sent a bill to the Nettie Corporation for managing the dealings with the bondholders over the past year, and this bill amounts to $400. So, the Nettie Corporation debits Service Charge Expense for $400, since it is getting the bank's services, and credits Cash, since it is sending the bank a check for this amount.

On April 1, 2004, the Trust Department of the bank announced that $6,650 from Bond Sinking Fund Cash account was being invested in stocks and bonds of other corporations. What book entry will be made for this? Also, what is the status of the accounts after these entries?

2004		$ (in dollars)	
April 1	Bond Sinking Fund Investments	6,650	
	Bond Sinking Fund Cash		6,650

Bonds Payable		
	3/1/99	50,000

Bond Sinking Fund Cash

3/1/2000	4,000	4/1/2000	4,000
3/1/2001	340		
3/1/2001	4,000	4/1/2001	4,340
3/1/2002	700	4/1/2002	2,000
3/1/2002	4,000		
3/1/2003	950		
3/1/2003	4,000	4/1/2003	5,000
3/1/2004	1,380		
3/1/2004	4,000	4/1/2004	6,650

Bond Sinking Fund Investments

4/1/2000	4,000
4/1/2001	4,340
4/1/2002	2,000
4/1/2003	5,000
4/1/2004	6,650

• PROBLEM 5–42

On March 1, 1999, the Nettie Corporation, through the Trust Department of the Broad Street National Bank, Chicago, sold $50,000 of 10-year, 7% bonds with a Sinking Fund provision. On March 1, 2000, the first year's Interest on the bonds was paid, and in accordance with the Bond Indenture, a Bond Sinking Fund was set up and run by the Trust Department of the Broad Street National Bank. Within a month thereafter, the Trust Department had invested the $4,000 in stocks and bonds of other corporations.

On March 1, 2001, the Trust Department announced that the stocks and bonds of these corporations had earned $340 Income for the Sinking Fund. Also on that date, the Nettie Corporation made a second $4,000 payment to the Bond Sinking Fund. On April 1, 2001, the Trust Department of the Broad Street National Bank notified the Nettie Corporation that all the money in the Sinking Fund Cash account had been invested in stocks and bonds of other corporations.

On March 1, 2002, the Trust Department of the Broad Street National Bank announced that the Bond Sinking Fund investments had earned $700 Income for the previous 12 months. Also on that date, the Nettie Corporation made a third $4,000 payment to the Bond Sinking Fund. On April 1, 2002, the Trust Department of the Broad Street National Bank announced that $2,000 of the $4,700 balance in the Sinking Fund Cash account had been invested in stocks and bonds of other corporations.

On March 1, 2003, the Trust Department of the Broad Street National Bank announced that the Bond Sinking Fund investments had earned $950 Income for the previous 12 months. Also on that date, the Nettie Corporation made a fourth $4,000 payment to the Bond Sinking Fund. On April 1, 2003, the Trust Department announced that $5,000 from the Bond Sinking Fund Cash account was being invested in stocks and bonds of other corporations.

On March 1, 2004, the Trust Department of the Broad Street National Bank announced that the Bond Sinking Fund investments had earned $1,380 Income for the previous 12 months. Also on that date, the Nettie Corporation made a fifth $4,000 payment to the Bond Sinking Fund. On April 1, 2004, the Trust Department announced that $6,650 from the Bond Sinking Fund Cash account was being invested in stocks and bonds of other corporations.

On March 1, 2005, the Trust Department of the Broad Street National Bank announced that the Bond Sinking Fund investments had earned $1,421 Income for the previous 12 months. Also on that date, the Nettie Corporation made a sixth $4,000 payment to the Bond Sinking Fund. On April 1, 2005, the Trust Department announced that $6,801 from the Bond Sinking Fund Cash account was being invested in stocks and bonds of other corporations. What entries will be made on the books of the Nettie Corporation on March 1 and April 1, 2005, and how will the accounts appear in the ledger after these entries have been made?

SOLUTION:

2005		$ (in dollars)	
March 1	Bond Sinking Fund Cash	1,421	
	Bond Sinking Fund Income		1,421

1	Bond Interest Expense	3,500	
	Cash		3,500
1	Bond Sinking Fund Cash	4,000	
	Cash		4,000
1	Service Charge Expense	400	
	Cash		400
April 1	Bond Sinking Fund Investments	6,801	
	Bond Sinking Fund Cash		6,801

Bonds Payable

	3/1/99	50,000

Bond Sinking Fund Cash

3/1/2000	4,000	4/1/2000	4,000
3/1/2001	340		
3/1/2001	4,000	4/1/2001	4,340
3/1/2002	700		
3/1/2002	4,000	4/1/2002	2,000
3/1/2003	950		
3/1/2003	4,000	4/1/2003	5,000
3/1/2004	1,380		
3/1/2004	4,000	4/1/2004	6,650
3/1/2005	1,421		
3/1/2005	4,000	4/1/2005	6,801

Bond Sinking Fund Investments

4/1/2000	4,000
4/1/2001	4,340
4/1/2002	2,000
4/1/2003	5,000
4/1/2004	6,650
4/1/2005	6,801

On March 1, 2005, the Trust Department of the Broad Street National Bank has notified the Nettie Corporation that the Bond Sinking Fund investments in stocks and bonds of other corporations have brought in $1,421 during the past 12 months. So, Nettie Corporation in the first entry debits Bond Sinking Fund Cash for this $1,421. This is a long-term Asset because even though it is Cash, it is not in the hands of the Nettie Corporation, but is in the hands of the Trust Department of the Broad Street National Bank. It is managed by them and is to be invested when a good investment opportunity comes along. The account Bond Sinking Fund Income is credited for $1,421 to show Revenue. This Revenue Account is taxable to the Nettie Corporation and must be reported on its Federal Income Tax return.

Each year the Nettie Corporation must remit to the Broad Street National Bank the Interest on the bonds for the year just ended. In this case it is an annual payment of $3,500 ($50,000 × 7%). The Trust Department of the Broad Street National Bank then mails this money to the various outstanding bondholders. So, on the Nettie Corporation books the account Bond Interest Expense is debited for $3,500 to show that the corporation is getting the use of the money. Cash is credited for $3,500 because a check is being mailed to the bank.

The Nettie Corporation also sends the Broad Street National Bank its sixth $4,000 payment to the Bond Sinking Fund, so the long-term Asset Account Sinking Fund Cash is debited because this money is added to the Sinking Fund and is still owned by the Nettie Corporation even though it is managed by the Broad Street National Bank. Cash is credited because a check for $4,000 is being mailed to the bank.

Next, the Broad Street National Bank sent a bill to the Nettie Corporation for managing the dealings with the bondholders over the past year, and this bill amounts to $400. So the Nettie Corporation debits Service Charge Expense for $400, since it is getting the bank's services, and credits Cash, since it is sending the bank a check for this amount.

On April 1, 2005, the Trust Department of the bank announced that $6,801 from the Bond Sinking Fund Cash account was being invested in stocks and bonds of other corporations, so Bond Sinking Fund Investments, a long-term Asset Account, was debited for $6,801. Also at this time, Bond Sinking Fund Cash was credited for $6,801, since this cash was being paid out for the investments. After this entry was made, the

Sinking Fund Cash account balance is zero, since all the Sinking Fund cash has now been invested. As of April 1, 2005, the Sinking Fund Investments account balance is $28,451.

• PROBLEM 5–43

On March 1, 1999, the Nettie Corporation, through the Trust Department of the Broad Street National Bank, Chicago, sold $50,000 of 10-year, 7% bonds with a Sinking Fund provision. On March 1, 2000, the first year's Interest on the bonds was paid, and in accordance with the Bond Indenture, a Bond Sinking Fund was set up and run by the Trust Department of the Broad Street National Bank. Within a month thereafter, the Trust Department had invested the $4,000 in stocks and bonds of other corporations.

On March 1, 2001, the Trust Department announced that the stocks and bonds of these corporations had earned $340 Income for the sinking fund. Also on that date, the Nettie Corporation made a second $4,000 payment to the Bond Sinking Fund. On April 1, 2001, the Trust Department of the Broad Street National Bank notified the Nettie Corporation that all the money in the Sinking Fund Cash account had been invested in stocks and bonds of other corporations.

On March 1, 2002, the Trust Department of the Broad Street National Bank announced that the Sinking Fund investments had earned $700 Income for the previous 12 months. Also on that date, the Nettie Corporation made a third $4,000 payment to the Bond Sinking Fund. On April 1, 2002, the Trust Department of the Broad Street National Bank announced that $2,000 of the $4,700 balance in the Sinking Fund Cash account had been invested in stocks and bonds of other corporations.

On March 1, 2003, the Trust Department of the Broad Street National Bank announced that the Sinking Fund investments had earned $950 Income for the previous 12 months. Also on that date, the Nettie Corporation made a fourth $4,000 payment to the Bond Sinking Fund. On April 1, 2003, the Trust Department announced that $5,000 from the Bond Sinking Fund Cash account was being invested in stocks and bonds of other corporations.

On March 1, 2004, the Trust Department of the Broad Street National Bank announced that the Sinking Fund investments had earned $1,380 Income for the previous 12 months. Also on that date, the Nettie Corporation made a fifth $4,000 payment to the Bond Sinking Fund. On April 1, 2004, the Trust Department announced that $6,650 from the Bond Sinking Fund Cash account was being invested in stocks and bonds of other corporations.

On March 1, 2005, the Trust Department of the Broad Street National Bank announced that the Sinking Fund investments had earned $1,421 Income for the previous 12 months. Also on that date, the Nettie Corporation made a sixth $4,000 payment to the Bond Sinking Fund. On April 1, 2005, the Trust Department announced that $6,801 from the Bond Sinking Fund Cash account was being invested in stocks and bonds of other corporations.

On March 1, 2006, the Trust Department of the Broad Street National Bank announced that the Sinking Fund investments had earned $1,950 Income for the previous 12 months. Also on that date, the Nettie Corporation made a seventh $4,000 payment to the Bond Sinking Fund. On April 1, 2006, the Trust Department announced that the entire $5,950 from the Bond Sinking Fund Cash acount was being invested in stocks and bonds of other corporations. What entries will be made on the books of the Nettie Corporation on March 1 and April 1, 2006, and how will the accounts appear in the ledger after these entries have been made?

SOLUTION:

2006		$ (in dollars)	
March 1	Bond Sinking Fund Cash	1,950	
	Bond Sinking Fund Income		1,950
1	Bond Interest Expense	3,500	
	Cash		3,500
1	Bond Sinking Fund Cash	4,000	
	Cash		4,000
April 1	Bond Sinking Fund Investments	5,950	
	Bond Sinking Fund Cash		5 ,950

Bonds Payable

	3/1/99	50,000

Bond Sinking Fund Cash

3/1/2000	4,000	4/1/2000	4,000
3/1/2001	340		
3/1/2001	4,000	4/1/2001	4,340
3/1/2002	700		
3/1/2002	4,000	4/1/2002	2,000
3/1/2003	950		
3/1/2003	4,000	4/1/2003	5,000
3/1/2004	1,380		
3/1/2004	4,000	4/1/2004	6,650
3/1/2005	1,421		
3/1/2005	4,000	4/1/2005	6,801
3/1/2006	1,950		
3/1/2006	4,000	4/1/2006	5,950

Bond Sinking Fund Investments

4/1/2000	4,000
4/1/2001	4,340
4/1/2002	2,000
4/1/2003	5,000
4/1/2004	6,650
4/1/2005	6,801
4/1/2006	5,950

On March 1, 2006, the Trust Department of the Broad Street National Bank has notified the Nettie Corporation that the Sinking Fund investments in stocks and bonds of other corporations have brought in $1,950 during the past 12 months. So, Nettie Corporation in the first entry debits Bond Sinking Fund Cash for this $1,950. This is a long-term Asset because even though it is cash, it is not in the hands of the Nettie Corporation, but is in the hands of the Trust Department of the Broad Street National Bank. It is managed by them and is to be invested when a good investment opportunity comes along. The account Bond Sinking Fund

Income is credited for $1,950 to show Revenue. This Revenue account is taxable to the Nettie Corporation and must be reported on its Federal Income Tax return.

Each year the Nettie Corporation must remit to the Broad Street National Bank the Interest on the bonds for the year just ended. In this case, it is an annual payment of $3,500 ($50,000 × 7%). The Trust Department of the Broad Street National Bank then mails this money to the various outstanding bondholders. So, on the Nettie Corporation books the account Bond Interest Expense is debited for $3,500 to show that the corporation is getting the use of the money. Cash is credited for $3,500 because a check is being mailed to the bank.

The Nettie Corporation also sends the Broad Street National Bank its seventh $4,000 payment to the Bond Sinking Fund, so the long-term Asset account Sinking Fund Cash, is debited because this money is added to the Sinking Fund and is still owned by the Nettie Corporation even though it is managed by the Broad Street National Bank. Cash is credited because a check for $4,000 is being mailed to the bank.

Next, the Broad Street National Bank sent a bill to the Nettie Corporation for managing the dealings with the bondholders over the past year, and this bill amounts to $410. The entry appears on the books as follows:

2006		$ (in dollars)
March 1	Service Charge Expense	410
	Cash	410

So, the Nettie Corporation debits Service Charge Expense for $410, since it is getting the bank's services, and credits Cash, since it is sending the bank a check for this amount.

On April 1, 2006, the Trust Department of the bank announced that $5,950 from the Bond Sinking Fund Cash account was being invested in stocks and bonds of other corporations, so Bond Sinking Fund Investments, a long-term Asset Account, was debited for $5,950. Also at this time, the Bond Sinking Fund Cash account was credited for $5,950, since this cash was being paid out for the investments.

After this entry was made, the Bond Sinking Fund Cash account balance is zero, since all the Bond Sinking Fund cash has now been invested. As of April 1, 2006, the Sinking Fund Investments account balance is $34,401.

• PROBLEM 5–44

On March 1, 1999, the Nettie Corporation, through the Trust Department of the Broad Street National Bank, Chicago, sold $50,000 of 10-year, 7% bonds with a Sinking Fund provision. On March 1, 2000, the first year's Interest on the bonds was paid, and in accordance with the Bond Indenture, a Bond Sinking Fund was set up and run by the Trust Department of the Broad Street National Bank. Within a month thereafter, the Trust Department had invested the $4,000 in stocks and bonds of other corporations.

On March 1, 2001, the Trust Department announced that the stocks and bonds of these corporations had earned $340 Income for the Bond Sinking Fund. Also on that date, the Nettie Corporation made a second $4,000 payment to the Bond Sinking Fund. On April 1, 2001, the Trust Department of the Broad Street National Bank notified the Nettie Corporation that all the money in the Sinking Fund Cash account has been invested in stocks and bonds of other corporations.

On March 1, 2002, the Trust Department of the Broad Street National Bank announced that the Sinking Fund investments had earned $700 Income for the previous 12 months. Also on that date, the Nettie Corporation made a third $4,000 payment to the Bond Sinking Fund. On April 1, 2002, the Trust Department of the Broad Street National Bank announced that $2,000 of the $4,700 balance in the Sinking Fund Cash account had been invested in stocks and bonds of other corporations.

On March 1, 2003, the Trust Department of the Broad Street National Bank announced that the Sinking Fund investments had earned $950 Income for the previous 12 months. Also on that date, the Nettie Corporation made a fourth $4,000 payment to the Bond Sinking Fund. On April 1, 2003, the Trust Department announced that $5,000 from the Bond Sinking Fund Cash account was being invested in stocks and bonds of other corporations.

On March 1, 2004, the Trust Department of the Broad Street National Bank announced that the Sinking Fund investments had earned $1,380 Income for the previous 12 months. Also on that date, the Nettie Corporation made a fifth $4,000 payment to the Bond Sinking Fund. On April 1, 2004, the Trust Department announced that $6,650 from the Bond Sinking Fund Cash account was being invested in stocks and bonds of other corporations.

On March 1, 2005, the Trust Department of the Broad Street National Bank announced that the Sinking Fund investments had earned $1,421 Income for the previous 12 months. Also on that date, the Nettie Corporation made a sixth $4,000 payment to the Bond Sinking Fund. On April 1, 2005, the Trust Department announced that $6,801 from the Bond Sinking Fund Cash account was being invested in stocks and bonds of other corporations.

On March 1, 2006, the Trust Department of the Broad Street National Bank announced that the Sinking Fund investments had earned $1,950 Income for the previous 12 months. Also on that date, the Nettie Corporation made a seventh $4,000 payment to the Bond Sinking Fund. On April 1, 2006, the Trust Department announced that the entire $5,950 from the Bond Sinking Fund Cash account was being invested in stocks and bonds of other corporations.

On March 1, 2007, the Trust Department of the Broad Street National Bank announced that the Sinking Fund investments had earned $2,358 Income for the previous 12 months. Also on that date, the Nettie Corporation made an eighth $4,000 payment to the Bond Sinking Fund. On April 1, 2007, the Trust Department announced that the entire $6,358 from the Bond Sinking Fund Cash account was being invested in stocks and bonds of other corporations. What entries will be made on the books of the Nettie Corporation on March 1 and April 1, 2007, and how will the accounts appear in the ledger after these entries have been made?

SOLUTION:

2007		$ (in dollars)	
March 1	Bond Sinking Fund Cash	2,358	
	Bond Sinking Fund Income		2,358
1	Bond Interest Expense	3,500	
	Cash		3,500
1	Bond Sinking Fund Cash	4,000	
	Cash		4,000
1	Service Charge Expense	420	
	Cash		420
April 1	Bond Sinking Fund Investments	6,358	
	Bond Sinking Fund Cash		6,358

Bonds Payable

		3/1/99	50,000

Bond Sinking Fund Cash

3/1/2000	4,000	4/1/2000	4,000
3/1/2001	340		
3/1/2001	4,000	4/1/2001	4,340
3/1/2002	700		
3/1/2002	4,000	4/1/2002	2,000
3/1/2003	950		
3/1/2003	4,000	4/1/2003	5,000
3/1/2004	1,380		
3/1/2004	4,000	4/1/2004	6,650
3/1/2005	1,421		
3/1/2005	4,000	4/1/2005	6,801
3/1/2006	1,950		
3/1/2006	4,000	4/1/2006	5,950
3/1/2007	2,358		
3/1/2007	4,000	4/1/2007	6,358

Bond Sinking Fund Investments

4/1/2000	4,000	
4/1/2001	4,340	
4/1/2002	2,000	
4/1/2003	5,000	
4/1/2004	6,650	
4/1/2005	6,801	
4/1/2006	5,950	
4/1/2007	6,358	

On March 1, 2007, the Trust Department of the Broad Street National Bank has notified the Nettie Corporation that the Sinking Fund investments in stocks and bonds of other corporations have brought in $2,358 during the past 12 months. So, Nettie Corporation in the first entry debits Bond Sinking Fund Cash for this $2,358. This is a long-term Asset because even though it is Cash, it is not in the hands of the Nettie Corporation, but is in the hands of the Trust Department of the Broad Street National Bank. It is managed by them and is to be invested when a good investment opportunity comes along. The account Bond Sinking Fund Income is credited for $2,358 to show Revenue. This revenue account is taxable to the Nettie Corporation and must be reported on its Federal Income Tax return.

Each year the Nettie Corporation must remit to the Broad Street National Bank the interest on the bonds for the year just ended. In this case it is an annual payment of $3,500 ($50,000 × 7%). The Trust Department of the Broad Street National Bank then mails this money to the various outstanding bondholders. So, on the Nettie Corporation books the account Bond Interest Expense is debited for $3,500 to show that the corporation is getting the use of the money. Cash is credited for $3,500 because a check is being mailed to the bank.

The Nettie Corporation also sends the Broad Street National Bank its eighth $4,000 payment to the Bond Sinking Fund, so the long-term Asset account Sinking Fund Cash is debited because this money is added to the Sinking Fund and is still owned by the Nettie Corporation even though it is managed by the Broad Street National Bank. Cash is credited because a check for $4,000 is being mailed to the bank.

Next, the Broad Street National Bank sent a bill to the Nettie Corporation for managing the dealings with the bondholders over the past year, and this bill amounts to $420. So, the Nettie Corporation debits Service Charge Expense for $420, since it is getting the bank's services, and credits Cash, since it is sending the bank a check for this amount.

On April 1, 2007, the Trust Department of the bank announced that $6,358 from the Bond Sinking Fund Cash account was being invested in stocks and bonds of other corporations, so Bond Sinking Fund Investments, a long-term Asset account, was debited for $6,358. Also at this time, Bond Sinking Fund Cash was credited for $6,358, since this Cash was being paid out for the investments.

After this entry was made, the Sinking Fund Cash account balance is zero, since all the Sinking Fund cash has now been invested. As of April 1, 2007, the Sinking Fund Investments account balance is $40,759.

• PROBLEM 5–45

On March 1, 1999, the Nettie Corporation, through the Trust Department of the Broad Street National Bank, Chicago, sold $50,000 of 10-year, 7% bonds with a Sinking Fund provision. On March 1, 2000, the first year's Interest on the bonds was paid, and in accordance with the Bond Indenture, a Bond Sinking Fund was set up and run by the Trust Department of the Broad Street National Bank. Within a month thereafter, the Trust Department had invested the $4,000 in stocks and bonds of other corporations.

On March 1, 2001, the Trust Department announced that the stocks and bonds of these corporations had earned $340 Income for the Sinking Fund. Also on that date, the Nettie Corporation made a second $4,000 payment to the Bond Sinking Fund. On April 1, 2001, the Trust Department of the Broad Street National Bank notified the Nettie Corporation that all the money in the Sinking Fund Cash account has been invested in stocks and bonds of other corporations.

On March 1, 2002, the Trust Department of the Broad Street National Bank announced that the Sinking Fund investments had earned $700 Income for the previous 12 months. Also on that date, the Nettie Corporation made a third $4,000 payment to the Bond Sinking Fund. On April 1, 2002, the Trust Department of the Broad Street National Bank announced that $2,000 of the $4,700 balance in the Sinking Fund Cash account had been invested in stocks and bonds of other corporations.

On March 1, 2003, the Trust Department of the Broad Street National Bank announced that the Sinking Fund investments had earned $950 Income for the previous 12 months. Also on that date, the Nettie Corporation made a fourth $4,000 payment to the Bond Sinking Fund. On April 1, 2003, the Trust Department announced that $5,000 from the Bond Sinking Fund Cash account was being invested in stocks and bonds of other corporations.

On March 1, 2004, the Trust Department of the Broad Street National Bank announced that the Sinking Fund investments had earned $1,380 Income for the previous 12 months. Also on that date, the Nettie Corporation made a fifth $4,000 payment to the Bond Sinking Fund. On April 1, 2004, the Trust Department announced that $6,650 from the Bond Sinking Fund Cash account was being invested in stocks and bonds of other corporations.

On March 1, 2005, the Trust Department of the Broad Street National Bank announced that the Sinking Fund investments had earned $1,421 Income for the previous 12 months. Also on that date, the Nettie Corporation made a sixth $4,000 payment to the Bond Sinking Fund. On April 1, 2005, the Trust Department announced that $6,801 from the Bond Sinking Fund Cash account was being invested in stocks and bonds of other corporations.

On March 1, 2006, the Trust Department of the Broad Street National Bank announced that the Sinking Fund investments had earned $1,950 Income for the previous 12 months. Also on that date, the Nettie Corporation made a seventh $4,000 payment to the Bond Sinking Fund. On April 1, 2006, the Trust Department announced that the entire $5,950 from the Bond Sinking Fund Cash account was being invested in stocks and bonds of other corporations.

On March 1, 2007, the Trust Department of the Broad Street National Bank announced that the Sinking Fund investments had earned $2,358 Income for the previous 12 months. Also on that date, the Nettie Corporation made an eighth $4,000 payment to the Bond Sinking Fund. On April 1, 2007, the Trust Department announced that the entire $6,358 from the Bond Sinking Fund Cash account was being invested in stocks and bonds of other corporations.

On March 1, 2008, the Trust Department of the Broad Street National Bank announced that the Sinking Fund investments had earned $2,503 Income for the previous 12 months. Also on that date, the Nettie Corporation made a ninth $4,000 payment to the Bond Sinking Fund. On April 1, 2008, the Trust Department announced that the entire $6,503 from the Bond Sinking Fund Cash account was being invested in stocks and bonds of other corporations. What entries will be made on the books of the Nettie Corporation on March 1 and April 1, 2008, and how will the accounts appear in the ledger after these entries have been made?

SOLUTION:

2008		$ (in dollars)	
March 1	Bond Sinking Fund Cash	2,503	
	Bond Sinking Fund Income		2,503
1	Bond Interest Expense	3,500	
	Cash		3,500

1	Bond Sinking Fund Cash	4,000	
	Cash		4,000
1	Service Charge Expense	420	
	Cash		420
April 1	Bond Sinking Fund Investments	6,503	
	Bond Sinking Fund Cash		6,503

Bonds Payable

		3/1/99	50,000

Bond Sinking Fund Cash

3/1/2000	4,000	4/1/2000	4,000
3/1/2001	340		
3/1/2001	4,000	4/1/2001	4,340
3/1/2002	700		
3/1/2002	4,000	4/1/2002	2,000
3/1/2003	950		
3/1/2003	4,000	4/1/2003	5,000
3/1/2004	1,380		
3/1/2004	4,000	4/1/2004	6,650
3/1/2005	1,421		
3/1/2005	4,000	4/1/2005	6,801
3/1/2006	1,950		
3/1/2006	4,000	4/1/2006	5,950
3/1/2007	2,358		
3/1/2007	4,000	4/1/2007	6,358
3/1/2008	2,503		
3/1/2008	4,000	4/1/2008	6,503

Sinking Fund Investments

4/1/2000	4,000
4/1/2001	4,340
4/1/2002	2,000
4/1/2003	5,000
4/1/2004	6,650
4/1/2005	6,801
4/1/2006	5,950
4/1/2007	6,358
4/1/2008	6,503

On March 1, 2008, the Trust Department of the Broad Street National Bank has notified the Nettie Corporation that the Sinking Fund investments in stocks and bonds of other corporations have brought in $2,503 during the past 12 months. So Nettie Corporation in the first entry debits Bond Sinking Fund Cash for this $2,503. This is a long-term Asset because even though it is Cash, it is not in the hands of the Nettie Corporation, but is in the hands of the Trust Department of the Broad Street National Bank. It is managed by them and is to be invested when a good investment opportunity comes along. The account Bond Sinking Fund Income is credited for $2,503 to show Revenue. This Revenue account is taxable to the Nettie Corporation and must be reported on its Federal Income Tax return.

Each year the Nettie Corporation must remit to the Broad Street National Bank the Interest on the bonds for the year just ended. In this case it is an annual payment of $3,500 ($50,000 × 7%). The Trust Department of the Broad Street National Bank then mails this money to the various outstanding bondholders. So, on the Nettie Corporation books the account Bond Interest Expense is debited for $3,500 to show that the corporation is getting the use of the money. Cash is credited for $3,500 because a check is being mailed to the bank.

The Nettie Corporation also sends the Broad Street National Bank its ninth $4,000 payment to the Bond Sinking Fund, so the long-term Asset account Bond Sinking Fund Cash is debited because this money is added to the Sinking fFund and is still owned by the Nettie Corporation even though it is managed by the Broad Street National Bank. Cash is credited because a check for $4,000 is being mailed to the bank.

Next, the Broad Street National Bank sent a bill to the Nettie Corporation for managing the dealings with the bondholders over the past year, and this bill amounts to $420. So, the Nettie Corporation debits Service Charge Expense for $420, since it is getting the bank's services, and credits Cash, since it is sending the bank a check for this amount.

On April 1, 2008, the Trust Department of the bank announced that $6,503 from the Bond Sinking Fund Cash account was being invested in stocks and bonds of other corporations, so Bond Sinking Fund Investments, a long-term Asset Account, was debited for $6,503. Also at this time, the Bond Sinking Fund Cash account was credited for $6,503, since this cash was being paid out for the investments.

After this entry was made, the Sinking Fund Cash account balance is zero, since all the Bond Sinking Fund cash has now been invested. As of April 1, 2008, the Sinking Fund Investments account balance is $47,262.

• PROBLEM 5–46

On March 1, 1999, the Nettie Corporation, through the Trust Department of the Broad Street National Bank, Chicago, sold $50,000 of 10-year, 7% bonds with a Bond Sinking Fund provision. On March 1, 2000, the first year's Interest on the bonds was paid, and in accordance with the Bond Indenture, a Bond Sinking Fund was set up and run by the Trust Department of the Broad Street National Bank. Within a month thereafter, the Trust Department had invested the $4,000 in stocks and bonds of other corporations.

On March 1, 2001, the Trust Department announced that the stocks and bonds of these corporations had earned $340 Income for the Sinking Fund. Also on that date, the Nettie Corporation made a second $4,000 payment to the Bond Sinking Fund. On April 1, 2001, the Trust Department of the Broad Street National Bank notified the Nettie Corporation that all the money in the Sinking Fund Cash account has been invested in stocks and bonds of other corporations.

On March 1, 2002, the Trust Department of the Broad Street National Bank announced that the Sinking Fund investments had earned $700 Income for the previous 12 months. Also on that date, the Nettie Corporation made a third $4,000 payment to the Bond Sinking Fund.

On April 1, 2002, the Trust Department of the Broad Street National Bank announced that $2,000 of the $4,700 balance in the Sinking Fund Cash account had been invested in stocks and bonds of other corporations.

On March 1, 2003, the Trust Department of the Broad Street National Bank announced that the Sinking Fund investments had earned $950 Income for the previous 12 months. Also on that date, the Nettie Corporation made a fourth $4,000 payment to the Bond Sinking Fund. On April 1, 2003, the Trust Department announced that $5,000 from the Bond Sinking Fund Cash account was being invested in stocks and bonds of other corporations.

On March 1, 2004, the Trust Department of the Broad Street National Bank announced that the Bond Sinking Fund investments had earned $1,380 Income for the previous 12 months. Also on that date, the Nettie Corporation made a fifth $4,000 payment to the Bond Sinking Fund. On April 1, 2004, the Trust Department announced that $6,650 from the Bond Sinking Fund Cash account was being invested in stocks and bonds of other corporations.

On March 1, 2005, the Trust Department of the Broad Street National Bank announced that the Sinking Fund investments had earned $1,421 Income for the previous 12 months. Also on that date, the Nettie Corporation made a sixth $4,000 payment to the Bond Sinking Fund. On April 1, 2005, the Trust Department announced that $6,801 from the Bond Sinking Fund Cash account was being invested in stocks and bonds of other corporations.

On March 1, 2006, the Trust Department of the Broad Street National Bank announced that the Bond Sinking Fund investments had earned $1,950 Income for the previous 12 months. Also on that date, the Nettie Corporation made a seventh $4,000 payment to the Bond Sinking Fund. On April 1, 2006, the Trust Department announced that the entire $5,950 from the Bond Sinking Fund Cash account was being invested in stocks and bonds of other corporations.

On March 1, 2007, the Trust Department of the Broad Street National Bank announced that the Bond Sinking Fund investments had earned $2,358 Income for the previous 12 months. Also on that date, the Nettie Corporation made an eighth $4,000 payment to the Bond Sinking Fund. On April 1, 2007, the Trust Department announced that the entire $6,358 from the Bond Sinking Fund Cash account was being invested in stocks and bonds of other corporations.

On March 1, 2008, the Trust Department of the Broad Street National Bank announced that the Bond Sinking Fund investments had earned $2,503 Income for the previous 12 months. Also on that date, the Nettie Corporation made a ninth $4,000 payment to the Bond Sinking Fund. On April 1, 2008, the Trust Department announced that the entire $6,503 from the Bond Sinking Fund Cash account was being invested in stocks and bonds of other corporations.

On March 1, 2009, the Trust Department of the Broad Street National Bank announced that the Bond Sinking Fund investments had earned $3,302 Income for the previous 12 months. Also on that date, the Nettie Corporation made the tenth and final $4,000 payment to the Bond Sinking Fund. This made a balance in the Bond Sinking Fund Cash account of $7,302 ($3,302 + $4,000). What entries will be made on the books of the Nettie Corporation on March 1, 2009, and how will the accounts appear in the ledger after these entries have been made?

SOLUTION:

2009		$ (in dollars)	
March 1	Bond Sinking Fund Cash	3,302	
	Bond Sinking Fund Income		3,302
1	Bond Interest Expense	3,500	
	Cash		3,500
1	Bond Sinking Fund Cash	4,000	
	Cash		4,000
1	Service Charge Expense	500	
	Cash		500

Bonds Payable

		3/1/99	50,000

Bond Sinking Fund Cash

3/1/2000	4,000	4/1/2000	4,000
3/1/2001	340		
3/1/2001	4,000	4/1/2001	4,340
3/1/2002	700		
3/1/2002	4,000	4/1/2002	2,000

3/1/2003	950		
3/1/2003	4,000	4/1/2003	5,000
3/1/2004	1,380		
3/1/2004	4,000	4/1/2004	6,650
3/1/2005	1,421		
3/1/2005	4,000	4/1/2005	6,801
3/1/2006	1,950		
3/1/2006	4,000	4/1/2006	5,950
3/1/2007	2,358		
3/1/2007	4,000	4/1/2007	6,358
3/1/2008	2,503		
3/1/2008	4,000	4/1/2008	6,503
3/1/2009	3,302		
3/1/2009	4,000		

On March 1, 2009, the Trust Department of the Broad Street National Bank has notified the Nettie Corporation that the sinking fund investments in stocks and bonds of other corporations have brought in $3,302 during the past 12 months. So, Nettie Corporation in the first entry debits Bond Sinking Fund Cash for this $3,302. This is a long-term Asset because even though it is Cash, it is not in the hands of the Nettie Corporation, but is in the hands of the Trust Department of the Broad Street National Bank. It is managed by them and is to be invested when a good investment opportunity comes along. The account Bond Sinking Fund Income is credited for $3,302 to show Revenue. This Revenue account is taxable to the Nettie Corporation and must be reported on its Federal Income Tax return.

Each year the Nettie Corporation must remit to the Broad Street National Bank the interest on the bonds for the year just ended. In this case it is an annual payment of $3,500 ($50,000 × 7%). The Trust Department of the Broad Street National Bank then mails this money to the various outstanding bondholders. So, on the Nettie Corporation books the account Bond Interest Expense is debited for $3,500 to show that the corporation is getting the use of the money. Cash is credited for $3,500 because a check is being mailed to the bank.

The Nettie Corporation also sends the Broad Street National Bank its tenth and final $4,000 payment to the Bond Sinking Fund, so the long-term Asset Account Sinking Fund Cash is debited because this money is added to the Sinking Fund and is still owned by the Nettie Corporation even though it is managed by the Broad Street National Bank. Cash is credited because a check for $4,000 is being mailed to the bank.

Next, the Broad Street National Bank sent a bill to the Nettie Corporation for managing the dealings with the bondholders over the past year, and this bill amounts to $500 because of the extra work the bank has to do not only to pay Interest but to pay off the bonds now at the end of the ten-year period. So, the Nettie Corporation debits Service Charge Expense for $500,0 since it is getting the bank's services, and credits Cash, since it is sending the bank a check for this amount.

Now, at the end of the tenth year, the Sinking Fund Investments account appears as follows:

Sinking Fund Investments

4/1/2000	4,000
4/1/2001	4,340
4/1/2002	2,000
4/1/2003	5,000
4/1/2004	6,650
4/1/2005	6,801
4/1/2006	5,950
4/1/2007	6,358
4/1/2008	6,503
	47,602

As can be seen in the Sinking Fund Investments account above, the cost price of the Bond Sinking Fund investments account is $47,602 as of April 1, 2008, and also, since no other investments have been made since that date, this is also the balance of that account on March 1, 2009, the maturity date of the bonds.

The Trust Department of the Broad Street National Bank sells all the investments at market price, which in this case is the same as cost price, and receives cash of $47,602, making the following book entry:

2009		$ (in dollars)
March 1	Sinking Fund Cash	$47,602
	Sinking Fund Investments	$47,602

This credit to the Sinking Fund Investments account closes it out. The debit of $47,602 to Sinking Fund Cash brings the balance of this account to $54,904. (As of March 1, 2009, the Sinking Fund Cash account carried a balance of $7,302.) This additional $47,602 brings the balance of the Sinking Fund Cash account to $54,904 ($7,302 + $47,602 = $54,904).

The Broad Street National Bank sends a letter to each of the holders of outstanding bonds asking that they send in their bond certificates. As the bond certificates come into the bank, the bank mails them checks for the maturity value of their bonds. This in total amounts to $50,000, and the bank notifies the Nettie Corporation which makes the following entry on its books:

2009		$ (in dollars)	
March 1	Bonds Payable	50,000	
	Sinking Fund Cash		50,000

The Sinking Fund Cash account then appears as follows:

Sinking Fund Cash			
3/1/2009	3,302		
3/1/2009	4,000		
3/1/2009	47,602	3/1/2009	50,000
	54,904		
3/1/2009 Balance	4,904		

The Trust Department of the Broad Street National Bank then closes out the Sinking Fund Cash account by sending the Nettie Corporation a check for the balance of this account, that is: $4,904. Upon receiving this check, the Nettie Corporation makes the following entry on its books:

2009		$ (in dollars)	
March 1	Cash	4,904	
	Sinking Fund Cash		4,904

CHAPTER 6

THE BALANCE SHEET

Basic Attacks and Strategies for Solving Problems in this Chapter. See pages 145 to 164 for step-by-step solutions to problems.

The Balance Sheet, also called the Statement of Financial Position, provides information about a company's Assets, Liabilities, and Owner's Equity. Next to the Income Statement, and possibly the Statement of Cash Flows, the Balance Sheet is probably the most important financial statement in the business world. People readily see the importance of the Income Statement and the Statement of Cash Flows, but the value of the Balance Sheet escapes many.

A Balance Sheet by itself is valuable, but it becomes much more valuable if it is compared with the Balance Sheet of the period immediately preceding. The reader can thereby tell whether or not his or her Assets are increasing or decreasing; whether or not his or her Liabilities are increasing or decreasing, and whether or not the Owners' Equity are increasing or decreasing and how much. Two Balance Sheets and their comparisons are just as valuable to a person, or to a married couple, as they are to a corporation. Thus, a Balance Sheet is an important means of delving into financial information and gaining a clear insight into one's financial affairs.

Contingent Liabilities (or "Maybe Liabilities") are possible increases in the corporation's debts: such as pending lawsuits. In case of Contingent Liabilities, most corporations make a footnote at the bottom of the Balance Sheet, notifying readers of these possible debts.

Some corporations deal in stock options. In cases where stock options have caused a definite debt or loss to the corporation, and where the amount of the loss can definitely be arrived at, the accountants often make an adjusting or correcting entry. Otherwise, they usually opt either to do nothing or to make a footnote at the end of the Balance Sheet.

Some examples of Contingent Liabilities are recall of merchandise and threatened expropriation of Assets, as well as risk of loss from catastrophes.

Often Balance Sheets are not published immediately at year end. Sometimes as much as two months elapse between the end of the fiscal year and the publishing and issuance of the Balance Sheet. How is the Balance Sheet affected if a business discovers that one of its customers has gone bankrupt immediately after year end? What will or should happen to the Balance Sheet if a major warehouse burns after the Balance Sheet date?

Today corporate pension liabilities are important with the issuance of Financial Accounting Standards Board pronouncements. How do a corporation's pension liabilities affect the Balance Sheet?

Because corporations do not always keep their own books according to Income Tax rules, they can sometimes defer some of their Income Tax liabilities to later years. How do corporations make these entries, and how do these affect the Balance Sheet?

The Balance Sheet closely affects the Statement of Cash Flows. How does the accountant set up this Statement of Cash Flows? After the Statement of Cash Flows has been made, how does the accountant reconcile the Net Cash Flow from Operating Activities with the Net Income?

This chapter attempts to answer all these questions and to give concrete examples of all these problems as well as answers to these questions.

Step-by-Step Solutions to Problems in this Chapter, "The Balance Sheet"

• PROBLEM 6–1

One of our clients, the Britt Company, has engaged us to fill out their financial statements for year's end. While working on their Balance Sheet, they notify us that the government has contested their Income Tax of 3 years ago in the amount of $10,000, so they have sent this $10,000 to the federal government under protest until the dispute can be settled. The Britt Company believes that some or all of this amount will be eventually recovered and recommends that we add at least $5,000 of this as Accounts Receivable.

SOLUTION:

Britt Company lawyers are not completely sure that the federal government will return any of the money. The court case stretches out, and no one knows what or when the judge will decide in the case.

Generally Accepted Accounting Principles do not encourage accountants to report gain Contingencies unless it is sure, or almost sure, that the Income will be received by the company. We decide not to put this potential $10,000 Income in the Balance Sheet and decide not even to place it in the Balance Sheet footnotes.

• PROBLEM 6–2

Rumor has it that friends of the Samuels Corporation are raising money to be given as gifts to the corporation. Our client, the Samuels Corporation, suggests that we place these potential gifts in the Asset section of the Balance Sheet.

SOLUTION:

After discussing these possible gifts with various corporation officers, we come to the conclusion that these gifts are not an absolute certainty. We decide not to add these amounts at the present time in the Asset section of the Samuels Corporation's Balance Sheet, or in the body of the Balance Sheet or as a footnote.

• PROBLEM 6–3

Cole Tire Company gives a warranty with each tire sold. The warranty promises buyers a new $70 tire replacement if the tires do not last a definite period of time. From past experience, about 10% of the warranties are used to obtain new tire replacements. During the past year, Cole Tire Company has sold 50,000 tires and thus has given out 50,000 warranties. How should these be handled?

SOLUTION:

An adjusting entry to accrue this Liability should be made if both of two requirements are met: (1) It is probable that some of these tires will need to be replaced and (2) The loss can be reasonably arrived at.

In this case, both these requirements seem to have been met, because in the case of the Cole Tire Company, 10% of the warranties have been used in the past, and each tire can be replaced for $70. We discuss this matter with the client and agree that since 10% of the tires have needed replace in the past, this is the logical figure to use for this year. Since the Cole Tire Company have sold 50,000 tires, 10% of 50,000 is 5,000 possible warranties that may be used. Since each warranty is worth $70, we multiply 5,000 by $70 to obtain a possible loss of $350,000.

The following adjusting entry is made on the books of the Cole Tire Company:

1997		($ in dollars)
December 31 Warranty Expense	350,000	
Warranties Payable		350,000

By debiting Warranty Expense for the $350,000 we expect to lose, we add this much to the Expenses in the end-of-year Income Statement, thus cutting down the Net Income by $350,000 and lowering our Income Tax legally and considerably.

By crediting Warranties Payable, we add $350,000 to our Liabilities in the Balance Sheet, because in all probability we will owe some or all of this as the warranties come in.

• PROBLEM 6-4

The Gordon Manufacturing Company has been our supplier for a number of years, and we have grown to depend on this supplier so that we can have small inventories and Just-in-Time purchasing. Without the ready and constant services of this supplier, our company would be in bad shape if Raw Materials were not received in time. A few months ago Gordon Manufacturing Company approached us with a problem. Because of Cash Flow problems, they have not been able to pay their own suppliers as rapidly as their suppliers have wished, and their suppliers have threatened to stop shipments. This, of course, would not only greatly harm the Gordon Manufacturing Company but would, in turn, harm our own company also. For years, our own company has paid its creditors on time and has never been in a financial bind. At the time of trouble, Gordon Manufacturing did not ask us for a loan but merely to guarantee that their credit purchases from one of their suppliers would eventually be paid. We did this. The amount of the guaranty was for $1,000. Where, if anyplace, should we put this on our company's year-end Balance Sheet?

SOLUTION:

We look over the practice of other accountants in this regard, conferring with them, and discover that some do one thing and some another, and that there is no certain rule on this. We finally decide to place this information in the footnote of the company's Balance Sheet.

• PROBLEM 6–5

One of our clients, the Bittersweet Company, had allowed their Accounts Receivable to reach the alarmingly high figure of $15,000. Naturally, it was seriously affecting their Cash Flow. They had sent out letters to their creditors, but to little avail. Finally, they decided to sell their Accounts Receivable to a factor for $12,000, but the factor insisted that the Bittersweet Company agree to repurchase these Accounts Receivable if the factor was not able to collect on these accounts. We are now preparing a Balance Sheet for the Bittersweet Company at year's end and wonder how to handle this guaranty.

SOLUTION:

In looking over present rules and past practice, we discover that there is no definite rule or practice to cover this situation, and that some firms handle it one way and some another. In other words, some firms do not mention these guaranties at all. Other firms place this information in footnotes of Balance Sheets, while other firms add these amounts to the Liability sections of their Balance Sheets.

In discussing this with our client, the Bittersweet Company, and with their factor, we come to the conclusion that there is a definite possibility that the Bittersweet Company might have to repurchase some of these accounts, but they have no idea how much or how many. We finally come to the conclusion that we will place this information as a footnote in the company's year-end Balance Sheet.

• PROBLEM 6-6

Our client, the Stamford Company, has notified all 10,000 of its stockholders that they will soon be receiving 10,000 stock options, one option for each share outstanding, allowing the stockholders to purchase a share of the Stamford Company stock, any time within the next 90 days, for $30 per share. The stock is now selling at $30 per share, but no one knows what it will be selling for during the next 90 days. Naturally, if the Market Value of the stock rises, the corporation would have to pay the difference between that price and the $30. What should we do about this as far as the company's Balance Sheet is concerned?

SOLUTION:

We discussed this situation with officers of the Stamford Company, with brokers, and with other accountants. There are no definite rules for this situation except that the exact details of the options should be revealed on the financial statement. The exact amount that the company would owe the stockholders cannot definitely be determined at this time. Perhaps the company will owe the stockholders nothing!

It is finally determined that this information should be added to the footnotes of the Balance Sheet but not to the body of the Balance Sheet itself.

• PROBLEM 6-7

One of our clients, the Rabid Fruit Company, has several products on the grocers' shelves. One of them is canned peaches. A customer has complained that one of the cans had spoiled peaches. Because of this complaint, our company has recalled from grocers' shelves $50,000 of canned peaches. How should this recall be handled on the Rabid Fruit Company's Balance Sheet at the end of the year?

SOLUTION:

The Financial Accounting Standards Board suggests that accountants classify Loss Contingencies as probable, reasonably probable, or remote.

In this case the $50,000 loss is more than probable, it is inherent, especially if it can be proved that it is probable that the Liability has occurred and that the loss can be reasonably estimated.

Since the company has called back the entire shipment of fruit, there will undoubtedly be some loss, and since the shipment of fruit can be judged at $25,000, it can be reasonably estimated. We therefore determine that an adjusting entry should be made as follows:

1997		($ in dollars)
December 31 Loss on Recall of Shipment	25,000	
Accounts Payable		25,000

The account Loss on Recall of Shipment is debited for $25,000, the value of the shipment recalled. This loss will be an added Expense on the Income Statement and will cut down the amount of the company's Net Income for the year, 1997, by $25,000, thus cutting down the company's Net Income Tax considerably.

The account Accounts Payable will be credited for $25,000 extra, thus adding $25,000 to the company's Total Liabilities on the Balance Sheet.

• PROBLEM 6–8

One of our clients, Pablo Construction Company, has a warehouse in Angola, which has been insured for $75,000. Because of the civil war there, the warehouse has fallen into the hands of the rebel government, and the latest rumors from Angola inform us that the rebel government will soon probably expropriate (take away) the warehouse from the Pablo Construction Company. Should this news affect the year-end Balance Sheet?

SOLUTION:

We look in accounting literature including information from the Accounting Principles Board and the Financial Accounting Standards Board, as well as from government agencies in this regard. It is found that there are no definite rules from similar cases, but that the Asset could be written off if expropriation is probable and reasonably estimable.

In this case, the news from Angola mentions that expropriation is probable, and we know that the worth of the warehouse is reasonably estimable—that is, $75,000.

Therefore, we decide to write off the warehouse on our year-end books as follows:

1997	($ in dollars)
December 31 Expropriation Loss	75,000
Expropriation Loss Payable	75,000

The account Expropriation Loss is an Expense account, and this will add $75,000 to the Total Expenses in our Income Statement. This will cut down the Net Income at the bottom of the Income Statement by $75,000, thus cutting down our Income Tax considerably.

The account Expropriation Loss Payable is a Liability account and will be placed in the Liability section of our Balance Sheet, thus adding $75,000 to the Total Liabilities in the Balance Sheet and cutting down by $75,000 the value of the Owners' Equity on the Balance Sheet.

• PROBLEM 6–9

One of our clients, the Worldwide Trading Corporation, has just purchased an office building in Bangladesh. They have had great trouble obtaining flood and wind damage insurance on this building. The reason is that much of the country is flooded almost every year, and there are often terrible windstorms that demolish most of the buildings on a regular scale. The Worldwide Trading Corporation has been turned down for insurance by several large insurance companies, and even Lloyds of London has refused to write a policy.

The company has considered self-insurance, which some experts say is "no insurance at all." The appraised value of this office building is $45,000. The corporate officers have approached us wondering how to handle this item on their Balance Sheet, and whether it would be possible to write off this $45,000 investment because of probable loss.

SOLUTION:

The accountants examine all accounting information possible, including textbooks on the subject. In this case, all authorities seem to agree that if the building can be insured by some existing insurance company, the Asset cannot be written off. They encourage the corporation to try all possible means of getting an actual insurance policy, and not to have self-insurance. If it is possible to get the building actually insured, there would be no write-off. However, if this is impossible, then the building could be written off as follows:

1998		($ in dollars)
December 31 Probable Loss	45,000	
Loss Payable		45,000

The Probable Loss account is an Expense, and this would add to the Total Expenses in the Income Statement and thus cut down by $45,000 the Net Income of the corporation for the year. However, since this loss has not actually occurred, it could not cut down the Net Income for Income Tax purposes.

Loss Payable would be a Liability in the Balance Sheet and would add to the Total Liabilities on the Balance Sheet and effectively cut down by $45,000 the Owners' Equity of the corporation on the Balance Sheet.

• PROBLEM 6–10

Two years ago Mrs. Elizabeth Marcy, age 85, was walking on the sidewalk in front of the Hart Corporation Home Office when she slipped on the ice and broke her leg. She was rushed by an emergency vehicle to a local hospital where, after much anguish, her leg was set. She suffered great pain and is suing the Hart Corporation, one of our clients, for $50,000. How should this be handled on the Hart Corporation's year-end books?

SOLUTION:

Accounting authorities have determined that pending or threatened litigation may be accrued if the suits are probable and the loss reasonably estimable. Hart lawyers suggest that they will fight the case, and even if the defendant wins, that there is little possibility that she could win the entire $50,000 for which she is suing.

Since the amount of loss is indefinite, we decide to mention the suit in the footnotes of the Balance Sheet. The other possibility is actually to make an adjusting entry for an amount which we think Hart Corporation might lose, as follows:

1997	($ in dollars)
December 31 Litigation Loss Expense	35,000
Litigation Loss Payable	35,000

The account Litigation Loss Expense is an Expense account which would be placed in the Expense section of the Income Statement. This would add $35,000 to the Total Expenses and deduct $35,000 from the reported Net Income of the corporation. However, since this is not an actual loss, it could not be done for Income Tax purposes, only for accounting purposes.

The account Litigation Loss Payable is a Liability account which would be placed in the Liability Section of the corporation's year-end Balance Sheet, thus adding $35,000 to the Total Liabilities of the corporation and cutting down the Owners' Equity of the corporation by $35,000.

• PROBLEM 6–11

This year, the driver of the delivery truck for the Sweden Corporation, one of our clients, this year got in a fistfight on the street with James Markham. Markham has threatened to sue Sweden Corporation for $50,000. Sweden Corporation's lawyers have checked with the court records and have found that so far no suit has been filed.

SOLUTION:

The Sweden Corporation must now determine whether or not there is a real probability that a suit will be filed, and the probability that they might lose the case. After interviewing the driver of the delivery truck and witnesses to the fight, it is determined that there is some possibility that a suit might be filed. At the time of the encounter, the driver of the delivery truck was actually in the employ of the Sweden Corporation. Since the fight did not break any bones of James Markham, and merely hurt his ego, Sweden lawyers surmise that the probability of an unfavorable outcome is minimal. Therefore, the accountants determine not to accrue the Expense. Another reason is that any possible loss at this point of time is not readily determinable. Since the accountants do not wish to publicize the case until there is actually a suit filed, the accountants determine not to mention this case in the footnotes of the Balance Sheet.

• PROBLEM 6–12

On November 17 of this year, one of our customers who owed us $30,000 declared bankruptcy. We made no entries on our books regarding this situation at that time. Now, on December 31, we wonder what, if anything, we should do before making our year-end Balance Sheet.

SOLUTION:

When phoning the bankruptcy lawyers regarding this situation, we discover that the customer will probably be able to pay 30% of its debts after going through bankruptcy court. Although this is merely an educated guess on the part of the lawyers, the company involved in the bankruptcy proceedings, the Enton Company, does have enough Assets to cover 30% of its debts, and it looks as if these Assets will be sold for their book value.

Our company is in the habit of using the Direct-Writeoff method of handling bad debts. Therefore, we take 30% of the money that this bankrupt customer owes us (30% × $30,000 = $9,000), and consider that perhaps the Enton Company will be able to pay us that amount. Next, we subtract the $9,000 from the amount owed, $30,000 ($30,000 − $9,000 = $21,000). It is therefore assumed that $21,000 will be lost, so we make the following adjusting entry on our books:

1997		($ in dollars)
December 31 Bad Debts Expense	21,000	
Accounts Receivable—Enton Co.		21,000

By debiting Bad Debts Expense, we increase the Expenses on our

Income Statement by $21,000, thus cutting down the Net Income by $21,000. This also cuts down the Income Tax owed considerably. The Enton Company account appears as follows:

Enton Company

1/2/97	30,000	12/31/97	21,000
Balance	9,000		

The balance of $9,000 in the Enton Company account on our books is the amount we hope to recover eventually at the end of bankruptcy proceedings.

• PROBLEM 6–13

On December 13, 1997, our Madison County plant burned to the ground. It was a complete loss. The plant building had originally been purchased for $100,000, and it had been depreciated over the years by the amount of $20,000, giving it a book value of $80,000. The building was insured for $60,000. The machinery was valued at $50,000 with Accumulated Depreciation of $20,000, giving it a book value of $30,000 and was completely covered by insurance. The furniture was valued at $10,000 and insured for $8,000. The inventory, a complete loss, was valued at $50,000 and completely insured. What adjusting entries should be made at year's end in this situation?

SOLUTION:

The first entry will have to do with the plant building's complete loss as follows:

1997			($ in dollars)
December 31	Accumulated Depreciation—Plant Building	20,000	
	Cash Refund from Insurance Policy	60,000	
	Loss on Plant Building	20,000	
	Plant Building		100,000

The Accumulated Depreciation—Plant Building account had a credit balance of $20,000, the total depreciation written off over the years. To get rid of this account, we now debit Accumulated Depreciation—Plant Building for $20,000. The building was insured for $60,000, and our corporation eventually receives a check from the insurance company for this amount, so we debit Cash for $60,000. The Plant Building is a complete loss, and this account has a debit balance of $100,000. So, to get rid of this account, we now credit Plant Building for $100,000. The difference of $20,000 is debited to a Loss on Plant Building account. This is an Expense account and will serve to cut down the Net Income for the business by the amount of $20,000.

Since the machinery was completely covered by insurance, the entry for adjusting the machinery accounts is as follows:

1997		($ in dollars)	
December 31	Accumulated Depreciation—Machinery	20,000	
	Cash Refund from Insurance Policy	30,000	
	Machinery		50,000

Prior to this entry just above, the Machinery account and the Accumulated Depreciation—Machinery account appeared on the company books as follows:

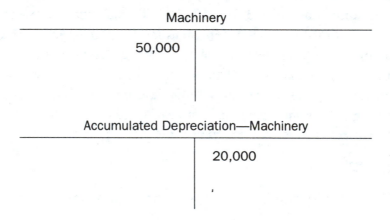

As can be seen from these accounts, the machinery was originally purchased for $50,000, and over the years had been depreciated by the amount of $20,000, giving it a book value of $30,000.

Following the adjusting entry, the Machinery and the Accumulated Depreciation—Machinery accounts appear as follows:

Machinery

50,000	50,000

Accumulated Depreciation—Machinery

20,000	20,000

As can be seen from the above accounts, they have both been closed out by the adjusting entry. The debit to Cash Refund from Insurance Policy shows the Cash Income from the insurance check of $30,000 for the machinery. This debit does not add to the Net Income of the business for tax purposes.

The newly purchased furniture had a debit of $10,000 on the books of the corporation, and none of it had as yet been depreciated. Since it was insured for $8,000, upon receipt of this $8,000 check from the insurance company, the following entry would be made on the books of our corporation:

1997		($ in dollars)
December 31 Cash	8,000	
Loss	2,000	
Furniture		10,000

The debit to Cash for $8,000 is made when the check is received from the insurance company. Furniture is credited for $10,000 to show the loss of furniture to the fire—a complete loss. This also closes out the Furniture account which had previously a debit balance of $10,000. The difference between the value of the furniture and the amount derived from the insurance company, $2,000, is debited to a Loss account ($10,000 − $8,000 = $2,000). This Loss account is an Expense which is placed on the Income Statement and tends to increase the total expenses suffered by the company in the amount of $2,000. This also cuts down the company's Net Income by $2,000 (or increases the loss by $2,000, if that is the case). This loss is deductible for Income Tax purposes.

Since the inventory of $50,000 was completely insured, when the check comes from the insurance company, the following entry is made on the corporation's books:

1997		($ in dollars)
December 31 Cash	5	0,000
Merchandise Inventory		50,000

The Cash debit of $50,000 is the insurance company's check. This does not increase Net Income or Income Taxes owed by the corporation. The Merchandise Inventory account is credited for $50,000 to show the loss of the inventory and to close out the Merchandise Inventory account.

• PROBLEM 6–14

Our fiscal year for the Brown Lumber Company ends on December 31, 1997. On that date, the Jones Company owes us $27,000. After year's end it takes us two months to prepare the Balance Sheet, and on February 2, the Jones Lumber Company declares bankruptcy. It looks as if the entire $27,000 owed to us by the Jones Company will be lost. Should we make an adjusting entry on our books going back to December 31, 1997? Should we report this on the December 31, 1997 Balance Sheet? If so, how?

SOLUTION:

Since the bankruptcy declaration wasn't until after the end of the company's year, no adjusting entry will be required on the books of the old year, 1997. A footnote in the Balance Sheet of December 31, 1997 should mention this bankruptcy, as follows: Our creditor, the Jones Co., which owes us $27,000 declared bankruptcy on February 2, 1998.

• PROBLEM 6–15

Our fiscal year for the Brown Lumber Company ends on December 31, 1997, and the Balance Sheet is dated for that date. However, it actually takes two months to compile the Balance Sheet information, which is then printed and mailed out to the public and the stockholders on about March 2, 1998. On February 16, a major warehouse burned down, causing a loss of approximately $150,000. How should this loss be handled on the Balance Sheet?

SOLUTION:

Since the fire occurred after the Balance Sheet date, it does not affect the body of the Balance Sheet. A footnote should be placed at the bottom of the Balance Sheet mentioning the possible loss of $150,000.

• PROBLEM 6–16

Let us say that one of the Brown Lumber Company warehouses burned down on December 30, 1997, and was a complete loss of $150,000. How will this be reported in the Balance Sheet, if at all? (uninsured)

SOLUTION:

Since the building burned down prior to the Balance Sheet date, it must be reported in the body of the Balance Sheet, under the Liabilities section. Usually, immediately after the tragedy, only an approximate figure can be given. However, this approximate figure should be added in the Liabilities section, thus adding $150,000 to the Liabilities. The adjusting entry could be as follows:

1997		($ in dollars)
December 30 Approximate Loss from Fire	150,000	
Loss Payable		150,000

The Approximate Loss from Fire account will be an added Expense in the year-end list of Expenses in the Income Statement. It will add $150,000 to the Total Expenses and, of course, deduct $150,000 from the

Net Income of the business for the year 1997. The Loss Payable account will be one of the Liabilities in the Balance Sheet and will add $150,000 to the Total Liabilities, thus cutting down the Owners' Equity account by $150,000.

• PROBLEM 6-17

The Hanstead Construction Company employees are members of a labor union, and they have threatened to strike, because the Hanstead Construction Company has no pension program. During the past few months, both union representatives and corporate executives have met together with representatives of insurance companies in an attempt to set up an equitable pension plan for the employees. Both the employees and the corporation plan to invest half of the required cost each year. The corporation's premium amount for the year just ended, 1997, is $120,000, which includes all present and future Liabilities of the pension plan as far as the corporation is concerned. The employees together invest another $120,000 which is taken out of their salaries gradually, according to the agreed-upon rules. How will this pension plan affect the Balance Sheet of the corporation for December 31, 1997?

SOLUTION:

An adjusting entry should be made on the books of the Hanstead Construction Company as follows:

1997		($ in dollars)
December 31 Pension Expense	120,000	
Pension Payable		120,000

The account Pension Expense adds to the Total Expenses in the Income Statement. It is fully deductible for Income Taxes and cuts down the corporate Income Taxes considerably, depending upon the tax bracket of the corporation.

Pension Payable will be a Liability in the Balance Sheet as of December 31, 1997. If this payment is due within a year, it will be listed under Current Liabilities. On the other hand, if the payment need not be made for over a year, it will be listed under long-term Liabilities. In either case, it will add $120,000 to the Total Liabilities, and cut down Owners' Equity by that amount.

• PROBLEM 6–18

The James Construction Company has Income Tax Expense at the end of 1997 of $30,000. This company has always depreciated its plant and equipment by the Straight-Line Method for its own book-keeping purposes. However, for Federal Income Tax purposes, it depreciates its plant and equipment by the Double Declining Method, which is legal, and which temporarily saves on Income Tax. In fact, for this year just ending, 1997, the company saves $5,000 by using the Double Declining method to compute its depreciation. How will this be recorded on the books of the James Construction Company?

SOLUTION:

The James Construction Company should make an adjusting entry as of the year's end as follows:

1997	($ in dollars)	
December 31 Income Tax Expense	30,000	
Income Tax Payable		25,000
Deferred Tax Liability		5,000

The Income Tax Expense account is debited for the full $30,000 that the James Construction Company would owe the federal government using the Straight-Line Method of depreciation for plant and equipment. This adds to the Expenses of the corporation on the Income Statement and cuts down the Net Income by $30,000, thus cutting down the Income Tax considerably.

The Income Tax Payable credit of $25,000 is a Current Liability, since it will have to be paid within a year, and will thus add $25,000 to the Current Liability section of the Balance Sheet. The account Deferred Tax Liability is a long-term Liability and should be placed under that section of the Balance Sheet. It will not have to be paid to the federal government immediately, not until some later year.

In March, when the corporation pays its Income Tax, the following entry will be made:

1998		($ in dollars)
March 15	Income Tax Payable	25,000
	Cash	25,000

The debit to the account Income Tax Payable of $25,000 will close this Current Liability account. The credit to Cash of $25,000 is made when the check for $25,000 is mailed to the federal government with the Income Tax forms.

If the corporation does not buy much new plant and equipment, the equipment and plant accounts will get older, and the time will come when the Liabilities will turn around and the Double Declining Balance Method will report less yearly depreciation than will the Straight-Line Method of depreciation. Let us say that this is true in the year of 1998. Let us say that the Income Tax in 1998 is $20,000 as computed by the Straight-Line Method of depreciation, while the Income Tax using the Double Declining Balance Method of depreciation is $25,000. The following entry would be made on the books of the James Construction Company at year's end:

1998		($ in dollars)
December 31	Income Tax Expense	20,000
	Deferred Tax Liability	5,000
	Income Tax Payable	25,000

The account Income Tax Expense is based on the way the company keeps its books—the Straight-Line Method of depreciation. So at the end of the year, 1998, this account is debited for $20,000. This cuts down the Net Income of the company in the Income Statement by $20,000.

The account Deferred Tax Liability has been carried on the books as a long-term Liability with a credit balance of $5,000. This debit of $5,000 to that account allows it to be closed out. The account Income Tax Payable is credited for the full $25,000, since that is the amount of money owed by the James Construction Company during 1998, using the Double Declining Balance Method of depreciation.

In March of 1999, when the corporation pays its Federal Income Tax, the following entry should be made:

1999		($ in dollars)
March 15	Income Tax Payable	25,000
	Cash	25,000

The account Income Tax Payable is a short-term Liability account, and it is closed out by this entry. Cash is credited because the firm is mailing a check to the federal government for this amount.

• PROBLEM 6-19

The accountant for the Marsh Construction Company is new on the job. He has been assigned to make a Statement of Cash Flows and knows that there are three sections: Operating Activities, Investing Activities, and Financing Activities. He has many transactions during the fiscal period having to do with Cash, but he doesn't know how to separate them into the above three classifications. We are asked to separate these items for the new accountant and to explain to him the differences between Operating Activities, Investing Activities, and Financing Activities so the new accountant will be able to ascertain these differences himself in the future.

Some of these items are as follows: Depreciation Expense; Sale of Plant Assets; Payment of Cash Dividend; Amortization of Intangibles; Gain on Sale of Plant Assets; Purchase of Equipment; Issuance of Common Stock of the Corporation; Redemption of Bonds; Purchase of Land; Decrease in Inventory; and Increase in Accounts Receivable.

SOLUTION:

Depreciation Expense	Operating Activity
Sale of Plant Assets	Investing Activity
Payment of Cash Dividend	Financing Activity
Amortization of Intangibles	Operating Activity
Gain on Sale of Plant Assets	Operating Activity
Purchase of Equipment	Investing Activity
Issuance of Common Stock	Financing Activity
Redemption of Bonds	Financing Activity
Purchase of Land	Investing Activity
Decrease in inventory	Operating Activity
Increase in Accounts Receivable	Operating Activity

(1) If the activity has to do with the day-to-day running of the business, it is classified as an Operating Activity.

(2) If the activity has to do with the purchase or sale of long-term Assets of the business, such as equipment, plant, or land, it is an investing activity.

(3) If the activity has to do with buying or selling the corporation's own stock or bonds, or paying its own dividends, it is a financing activity.

• PROBLEM 6–20

The Net Income for the Harmond Construction Company for the year 1997 is $135,000, and the Net Cash provided by Operating Activities is $182,000. How can one reconcile these two figures?

SOLUTION:

Reconciliation of Net Income with Net Cash Flow from Operating Activities

Net Income		$135,000
Depreciation Expense	15,000	
Increase in Accounts Receivable	(5,000)	
Decrease in Prepaid Expenses	7,000	
Increase in Accounts Payable	30,000	
		47,000
Net Cash Provided by Operating Activities		$182,000

The Net Income is figured by the accrual basis of accounting while the Net Cash provided by Operating Activities is figured on the Cash Basis of accounting. In this reconciliation, we begin with the Net Cash Income of $135,000. To it we add back the depreciation Expense, because depreciation Expense was deducted from sales in the Income Statement to compute Net Income; yet depreciation does not take any Cash in the current year.

Accounts Receivable increased by $5,000. This means that we sold $5,000 more merchandise on account than we received in Cash, so it cuts down Cash by $5,000.

Prepaid Expenses includes such items as prepaid insurance and prepaid rent. These items have decreased by $7,000, which means that we have used up more of these items than we have purchased, thus increasing Cash by $7,000.

Accounts Payable has increased by $30,000. This means that we have purchased $30,000 more on account than we have paid off during the period, so this saves $30,000 cash that we would not have otherwise had.

CHAPTER 7

INTEREST AND MONEY'S VALUE

Basic Attacks and Strategies for Solving Problems in this Chapter. See pages 166 to 207 for step-by-step solutions to problems.

In the Middle Ages the charging of Interest was a crime and a sin. But times have changed, and now money is paid for the use of money. Even notes without an Interest Rate have an imputed or inherent Interest which must be taken into account. Interest is principal times rate times time. Time must elapse before Interest can be charged. The longer the period of time, the more the principal, and the higher the rate, the higher the Interest. Thus, the Future Value of money is always higher than the Present Value of money; or to put it another way—the Present Value of money is always less than the Future Value of money. And this is due to Interest.

In the chapter, two Present Value Tables are introduced: **The Present Value of a Single Sum**, and **The Present Value of an Ordinary Annuity of 1**. Two Future Value Tables are also introduced: **The Future Amount of a Single Sum**, and **The Future Amount of an Ordinary Annuity of 1**. Detailed instructions are given as to how to compute Present Value and Future Value.

Then more difficult types of problems come into view, such as determining the price of bonds sold at a discount, and book entries for bonds sold at a discount, including Interest Payment entries, and maturity date entries. Then bonds sold at a premium are discussed. Book entry items are given for bonds sold at a premium. "T Account" examples of ledger pages are also shown.

Examples of bonds sold at face value are given, as well as entries to pay brokers' fees. Several methods of figuring Interest are shown including figuring by days, months, and years. Examples are given showing finding the maturity date of a note. Journal entries are given showing entries when the money is borrowed, along with adjusting and closing entries at year's end, reversing entries on the first day of the year, and the final entry when the note is paid off. This is done for the books of the borrower and the books of the lender, and these entries are explained in detail. So-called zero-interest notes are defined, and examples given, along with journal entries, and "T-Account" examples, from the viewpoint of both the borrower and the lender.

Compound Interest is discussed, beginning with a simple compounding problem. Tables are shown, and ways to use the table given simply worded. More complicated problems are then constructed, such as a college fund for a baby and setting up a retirement fund for an older person.

More complicated problems are then introduced, such as a corporation's desire to retire an issue of Preferred Stock. However, it is really only the dollar figures that are larger, and it is hoped that even these problems are explained simply enough to be understandable to the non-accountant. Regarding dividend payment by the corporation, the Dates of Declaration, Record, and Payment are discussed.

Finally a discussion explaining how to determine the Present Value of a corporation's pension Liability to its employees.

The whole chapter is in Question-and-Answer Format. The author has explained each question in great detail that most of the troubles that the reader would have can be solved with the simple explanations.

Step-by-Step Solutions to Problems in this Chapter, "Interest and Money's Value"

• PROBLEM 7–1

What is meant by the Future Value of money and the Present Value of money?

Table A–1
Present Value of 1 (Present Value of a Single Sum)

Periods	2%	3%	4%	5%	6%
1	.98039	.97087	.96154	.95238	.94340
2	.96117	.94260	.92456	.90703	.89000
3	.94232	.91514	.88900	.86384	.83962
4	.92385	.88849	.85480	.82270	.79209
5	.90573	.86261	.82193	.78353	.74726
6	.88797	.83748	.79031	.74622	.70496
7	.87056	.81309	.75992	.71068	.66506
8	.85349	.78941	.73069	.67684	.62741
9	.83676	.76642	.70259	.64461	.59190
10	.82035	.74409	.67556	.61391	.65839
11	.80426	.72242	.64958	.58468	.52679
12	.78849	.70138	.62460	.55684	.49697
13	.77303	.68095	.60057	.53032	.46884
14	.75788	.66112	.57748	.50507	.44230
15	.74301	.64186	.55526	.48102	.41727
16	.72845	.62317	.53391	.45811	.39365
17	.71416	.60502	.51337	.43630	.37136
18	.70016	.58739	.49363	.41552	.35034
19	.68643	.57029	.47464	.39573	.33051
20	.67297	.55368	.45639	.37689	.31180

SOLUTION:

If we are to get $100 one year from now, that is the Future Value. The Present Value is a lesser figure dependent on the Interest Rate. For instance, if the going Interest Rate is 6%, the Present Value of $100 a year from now is $94.34. We get this by looking up a single sum of 1 and looking under 1 in the period column and under 6% to get in a Present Value table of .9434. Then we multiply $100 by .9434 and get $94.34. Thus, if we are promised $100 a year from now and the Interest Rate is 6%, it is worth $94.34 now. The Present Value is always less than the Future Value because of the Interest.

• PROBLEM 7-2

The Interest Rate is 6%. Our rich uncle promises us $100 10 years from now. How much is this promise worth right now?

SOLUTION:

We look up in a Present Value table of a single sum of 1, and look under 6% and under 10 periods, discovering a figure as follows: .65839. Then we multiply $100 times .65839 to get $65.839. This means that $100 due us 10 years from now is only worth $65.84 today. The further away the Future Value is, the lower the Present Value.

• PROBLEM 7-3

Present Value is what Future Value is worth now. Let us say we have a zero-interest bond that will mature in 20 years and will be worth $10,000 at that time. What is this bond worth now?
Going Interest Rate is 5%.

SOLUTION:

$3,768.90. This figure is computed by looking at the table for Present Value of 1 (Present Value of a Single Sum). This means that we desire a single sum of money that is worth so much at a Future date. We bring this down to Present Value (a smaller sum) by looking at the table above. Looking down the left side of the table with the column entitled "Periods" we look for 20 periods. Looking along the top of the table for 5%, and coming down that column to the "20 periods" we read the figure ".37689." This means that if we multiply any Future Value by 37.689%, we will get the Present Value of that figure. Why is the percentage figure so low? Because it will take so many years until we get the money.

In this case the zero Interest Rate bonds do not mature until 20 years from now. At that time they will mature, and the maturity value is $10,000. But how much are they worth now? What is the Present Value of these $10,000 bonds?

We multiply the figure from the table (.37689) by the maturity value of the bonds ($10,000). Or, $10,000 × .37689 = $3,768.90. Thus, if the Interest Rate is 5% today, we could buy $10,000 maturity value bonds that mature in 20 years for $3,768.90. These bonds pay no Interest, since they are appreciation bonds. There are two reasons why the purchase price (or Present Value) is so low. One reason is they pay no Interest so there has to be appreciation of value. The other reason is that the maturity date is so far in the future—20 years of waiting. The longer one has to wait, the more the bond appreciates or increases in value. This procedure determines the Present Market Value. Of course, during the intervening years the market rate is bound to change.

• PROBLEM 7–4

The Large Corporation issued $50,000 worth of bonds to build a new factory on January 1, 2000. These are 5% term bonds, due 5 years later, or January 1, 2005, with Interest Payable each July 1 and January 1. Because investors required an effective Rate of Return of 6%, the bonds sold at a discount. At what price were the bonds actually sold?

SOLUTION:

Maturity Value of the Bonds Payable	$50,000.00
Present Value of $50,000 due in 5 years at 6%,	
Interest Payable Semi-Annually (See Table	
A-1. Look up 10 periods, or 10 half-	
years and 3%.) This equals .74409.	
Thus, $50,000 × .74409 =	$37,204.50
Semi-Annual Interest is $1,250.	
($50,000 × 5% × 1/2 = $1,250.)	
Present Value of $1,250 Interest Payable	
Semi-Annually for 5 years at 6%	
annually (Table A-2. Look up 10	
periods, or 10 half-years and 3%.)	
This equals 8.53020	
($1,250 × 8.53020 = $10,662.75)	$10,662.75
Proceeds from the Sale of the Bonds	−47,867.25
Discount on Bonds Payable	2,132.75

Table A-2
Present Value of an Ordinary Annuity of 1

Periods	2%	3%	4%	5%	6%
1	.98039	.97087	.96154	.95238	.95238
2	1.94156	1.91347	1.88609	1.85941	1.83339
3	2.88388	2.82861	2.77509	2.72325	2.67301
4	3.80773	3.71710	3.62990	3.54595	3.46551
5	4.71346	4.57971	4.45182	4.32948	4.21236
6	5.60143	5.41719	5.24214	5.07569	4.91732
7	6.47199	6.23028	6.00205	5.78637	5.58238
8	7.32548	7.01969	6.73274	6.46321	6.20979
9	8.16224	7.78611	7.43533	7.10782	6.80169
10	8.98259	8.53020	8.11090	7.72173	7.36009
20	16.35143	14.87747	13.59033	12.46221	11.46992
30	22.39646	19.60044	17.29203	15.37245	13.76483
40	27.35548	23.11477	19.79277	17.15909	15.04630

Table A-3
Present Value of an Ordinary Annuity of 1

Periods	2-1/2%
1	.97561
2	1.92742
3	2.85602
4	3.76197
5	4.64583
6	5.50813
7	6.34939
8	7.17014
9	7.97087
10	8.75206
20	15.58916
30	20.93029
40	25.10278

The going rate (also known as Effective Rate) of Interest at any one time, in the nation, depends on the supply and demand of money. At the time of this problem, the lenders demanded a yearly Rate of Return of 6%. The bond had been printed at an earlier date and only paid a 5% Rate of

Return. This was not enough to satisfy the investors, so the value of the bond dropped from the maturity value (also face value) of $50,000 to only $47,867.25.

Since Interest is paid semi-annually, there are ten periods or ten half-years. (Five years times 1/2 = 10 half years.) In order to get the Present Value of the $50,000 payment five years from the issuance date of the bond, we look in Table A-l, the Table for the Present Value of 1, or the Present Value of a Single Sum. Look down the Periods column for 10 periods (in this case, 10 half-year periods), and look at the 3% column, since 3% is half of the annual 6% required by the investors. This gives you the figure .74409, meaning that the Present Value is only 74.409% of the maturity value. We then multiply .74409 by the $50,000 maturity value to get $37,204.50, which is the Present Value of the $50,000 maturity value of the bond.

But a bond pays more than the maturity value. It also pays Interest every half year. What is the Present Value of these Interest Payments? In order to compute this figure, we must first determine the Interest Income every half year. This is computed by multiplying the maturity value of the bonds by the Interest Rate printed on the face of the bond times 1/2. The Interest Rate printed on the face of the bond is always the annual rate, so in order to determine a half year's rate, we must multiply this by 1/2. The computation is $50,000 × 5% × 1/2 = $1,250. This means that the corporation will have to mail interest checks every six months amounting to $1,250.

How much is the Total Interest over the life of the bonds? The bonds' life is 5 years or 10 half years, so we multiply the $1,250 Semi-Annual Interest by 10 half years ($1,250 × 10 =$12,500), the Total Interest to be paid, gradually, over the 5-year period. Now we determine its Present Value, or what it is worth right now. Since these are not lump-sum payments, but rather equal payments every half year, we look in the annuity table, since regular payments of regular amounts of money are called annuities.

Looking in Table A-2—Present Value of an Ordinary Annuity of 1, we look up 10 periods and 3%. Ten periods are the ten half years or the life of the bonds, and 3% is half the 6% annual Interest required of the investors. Since the bonds are payable every half year, we are using the 3% half-year Interest which is the same as the 6% annual Interest. Using Table A-2 under the Periods column for 10 periods and looking under the

3% column, we get the figure: 8.53020. Then we multiply the $1,250 semi-annual interest by 8.53020 ($1,250 × 8.53020 = $10,662.75). This $10,662.75 is the Present Value of all the Semi-Annual Interest payments.

The next step is adding the Present Value of the maturity value of the bonds ($37,204.50) and the Present Value of all the Interest Payments ($10,662.75) to get the figure $47,867.25. This is the amount that the investors pay for the bonds. The final step is to subtract the amount paid for the bonds, $47,867.25, from the face value of the bonds, $50,000.00, to get the discount on the bonds. $2,132.75 ($50,000 − $47,867.25 = $2,132.75). This discount is the amount that the Large Company loses by selling the bonds at less than face value.

• PROBLEM 7–5

What entry does the Large Company make on their books when they sell the bonds at a discount?

SOLUTION:

2000		($ in dollars)	
January 1	Cash	47,867.25	
	Discount on Bonds Payable	2,132.75	
	Bonds Payable		50,000

Cash is debited for $47,867.25, since this is all the money that the Large Company received from selling the bonds. The money will be used to build the factory. Discount on Bonds Payable is debited for $2,132.75, the amount the Large Company lost. This discount account is a Contra-Liability and will have to be amortized (written off) over the life of the bonds. Bonds Payable is credited for $50,000. This $50,000 is the face value of the bonds. It is also the maturity value of the bonds, or the amount that the Large Company will have to pay the bondholders 5 years from now.

• PROBLEM 7-6

What entry does the Large Company make on its books on July 1, at the first Interest-Payment date?

SOLUTION:

2000			($ in dollars)
July 1	Bond Interest Expense	1,250	
	Cash		1,250
1	Bond Interest Expense	213.27	
	Discount on Bonds Payable		213.27

As seen from the entries immediately above, it takes two entries on the Interest-Payment date. The first one shows the payment of the Interest, and the second one shows the Amortization of the discount.

The Semi-Annual Interest is computed by using the Interest Rate printed on the face of the bond, which in this case is 5%. Since it is for only half a year, we also multiply by 1/2. ($50,000 × 5% × 1/2 = $1,250.) Bond Interest Expense is debited because the Large Company is getting the use of the investors' money. Cash is credited for $1,250 because Interest checks totalling this amount are being mailed to the various bondholders.

Discount on Bonds Payable is a Contra-Liability account with a debit balance of $2,132.75, the amount lost by the Large Company, because it sold the bonds at a price that much below the face value of the bonds. This account must be amortized, or gradually written off, over the 5-year life of the bonds. It is actually written off over the 10 half-years because there are ten half-year Interest Payments. In order to compute this figure, we divide the $2,132.75 by 10 to get $213.27. The account, Bond Interest Expense, is debited for $213.27 because this Amortization entry adds to the costs of the Large Company doing business. The account, Discount on Bonds Payable, is credited in order to cut down on the value of this account. The Discount on Bonds Payable, after the above entry, will appear as follows:

Discount on Bonds Payable	
2,132.75	213.27
1,919.48	

The $2,132.75 is the amount the Large Company originally lost because the bonds were sold too cheaply. The $213.27 is the first 6 months' Amortization. The $1,919.48 is the amount that is still left to be amortized, often called the unamortized amount. Each six months another Amortization entry will be made, but at the end of the next six months, it will be for $213.28, to take care of the odd amount.

• PROBLEM 7-7

What entry or entries does the Large Company make on their books at maturity date?

SOLUTION:

2005			($ in dollars)
January 1	Bond Interest Expense	1,250	
	Cash		1,250
1	Bond Interest Expense	213.28	
	Discount on Bonds payable		213.28

2005			($ in dollars)
January 1	Bonds Payable	50,000	
	Cash		50,000

As seen above, there are actually three entries that the Large Company needs to make on the maturity date, which in this case is January 1, 2005. The first entry, debiting Bond Interest Expense and crediting cash, is the final entry for the Interest Expense when the company sends out its final Interest Payment to the various bondholders. It debits Bond Interest Expense because the company is getting the use of the investors' money for these past six months. It credits Cash because it is mailing out the Interest checks.

The second entry is the final entry to amortize the account, Discount on Bonds Payable. The $213.28 is debited to bond Interest Expense because the amount of money the company lost by selling the bonds too cheaply is an Expense to the company. The account, Discount on Bonds Payable, is credited to close out this account. This account will appear on maturity date as follows:

Discount on Bonds Payable

2,132.75	213.27
	213.28
	213.27
	213.28
	213.27
	213.28
	213.27
	213.28
	213.27
	213.28
	2,132.75

The third and final entry of the series debits Bonds Payable for $50,000. This is the face value and the maturity value of the bonds outstanding. On maturity date the bondholders bring or mail their bonds back to the company, so the company debits Bonds Payable. The company then sends the bondholders the maturity value of the bonds, as checks. So the company credits Cash for $50,000.

• PROBLEM 7-8

The Large Corporation issued $50,000 worth of bonds to build a new factory on January 1, 2002. These are 6% term bonds, due 5 years later, or January 1, 2007, with Interest Payable each July 1 and January 1. Between the years 2000 and 2002 the effective Rate of Interest dropped to 4%, causing the bonds to be sold at a premium. The reason the bonds sell at a premium in this case is that the rate printed on the face of the bonds—6%—is higher than the effective market rate of 4%. At what price were the bonds actually sold?

SOLUTION:

Maturity Value of the Bonds Payable	$50,000.00
Present Value of $50,000 due in 5 years at 4%	
Interest Payable Semi-Annually (See Table A-1).	
(Look up 10 periods, or 10 half-years and 2%.)	
This equals .82035. Thus, $50,000 × .82035 = $41,017.50	
Semi-Annual Interest is $1,500.	
($50,000 × 6% × 1/2 = $1,500)	
Present Value of $1,500 Interest Payable	
Semi-Annually for 5 years at 4% annually	
(Table A-2) (Look up 10 periods, or	
10 half-years and 2%.) This equals 8.98259.	
($1,500 × 8.98259 = 13,473.885) $13 473.885	
Proceeds from Sale of Bonds	$54,491.385
Premium on Bonds Payable	$ 4,491.385

The going rate (also known as Effective Rate) of Interest at any one time, in the nation, depends on the supply and demand of money. At the time of this problem, January 1, 2002, the lenders demanded a yearly Rate of Return of only 4%. The bond had been printed at an earlier date and paid a 6% Rate of Return. This was more than enough to satisfy the investors, so the value of the bond increased from the maturity value (also the face value) of $50,000 to $54,491.385.

Since Interest is paid semi-annually, there are ten periods or ten half-years (five years times 1/2 = 10 half years). In order to get the Present Value of the $50,000 payment five years from the issuance date of the bond, we look at Table A-l, the Table for the Present Value of 1, or the Present Value of a Single Sum. Look down the Periods column for 10 periods (in this case, 10 half-year periods), and look at the 2% column, since 2% is half of the annual 4% required by the investors. This gives us the figure .82035, meaning that the Present Value is only 82.035% of the maturity value. We then multiply .82035 by the $50,000 maturity value to get $41,017.50, which is the Present Value of the $50,000 maturity value of the bond.

But a bond pays more than the maturity value. It also pays Interest every half year. What is the Present Value of these Interest payments? In order to compute this figure, we must first determine the Interest Income every half year. This is computed by multiplying the maturity value of the bonds by the Interest Rate printed on the face of the bond times 1/2. The Interest Rate printed on the face of the bond is always the annual rate, so in order to determine a half year's rate, we must multiply this by 1/2. The computation is $50,000 × 6% × 1/2 = $1,500. This means that the corporation will have to mail Interest checks every six months amounting to $1,500.

How much is the Total Interest over the life of the bonds? The bonds' life is 5 years or 10 half years, so we multiply the $1,500 Semi-Annual Interest by 10 half years ($1,500 × 10 = $15,000), the Total Interest to be paid, gradually, over the 5-year period. Now we must bring this $15,000 down to size and determine its Present Value, or what it is worth right now. Since these are not lump-sum payments, but rather, equal payments every half year, we must look in the annuity table, since regular payments of regular amounts of money are called annuities.

Looking in Table A-2—Present Value of an Ordinary Annuity of 1, we look up 10 periods and 2%. Ten periods are the ten half years or the life of the bonds, and 2% is half the 4% annual Interest required of the investors. Since the bonds are payable every half year, we are using the 2% half-year Interest which is the same as the 4% annual Interest. Using Table A-2 under the Periods column for 10 periods and looking under the 2% column, we get the figure 8.98259. Then we multiply the $1,500 Semi-Annual Interest by 8.98259 ($1,500 × 8.98259 = $13,473.885). This $13,473.885 is the Present Value of all the Semi-Annual Interest Payments.

The next step is adding the Present Value of the maturity value of the bonds ($41,017.50) and the Present Value of all the Interest Payments ($13,473.885) to get the figure $54,491.385.

This is the amount that the investors pay for the bonds. The final step is to subtract the face value of the bonds, $50,000.00, from the amount paid for the bonds, $54,491.385, to get the Premium on the bonds, which in this case is $4,491.385 ($54,491.385 − $50,000.00 = $4,491.385.) This premium is the extra amount that the Large Company gains because the bonds were sold for more than the face value. The chief reason that the bonds were sold at more than their face value was because the Interest Rate printed on the face of the bonds, 6%, was higher than the effective or going Interest Rate in the nation at the time, 4%.

• PROBLEM 7–9

What entry is made on the company books when these bonds are sold at a premium?

SOLUTION:

2002		($ in dollars)	
January 1	Cash	54,491.39	
	Premium on Bonds Payable		4,491.39
	Bonds Payable		50,000.00

Because the bonds were sold at a premium, the company received $54,491.39 instead of the $50,000, so Cash is debited for the full amount of $54,491.39. The Premium or reward for the company in this case is $4,491.39, the difference between the amount of Cash actually received and the maturity value of the bonds ($54,491.39 – $4,491.39 = $50,000).

The account, Premium on Bonds Payable, was credited for this amount, $4,491.39. The Premium on Bonds Payable account is considered to be a Liability, and it is amortized through Bond Interest Expense every six months over the life of the bonds.

The account, Bonds Payable, is credited for $50,000. This is the amount printed on the face of the bonds and is also the total maturity value of the bonds.

• PROBLEM 7–10

What entry is made on the company books six months after the bonds are sold?

SOLUTION:

2002		($ in dollars)	
July 1	Bond Interest Expense	1,500.00	
	Cash		1,500.00
1	Premium on Bonds Payable	449.14	
	Bond Interest Expense		149.14

Two entries are made at the end of six months after the bonds are sold. The first entry is to show the payment of six months' Interest. In this case the Interest is $1,500, computed as follows: ($50,000 × 6% × 1/2 = $1,500). The $50,000 is the maturity value of the bonds. The 6% rate is the Interest Rate printed on the face of the bonds, also known as the Coupon Rate. It is also multiplied by 1/2 because it is one-half of a year's Interest.

In the first of the two entries, the account, Bond Interest Expense, is debited for the $1,500, because the company is getting the use of the $50,000. Cash is credited for $1,500 because checks for that amount are being mailed out to the various bondholders.

In the second of the two entries, the account, Premium on Bonds Payable, is debited for $449.14. This amortizes or writes off 1/10 of the premium. As was noted earlier, the premium on Bonds Payable was $4,491.39, and the life of the bonds is five years (or 10 half years.) So each half year the premium is written off by 1/10 of its value, and 1/10 of $4,491.39 is $449.14. Also, the account, Bond Interest Expense, is credited for $449.14, since the premium cuts down the Bond Interest Expense.

• PROBLEM 7-11

How does the account, Premium on Bonds Payable, appear on the books of the Large Corporation after the first six months of the bonds' life have elapsed?

SOLUTION:

Premium on Bonds Payable

2002		2002	
July 1	449.14	January 1	4,491.39
		Balance	4,042.25

The January 1, 2002 entry shows the original premium on Bonds Payable of $4,491.39, the extra amount the Large Corporation earned by selling the bonds for that amount over the face value. The July 1, 2002 entry shows the Amortization entry at the end of the first six months of the bonds' lives, for $449.14, or 1/10 of the value of the premium. The credit balance of $4,042.25 shows the unamortized premium, or the amount of the premium not yet written off.

• PROBLEM 7-12

What entry or entries are made on the books of the Large Corporation at the maturity date of the bonds?

SOLUTION:

2007			($ in dollars)
January 1	Bond Interest Expense	1,500.00	
	Cash		1,500.00
1	Premium on Bonds Payable	449.14	
	Bond Interest Expense		449.14
1	Bonds Payable	50,000.00	
	Cash		50,000.00

There are three entries that need to be made on the books of the Large Corporation at the maturity date of the bonds. The first one is the final Semi-Annual Interest Payment of $1,500. The Semi-Annual Interest Payment is computed as follows: $50,000 \times 6\% \times 1/2 = \$1,500$. It will be noted that the Coupon Rate of Interest (the rate printed on the face of the bonds), *not* the Effective Rate of Interest, is used in this computation.

The account, Bond Interest Expense, is debited because the Large Corporation has received the use of the $50,000 during these last six months. Cash is credited because the corporation is mailing Interest checks to the various bondholders at this time.

The second of the three entries is the Amortization entry to write off the balance of the Premium on Bonds Payable account. That account was originally credited for $4,491.39, and at the end of each of the 10 half-year periods the account was debited for 1/10 of that figure, or $4,042.25. So Premium on Bonds Payable is debited for $449.14. This is the tenth and final entry and will close out the account. Bond Interest Expense is credited for $449.14 because the Premium, or reward to the company, cuts down the Bond Interest Expense.

The third of the three entries shows the receipt of the bonds by the Large Corporation, and the final payment of the money borrowed, to the bondholders of the corporation. The Large Corporation or its bank trustee has previously sent a letter to the bondholders notifying them of the approaching maturity date and requesting that they mail in their bond certificates. Those bondholders who fail to mail in their bond certificates do not receive their money, and also, after the maturity date, they receive no more interest. Let us assume, therefore, that all the Bond Certificates have been mailed back to the corporation. Thus, the corporation debits the account, Bonds Payable, for the maturity value (which is also the face value) of the bonds—$50,000. It then mails checks to the bondholders so credits Cash for $50,000.

• PROBLEM 7-13

How does the account, Premium on Bonds Payable, appear on the books of the Large Corporation after the maturity date of the bonds?

SOLUTION:

Premium on Bonds Payable

2002		2002	
July 1	449.14	January 1	4,491.39
2003			
January 1	449.13		
2003			
July 1	449.14		
2004			
January 1	449.14		
2004			
July 1	449.14		
2005			
January 1	449.14		

2005	
July 1	449.14
2006	
January 1	449.14
2006	
July 1	449.14
2007	
January 1	449.14
	4,491.39

As can be seen from the "T" account above, the Liability account, Premium on Bonds Payable is written off over the life of the bonds. The premium was originally $4,491.39, and 1/10 of this figure is written off each half year over a period of 5 years (10 half years).

• PROBLEM 7-14

The Large Corporation issued $50,000 worth of bonds to build a new factory on January 1, 2009. These are 6% bonds, due 5 years later, or on January 1, 2014, with Interest Payable each July 1 and January 1. Between the years 2002 and 2009, the effective Rate of Interest increased to 6%, causing the bonds to be sold at Par. The reason the bonds sell at Par in this case is that the rate printed on the face of the bonds—6%—is the same as the effective Market Rate of 6%. At what price were the bonds actually sold?

SOLUTION:

$50,000. When the effective Market Rate is the same as the Coupon Rate (rate printed on the face of the bonds), then the bonds are sold at Par, which is the exact amount printed on the face of the bonds, and which is also the maturity value—in this case, $50,000.

• PROBLEM 7–15

What entry is made on the books of the Large Corporation on the date that the bonds are sold?

SOLUTION:

2009		($ in dollars)	
January 1	Cash	50,000	
	Bonds Payable		50,000

The Large Corporation is receiving a $50,000 loan from the bondholders, so the account, Cash, is debited for that amount. The corporation at the same time is sending bonds to the new bondholders, the face amount of which is also $50,000; so the account, Bonds Payable, is credited for $50,000.

• PROBLEM 7–16

How are brokers' fees handled on the books of the Large Corporation?

SOLUTION:

2009		($ in dollars)	
January 1	Brokerage Expense	1,000	
	Cash		1,000

Let us assume that the brokers that sell the bonds to the public charge the Large Corporation $1,000 for selling the bonds. This is a deductible Expense to the corporation, so Large Corporation debits Brokerage Expense. The corporation is getting the use of the brokers' services. The corporation also credits Cash for $1,000 since it sends the brokerage firm a check for that amount.

• PROBLEM 7–17

The Smith Construction Company needs money to construct an office building. They believe the building will be constructed at a cost of $10,000, and that they will be able to pay this off in 4 years. The banker agrees to this, and the officers of the Smith Construction Company sign a $5,000 note at 8% for 5 years. What is the Interest on the note?

SOLUTION:

$2,000. Interest is a combination of Principal times Rate times Time. If there is no Time, there is no Interest. In this case, the Principal is the amount of money borrowed, or $5,000. The Rate is 8%, and the Time is 5 years. In order to compute the Interest, one multiplies the $5,000 by the Rate of 8% to get $400. This is one year's Interest. Then one multiplies the $400 by 5 years to get $2,000.

• PROBLEM 7–18

The Elmand Corporation needs money to pay current debts. They immediately need $1,500 and believe they can pay this back in 120 days. How much Interest will they have to pay if the bank charges 9%?

SOLUTION:

$45. Interest is Principal times Rate times Time. In this case, the Principal or amount borrowed is $1,500, and the Rate is 9%, and the Time is 120 days. First, we multiply the Principal of $1,500 times 9% ($1,500 × .09 = 135). The $135 is the yearly Interest. But we are borrowing the money for only 120 days, so we use the fraction 120/360, or 1/3 of a year. Businessmen and especially bankers are allowed by law to use a 360 day year because it is near enough to the 365 1/4 day year, and it is easier to compute. Then we multiply the $135 yearly Interest by 1/3 of a year to get the answer, $45.

• PROBLEM 7-19

The Hinton Company was behind in paying its current Liabilities. The officers decided to go to the bank and borrow $2,000 for 8 months, at which time it was determined the company would have sufficient working capital to pay its debts. The banker charged the going Rate of Interest of 5%. How will the Interest be figured?

SOLUTION:

Interest is computed by multiplying Principal by Rate by Time. In this case, we multiply the Principal or amount borrowed of $2,000 by 5% ($2,000 × .05 = $100), and $100 is the amount of Interest for a year. But this loan is only for 8 months, or 8/12 of a year. The fraction 8/12 can be reduced to 2/3, so it is for 2/3 of a year. Multiply 2/3 by $100 to get $66.67, the amount of the Interest on this note ($100 × 2/3 = $66.67).

• PROBLEM 7-20

The Hinton Co. borrowed $2,000 for 8 months at 5%. The Interest to be paid was $66.67. What was the maturity value of the note?

SOLUTION:

The maturity value of the note is the face value plus the Interest expense. In this case the face value of the note is $2,000 and the Interest Expense is $66.67, so the maturity value of the note is $2,066.67.

• PROBLEM 7-21

On January 16, 2000 the Bascomb Corporation borrowed $10,000 from the First National Bank of Beacon City by signing a $10,000 note at 5% for 90 days. What is the maturity date of the note?

SOLUTION:

April 15.

It is possible to count 90 days ahead on a calendar, but this is extremely time consuming when the average knowledgeable individual can figure this out with a short computation. Of course, in order to do so, one most know the number of days in each month. One of the easiest ways to remember these facts is by memorizing the following poem:

> Thirty days hath September,
> April, June, and November.
> All the rest have thirty-one
> Except February having twenty-eight,
> Except one year in four
> Having one day more.

But which year is leap year? Leap years are years divisible by four and are years when there is a presidential election.

The computation of the Maturity Date of this note is to put down on paper the number of days in the month in which the note was signed. In this case the month is January, which has 31 days, so "31" is placed on the paper. The next step is to subtract the date of the note, 16. The difference is 15 days, the number of days that the note will run in January. Thus, the first part of the computation is as follows:

> 31 days in January
> −16 day of January—date of note
> 15 days that the note runs in January

The next step is to determine the days that the note runs in the following month, which is February. Usually February has 28 days, but it has 29 days in leap year. Is the year 2000 a leap year? The usual rule is that if the year is divisible by 4, then it is a leap year. However, the Gregorian Calendar has an additional rule that a century year, in order to be a leap year, also has to be divisible by 400. It turns out, then, that the year 2000 is not only divisible by 4, but also by 400, and it is therefore a leap year. (It will be noted that the century years 2100, 2200, and 2300, though divisible by 4, are not leap years. For this reason, the Julian Calendar of Russia keeps getting further behind the other nations of the world, which are mainly on the Gregorian Calendar, because the Julian calendar does not have the 400 rule. The Julian Calendar is now 13 days behind the

Gregorian Calendar, and in the year 2100 will slip to 14 days behind the Gregorian Calendar, since in 2100 the Julian Calendar will have a February 29 while the Gregorian Calendar will not. (The year is not exactly 365 days long. It is somewhat less than that, and without the 400 rule the calendar year will be too short and will not accurately measure an earthly year.)

Getting back to the computation, since the year 2000 is a leap year under the Gregorian Calendar, we will add 29 days for February of the year 2000. Now we have 15 days that the note runs in January and 29 days running in February. Does the total of these two figures come within 30 days of the 90 days that the note runs? No; 15 and 29 add up to 44, which is not within a month of 90 days. So it is time to add another month to the computation. The next month is March, and since March has 31 days, we add 31. to Now we re-add 16 days that the note runs in January, 29 days in February, and 31 days in March. This adds up to a total of 75 days. Is 75 days within a month of the total of 90 days? Yes, if we subtract 75 days from 90 days, we get 15 days. The next month is April, so the maturity date of the note is April 15.

Thus, the computation of the maturity date of the note will appear as follows:

```
     31 days in January
   –16 date of note, January 16, 2000
     15 days that the note runs in January
     29 days in February in the year 2000
     31 days in March
     75 days
     90 day note
   –75 days accounted for thus far
     15 of April, maturity date of note.
```

• PROBLEM 7–22

On January 16, 2000, the Billings Company borrows $2000 from the Tracy National Bank at 7% Interest for 560 days. What is the Maturity Date of the note? How much Interest will need to be paid? What is the maturity value of the note? What entries will have to be made on the books of the borrower? What entries will have to be made on the books of the lender?

SOLUTION:

31 days in January

– 16 (January 16, date of note)

15 days that the note runs in January

29 days in February in the year 2000

31 days in March

30 days in April

31 days in May

30 days in June

166 days accounted for thus far

365 days in the non-leap year of 2001

531 days accounted for thus far

560 day note

–531 days accounted for thus far

29 days more to be accounted for Maturity date—July 29, 2001

There are 31 days in January, the month in which the money is borrowed. The money was borrowed on January 16, so 16 is subtracted from 31 to give a remainder of 15. Thus, the note runs 15 days during January. It also runs 29 days in February, 31 days in March, 30 days in April, 31 days in May, 30 days in June, for a total thus far of 166 days. Since the note runs for more than a year, the number 365 is added, because there are 365 days in a non-leap year, and the year 2001 is not a leap year. This gives a total of 531 days to be accounted for to this point in the computation. The final step is to subtract the 531 days accounted for from the 560 days of the note, to get 29 days. Going 29 days into the next month, which happens to be July, we find that the Maturity Day or Date of the note is July 29 of the following year, or the year 2001.

The second part of the problem is to compute the Interest on the note.

The note is for $2,000 at 7% for 560 days. First, we multiply the 7% by $2,000, as follows: 2,000 × .07 = $140. Using the banker's 360-day year, and the number of days in the note, 560, we derive the following fraction: 560/360. Multiplying 560/360 times $140, we get $217.77, the amount of Interest on the note.

The third part of the problem is to compute the maturity value of the note. The maturity value is the face value plus the Interest. We add the face value of $2,000 and the Interest of $217.77 to get the maturity value of $2,217.77 ($2,000 + $217.77 = $2,217.77).

The fourth part of the problem is making the entries on the books of the borrower. They are as follows:

Billings Company Books

2000		($ in dollars)	
January 16	Cash	2,000.00	
	Notes Payable		2,000.00
	Borrowed $2000 from bank and signed note for $2000.		
December 31	Interest Expense	136.11	
	Interest Payable Adjusting Entry		136.11
31	Income Summary	136.11	
	Interest Expense Closing Entry		136.11
2001		($ in dollars)	
January 1	Interest Payable	136.11	
	Interest Expense Reversing Entry		136.11
July 28	Notes Payable	2,000.00	
	Interest Expense	217.77	
	Cash		2,217.77
	Paid off the note plus interest.		

The fifth part of the problem is making the entries on the books of the lender, the Tracy National Bank.

Tracy National Bank Books

2000			($ in dollars)
January 16	Notes Receivable—Billings Company	2,000.00	
	Cash		2,000.00
	Billings Co. borrowed $2,000 from bank and signed a 7% note.		
December 31	Interest Receivable	136.11	
	Interest Income Adjusting Entry		136.11

2000			($ in dollars)
December 31	Interest Income	136.11	
	Income Summary Closing Entry		136.11

2001			($ in dollars)
January 1	Interest Income	136.11	
	Interest Receivable Reversing Entry		136.11
July 28	Cash	2,217.77	
	Notes Receivable—Billings Company		2,000.00
	Interest Income		217.77

Explanation of the Entries on the Books of the Billings Company

On January 16, 2000, the Billings Company borrowed $2,000 from the Tracy National Bank. So they debited Cash for $2,000. At this time they wrote a $2,000 note to the bank and credited Notes Payable for $2,000 on their books.

On December 31, 2000, an adjusting entry was made debiting an Expense account entitled Interest Expense for $136.11, and crediting a Liability account entitled Interest Payable for $136.11. The figure, $136.11, is the amount of Interest accrued or built up on the note during the year, between the date the note was signed, January 16, 2000, and the end of the year, December 31, 2000. This Interest is computed as follows: $2,000 \times 7\% \times 350/360 = \$136.11$.

The 350 is the number of the days that the note has run so far, as follows: 15 days that the note has run between January 16, the date the note was signed, and the 31st of January; 29 days in February because the year 2000 is a leap year, 31 days in March, 30 days in April, 31 days in May, 30 days in June, 31 days in July, 31 days in August, 30 days in

September, 31 days in October, 30 days in November, and 31 days in December. These figures all add up to 350 days, which is the numerator of the fraction. The denominator of the fraction is 360 days and is legally used as the bankers' year.

This adjusting entry at year's end is necessary because the built-up Interest must be shown on the corporate books for Income Tax purposes. Even though the Cash has not yet been paid, the Interest Expense for the old year must be debited to the Expense account entitled Interest Expense. This legally cuts down the company's Net Income, thus cutting down the company's Income Tax by $136.11. In the adjusting entry the Liability account, Interest Payable, is credited because the company owes $136.11 which has not as yet been paid to the bank. This Interest Payable account will appear in the Liability section of the Billings Company's Balance Sheet at the end of the year, 2000.

The closing entry debits Income Summary, a catch-all account at year's end and credits Interest Expense. This closes out Interest Expense, a temporary account, since all temporary accounts must be closed out into Income Summary at year's end.

The reversing entry on January 1, 2001, debits Interest Payable to close out that account and credits Interest Expense so that the old year's Interest will not appear on the new year's books.

Finally, on July 28, 2001, the Billings Company pays the Tracy National Bank the maturity value of the note, $2,217.77, by crediting Cash for that amount. In return the Billings Company receives its note back from the bank marked "paid." The face value of the note is $2,000, so the Billings Company debits Notes Payable for $2,000. The Total Interest Expense for the entire 560 days that the note runs is $217.77, so the account, Interest Expense is debited for this amount. It is debited because the Billings Company has received the use of this money.

Explanation of the entries on the books of the Bank

On January 16, 2000, the Tracy National Bank lent the Billings Company $2,000 and received a note from the Billings Company for that amount. They debited Notes Receivable—Billings Company for $2,000 and credited Cash for $2,000; this was the amount that they lent to Billings.

On December 31, 2000, an adjusting entry was made debiting an Asset account, Interest Receivable, for $136.11 and crediting a Revenue account, Interest Income, for $136.11. The figure, $136.11, is the amount of Interest accrued or built up on the note during the year, between the date the note was signed, January 16, 2000, and the end of the year, December 31, 2000. This Interest is computed as follows: $2,000 × 7% × 350/360 = $136.11:

The 350 is the number of the days that the note has run so far, as follows: 15 days that the note has run between January 16, the date the note was signed, and the 31st of January; 29 days in February because the year 2000 is a leap year, 31 days in March, 30 days in April, 31 days in May, 30 days in June, 31 days in July, 31 days in August, 30 days in September, 31 days in October, 30 days in November, and 31 days in December. These figures all add up to 350 days, which is the numerator of the fraction. The denominator of the fraction is 360 days and is legally used as the bankers' year.

This adjusting entry at year's end is necessary because the built-up Interest must be shown on the corporate books for Income Tax purposes. Even though the Cash has not yet been received, the Interest Income for the old year must be credited to the Revenue account, Interest Income, and added to the Income of the business for the old year, to be reported on the annual report's Income Statement and reported to the government on the Income Tax return of the business. The Asset account, Interest Receivable, is debited because in effect the business owns the money that it has earned but has not yet received.

The closing entry credits Income Summary, a catch-all account to which all temporary accounts are closed at year's end. The credit balance of Interest Income is closed out by debiting Interest Income for that amount.

The reversing entry on January 1, 2001, debits Interest Income so that the old year's Interest will not appear on the new year's books. It credits Interest Receivable to close out that account.

Finally, on July 28, 2001, the Tracy National Bank receives the maturity value of the note, $2,217.77, and debits Cash for this amount. It returns the note marked paid to the Billings Company, so credits Notes Receivable—Billings Company for the face value of the note, in this case, $2,000. The difference, $217.77, is credited to Interest Income, because this is the amount earned by the bank over the life of the note, and it must be added to the bank's Income and reported in the bank's Income Statement for the year 2001 and on the bank's Income Tax return for the year 2001.

The Tracy National Bank's Interest Income account, in so far as this note with the Tracy National Bank is concerned, would appear as follows:

Interest Income

2000		2000	
Dec. 31	136.11	Dec. 31	136.11
2001		2001	
Jan. 1	136.11	July 28	217.77
		Balance	81.66

The amount of $136.11 is the portion of the $217.77 Total Interest Revenue that was earned in the year, 2000. The $81.66 is the portion of the $217.77 Total Interest Revenue that was earned in the year, 2001.

Answers

What is the Maturity Date of the note?	July 29, 2001
How much Interest will need to be paid?	$217.77
What is the maturity value of the note?	$2,217.77

• PROBLEM 7–23

How can there be Zero-Interest notes in the business world?

SOLUTION:

Zero-Interest notes really contain an Interest element. So-called Zero-Interest notes have a higher face value than borrowing value, and the difference between the two is the Interest, but it is called Discount.

• PROBLEM 7-24

Give examples of Zero-Interest notes?

SOLUTION:

On January 16, 2000, the Billings Company borrows $2,000 from the Tracy National Bank for 560 days, but it signs a note for the maturity value of $2,217.77. What entries are made on the books of the Billings Company?

Billings Company Books

2000		($ in dollars)	
January 16	Cash	2,000.00	
	Discount on Notes Payable	217.77	
	Notes Payable		2,217.77
	Borrowed $2,000 from Tracy National Bank but signed a note for the maturity value of $2,217.77.		
December 31	Interest Expense	136.11	
	Discount on Notes Payable		136.11
	To record accrued Interest.		
31	Income Summary	136.11	
	Interest Expense		136.11
	To close out the Interest Expense account at year's end.		

2001		($ in dollars)	
July 28	Interest Expense	81.66	
	Discount on Notes Payable		81.66
	To record Interest on the note during the year 2001.		
28	Notes Payable	2,217.77	
	Cash		2,217.77

A Zero-Interest note shows the maturity value of $2,217.77, but the amount actually borrowed is only $2,000.00. So the difference of $217.77 ($2,217.77 − $2,000.00 = $217.77) is Imputed Interest, sometimes called Built-In Interest. The rate is 7% as follows: $2,000 × 7% × 560/360 = $217.77.

The difference between the maturity value of the note ($2,217.77) and the amount borrowed ($2,000) is $217.77, and is called Discount on Notes Payable. The entry on January 16, 2000, the date when the money is borrowed, debits Cash for $2,000, the amount borrowed, since we get this money from the bank. The Contra-Liability account, Discount on Notes Payable, is debited for the $217.77. Notes Payable is credited for $2,217.77, the maturity value of the note, since that is also the face value of the note.

On December 31, 2000, 350 days after the money was borrowed, an adjusting entry is made on the books to record the amount of Interest accrued or built up. At this time the note has run 350 days, so the following computation is made: $2,000 \times 7\% \times 350/360 = \$136.11$. So on the books the account, Interest Expense, is debited for $136.11, because the Billings Company owes this amount for having the use of the $2,000 during this time. The Contra-Liability account, Discount on Notes Payable, is credited for $136.11 to show the accrual of this Interest. At the end of the year 2000, the Discount on Notes Payable account appears as follows on the books of the Billings Company:

Discount on Notes Payable			
2000		2000	
January 16	217.77	December 31	136.11
	81.66		

The original debit of $217.77 is the difference between the face value of the note and the amount of money borrowed, sometimes called the Imputed Interest, for the entire 560 days which the note runs. The credit on December 31 of $136.11 is the amount of Interest incurred on the note between the date the money was borrowed (January 16, 2000) and the end of the year (December 31, 2000). The balance of the account, $81.66, is the amount of Interest yet to be incurred, in this case the amount to be incurred between December 31, 2000, and the Maturity Date of the note, July 28, 2001.

The closing entry on December 31, 2000, debits the catch-all account, Income Summary for $136.11 and credits Interest Expense for the same amount. This closes out the Interest Expense, which is a temporary account, and brings it down to zero.

On the Maturity Date, July 28, 2001, Interest Expense is debited for $81.66, the amount of Interest incurred between January 1, 2001 and July 28, 2001. The account, Discount on Notes Payable, is credited for the $81.66 Interest. This serves to close out the Discount on Notes Payable account, as follows:

Discount on Notes Payable			
2000		2000	
January 16	217.77	December 31	136.11
		2001	
		July 28	81.66
			217.77

The final entry on July 28, 2001, debits Notes Payable and credits Cash for $2,217.77, the maturity value of the note. Notes Payable is debited, because the Billings Company receives its note marked paid, the face value of which is $2,217.77. On that date it pays the bank the same amount so credits Cash.

Tracy National Bank Books

2000			($ in dollars)
January 15	Notes Receivable	2,217.77	
	Discount on Notes Receivable		217.77
	Cash		2,000.00
	Bank lends money to Billings Company.		
December 31	Discount on Notes Receivable	136.11	
	Interest Revenue		136.11
	To record accrued Interest Income at year's end.		
31	Interest Revenue	136.11	
	Income Summary		136.11
	To close out Interest Revenue account at year's end.		

2001			($ in dollars)
July 28	Discount on Notes Receivable	81.66	
	Interest Revenue		81.66
	To record Interest Income for the year 2001		

July 28	Cash	2,217.77	
	Notes Receivable		2,217.77
	To record customer's payment and		
	bank's receipt of the maturity value of the		
	note on the Maturity Date		

The bank's book entry on January 15, 2000, the date that it lent $2,000 to the Billings Company, debits Notes Receivable for $2,217.77, because on that date the Billings Company signed a note for that amount and the bank received the note. Cash is credited for $2,000, because this is the amount that was lent to the Billings Company. The difference, $217.77, is Imputed Interest and is credited to the account, Discount on Notes Receivable, which is a Contra-Asset account with a credit balance.

On December 31, 2000, the accrued or built-up Interest is computed to be $136.11 ($2,000 × 7% × 350/360 = $136.11). Discount on Notes Receivable is debited for $136.11 to decrease this Contra-Asset account, and Interest Revenue is credited for $136.11 to show the built-up Revenue. This Revenue must be reported for the year 2000 even though it hasn't been received, because it has been earned by the bank during the 350 days from January 15, 2000 through December 31, 2000.

There is also a closing entry on December 31, 2000, to close out the temporary account known as Interest Revenue. This is accomplished by debiting Interest Revenue for $136.11 and thus closing out this account which previously had had a credit balance. Income Summary account is credited.

On the maturity date, July 28, 2001, Discount on Notes Receivable is debited for $81.66 to close out this account. Interest Revenue is credited for $81.66, the Interest earned by the bank between January 1, 2001 and July 28, 2001. After this entry has been posted, the Discount on Notes Receivable account appears as follows on the books of the Tracy National Bank:

Discount on Notes Receivable			
2000		2000	
December 31	136.11	January 15	217.77
2001			
July 28	81.66		
	217.77		

The final entry on the Maturity Date of July 28, 2001 debits Cash for $2,217.77, because on this date the bank receives this amount from the Billings Company in repayment of the loan. The bank credits Notes Receivable because it then returns to Billings Company its $2,217.77 note marked paid.

• PROBLEM 7–25

If we invested $500 today at 6%, how much would we have three years from now?

SOLUTION:

$595.51. This problem can be worked either by compounding Interest mathematically or with a Future Amount of 1 Table. Let us do this problem first by compounding Interest:

At the beginning of the first year, we invest $500. At the end of the first year we have earned $30 Interest ($500 × 6% = $30). We therefore have a total investment of $530 ($500 + $30 = $530).

During the second year the $530 stays invested. At the end of the second year we have earned Interest for the second year of $31.80 ($530 × 6% = $31.80). We therefore have a total investment of $561.80 ($530 + $31.80 = $561.80).

During the third year the $561.80 stays invested. At the end of the third year we have earned Interest for the third year of $33.71 ($561.80 × 6% = $33.71).

At the end of the third year we therefore have a total investment of $595.51 ($561.80 + $33.71 = $595.51).

From the above compound Interest computations it can be seen that over a three-year period the original investment has grown from $500.00 to $595.51, or a Total Interest Income over the three years of $95.51.

In order to keep from having to compute these trying computations each time that compound Interest is desired, mathematicians have compiled a Table of the Future Amount of 1—Future Amount of a Single Sum. Part of this table is shown below:

Table B
Future Amount of 1 (Future Amount of a Single Sum)

Periods	2%	2-1/2%	3%	4%	5%	6%
1	1.02000	1.02500	1.03000	1.04000	1.05000	1.06000
2	1.04040	1.05063	1.06090	1.08160	1.10250	1.12360
3	1.06121	1.07689	1.09273	1.12486	1.15763	1.19102
4	1.08243	1.10381	1.12551	1.16986	1.21551	1.26248
5	1.10408	1.13141	1.15927	1.21665	1.27628	1.33823
6	1.12616	1.15969	1.19405	1.26532	1.34010	1.41852

Looking at Table B, just above, for the Future Amount of a Single Sum, and looking down the Periods column for 3 periods (in this case, 3 years) and looking over at the 6% column, we see a figure 1.19102. We then multiply our original $500 investment by this figure to get $595.51 ($500 × 1.19102 = $595.51). This is the same answer that we found using the compound Interest method, but is much easier with the Table. The figure, 1.19102, means that over the three-year period our investment has grown a little over 19%, and therefore the total amount invested is now 119.102% of the original investment.

• PROBLEM 7-26

We have found a safe investment that pays a 6% return. Our daughter will be ready for college in 5 years. We believe it will be possible for us to save $1,000 each year for her college fund and that we could put this money in the 6% investment at the end of each year for five years. How much would our daughter have in her fund at the end of five years, when she is ready to begin college?

SOLUTION:

The easiest and best way to work this problem is to look into a table entitled Future Amount of an Annuity of 1. We will call this Table C, as follows:

Table C
Future Amount of an Annuity of 1

Periods	2%	2-1/2%	3%	4%	5%	6%
1	1.00000	1.00000	1.00000	1.00000	1.00000	1.00000
2	2.02000	2.02500	2.03000	2.04000	2.05000	2.06000
3	3.06040	3.07563	3.09090	3.12160	3.15250	3.18360
4	4.12161	4.15252	4.18363	4.24646	4.31013	4.37462
5	5.20404	5.25633	5.30914	5.41632	5.52563	5.63709
6	6.30812	6.38774	6.46841	6.63298	6.80191	6.97532

Looking at Table C, just above, and down the Periods column for 5 periods (in this case, 5 years), and coming over to the 6% column, we see the figure 5.63709. Since we are planning to invest $1,000 at the end of each year for 5 years, we multiply $1,000 by 5.63709 to get $5,637.09. This means that if we did invest our $1,000 at the end of each year for the next five years, our daughter would have $5,637.09 in her college fund.

• PROBLEM 7–27

Our new grandson, Robert William, has just been born, and we want to be sure that he attends college. We decide to put $500 into a safe investment fund at the end of each year for the next 18 years. This fund earns 5% Interest. How much will our grandson have in his college fund when he becomes 18 years of age?

SOLUTION:

The easiest and best way to work this problem is to look into a table entitled Future Amount of an Ordinary Annuity of 1.

We will call this part of the table, Table D, as follows:

Table D
Future Amount of an Ordinary Annuity of 1

Periods	2%	2-1/2%	3%	4%	5%	6%
18	21.41231	22.38635	23.41444	25.64541	28.13238	30.90565

Looking in Table D, just above, which is set up for the eighteenth period, and looking across to the 5% Column, we see the figure 28.13238. Since we plan to invest $500 at the end of each year for the next 18 years, we multiply $500 by 28.13238 to get $14,066.19 ($500 × 28.13238 = $14,066.19).

This means that there will be $14,066.19 in our grandson's college account when he reaches age 18, if the investment continues to pay 5% during all those years, and if we regularly place $500 in the account at the end of each year for the next 18 years.

• PROBLEM 7–28

Our new grandson, Robert William, has just been born, and we want to be sure that he attends college. We may not live long enough to make regular annual payments, so we decide to invest a single sum of $5,000 into a safe fund that pays 6% Interest regularly. How much will Robert William have in the fund when he reaches age 18, whether his grandparents live or die?

SOLUTION:

The easiest and best way to work this problem is to look into a table entitled Future Amount of 1 (Future Amount of a Single Sum). The first six periods of this table were presented earlier as Table B, but that table contained only 6 periods, or the first 6 years. Below is the same table, but with figures for the 18th year. We will call this Table B-1.

Table B-1
Future Amount of 1 (Future Amount of a Single Sum)

Periods	2%	2-1/2%	3%	4%	5%	6%
18	1.42825	1.55966	1.70243	2.02582	2.40662	2.85434

Looking at Table B-l, just above, which contains figures for the eighteenth year, we look over to the 6% column, because our investment pays 6%, and see the figure 2.85434. We then multiply our investment of $5,000 by 2.85434 to get $14,271.70. ($5,000 × 2.85434 = $14,271.70). No matter whether we grandparents live or die, our grandson will have $14,271.70 in his college account when he reaches age 18, 18 years from now, if the investment continues to pay 6%.

• PROBLEM 7–29

James Arbor runs his own business which is doing well, but he has nothing in a retirement fund. He is age 55, and would like to retire in 10 years when he reaches age 65. James believes he could save up $8,000 each year to place into the fund, which pays 10% interest. He would like to have $100,000 in the fund 10 years from now. How close will he come to the $100,000 if he places $8,000 in the fund at the end of each year?

SOLUTION:

In order to solve this problem we should make use of the table entitled Future Amount of an Ordinary Annuity of 1, looking at the 10% level for 10 years. The figures we will need are presented below in a table which we will call Table E:

Table E
Future Amount of an Ordinary Annuity of 1

Periods	8%	9%	10%	11%	12%
10	14.48656	15.19293	15.93743	16.72201	17.54874

In the above table, which shows some of the figures for ten periods, in this case for ten years, and looking across to the 10% column, we find the number 15.93743. Since James Arbor figures that he could save $8,000 each year toward his retirement fund, we multiply this $8,000 by 15.93743, getting $127,499.44. ($8,000 × 15.93743 = $127,499.44). This means that if Arbor actually saved $8,000 each year, and at the end of the year invested it in a safe investment that paid a steady 10% annual Interest, he would have $127,499.44 at the end of ten years.

However, Arbor mentioned previously that he desired only $100,000 at the end of ten years. This would mean that Arbor would need to invest something less than $8,000 each year in order to attain his desired goal. How much would he have to invest each year in order to get exactly the $100,000 desired at the end of ten years?

This computation is made by dividing $100,000 by 15.93743. The answer is $6,274.54 ($100,000 divided by 15.93743 = $6,274.54). Thus, if James Arbor saved only $6,274.54 each year, and at the end of each year invested this amount in a safe investment at 10% return, he would have exactly $100,000 in his investment account ten years from now.

• PROBLEM 7–30

The Brown Construction Corporation sees increased business opportunities on the horizon, but its present factory is too small. It needs $75,000 immediately to build a new factory and place machines therein. Investment counsellors have suggested that the Corporation sell $75,000 worth of 9% Preferred Stock. The advantages of Preferred Stock, of course, are that Dividends do not have to be paid in bad times, especially if the stock is Non-Cumulative; also, most Preferred Stock has no Maturity Date, so the stock does not ever need to be retired.

What entries need to be made when the stock is sold? What entries are made each quarter when the dividends are paid? How much money will need to be put aside each year in a sinking fund if we decide to retire the Preferred Stock issue in 20 years? What entry or entries will need to be made 20 years from now when we pay off the amount borrowed?

SOLUTION:

Let us assume that we successfully sell $75,000 worth of Non-Cumulative Preferred Stock in our Brown Construction Corporation. The entry would be as follows:

2002		($ in dollars)	
January 2	Cash	75,000	
	Preferred Stock		75,000

Let us also assume that $75,000 is both the Market Value and the Par Value of the stock. Three months elapse, and it is time to declare a dividend on the Preferred Stock. The Board of Directors of the Brown Construction Corporation vote the dividend. Following is the entry made on the books of the corporation on the dividend declaration date:

2002		($ in dollars)	
April 1	Retained Earnings	1,687.50	
	Dividends Payable		1,687.50

The $6,750 figure is determined by multiplying the $75,000 Par Value of the Preferred Stock issue outstanding by the 9% Interest figure on the face of the stock certificates ($75,000 × 9% = $6,750). $6,750 is one year's dividends. But this is a quarterly dividend, so we divide $6,750 by 4 to get $1,687.50.

On April 15, the Cash dividend is mailed to all Preferred Stockholders whose names are on the books on the date of record, April 8, 2002. The following entry is made on April 15, the date the checks are mailed out:

2002		($ in dollars)
April 15	Dividends Payable	1,687.50
	Cash	1,687.50

On April 1, the account, Retained Earning, is debited for $1,687.50, thus cutting down the Retained Earnings account by that amount. Retained Earnings account balance is the past profits that have been plowed back into the business. These past profits are decreased when a dividend is declared. Dividends Payable is a current Liability account showing that the corporation owes the Preferred Stockholders that amount of money, in this case, $1,687.50.

On April 15, Dividends Payable account is debited in the amount of $1,687.50 to close out that account, because the Preferred Stockholders are being paid and the corporation no longer owes them the money. Cash is credited because the dividend checks are being mailed out.

How much money will need to be put aside each year in a sinking fund if we decide to retire the Preferred Stock issue in 20 years? Let us say the going Interest Rate (Market Interest Rate) is 9%.

In order to solve this problem, we will have to look at the table entitled Future Amount of an Ordinary Annuity of 1, looking at 20 years and at the 9% level. Let us call this Table F.

Table F
Future Amount of an Ordinary Annuity of 1

Periods	8%	9%	10%	11%	12%
20	45.76196	51.16012	57.27500	64.20283	72.05244

In the above table, which shows some of the figures for 20 periods, in this case for twenty years, and looking across to the 9% column, we find the figure 51.16012. Since the future amount that we must save is $75,000 to retire this issue of Preferred Stock, we divide $75,000 by 51.16012 to get $1,465.99, the amount we will have to put aside at the end of each year in order to have $75,000 at the end of 20 years. We must also assume that the investment is safe and that it will earn a 9% return consistently over the 20 years.

What entry or entries will need to be made 20 years from now when we pay off the amount borrowed?

Let us assume that we make the $1,465.99 payments at the end of each year for 20 years and that the Interest Rate remains 9%. In this case we will have the $75,000 needed to retire the issue of Preferred Stock.

2020		($ in dollars)	
January 2	Preferred Stock	75,000	
	Cash		75,000

The year is 2020, twenty years following the year that the Preferred Stock was sold. A letter is sent to all the holders of Preferred Stock mentioning that the shares are to be retired on that date. If the stockholders do not send in their shares, they will not receive the liquidation amount; neither will they receive any further dividends on the stock.

It is assumed, then, that all the Preferred Stock certificates are received by the corporation. To show this, we debit Preferred Stock for the Par Value of $75,000. We send out checks to the Preferred Stock holders for this amount, so credit Cash for $75,000.

• PROBLEM 7–31

The Fable Manufacturing Company plans to buy a fleet of trucks which will cost them $500,000. In order to raise this money, financial counsellors have suggested that they sell $500,000 worth of bonds, at the going Market Rate of 12%. What is the Present Value of the $500,000 Bond Issue, and what is the Present Value of all the future Interest payments?

SOLUTION:

In order to compute the Present Value of a single figure, it is necessary to look into a table entitled, Present Value of 1 (Present Value of a Single Sum). Let us call this Table F.

Table F

Periods	8%	9%	10%	11%	12%
10	.46319	.42241	.38554	.35218	.32197

These are 10-year bonds with 12% Interest Rate printed on the face of the bonds. The going or effective Interest Rate is also 12%. The Maturity Date of the bonds is 10 years hence. Looking up in Table F under 10 periods (in this case, 10 years), and looking over at the 12% column, we see the figure .32197. We then multiply .32197 by the $500,000 face value of the bonds to get $160,985, which is the Present Value of the $500,000 borrowed. The Present Value is always less than the Future Value.

What is the Present Value of all future Interest payments? Let us assume that these bonds pay Interest annually and that they pay Interest of 12%. To compute the annual Interest Payment we multiply the $500,000 face value of the bonds by the 12% Interest to get $60,000 ($500,000 × 12% = $60,000). This Interest is to be paid every year for 10 years, so the Total Interest to be paid over the life of the bonds is $600,000 ($60,000 × 10 years = $600,000).

In order to compute the Present Value of all these Interest Payments, we look in a table entitled, Present Value of an Ordinary Annuity of 1. Let us call this Table G.

Table G

Periods	10%	11%	12%	15%
10	6.14457	5.88923	5.65022	5.01877

Looking at Table G under 10 periods (in this case 10 years) and looking over to the 12% column, we find the number 5.65022. Since the annual Interest Payment is $60,000 per year, we multiply the $60,000 by 5.65022 to get $339,013.20, the Present Value of all the future Interest Payments. It will be noted that the total value of all the future Interest Payments is $600,000 ($60,000 yearly Interest times 10 years = $600,000). The Future Value is always greater than the Present value.

• PROBLEM 7–32

The Vision Construction Company has signed a union contract setting up a pension fund for employees at 2% of all future salaries. At present the total yearly wages of all employees is $1,000,000, and it is assumed that this level of business will continue for the next 20 years or more. What is the value of the company's pension Liability over the next 20 years, and what is the Present Value of this 20-year Liability? The effective Interest Rate is 9% and it is assumed this will continue.

SOLUTION:

What is the value of the company's pension Liability over the next 20 years? The total wages are $1,000,000 per year, and the company promised that 2% of these will be placed in a retirement fund each year. This is $20,000 ($1,000,000 × 2% = $20,000). And $20,000 for 20 years is $400,00 ($20,000 × 20 years = $400,000).

What is the Present Value of the company's $400,000 pension fund Liability if the Time Value is 20 years and the percent is 9%?

We look in a table entitled, Present Value of an Ordinary Annuity of 1. Let us call this Table H.

Table H

Periods	8%	9%	10%	11%
20	9.81815	9.12855	8.51356	7.96333

Looking at Table H for 20 periods (in this case, 20 years) and looking under the 9% column, we see the figure 9.12855. The yearly pension Liability for the Vision Construction Company is $20,000 ($1,000,000 annual wages times 2% = $20,000). So we multiply $20,000 by 9.12855 to get $182,571, which is the Present Value of the $400,000 ($20,000 × 9.12855 = $182,571).

CHAPTER 8

CASH AND RECEIVABLES

> **Basic Attacks and Strategies for Solving Problems in this Chapter. See pages 210 to 247 for step-by-step solutions to problems.**

Cash is different from other Assets, in that anyone who has it, owns it. If we pick up a $10 bill on the streets, it is ours. On the other hand, a note or a check is usually made out to an individual, and another person finding the note or check on the street cannot usually claim it as his or hers. Therefore, Cash has to be guarded carefully by such means as placing it in a safe place such as a bank, a safety deposit box, or a cash register. Also, the successful business person will use internal control to be sure that customers and employees don't "rob him blind." This chapter regarding Cash and receivables should help readers understand how business persons deal with Cash and receivables in practical business situations.

One of the most important parts of running any business is reconciling a bank statement. Although this is a fairly simple procedure, it is surprising how many people do not reconcile their bank statements because they do not take the time, or because they do not know how to reconcile and cannot see any value in it.

Even fewer people are familiar with Petty Cash accounts, Petty Cash drawers, Petty Cash vouchers, and the imprest system for controlling Petty Cash

Accountants handle bad debts by methods almost completely unknown to the general public. There are two major methods of handling bad debts: (1) the Direct Write-Off Method and (2) the Allowance Method. These are explained in the chapter.

The Allowance Method of handling bad debts is complicated by the fact that there are two methods of estimating bad debts: (1) the percent of credit sales method and (2) the aging of Accounts Receivable method. Detailed examples of computing both methods are given, along with general journal entries and "T" account balances. Not only are entries given for estimating bad debts at year's end, but entries are given for writing off accounts when bankruptcies occur. Entries are also shown when customers return after having had their accounts written off, and when these customers finally pay their bills at a later time.

Accounts Receivable are a special concern for business people, especially when they go unpaid for long periods of time. Some lines of business, such as furniture and textiles, sell their Accounts Receivable to collection agencies called **Factors**. There are several types of such agreements that are explained in the chapter.

Step-by-Step Solutions to Problems in this Chapter, "Cash and Receivables"

• PROBLEM 8–1

Martha Hanson received her bank statement at the end of the month. It showed that she had a bank balance of $5,000. But her check stub balance showed $6,000. She comes to her accountant and asks him or her to explain the discrepancy.

Along with the bank statement are 10 cancelled checks and several deposit slips, one debit memorandum for $100, one credit memorandum for $300, and one insufficient funds check for $3600. Reconcile Martha's bank statement.

SOLUTION:

Reconciling a bank statement immediately upon receipt is important for every business or person. The bank usually gives the customer a 10-day grace period to find any bank mistakes. Also, if the customer has made a mistake, he or she should correct it on the books to prevent future

Martha Hanson
Bank Statement Reconciliation
December 31, 2000

Bank Balance	$5,000.00
Deposits in Transit ($400 and $200)	+ 600.00
Subtotal	5,600.00
Outstanding Checks	− 3,000.00
Revised Balance	$2,600.00
Book Balance	$6,000.00
Plus Note Collected by Bank (credit memorandum)	+ 300.00
	$6,300.00
Subtotal	
Less Service charge of bank	− 100.00
Subtotal	6,200.00
Insufficient Funds Check	− 3,600.00
Revised Balance	$2,600.00

checks bouncing. And usually when one check bounces, many checks bounce.

The bank statement reconciliation is started with a three-line heading. The first line gives the name of the person or business. In this case, the name of the person is Martha Hanson. The second line gives the name of the statement—in this case, Bank Statement Reconciliation. The third line gives the date.

The body of the reconciliation is in two parts: the bank part and the customer part. The bank part begins with the figure that the bank has on the bank statement, which, in this case, is $5,000. The next line is entitled Deposits in Transit. Some people use the term Unrecorded Deposits. These are deposits that the customer has made during the month that the bank, for some reason, has not recorded on its books. Usually, the deposits are the ones made at the end of the period and which the bank has not yet had time to place on its books. In this case, we have two deposits in transit: one for $400 and one for $200, or a total of $600. Deposits in transit are discovered by comparing the deposits recorded on the bank statement with the deposits recorded on the company books or on the personal check stubs. In this case, the two unrecorded deposits are on the check stubs of the customer but have not yet been placed or recorded on the books of the bank. When these two unrecorded deposits are placed on the bank books, they will be added to the amount that the customer has deposited in the bank; so the $600 (total of $400 and $200) is added to the bank balance in the reconciliation.

The next step is to compute the total dollar value of the outstanding checks. Outstanding checks are those checks that have been written but have not come back through the bank and been mailed to the customer along with the bank statement. The outstanding checks are determined as follows: take the individual canceled checks that have been returned with the bank statement and compare these with the checks recorded in the Cash Payments Journal or in the check stubs. Usually, a check mark is made in the Cash Payments Journal or in the check stubs for each canceled check. After this has been accomplished, the written check amounts that do not have check marks beside them are the outstanding checks, or the checks that have not yet been returned to the customer by the bank. These checks are then added up, and the total dollar value of these outstanding checks is subtracted in the bank reconciliation. The reason that they are subtracted is that when they finally do come through the bank, the bank will subtract their face value from the amount the customer has in the bank.

In the case of Martha Hanson, she had outstanding checks amounting to $3,000; so $3,000 is subtracted from her bank balance in the reconciliation report.

This gives Martha Hanson a revised Balance of $2,600.

The next step is to look at Martha's book balance. This is either the balance of her cash journal or the running balance in her check stubs. We begin with her book balance of $6,000. Along with the bank statement, Martha has received a Credit Memorandum from the bank. This is a slip of paper mentioning that the bank is crediting Martha's account for $300 because one of her notes was collected by the bank, from a customer, Many times, when a customer cannot or will not pay, or is slow to pay, a business person will send the Note Receivable to the bank and ask the bank to collect it. This often encourages the debtor to pay promptly, because most persons want to keep their bank credit in good shape. So let us say that some time ago, Martha Hanson gave a customer's note to the bank for collection. The bank has collected the $300 note and placed the $300 in Martha Hanson's account. So toward the bottom of the reconciliation, we add $300 to Martha's bank balance. In one way, banks keep books opposite to the way other businesses keep books. To banks, the customers are creditors, because the banks owe the customers the money deposited in the banks. These customer-creditors are Liabilities to the bank, and so customer accounts have credit balances. When these balances increase, the bank credits the account. On the contrary, when the accounts decrease, the bank debits the account. So a bank credit memorandum shows an increase in the customer's account and a bank debit memorandum shows a decrease in the customer's account. In the case of the note collected by the bank, it is a credit memorandum and a $300 increase in the customer's bank balance is recorded in the Reconciliation.

But there is also a debit memorandum. This is a service charge or several service charges from the bank for services that the bank has rendered to the customer (depositor). In this case, all the service charges for the period add up to $100; so in the reconciliation $100 is subtracted from the bank balance.

Along with the bank statement is a debtor's insufficient funds check for $3600. An insufficient funds check is also called a "bounced check." Let us say that one of Martha Hanson's customers (debtors) owed her $3600, and he gave her his check for that amount. She then deposited the $3600 check in her bank account and the bank gave her credit for it. Later it was discovered that the customer did not have this much money in his personal bank account; so the bank returned or bounced the check, sending it back to Martha Hanson and debiting or deducting $3600 from her account in the bank. Since this is a decrease in Martha's balance, we deduct the $3600 from her book balance in the bank reconciliation. This brings Martha's account down to $2600 Revised Balance, which is the same as the $2600 revised balance in the first half of the Reconciliation. This makes the reconciliation balance, and Martha revises her books to show the amount of $2600, or she revises her check stub running balance to show this amount.

If this procedure does not show a balance, her next step is to go over the bank statement and try to find a mistake in the bank's figures. Of course, if she finds a mistake in the bank's figures, she should phone the bank immediately.

• PROBLEM 8-2

The Brown Manufacturing Corporation has the following balances in the following accounts: Checking Account Cash $5,000; Savings Account Cash $300; Petty Cash $100; Money orders on hand $500; certified checks on hand $150; Bank drafts on hand $100; Postdated Checks on hand $500; IOU's on hand $50; Postage stamps on hand $37; Travel Advances to employees $580; Change Fund $900. How much Cash does Brown Manufacturing Corporation have on hand, and how should the other items be classified in the Balance Sheet?

SOLUTION:

$7,050 Cash, composed of: Checking Account Cash $5,000; Savings Account Cash $300; Petty Cash $100; Money orders on hand $500; certified checks on hand $150; Bank drafts on hand $100; and Change Fund $900. Total $7,050.

Postdated checks are considered Accounts Receivable; IOU's are considered Accounts Receivable; Postage Stamps are considered Office Supplies; Travel Advances to employees that are taken out of employees' salaries are considered Receivables; Travel advances not taken out of employees' salaries are Prepaid Expenses.

• PROBLEM 8-3

James Brookings runs Brookings Clothing Store. In the past, using a voucher system and paying all bills by check, he has maintained tight control over Cash. He has decided to set up a Petty Cash System and has several questions to ask his accountant: Is Petty Cash an Asset account? When Petty Cash comes in, do you debit Petty Cash; and when Petty Cash goes out, do you credit Petty Cash? How much should I place in the Petty Cash account?

SOLUTION:

Yes, Petty Cash is a Current Asset account and has a debit balance.

No, when Petty Cash comes in, you shouldn't debit Petty Cash; and when Petty Cash goes out, you shouldn't credit Petty Cash. In other words, you do not treat a Petty Cash account the same way you treat Cash. If you do it that way, you lose internal control of Petty Cash; so the boss does not know what is happening to the Cash itself in the Petty Cash drawer.

The owner himself or herself should decide how much Cash to place in the Petty Cash account, with this amount being placed in the Petty Cash drawer. Some firms use $100, some $150, some $200, and so on.

• PROBLEM 8–4

How do you get internal control of Petty Cash?

SOLUTION:

By using the Imprest System. When the owner begins to set up a Petty Cash System, he or she decides how much should be in the Petty Cash drawer. Let us say he decides on $100. He writes a check, taking $100 out of his regular bank account and placing this $100 in his Petty Cash drawer, probably part of his cash register in the store. At the same time, he makes the following entry in his books:

2002		($ in dollars)	
January 2	Petty Cash	100	
	Cash in Bank		100

Petty Cash is one of the Cash accounts. It has a debit balance, and it is a Current Asset, just as the Cash account is a current asset. Petty Cash is debited, because this amount is placed in the Petty Cash drawer. Cash in Bank or just Cash is credited, because this amount has been taken out of the owner's account in the bank.

The Petty Cash account will appear as follows on the Owner's books.

Petty Cash

2002	
January 2	100

The Imprest System means that the $100 debit in the Petty Cash account is impressed in the account. It stays there and never leaves. (Of course, if the owner later decided to change the amount of money in the account, or perhaps do away with the account entirely, he or she could do this.) But usually the $100 will stay permanently in the account. This is one of the reasons the boss has **Internal Control** over the account.

The owner also has **Petty Cash Vouchers** printed. They could appear as follows:

Brookings Clothing Store
Petty Cash Voucher

Amount _____

ACCOUNT DEBITED _____

Date _____

Signature of recipient of Cash _____

Signature of Manager _____

The use of the Petty Cash Vouchers is another means of internal control for the manager. When paying Petty Cash amounts from the Petty Cash drawer, each clerk must fill out a Petty Cash voucher and have both the recipient and the manager sign the voucher. The clerk then files the completed voucher in the Petty Cash drawer. At any time, the manager can open the drawer, and the amounts of the vouchers plus the amount of Cash in the drawer should add up to the $100.

If the year is coming to an end, or if the Petty Cash drawer cash is running low, the manager can replenish the Petty Cash as follows:

Let us say that only $5 remains in the Petty Cash drawer and that the Petty Cash vouchers add up to $95. The owner takes the vouchers out of the drawer and puts them in various piles, depending on the types of Expenses or Assets purchased with the Petty Cash. He then adds up the vouchers in each pile and makes an entry in his journal similar to the following:

2002			($ in dollars)
February 15	Office Supplies Expense	46.50	
	Store Supplies Expense	30.00	
	Stamps	18.50	
	Cash in Bank		95.00
	To replenish the Petty Cash fund		

The vouchers are then filed in a file drawer; a check is written for $95; and $95 is taken out of the regular Cash bank account and placed in the Petty Cash drawer along with the $5 that is still in the drawer, making a total of $100 Cash.

It will be noted that the various Expense and Asset accounts are debited because the Brookings Clothing Store got the use of them. Cash in Bank is credited, because $95 is taken out of the firm's regular Cash account. Petty Cash is not touched. It is imprest and remains the same. This Imprest System, plus the use of vouchers, gives the owner internal control and prevents customers and employees from stealing from the Petty Cash fund.

Let us say the owner wishes to increase the Petty Cash fund from $100 to $150. He would make the following entry:

2002		($ in dollars)
March 1	Petty Cash	50
	Cash in Bank	50
	To increase Petty Cash	

After this entry has been made, the Petty Cash account in the ledger would appear as follows:

Petty Cash

2002		
January 2	100.00	
2002		
March 1	50.00	
	150.00	

Let us say that in later years the owner decided to lower the amount of Cash in the Petty Cash drawer from $150 to $75. This could be accomplished by the following entry:

2004		($ in dollars)
September 1 Cash in Bank		75.00
Petty Cash		75.00
To decrease Petty Cash		

After this entry has been made, the Petty Cash account in the ledger would appear as follows:

Petty Cash

2002				
January 2	100.00	2004		
		September 1	75.00	
2002				
March 1	50.00			
	150.00			
Balance	75.00			

• PROBLEM 8–5

What are the two methods of handling bad debts in the business world? Which method is best and why?

SOLUTION:

The two methods by which accountants handle bad debts in the business world are as follows:

1. The Direct Write-Off Method

2. The Allowance Method

The Direct Write-Off Method is favored by the Internal Revenue Service. In fact, it is the only method the IRS will accept at the present time. This is because the account, Bad Debts Expense, is not debited until the time when it appears that the debt will never be collected, such as the time when a customer goes bankrupt or leaves the area and it looks as if he or she will never repay the debt.

The Allowance Method is favored by the accountants, because the account, Bad Debts Expense, is debited at the end of each month or each year for the amount that the owner thinks he or she will lose in bad debts. Accountants favor the Allowance Method because Bad Debts Expense is deducted in the year when the merchandise was sold, not in the year when the customer goes bankrupt. By deducting the bad debts Expense in the year in which the merchandise was sold, one subtracts the proper Expenses from the proper Revenue to get the proper Net Income for the year.

• PROBLEM 8–6

If accountants do not agree with the Internal Revenue Service on the best method to follow in handling bad debts, how can businesses decide what method to follow and how to handle bad debts in their books?

SOLUTION:

Many businesses have switched to the Direct Write-Off Method so that they will not get in trouble with the Internal Revenue Service.

Other businesses keep two sets of books: they use the Allowance Method for their regular set of books that they keep for their stockholders and for their annual reports; and they keep another set of books for Income Tax purposes.

• **PROBLEM 8–7**

The Jacobson Clothing store sells to many of their customers on account. Most of the customers pay promptly, but a few are slow to pay, and even fewer never pay. How does Jacobson Clothing Company handle bad debts at the end of the year, at the time they discover that the particular customer won't pay, and at a later date when the customer surprises them and finally pays his or her debt after the company has written it off?

Let us assume that in the year 1999, customer Raymond Harrison has purchased $800 worth of clothing, for which he has not paid, as the year ends. What entry is made on the books of the Jacobson Clothing Store at year's end? At a later date, when we hear Harrison has gone bankrupt? And, at an even later date, when Harrison comes into the store unexpectedly and pays us?

SOLUTION:

1999	($ in dollars)
December 31 (No entry)	

In the Direct Write-Off method of accounting for bad debts, there is no Allowance for Doubtful Accounts. The business makes no year-end entries and does not have to guess how much is going to be lost.

On March 31, 2000, we hear that Raymond Harrison has gone bankrupt and it looks as if we will not get paid the $800 he owes us on account. So we make the following entry:

2000		($ in dollars)	
March 31	Bad Debts Expense	800	
	Accounts Receivable—Raymond Harrison		800

As can be seen in the entry above, Bad Debts Expense is debited for $800 only when we learn that we will probably never receive the money because the customer has gone bankrupt. The Internal Revenue Service favors this method, because we don't subtract the loss until we are sure that we have actually lost the money. Accounts Receivable—Raymond Harrison is credited, and this closes out the Harrison account on our books. Although Harrison really still owes us the money, it looks as if we will never collect it; so we write him off. We mark his account **Bankrupt** so that in later years we will never sell him any more clothing on account.

Theoretically, the accounting profession does not favor this method, because we sold Harrison the merchandise in the year 1999 but did not debit Bad Debts Expense until the year 2000 when Harrison went bankrupt. So the Bad Debts Expense is subtracted in the Income Statement of the wrong year.

Let us say that in September of the year 2000, Harrison receives a great deal of money from his rich uncle and comes into our store and pays us the $800. How do we handle this on our books?

Our books are not set up for this occasion; so it takes two entries to handle the matter, as follows:

2000	($ in dollars)	
September 14 Accounts Receivable—Harrison	800	
Bad Debts Expense		800
To reinstate the account		
14 Cash	800	
Accounts Receivable—Harrison		800
To show the receipt of Cash		

The first of these two entries is called "Reinstating the account." It turns around the entry of March 31. Accounts Receivable—Harrison is debited so that the account of Harrison is no longer closed. It is open again and Harrison owes us the money according to the books. Bad Debts Expense is credited for $800; so this does away with the Bad Debts Expense and Harrison is no longer a bad debt.

The second of these two entries debits Cash for $800 because we are receiving the money from Harrison. We credit Accounts Receivable—Harrison to show that Harrison no longer owes us money and we cancel his debt. As we write him off, we could write off the word Bankrupt to show that the man pays his debts.

The Jacobson Clothing store sells to many of their customers on account. Most of the customers pay promptly, but a few are slow to pay, and even fewer never pay. How does Jacobson Clothing Company handle bad debts, at the end of the year, at the time it is discovered that the particular customer won't pay, and at a later date when the customer surprises us and finally pays his or her debt after it has been written off? What type of account is Allowance for Doubtful Accounts, and how is it used?

Let us assume that in the year 1999, customer Raymond Harrison has purchased $800 worth of clothing for which he has not paid as the year ends. What entry is made on the books of the Jacobson Clothing Store at year's end? How is the amount of this entry determined? What entry is made at a later date when we hear that Harrison has gone bankrupt? What entry is made at an even later date when Harrison comes into the store unexpectedly and pays us?

SOLUTION:

1999		($ in dollars)
December 31 Bad Debts Expense	5,100	
Allowance for Doubtful Accounts		5,100

The above entry is the adjusting entry made for bad debts at the end of the year. Bad Debts Expense is debited for the amount of money we think we are going to lose. There are two methods of determining this figure:

1. The percent of credit sales method

2. The Aging of Accounts Receivable method

First, let us discuss the (1) percent of credit sales method. Let us assume that a year ago our total credit sales amounted to $181,000, of which $5,430 was uncollectible last year and this year. We therefore divide $5,430 by $181,000 to get 3%. Thus, about 3% of our credit sales have been uncollectible. We assume that same figure will hold true for this year's credit sales. However this past year, the year 2000, our credit sales have amounted to only $170,000. So we multiply $170,000 by 3% to get $5,100. So we guess we will lose $5,100 and use this figure in our adjusting entry at year's end. This is just a guess, but it is an educated guess.

Second, let us discuss the Aging of Accounts Receivable Method. This is more complicated but more accurate. We list, in a table, all our credit customers that owe us money, the amount owed, and the time length that they have owed us, as follows:

Customer Name	Amount Owed	New Debt	0 to 30 days	30 to 90 days	90 to 180 days	Over 180 days
Anderson, James	$350	$100		$150		$100
Bangor, Mary	150		100		50	
Hanson, Art	100				100	
Johnson, Harry	125	75		50		
Nieman, Roger	290	200				90
Zach, John	500	500				
Totals	$1,515	875	100	200	150	190

As can be determined by the above table, there are seven customers who owe us money at year's end. The total Accounts Receivable is $1,515 of which Anderson owes $350, Bangor $150, Hanson $100, Johnson $125, Nieman $290, and Zach $500. Of the $1,515 owed us, $875 is new debt, which has probably just been incurred this month when customers bought merchandise from us on account. $100 is 0 to 30 days old, $200 is 30 to 90 days old, $150 is 90 to 180 days old, and $190 is over 180 days old.

The second table turns the first table on its side, as follows:

Age of Debt	Amount	Percent Lost	Amount Lost
New Debt	$875	2%	$17.50
0 to 30 days	100	5%	5.00
30 to 90 days	200	15%	30.00
90 to 180 days	150	30%	45.00
Over 180 days	190	50%	95.00
	$1,515		$192.50

As can be seen from the table above, we multiply $875 by 2% to get $17.50; we multiply $100 by 5% to get $5, and so forth. But where do we get the column, Percent Lost? These are educated guesses from past experience. Let us say that in the past we have lost about 2% of our so-called "new debt." We have lost 5% of our 0 to 30 day debt; we have lost 15% of our 30 to 90 day debt and so forth. As can be seen from the Percent Lost column in the table above, the longer the debt has gone unpaid, the higher the estimated percentage of loss.

Looking at the lower right hand corner of the table above, we see that the amount lost total is $192.50. That means that the Allowance for Doubtful Accounts should, at the end of the period, be adjusted so that it will end the period with a credit balance of $192.50. Let us say that before this adjusting entry is made, the Allowance for Doubtful Accounts account has a credit balance of $150.00. This means we will have to adjust the Allowance account for $42.50 more to bring it up to the balance of $192.50 ($192.50 – $150.00 = $42.50).

So the adjusting entry at the end of the period will appear in the journal as follows:

2000		($ in dollars)
December 31 Bad Debts Expense	42.50	
Allowance for Doubtful Accounts		42.50

The Allowance for Doubtful Accounts will appear in the ledger as follows:

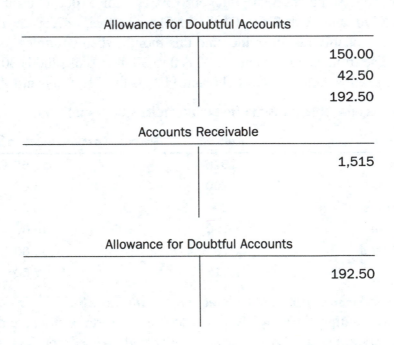

Allowance for Doubtful Accounts

	150.00
	42.50
	192.50

Accounts Receivable

| | 1,515 |

Allowance for Doubtful Accounts

| | 192.50 |

Accounts Receivable is a Current Asset account. Its total, $1,515, is the amount that all the customers owe the Jacobson Clothing Store at the end of the year. Allowance for Doubtful Accounts is a Contra-Liability account. Its balance $192.50 is the amount we believe we are going to lose after having carefully aged the Accounts Receivable. In other words, we will be lucky to collect $1,322.50, the difference between these two figures ($1,515 − $192.50 = $1,322.50).

One of our customers, Harry Johnson, who owes us $125, goes bankrupt on April 1, 2001. What entry do we make to write off this customer?

2001		($ in dollars)
April 1	Allowance for Doubtful Accounts	125
	Accounts Receivable—Harry Johnson	125
	To write off Harr Johnson's account	

When a customer actually goes bankrupt, we debit Allowance for Doubtful Accounts. The Allowance for Doubtful Accounts account credit balance is something like squirrels storing up nuts in the fall. We have stored up the $192.50 that we think we are going to lose. Then when a customer goes bankrupt, we debit the Allowance for Doubtful Accounts account. This is something like squirrels finding the hidden nuts in the middle of the winter. At year's end, we guess we will lose $192.50; and sure enough, as of the first of the next April, we have lost part of this amount—$125.

This is how the Allowance for Doubtful Accounts account looks after the write-off entry.

Allowance for Doubtful Accounts	
125.00	192.50
	67.50

In the above Allowance "T Account," the $192.50 was the amount we thought we were going to lose. The debit of $125 is the amount we actually lost when one of our customers, Harry Johnson, went bankrupt. The difference of $67.50, the present balance, is the amount we have yet to lose if other customers go bankrupt.

But what happens if other customers go bankrupt? It would certainly then be possible to have a debit balance in Allowance for Doubtful Accounts.. Let us assume that Art Hanson, on June 1, goes bankrupt, and he owes us $100. We would then make the following entry:

2001		($ in dollars)
June 1	Allowance for Doubtful Accounts	100
	Accounts Receivable—Art Hanson	100

How would the Allowance for Doubtful Accounts account appear after making this entry?

Allowance for Doubtful Accounts

125.00	192.50
100.00	
225.00	
32.50	

As can be seen from the Allowance account just above, it now has a debit balance of $32.50, because customers owing us a total of $225 went bankrupt when we thought we were only going to lose $192.50. It should then be feasible for us to make a higher adjusting entry or guess at the end of the following year.

Let us now assume that on September 1, 2001, Art Hanson drops by the store and pays us the $100 he owes us. Our books are not set up to handle this contingency; so it takes us two entries to cover this situation, as follows:

2001		($ in dollars)
September 1	Accounts Receivable—Art Hanson	100
	Allowance for Doubtful Accounts	100
	To reinstate Hanson's account	
1	Cash	100
	Accounts Receivable-Art Hanson	100
	To show the receipt of Cash	

The first entry debits Accounts Receivable, Art Hanson, for $100 to reinstate his account. It shows that he now owes us the $100 again. The Allowance for Doubtful Accounts is credited for $100, because we no longer have to take $100 out of this account.

The second entry debits cash, because we are receiving $100 from the customer, Art Hanson. Accounts Receivable—Art Hanson is credited, because we are giving Hanson credit for his payment and closing out his account.

Art Hanson's account in the Accounts Receivable subsidiary ledger would appear as follows:

Art Hanson

2000		2001	
June 1	100	June 1	100

Bankrupt

2001		2001	
September 1	100	September 1	100
Reinstatement		Repayment	

In examining Art Hanson's account just above, the debit to Hanson's account on June 1, 2000 for $100 was at the time that Hanson purchased clothing at the Jacobson Clothing Store. His account is debited because he owes us the money. The credit entry for $100 on June 1, 2001 was the date that Hanson went bankrupt, and we wrote him off by crediting his account for $100, the amount owed. Although this closed his account, we wrote the word Bankrupt by his name so that in the future we would not sell him any more clothes or other merchandise on account.

The debit entry for $100 on September 1, 2001 is the reinstatement of Art Hanson's account on the date he pays us. Reinstatement means that Hanson owes us $100 again and we are writing off the term, Bankrupt. The credit entry of $100 on September 1, 2001 shows that he has repaid us the debt and we are giving him credit for this $100 cash we have received from him. This also closes his account again, but he is now a customer in good standing.

• PROBLEM 8–9

The James Computer Company sells for Cash and on account. At the end of the year 2000, they discover that their Accounts Receivable amount to $300,000 and they are short of Cash. After talking with their banker, they are advised to assign their Accounts Receivable over to the banker for a loan of $100,000. This is a general assignment, and the James Computer Company continues to collect the money from the Accounts Receivable but turns over the collections to the bank until the $100,000 and interest are paid. What entry does the James Computer Company make on its books at this time?

SOLUTION:

2000		($ in dollars)
December 31 Cash	100,000	
Notes Payable		100,000

In the above entry, Cash is debited because a loan of $100,000 Cash is received from the bank. The James Computer Company signs a note for $100,000 and gives it to the bank. Let us say the note is for 8%, and for a year. Since this is a general assignment, no other entries are made at this time.

• PROBLEM 8–10

The James Computer Company sells for Cash and on account. At the end of the year 2000 they discover that their Accounts Receivable amount to $300,000 and they are short of Cash. After talking with their banker, they are advised to assign their Accounts Receivable of $300,000 over to the banker for a loan of $100,000. This is a general assignment, and the James Computer Company continues to collect the money from the Accounts Receivable but turns over the collections to the bank until the $100,000 and Interest are paid. Let us say that on February 1, 2001, the James Computer Company receives $25,000 from customers. What entry or entries should it make on its books?

SOLUTION:

2001			($ in dollars)
February 1	Cash	25,000	
	Accounts Receivable		25,000
	Received payments from customers		
1	Notes Payable	25,000	
	Cash		25,000
	Turned the $25,000 over to the bank		
1	Interest Expense	666	
	Cash		666

In the first entry above, Cash is being received from customers, so Cash is debited for $25,000. Accounts Receivable is credited for $25,000 because the customers now owe the James Computer Company that much less.

In the second entry above, the James Computer Company immediately turns over this $25,000 to the bank; so it debits Notes Payable for $25,000 because its debt to the bank is that much less. It credits Cash because it is paying $25,000 to the bank.

In the third entry above, the James Computer Company is paying one month's Interest to the bank, computed as follows:

$$\$100,000 \times 8/100 \times 1/12 = \$666$$

Interest Expense is debited for $666 because the James Computer Company has had the use of the $100,000 for a month. Cash is credited for $666 because that is the amount that the James Computer Company is paying the bank for the Interest.

• PROBLEM 8–11

The James Computer Company sells for Cash and on account. At the end of the year 2000 they discover that their Accounts Receivable amount to $300,000 and they are short of Cash. After talking with their banker, they are advised to assign their Accounts Receivable of $300,000 over to the banker for a loan of $100,000. This is a general assignment, and the James Computer Company continues to collect the money from the Accounts Receivable but turns over the collections to the bank. On February 1, 2001, the James Computer Company received $25,000 from customers which they turned over to the bank and also paid the bank one month's Interest. On March 1, 2001, the James Computer Company received $200,000 from customers and used part of this money to repay the remainder of their debt to the bank plus Interest. What entry or entries should it make on its books?

SOLUTION:

2001			($ in dollars)
March 1	Cash	200,000	
	Accounts Receivable		200,000
	Received payments from customers		
1	Notes Payable	75,000	
	Cash		75,000
	Turned over$75,000 as full payment		
	of bank loan		
1	Interest Expense	500	
	Cash		500

In the February 1 entry, the $100,000 loan had been paid down to $75,000. Now with the receipt of $200,000 from customers, the James Computer Company has more than enough money to pay off its debt to the bank.

The first entry debits Cash for the $200,000 collected from the customers. Accounts Receivable is credited for $200,000 because the customers now owe the James Computer Company $200,000 less than previously.

The second entry shows the James Computer Company paying the bank the $75,000 it still owes on the note. It then receives the note marked paid from the bank; so Notes Payable is debited for $75,000. Cash is credited for $75,000 to show that the James Computer Company is paying the bank this amount.

The third entry shows that the James Computer Company is paying the bank one month's Interest, computed as follows:

$75,000 × 8% × 1/12 = $500.

So Interest Expense is debited for $500 because the James Computer Company had the use of the $75,000 during the month of February. Cash is credited for $500 because the James Computer Company is paying this amount to the bank.

As soon as the bank receives the payment in full along with the Interest, the bank ends the $300,000 assignment of Accounts Receivable. Since it is a general assignment, no book entries have to be made for this.

• PROBLEM 8-12

The Swisher Furniture Company is short of Cash and long on Accounts Receivable. In fact, they need $600,000 Cash to pay their debts and to have enough working capital to continue. After discussing their financial problems with the bank, they are advised that the bank will lend them this large amount of money, $600,000, if they will make a specific assignment of $800,000 of their Accounts Receivable to the bank. The company agrees upon this. The Interest Rate is 9%. What entry or entries are made on the Swisher Furniture Company books on July 1, 2001, when the money is borrowed?

SOLUTION:

2001		($ in dollars)	
July 1	Cash	600,000	
	Discount on Notes Payable	4,500	
	Notes Payable		604,500
1	Accounts Receivable Assigned	800,000	
	Accounts Receivable		800,000

In the first entry above, Cash is debited for $600,000 on the books of the Swisher Furniture Company as the company receives the $600,000 loan from the bank. The Contra-Liability account, Discount on Notes Payable, is debited for one month's Interest, computed as follows: $600,000 × 9% = $54,000; $54,000 divided by 12 months = $4,500. Thus, the Discount on Notes Payable is debited for $4,500. Notes Payable is credited for the $604,500 total, and that is also the face value of the note. ($600,000 + $4,500 = $604,500).

Since a large amount of money is being borrowed, the bank has insisted on a specific assignment of Accounts Receivable. And the assignment ($800,000) is quite a bit higher than the amount borrowed ($600,000). To show the assignment, an Asset account entitled Accounts Receivable Assigned is set up and debited for $800,000. Accounts Receivable is credited for $800,000. Let us assume that before the assignment the Swisher Furniture Company had Accounts Receivable totaling $900,000. If this is true, the Accounts Receivable account and the Accounts Receivable Assigned account would appear as follows on the books of the Swisher Corporation:

Accounts Receivable

Balance	6/30/01	900,000	7/1/01		800,000
		100, 000			

Accounts Receivable Assigned

7/1/01	800,000	

As can be seen from looking at the two above accounts, on June 30 the Accounts Receivable account had a debit balance of $900,000. With the borrowing of $600,000 from the bank, the Swisher Furniture Company assigned $800,000 of its Accounts Receivable to the bank; thereafter the balance of Accounts Receivable (unassigned) is $100,000. The second Asset account, Accounts Receivable Assigned, shows the $800,000 balance.

• PROBLEM 8-13

The Swisher Furniture Company was short of Cash and long on Accounts Receivable. They needed $600,000 cash to pay their debts and to have enough working capital to continue operating their business. After discussing their financial problems with the bank, they were advised that the bank would lend them this large amount of money, $600,000, if they would make a specific assignment of $800,000 of their Accounts Receivable to the bank; and the going Interest Rate is 9%. This was done; and the Swisher Furniture Company received the $600,000 loan from the bank. Two weeks later, the Swisher Furniture Company received $200,000 payment from customers and turned this money over to the bank. What entries should be made on Swisher Furniture Company books?

SOLUTION:

2001			($ in dollars)
July 15	Cash	200,000	
	Accounts Receivable Assigned		200,000
	Cash received from customers		
15	Notes Payable	200,000	
	Cash		200,000

In the first entry above, $200,000 Cash was received from customers; so the account, Cash, was debited for that amount. The Asset account, Accounts Receivable Assigned, was credited for $200,000, bringing its balance down to $600,000.

In the second entry above, the $200,000 received from customers was immediately turned over to the bank in partial payment of the note; so Notes Payable is debited for $200,000 because we now owe less on the note; and Cash is credited for $200,000 because we are paying the bank that amount.

• PROBLEM 8-14

The Swisher Furniture Company was short of Cash and long on Accounts Receivable. They needed $600,000 Cash to pay their debts and to have enough working capital to continue operating their business. After discussing their financial problems with the bank, they were advised that the bank would lend them this large amount of money, $600,000, if they would make a specific assignment of $800,000 of their Accounts Receivable to the bank, with the going Interest Rate of 9%. This was done, and the Swisher Furniture Company received the $600,000 loan from the bank. Two weeks later, the Swisher Furniture Company collected $200,000 from customers and immediately turned this money over to the bank as partial payment on their loan.

During the second half of July, the Swisher Furniture Company received other payments of $350,000 from customers and wrote off the other $50,000 as bad debts. What entries should be made on the Swisher books?

SOLUTION:

2001			($ in dollars)
July 31	Cash	350,000	
	Allowance for Doubtful Accounts	50,000	
	Accounts Receivable Assigned		400,000
	Cash received from customers and		
	some accounts written off		
31	Notes Payable	404,500	
	Cash		404,500
	To pay off the remainder of the note		
31	Interest Expense	4,500	
	Discount on Notes Payable		4,500
	To show interest expense		
	on the money borrowed		
31	Accounts Receivable	200,000	
	Accounts Receivable Assigned		200,000
	To close out the Assigned account		

On the first of the above four entries, Cash is debited for $350,000 because this much was collected by Swisher Furniture Company from customers during the last half of July. Allowance for Doubtful Accounts is debited for $50,000 because this is written off as bad debts. Accounts Receivable Assigned asset account is credited for $400,000 to show a decrease in this account.

In the second of the above four entries, the Swisher Furniture Company has decided to pay off the remainder of the debt to the bank, in the amount of $404,500. They receive their Note Payable marked paid from the bank; so debit Notes Payable for $404,500. They credit Cash for $404,500 because this amount is being paid to the bank at this time.

In the third of the above four entries, Interest Expense is being recorded, so Interest Expense is debited for $4,500 ($600,000 × 9% = $54,000, $54,000 divided by 12 months = $4,500.) Discount on Notes Payable is credited for $4,500 to close out this account.

In the fourth of the above four entries, Accounts Receivable is debited for $200,000 because Accounts Receivable Assigned is being closed out into Accounts Receivable. On the other hand, Accounts Receivable Assigned is credited for $200,000 to close it out. Accounts Receivable Assigned is a temporary Asset account which is open only during the life of the loan. Since the loan is now being paid in full, this account is being closed out.

The various "T" accounts in the general ledger of the Swisher Furniture Company appear as follows after these entries are made:

Notes Payable

2001		2001	
July 15	200,000	July 1	604,500
2001			
July 31	404,500		
	604 500		

Accounts Receivable

Balance	6/30/01	900,000	7/1/01	800,000
	7/31/01	200 000		
		1,100, 000		
Balance	7/31/01	300,000		

Accounts Receivable Assigned

7/1/01	800,000	7/15/01	200,000
		7/31/01	400,000
		7/31/01	200 000
			800 000

Discount on Notes Payable

7/1/01	4,500	7/31/01	4,500

Explaining the Notes Payable account above, on July 1, 2001, the Swisher Furniture Company signed a note for $604,500. On July 15, 2001, they repaid $200,000 of this note; and on July 31, 2001, repaid the remaining $404,500 on the note.

Explaining the Accounts Receivable account above, on June 30, 2001, the balance (debit balance) was $900,000. On July 1, 2001, $800,000 of the $900,000 was assigned to the bank. On July 31, 2001, the Accounts Receivable Assigned was closed out into Accounts Receivable, thus debiting Accounts Receivable for $200,000. Thus the Accounts Receivable account has a final balance of $300,000.

Explaining the Accounts Receivable Assigned account above, on July 1, 2001, this temporary Asset account was set up when $800,000 of Swisher Furniture Company Accounts Receivable was assigned to the bank. At this time, Accounts Receivable Assigned was debited for $800,000. On July 15, 2001, when Swisher Furniture Company paid off part of its loan, Accounts Receivable Assigned was credited for $200,000. On July 31, 2001, when Swisher Furniture Company paid off the remainder of its debt to the bank, Accounts Receivable Assigned was credited for $400,000. Finally, on July 31, 2001, the remaining $200,000 balance in Accounts Receivable Assigned was closed out by crediting Accounts Receivable Assigned for $200,000.

Explaining the Discount on Notes Payable account above, on July 1, 2001, the Swisher Furniture Company borrowed $600,000 from the bank but was forced to sign a note for $604,500. The difference, $4,500, was debited to Discount on Notes Payable, a Contra-Liability account. Finally, on July 31, 2001, when the note was paid in full, Interest Expense was debited for the $4,500 and Discount on Notes Payable was credited for $4,500, thus closing out the account.

• PROBLEM 8–15

The James Textile Corporation is long on Accounts Receivable and short of Cash. James Textile sells $300,000 of its Accounts Receivable to a factor, receiving $276,000 Cash. What entry does James Textile Corporation make on its books and why?

SOLUTION:

James Textile Corporation Books

2005		($ in dollars)	
February 1	Cash	276,000	
	Factor Expense	15,000	
	Interest Expense	9,000	
	Accounts Receivable		300,000
	Selling accounts to Factor		
	without recourse		

Factors are finance companies that buy receivables for a fee and then collect directly from customers. These are common in furniture and textile businesses. Selling without recourse means that if the factor cannot collect, he cannot give the Accounts Receivable back to the James Textile Corporation. Because of this, the fees are somewhat high.

Cash is debited because the James Textile Corporation is receiving $276,000 from the factor. Factor Expense is debited for $15,000 because this is the amount the factor charges for collecting the Accounts Receivable and taking these receivables off the hands of the James Textile Corporation. Interest Expense is charged for $9,000. The factor must borrow this money until he can collect the bills, and so he passes this Interest Expense on to the James Textile Corporation. Finally, Accounts Receivable is credited, because $300,000 worth of receivables are being turned over to the factor.

Now let us see how this sale or purchase of Accounts Receivable is shown on the books of the factor:

• PROBLEM 8-16

The Broadmore Factor Collection Agency purchases Accounts Receivable from James Textile Corporation. James Textile turns over $300,000 Accounts Receivable but receives only $276,000 Cash. How is this recorded on the books of Broadmore Factor Collection Agency?

SOLUTION:

Broadmore Factor Collection Agency Books

2005		($ in dollars)
February 1	Accounts Receivable	300,000
	Due from James Textiles	15,000
	Financing Revenue	9,000
	Cash	276,000
	Purchased Accounts Receivable	
	from James Textile Corporation.	

Purchasing Accounts Receivable without recourse is a dangerous procedure for the purchaser, in this case the Broadmore Factor Collection Agency. This is so, because if Broadmore cannot collect from the Accounts Receivable, this factor has no recourse—it cannot give the Accounts Receivable back to James Textile Corporation. Broadmore is thus forced to charge quite a heavy fee. Broadmore also must produce Cash immediately to pay James Textile Corporation. It must usually borrow, and this means there will be Interest charges also.

When Broadmore Factor Collection Agency purchases the Accounts Receivable, it debits Accounts Receivable for $300,000, the total of the receivables it purchases. Then it credits an account entitled Due from James Textiles for $15,000. This is a Revenue account and is the major fee that Broadmore charges for its purchase of the receivables. However, there is another fee also, and this is called Financing Revenue, which is the total Interest charges that Broadmore Factor Collection Agency must pay for borrowing the money used to pay James Textiles. So, Financing Revenue is credited for $9,000. Finally, Cash is credited for $276,000 when Broadmore pays James Textiles.

• PROBLEM 8–17

James Textile Corporation needs money; so it sells $300,000 worth of its Accounts Receivable to Broadmore Factor Collection Agency **With Recourse**. This means that if the debtors fail to pay the collection agency, the James Textile Corporation will pay Broadmore Factor Collection Agency the difference. Since there is no danger of loss to the Broadmore Factor Collection Agency, the Broadmore Factor feels it can charge a lower fee of only $6,000, instead of $15,000. What entry is made on the books of the James Textile Corporation when the sale is made?

SOLUTION:

James Textile Corporation Books

2005			($ in dollars)
February 1	Cash	285,000	
	Factor Expense	6,000	
	Interest Expense	9,000	
	Accounts Receivable		300,000
	Selling accounts to factor with recourse		

Factors are finance companies that buy receivables for a fee, then collect directly from customers. Selling with recourse means that if the factor cannot collect, he can give the Accounts Receivable back to the selling corporation.

Cash is debited for $285,000, because the James Textile Corporation is receiving that amount from the factor. Factor Expense is debited for only $6,000, the factor fee. Interest Expense is debited for $9,000, because the factor has to borrow money to pay the James Textile Company; and the factor is passing this fee on to the textile company. Accounts Receivable is credited for $300,000, the amount of the receivables being turned over to the factor.

• PROBLEM 8–18

The Broadmore Factor Collection Agency purchases Accounts Receivable from James Textile Corporation. James Textile turns over $300,000 worth of Accounts Receivable but receives only $285,000 cash. How is this recorded on the books of the Broadmore Factor Collection Agency?

SOLUTION:

Broadmore Factor Collection Agency Books

2005		($ in dollars)
February 1	Accounts Receivable	300,000
	Due from James Textile	6,000
	Financing Revenue	9,000
	Cash	285,000
	Purchased Accounts Receivable with recourse	

Purchasing Accounts Receivable with recourse is not as dangerous a procedure for the purchaser as is purchasing without recourse, because in case Broadmore cannot collect, it can turn the receivables back to the James Textile Corporation for collection.

When Broadmore Factor Collection Agency purchases the accounts receivable, it debits Accounts Receivable for $300,000, the amount of receivables turned over by James Textile Corporation. It credits a Revenue account entitled Due from James Textile for $6,000, which is the factor fee. It also credits another Revenue account entitled Financing Revenue. This is an extra amount charged the James Textile Corporation because Broadmore needs to borrow the money used to pay James and must pay interest on this money borrowed.

• PROBLEM 8-19

When receivables are transferred **With Recourse**, the Financial Accounting Standards Board considers this a sale if (l) the transferor surrenders control of the future economic benefits of the receivables and (2) the transferor's obligation under the recourse provisions can be reasonably estimated, and (3) the transferee cannot require the transferor to repurchase the receivables. Let us say that all of these three requirements cannot be met in the transaction. This means that the transaction is a **Borrowing** of Accounts Receivable, and not a **Sale** of Accounts Receivable. What entries will be made on the James Textile Corporation books under conditions of borrowing Accounts Receivable?

SOLUTION:

James Textile Corporation Books

2005			($ in dollars)
February 1	Cash	285,000	
	Factor Expense	6,000	
	Interest Expense	9,000	
	Liability on Transferred		
	Accounts Receivable		300,000

The account credited is a Current Liability account entitled Liability on Transferred Accounts Receivable. If the factor finally collects on all the accounts, the following entry would be made on the books of the James Textile Corporation:

2005			($ in dollars)
April 1	Liability on Transferred		
	Accounts Receivable	300,000	
	Accounts Receivable		300,000

Accounts Receivable are turned over to the factor legally only after the factor collects on all accounts.

On the other hand, if the factor collects only $200,000 of the $300,000, the following entry could be made:

2005			($ in dollars)
April 1	Liability on Transferred Accounts Receivable	300,000	
	Cash		100,000
	Accounts Receivable		200,000

In this case, since the entry is a borrowing, and not a true sale, the Accounts Receivable are not turned over to the factor until the factor collects on the Accounts Receivable. In this case, the factor only collected $200,000 of the Accounts Receivable; so only that amount was turned over to the factor by a $200,000 credit to Accounts Receivable. In the above entry, the Liability on Transferred Accounts Receivable is debited for $300,000 to close out that account. Also, Cash is credited for $100,000, since James Textile would have to pay the factor for the receivables not collected and James Textile would receive these Receivables back and try to collect them themselves.

• PROBLEM 8-20

Our Burton Construction Company sold 5 acres of unneeded land to the Bigelow Lumber Company. Several years ago, we had purchased that land for $10,000. It has an appraised value of $12,000, and the Bigelow Lumber Company has given us their 5-year note for face value of $15,000. The note shows no Interest. How do we record this in our books?

SOLUTION:

Burton Construction Company books

2005			($ in dollars)
March 1	Notes Receivable	15,000	
	Discount on Notes Receivable		3,000
	Land		10,000
	Gain on Sale of Land		2,000

The Note Receivable that we are getting from the Bigelow Lumber Company has a face value of $15,000; so we debit Notes Receivable for that amount. However, the appraised value of the land, which we will consider the fair Market Value, is only $12,000. It is therefore assumed that the $3,000 difference between $15,000 and $12,000 is Imputed Interest. Therefore a Contra-Asset account, Discount on Notes Receivable, is credited for this Imputed Interest in the amount of $3,000. We had originally purchased this land for $10,000 and it is still debited for $10,000 on our books. In order to close out this account, we credit Land for $10,000. In order to make the debits equal the credits, we credit Gain on Sale of Land, a Revenue Account, for $2,000. The note shows no Interest, but the interest is really the $3,000.

• PROBLEM 8-21

> Our Burton Construction Company sold 5 acres of unneeded land to the Bigelow Lumber Company. Several years ago we had purchased that land for $10,000. It has an appraised value of $12,000; and the Bigelow Lumber Company has given us their 5-year note for face value of $15,000. The note shows no Interest. However, we figure the Imputed Interest is the difference between the $15,000 face value of the note and the $12,000 appraised value. Therefore, in the entry recording the sale of land, we credited a Contra-Asset account, Discount on Notes Receivable. How is this note written off each year?

SOLUTION:

Burton Construction Company books

2006		($ in dollars)
March 1	Discount on Notes Receivable	600
	Interest Revenue	600

At the end of each year that we hold the note, for the next five years, we debit Discount on Notes Receivable for $600 and credit Interest Revenue for $600. Discount on Notes Receivable is debited for $600 (1/5 the original discount) so that the $3,000 can gradually be written off over the five year period. Interest Revenue is credited, because it shows that we have earned $600 during this year. The actual earnings (Interest Revenue) were the $3,000 difference between the face value of the note ($15,000) and the appraisal value of the note ($12,000), but this Interest Revenue is being spread over the five-year life of the note.

• PROBLEM 8–22

Dr. James Smith performed medical services for Bower Construction Company over a period of time. On June 1, 2001, the Bower Construction Company gave Dr. Smith a $2,000 note due in 5 years with Interest at 2%. What entry should Dr. Smith make on his books?

SOLUTION:

The amount of money Dr. Smith earned is difficult to determine from the problem. The 2% Interest on the note is far too low. It is determined that the effective Interest Rate on other notes is now around 6%; so this interest should be used in the Present Value computations.

Face value of the note		$2,000.00
Present Value of note for 5 years at 6% = .74726		
.74726 × $2,000 =	$1,494.52	
Interest computation:		
$2,000 face value of note		
× .02 (Interest on face of note)		
$40. yearly Interest on note		
Present Value of interest over 5 years:		
4.21236 × $40 = $168.49	168.49	
Present Value of note and Interest	$1663.01	1,663.01
Discount on Notes Receivable		336.99

In order to find the Present Value of the $2,000 note for 5 years at 6%, we look in the Table for the Present Value of 1—Present Value of a Single Sum for 5 periods at 6% and find the figure .74726 and multiply this by the $2,000 face value of the note to get $1,494.52, the Present Value of the face value of the note.

In order to find the Present Value of all the Interest Payments, we first compute the value of the yearly Interest Payments by multiplying the face value of the note, $2,000, by the Interest Rate on the face of the note, 2% ($2,000 × 2% = $40 yearly interest.) The Total Interest over the five years would be $40 × 5 years = $200. What is the Present Value of this $200 Total Interest? We look in the table of the Present Value of an Ordinary Annuity of 1 to discover the figure 4.21236 (5 years at 6%).

We then multiply the 4.21236 by the $40 yearly Interest to get $168.49, the Present Value of all future Interest Receipts (4.21236 × $40 = $168.49).

The $1,494.52 Present Value of the face value of the note is then added to the $168.49 Present Value of all future Interest Receipts to get $1,663.01, the Total Present Value of both the face value of the note and the future Interest Receipts. Next, the $1,663.01 is subtracted from the $2,000 face value of the note to get the $336.99 discount.

The doctor's journal entry would be as follows:

2001		($ in dollars)
June 1	Notes Receivable	2,000.00
	Discount on Notes Receivable	336.99
	Revenue	1663.01

Discount on Notes Receivable is a Contra-Asset account in the Balance Sheet. It is amortized each year through Interest Revenue as follows:

2002		($ in dollars)
June 1	Discount on Notes Receivable	67.40
	Interest Revenue	67.40

$67.40 is 1/5 of the $336.99 balance of the Discount on Notes Receivable account; so 1/5 of the Discount balance is written off each year for five years. Five of the above entries will therefore close out the Discount on Notes Receivable account. Interest Revenue is credited each year, because discount on Notes Receivable is really Revenue; and this is a method of spreading the Interest Revenue over the 5-year life of the note.

• PROBLEM 8–23

What is the going Interest Rate if the Future Value of a loan is $9,000, the Present Value is $5,849.37, and the length of time is 5 years?

SOLUTION:

Part of a Table for the Present Value of a Single Sum

Periods	6%	8%	9%	10%	11%
5	.74726	.68058	.64993	.62092	.59345

When both the Future and Present Values of a loan are known, as well as the length of time of the loan, and when the going Interest Rate is desired, one should look up the table entitled Table for the Present Value of a Single Sum. First we look under the heading entitled Periods for the number of periods (in this case years) of the loan. Then we divide the Present Value of the loan ($5,849.37) by the Future Value of the loan ($9,000.00), to get .64993. (This means that the Present Value of the loan is 64.993% of the future value of the loan.) Next, we look in the table for a figure of or approximating .64993. In this case we find the figure .64993 and then look up the vertical column to find 9%. This means that the going Interest Rate is 9%.

• PROBLEM 8–24

James Hanwich plans to place $1,200 in an annuity at the end of every year for 10 years and wants about $20,066.412 at the end of that time. What will the Interest Rate have to be in order for him to do this?

SOLUTION:

Part of a Table for the Future Amount of an Ordinary Annuity of 1

Periods	8%	9%	10%	11%	12%	15%
10	14.48656	15.19293	15.93743	16.72201	17.54874	20.30372

James Hanwich divides the future value of $20,066.412 by the amount of yearly annuity ($1,200) to get 16.72201. This means that over the 10-year period, the Present Value of $1,200 will increase over 16 times. Looking at the Table for the Future Amount of an Ordinary Annuity of 1, we look at the 10th period line, since the annuity payments will be 10, 1 each year for 10 years. Then we look across that line for the number equal to or almost equal to the 16.72201 computed above. When we come to this figure, we look up the column to the percentage at the top of the column, which would be 11% in this case.

This means that if James Hanwich invests $1,200 per year at the end of each year for 10 years, he will have $20,066.412 at the end of this time if the Interest Rate is 11%.

CHAPTER 9

INVENTORIES

> **Basic Attacks and Strategies for Solving Problems in this Chapter. See pages 251 to 284 for step-by-step solutions to problems.**

Many businesses have a majority of their investment tied up in inventory. Therefore, care of inventory is highly important to the successful business. Inventory, of course, is what a mercantile business buys, in order to sell at a higher price and make a profit. Inventory for a manufacturing business is what it manufactures then sells in order to make Income. In either case, the whole success of the business is based on caring for and selling its product.

A business must protect its inventory from being stolen or from being destroyed by flood, fire, water, or some other calamity. It must also protect inventory from rust, freeze, and sometimes heat so that it is in proper condition to be sold.

Sometimes it is difficult to tell what is inventory and what is not. For instance, goods in transit at year's end are only considered inventory if they are still legally owned by the company in question. Goods on consignment are still owned by the consignor, even though the consignee has physical possession of them.

Even though a vendor firm has a liberal returns policy, if merchandise has changed hands and title, it is owned by the purchaser, not the seller. Freight charges are not included in inventory, but in a separate Cost account. They are eventually added to inventory to become merchandise available for sale figures. Even installment sales are still listed on the books of the vendor as inventory, because usually title does not pass in an installment sale until the vendor receives the final cash from the buyer.

Usually supplies are not considered inventory because supplies are used by the business itself and are not meant to be sold. Of course in an office supplies company, where the supplies are meant to be sold, they would be considered inventory.

In a manufacturing business, raw materials and goods in process are both considered to be inventories. They are so important that the first part of an Income Statement of a manufacturing firm is taken up with these inventories.

Even on the wholesale level it is important for business that bills be paid on time, so various discounts are given. Some businesses record purchases at gross; but others, being certain that they will take advantage of all purchase discounts, record purchases at net. This is also done with sales discounts in recording sales either Gross or Net. The Net Method of recording sales and purchases works well as long as the company pays bills within the discount period. If it neglects this, more complications set in, such as adjusting entries at year's end by debiting an Expense account entitled Purchases Discounts Lost.

Probably the most important End-of-Month Statement that a business must compute is the Income Statement, because it shows the company's Net Profit or Net Loss for the period. This must be compared with last month's, last quarter's, or perhaps last year's Income Statement to see if the company is doing better or worse financially. Then Revenues and Expenses for this month and last month must be compared in order to see what items have done better and where things have gone awry.

But an Income Statement cannot be completed unless the dollar value of the ending inventory is known. And how can that figure be computed? There are at least six different ways, as follows:

1. Periodic Inventory Method using First In First Out Computations

2. Periodic Inventory Method using Last In First Out Computations

3. Periodic Inventory Method using Average Cost Computations

4. Perpetual Inventory Method using First In First Out Computations

5. Perpetual Inventory Method using Last In First Out Computations

6. Perpetual Inventory Method using Moving Average Computations

In order to show how the ending inventory is computed under each of these six conditions, a simple problem using one item of inventory is illustrated in the chapter, figuring the dollar value of the Ending Inventory and the Cost of Goods Sold using each of the above six methods.

If the Cost of Goods Sold changes, then naturally the Gross Profit figure changes. The Gross Profit is computed in each instance by subtracting the ending inventory from the merchandise available for sale.

Step-by-Step Solutions to Problems in this Chapter, "Inventories"

• PROBLEM 9–1

The Arthur Company had extra money it did not immediately need, so it invested this money temporarily in mutual funds. The amount was $10,000. Could this be considered inventory?

SOLUTION:

No, temporary investments are under Current Assets in the Balance Sheet, under Temporary Investments, and not under Merchandise Inventory.

• PROBLEM 9–2

The Hanson Construction Company had factory supplies. Could these be placed in inventory?

SOLUTION:

Yes, while these supplies are being stored prior to use, they could be placed in Raw Materials Inventory.

• PROBLEM 9–3

On Deember 28, the Jacobson Manufacturing Company purchased merchandise f.o.b. shipping point. At midnight on December 31, the goods were still in transit. Should Jacobson Manufacturing Company include this as merchandise in their End-of-Year Balance Sheet?

SOLUTION:

Yes. The terms of the shipment were F.O.B. shipping point. This means that as soon as the goods left the vendor's warehouse on December 28, they were legally the property of the Jacobson Manufacturing Company. So they definitely should be included in Merchandise Inventory on the December 31 Balance Sheet.

• PROBLEM 9–4

The March Manufacturing Company on December 28 purchased merchandise F.O.B. destination. At midnight on December 31, the goods were still in transit. Should March Manufacturing Company include this as merchandise in their End-of-Year Balance Sheet?

SOLUTION:

No. The terms of the shipment were F.O.B. destination. This means that the goods belong to the vendor until they reach March Manufacturing Company's unloading dock. On December 31 they have not yet reached the unloading dock, so they do not yet legally belong to the March Manufacturing Company and should not be included as Merchandise Inventory on the End-of-Year Balance Sheet.

• PROBLEM 9–5

The Stecklen Manufacturing Company has merchandise on consignment at Breck Brothers Store. Should this merchandise be included as Merchandise inventory in the Stecklen Manufacturing Company's End-of-Year Balance Sheet?

SOLUTION:

Yes, goods on consignment belong to Stecklen Manufacturing Company, the consignor.

• PROBLEM 9–6

The Richardson Manufacturing Company sold merchandise on December 30, terms F.O.B. destination. At midnight on December 31, these goods had not yet reached the customer. Should these be on the End-of-Year inventory of the Richardson Manufacturing Company?

SOLUTION:

Yes. The terms of the sale are F.O.B. destination, which means that the goods belong to the Richardson Manufacturing Company until they reach the customer. Since at year's end they are still in transit and have not reached the customer, they still legally belong to the Richardson Manufacturing Company and still should be listed on the Richardson Balance Sheet as Merchandise Inventory.

• PROBLEM 9–7

The Jones Steel Corporation purchased merchandise F.O.B. destination on December 29. As of year's end, the goods had not yet arrived on the Jones' loading and unloading dock. Should these goods be listed as Merchandise Inventory on the books of the Jones Steel Corporation in the End-of-Year Balance Sheet?

SOLUTION:

No. Since the terms of the contract are F.O.B. destination, the Jones Steel Corporation does not gain ownership of the merchandise until it arrives on their unloading dock. As of midnight on December 31, these goods had not yet arrived so they should not be listed.

• PROBLEM 9-8

The Jason Company has sold merchandise to the Gypsum Construction Company, but the Jason Company has a liberal returns policy and accepts returns in good condition. This sale was made on December 31. Should these goods be listed as Merchandise Inventory on the Balance Sheet of the Jason Company at year's end?

SOLUTION:

No. It is true that the returns policy is liberal, but as long as an honest sale has been made, this merchandise as of year's end belongs to Gypsum Construction Company, not to the Jason Company.

• PROBLEM 9-9

The Ryder Company on December 30 sold merchandise to the Quarter Company F.O.B. shipping point. Should this merchandise be included in the Merchandise Inventory of the Ryder Company's Balance Sheet at year's end?

SOLUTION:

No. The terms of the sale are F.O.B. shipping point, which means that on December 30, when the goods left the Ryder Company loading dock, they then belonged to Quarter Company.

• PROBLEM 9–10

The Bruce Company has completed making brooms which are still stored on the Bruce Company property. These brooms have not yet been sold as of year's end. Should they be included in Bruce Company's Year-End Inventory?

SOLUTION:

Yes. They are part of the Finished Goods Inventory and should be included since they have not yet been sold.

• PROBLEM 9–11

The Jones Company has purchased raw materials for use in the factory. The freight charges on these goods come to $100. Should this $100 be included in Inventory?

SOLUTION:

No. They should be placed in Freight In, a Cost account. This will be figured into the Cost of Goods Sold, but is separate from Inventory.

• PROBLEM 9–12

The Jason Manufacturing Company has labor costs during December of $50,000. This is work on goods that have not yet been sold, and the manufacturing process on these goods is not yet complete either. Should these costs be added to Inventory?

SOLUTION:

Yes. These should be added to Work in Process Inventory because the goods have not yet been completely manufactured.

• PROBLEM 9–13

> The Burch Company on December 31 made installment sales of $10,000. Should these be listed on the Year-End Balance Sheet of the Burch Company as Merchandise Inventory?

SOLUTION:

Yes, most installment sales are made through the use of a Conditional Sales Contract which does not allow title to pass to the purchaser until the last installment payment is made. This is to allow the vendor to reclaim the merchandise if the customer defaults. Therefore, the Burch Company still legally owns the merchandise, and it should be listed as an Asset on the Burch Company Balance Sheet at year's end.

• PROBLEM 9–14

> The Rostov Company holds goods on consignment from the Flint Corporation. Rostov Company is attempting to sell these goods. When there is a sale, the Rostov Company remits a portion of the sale to the Flint Corporation. As of the end of the year, the dollar value of these consigned goods is $50,000. Should Rostov Company list this $50,000 as Merchandise Inventory on its Year-End Balance Sheet?

SOLUTION:

No. Goods on consignment are legally owned by the consignor, not the consignee. Therefore, the Rostov Company should not list the $50,000 as Inventory on its books.

• PROBLEM 9-15

The Randolph Company has $150 worth of office supplies in its office supplies closet. Should these be listed as Merchandise Inventory in the Asset section of its Year-End Balance Sheet?

SOLUTION:

No. Although Office Supplies and Merchandise Inventory are both Current Assets, they should be listed separately. Merchandise Inventory is goods used for sale, while Office Supplies are used in the company. Of course, if a firm is in the office supplies business and is selling office supplies, the office supplies up for sale would be Merchandise Inventory.

• PROBLEM 9-16

The Smith Corporation has materials on hand that have not yet been placed into production, and this is a manufacturing firm. Would these be considered Inventory?

SOLUTION:

Yes. A manufacturing firm would consider materials not yet placed into production as Raw Materials Inventory.

• PROBLEM 9-17

Brooklyn Corporation is a hardware store. During the month of March their sales were $50,000; Sales Returns $2,000; Beginning Inventory March 1 $30,000; March Purchase Returns $500; March Purchases Discounts $200; Transportation In $100; Ending Inventory March 31 $8,000; and Gross Profit $20,600. Compute the following: Net Sales, Purchases, Cost of Goods Purchased, and Cost of Goods Sold. How would these look in an Income Statement?

SOLUTION:

The easiest way to solve this problem and make meaning of it is to set up the accounts as they would appear in the Balance Sheet of a mercantile firm, as follows:

Sales			$50,000
Less Sales Returns			2,000
Net Sales			
Beginning Inventory		30,000	
Purchases	6,000		
Less: Purchases Returns	500		
Purchase Discounts	200		
Net Purchases			
Plus: Transportation In	100		
Cost of Goods Purchased			
Cost of Goods Available for Sale			
Less: Ending Inventory		8,000	
Cost of Goods Sold			
Gross Profit			20,000

The Net Sales figure is computed by subtracting the $2,000 Sales Returns from the $50,000 Sales in order to arrive at $48,000.

The Purchases Returns of $500 and the Purchase Discounts of $200 are added together to get deductions of $700.

Deduct Gross Profit of $20,600 from Net Sales of $48,000 to get Cost of Goods Sold of $27,400. Add Cost of Goods Sold of $27,400 plus Ending Inventory of $8,000 to get Cost of Goods Available for Sale of $35,400. Deduct Beginning Inventory of $30,000 from Cost of Goods Available for Sale of $35,400 to get Cost of Goods Purchased of $5,400. Deduct Transportation In of $100 from Cost of Goods Purchased of $5,400 to get Net Purchases of $5,300. The total of Purchases Returns and Purchase Discounts is $700—so add this $700 to the Net Purchases of $5,300 to get Purchases of $6,000. Following these computations, the top section of the March Balance Sheet will appear as follows:

Sales		50,000	
Less: Sales Returns		−2,000	
Net Sales			48,000
Beginning Inventory		30,000	
Purchases	6,000		
Less: Purchases Returns	500		
Purchase Discounts	200		
	− 700		
Net Purchases	5,300		
Plus: Transportation In	+ 100		
Cost of Goods Purchased	5,400	5,400	
Cost of Goods Available for Sale		35,400	
Less: Ending Inventory		− 8,000	
Cost of Goods Sold		27,400	27,400
Gross Profit			20,600

• PROBLEM 9-18

Here are some of the accounts appearing in the Trial Balance of the Brown Corporation at the end of the year 2000:

Raw Materials Inventory on Jan. 1, 2000:	$38,000
Raw Materials Purchased in year 2000:	60,000
Raw Materials Inventory on Dec. 31, 2000:	33,000
Work in Process Inventory on Jan. 1, 2000:	40,000
Direct Labor incurred during the year 2000:	80,000
Manufacturing Overhead during the year 2000:	90,000
Work in Process Inventory on Dec. 31, 2000:	60,000
Finished Goods Inventory Jan. 1, 2000:	55,000
Finished Goods Inventory Dec. 31, 2000:	65,000
Sales during the year 2000:	398,000
General and Administrative Expenses during the year:	60,000

Give the closing entries to show how much Raw Material was taken from the raw materials warehouse to the factory; how much finished product left the factory for the finished goods warehouse; and how much Cost of Goods Sold left the finished goods warehouse to be sold.

SOLUTION:

Add the beginning Raw Materials Inventory on January 1, 2000 of $38,000 to the purchases of Raw Materials totaling $60,000 to get Raw Materials Available for Sale of $98,000. Deduct the ending Raw Materials Inventory of $33,000 from the Raw Materials Available for Sale of $98,000 to get $65,000, which is the dollar value of the raw materials leaving the raw materials warehouse for the factory during the year 2000.

The journal entry to show the materials leaving the raw materials warehouse and entering the factory is as follows:

Work in Process Inventory	65,000
Raw Materials Inventory	65,000

The Direct Materials of $65,000 and the Direct Labor of $80,000 and the Manufacturing Overhead of $90,000 are added together to get Total Cost of Goods Manufactured of $235,000. The Total Cost of Goods Manufactured of $235,000 plus the beginning Work in Process Inventory of $40,000 are added together to get Total Cost of Goods Manufactured plus beginning Work in Process Inventory of $275,000. The ending Work in Process Inventory of $60,000 is subtracted from the $275,000 to get Cost of Goods Manufactured of $215,000.

The journal entry to show the finished product leaving the factory and entering the finished goods warehouse is as follows:

Finished Goods Inventory	215,000
Work in Process Inventory	215,000

The beginning Finished Goods Inventory of $55,000 and the Cost of Goods Manufactured of $215,000 are added to get Finished Goods Available for Sale of $270,000. The ending Finished Goods Inventory of $65,000 is subtracted from the Finished Goods Available for Sale of $270,000 to get Cost of Goods Sold of $205,000.

The journal entry to show the Cost of Goods Sold as the merchandise leaves the finished goods warehouse to be sold is as follows:

Cost of Goods Sold	205,000
Finished Goods	205,000

At the end of the year 2000, the three Inventory accounts (Raw Materials Inventory, Work in Process Inventory, and Finished Goods Inventory) appear as follows:

Raw Materials Inventory

Inv. 1/1/2000	38,000		
Raw Mat. Purchases	60,000	Material Used	65,000
Raw Mat. Available	98,000		
Inventory 12/31/2000	33,000		

Work in Process Inventory

Inventory 1/1/2000	40,000		
Direct Materials	65,000		
Direct Labor	80,000	Cost of Goods	
Manufacturing Overhead	90,000	Manufactured	215,000
Total	275,000		
Inventory 12/31/2000	60,000		

Finished Goods Inventory

Inventory 1/1/2000	55,000		
Cost of Goods		Cost of Goods	
Manufactured	215,000	Sold	205,000
Available	270,000		
Inventory 12/31/2000	65,000		

The Raw Materials at the beginning of the year were determined to be $38,000. During the year $60,000 of Raw Materials were purchased from vendors, thus giving a total of $98,000 worth of Raw Materials available for sale. Some of these were sold and the rest remained in the Raw Materials Inventory at the end of the year. The unsold Raw Materials at year's end amounted to $33,000, so this $33,000 is subtracted from the $98,000 Raw Materials Available for Sale to get $65,000—the value of the Raw Materials that were used and went from the Raw Materials warehouse to the factory.

The Factory account is called Work in Process Inventory. At the beginning of the year 2000, there was a Beginning Inventory (partially finished merchandise in the factory) of $40,000. To this is added the

$65,000 worth of Direct Materials that came over from the Raw Materials warehouse, the Direct Labor of $80,000, and the Manufacturing Overhead (all the other costs on the factory such as machine depreciation, indirect labor, indirect materials, heat, light, rent) of $90,000, to get a total of $275,000. At year's end some of the goods had been finished and sent on to the Finished Goods Warehouse, and the rest of the goods were not finished and remained in the Work in Process Inventory. So we subtract the $60,000 partially finished goods in the Work in Process Inventory from the total costs of $275,000 to get $215,000, the Cost of Goods Manufactured.

The Finished Goods Inventory contains the completed product. These products wait in the Finished Goods warehouse until they are sold.

On January 1, 2000, there are finished products in the Finished Goods Warehouse amounting to $55,000. During the year 2000, $215,000 worth of finished products enter the Finished Goods warehouse from the factory. These are called Cost of Goods Manufactured.

Our next step is to add the $215,000 Cost of Goods Manufactured to the $55,000 beginning Finished Goods Inventory to get $270,000 Goods Available for Sale.

Of the Goods Available for Sale, they are either sold or still unsold. As of December 31, 2000, there are still $65,000 worth of merchandise unsold and remaining in the Finished Goods warehouse.

Our next step is to subtract the $65,000 ending Finished Goods Inventory from the $270,000 Finished Goods Available for Sale, to get $205,000 Cost of Goods Sold.

• PROBLEM 9–19

> The Hinton Manufacturing Company purchased goods billed at $12,500 subject to a Cash discount of 2/10; n/30 on June 1, 2000. On June 19, 2000, they purchased goods from the same company, Lanton Company, for $10,000 subject to a Cash discount of 2/10; n/30. On June 23 they paid the invoice of June 1. On June 27 they purchased from Lanton Company goods billed at $5,300 subject to a Cash discount of 2/10; n/30. Give journal entries if purchases are recorded at Net, then at Gross.

SOLUTION:

Purchases at Net Amounts—Hinton Books

2000		($ in dollars)	
June 1	Purchases	12,250	
	Accounts Payable—Lanton		12,250
	Purchased merchandise at Net		
19	Purchases	9,800	
	Accounts Payable—Lanton		9,800
23	Accounts Payable—Lanton	12,250	
	Discounts Lost	250	
	Cash		12,500
	Paid debt after discount date		
27	Purchases	5,194	
	Accounts Payable—Lanton		5,194
	Purchased merchandise at Net		

Purchases at Gross Amounts—Hinton Books

2000		($ in dollars)	
June 1	Purchases	12,500	
	Accounts Payable—Lanton		12,500
	Purchased merchandise at Gross		
19	Purchases	10,000	
	Accounts Payable—Lanton		10,000
	Purchased merchandise at Gross		
23	Accounts Payable—Lanton	12,500	
	Cash		12,500
	Paid debt after discount date		
27	Purchases	5,300	
	Accounts Payable—Lanton		5,300
	Purchased merchandise at Gross		

Sales at Net Amounts—Lanton Books

2000		($ in dollars)	
June 1	Accounts Receivable—Hinton	12,250	
	Sales		12,250
	Sold merchandise; recorded at Net		
19	Accounts Receivable—Hinton	9,800	
	Sales		9,800
	Sold merchandise; recorded at Net		
23	Cash	12,500	
	Gain		250
	Accounts Receivable—Hinton		12,250
	Received payment after discount period		
27	Accounts Receivable—Hinton	5,194	
	Sales		5,194
	Sold merchandise; recorded at Net		

Sales at Gross Amounts—Lanton Books

2000		($ in dollars)	
June 1	Accounts Receivable—Hinton	12,500	
	Sales		12,500
	Sold merchandise; recorded at Gross		
19	Accounts Receivable—Hinton	10,000	
	Sales		10,000
	Sold merchandise; recorded at Gross		
23	Cash	12,500	
	Accounts Receivable—Hinton		12,500
	Received cash after discount period		
27	Accounts Receivable—Hinton	5,300	
	Sales		5,300
	Sold merchandise; recorded at Gross		

The Hinton Company has decided to record all purchases at Net instead of at Gross, since it plans to make all payments for purchases within the discount period, which usually amounts to 10 days. On June 1, it makes a $12,500 purchase, but the vendor offers a 2% discount if the bill is paid within 10 days. Supposing they will be able to do this, the Hinton Company deducts the 2% (2% × $12,500 = $250), or $250, from the $12,500 purchase to get $12,250, and debits Purchases for $12,250 and credits Accounts Payable—Lanton for $12,250. If they had done it by the gross method, they would have debited Purchases for the full $12,500 and credited Accounts Payable—Lanton for the full $12,500.

Also on June 19, Hinton Company makes another purchase from Lanton, this time for $10,000, again with a 2% discount if paid within 10 days. Two percent of $10,000 is $200, and this $200 is deducted from $10,000 to make a Net amount of $9,800. So the account Purchases is debited for $9,800 and Accounts Payable—Lanton is credited for $9,800. If the gross method had been used, Purchases would have been debited for $10,000 and Accounts Payable—Lanton would have been credited for $10,000.

On June 23 Hinton pays for the June 1 purchase, but June 23 is more than 10 days after June 1, so the full Gross price of $12,500 must be paid rather than the Net amount of $12,250. So in the Net method, the account, Accounts Payable—Lanton is debited for $9,800 (the Net amount) to close out that figure. The Expense account Discounts Lost is debited for the $250 which is the amount lost because the bill was paid after the discount date. And Cash is credited for the full Gross amount of $12,500.

On June 27, Hinton buys more merchandise for a Gross price of $5,300. Two percent of $5,300 is $106. This $106 is subtracted from $5,300 to get a Net price of $5,194. So, keeping books by the Net method, we debit the Purchases account for $5,194 and credit Accounts Payable—Lanton for $5,194.

What is shown on the Lanton Books? Lanton is the seller. Lanton too can keep records of his sales either by the Gross method or the Net method. On June 1, using the Net method, Lanton debits Accounts Receivable—Hinton for $12,250 (the Net price) and credits Sales for $12,250. If he had been keeping books by the Gross method, he would have debited Accounts Receivable—Hinton for $12,500 and credited Sales for $12,500.

For the June 19 entry, on the Net method, Lanton would debit Accounts Receivable—Hinton for the $9,800 and credited Sales for $9,800. If he had used the Gross method he would have debited Accounts Receivable-Hinton for the full amount of $10,000 and credited Sales for $10,000.

On June 23 he finally receives the payment for the first sale, but it is later than the 10-day discount period, so he receives the full amount of $12,500 under both methods. Under the Net method, Cash is debited for $12,500. A Revenue account entitled Gain is credited for $250 (the amount that the seller Lanton gains by having to wait until after the discount period to receive the money). Accounts Receivable—Hinton is credited for $12,250, the Net amount, to close out this figure on the books. Under the Gross method on June 23, Cash is debited for the gross amount of $12,500 and Accounts Receivable—Hinton is credited for $12,500 to close out this figure on the books.

The final entry on June 27 is another sale to Hinton. If the Net method is used, Accounts Receivable—Hinton is debited for the Net amount of the sale, $5,194, and Sales is credited for $5,194. If the Gross method is used, Accounts Receivable—Hinton is debited for the Gross amount of $5,300 and Sales account is credited for $5,300.

• PROBLEM 9–20

The Hinton Manufacturing Company purchased goods billed at $10,000 from the Lanton Company on June 19, 2000, subject to a Cash discount of 2/10; n/30. They kept records at the Net amount so they made the following entry:

2000		($ in dollars)
June 19	Purchases	9,800
	Accounts Payable-Lanton	9,800
	Purchased merchandise at Net	

The $9,800 is 98% of the Gross amount of $10,000.

At the end of June, on June 30, the invoice remains unpaid and the 10-day discount period has elapsed. What adjusting entry should the Hinton Manufacturing Company make on its books?

SOLUTION:

2000		($ in dollars)
June 30	Purchases Discounts Lost	200
	Accounts Payable	200

The $200 is the difference between the Gross amount of the purchase ($10,000) and the net amount of the purchase ($9,800). In the June 19 entry, Accounts Payable was credited for only $9,800 because it was assumed that the purchase would be paid for within the discount period so only the $9,800 would be owed. However, since the discount period, of 10 days has elapsed without payment, the Accounts Payable account should be increased by $200 to show that the full $10,000 is owed. This is done by the above adjusting entry on June 30, crediting Accounts Payable for $200. The Expense account, Purchases Discounts Lost, is debited for the $200, because this is an added expense to the Hinton Manufacturing Company for not paying for the purchases within the 10-day discount period.

• PROBLEM 9-21

The Brown Company sells one product. Presented below is information for the year 2000 for this company.

1/1/2000	Beginning Inventory	50 units @ $5	=	$250
3/10/2000	Sale	10 units @ $8		
3/25/2000	Purchase	80 units @ $6	=	480
5/10/2000	Sale	100 units @ $9		
8/7/2000	Purchase	15 units @ $7	=	105

What is the dollar value of the Ending Inventory using the Periodic Inventory Method? (First In First Out Method)

SOLUTION:

In using the Periodic Inventory Method, only the Beginning Inventory and the purchases are considered, not the sales. Following is the information about the Beginning Inventory and purchases, leaving out the sales:

1/1/2000	Beginning Inventory	50 units @ $5	=	$250
3/25/2000	Purchase	80 units @ $6	=	$480
8/7/2000	Purchase	15 units @ $7	=	$105
Total units available for sale and their dollar value:		145		$835
Number of units sold		−110		
Number of units unsold (in Ending Inventory)		35		

As seen from the computations immediately above, there is the Beginning Inventory of 50 units, the March purchase of 80 units, and the August purchase of 15 units. These add up to a total of 145 units available for sale. From the information in the question, we see that the March sale was 10 units and the May sale was 100 units, or a total of 110 units. Next, we subtract the 110 units sold from the 145 units available for sale to get 35 units in the Ending Inventory.

The next step is to ascertain the dollar value of the Ending Inventory of 35 units, using the First In First Out computation. In the First In First Out Method the units in the Beginning Inventory and early purchases are sold first. This means that the Ending Inventory is made up of the later purchases. In order, then, to determine the dollar value of the Ending Inventory by the First In First Out computation, one must **Start at the Bottom** of the above table and work up until one reaches the 35 units in the Ending Inventory. This is done as follows:

Determining the Dollar Value of the Ending Inventory
Using the First In First Out Method

Units from the 8/7/2000		
purchase	15 units @ $7 =	$105
Some units from the		
3/25/2000 purchase	20 units @ $6 =	$120
Ending inventory (FIFO)	35 units	$225

Working backwards up the previous table until 35 units of Ending Inventory are reached, we start with the August 7, 2000 purchase of 15 units @ $7 = $105. Then we move up to the March 25, 2000 purchase. Subtracting 15 units of the August 7, 2000 purchase from the 35 units of the Ending Inventory, we discover that we need 20 more units. These are all taken from the March 25, 2000 purchase at $6. So we multiply the 20 units additional that are needed by the $6 per unit in the March 25 inventory, to get $120. Next, we add the $105 and the $120 to get $225, which is the dollar value of the 35 units in the Ending Inventory, using the First In First Out Method.

• PROBLEM 9–22

The Brown Company sells one product. Presented below is information for the year 2000 for this company.

1/1/2000	Beginning Inventory	50 units @ $5	=	$250
3/10/2000	Sale	10 units @ $8		
3/25/2000	Purchase	80 units @ $6	=	$480
5/10/2000	Sale	100 units @ $9		
8/7/2000	Purchase	15 units @ $7	=	$105

In the previous problem (Problem 9–21), it was computed that there were 145 units available for sale and that there were 35 units in the Ending Inventory of unsold units. It was also computed that the dollar value of the 145 units available for sale was $835 and that the dollar value of the 35 units in the Ending Inventory was $225, using the FIFO Method of computation. How much was the Cost of Goods Sold?

SOLUTION:

If one subtracts the dollar value of the Ending Inventory (unsold units) from the dollar value of the units available for sale, one will get the dollar value of the units sold, at cost price. The reason that it will be at cost price is because in the computations we have kept the sales prices separate from the cost prices. The Beginning Inventory is kept at cost price, and the purchases are at cost price. The computation of the dollar value of the Cost of Goods Sold is as follows:

Total units available for sale and their dollar value	145 units	$835
Number of units unsold (ending inventory) and their dollar value	– 35 units	–$225
Cost of Goods Sold	110 units	$610

• PROBLEM 9-23

The Brown Company sells one product. Presented below is information for the year 2000 for this company. Compute the dollar value of the Ending Inventory using the LIFO method. Number of units sold during the year 2000:

Beginning Inventory and Purchases

1/1/2000	Beginning Inventory	50 units @ $5	=	$250
3/25/2000	Purchase	80 units @ $6	=	$480
8/7/2000	Purchase	15 units @ $7	=	$105
Total units available for sale				
and their dollar value		145 units		$835

SOLUTION:

As seen from the computations immediately above, there is the Beginning Inventory of 50 units, the March purchase of 80 units, and the August purchase of 15 units. These add up to a total of 145 units available for sale. From the information in the question, we determine to compute the number of units in the Ending Inventory (unsold). As seen above, there are 145 units available for sale, and of these, 110 units were sold. There are, therefore, 35 units unsold in the Ending Inventory (145 units – 110 units = 35 units).

The next step is to ascertain the dollar value of the Ending Inventory of 35 units, using the Last In First Out computation. In the Last In First Out computation, the last units purchased are sold first. This means that the ending inventory is derived from the earliest purchased units. So in order to compute the dollar value of the ending inventory by the Last In First Out computation, we need to start **At the Top** of the above table and work down, until we reach the 35 unsold units in the Ending Inventory, as follows:

1/1/2000	Ending Inventory at Beginning			
	Inventory price	35 units @ $5	=	$175

There are 50 units in the Beginning Inventory that were purchased at $5 per unit. But in this computation we are interested in only 35 of these units that have still been unsold at year's end. So we multiply the 35 units by the $5 price to get $175, the dollar value of the Ending Inventory.

• PROBLEM 9-24

The Brown Company sells one product. Presented below is information for the year 2000 for this company:

1/1/2000	Beginning Inventory	50 units @ $5	=	$250
3/25/2000	Purchase	80 units @ $6	=	$480
8/7/2000	Purchase	15 units @ $7	=	$105
Total units available for sale				
and their dollar value		145 units		$835

What is the dollar value of the Cost of Goods Sold, using the Periodic Inventory Method, using Last In First Out computations?

SOLUTION:

Total units available for sale and their dollar value	145 units	$835
Less Ending Inventory (LIFO)	35 units	− 175
Cost of Goods Sold (LIFO)	105 units	$660

As previously computed, there were 145 units available for sale at $835 cost. Of these available units, during the year they are either sold or else they remain in the Ending Inventory unsold. In Problem 9-23, the Ending Inventory of 35 units was computed, using the Last In First Out computations, to be $175. Therefore, we subtract the $175 value of the unsold units from the $835 value of the units available for sale to get the $660 value of the units sold. Since we have kept cost prices separate from selling prices, and this is the cost price, we can call the $660 the Cost of Goods Sold, LIFO method.

• PROBLEM 9-25

The Brown Company sells one product. Presented below is information for the year 2000 for this company:

Beginning Inventory and Purchases

1/1/2000	Beginning Inventory	50 units @ $5	=	$250
3/25/2000	Purchase	80 units @ $6	=	$480
8/7/2000	Purchase	15 units @ $7	=	$105
Total units available for sale and their dollar value		145 units		$835

Compute the dollar value of the ending inventory by the Periodic Inventory Method, using the **Average Cost** computation.

SOLUTION:

We have 145 units available for sale at a total cost of $835. The first step in computing the dollar value of the Ending Inventory by the Average Cost computation is to divide the $835 total cost by the 145 units to get $5.758620689 average cost per unit.

The second step is to multiply the $5.758620689 average cost per unit by the 35 units in the Ending Inventory to get $201.5517241, the dollar value of the Ending Inventory by the Average Cost computation. This will, of course, be rounded off to $201.55.

Step 1: Divide $835 by 145 units = $5.758620689

Step 2: $5.758620689 × 35 = $201.55

• PROBLEM 9–26

The Brown Company sells one product. Presented below is information for the year 2000 for this company:

1/1/2000	Beginning Inventory	50 units @ $5	=	$250
3/25/2000	Purchase	80 units @ $6	=	$480
8/7/2000	Purchase	15 units @ $7	=	$105
Total units available for sale and their dollar value		145 units		$835

What is the dollar value of the Cost of Goods Sold, using the Periodic Inventory Method, using the **Average Cost** Method?

SOLUTION:

As previously computed, there were 145 units available for sale at $835 cost. Of these available units, during the year they are either sold or else they remain in the Ending Inventory unsold. In Problem 9-25, the Ending Inventory of 35 units was computed, using the **Average Cost** computation, to be $201.55. Therefore, we subtract the $201.55 value of the unsold units in the Ending Inventory from the $835 value of the units available for sale to get the $633.45 value of the units sold. Since we have kept cost prices separate from selling prices, and this is the cost price, we can call the $633.45 the Cost of Goods Sold, **Average Cost** computation.

• PROBLEM 9–27

The Brown Company sells one product. Presented below is information for the year 2000 for this company:

1/1/2000	Beginning Inventory	50 units @ $5	=	$250
3/10/2000	Sale	10 units @ $8		
3/25/2000	Purchase	80 units @ $6	=	$480
5/10/2000	Sale	100 units @ $9		
8/7/2000	Purchase	15 units @ $7	=	$105

What is the dollar value of the Ending Inventory using the **Perpetual Inventory** Method, using the First In First Out computation?

SOLUTION:

The **Perpetual Inventory** Method differs from the **Periodic Inventory** Method of computing the dollar value of Ending Inventory in that under the Perpetual Inventory Method, every time there is a sale, the units in the sale are subtracted from the units on hand, and a new dollar value of inventory is computed. Under the Periodic Inventory, on the other hand, the units sold are not subtracted from units available until the end of the fiscal period.

The computation of the dollar value of the Ending Inventory using the Perpetual Inventory Method, and using the First In First Out computation of computation follows:

Perpetual Inventory Method
First In First Out Computation

Date	In	Out	Balance
1/1/2000			50 units @ $5=$250
3/10/2000		10 units @ $5=$50	40 units @ $5=$200
3/25/2000	80 units @ $6=$480		80 units @ $6=$480
5/10/2000		40 units @$5=$200	
		60 units @$6=$360	20 units @ $6=$120
8/7/2000	15 units @ $7=$105		15 units @ $7=$105

The Perpetual Inventory item is kept in a computer data base or on a storage card similar to the one above, with Date, In, Out, and Balance. On January 1, 2000, this item consisted of 50 units at $5 = $250. On March

10, 2000, 10 units were sold. These were units purchased at $5 per unit, and all these figures are at cost, not at sales price. Thus, 10 units are going out of inventory at a cost of $5 per unit, or $50. Subtracting the 10 units from the 50 units previously on hand, the balance is 40 units at $5 or $200.

On March 25, 2000, 80 units more are purchased, but this time at a higher price—$6 per unit, making it a cost of $480 (80 units × $6 = $480). This is added to the balance. The previous balance had been 40 units at $5 = $200. Now to this we add 80 units at $6 = $480.

On May 10, 2000, 100 units are sold. Since this is the First In First Out Method, the 40 units purchased at $5 per unit will be sold first. Therefore, under the **Out** column, there are 40 units @ $5 = $200.

We still need 60 more units to make the 100 units being sold (100 − 40 = 60). The only units we still have left are those previously purchased at $6 per unit, so we take out 60 units at $6 = $360. All of this is subtracted from the previous inventory, so all that is left in the Balance column is 20 units @ $6 = $120.

On August 7, 2000, 15 units of the same item are purchased at $7 = $105. This is then added to the balance. So the balance at year's end is as follows:

$$
\begin{array}{ll}
20 \text{ units @ } \$6 = & \$120 \\
\underline{15 \text{ units @ } \$7 =} & \underline{\$105} \\
35 \text{ units} & \$225
\end{array}
$$

Thus, the dollar value of the 35 units in the Ending Inventory as of December 31, 2000 is $225 under the **Perpetual Inventory** Method, using First In First Out computation.

• PROBLEM 9–28

The Brown Company sells one product. Presented below is information for the year 2000 for this company:

Ending Inventory, Perpetual Inventory Method, FIFO $225

What is the dollar value of the Cost of Goods Sold, using the Perpetual Inventory Method, and using the First In First Out computation?

SOLUTION:

Total units available for sale and their dollar value	145 units	$835
Less: Ending Inventory, Perpetual Inventory Method,		
FIFO Computation	– 35 units	– $225
Cost of Goods Sold	105 units	$610

Thus, the Cost of Goods Sold is $610, using the Perpetual Inventory Method and the First In First Out computation.

Another method of computing the Cost of Goods Sold under the Perpetual Inventory Method is to list the cost price of each item as it is sold, as follows:

March 10, 2000	10 units out @ $5	=	$ 50
May 5, 2000	40 units out @ $5	=	$200
May 5, 2000	60 units out @ $6	=	$360
Cost of Goods Sold			$610

• PROBLEM 9–29

The Brown Company sells one product. Presented below is information for the year 2000 for this company:

1/1/2000	Beginning Inventory	50 units @ $5	=	$250
3/10/2000	Sale	10 units @ $8		
3/25/2000	Purchase	80 units @ $6	=	$480
5/10/2000	Sale	100 units @ $9		
8/7/2000	Purchase	15 units @ $7	=	$105

What is the dollar value of the ending inventory using the **Perpetual Inventory** Method, and using the Last In First Out computation?

SOLUTION:

The **Perpetual Inventory** Method differs from the **Periodic Inventory** Method of computing the dollar value of Ending Inventory in that under the Perpetual Inventory Method, every time there is a sale, the units in the sale are subtracted from the units on hand, and a new dollar value of inventory is computed. Under the Periodic Inventory, on the other hand, the units sold are not subtracted from the units available until the end of the fiscal period.

The computation of the dollar value of the ending inventory using the Perpetual Inventory Method, and using the Last In First Out computation follows:

**Perpetual Inventory Method
Last In First Out Computation**

Date	In	Out	Balance
1/1/2000			50 units @ $5=$250
3/10/2000		10 units @ $5=$50.00	40 units @ $5=$200
3/25/2000	80 units @ $6=$480		80 units @ $6=$480
5/10/2000		80 units @ $6=$480	
		20 units @ $5=$100	20 units @ $5=$100
8/7/2000	15 units @ $7=$105		15 units @ $7=$105

The Perpetual Inventory item is kept in a computer data base or on a storage card similar to the one above, with Date, In, Out, and Balance. On January 1, 2000, this item consisted of 50 units at $5 = $250. On March 10, 2000, 10 units were sold. These were units purchased at $5 per unit, and all these figures are at cost, not at sales price. Thus, 10 units are going out of inventory at a cost of $5 per unit, or $50. Subtracting the 10 units from the 50 units previously on hand, the balance is 40 units at $5 or $200.

On March 25, 2000, 80 units more are purchased, but this time at a higher price—$6 per unit, making it a cost of $480 (80 units × $6 = $480). This is added to the balance . The previous balance had been 40 units at $5 = $200. Now to this we add 80 units at $6 = $480

On May 10, 2000, 100 units are sold. Since this is the Last In First Out Method, the 80 units purchased on March 25 will be sold first. These 80 units were purchased at $6 per unit for $480 (80 × $6 = $480). But 100 units are leaving, so we will need another 20 units (100 − 80 = 20). These 20 units will have to come from the original inventory which was purchased at $5 per unit, for a total of $100 (20 × $5 = $100).

After the 100 units have gone out, there are only 20 units left in inventory, and these will be at the price of $5 per unit, or a value of $100 (20 × $5 = $100).

On August 7, 2000, 15 more units of the item are purchased at $7 per unit for a value of $105 (15 × $7 = $105). There are, then, the following entries in the inventory at year's end:

      20 units @ $5 = $100
      15 units @ $7 = $105
      ───   ────
       35             $205

Thus, the dollar value of the Ending Inventory using the Perpetual Inventory Method and the Last In First Out computation is 35 units for $205.

• PROBLEM 9–30

The Brown Company sells one product. Presented below is information for the year 2000 for this company:

Ending Inventory, Perpetual Inventory Method, LIFO $205

What is the dollar value of the Cost of Goods Sold, using the Perpetual Inventory Method, and using the Last In First Out computation?

SOLUTION:

Total units available for sale and their dollar value	145 units	$835
Less: Ending Inventory, Perpetual Inventory Method,		
LIFO Computation	– 35 units	–$205
Cost of Goods Sold	105 units	$630

Thus, the Cost of Goods Sold is $630, using the Perpetual Inventory Method and the Last In First Out computation.

Another method of computing the Cost of Goods Sold under the Perpetual Inventory Method is to list the cost price of each item as it is sold, as follows:

March 10, 2000	10 units out @ $5	=	$ 50
May 5, 2000	80 units out @ $6	=	$480
May 5, 2000	20 units out @ $5	=	$100
Cost of Goods Sold			$630

• PROBLEM 9–31

The Brown Company sells one product. Presented below is information for the year 2000 for this company:

1/1/2000	Beginning Inventory	50 units @ $5	=	$250
3/10/2000	Sale	10 units @ $8		
3/25/2000	Purchase	80 units @ $6	=	$480
5/10/2000	Sale	100 units @ $9		
8/7/2000	Purchase	15 units @ $7	=	$105

What is the dollar value of the Ending Inventory using the **Perpetual Inventory** Method and using the Average Cost computation, sometimes called the Moving Cost omputation (Moving Average Computation)?

SOLUTION:

The **Perpetual Inventory** Method differs from the **Periodic Inventory** Method of computing the dollar value of Ending Inventory in that under the Perpetual Inventory Method, every time there is a sale, the units in the sale are subtracted from the units on hand, and a new dollar value of inventory is computed. Under the Periodic Inventory, on the other hand, the units sold are not subtracted from the units available until the end of the fiscal period.

The computation of the dollar value of the Ending Inventory using the Perpetual Inventory Method, and using the Average Cost Computation (Moving Average Computation) follows:

Perpetual Inventory Method
Moving Average Computation

Date	In	Out	Balance
1/1/2000			50 units@$5=$250
3/10/2000		10 units@$5=$50	40 units@$5=$200
3/25/2000	80 units@$6=$480		120 units @$5.67=$680
5/10/2000		100 units@$5.67=$567	20 units@$5.67=$113
8/7/2000	15 units@$7=$105		35 units@$6.2285=$218

On the first day of the year 2000, there were 50 units on hand that had been purchased for $5 per unit, totaling $250 (50 × $5 = $250). On

March 10, 2000, 10 of these units were sold, leaving a balance of 40 units on hand which were previously purchased for $5, totaling $200 (40 × $5 = $200).

On March 25, 2000, 80 more units of the item were purchased at $6 per unit for $480. Adding the previous balance of 40 units to the new purchase of 80 units, we now have 120 units in the new balance. Adding the $200 cost value of the previous balance to the $480 cost of the new purchase, we now have up to $680, the cost price of the merchandise on hand at the end of the day, March 25, 2000. In order to get the unit cost, we divide the total cost of the inventory, $680, by the number of units in the inventory, 120, to get $5.67 per unit. This is the Moving Average.

On May 10, 2000, we sell 100 units, and multiply this figure by the Moving Average per unit of $5.67, to get $567, the cost of the inventory moving out. This leaves 20 units in the inventory at the end of May 10, 2000 (120 units − 100 units = 20 units). These 20 units have a cost of $5.67 per unit or $113 (20 × $5.67 = $113).

On August 7, 2000, 15 more units are purchased at $7 per unit for a total cost of $105 (15 × $7 = $105). The 20 units in the previous inventory are added to the 15 units newly purchased to give an Ending Inventory of 35 units. The previous dollar value of the inventory was $113, and this is added to the purchase price of $105 to get a total Ending Inventory of $218 ($113 + $105 = $218).

Thus, the Ending Inventory using the Perpetual Inventory Method and the Moving Average computation is $218.

• PROBLEM 9–32

The Brown Company sells one product. Presented below is information for the year 2000 for this company:

Ending Inventory, Perpetual Inventory Method,
   Moving Average Computation $218

What is the dollar value of the Cost of Goods Sold, using the Perpetual Inventory Method, and using the Moving Average computation?

SOLUTION:

Total units available for sale and their dollar value	145 units	$835
Less: Ending Inventory, Perpetual Inventory Method,		
Moving Average Computation	−35 units	− 218
Cost of Goods Sold	105 units	$617

Thus, the Cost of Goods Sold is $617, using the Perpetual Inventory Method and the Moving Average computation.

Another method of computing the Cost of Goods Sold under the Perpetual Inventory Method is to list the cost price of each item as it is sold, as follows:

March 10, 2000	10 units out @ $5.00	=	$ 50
May 5, 2000	100 units out @ $5.67	=	$567
Cost of Goods Sold			$617

• PROBLEM 9–33

The Brown Company sells one product. Presented below is information for the year 2000 for this company:

1/1/2000	Beginning Inventory	50 units @ $5	=	$250
3/10/2000	Sale	10 units @ $8		
3/25/2000	Purchase	80 units @ $6	=	$480
5/10/2000	Sale	100 units @ $9		
8/7/2000	Purchase	15 units @ $7	=	$105

What is the dollar value of the gross profit, first using the Periodic Inventory Method, with FIFO, LIFO, and Average Cost computations, then using the Perpetual Inventory Method, with FIFO, LIFO, and Moving Average Computations?

SOLUTION:

First the total dollar value of the sales for the year are determined, then the gross profit (**periodic, FIFO**) as follows:

3/10/2000 Sale	10 units @ $8	=	$ 80	
5/10/2000 Sale	100 units @ $9	=	$900	
Total Sales			$980	$980
Available for sale	145 units		$835	
Ending Inventory (FIFO)				
(From Prob. 9–22)	35 units		$225	
Cost of Goods Sold	105 units		$610	– $610
Gross Profit (Periodic Method, FIFO)				$370

Determination of Gross Profit (Periodic, LIFO)

3/10/2000 Sale	10 units @ $8	=	$ 80	
5/10/2000 Sale	100 units @ $9	=	$900	
Total Sales			$980	$980
Available for sale	145 units		$835	
Ending Inventory (LIFO)				
(From Prob. 9–24)	35 units		$175	
Cost of Goods Sold	105 units		$660	– $660
Gross Profit (Periodic Method, LIFO)				$320

Determination of Gross Profit (Periodic, Average Cost)

3/10/2000 Sale	10 units @ $8	= $ 80	
5/10/2000 Sale	100 units @ $9	= $900	
Total Sales		$980	$980.00
Available for sale	145 units	$835.00	
Ending Inventory (Average cost)			
(From Prob. 9–25)	35 units	$201.55	
Cost of Goods Sold	105 units	$633.45	–$633.45
Gross Profit Periodic Method (Average Cost)			$246.55

Determination of Gross Profit (Perpetual, FIFO)

3/10/2000 Sale	10 units @ $8	=	$ 80	
5/10/2000 Sale	100 units @ $9	=	$900	
Total Sales			$980	$980
Available for sale	145 units		$835	
Ending Inventory (Perpetual, FIFO)				
(From Prob. 9–27)			$225	
Cost of Goods Sold	105 units		$610	– $610
Gross Profit (Perpetual, FIFO)				$350

Determination of Gross Profit (Perpetual, LIFO)

3/10/2000 Sale	10 units @ $8	=	$ 80	
5/10/2000 Sale	100 units @ $9	=	$900	
Total Sales			$980	$980
Available for sale	145 units		$835	
Ending Inventory (Perpetual, LIFO)				
(From Prob. 9–29)			$205	
Cost of Goods Sold	105 units		$630	– $630
Gross Profit (Perpetual, LIFO)				$350

Determination of Gross Profit (Perpetual, Moving Average)

3/10/2000 Sale	10 units @ $8	=	$ 80	
5/10/2000 Sale	100 units @ $9	=	$900	
Total Sales			$980	$980.00
Available for sale	145 units		$835	
Ending Inventory				
(Perpetual, Moving Average)				
(From Prob. 9–31)	35 units		$218	
Cost of Goods Sold	105 units		$617	–$617.00
Gross Profit (Perpetual, Moving Average)				$363.00

• PROBLEM 9–34

On January 2, 1996, the James Construction Company purchased land for $10,000. On January 2, 1998, the James Construction Company purchased adjacent land for $3,000. How much are these two pieces of land worth today?

SOLUTION:

Because of constant inflation in the United States, one must use price-level indexes to compute the dollar value of goods or of real estate purchased in the past, in order to bring these values up to today's inflated values. These price indexes are computed by the federal government. Any year can be used as the base year with the value of 100, or 100%.

Let us then use the year 1996 as the base year and assign it a value of 100. Between January 1, 1996 and January 1, 1998, let us say, inflation rose 20%, so if 1996 had a value of 100, then 1998 would have a value of 120. Let us say that inflation rose even more between 1998 and the year 2000, so that average prices were 60% higher on January 1, 2000 than they were on January 1, 1996. So if 1996 had a value of 100, then the year 2000 would have a value of 160.

In order to change prices of previous years into today's inflated prices, we multiply the purchase price by a fraction, the numerator of which is the index for current prices and the denominator of which is the index for prices that were in effect at the date related to the amount being restated.

So the computations would be as follows:

```
Purchase of land 1/2/96  $10,000 ($10,000 × 160/100) = $16,000
Purchase of land 1/2/98  $ 3,000 ($ 3,000 × 160/120) = $ 4,000
                                                        $20,000
```

The original land was purchased for $10,000 and the later piece of land was purchased for $3,000, or a total of $13,000. As of January 1, 2000, the two pieces of land together are worth $20,000 in inflated prices, as follows:

The original price of the first piece of land purchased was $10,000. This amount is multiplied by the fraction 160/100.

The numerator of the fraction is the price index as of today's date. (Let us assume that this date is January 1, 2000.) Since inflation has increased prices 160% since the date the original piece of land was purchased, the numerator figure is 160. The denominator figure is the price index as of the date the first piece of land was purchased, January 2, 1996, 100. Multiplying $10,000 by 160/100 gives $16,000 which is the value of the first piece of land at today's inflated prices.

The second piece of land, purchased for $3,000, was bought on January 2, 1998. The numerator of the fraction is 160, which is the price index today (January 1, 2000), and the denominator of the fraction is 120, the price index on January 2, 1998, the date when the second piece of land was purchased. This computation gives $4,000 which is the inflated price of the second piece of land in terms of today's prices.

Thus, the first piece of land should be worth $16,000 today, and the second piece of land should be worth $4,000 today, for a total of $20,000.

CHAPTER 10

DETERMINATION OF ENDING INVENTORIES

Basic Attacks and Strategies for Solving Problems in this Chapter. See pages 287 to 321 for step-by-step solutions to problems.

There are two chapters devoted to inventory because of its importance in most businesses. This chapter addresses the computation of Ending Inventories by various methods. The dollar value of Ending Inventories is on both the Income Statement and the Balance Sheet of corporations' Annual Reports and Interim Statements.

The dollar value of Ending Inventories is extremely important and much time is spent attempting to get an actual count of the Ending Inventory in items. This figure is then translated into dollar values. An accurate item number count and, thus an accurate dollar value determination, determines Total Assets and Total Net Income. If the Net Income is not determined accurately, then the Income Tax cannot be determined accurately. The Income Tax many states impose on inventories must also be accounted for.

To complicate things further, the accounting profession and the government allow merchants to keep inventory at cost, at market, and at "lower of cost or market," as long as they follow one of these methods consistently. If the merchant chooses to follow the "lower of cost or market" computation (which is the most utilized of the methods), the merchant may keep inventory according to individual items, according to major categories, or according to total inventory—again, as long as the merchant sticks to one of these methods consistently. Additionally, merchants may use either the **Periodic System** or the **Perpetual System** of inventory computation. Each of these methods and sub-methods shows different figures on both the Income Statement and Balance Sheet presentations.

Also, some merchants use the cost price as the base of 100% and compute sales as a certain percentage of cost, while others use the sales price as the base of 100% and compute cost as a percentage of sales.

Many business owners do not count inventory until the end of the year because of the cost involved in doing so. Yet, they need to know the Ending Inventory in items *and* in dollars in order to compute Net Income on quarterly statements for the use of management and to send to stockholders. There are two methods used widely to compute Ending Inventory without actually counting; the **Gross Profit Method** and the **Retail Inventory Method**. The Gross Profit Method is easier and does not require as much record keeping. It is merely an estimate, though, and the results are not approved by either the Internal Revenue Service or the accounting profession. In interim statements, however, this method is acceptable if accompanied by a footnote showing the reader that the Ending Inventory was determined by the Gross Profit Method.

The Retail Inventory Method is approved by the Internal Revenue Service and the accounting profession because of its accuracy. It more clearly determines the dollar value of the Ending Inventory. Records of Beginning Inventories and purchases must be kept not only by cost, but by retail price. Sales records must also be kept at retail price.

There are different methods for determining the dollar value of various items in a department store for Ending Inventory purposes. One technique is to determine the Designated Market Value and use this as the replacement cost if it is between the floor price and the ceiling price. However, if the replacement cost (the Designated Market Value) is above the ceiling price, then the ceiling price is used; and if the replacement cost is below the floor price, then the floor price is used.

Accountants can compare the cost value of an inventory item with the Designated Market Value of the item on three bases: individual items, major categories, and total inventory.

General journal entries can be made for inventories using both the Periodic System and the Perpetual System of recording items. With increased computer usage in the average and small businesses, inventory is more often kept by the Perpetual System, keeping the inventory up to date at all times. However, because of pilferage, depreciation, rot, rust, and other negative elements, the inventory still has to be counted at the end of the year to be sure the number of items in the books is the same as the number of items in the storehouse.

Since some entrepreneurs keep records with cost as the basis and other entrepreneurs keep records with sales as the basis, accountants must know how to change percentages from those based on sales to those based on cost, and vice versa.

Also presented in this chapter are the methods in which accountants compute the dollar value of ending inventory lost in a fire, how ending inventory is computed by the Retail Inventory Method, and markups, markup cancellations, markdowns, and markdown cancellations affect the computation of ending inventory using the Lower of Cost or Market Assumption.

Step-by-Step Solutions to Problems in this Chapter, "Determination of Ending Inventories"

• PROBLEM 10–1

The James Brothers Wholesale Grocery warehouse provides wholesale grocery items to a chain of grocery stores in a wide area. Many of these items change in price due to rotting, damage, and price level changes. How will these items that are on hand at the end of the year be valued in the inventory on the balance sheet? Following are five fruit items with Replacement Cost, Net Realizable Value, or Ceiling, and Net Realizable Value Less Normal Profit Margin, or Floor.

Various Values of Five Grocery Inventory Items

Item	Replacement Cost	Net Realizable Value (Ceiling)	Net Realizable Value Less Normal Profit Margin (Floor)
Bananas	$60,000	$80,000	$74,000
Peaches	64,000	75,000	60,000
Pears	30,000	25,000	20,000
Oranges	25,000	50,000	30,000
Lemons	75,000	67,000	60,000

What is the Designated Market Value of each item, and why was this value chosen?

SOLUTION:

Choosing the Designated Market Value
for Five Grocery Inventory Items

Item	Replacement Cost	Net Realizable Value (Ceiling)	Net Realizable Value Less Normal Profit Margin (Floor)	Designated Market Value
Bananas	$60,000	$80,000	$74,000	$74,000
Peaches	64,000	75,000	60,000	64,000
Pears	30,000	25,000	20,000	25,000
Oranges	25,000	50,000	30,000	30,000
Lemons	75,000	67,000	60,000	67,000

The **Replacement Cost** is the price at which the item could be purchased for today. The **Net Realizable Value** is the selling price less the cost of selling the item. This is also called the Ceiling, because it is the highest price at which this item of inventory could be listed at. Any higher price would be unrealistic. The **Net Realizable Value Less Normal Profit Margin** is the selling price less the cost of selling the item less the normal profit. This is also called the Floor, since any price lower than this would be unrealistic.

The **Designated Market Value** is the middle price of the first three listed, and this is explained for each item as follows:

For the Bananas, the price has really gone down. Notice that the **Replacement Cost**, or the cost of today replacing these bananas on the store shelves, would be only $60,000, while the ceiling is $80,000 and the floor is $74,000. Since the Replacement Cost is even lower than the Floor, the Floor price of $74,000 is chosen as the Designated Market Value.

For the Peaches, the **Replacement Cost** is $64,000. This is a price partway between the Ceiling ($75,000) and the Floor ($60,000). Since it is between the two, it is chosen as the Designated Market Value.

For the Pears, the **Replacement Cost** is $30,000. The price has really increased on pears, and the Replacement Cost is higher than either the Floor or the Ceiling, and it must not be higher than the ceiling. Therefore, the Ceiling price of $25,000 is chosen as the Designated Market Value.

For the Oranges, the **Replacement Cost** is $25,000. The price is really low to replace the oranges in fact, the Replacement Cost of $25,000 is lower than the Floor price of $30,000. It cannot be below the Floor, therefore, the floor price of $30,000 is chosen as the Designated Market Value for oranges.

For the Lemons, the **Replacement Cost** is $75,000. The price of lemons has really risen, because the Replacement Cost for lemons is $75,000, which is even higher than the Ceiling price of $67,000. It cannot be higher than the Ceiling, so the Ceiling price of $67,000 is chosen as the Designated Market Value.

• PROBLEM 10–2

In the previous problem the Designated Market Value of bananas was found to be $74,000; peaches $64,000; pears $25,000; oranges $30,000; and lemons $67,000. Using Lower of Cost or Market comparisons, how might the inventories of these fruits be listed on the Balance Sheet?

SOLUTION:

James Brothers Wholesale Grocery
Methods of Applying Lower of Cost or Market

Item	Cost	Designated Market	Lower of Cost or Market By: Individual Items	Major Categories	Total Inventory
Citrus Fruits:					
Oranges	$32,000	$30,000	$30,000		
Lemons	63,000	67,000	63,000		
Total Citrus	95,000	97,000		95,000	
Other Fruits:					
Bananas	$75,000	$74,000	$74,000		
Peaches	55,000	64,000	55,000		
Pears	30,000	25,000	25,000		
Total Other	160,000	163,000		160,000	
Total	255,000	260,000	247,000	255,000	255,000

The Designated Market Value was computed in the previous problem to be the Replacement Cost if the Replacement Cost was between the Floor Value and the Market Value. However, if the Replacement Cost was lower than the Floor value, the Floor value would be used as the Designated Market Value. On the other hand, if the Replacement Cost was higher than the Ceiling Value, the Ceiling Value would be used as the Designated Market Value. Now, in this present problem, we compare the original cost of the item with the Designated Market Value to see which of the two is lower. The trouble is that there are three ways of doing this as follows: (1) the lower of cost or market comparing individual items, (2) the lower of cost or market comparing major categories, and (3) the total inventory.

In the first method, the Lower of Cost or Market comparing individual items, each of the five fruits is separately compared to determine the lower of the two prices. For instance, the Cost price of oranges is $32,000 and the designated Market price of oranges is $30,000. So the lower of the two, $30,000, is used in the third column. The Cost price of lemons is $63,000 and the designated Market price of lemons is $67,000. So the lower of the two, $63,000, is used in the third column. The cost price of bananas is $75,000 and the designated Market price of bananas is $74,000. So the lower of the two, $74,000, is used in the third column. The Cost price of peaches is $55,000 and the designated Market price of peaches is $64,000, so the lower of the two, $55,000, is used in the third column. The Cost price of pears is $30,000 and the designated Market price of pears is $25,000. So the lower of the two, $25,000, is used in the third column. The total of the third column, $247,000 is the amount to be used in the inventory of these fruits if the business has consistently kept its inventory by the Lower of Cost or Market method using individual inventory items.

However, some firms keep their books using Lower of Cost or Market by major categories, and this method is acceptable by accountants. For this purpose the fruits have been divided into the following categories: (1) citrus fruits, and (2) other fruits. The Cost price of the Total Citrus is $95,000 and the Designated Market Value of Total Citrus is $97,000. So the lower of the two, $95,000, is placed in the fourth column. The Cost price of Other Fruits is $160,000 and the Designated Market Value is $163,000. So the lower of the two, $160,000, is placed in the fourth column. Then the two figures in the fourth column ($95,000 and

$160,000) are added to derive $255,000, the Lower of Cost or Market by major categories.

However, some firms keep their books using Lower of Cost or Market by total inventory. The Total Cost Price of all five fruits is $255,000 and the Total Designated Market Value of all five fruits is $260,000. So the lower of the two, $255,000, is placed in the rightmost column as the value of the Total Inventory.

Any one of these methods, Lower of Cost or Market by individual items, Lower of Cost or Market by major categories, or Lower of Cost or Market by total inventory is acceptable for accountants; but whichever of the three methods is chosen should be used consistently by the business from year to year. If this is done, the profits of the business will be reflected accurately and the taxes apportioned properly.

• PROBLEM 10-3

The Smith Grocery Corporation has the following Beginning and Ending Inventory figures.

Inventory	At Cost	At Market
Beginning	$50,000	$50,000
Ending	60,000	58,000

On January 1, 2000, the Total Inventory for the grocery store was $50,000. This is the Cost price, and because of the high inventory turnover in the grocery business, this was also the replacement price known as market. A year later, on December 31, 2000, the inventory was counted up and determined to have a Cost price of $60,000. Due to a decline in wholesale prices, this inventory could be replaced for $58,000, or a figure $2,000 less than the Ending Inventory at Cost price ($60,000 − $58,000 = $2,000).

Under the Periodic System, what entries should be made on the grocery company books if the grocery company has been consistently keeping inventory records at Lower of Cost or Market?

SOLUTION:

Entry 1:   ($ in dollars)

Income Summary		50,000	
Merchandise Inventory			50,000
To close out Beginning Inventory			

Entry 2:

Merchandise Inventory		60,000	
Income Summary			60,000
To record the Ending Inventory at Cost price			

Entry 3:

Loss Due to Market Decline of Inventory		2,000	
Allowance to Reduce Inventory to Market			2,000

The date of all three of the above entries is December 31, 2000. The first entry, debiting Income Summary and crediting Merchandise Inventory for $50,000, closes out the old Merchandise Inventory because all during the year, under the Periodic System, the Merchandise Inventory account has had a debit balance of $50,000, reflecting the Beginning inventorycount as of the first of the year. The credit to Merchandise Inventory of $50,000 effectively closes this account out.

The second entry, also dated December 31, 2000, debits Merchandise Inventory and credits Income Summary for $60,000, the new Ending Inventory at cost price. This effectively puts the $60,000 in the Merchandise Inventory account at year's end and brings the account up to date.

The third entry, also dated December 31, 2000, debits Loss Due to Market Decline of Inventory for $2,000 and credits Allowance to Reduce Inventory to Market for $2,000. The $2,000 is the difference between the Ending Inventory at cost ($60,000) and the ending inventory at market ($58,000) ($60,000 – $58,000 = $2,000). The account Loss Due to Market Decline of Inventory is an Expense account which is deductible in the Income Statement in determining Net Iincome. The account Allowance to Reduce Inventory to Market is a Contra-Asset account, and would appear just beneath Merchandise Inventory on the Balance Sheet.

• PROBLEM 10-4

The Smith Grocery Corporation has the following Beginning and Ending Inventory figures:

Inventory	At Cost	At Market
Beginning	$50,000	$50,000
Ending	60,000	58,000

On January 1, 2000, the Total Inventory for the grocery store was $50,000. This is the Cost price, and because of the high inventory turnover in the grocery business, this was also the replacement price known as Market. A year later, on December 31, 2000, the inventory was counted up and determined to have a Cost price of $60,000. Due to a decline in wholesale prices, this inventory could be replaced for $58,000, or a figure $2,000 less than the Ending Inventory at cost price ($60,000 – $58,000 = $2,000).

Under the Perpetual System, what entries should be made on the grocery company books if the grocery company has been consistently keeping inventory records at Lower of Cost or Market?

SOLUTION:

Method One:		($ in dollars)
Cost of Goods Sold	2,000	
Merchandise Inventory		2,000 ·

Method Two:		
Loss Due to Market Decline of Inventory	2,000	
Allowance to Reduce Inventory to Market		2,000

Accounting is an art, not a science, and sometimes there is more than one way to handle a situation. The first method illustrated above debits Cost of Goods Sold and credits Merchandise Inventory for the $2,000 difference between the Ending Inventory cost price and the Ending Inventory Market Price. The debit to Cost of Goods Sold increases this account, and it thus appears $2,000 higher in the Income Statement than it would otherwise. The credit of $2,000 to Merchandise Inventory cuts the inventory by $2,000 and brings the inventory figure down from Cost price to market price in the ledger and also in the Asset section of the Balance Sheet.

On the other hand, the second method illustrated above debits an Expense account entitled Loss Due to Market Decline of Inventory by $2,000. This Expense account will be placed with the other expenses in the Income Statement. The account, Allowance to Reduce Inventory to Market, is a Contra-Asset account which will be deducted from Merchandise Inventory in the Asset section of the Balance Sheet.

In the Perpetual Inventory Method the account Merchandise Inventory is debited whenever merchandise is purchased, as follows:

Merchandise Inventory	500
Cash (or Accounts Payable)	500

Also, the account Merchandise Inventory is credited for the Cost price whenever an item is sold, as follows:

Cost of Goods Sold	500
Merchandise Inventory	500

So, since Merchandise Inventory is debited all throughout the year, whenever inventory is purchased, and since Merchandise Inventory is credited for the Cost price all throughout the year, whenever merchandise inventory is sold, there is no need (as there is in the Periodic System) to close out Merchandise Inventory into Income Summary at the end of the year under the Perpetual Inventory Method.

Under the first method, the Merchandise Inventory is credited for the entire $2,000, bringing the account at the end of the year down to $58,000 on the Balance Sheet. The part of the balance sheet containing Merchandise Inventory would appear as follows:

Current Assets:		
Cash	15,000	
Notes Receivable	3,000	
Accounts Receivable	8,000	
Merchandise Inventory	58,000	
Prepaid Insurance	2,000	
Total Current Assets		$86,000

Under the first method, with the Merchandise Inventory credited for the entire $2,000, the Ending Inventory in the Income Statement shows the Lower of Cost or Market inventory figure of $58,000, as follows:

Sales		$300,000
Cost of Goods Sold:		
Inventory, January 1	$50,000	
Purchases	75,000	
Merchandise Available for Sale	$125,000	
Less: Ending Inventory (at Market which is lower than Cost)	–58,000	
Cost of Goods Sold		67,000
Gross Profit on Sales		$233,000

On the other hand, under Method Two, the ending Merchandise Inventory remains at the higher figure of $60,000, and an Expense account entitled Loss Due to Market Decline of Inventory is debited for $2,000 and a Contra-Asset account entitled Allowance to Reduce Inventory to Market is credited for $2,000. If this Method Two is used, the part of the Balance Sheet containing Merchandise Inventory would appear as follows:

Current Assets:			
Cash		15,000	
Notes Receivable		3,000	
Accounts Receivable		8,000	
Merchandise Inventory	60,000		
Less: Allowance to Reduce			
Inventory to Market	–2,000	58,000	
Prepaid Insurance		2,000	
Total Current Assets			$86,000

As seen in comparing this Current Asset section of the Balance Sheet with the previous one, the higher ending Merchandise Inventory of $60,000 is brought down from Cost to Market by subtracting the contra-asset account of $2,000 entitled Allowance to Reduce Inventory to Market.

Under the second method, an Expense account entitled Loss Due to Market Decline of Inventory is debited. This account is also shown in the partial Income Statement as follows:

Sales	$300,000
Cost of Goods Sold:	
Inventory, January 1	$50,000
Purchases	75,000
Merchandise Available for Sale	$125,000
Less: Ending Inventory (at cost)	– 60,000
Cost of Goods Sold	65,000
Gross Profit on Sales	$235,000
Less: Loss due to Market decline of inventory	– 2,000
Adjusted Gross Profit on Sales	$233,000

As can be seen from the partial Income Statement above, the Ending Inventory is put down at full cost of $60,000, then the $2,000 loss due to market decline of inventory is subtracted further down the Income Statement, so the last line—Adjusted Gross Profit on Sales comes out at $233,000, just as it did under the first method.

• PROBLEM 10–5

The inventory of the Jerome Company is made up of the following items:

Item No.	Quantity	Cost per unit	Cost to Replace per unit
1	900	$ 85	$ 90
2	700	65	63
3	600	81	78
4	300	200	205
5	1700	12	9
6	200	6	4
7	200	3	2

Lower of Cost or Market prices, Lower of Cost or Market.

SOLUTION:

Item No.	Quantity	Cost per Unit	Total Cost	Cost to Replace per Unit	Total Market (Cost to Replace)
1	900	$ 85	$76,500	$90	$ 81,000
2	700	65	45,500	63	44,100
3	600	81	48,600	78	46,800
4	300	200	60,000	205	61,500
5	1700	12	20,400	9	15,300
6	200	6	1,200	4	800
7	200	3	600	2	400

Looking at the above table, the quantity times the cost per unit equals the total cost. The quantity times the cost to replace per unit equals the total Market, sometimes called the total Cost to replace.

The next step is to compare the total Cost with the total Market to determine the lower of the two, as follows:

Item No.	Total Cost	Total Market	Lower of Cost or Market by Items	
1	$76,500	$81,000	$76,500	
2	45,500	44,100	44,100	
3	48,600	46,800	46,800	
4	60,000	61,500	60,000	
5	20,400	15,300	15,300	
6	1,200	800	800	
7	600	400	400	
Totals	$252,800	$249,900		$249,900
Lower of Cost or Market, Each Item		$243,900		

Two methods are used to determine Lower of Cost or Market.

Lower of Cost or Market, Totals $249,900

There are two methods in the above table to determine Lower of Cost or Market: the first method is by comparing each of the seven individual items. The second method is just comparing the totals.

For instance, in the item-by-item method for Item 1, we compare the $76,500 Total Cost with the $81,000 Total Market Value. Obviously, the $76,500 is the lower of the two figures, so that amount is carried over into the third column, entitled Lower of Cost or Market by Items. In the item-by-item method for Item 2, we compare the $45,500 Total Cost with the $44,100 Total Market Value. Obviously, the $44,100 is the lower of the two figures, so that amount is carried over into the third column, entitled Lower of Cost or Market by Items. This is done with each of the items, comparing the Total Cost figure with the Total Market figure and bringing the lower of the two figures over to the Lower of Cost or Market by Items column. Finally, all the figures in the Lower of Cost or Market by Items column are added to get the total of $243,900, which is the total for the Lower of Cost or Market, comparing each item.

The other method is comparison of the totals. For instance, first the total Cost column is added, getting the total of $252,800. Next, the total Market column is added, getting the total of $249,900. These two figures are compared, and the lower of the two (in this case, $249,900) is determined to be the answer.

There are two methods and two answers in this computation. The total for Lower of Cost or Market by comparing each item is $243,900 and the total for Lower of Cost or Market by merely comparing the total Cost with the total Market is $249,900. The total for Lower of Cost or Market by comparing each item is a lower figure than is the total for Lower of Cost or Market by merely comparing the total Cost with the total Market. Why the difference? Why is this? And is this always the case?

The reason for the difference in the figures is that in the first computation, each item is compared individually while in the second computation only the totals are compared. So naturally the dollar outcomes will be different. Will the individually compared items method always result in a lower figure? Yes, because the lower figure is continuously chosen in each of the cases.

What does this outcome mean for accounting? The Internal Revenue Service allows either method, but the method chosen must be used consistently so the government will get its correct portion of any Net Profit that the business may earn.

• PROBLEM 10-6

Each of the following Gross Margin percentages is expressed in terms of sales. Indicate the Gross Profit Margin percentages in terms of Cost.

1. 25%
2. 20%
3. $33^1/_3$%
4. $37^1/_2$%

SOLUTION:

Part 1

Let us assume that we sold a small radio for $120, and the wholesale cost of this item was $90. Then the Gross Profit of this item would be $30, as follows: $120 – $90 = $30.

Another way to set this computation up would be as follows:

Sales Price	$120
Cost Price	– 90
Gross Margin	$ 30

Finding the Gross Profit Percentage and the Cost Percentage. The Gross Profit Percentage in terms of sales means that the sales figure is considered the base or 100%, as follows:

Sales Price	$120	100%
Cost Price	– 90	
Gross Margin	$ 30	

What is the Gross Margin Percentage when the sales price is considered 100%? The sales price is the divisor and the Gross Margin is the dividend as follows: $30 ÷ $120 = 25%.

Sales Price	$120	100%
Cost Price	– 90	75%
Gross Margin	$ 30	25%

As can be seen above, if the Gross Margin is 25% of sales, we subtract the 25% from the 100% to get 75%, the percent that the Cost is of the sales (100% – 25% = 75%).

The first part of the question gives the Gross Margin as 25% of sales, and they want the Gross Margin Percentage in terms of Cost. Using the same figures as those used above, that is: $120 for sales, $90 for Cost, and $30 for Gross Margin, we now make the base the cost price of $90 and call that arbitrarily 100% as follows:

Sales Price	$120	
Cost Price	− 90	100%
Gross Margin	$ 30	

With the $90 Cost price the base, what percent of the Cost price is the Gross Profit? We use the base price, $90 as the divisor and the Gross Margin figure, $30, as the dividend as follows: $30 ÷ by $90 = $33^1/_3\%$. This can be set up as follows:

Sales Price	$120	
Cost Price	− 90	100 %
Gross Margin	$ 30	$33^1/_3\%$

What is the sales price percentage? Since the Gross Margin of $30 plus the Cost price of $90 adds up to the sales price of $120, we can do the same for the percentages, as follows. We add the Gross margin Percentage of $33^1/_3\%$ and the Cost price percentage of 100% to get the sales price percentage of $133^1/_3\%$. This can be set up as follows:

Sales Price	$120	$133^1/_3\%$
Cost Price	− 90	100 %
Gross Margin	$ 30	$33^1/_3\%$

Thus, the answer to the first part of the program is as follows: if the Gross Margin percentage in terms of sales is 25%, then the Gross Margin percentage in terms of Cost is $33^1/_3\%$.

Part 2

Let us assume that we sold a used car that we sold brought $250, and that the Cost of this used car to us was $200. Then the Gross Profit to us would be $50, as follows: $250 − $200 = $50.

Another way to set up this computation would be as follows:

Sales Price	$250
Cost Price	− 200
Gross Margin	$ 50

Finding the Gross Profit percentage and the Cost percentage. The Gross Profit percentage in terms of sales means that the sales figure is considered the base or 100%, as follows:

Sales Price	$250	100%
Cost Price	– 200	
Gross Margin	$ 50	

What is the Gross Margin percentage when the sales price is considered 100%? The sales price is the divisor and the Gross Margin is the dividend as follows: $50 ÷ $250 = 20%. This can be presented graphically as follows:

Sales Price	$250	100%
Cost Price	– 200	
Gross Margin	$ 50	20%

As can be seen above, if the Gross Margin is 20% of sales, we subtract the 20% from the 100% to get 80%, the percent that the cost is of the sales (100% – 20% = 80%).

The second part of the question gives the Gross Margin as 20% of sales, and they want the Gross Margin percentage in terms of cost. Using the same figures as those used above, that is: $250 for sales, $200 for cost, and $50 for Gross Margin, we now make the base the cost price of $200 and call that arbitrarily 100% as follows:

Sales Price	$250	
Cost Price	– 200	100%
Gross Margin	$ 50	

With the $200 cost price as the base, what percent of the cost price is the Gross Margin? We use the base price, $200, as the divisor and the Gross Margin figure, $50, as the dividend as follows: $50 ÷ $200 = 25%, which could be set up as follows:

Sales Price	$250	
Cost Price	– 200	100%
Gross Margin	$ 50	25%

What is the sales price percentage? Since the Gross Margin of $50 plus the Cost Price of $200 adds up to the sales price of $250, we can do the same for the percentages, as follows. We add the Gross Margin percentage of 25% and the cost price percentage of 100% to get the sales price percentage of 125%. This can be set up as follows:

Sales Price	$250	125%
Cost Price	– 200	– 100%
Gross Margin	$ 50	25%

Thus, the answer to the second part of the program is as follows: if the Gross Margin percentage in terms of sales is 20%, then the Gross Margin percentage in terms of cost is 25%.

Part 3

Let us assume that a stove that we have just sold has brought us $135, and that the cost of this stove to us was $90. Then the Gross Profit to us would be $45, as follows: $135 – $90 = $45.

Another way to set up this computation would be as follows:

Sales Price	$135
Cost Price	– 90
Gross Margin	$ 45

Finding the Gross Profit percentage and the Cost percentage. The Gross Profit percentage in terms of sales means that the sales figure is considered the base or 100%, as follows:

Sales Price	$135	100%
Cost Price	– 90	
Gross Margin	$ 45	

What is the Gross Margin percentage when the sales price is considered 100%? The sales price is the divisor and the Gross Margin is the dividend as follows: $45 \div $135 = 33\frac{1}{3}\%$.

This can be presented graphically as follows:

Sales Price	$135	100	%
Cost Price	– 90		
Gross Margin	$ 45	$33\frac{1}{3}\%$	

As can be seen above, if the Gross Margin is $33\frac{1}{3}\%$ of sales, we subtract the $33\frac{1}{3}\%$ from the 100% to get $66\frac{2}{3}\%$, the percent that the cost is of the sales. This can be presented graphically as follows:

Sales Price	$135	100 %
Cost Price	– 90	$66^2/_3\%$
Gross Margin	$ 45	$33^1/_3\%$

The third part of the question gives the Gross Margin as $33^1/_3\%$ of sales, and they want the gross margin percentage in terms of cost. Using the same figures as those used above, that is: $135 for sales, $90 for cost, and $45 for Gross Margin, we now make the base the Cost price of $90 and call that arbitrarily 100% as follows:

Sales Price	$135	
Cost Price	– 90	100%
Gross Margin	$ 45	

With the $90 Cost price as the base, what percent of the Cost price is the Gross Margin? We use the base price, $90, as the divisor and the Gross Margin figure, $45, as the dividend as follows: $45 ÷ $90 = 50%, which could be set up as follows:

Sales Price	$135	
Cost Price	– 90	100%
Gross Margin	$ 45	50%

What is the sales price percentage? Since the Gross Margin of $45 plus the Cost price of $90 adds up to the sales price of $135, we can do the same for the percentages, as follows: we add the Gross Margin percentage of 50% and the Cost price percentage of 100% to get the sales price percentage of 150%. This can be set up as follows:

Sales Price	$135	150%
Cost Price	– 90	– 100%
Gross Margin	$ 45	50%

Thus, the answer to the third part of the program is as follows: if the Gross Margin percentage in terms of sales is $33^1/_3\%$, then the Gross Margin percentage in terms of cost is 50%.

Part 4

Let us assume a chair that we have just sold has brought us $144, and that the Cost of this chair to us was $90. Then the Gross Profit to us would be $54, as follows: $144 – $90 = $54.

Another way to set up this computation would be as follows:

Sales Price	$144
Cost Price	− 90
Gross Margin	$ 54

Finding the Gross Profit Percentage and the Cost Percentage. The Gross Profit Percentage in terms of sales means that the sales figure is considered the base or 100%, as follows:

Sales Price	$144	100%
Cost Price	− 90	
Gross Margin	$ 54	

What is the Gross Margin Percentage when the sales price is considered 100%? The sales price is the divisor and the Gross Margin is the dividend as follows: $54 ÷ $144 = $37\frac{1}{2}$%. This can be presented graphically as follows:

Sales Price	$144	100 %
Cost Price	− 90	
Gross Margin	$ 54	$37\frac{1}{2}$%

As can be seen above, if the Gross Margin is $37\frac{1}{2}$% of sales, we subtract the $37\frac{1}{2}$% from the 100% to get $62\frac{1}{2}$%, the percent that the cost is of the sales. This can be presented graphically as follows:

Sales Price	$144	100 %
Cost Price	− 90	$62\frac{1}{2}$%
Gross Margin	$ 54	$37\frac{1}{2}$%

The fourth part of the question gives the Gross Margin as $37\frac{1}{2}$% of sales, and they want the gross margin percentage in terms of Cost. Using the same figures as those used above, that is: $144 for sales, $90 for Cost, and $54 for Gross Margin, we now make the base the Cost price of $90 and call that arbitrarily 100% as follows:

Sales Price	$144	
Cost Price	− 90	100%
Gross Margin	$ 54	

With the $90 Cost price as the base, what percent of the Cost price is the Gross Margin? We use the base price, $90, as the divisor and the Gross Margin figure, $54, as the dividend as follows: $54 ÷ $90 = 60%, which could be set up as follows:

Sales Price	$144	
Cost Price	– 90	100%
Gross Margin	$ 54	60%

What is the sales price percentage? Since the Gross Margin of $54 plus the Cost price of $90 adds up to the sales price of $144, we can do the same for the percentages, as follows: we add the Gross Margin percentage of 60% and the Cost price percentage of 100% to get the sales price percentage of 160%. This can be set up as follows:

Sales Price	$144	160%
Cost Price	– 90	– 100%
Gross Margin	$ 54	60%

Thus, the answer to the fourth part of the program is as follows: if the Gross Margin Percentage in terms of sales is $37\frac{1}{2}\%$, then the Gross Margin Percentage in terms of cost is 60%.

• PROBLEM 10-7

The Saturn Wholesale Grocery Company finds itself at the end of a quarter of a year in need to publish an interim Income Statement for the use of management so that it can send a quarterly report to stockholders. However, one of the major items in an Income Statement is the dollar value of the Ending Inventory. Without this figure an Income Statement cannot be made, and no Net Income can be computed. Yet the company has neither the time nor the money to close down and take a physical inventory. Following are some of the dollar figures for the first quarter of the year 2000:

Inventory, January 1, 2000	$130,000
Purchases (Gross)	658,000
Freight In	2,000
Sales	503,000
Sales Returns	3,000

From past experience, it is known that the Saturn Wholesale Grocery Company's Gross Margin has consistently equaled 20% of sales. Estimate the dollar value of the Ending Inventory on March 31, 2000.

SOLUTION:

Beginning Inventory (at Cost)		$130,000
Purchases (at Cost)	$658,000	
Freight In	2,000	660,000
Merchandise Available for Sale (at Cost)		$790,000
Sales (at Selling Price)	$503,000	
Less Sales Returns	– 3,000	
Net Sales	$500,000	
Less Estimated Gross Margin (20% of $500,000)	– 100,000	
Approximate Cost of Goods Sold		$ 400,000
Approximate Ending Inventory at cost		$ 390,000

The above computation shows that the approximate Ending Inventory at Cost price is $390,000. This is computed by adding the Beginning Inventory at Cost ($130,000) and the Purchases at Cost ($658,000) and the Freight In ($2,000) to get Merchandise Available for Sale at Cost ($790,000). Next, the sales figure for the period January 1, 2000 through March 31, 2000 of $503,000 is put down. From this is subtracted the Sales Returns of $3,000, giving the Net Sales for the period of $500,000 ($503,000 – $3,000 = $500,000). These figures are at selling price.

From past experience, we know that the Saturn Wholesale Grocery Company's Gross Margin has consistently equaled 20% of sales. Since sales for the quarter (Net sales) have been $500,000, we multiply this by 20% to get the Estimated Gross Margin of $100,000 (20% × $500,000 = $100,000). Next, we subtract the Estimated Gross Margin of $100,000 from the Net Sales of $500,000 in order to get the Approximate Cost of Goods Sold of $400,000. Finally, we subtract the Approximate Cost of Goods Sold of $400,000 from the Merchandise Available for Sale of $790,000 to get the Approximate Ending Inventory at cost of $390,000.

• PROBLEM 10-8

In the previous problem, we computed the Approximate Ending Inventory for the first quarter of the year 2000 for the Saturn Wholesale Grocery Company as $390,000. If the Saturn Wholesale Grocery Company's Operating Expenses for the quarter are $80,000, what is the company's Net Income for the first quarter of the year 2000?

SOLUTION:

Saturn Wholesale Grocery Company
Income Statement
For the Quarter Ended March 31, 2000

Gross Sales		$503,000	
Less: Sales Returns and Allowances		− 3,000	
Net Sales			$500,000
Merchandise Inventory			
January 1, 2000		$130,000	
Purchases	$658,000		
Freight In	2,000	660,000	
Merchandise Available for Sale		790,000	
Less: Approximate Ending Inventory,			
March 31, 2000		390,000	
Approximate Cost of Goods Sold			400,000
Approximate Gross Profit			100,000
Less: Operating Expenses			− 80,000
Net Income (Approximate)			20,000

The above Income Statement for Saturn Wholesale Grocery Company shows how the Approximate Ending Inventory figure can be used in computing the approximate Net Income for a quarterly Income Statement. As can be seen above, the first part of the Income Statement is similar to any other Income Statement, with the heading, and the first part of the body of the Income Statement including the Gross Sales, and deducting the Sales Returns and Allowances, to get the Net Sales. Then the Beginning Merchandise Inventory is presented, followed by the Purchases and Freight In. The total of these items gives the Merchandise Available for Sale of $790,000. Then we deduct the approximate Ending Inventory of $390,000 (this figure is derived from the previous problem). This then gives the approximate Cost of Goods Sold of $400,000. Then the approximate Cost of Goods Sold of $400,000 is subtracted from the Net Sales of $500,000 to give the approximate gross profit of $100,000. Finally, we subtract the Operating Expenses of $80,000 from the approximate gross profit of $100,000 to get the approximate Net Income of $20,000 ($100,000 – $80,000 = $20,000).

But is the approximate Cost of Goods Sold good enough? Isn't it true that once we approximate the Ending Inventory, that almost all the items below that in the Income Statement are mere approximations? That is true. But if the fact that the Gross Margins in past Income Statements have consistently been equal to 20% of the sales prices, then this approximation is probably close. After all, this is merely an interim (quarterly) report. As long as the fact that the Gross Profit Method was used in computing the approximate Ending Inventory is placed in a footnote to the Income Statement, this is satisfactory for accounting purposes, and it certainly saves all the time and expense it would take to actually count the inventory in the wholesale grocery company at the end of each quarter.

This method of computing Ending Inventory certainly would not do for an End-of-Year Income Statement. At least once a year, preferably at year's end, an actual count of the inventory would have to be taken to get an accurate Income Statement that would actually reflect the financial condition of the business at that time.

• PROBLEM 10-9

The Saturn Wholesale Grocery Company finds itself at the end of a quarter of a year and in need to publish an interim Income Statement for the use of management and so that it can send a quarterly report to stockholders. However, one of the major items in an Income Statement is the dollar value of the Ending Inventory. Without this figure, an Income Statement cannot be made, and no Net Income can be computed. Yet, the company has neither the time nor the money to close down and take a physical inventory. Following are some of the dollar figures for the first quarter of the year 2000:

Inventory, January 1, 2000	$130,000
Purchases (Gross)	658,000
Freight In	2,000
Sales	503,000
Sales Returns	3,000

From past experience, it is known that the Saturn Wholesale Grocery Company's Gross Margin has consistently equaled 20% of merchandise available for sale. Estimate the dollar value of the Ending Inventory on March 31, 2000.

SOLUTION:

Beginning Inventory (at Cost)		$130,000
Purchases (at Cost)	$658,000	
Freight In	2,000	660,000
Merchandise Available		
for Sale (at cost)		790,000
Approximate percent that the Gross Margin		
is of Merchandise Available for Sale		× 20%
Approximate Gross Margin		158,000
Net Sales		500,000
Approximate Gross Margin (from above)		– 158,000
Approximate Cost of Goods Sold		342,000
Merchandise Available for Sale (from above)		790,000
Less: Approximate Cost of Goods Sold		
(from above)		– 342,000
Approximate Ending Inventory		448,000

• PROBLEM 10–10

In the previous problem, we computed the Approximate Ending Inventory for the first quarter of the year 2000 finding the Gross Margin as a certain percent of merchandise available for sale, and then computing the Approximate Ending Inventory to be $448,000. If the Saturn Wholesale Grocery Company's Operating Expenses for the quarter are $80,000, what is the company's Net Income for the first quarter of the year 2000?

SOLUTION:

Saturn Wholesale Grocery Company
Income Statement
For the Quarter Ended March 31, 2000

Gross Sales		503,000	
Less: Sales Returns and Allowances		– 3,000	
Net Sales			$500,000
Merchandise Inventory			
January 1, 2000		$130,000	
Purchases	$658,000		
Freight In	2,000	660,000	
Merchandise Available			
for Sale		790,000	
Less: Approximate Ending Inventory,			
March 31, 2000		– 448,000	
Approximate Cost of Goods Sold		342,000	
Approximate Gross Profit (Gross Margin)		158,000	
Less: Operating Expenses			80,000
Net Income (Approximate)			78,000

The above Income Statement for Saturn Wholesale Grocery Company shows how the Approximate Ending Inventory figure can be used in computing the approximate Net Income for a quarterly Income Statement. As can be seen above, the first part of the Income Statement is similar to any other Income Statement, with the heading, and the first part of the body of the Income Statement including the Gross Sales, and deducting the Sales Returns and Allowances, to get the Net Sales. Then the Beginning Merchandise Inventory is presented, followed by the Purchases and

Freight In. The total of these items gives the Merchandise Available for Sale of $790,000. From this we deduct the approximate Ending Inventory of $448,000 (this figure is derived from the previous problem). This then gives the Approximate Cost of Goods Sold of $342,000. Then the Approximate Cost of Goods Sold of $342,000 is subtracted from the Net Sales of $500,000 to give the Approximate Gross Profit of $158,000. Finally, we subtract the Operating Expenses of $80,000 from the Approximate Gross Profit of $158,000 to get the Approximate Net Income of $78,000 ($158,000 – $80,000 = $78,000).

But is the Approximate Cost of Goods Sold good enough? Isn't it true that once we approximate the Ending Inventory, that almost all the items below in the Income Statement are mere approximations? That is true. But if the fact that the Gross Margins in past Income Statements have consistently been equal to 20% of the Merchandise Available for Sale, then this approximation is probably close. After all, this is merely an interim (quarterly) report. As long as the fact that the Gross Profit Method was used in computing the approximate Ending Inventory is placed in a footnote to the Income Statement, this is satisfactory for accounting purposes, and it certainly saves all the time and expense it would take to actually count the inventory in the wholesale grocery company at the end of each quarter. This method of computing Ending Inventory certainly would not do for an End-of-Year Income Statement. At least once a year, preferably at year's end, an actual count of the inventory would have to be taken to get an accurate Income Statement that would actually reflect the financial condition of the business at that time.

• PROBLEM 10–11

The insurance company of the Smith Wholesale Grocery Company requires an estimate of the Cost of Goods lost by a fire on February 25, 2000. Merchandise in the beginning inventory on January 1, 2000, totaled $40,000. Purchases between January 1, 2000 and the date of the fire (February 25) were $70,000. Purchases Returns were $5,000. Freight In was $1,000. Sales were made at 25% above Cost, and the total sales between January 1 and February 25, 2000, were $75,000. The merchandise was completely destroyed in the fire. What was the dollar value of the merchandise lost?

SOLUTION:

Smith Wholesale Grocery Company
Computation of Ending Inventory Lost in Fire
February 25, 2000

Sales (January 1, 2000, through		
February 25, 2000)		$75,000
Beginning Inventory		
(January 1, 2000)		$40,000
Purchases	$70,000	
Purchases Returns	– 5,000	
Net Purchases	65,000	
Plus: Freight In	1,000	
Cost of Merchandise Purchased		66,000
Merchandise Available for Sale		106,000
Sales were made at 25% above Cost		
(100% + 25% = 125%),		
and sales were $75,000		
$75,000 divided by 125%		
= $60,000 Cost of Goods Sold		
Merchandise Available for Sale (from above)		$106,000
Less: Cost of Goods Sold (from above)		– 60,000
Ending Inventory, February 25, 2000		
Dollar Value of inventory lost in fire		$ 46,000

When a fire occurs in a warehouse, usually the building itself is covered by fire insurance. Also, hopefully, the merchandise is covered by merchandise insurance. However, it is not always known exactly what the dollar value is of the merchandise that was lost in the fire. Therefore, after a fire, the accountant must come up with a dollar figure for the merchandise that was lost, and this figure must be backed by information backed by paper work. Hopefully, the sales have been rung up on the cash register or there are invoices in the safe showing the sales. In this case the amount of sales between January 1 and February 25, the date of the fire, are known to be $75,000. Hopefully, a Beginning Inventory was taken on the first of the year and these inventory papers are in the safe. This Beginning Inventory amounts, in this case, to $40,000. Let us also hope that in the safe are invoices for purchases made between January 1 and February 25, and these purchases of merchandise amount to $70,000 with $5,000 in purchases returns, or Net purchases of $65,000 ($70,000 − $5,000 = $65,000). The Freight In amounts to $1,000 and should also be backed by receipts. Adding the freight in of $1,000 to the Net purchases of $65,000, we now have $66,000 Cost of Merchandise Purchased ($1,000 + $65,000 = $66,000). Next, the $66,000 Cost of Merchandise Purchased is added to the $40,000 Beginning Inventory to give $106,000 Merchandise Available for Sale.

The Smith Wholesale Grocery Company is in the habit of selling its merchandise at 25% above Cost. Therefore, the Cost figure is used as the base in the computation or 100%. Since the Cost is arbitrarily used as 100% and the sales price is 25% higher than this, we add 100% to 25% to get 125%, which is the sales price in terms of 100% Cost. We know that the sales are $75,000 and that the sales price is 125% of the Cost price. Is it possible to figure the Cost of Goods Sold? Yes, this can be done by dividing the $75,000 sales by 125% ($75,000 ÷ 125% = $60,000 Cost of Goods Sold).

Next, we take the $106,000 Merchandise Available for Sale (previously computed) and deduct the $60,000 Cost of Goods Sold to get the Ending Inventory on February 25, 2000, of $46,000. This is the amount of inventory lost in the fire.

It will be necessary for the accountant, if asked, to show the insurance company representative the **Computation of Ending Inventory Lost in Fire** and any paper work requested.

• PROBLEM 10-12

The Rossville Book Company does not have time to inventory all its books at the end of the second quarter of the year. It wishes to compute the Ending Inventory on June 30, 2000, using the Retail Inventory Method, since this method is approved by the Internal Revenue Service as a way to determine Ending Inventory without actually taking a physical count. The business has been careful to keep not only retail records but also cost records, as follows:

	At Cost	At Retail
Beginning Inventory, April 1, 2000	$12,000	$18,000
Purchases (April 1–June 30)	60,000	70,000
Sales (April 1–June 30)	$60,000	

What is the Ending Inventory in dollars on June 30, 2000?

SOLUTION:

Rossville Book Company
Computation of Ending Inventory by Retail Inventory Method
For Quarter Ended June 30, 2000

	At Cost	At Retail
Beginning Inventory, April 1, 2000	$12,000	$18,000
Purchases (April, May, June)	60,000	70,000
Merchandise Available for Sale	72,000	88,000
Less: Sales (April, May, June)		60,000
Ending Inventory (at Retail) 6/30/2000		28,000
($72,000 ÷ $88,000 = 81.818%)		
$28,000 × .81818 = $22,909		
Ending Inventory (at Cost) 6/30/2000		$22,909

The Beginning Inventory at Cost is $12,000 and the Purchases at Cost are $60,000. These add up to Merchandise Available for Sale at Cost price of $72,000 (12,000 + $60,000 = $72,000).

The Beginning Inventory at Retail is $18,000 and the Purchases at Retail are $70,000. These add up to Merchandise Available for Sale at Retail Price of $88,000. The Merchandise Available for Sale at Cost price of $72,000 is divided by the Merchandise Available for Sale at Retail price of $88,000 to give 81.818%, also written as .81818. This means that the Merchandise Available for Sale at Cost price is 81.818% of the Merchandise Available for Sale at Retail price.

The sales for the quarter of $60,000 are subtracted from the Merchandise Available for Sale at Retail price of $88,000 to get the Ending Inventory at Retail price of $28,000. But most inventories are kept at Cost price and not at Retail price. How does one then determine the dollar value of the Ending Inventory at cost price?

We have computed that the Merchandise Available for Sale at Cost price is 81.818% of the Merchandise Available for Sale at Retail price. Therefore, it is necessary to multiply the Ending Inventory figure at Retail price ($28,000 by this percentage (81.818%) to get the Ending Inventory at Cost price ($22,909) ($28,000 × .81818 = $22,909).

The advantage of this Retail inventory method over the previous Gross Profit Method is that the Retail inventory method is approved by the Internal Revenue Service and the Gross Profit method is not. The Gross Profit Method, after all, is merely an estimate whereas the Retail Inventory Method is an exact figure.

The disadvantage of the Retail Inventory Method over the Gross Profit Method is that the Beginning Inventory and the Purchases must be kept at both Retail and Cost prices, whereas for the Gross Profit Method, the Beginning Inventory and Purchases are needed at only the Cost price.

• PROBLEM 10–13

The Rudyard Radio and Television Store does not have the time nor the money to take an inventory, so it wishes to compute Ending Inventory by the Retail Inventory Method. It has kept both Cost and Retail records of its Beginning Inventory and its Purchases. But it has also had Markups, Markup Cancellations, Markdowns, and Markdown Cancellations as follows:

		At Cost	At Retail
Beginning Inventory		$ 700	$ 900
Purchases		10,000	15,000
Merchandise Available for Sale		10,700	15,900
Markups	$3,000		
Markup Cancellations	2,000		
Markdowns	1,500		
Markdown Cancellations	1,000		

Compute the Ending Inventory for the year 2000 at cost price.

SOLUTION:

The Rudyard Radio and Television Store has done well to keep both its Beginning Inventory and its Purchases at both Cost and Retail prices, as well as keeping records of its Markups, Markup Cancellations, Markdowns, and Markdown Cancellations. Although the Markdown Cancellations are subtracted from the Markdowns, and the Net Markdowns are subtracted from the Costs at retail, a Net Markdown is not considered in the calculation of the Cost-to-Retail ratio, as follows:

Rudyard Radio and Television Store
Computation of Ending Inventory at Cost Price
by the Retail Inventory Method, Lower of Cost or Market

	Cost		Retail
Beginning Inventory, 1/1/2000	$ 700		$ 900
Purchases (1/1/2000 – 12/31/2000)	10,000		15,000
Merchandise Available for Sale	10,700		15,900
Markups		$3,000	
Less: Markup Cancellations		– 2,000	

Net Markups		+ 1,000
Subtotal	10,700	16,900
Markdowns	$1,500	
Less: Markdown Cancellations	– 1,000	
Net Markdowns		– 500
Sales Price of Goods Available		16,400
Sales (at Retail)		– 12,000
Ending Inventory at Retail		4,400

The Subtotals show $10,700 at Cost and
$16,900 at Retail; Divide $10,700 by
$16,900 to get 63.3%

Multiply Ending Inventory at Retail of $4,400
by 63.3% to get $2,785.20 Ending Inventory at Cost

Ending Inventory at Cost	$2,785.20

The Retail Inventory Method has a special advantage. It is approved by the Internal Revenue Service and by the accounting profession as a method of computing Ending Inventory without having to take a physical inventory. (This is not true of the Gross Profit Method of computing Ending Inventory.) The disadvantage of the Retail Inventory Method of computing Ending Inventory is that the business owner must keep records at both Cost and Retail prices.

The Rudyard Radio and Television Store has done this: it has kept records at both Cost and Retail prices. For instance, the Cost price of the Beginning Inventory was $700 and the Cost price of the Purchases of inventory during the year was $10,000. These added together give Merchandise Available for Sale at Cost price of $10,700. The Retail price of the Beginning Inventory was $900 and the Retail Price of the Purchases of Inventory during the year was $15,000. These added together give Merchandise Available for Sale at Retail Price of $15,900.

During the year some Retail stores have markups. These are increases in prices. Later in the year, if the items are not selling as rapidly as expected, they can be marked down again. These are called Markup Cancellations. During the year 2000, the Rudyard Radio and Television Store had markups of $3,000 and Markup Cancellations of $2,000, giving Net markups of $1,000 ($3,000 – $2,000 = $1,000).

As can be seen from the previous table, these Net Markups of $1,000 are added to the Merchandise Available for Sale at Retail price ($15,900) to give a subtotal of $16,900 ($15,900 + $1,000 = $16,900). Since among retail store owners, markdowns are considered a current loss and are not involved in the calculation of the Cost-to-Retail ratio, we now use this subtotal after having added the Net markup to compute the Cost-to-Retail ratio. It will be noticed that the subtotal at Retail price is $16,900 and the subtotal at Cost price is $10,700. So we divide the $10,700 by the $16,900 to get 63.3%. This means that at that point of the computation (before figuring markdowns and Markdown Cancellations) the Cost price is 63.3% of the Retail price.

The markdowns are used when an item is not selling or when it may have lost some of its value due to such things as rust, freezing, depreciation, age, or fire, among other things. In the case of the Rudyard Radio and Television Store, the markdowns for the year 2000 were $1,500 and the Markdown Cancellations were $1,000. A Markdown Cancellation is where the previous markdown is later marked back up. This gives Net markdowns of $500 ($1,500 – $1,000 = $500). Next, the Net Markdowns of $500 are subtracted from the Retail subtotal figure of $16,900 to get $16,400, the Sales Price of Goods Available ($16,900 – $500 = $16,400).

Next, the Sales at Retail ($12,000) are subtracted from the Sales Price of Goods Available ($16,400) to get the Ending Inventory at Retail ($4,400) ($16,400 – $12,000 = $4,400). Two paragraphs above this it was explained that the Cost price is 63.3% of the sales price at the point before figuring in Markdowns and Markdown Cancellations. We now multiply the Ending Inventory at Retail ($4,400) by this 63.3% to get $2,785.20, the Ending Inventory at Cost ($4400 × 63.3% = $2,785.20).

• PROBLEM 10–14

The Rudyard Radio and Television Store does not have the time nor the money to take an inventory, so it wishes to compute Ending Inventory by the Retail Inventory Method. It has switched from the First In First Out Method of computing the dollar value of Ending Inventory to the Last In First Out Method of computing the dollar value of Ending Inventory, for Income Tax reasons. It now wishes to use the Last In First Out Method in computing Ending Inventory by the Retail Inventory Method. It has kept both Cost and Retail records of its Beginning Inventory and its Purchases. But it has also had Markups, Markup Cancellations, Markdowns, and Markdown Cancellations as follows:

		At Cost	At Retail
Beginning Inventory		$ 700	$ 900
Purchases		10,000	15,000
Merchandise Available for Sale		10,700	15,900
Markups	$3,000		
Markup Cancellations	2,000		
Markdowns	1,500		
Markdown Cancellations	1,000		

Compute the Ending Inventory for the year 2000 at Cost price.

SOLUTION:

The Rudyard Radio and Television Store has done well to keep both its Beginning Inventory and its Purchases at both Cost and Retail prices, as well as keeping records of its Markups, Markup Cancellations, Markdowns, and Markdown Cancellations. In this Last In First Out Method of computing Ending Inventory, a Net Markdown is considered in the calculation of the Cost-to-Retail ratio, because this is a **Cost Method**, not a Cost-or-Market-whichever-is-lower method. Also, in this Last In First Out Method of computing Ending Inventory, the Beginning Inventory **Is Not** added in while computing the Cost-to-Retail ratio, because under the Last In First Out approach, it is concerned only with the additional layer and not with the Beginning Inventory.

Rudyard Radio and Television Store
Computation of Ending Inventory at Cost Price
by the Retail Inventory Method
Last In First Out Computation

	Cost		Retail
Beginning Inventory, 1/1/2000	$ 700		$ 900
Purchases (1/1/2000–12/31/2000)	10,000		15,000
Markups		$3,000	
Less: Markup Cancellations		– 2,000	
Net Markups			+ 1,000
Markdowns		$1,500	
Markdown Cancellations		– 1,000	
Net Markdowns			(500)
Total (excluding Beginning Inventory)	$10,000		$15,500
Total (including Beginning Inventory)	$10,700		$16,400
Net Sales (at Retail)			– 12,000
Ending Inventory (at Retail)			4,400
($10,000 ÷ $15,500 = 64.516%)			
($4,400 × 64.516% = $2,838.704)			
Ending Inventory (at Cost)			$2,838.70

In the Last In First Out Computation of Retail Inventory Method, the Beginning Inventory is not figured into the Cost-to-Retail ratio, but it is figured into the Total Goods Available for Sale. Thus, looking at the previous table, the Beginning Inventory of $700 cost and $900 Retail price has a double line below it, indicating that it is not immediately added into the computations below.

Next, the Purchases at Retail ($15,000) are added to the Net Markups ($1,000) as follows: $15,000 + $1,000 = $16,000. Then the Net Markdowns ($500) are subtracted as follows: $16,000 – $500 = $15,500. This is the Total Merchandise Available for Sale excluding the Beginning Inventory, and it amounts to $10,000 at Cost and $15,500 at Retail. Next, the $10,000 is divided by the $15,500 to get 64.516%. This means that at this point in the computation, the Cost price is 64.516% of the Retail price.

Since the Beginning Inventory is needed in figuring the Total Merchandise Available for Sale, the Beginning Inventory is next added in as follows: at Cost price the $10,000 Purchases are added to the $700 Beginning Inventory to get $10,700 Total Merchandise Available for Sale including the Beginning Inventory ($10,000 + $700 = $10,700). At Retail price the $15,000 Purchases are added to the $900 Beginning Inventory and added to the $1,000 Net Markups and then the Net Markdowns of $500 are deducted, giving $16,400 Total Goods Available for Sale at Retail price including the Beginning Inventory ($900 + $15,000 + $1,000 − $500 = $16,400).

The next step is to deduct the Net Sales at Retail price of $12,000 from the Total Merchandise Available for Sale at Retail price of $16,400, to get the Ending Inventory at Retail price of $4,400 ($16,400 − $12,000 = $4,400).

In the third paragraph above, it was explained that the Cost price is 64.516% of the Retail price. So the next step is to multiply the $4,400 Ending Inventory at Retail price by the Cost-to-Retail percentage of 64.516% to get the Ending Inventory at Cost price of $2,838.704 ($4,400 × 64.516% = $2,838.70). The reason for this computation is that Merchandise Inventories in most businesses are kept at Cost, not at Retail price.

CHAPTER 11

LONG-TERM ASSETS

Basic Attacks and Strategies for Solving Problems in this Chapter. See pages 327 to 349 for step-by-step solutions to problems.

Long-Term Assets in a business often consist of such items as Land, Building, Business Trucks and Cars, Furniture, Equipment, and Machinery. These Assets are kept over a year and are used in the actual operation of the business. They are also listed in the Balance Sheet. Many times these items, of necessity, must be lumped together as Balance Sheet items to shorten the length of the Balance Sheet. For example, all the different kinds of Furniture are lumped together and totaled in the Balance Sheet. The same would be true of Machinery, of Trucks, of Business Cars; and even the various buildings would be lumped together as Buildings. Sometimes Long-Term Investments are part of the Long-Term Assets, but more appropriately, the Long-Term Investments have a separate section of the Balance Sheet entitled *Investments*. This is a better arrangement, because Investments in other firms are using extra unneeded cash and are not really a necessary part of the Day-to-Day operation of a specific business.

It should not be assumed that there would be many problems regarding Long-Term Assets, but these items are usually expensive and extremely necessary to the successful operation of any business. Since the dollar value is so high, the decisions regarding these Long-Term Assets, such as whether to expense them or put them in the Long-Term Asset section of the Balance Sheet, are terribly important, not only as proper accounting procedures, but also for proper Income Tax reporting.

The chapter begins with the purchase of Land and its appraisal price versus its Cost Price, with the Cost Price being preferred. Next, costs of attorney fees, title fees, and grading land are debited to Land. Also, costs of assuming a mortgage should be debited to Land. The necessity of separating the Land account from the Building account is stressed for depreciation of the building and for tax reasons. Special assessment and land improvements are also discussed.

Temporary improvements in the land (such as paving the parking lot) and permanent improvements (such as planting trees) are handled in different ways, and these are explained. For instance, when does a Land Improvement get debited to Land, and when does a Land Improvement get debited to Land Improvement? Why the difference? How does this decision affect tax computation? Also, when does one debit Land and when does one debit Investments? How are building permits handled? What do you do if you purchase land with an old, unwanted building on it?

How does the accountant handle the purchase of factory equipment and the costs of moving this equipment from the railroad siding to the plant site? After the machine has been put in place, how are the costs of trial runs charged?

What is the difference between Expensing and Capitalizing? Why is this important?

If a company is working on a Long-Term contract, such as building a ship or a highway or a bridge, and needs to borrow money from the bank for its Business Expenses, what account is charged (debited) When the company pays Interest to the bank? If the company accidentally borrows too much money from the bank, does it put this extra money into some type of investment account? Then this investment account pays Interest or dividends. Of course cash would be debited, but what account would be credited?

More and more, companies are issuing stock to buy large Assets. Should the accountant debit the value of the Asset purchased or use the value of the stock given?

If a company has Assets on hand that cost a certain amount of money and these Assets are traded for other Assets, how is the transaction handled on the corporation books (at the cost of the old Asset traded in, or at the cost of the new Asset purchased)?

What if both Cash and a Non-Interest-bearing note are given in exchange for an Asset, and the note is for a certain term but has no Interest? Is there Imputed or Hidden Interest? If so, how much?

When purchasing a big-ticket item, does one record the list price or the purchase price? If a company builds its own large Asset, such as a Railroad Car, Equipment, or Machinery, does the firm list merely the material and labor costs, or does it also add Manufacturing Overhead? Can it also list Imputed profits?

When a firm installs a newly-purchased machine in its factory, how does it handle installation costs? Are they debited to an Expense account or to an Asset account?

Many times, when land or land and buildings are bought, the lawyer insists on an abstract of title search to assure the purchaser that he or she is getting the land free from previous mortgages or other claims. How are the costs of these title searches handled on the books of the purchasing corporation? What about survey costs? To what account will they be debited?

If the Raw Materials warehouse is running over and Raw Materials must be stored elsewhere, to what account are these storage costs charged (debited)?

Lately, many large banks have made loans to third-world countries in the belief that lower tariffs and increased world trade will make these countries prosperous and able to pay their debts. Often, the countries are unable to pay and the banks must lose all or part of their original loans. How do banks handle these situations in their journals and in their Balance Sheets?

If a firm buys both land and building of another firm and gives stock in return, does it record the purchase at the original values of the land and building, at the Par Value of the stock, or at the Market Value of the stock? Also, how is this transaction recorded on the books of the seller?

Not only do individuals trade in their personal cars and trucks, but businesses also do this. In this chapter, we are interested in businesses trading in their old trucks plus cash for newer trucks. Is the list price of the newer trucks debited, or is some other figure debited on the books of the trading corporation?

Long-Term Assets in a business often consist of such items as Land, Building, Business Trucks and Cars, Furniture, Equipment, and Machinery. These Assets are kept over a year and are used in the actual operation of the business. They are also listed on the Balance Sheet. Many times these items must be lumped together as Balance Sheet items to shorten the length of the Balance Sheet. For example, all the different kinds of furniture are lumped together and totaled in the Balance Sheet. The same would be true of Machinery, Trucks, and Business Cars; even the various buildings would be lumped together as buildings. Sometimes Long-Term Investments are part of the Long-Term Assets, but more appropriately, the Long-Term Investments have a separate section of the Balance Sheet called *Investments*. This is a better arrangement, because Investments in other firms are using extra unneeded cash, and are not really a necessary part of the Day-to-Day operation of a specific business.

It should not be assumed that there are many problems regarding Long-Term Assets, although these items are usually expensive and extremely necessary to the successful operation of any business. Since the dollar value is so high, the decisions regarding these Long-Term Assets, such as whether to expense them or put them in the Long-Term Asset section of the Balance Sheet, are terribly important because one must abide by proper accounting procedures, as well as proper Income Tax reporting procedures.

When land is purchased, its appraisal price is compared to its Cost Price, the Cost Price being preferred. The purchase price of land includes the cost of land grading and the cost of assuming a mortgage. (Often mortgaged property is purchased, and when this is done, the new owner often not only takes over the property but takes over the mortgage also.)

The necessity of separating the Land account from the Building account must be stressed, for depreciation of the building and for tax reasons. Often, the local taxing authority (such as City, Township, or County) will place a special assessment on a piece of business or residential property. This is an extra tax over a period of years to pay for such things as street paving, sidewalk paving, or sewer work.

Temporary improvements in land (such as paving parking lots) and permanent improvements in the land (such as planting trees) are handled by debiting **Land Improvements**.

The costs of Machinery before it is put in place, such as Freight Costs, are debited to Machinery. After the machine has been put in place and is running satisfactorily, any costs (such as repairs) are debited to Expense accounts.

The difference between Expensing and Capitalizing is that if an account is expensed, it cuts down on the Net Income for the month and thus cuts down on the Income Tax. On the other hand, if a purchase of a Long-Term Asset is capitalized, an Asset account (such as Building) is debited, and it must gradually be expensed through depreciation.

Many times, when Land is bought, or Land and Buildings are purchased at the same time, the lawyer insists on an abstract of title search to assure the purchaser that he or she is getting the land free from previous mortgages or other claims. These search fees should be added to the cost of the Asset.

Sometimes, many large banks have made loans to third-world countries in the belief that lower tariffs and increased world trade will make these countries prosperous and able to pay their debts. Often, the countries are unable to pay and the banks must lose all or part of their original loans. Banks could write these loans off all at once by debiting a Loss Expense account, or they could write them off gradually over a period of years.

Temporary improvements are such things as patching a roof to keep out the rain. This sort of thing might be expected to last less than a year and could be expensed by debiting Repair Expense and crediting Cash. On the other hand, a more permanent improvement like a new roof could be debited to Building and credited to Cash.

Step-by-Step Solutions to Problems in this Chapter, "Long-Term Assets"

• PROBLEM 11-1

When buying Land, should Land be recorded on the books at Appraisal Price or at Cost Price?

SOLUTION:

At Cost Price. The Cost Price is definitely determinable while the Appraisal Price is an estimate.

• PROBLEM 11–2

When buying real estate, there are closing costs which usually include attorneys' fees, title fees, recording fees at the court house, grading land, filling and clearing land, improving land. Should these costs be debited to Land or to some other account such as Attorneys' Fees?

SOLUTION:

They should be debited to the Land because they add value to the Land and probably the Land would not have been purchased without the idea of grading, clearing, or whatever.

• PROBLEM 11–3

Sometimes Land is purchased from a purchaser who has a mortgage on the property, and the new purchaser assumes this mortgage, or takes it over. Should the costs of assuming this mortgage be debited to the Land or to some other account?

SOLUTION:

The costs of assuming a mortgage should be debited to the Land account, since the mortgage is on the Land. However, if the mortgage is on the building, the Building account should be debited.

• PROBLEM 11–4

Why is it so important to differentiate between Land and Building in making the journal entries? Aren't Land and Building purchased at the same time and usually for one total price?

SOLUTION:

Land and Building are usually purchased at the same time and usually for one total price. However, an assessor (usually a local banker or real estate agent) who knows the value of local property should look over the Land and Building and determine what portion of the purchase price is allocable to the Land and what portion of the purchase price is allocable to the Building. The assessor should put this in writing and the purchaser should keep this information on file for tax purposes.

• PROBLEM 11-5

How does the separation of the Land Account from the Building Account affect the taxes of the entrepreneur?

SOLUTION:

Building is depreciable and Land is not depreciable. In an adjusting entry at the end of each year, Depreciation Expense is debited and Accumulated Depreciation is credited for the amount of the yearly depreciation, as follows:

2000		($ in dollars)
December 31 Depreciation Expense	500	
Accumulated Depreciation—Building		500

This Depreciation Expense is listed in the Income Statement as one of the expenses; and it effectively cuts down on the Net Income for the year, legally, and this cuts down on the Income Tax. On the other hand, if the amount is debited to Land account, there is no way it can be depreciated legally. But doesn't land depreciate? Isn't there water and wind erosion that decreases the value of land? This may be, but it isn't taken into account legally. The only way to cut taxes because of any possible wind or water erosion to land would be if the land is later sold at a loss (which is an Expense Account); and, at that time, the loss could be deducted from Revenue to show a lower Net Income and would thus result in a lower Income Tax that year.

• PROBLEM 11–6

Special assessments are levied by the local taxing authority (such as City, Township, or County) for such improvements as city pavements, street lights, and sewers. Should these special assessments be debited to Land or to Land Improvements?

SOLUTION:

They should be debited to the Land account because the city pavements, street lights, and sewers are maintained by the local government.

• PROBLEM 11–7

If the owner or the business makes permanent improvements, such as landscaping, should this be debited to the Land Account or to Land Improvements?

SOLUTION:

Permanent improvements, such as landscaping, should be debited to the Land Account, because permanent improvements are not depreciated.

• PROBLEM 11–8

What is the difference between the Land Account and the Land Improvements Account?

SOLUTION:

The Land Account cannot be depreciated, while the Land Improvements Account can be depreciated.

• PROBLEM 11-9

What type of things can be debited to the Land Improvements account?

SOLUTION:

Temporary improvements which wear out over a period of time, such as paved parking lots, private drives, and fences.

• PROBLEM 11-10

Is there any time when the purchase of Land is not debited to the Land account?

SOLUTION:

Yes, if the purchase of Land is for speculation: that is, for the purpose of holding and later, hopefully selling at a profit, then one could debit Investments. But if Land is purchased for use in a business, the Land Account should be debited.

• PROBLEM 11-11

If Land is purchased for speculation and the Investment account is debited for the purchase price of the Land, can this account be depreciated?

SOLUTION:

No. Neither the Land account nor the Investment account can be depreciated.

• PROBLEM 11–12

When a Building is being constructed, should the cost of a Building permit be expensed or debited to the Building Account?

SOLUTION:

It should be debited to the Building Account. It cannot be totally expensed in the year the Building is constructed. The only way to deduct it as an expense is gradually through Building Account depreciation.

• PROBLEM 11–13

If Land is purchased with an old Building on it and the new owner then tears down the old Building to make way for new construction, how should the cost of razing the Building be handled? Can this cost be debited to an Expense Account, a Building Account, or the Land Account?

SOLUTION:

If the Land was purchased because of the location and area, and not for the Building, the cost of tearing down the Building should be debited to the Land Account, because it was the Land that was valuable, not the Building.

• PROBLEM 11–14

A large piece of Factory Equipment is being purchased. It must be transported to the factory site, hoisted to the third floor, and cemented into the floor. Can these costs be expensed; or do they have to be debited to the Equipment Account?

SOLUTION:

They have to be debited to the Equipment Account. All costs of getting the Assets into usable condition for business purposes are debited to the Asset Account. The expense of doing this can only be recovered by depreciation.

• PROBLEM 11-15

A large piece of Factory Equipment, a broom-making machine, has been placed in the factory. Trial runs are made to be sure that the machine is in proper working condition. Can the costs of these trial runs be expensed immediately, or should they be debited to an Asset Account?

SOLUTION:

The cost of trial runs should be debited to the Machine or to the Equipment account. These costs can then be recovered over the years of life of the machine through debiting Depreciation Expense in the adjusting entries at the end of each year.

• PROBLEM 11-16

The Hanson Broom Company employees construct a broom-making machine for future use in the factory. Materials total $10,000; Labor $20,000; and Overhead (heat, lights, rent) $3,000. How should these costs be allocated on the books?

SOLUTION:

There are several approaches that could be made. The first one is to debit the Machine Account for the $10,000 Materials and the $20,000 Labor, and not use the $3,000 Overhead. This is assuming that the Overhead would be used for other purposes anyway. The second approach would be to count the $10,000 Materials, the $20,000 Labor, and also the $3,000 Overhead and debit the Machine Account for the entire $33,000 (instead of merely $30,000). This would put the entire cost of Building the Equipment in the Machine Account. The third approach would be to allocate the cost of lost production to the Machine Account. Let us say that if the employees hadn't built the machine themselves, the costs of Material, Labor, and Overhead perhaps would have amounted to $20,000. So we would debit Machine for $20,000. This is a mere estimate.

All three approaches are legal, but the second approach is most often used because it gives the most accurate record and it can be proven for tax purposes most easily.

• PROBLEM 11–17

The Martin Shipbuilding Company is building a ship under contract which will cost $500,000 to build and is to be sold under contract for $600,000. Martin will receive no money from the buyer until the ship is completed. As construction continues and costs mount, Martin will borrow money from the bank to cover Material, Labor, and Overhead. Each month Martin will make Interest payments to the bank. Should Martin debit Interest Expense or should Martin debit the Asset account, Ship?

SOLUTION:

Martin should debit the Asset Account, Ship, for Interest paid to finance work under construction. Thus, the Interest paid to the bank adds to the cost of building the ship. All accountants do not agree on this, but most do. A minority of accountants would debit Interest Expense. It is legal to do it either way.

• PROBLEM 11–18

The Martin Shipbuilding Company knew it would need $2,000 to pay Interest on money it planned to borrow for expenses of building a ship. So it borrowed $2,000 from the bank. Not needing this money immediately, it invested it in mutual funds. Should the dividends from these mutual funds be credited to an Income Account or should they be capitalized (deducting from the Asset Account, Ship)?

SOLUTION:

The dividends from the mutual fund investment are temporary and should be credited to an Income Account.

• PROBLEM 11–19

The Langer Transportation Company purchased a bus with a list price of $40,000. Instead of giving the vendor cash, it was agreed to give the vendor stock in the Langer Transportation Company. The vendor was given 500 shares of Langer stock, and the Par Value of this stock is $20 and the Market Value is $58. What entry should be made on the books of the Langer Transportation Company to record this purchase?

SOLUTION:

Bus	29,000	
Common Stock		10,000
Paid-In Capital		19,000

It is true that the list price of the bus was $40,000. Then why isn't Bus debited for $40,000? Because 500 shares of stock with a Market Value of $58 was given for the bus. And 500 shares @ $58 = $29,000. So, in reality, the Langer Transportation Company is getting the bus for $29,000, not for the list price of $40,000.

It is the accounting rule that Common Stock is kept on the books of the corporation issuing the Common Stock, at Par Value. So we multiply the 500 shares by the Par Value per share $20 per share to get $10,000 ($500 × $20 = $10,000). Thus, the account Common Stock is credited for $10,000. Finally, the difference, $19,000, is credited to Paid-In Capital ($29,000 − $10,000 = $19,000).

• PROBLEM 11-20

The Langer Transportation Company purchased a bus with a List Price of $50,000. This was acquired for a number of engines which the Langer Transportation Company has in its inventory and which originally cost the company $40,000 and would have been sold for $45,000. What entry or entries should the Langer Transportation Company make on its books?

SOLUTION:

Bus	40,000	
Engines		40,000

It is true that the List Price of the bus was $50,000, but the Langer Transportation Company did not pay $50,000 for the bus; it merely traded some engines which the Langer Transportation Company had purchased for $40,000. It is true that the Selling Price of the engines is $45,000, but these engines are kept in inventory at Cost Price, not at Selling Price; so the Langer Transportation Company is only giving up $40,000 worth of value. The credit of $40,000 to the Engines account effectively closes out this account. Buses are debited for $40,000, the amount that the Langer Transportation Company gave up to acquire the bus.

• PROBLEM 11-21

The Langer Transportation Company purchased a bus with a List Price of $30,000. It is acquired with a down payment of $4,000 cash and a Non-interest-bearing note with a face amount of $30,000. This note is due in one year. The normal Interest Rate at the bank now is 9%. What entry should be made on the books of the Langer Transportation Company to record this purchase?

SOLUTION:

Bus	31,300	
Interest Expense	2,700	
Cash		4,000
Notes Payable		30,000

If the bus' List Price is $30,000, why isn't the Bus Account debited for $30,000? It is not because more than this amount was given for the bus. Cash of $4,000 in a down payment was given, and a Note Payable of $30,000 was also given. There was not any Interest mentioned on the face of the note, but the going Interest Rate at the bank at this time was 9%. When no Interest is mentioned in an Arm's-Length Business Transaction, an Imputed or Hidden Interest is still there. Since the note runs one year, in order to get the hidden Interest, we multiply the face value of the note ($30,000) by the 9% going Interest Rate to get $2700 real Interest Expense. Thus, the account Interest Expense is debited for $2,700; Cash (down payment) is credited for $4,000; and Notes Payable is credited for the face value of the note, $30,000. Why is Bus debited for $31,300? This is a "Plug figure" computed by adding the two credits and subtracting the debit as follows: $30,000 + $4,000 − $2,700 = $31,300. This means that if the Interest Expense is taken into account on the one-year note, the Langer Transportation Company is really paying $31,300 for the bus, not $30,000.

• PROBLEM 11–22

The Langer Transportation Company purchased a bus with a List Price of $25,000 but paid only $22,000 cash. What entry should be made on the books of the Langer Transportation Company to record this purchase?

SOLUTION:

Bus	22,000	
Cash		22,000

The List Price of the bus is different from the amount paid. Since the

Langer Transportation Company had to pay only $22,000 for the bus, this was the Cost Price of the bus to them and the amount for which Bus should be debited on the books. One of the rules of accounting is the Cost Rule, that is, that items purchased by a business should be recorded at Cost.

• PROBLEM 11-23

The Santa Fe Railroad Company had its own workers construct siding track for a 10-mile stretch parallel to the main line track. Material costs were $20,000; Direct Labor costs were $30,000; and Overhead costs were $25,000. What amount should the railroad put on its books for the asset Siding?

SOLUTION:

Choice 1:

Material	$20,000
Direct Labor	30,000
Manufacturing Overhead	25,000
Total	$75,000

Choice 2:

Material	$20,000
Direct Labor	30,000
Total	$50,000

The Material and the Direct Labor are easily computable, since there is a paper trail for the purchases of Material and the payment of the Direct Labor. However, much of the Manufacturing Overhead is not directly applicable to the project and might have to be paid out whether the project was undertaken or not. Either of the above choices is correct. The first one adds the Material Costs, the Direct Labor Costs, and the Estimated Manufacturing Overhead Costs, giving a grand total of $75,000.

The second one adds the Material Costs and the Direct Labor Costs, giving a grand total of only $50,000. Either method is acceptable for accounting purposes.

• PROBLEM 11-24

The Santa Fe Railroad Company had its own workers construct siding track for a 10-mile stretch parallel to the main line track. Material Costs were $20,000; Direct Labor Costs were $30,000; Overhead Costs were $25,000. The Santa Fe Railroad accountants determined that if the work had been contracted out, the contractor would also add a 20% profit for the work ($20,000 + $30,000 + $25,000 = $75,000; $75,000 × 20% = $15,000 profit.)

Material	$20,000
Direct Labor	30,000
Manufacturing Overhead	25,000
Imputed Profits	15,000
	$90,000

How should the Asset Account, Siding, dollar value appear on the books?

SOLUTION:

Either as $50,000, the cost of the Direct Material and the Direct Labor, or as $75,000, the cost of the Direct Material and the Direct Labor and the Manufacturing Overhead.

Imputed Profits means profits that would have been charged if the work had been contracted out. Since the work has not been contracted out and the work was done by the railroad employees themselves, there are no profits and these should not be added to the cost of the Asset, Siding.

• PROBLEM 11-25

A new broom-making machine was purchased for the factory of the Devon Broom Corporation at a cost of $50,000, delivered to the local freight station. It cost $300 for the van to move the machine from the freight station to the factory building. It cost $100 to lift the machine through the factory window and to cement the machine into the factory floor. Should the $300 Moving Costs and the $100 Cementing and Window Costs be expensed immediately or should they be added to the cost of the machine?

SOLUTION:

The $300 Moving Costs and the $100 Cementing and Window Costs were incurred before the machine was in actual operation; so they should be debited to the Asset Account, Machine, or to the Asset Account, Equipment.

• PROBLEM 11-26

The Mason Manufacturing Company is in the process of purchasing a piece of land for a new factory building. The company's lawyer has advised them that before the company signs the purchasing papers, they give him (the lawyer) the opportunity to conduct a title search at the abstract company. An abstract is a history of the property going back to the early days. For instance, many properties in the Midwest go back to the Louisiana Purchase. These searches assure the new buyer that he or she has clear title to the property and that no one in the future will try to claim title to the property after it has been purchased by the new buyer. The fees for the title search are $300. Should this $300 be expensed by debiting to an Expense Account, to Building, or to Land?

SOLUTION:

It should be debited to Land.

There is no building on the property; so it cannot be debited to Building. Costs of buying the Land before it is ready for use by the new buyer are properly debited to Land, not to an Expense Account.

• PROBLEM 11–27

The Mason Manufacturing Company has recently purchased Land and is getting ready to construct a new factory on this land. A survey crew has been hired to survey the Land to determine the proper location of the new building and any drainage problems that may occur. Should the costs of the survey be debited to an Expense, Land, or Building Account?

SOLUTION:

To the Building Account. The purpose of the survey is to get ready to build the Building; so Building should be debited for these costs. The Land has already been purchased. The Expense Accounts are only debited after the Building has been put into use. Costs having to do with the building before and during its construction should be debited to the Asset Account, Building.

• PROBLEM 11–28

The Mason Manufacturing Company has recently purchased Land and constructed a new factory building on that land. Direct Material for use in the factory is being stored in a nearby warehouse, not owned by the company, for use in the manufacturing process. How should this Material Cost for storage be handled? Should it be debited to some Expense Account or to some Asset Account, and to which one?

SOLUTION:

Choice 1: Debit the Materials Inventory Account, because these are materials used in the Manufacturing Process; so the cost of storage of these materials should increase the dollar value in the Materials Inventory Account.

Choice 2: Debit Storage Expense, a subsidiary account to Manufacturing Overhead Control. These are extra costs and are Overhead.

Choice 1 appears better, because it is allocating Storage Costs of Materials to the Materials Inventory Account. However, Choice 2 is not wrong, because these extra outside Storage Expenses could also be considered Overhead. These are internal accounting procedures within the company and do not really concern either the customers, the stockholders, or the government. Regardless of the way in which it is allocated, it will not affect the amount of taxes that the company pays. It will all be totaled in Cost of Goods Sold in the accounting period in which the manufactured goods are eventually sold.

• PROBLEM 11–29

The Mason Manufacturing Company has recently purchased Land and is in the process of constructing a new factory building. Should the construction costs be expensed, debited to Land, or debited to Building?

SOLUTION:

The new construction costs should be debited to Building because they are going to erect the building. Expenses are not debited until the building is finished and ready for the use for which it was built.

• PROBLEM 11–30

The First National Bank of Jamestown lent a Third-World nation $100,000. What entry should it make for this loan?

SOLUTION:

Long-Term Notes Receivable	100,000	
Cash		100,000

• PROBLEM 11–31

The First National Bank of Jamestown lent a Third-World nation $100,000, debiting the Asset Account Long-Term Notes Receivable for $100,000 and crediting Cash for $100,000. After several years, the economy of the nation has deteriorated and the nation asks the bank for more time to pay the loan. It also looks as if much of the loan will never be repaid. What entry should the bank make at this juncture?

SOLUTION:

The First National Bank of Jamestown should try to determine how much money it thinks it will lose from the loan. In other words, how much can be eventually collected? Let us assume they come to the conclusion that they will be able to collect $80,000 and that the other $20,000 will be lost ($80, 000 + $20, 000 = $100, 000).

Bad Debts Expense	20,000	
Allowance for Doubtful Accounts		20,000

• PROBLEM 11–32

The First National Bank of Jamestown loaned a Third-World nation $100,000 by debiting Notes Receivable $100,000 and crediting Cash for $100,000. Several years later, the economy of the nation deteriorated and the nation asked the bank for more time to pay the loan. The bank came to the conclusion that it would lose at least $20,000; so it made an entry on its books debiting Bad Debts Expense for $20,000, crediting Allowance for Doubtful Accounts for $20,000 during the year 2000. How would this appear on the Balance Sheet of the First National Bank of Jamestown on December 31, 2000?

SOLUTION:

Notes Receivable (Long Term)	100,000	
Less: Allowance for Doubtful Accounts	–20,000	80,000

This presentation shows that although the debt is $100,000, the bank has written off $20,000 and will be lucky to collect the remaining $80,000.

• PROBLEM 11–33

The Jason Company has just gone out of business. A former competitor of the Jason Company, the Langston Company, has offered to buy the Building and Land from the Jason Company, giving the Jason Company 100,000 shares of Langston Company stock. The Land and Building are listed on the Jason Company books as follows:

Land	$150,000
Building (Net)	100,000
Total	$250,000

The Common Stock of the Langston Company has a Par Value of $1 per share and a Market Value of $2 per share. Both the Langston Company and the Jason Company agree to the trade. How will this trade be recorded on the Langston Company books and why?

SOLUTION:

Land	120,000	
Building	80,000	
Common Stock		100,000
Paid-In Capital on Common Stock		100,000

The Common Stock of the Langston Company has a Market Value of $2 per share; and 100,000 shares of Langston Common Stock are being issued. This is a total value of $200,000. (100,000 shares × $2 = $200,000). Therefore, it is assumed that the Land and Building together are worth this much, or $200,000. Note that the Jason Company had the land listed for $150,000 and the Building listed for $100,000, or a total of $250,000, not $200,000. It will also be noted that the Land Cost as listed by Jason Company is 3/5 or 60% of the total as follows: 60% of $250,000 = $150,000, the price of the land on the Jason Company books. It will also be noted that the Building Cost as listed by Jason Company is 2/5 or 40% of the total as follows: 40% of $250,000 = $100,000 the price of the building on the Jason Company books. Thus, the Jason Company believes that the Land Cost amounts to 60% of the cost of both the land and building together; and the Building Cost amounts to 40% of the cost of both the Building and Land together.

Since the Market Value of the stock that the Langston Company is giving amounts to only $200,000, we multiply the $200,000 by 60% to get the new cost of the land to be recorded as a debit to Land on the books of the Langston Company. We also multiply the $200,000 by 40% to get the new cost of the building to be recorded as a debit to Building on the books of the Langston Company.

$200,000 × 60% = $120,000

$200,000 × 40% = $ 80,000

Common Stock is always put down on the books of the issuing company at Par Value, if the stock has a Par Value. If the stock does not have a Par Value, but has a Stated Value, the Common Stock is always entered on the books of the issuing company at Stated Value. (If the stock does not have either Par Value or Stated Value, Common Stock is put down on the books of the issuing company at Market Value.)

Since the Par Value of the Common Stock of the Langston Company is worth $1 a share and since the company is issuing 100,000 shares, the company credits Common Stock on its books for $100,000 (100,000 shares × $1 per share = $100,000). Subtracting the debits totalling $200,000 (Land $120,000 + Building $80,000 = $200,000) from the credit to Common Stock of $100,000, we get another $100,000 ($200,000– $100,000 = $100,000). This extra $100,000 is credited on the books of Langston Company to an account entitled Paid-In Capital on Common stock. This $100,000 is the difference between the Market Value of the stock issued ($200,000) and the Par Value of the stock issued ($100,000).

• PROBLEM 11–34

The Jason Company is in the process of going out of business during the year 2000. A former competitor of the Jason Company, the Langston Company, has offered to buy Jason's building and land for 100,000 shares of Langston Company stock. The land and building are listed on the Jason Company books as follows:

Land	$150,000
Building (Net)	100,000
Total	250,000

The Common Stock of the Langston Company has a Par Value of $10 per share and a Market Value of $2 per share. Both the Langston Company and the Jason Company agree to the deal. How will this deal be recorded on the Jason Company books and why?

SOLUTION:

Investment in Langston Company Stock	200,000	
Loss on trade	50,000	
Land		150,000
Building		100,000

The Jason Company is buying stock in the Langston Company, and the Market Value of this stock is $2 per share, and there are 100,000 shares coming to the Jason Company. This is a total of $200,000 (100,000 shares × $2 = $200,000); so the Jason Company debits the Asset Account,

Investment, in Langston Company Stock for the $200,000. It is giving Land, valued on its books at $150,000, and Building, with the Net Value on its books (original Cost Price of the building less accumulated depreciation) of $100,000. This is a total of $250,000 ($150,000 + $100,000 = $250,000). The Jason Company is giving Assets valued on its books at $250,000 for stock, Market Value of which is only $200,000. This means that the Jason Company is losing $50,000. So the account **Loss** On Trade (an Expense Account) is debited for $50,000. This is an expense which the Jason Company can use as a regular expense in its Income Statement to cut down its Net Income for the year 2000 and thus cut down its Income Tax.

Why would the Jason Company enter into an agreement whereby it stands to lose $50,000? Perhaps the Land and Building on its books are overpriced. Perhaps they are located in a declining section of the city where property values are being lowered. Or perhaps the owner of the Jason Company cannot quickly sell the property for a higher price. Or perhaps the owner of the Jason Company wants to get out of the responsibilities of running his own business, would like to turn things over to another firm, and live on the dividends from the Langston Company stock. Or perhaps the owner of the Jason Company will eventually sell his Langston Company stock if it increases in value. There are all sorts of reasons for this.

• PROBLEM 11–35

The Harlan Trucking Company has several old trucks that it originally purchased for $100,000. Accumulated depreciation on these trucks as of December 31, 2000, amounts to $20,000, and the accounts on the Harlan Trucking Company books appear as follows:

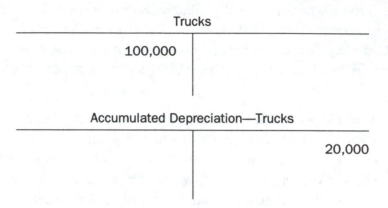

Trucks

| 100,000 | |

Accumulated Depreciation—Trucks

| | 20,000 |

The old trucks are becoming unreliable. So the company representatives decide to trade these old trucks in for some newer trucks, but to get the deal, the Harlan Trucking Company must pay the used car company $10,000 in addition to the old trucks. What entry will the Harlan Trucking Company make on its books and why?

SOLUTION:

Trucks (newer)	90,000	
Accumulated Depreciation—Trucks	20,000	
Trucks (Old)		100,000
Cash		10,000

In order to close out the account, Trucks, we must credit Trucks (Old) for the $100,000 balance. Also, the account Accumulated Depreciation—Trucks, has a credit balance of $20,000. In order to close out this credit balance, we must debit Accumulated Depreciation—Trucks, for $20,000. Since we are paying the used car company $10,000, we credit Cash for $10,000. Where do we get the $90,000 debit to Trucks (newer)? This is a "plug figure" derived by adding the two credit figures and deducting the debit figure as follows: 100,000 + $10,000 = $110,000; $110,000 − $20,000 = $90,000. Another way of computing the $90,000 value of the newer trucks on our books is to add the Book Value of the old trucks and the Cash amount paid. The Book Value of the old trucks is their Original Cost ($100,000) less the accumulated depreciation over the years ($20,000). ($100,000–$20,000 = $80,00.) Thus, the Book Value of the old trucks is $80,000. To this, add the Cash boot of $10,000 to get $90,000 ($80,000 + $10,000 = $90,000).

CHAPTER 12

DEPRECIATION, DEPLETION, AND AMORTIZATION

> **Basic Attacks and Strategies for Solving Problems in this Chapter. See pages 353 to 394 for step-by-step solutions to problems.**

Depreciation, Depletion, and Amortization are three legal Cost Recovery Systems used by accountants to reduce the value of various Assets as they wear out or are depleted. This is done either at the end of the year or end of the month through adjusting entries that, at the same time, debit Expense Accounts, thus adding to Legal Expenses and cutting down Net Incomes on the books in order to cut Income Tax.

It is common knowledge that Assets, such as Trucks, wear out with use. However, Depreciation systems, as such, and Depreciation tables are practically an enigma to the general public. One of the chief reasons the public take their taxes to accountants, rather than trying to do taxes themselves, is their unfamiliarity with methods of Depreciation, Depletion, and Amortization. Government laws, in particular, have made these systems complicated. As in the case of the recent MACRS tables, the federal government attempted to make computation easier, but has, instead, intimidated the general public.

MACRS is an acronym for **Modified Accelerated Cost Recovery System**. A Cost Recovery System is a method of Depreciation, turning the cost of a previously purchased Asset into an expense over a period of time. Accelerated means that a Depreciation method is chosen, which makes the Depreciation largest in the early years of the Asset's life and then gradually reduces this to smaller amounts of Depreciation each year. In 1986, Congress modified the previously existing **ACRS, Accelerated Cost Re-**

covery System. Deciding that ACRS was too accelerated, Congress modified it so that deductions allowed in the early years of an Asset's life were reduced.

There are definite distinctions between Depreciation, Depletion, and Amortization.

Depreciation is the systematic reduction in value of equipment—tangible Assets, such as buildings, trucks, furniture, and machinery.

Depletion is the progressive usage of wasting Assets, such as oil wells, natural gas wells, coal mines, and iron mines.

Amortization is the methodical reduction of the costs of intangible Assets, such as patents, copyrights, trade marks, and goodwill.

There are five legal methods of depreciation: Straight Line, Units of Output, Working Hours, Sum-of-Years-Digits, and Double-Declining-Balance.

Congress makes Depreciation different by setting up its own Depreciation systems, such as ACRS and MACRS. Congress may also require business people to depreciate using the 150% Declining Balance method, instead of the 200% Declining Balance method (Double Method).

Buildings are the best examples of the proper use of the Straight-Line method of Depreciation, because buildings usually wear out over time.

Factory machines are excellent examples of the Working Hours method of Depreciation. This method allows the greatest dollar amounts of Depreciation during the years when the machine has the greatest number of working hours.

The Units-of-Output method of Depreciation is similar to the working hours method. However, the greatest dollar value of Depreciation is instead calculated in relation to the greatest number of finished units.

The Sum-of-Years-Digits method of Depreciation might be used to depreciate a fleet of business cars. This is an accelerated method of Depreciation; cars are an excellent example because they depreciate the most in the first year of life.

When given a choice, taxpayers often switch from using the MACRS method to the Straight-Line method of Depreciation after half of the property's expectant life is complete.

Step-by-Step Solutions to Problems in this Chapter, "Depreciation, Depletion, and Amortization"

• PROBLEM 12–1

On January 1, 2000, the Sands Manufacturing Company purchased an expensive piece of equipment for its factory at a cost of $215,000. It was estimated that this equipment would last 9 years, at which time it would have a scrap value of $15,000. From past experience with similar equipment, it was also estimated that during the life of the equipment it would produce 1,000,000 units and work approximately 30,000 hours. On December 31, 2000, it was determined that during the entire year of 2000, the equipment ran 3,000 hours and produced 100,000 units of finished product. Compute the Depreciation for the year 2000 under the following five methods:

(1) Straight Line Depreciation
(2) Units of Output method of Depreciation
(3) Working Hours method of Depreciation
(4) Sum-of-Years-Digits method of Depreciation
(5) Double-Declining-Balance method of Depreciation

SOLUTION:

(1) Straight Line Method of Depreciation—$22,222 for the year 2000, computed as follows:

> $215,000 purchase price of equipment
>
> − 15,000 scrap value at end of 9 years
>
> $200,000 to be depreciated over the 9-year period

Next, divide the 9 year estimated usable life of the equipment into the $200,000 to be depreciated to get $22,222 Depreciation during the year 2000.

(2) Units-of-Output Method of Depreciation—$20,000 for the year

> $215,000 purchase price of equipment
> − 15,000 scrap value at end of 9 years
> $200,000 to be depreciated over the 9-year period.

It was estimated that during the life of the equipment it would produce 1,000,000 units of finished product. So the next step is to divide the 1,000,000 units into the $200,000 to be depreciated to get a Depreciation figure of $.20 per unit.

During the entire year of 2000, the equipment produced 100,000 units of finished product. So the next step is to multiply the 100,000 completed units by the Depreciation figure of $.20 per unit to get $20,000 depreciation for the year 2,000 using the Units-of-Output Method of Depreciation (1,000,000 units divided into $200,000 = $.20; 100,000 completed units × $.20 = $20,000).

(3) Working Hours Method of Depreciation—$20,010 Depreciation for the first year.

> $215,000 purchase price of equipment
> − 15,000 scrap value at end of 9 years
> $200,000 to be depreciated over the 9-year period.

It was estimated that during the life of the equipment it would work approximately 30,000 hours. So the next step is to divide the $200,000 to be depreciated over the 9-year period by the 30,000 work hours in the life of the equipment to get $6.67 Depreciation per hour.

During the year 2000, the equipment ran 3,000 hours. So the next step is to multiply the $6.67 Depreciation per hour by the 3,000 hours that the machine actually ran during the year 2000 to get $20,010 Depreciation for that year. ($200,000 divided by 30,000 hours = $6.67; and $6.67 × 3000 hours = $20,010 Depreciation for the year 2000.)

(4) Sum-of-Years-Digits Method of Depreciation—$40,000 Depreciation for the first year (in this case the year 2000).

> $215,000 purchase price of equipment
> − 15,000
> $200,000 to be depreciated over the 9-year period.

The next step is to determine the fraction of the $200,000 to multiply by the $200,000 to get the first year's Depreciation. This is accomplished by taking the 9-year life of the equipment and adding the following figures: $9 + 8 + 7 + 6 + 5 + 4 + 3 + 2 + 1 = 45$. Thus, the number 45 is the denominator of the fraction. The numerator for the first year is the length of life of the equipment: in this case, 9. So the fraction for the first year (the year 2000) is 9/45. Thus, we multiply 9/45 by the $200,000 to be depreciated over the 9-year period to get $40,000, the first year's Depreciation by the Sum-of-Years-Digits method.

(5) The Double-Declining-Balance Method of Depreciation—$47,777 Depreciation for the first year (in this case the year 2000).

The Double-Declining-Balance Method of Depreciation is the only one of the Depreciation methods that does not first deduct the scrap value from the cost. Instead, the original cost is used as the starting point. The number of years of estimated life is divided into 100%. Thus, the 9 year life is divided into 100, to get 11.111% (100 divided by $9 = 11.111$). Because this is the Double Declining Balance method, the 11.111% is then multiplied by 2, giving 22.222% or .22222. There is really no reason for multiplying by 2, except that Congress has allowed accountants to do this in computing this method of Depreciation, thus giving greater Depreciation in the early years of the life of the equipment being depreciated.

Next, the $215,000 original cost of the equipment is multiplied by the 22.222% to give $47,777 Depreciation during the first year's life of the equipment ($215,000 × .22222 = $47,777).

Let us now compare the amounts of Depreciation for the first year by all five methods of depreciation, as follows:

Straight-Line Method	$22,222
Units of Output Method	$20,000
Working Hours Method	$20,010
Sum-of-Years-Digits Method	$40,000
Double-Declining-Balance Method	$47,777

What conclusions can be drawn from the above first-year computations? It will be noted that the Double-Declining-Balance Method of Depreciation gives the greatest amount of Depreciation for the first year of the equipment's life. It will also be noted that the Sum-of-Years-Digits Method of Depreciation gives the second greatest amount of Depreciation for the first year of the equipment's life. These two methods are especially useful for items that depreciate rapidly at first. As we know, when we drive a new car off the lot after purchasing it, the car loses a great deal of value. This would also be true of jeeps and trucks. So the Double-Declining-Balance Method and the Sum-of-Years-Digits Method are especially useful for depreciating business cars and trucks. (Why just business cars and trucks? Why not personal cars and trucks? The federal government does not allow personal cars and trucks to be depreciated. That is, depreciation cannot be deducted as a personal expense.)

What conclusions can be drawn from the first-year computations regarding the Working Hours Method and the Units-of-Output Method of Depreciation? Since the Depreciation amount increases during the years when the equipment is worked harder, these methods depend on the use of the equipment, not on the years of life. So, in a year of great use, these methods might show Depreciation dollar figures even greater than those of the Double-Declining-Balance Method and the Sum-of-Years-Digits Method. Therefore, the Working Hours Method and the Units-of-Output Method are good for factory machine Depreciation.

What conclusions can be drawn from the Straight-Line method of Depreciation? This is the first and oldest method, and its use is best for Assets that depreciate over a period of time, such as buildings.

All five methods are legal for Income Tax purposes.

• PROBLEM 12-2

The Total Manufacturing Corporation has just built a new factory on land previously owned by the corporation. The cost of the building itself was $50,000. Appraisers calculate that the building should last 20 years and have no Residual Value at the end of that time. What method of Depreciation should be used?

SOLUTION:

The Straight-Line Method of Depreciation.

A factory building depreciates greatly over a period of time, and the Straight-Line method allows the same amount of Depreciation each year. On the contrary, the Unit-of-Output method of Depreciation is best for factory machinery, as is the Working-Hour method of Depreciation, because these methods increase the Depreciation as the Asset is used more fully in a particular year. On the other hand, the Sum-of-Years-Digits method of Depreciation and the Double-Declining-Balance method of depreciation are best to depreciate Assets that lose value the most in the beginning years of use, such as business cars and trucks.

Therefore, the Straight-Line Method of Depreciation is best for Depreciating a business building.

• PROBLEM 12–3

The Total Manufacturing Corporation has just built a new factory on land previously owned by the corporation. The cost of the building itself was $50,000. Appraisers calculate that the building should last 20 years and have no residual value at the end of that time. Set up a Depreciation table for this Asset for the period of 20 years and then explain the Depreciation table.

SOLUTION:

Since the Residual or Scrap Value is zero, the Cost Price of the building ($50,000) is the same price as the Book Value of the building ($50,000). The first column of the table represents the year, but the first line begins with year zero, and shows the $50,000 book value at the beginning of the year, immediately after the building was constructed. The Depreciation column shows the yearly Depreciation of $2,500, computed as follows: $50,000 cost divided by 20 years use = $2,500 yearly Depreciation according to the Straight-Line method. The accumulated Depreciation is the sum of all the Depreciation in the previous years and in the present year. At the date construction was completed, there was not yet any Depreciation to accumulate; so the entry is zero. At the end of the first year, the Depreciation was $2,500; so the accumulated depreciation was also $2,500. (See the following table.)

Each year thereafter, the accumulated Depreciation column increases by $2500, the steady amount of the annual Depreciation according to the Straight-Line method. The rightmost column is the Book Value column. At time of purchase, the Book Value ($50,000) is the same as the Construction Cost of the building ($50,000). Each year, the Book Value drops by the amount of the annual Depreciation ($2,500) until, at the end of the 20th year, the Book Value is zero since there is no Residual (Scrap) Value. On the other hand, at the end of the 20th year, the Accumulated Depreciation column shows a balance of $50,000, the total of all the Depreciation that has accumulated over the 20 years at $2500 per year.

Table 1
The Total Manufacturing Company
Depreciation Schedule for New Factory Building

Year	Depreciation	Accumulated Depreciation	Book Value
0	$ 0	$ 0	$ 50,000
1	2,500	2,500	47,500
2	2,500	5,000	45,000
3	2,500	7,500	42,500
4	2,500	10,000	40,000
5	2,500	12,500	37,500
6	2,500	15,000	35,000
7	2,500	17,500	32,500
8	2,500	20,000	30,000
9	2,500	22,500	27,500
10	2,500	25,000	25,000
11	2,500	27,500	22,500
12	2,500	30,000	20,000
13	2,500	32,500	17,500
14	2,500	35,000	15,000
15	2,500	37,500	12,500
16	2,500	40,000	10,000
17	2,500	42,500	7,500
18	2,500	45,000	5,000
19	2,500	47,500	2,500
20	2,500	50,000	0

• PROBLEM 12-4

The Total Manufacturing Corporation has just built a new factory on land previously owned by the corporation. The cost of the building itself was $52,000. Appraisers calculate that the building itself should last 20 years and at the end of that time have a $2,000 Residual Value. Set up a Depreciation table for this Asset for the period of 20 years, and explain the Depreciation table.

SOLUTION:

Since the Residual or Scrap Value is $2,000 and the Cost Price of the building is $52,000, the amount to be depreciated will be $50,000 ($52,000 − $2,000 = $50,000).

Table 2
The Total Manufacturing Company
Depreciation Schedule for New Factory Building

Year	Depreciation	Accumulated Depreciation	Book Value
0	$ 0	$ 0	$ 52,000
2	2,500	5,000	47,000
3	2,500	7,500	44,500
4	2,500	10,000	42,000
5	2,500	12,500	39,500
6	2,500	15,000	37,000
7	2,500	17,500	34,500
8	2,500	20,000	32,000
9	2,500	22,500	29,500
10	2,500	5,000	27,000
11	2,500	27,500	24,500
12	2,500	30,000	22,000
13	2,500	32,500	19,500
14	2,500	37,500	17,000
15	2,500	37,500	14,500
16	2,500	40,000	12,000
17	2,500	42,500	9,500
18	2,500	45,000	7,000
19	2,500	47,500	4,500
20	2,500	50,000	2,000

On line 0 of the table (Table 2), since the factory has just been built, there is not yet Depreciation nor accumulated Depreciation. The Book Value column shows the Cost Price of $52,000. At the end of the first year, the Depreciation column shows the year's Depreciation under the Straight-Line method of $2,500; and since there has been no previous accumulated Depreciation, the Accumulated Depreciation column also shows a balance of $2,500. The Book Value column at the end of the first year shows a balance of $49,500 ($52,000 cost less $2,500 first year's Depreciation = $49,500).

Each successive year, the Depreciation column shows an annual Depreciation of $2,500 ($50,000 amount to be Depreciated divided by 20 years life of building = $2,500 annual Depreciation under the Straight-Line Method). Each year, the Accumulated Depreciation column adds another $2500, until by the 20th year, the total amount to be Depreciated (in this case, $50,000) has been accumulated. Finally, in the rightmost column, the Book Value column, the cost amount of $52,000 has decreased regularly by the amount of annual Depreciation ($2,500) so that, by the 20th year, the balance in the Book Value column is $2,000, the amount of the estimated Residual Value.

• PROBLEM 12-5

The James Broom Works manufactures and sells brooms. In the year 2000, on January 2, the James Broom Works purchased and installed a broom-making machine at a cost of $11,000. From past experience with this type of Asset, it was estimated that the machine would last 50,000 hours and would have a Residual or Scrap Value of $1,000 at the end of that time. Why should the Working-Hours Method of Depreciation be chosen?

SOLUTION:

The Working-Hours Method of Depreciation adapts itself best to a broom-making machine. For instance, the number of estimated hours of life is known or at least can be guessed accurately from past experience. Also, the machine depreciates through use, so that, in the years when it is seldom used, it will not depreciate much, and, in the years in which it is greatly used, it will depreciate greatly.

On the other hand, the Straight-Line Depreciation method is best adapted to Assets that depreciate regularly over a period of time. The Sum-of-Years-Digits method and the Double Declining Balance methods of Depreciation are best adapted to Assets that depreciate most in the first year or two of use.

The Units-of-Output method would also be good for depreciating this broom-making machine, but since the number of units produced during the life of the machine has not been estimated, this method will not be used in this instance.

• PROBLEM 12–6

The James Broom Works manufactures and sells brooms. In the year 2000, on January 2, the James Broom Works purchased and installed a broom-making machine at a cost of $11,000. From past experience with this type of Asset it was estimated that the machine would last 50,000 hours and would have a Residual or Scrap Value of $1,000 at the end of that time. Show a Depreciation table for this machine and explain the table.

SOLUTION:

The broom-making machine was purchased for $11,000 and it was estimated that its Residual Value is $1,000; therefore, the amount to be depreciated is $10,000 ($11,000 – $1,000 = $10,000). From past experience, it is estimated that the broom-making machine will run 50,000 hours in its lifetime.

The next step is to compute the amount of Depreciation per hour. This is done by dividing the amount to be depreciated ($10,000) by the estimated number of hours of life of the machine (50,000 hours) to get $.20 per hour Depreciation ($10,000 divided by 50,000 hours = $.20 per hour).

Looking at the following table, we see that at the time of purchase, on January 2, 2000, the Book Value of the machine is the same as the Purchase Price of the machine—$11,000.

At the end of the year 2000, the machine had been used for 15,000 hours; so we multiply 15,000 hours by the previously computed Depreciation rate of $.20 per hour to get $3,000 that year. Since there had been no previously accumulated Depreciation, the Accumulated Depreciation column also has a figure of $3,000, the first year's Depreciation. Finally, the Book Value column shows $8,000, the Cost Price of $11,000 less the first

Table 3
James Broom Works
Depreciation Schedule for
Broom-Making Machine
Purchased January 2, 2000

Year	Hours Used	× Rate	= Depreciation	Accumulated Depreciation	Book Value
0					$11,000
2000	15,000	$.20	$3,000	$3,000	8,000
2001	10,000	.20	2,000	5,000	6,000
2002	5,000	.20	1,000	6,000	5,000
2003	3,000	.20	600	6,600	4,400
2004	10,000	.20	2,000	8,600	2,400
2005	7,000	.20	1,400	10,000	1,000

year's Depreciation of $3,000. This means that the machine is probably worth around $8,000 at the end of the first year. However, it does not mean that the machine could necessarily be sold for $8,000 at the end of the first year. It might be sold for more or less than $8,000, or perhaps at $8,000. The Book Value is merely an estimated figure, as is the Depreciation. However, the estimated Depreciation figure of $3,000 for the first year can be legally deducted as an expense on the Income Statement for Depreciation purposes.

At the end of the year 2001, the machine had been used during that year for 10,000 hours; so we multiply 10,000 hours by the previously computed Depreciation rate of $.20 per hour to get $2,000 that year. Looking over to the Accumulated Depreciation column, we see that it already has a $3,000 balance; so we add the additional $2,000 for the year 2001 to get a running balance of $5,000 in the Accumulated Depreciation column. The Book Value at the end of the year 2000 was $8,000; so we now deduct the $2,000 depreciation for the year 2001 to get a running balance of $6,000 for the book value at the end of the year 2001. The Book Value is merely an estimated figure as is the depreciation. However, the estimated Depreciation figure of $2,000 for the second year can be legally deducted as an expense on the Income Statement for Depreciation purposes.

At the end of the year 2002, the machine had been used during that year for 5,000 hours; so we multiply 5,000 hours by the previously computed Depreciation rate of $.20 per hour to get $1,000 that year. Looking over to the Accumulated Depreciation column, we see that it already has a $5,000 balance; so we add the additional $1,000 for the year 2002 to get a running balance of $6,000 in the Accumulated Depreciation column.

The Book Value at the end of the year 2001 was $6,000; so we now deduct the $1,000 Depreciation for the year 2002 to get a running balance of $5,000 for the Book Value at the end of the year 2002. The Book Value is merely an estimated figure, as is the Depreciation. However, the estimated Depreciation figure of $1000 for the third year can be legally deducted as an expense on the Income Statement for Depreciation purposes.

At the end of the year 2003, the machine had been used during that year for 3,000 hours; so we multiply 3,000 hours by the previously computed Depreciation rate of $.20 per hour to get $600 for the year 2003. Looking over to the Accumulated Depreciation column, we see that it already has a $6,000 balance; so we add the additional $600 for the year 2003 to get a running balance of $6,600 in the Accumulated Depreciation column. The Book Value at the end of the year 2002 was $5,000; so we now deduct the $600 Depreciation for the year 2003 to get a running balance of $4,400 for the book value at the end of the year 2003. The book value is merely an estimated figure, as is the Depreciation. However, the estimated Depreciation figure of $600 for the fourth year can be legally deducted as an expense on the Income Statement for Income Tax purposes.

At the end of the year 2004, the machine had been used during that year for 10,000 hours; so we multiply the 10,000 hours by the previously computed Depreciation rate of $.20 per hour to get $2,000 for the year 2004. Looking over to the Accumulated Depreciation column, we see that it already has a $6,600 balance; so we add the additional $2,000 for the year 2004 to get a running balance of $8,600 in the Accumulated Depreciation column. The Book Value at the end of the year 2003 was $4,400; so we now deduct the $2,000 Depreciation for the year 2004 to get a running balance of $2,400 for the book value at the end of the year 2004. The book value is merely an estimated figure, as is the Depreciation. However, the estimated Depreciation figure of $2,000 for the fifth year can be legally deducted as an expense on the Income Statement for Income Tax purposes.

At the end of the year 2005, the machine had been used during that year for 7,000 hours; so we multiply the 7,000 hours by the previously computed Depreciation rate of $.20 per hour to get $1,400 for the year 2005. Looking over to the Accumulated Depreciation column, we see that it already has an $8,600 balance, so we add the additional $1,400 for the year 2005 to get a running balance of $10,000 in the Accumulated Depreciation column. This $10,000 is the total amount to be depreciated as estimated when the machine was originally purchased. The Book Value at the end of the year 2004 was $2,400; we now deduct the $1,400 Depreciation for the year 2005 to get a running balance of $1,000 for the book value at the end of the year 2005. The Book Value of $1,000 is the same as the estimated Residual Value that we used when the machine was originally purchased. This means that the machine has been depreciated as far as possible. Of course, if the machine is still in good working order, it can continue to be used further. Perhaps the original estimates were wrong. But if the original estimates were not wrong and the machine continues to be used after the 50,000 working hours have been run, then no more Depreciation in future years can be taken.

• PROBLEM 12-7

The James Broom Works manufactures and sells brooms. In the year 2000, on January 2, the James Broom Works purchased and installed a broom-making machine at a cost of $11,000. From past experience with this type of Asset, it was estimated that the machine would be able to produce 100,000 brooms during its lifetime and would have a Residual or Scrap Value of $1,000 at the end of that time. Show a Depreciation table for this machine and explain the table.

SOLUTION:

The broom-making machine was purchased for $11,000 and it was estimated that its Residual Value would be $1,000; therefore, the amount to be depreciated is $10,000 ($11,000 − $1,000 = $10,000). From past experience, it is estimated that the broom-making machine will be able to produce 100,000 brooms during its lifetime.

The next step is to compute the amount of Depreciation per broom manufactured. This is done by dividing the amount to be depreciated ($10,000) by the estimated number of brooms the machine would be able to produce during its lifetime (100,000), getting $.10 Depreciation per broom. ($10,000 divided by 100,000 brooms = $.10 Depreciation per broom.)

Table 4
James Broom works
Depreciation Schedule for Broom-Making Machine
Purchased January 2, 2000

Year	Number of Brooms Produced	Depreciation Amount per Broom	Depreciation Amount for the Year	Accumulated- Depreciation	Book Value
					$11,000
2000	20,000	$.10	$2,000	$2,000	$ 9,000
2001	14,000	.10	1,400	3,400	7,600
2002	3,000	.10	300	3,700	7,300
2003	8,500	.10	850	4,550	6,450
2004	10,000	.10	1,000	5,550	5,450
2005	15,000	.10	1,500	7,050	3,950
2006	7,000	.10	700	7,750	3,250
2007	18,000	.10	1,800	9,550	1,450
2008	1,000	.10	100	9,650	1,350
2009	3,500	.10	350	10,000	1,000
Totals	100,000			$10,000	

Looking at the above table, we see that at the time of purchase, on January 2, 2000, the Book Value of the machine is the same as the purchase price of the machine—that is, $11,000.

At the end of the year 2000, the machine, had produced 20,000 brooms; so we multiply the 20,000 brooms by the $.10 Depreciation per broom (previously computed) to get $2,000 Depreciation for the year. Since there had been no previously accumulated Depreciation, the Accumulated Depreciation column also has a figure of $2,000 for the first year's Depreciation. Finally, the Book Value column shows $9,000, the Cost Price of $11,000 less the first year's Depreciation of $2,000. This means that the machine is probably worth around $9,000 at the end of the first year. However, it does not mean that the machine could necessarily be sold for $9,000 at the end of the first year. It might be sold for more or less than $9,000, or perhaps for $9,000. The Book Value is merely an estimated figure, as is the Depreciation. However, the estimated Depreciation figure of $2,000 for the first year can be legally deducted as an expense on the Income Statement for Depreciation purposes.

At the end of the year 2001, the machine has been used to manufacture 14,000 more brooms; so we multiply the 14,000 brooms by the previously computed Depreciation amount of $.10 per broom to get $1,400 Depreciation for that year.

The $1,400 is added to the $2,000 previously accumulated Depreciation to get a balance of $3,400 accumulated Depreciation. Finally, the Book Value column shows $7,600, which is the Cost Price of $11,000 less the accumulated Depreciation of $3,400. This means that the machine is probably worth around $7,600 at the end of the second year. However, it does not mean that the machine could necessarily be sold for $7,600 at that time. It might be sold for more or less than $7,600, or perhaps for $7,600. The Book Value is merely an estimated figure, as is the Depreciation. However, the estimated Depreciation figure of $1,400 for the second year can be legally deducted as an expense on the Income Statement for Depreciation and for Income Tax purposes.

At the end of the year 2002, the machine has been used to manufacture 3,000 more brooms; so we multiply the 3,000 brooms by the previously computed Depreciation amount of $.10 per broom to get $300 Depreciation for that year. The $300 is added to the $3,400 previously accumulated Depreciation to get a balance of $3,700 accumulated Depreciation. Finally, the Book Value column shows $7,300, which is the Cost Price of $11,000 less the accumulated Depreciation of $3,700. This means that the machine is probably worth around $7,300 at the end of the third year. However it does not mean that the machine could necessarily be sold for $7,300 at that time. It might be sold for more or less than $7,300, or perhaps for $7,300. The Book Value is merely an estimated figure as is the Depreciation. However, the estimated Depreciation figure, of $300 for the third year can be legally deducted as an expense on the Income Statement for Income Tax purposes.

At the end of the year 2003, the machine has been used to manufacture 8,500 more brooms; so we multiply the 8,500 brooms by the previously computed Depreciation amount of $.10 per broom to get $850 Depreciation for that year. The $850 is added to the $3,700 previously accumulated Depreciation to get a balance of $4,550 accumulated Depreciation. Finally, the Book Value column shows $6,450, which is the cost price of $11,000 less the accumulated Depreciation of $4,550. This means that the machine is probably worth around $6,450 at the end of the fourth year. However, it does not mean that the machine could necessarily be sold for $6,450 at that time. It might be sold for more or less than $6,450, or perhaps for $6,450. The Book Value is merely an estimated figure, as is the Depreciation. However, the estimated Depreciation figure of $850 for the fourth year can be legally deducted as an expense on the Income Statement for Income Tax purposes.

At the end of the year 2004, the machine has been used to manufacture 10,000 more brooms; so we multiply the 10,000 brooms by the previously computed Depreciation amount of $.10 per broom to get $1,000 Depreciation for that year. The $1,000 is added to the $4,550 previously accumulated Depreciation to get a balance of $5,550 accumulated Depreciation. Finally, the Book Value column shows $5,450, which is the Cost Price of $11,000 less the accumulated Depreciation of $5,550. This means that the machine is probably worth around $5,450 at the end of the fifth year. However, it does not mean that the machine could necessarily be sold for $5,450 at that time. It might be sold for more or less than $5,450, or perhaps for $5,450. The Book Value is merely an estimated figure, as is the Depreciation. However, the estimated Depreciation figure of $1,000 for the fifth year can be legally deducted as an expense on the Income Statement for Income Tax purposes.

At the end of the year 2005, the machine has been used to manufacture 15,000 more brooms; so we multiply the 15,000 brooms by the previously computed Depreciation amount of $.10 per broom to get $1,500 Depreciation for that year. The $1,500 is added to the $5,550 previously accumulated Depreciation to get a balance of $7,050 accumulated Depreciation. Finally, the Book Value column shows $3,950, which is the Cost Price of $11,000 less the accumulated Depreciation of $7,050. This means that the machine is probably worth around $3,950 at the end of the sixth year. However, it does not mean that the machine could necessarily be sold for $3,950 at that time. It might be sold for more or less than $3,950, or perhaps for $3,950. The Book Value is merely an estimated figure, as is the Depreciation. However, the estimated Depreciation figure of $1,500 for the sixth year can be legally deducted as an expense on the Income Statement for Income Tax purposes.

At the end of the year 2006, the machine has been used to manufacture 7,000 more brooms; so we multiply the 7,000 brooms by the previously computed Depreciation amount of $.10 per broom to get $700 Depreciation for that year. The $700 is added to the $7,050 previously accumulated Depreciation to get a balance of $7,750 accumulated Depreciation. Finally, the Book Value column shows $3,250, which is the Cost Price of $11,000 less the accumulated Depreciation of $7,750. This means that the machine is probably worth around $3,250 at the end of the seventh year. However, it does not mean that the machine could necessarily be sold for $3,250 at that time. It might be sold for more or less than $3,250, or perhaps for $3,250. The Book Value is merely an estimated figure, as is the Depreciation. However, the estimated Depreciation figure of $700 for the seventh year can be legally deducted as an expense on the Income Statement for Income Tax purposes.

At the end of the year 2007, the machine has been used to manufacture 18,000 more brooms; so we multiply the 18,000 brooms by the previously computed Depreciation amount of $.10 per broom to get $1,800 Depreciation for that year. The $1,800 is added to the $7,750 previously accumulated Depreciation to get a balance of $9,550 accumulated Depreciation. Finally, the Book Value column shows $1,450, which is the Cost Price of $11,000 less the accumulated Depreciation of $9,550. This means that the machine is probably worth around $1,450 at the end of the eighth year. However, it does not mean that the machine could necessarily be sold for $1,450 at that time. It might be sold for more or less than $1,450, or perhaps for $1,450. The Book Value is merely an estimated figure, as is the Depreciation. However, the estimated Depreciation figure of $1,800 for the eighth year can be legally deducted as an expense on the Income Statement for Income Tax purposes.

At the end of the year 2008, the machine has been used to manufacture, 1,000 more brooms; so we multiply the 1,000 brooms by the previously computed Depreciation amount of $.10 per broom to get $100 Depreciation for that year. The $100 is added to the $9,550 previously accumulated Depreciation to get a balance of $9,650 accumulated Depreciation. Finally, the Book Value column shows $1,350, which is the Cost Price of $11,000 less the accumulated Depreciation of $9,650. This means that the machine is probably worth around $1,350 at the end of the ninth year. However, it does not mean that the machine could necessarily be sold for $1,350 at that time. It might be sold for more or less than $1,350, or perhaps for $1,350. The book value is merely an estimated figure, as is the Depreciation. However, the estimated Depreciation figure of $100 for the ninth year can be legally deducted as an expense on the Income Statement for Income Tax Purposes.

At the end of the year 2009, the machine has been used to manufacture 3,500 more brooms; so we multiply the 3,500 brooms by the previously computed Depreciation amount of $.10 per broom; to get $350 Depreciation for that year. The $350 is added to the $9,650 previously accumulated depreciation to get a balance of $10,000 accumulated Depreciation. This $10,000 is the total amount to be Depreciated, which is the $11,000 cost of the machine less the $1,000 Residual Value of the machine ($11,000 − $1,000 = $10,000). The balance of the accumulated Depreciation account is $10,000 at the end of the tenth year, in this case, December 31, 2009; and all the allowed Depreciation has been accumulated. Finally, the Book Value column shows $1,000, which is the Cost Price of $11,000 less the accumulated Depreciation of $10,000. This means that the machine is probably worth around $1,000 at the end of the tenth year. However, it does not mean that the machine could necessarily be sold for $1,000 at that time. It might be sold for more or less than $1,000, or perhaps exactly for $1,000. The Book Value is merely an estimated figure, as is the Depreciation. However, the estimated Depreciation figure of $350 for the tenth year can be legally deducted as an expense on the Income Statement for Income Tax Purposes. The Book Value at the end of the tenth year shows $1,000, which is the same amount as the estimated Scrap Value ($1,000). The Depreciation is at an end for this machine. Looking at the column entitled, "Number of Brooms Produced," we add up all the figures in that column and derive a total of 100,000 brooms, which is the total number of brooms that we originally estimated could be produced during the life of the machine.

But what if the machine is still in working order and can produce more brooms? The accountant here has two options: he or she can stop depreciating, or he or she can continue depreciating the remaining Scrap Value. If the accountant chooses the former option, there will be no more Depreciation Expense for the following year (in this case, the year 2010). If the accountant chooses the latter option, he can still depreciate the remaining $1,000, in this case 10,000 brooms. (10,000 brooms times $.10 Depreciation per broom = $1,000.) If the latter option is chosen and the extra $1,000 is depreciated, the Book Value of the machine drops to zero and the accountant can show no loss when the machine is finally scrapped. (On the other hand, if the accountant chooses the former option and does not depreciate the extra $1,000, this $1,000 could be debited as a Loss Expense when the machine is finally discarded.)

• PROBLEM 12-8

The Hamlin Car Rental Agency purchased a fleet of 5 rental cars for a total price of $100,000. It is estimated that after using these cars for a period of 4 years, there will be no Residual Value. Since these business cars depreciate the most rapidly during their first year of use, it has been decided to use the Sum-of-Years-Digits method to depreciate these cars. Set up a Depreciation schedule for these cars and explain the schedule.

SOLUTION:

The first step is to deduct the Residual Value from the cost in order to determine the amount to be depreciated. Since, in this case, there is no Residual Value, the amount to be depreciated ($100,000) is the same as the Cost Price of the fleet ($100,000).

The next step is to determine the fraction to multiply by the total amount to be depreciated. The denominator of the fraction is determined by the length of estimated life of the Asset (in this case, the length of life of the fleet of cars—4 years). This is done by adding the length of life (4 years) plus the length of life less one (3 years) plus the length of life less 2 (2 years) and so on, as follows in this case: 4 + 3 + 2 + 1 = 10. Thus, the denominator of the fraction is 10. The numerator of the first year's fraction is the length of life (estimated) of the Asset (in this case 4 years). The numerator for the second year is the length of life of the Asset less one (3 years). The numerator for the third year is the length of life of the Asset less 2 (2 years). The numerator for the fourth year is the length of life of the Asset less 3 (1 year) as follows:

Fraction for the first year of Asset life:	4/10
Fraction for the second year of Asset life:	3/10
Fraction for the third year of Asset life:	2/10
Fraction for the fourth year of Asset life:	1/10

Each of these fractions are multiplied by the **Amount To Be Depreciated**, which in this case (since there is no Residual Value) is the Cost Price of the fleet of rental cars ($100,000).

The Depreciation schedule follows:

Table 5
Hamlin Car Rental Agency
Depreciation Schedule for Fleet of Five Cars
Purchased January 2, 2000

Sum-of-Years-Digits Method of Depreciation

Year	Fraction	Amount to be Depreciated	Yearly Depreciation	Accumulated Depreciation	Book Value
					$100,000
2000	4/10 × $100,000	$40,000	$40,000	60,000	
2001	3/10 × $100,000	$30,000	70,000	30,000	
2002	2/10 × $100,000	$20,000	90,000	10,000	
2003	1/10 × $100,000	$10,000	100,000	0	

At the beginning of the year 2000, the 5 business cars are purchased for $100,000. These must be business cars, since personal cars cannot legally be depreciated.

During the year 2000, 4/10 of the amount to be depreciated is used as the yearly Depreciation: in this case, $40,000. Since there was no previously accumulated Depreciation, this yearly Depreciation figure of $40,000 is also entered as the balance of the Accumulated Depreciation account at the end of the year 2000. The Book Value has dropped to $60,000 ($100,000 original cost $40,000 first-year Depreciation = $60,000 book value as of December 31, 2000).

During the year 2001, 3/10 of the amount to be depreciated ($100,000) is used as the yearly Depreciation: in this case, $30,000. Since the previous balance of the Accumulated Depreciation account was $40,000, this second year's Depreciation amount of $30,000 is added to the $40,000 to make a running balance at the end of the year 2001 in the Accumulated Depreciation account of $70,000. In the final Book Value column, the Book Value has dropped to $30,000 ($100,000 Cost Price less $70,000 balance in the accumulated Depreciation account = $30,000 Book Value at the end of year 2001).

During the year 2002, 2/10 of the amount to be depreciated ($100,000) is used as the yearly Depreciation: in this case, $20,000. Since the previous balance of the Accumulated Depreciation account was $70,000, this third year's Depreciation amount of $20,000 is added to the $70,000 to make a running balance at the end of the year 2002 in the

Accumulated Depreciation account of $90,000. In the final Book Value column, the Book Value has dropped to $10,000 ($100,000 Cost Price less $90,000 balance in the accumulated Depreciation account = $10,000 Book Value at the end of the year 2002).

During the year 2003, 1/10 of the amount to be depreciated ($100,000) is used as the yearly Depreciation: in this case, $10,000. Since the previous balance of the Accumulated Depreciation account was $90,000, this fourth year's Depreciation amount of $10,000 is added to the $90,000 to make a running balance at the end of the year 2003 in the Accumulated Depreciation Account of $100,000. This final balance of $100,000 is equal to the Purchase Price of the fleet of trucks; so this shows that in the four years (2000 – 2004) the entire cost of the fleet of trucks has been depreciated. In the final Book Value column, the Book Value has dropped to 0 ($100,000 cost price less $100,000 Accumulated Depreciation). ($100,000 – $100,000 = 0).

• PROBLEM 12-9

The Brown Car and Truck Rental Agency purchased a truck for $21,000. From past experience, it was determined that this truck would have a business life of five years and a Residual or Scrap Value at the end of that time of $1,000. Since trucks depreciate the most rapidly during their first year of use, it was decided to use the Sum-of-Years-Digits method of Depreciation. Set up a Depreciation schedule for this truck and explain the schedule.

SOLUTION:

The first step is to deduct the Residual Value from the cost of the truck in order to determine the amount to be depreciated. In this case, the Residual Value has been determined to be $1,000 and the cost of the truck was $21,000. So the $1,000 was subtracted from the $21,000 to get the amount to be depreciated—in this case, $20,000 ($21,000 – $1,000 = $20,000).

The next step is to determine the fraction to multiply by the total amount to be depreciated. The denominator of the fraction is determined by the length of estimated life of the Asset (in this case, the length of life of the truck—5 years). This is done by adding the length of life (5 years) plus the length of life less one (4 years) plus the length of life less 2 (3 years) and so on, as follows in this case: 5 + 4 + 3 + 2 + 1 = 15. Thus, the denominator of the fraction is 15. The numerator of the first year's fraction is the length of life (estimated) of the Asset (in this cas,e 5 years). The numerator for the second year is the length of life of the Asset less one (4 years). The numerator for the third year is the length of life of the Asset less 2 (3 years). The numerator for the fourth year is the length of life of the Asset less 3 (2 years). The numerator for the fourth year is the length of life of the Asset less 4 (1 year) as follows:

Fraction for the first year of Asset life: 5/15

Fraction for the second year of Asset life: 4/15

Fraction for the third year of Asset life: 3/15

Fraction for the fourth year of Asset life: 2/15

Fraction for the fifth year of Asset life: 1/15

Each of the fractions are multiplied by the Amount To Be Depreciated, which in this case is $20,000, the Cost Price less the Residual Value ($21,000 – $1,000 = $20,000).

The table follows:

Table 6
Brown Car and Truck Rental Agency
Depreciation Schedule for Business Truck
Purchased January 2, 2000

Sum-of-Years-Digits Method of Depreciation

Year	Fraction	Amount to be Depreciated	Yearly Depreciation	Accumulated Depreciation	Book Value
					$21,000
2000	5/15	$20,000	$6,667	$6,667	14,333
2001	4/15	20,000	5,333	12,000	9,000
2002	3/15	20,000	4,000	16,000	5,000
2003	2/15	20,000	2,667	18,667	2,333
2004	1/15	20,000	1.333	20,000	1,000

The Brown Car and Truck Rental Agency purchased a business truck for $21,000. At the time, it was determined that the useful life of the truck would be about 5 years, and that at the end of that time its Residual or Scrap Value would be $1,000.

During the year 2000, the first year of use, the truck is figured to depreciate 5/15 of $20,000 or $6,667. It will be noted that the greatest amount of yearly Depreciation is in the first year of the truck's life; and thereafter, the dollar amount of Depreciation drops. Since there was no previous accumulated Depreciation, this $6,667 figure is carried over to the Accumulated Depreciation column. The Book Value at the end of the year 2000 is $14,333, computed as follows: $21,000 cost less $6,667 = $14,333 Book Value. This does not necessarily mean that the truck could be sold for that amount of money.

During the year 2001, the second year of use, the truck is figured to depreciate 4/15 of $20,000, or $5,333. It will be noted that the second greatest amount of yearly Depreciation is taken in this second year of the truck's use. The previous balance of the Accumulated Depreciation account was $6,667; so the $5,333 latest year's Depreciation is added to this to make a running balance of $12,000 in the Accumulated Depreciation account at the end of the year 2001. The Book Value at the end of the year 2001 is $9,000, figured by deducting the balance of the Accumulated Depreciation Account ($12,000) from the $21,000 original cost ($21,000 – $12,000 = $9,000).

During the year 2002, the third year of use, the truck is figured to depreciate 3/15 of $20,000, or $4,000. The previous balance of the Accumulated Depreciation Account was $12,000; so the $4,000 latest year's Depreciation is added to this to make a running balance of $16,000 in the Accumulated Depreciation Account at the end of the year 2002. The Book Value at the end of the year 2002 is $5,000, figured by deducting the balance of the Accumulated Depreciation Account ($16,000) from the $21,000 original cost ($21,000 – $16,000 = $5,000).

During the year 2003, the fourth year of use, the truck is figured to depreciate 2/15 of $20,000, or $2,667. The previous balance of the Accumulated Depreciation Account was $16,000; so the $2,667 latest year's Depreciation is added to this to make a running balance of $18,667 in the Accumulated Depreciation Account at the end of the year 2003. The Book Value at the end of the year 2003 is $2,333, figured by deducting the balance of the Accumulated Depreciation account ($18,667) from the $21,000 original cost ($21,000 – $18,667 = $2,333).

During the year 2004, the fifth year of use, the truck is figured to depreciate 1/15 of $20,000, or $1,333. The previous balance of the Accumulated Depreciation Account was $18,6675; so the $1,333 latest year's Depreciation is added to this to make a running balance of $20,000 in the Accumulated Depreciation Account at the end of the year 2004. This $20,000 is the total amount set at the purchase date for the Depreciation; so the truck should not be depreciated beyond the 5th year in this case. The Book Value at the end of the year 2004 is $1,000, figured by deducting the balance of the Accumulated Depreciation account $20,000 from the $21,000 original cost ($21,000 − $20,000 = $1,000). The Book Value has thus been brought down to $1,000, which is also the Residual or Scrap value of the truck.

If the truck is still usable, the accountant has two choices: he or she may continue to depreciate this $1,000, or he or she may continue to use the truck without depreciating further. If the $1,000 is depreciated out, then there can be no Loss Expense debited when the truck is finally junked. However, if the Depreciation had been stopped at the end of the fifth year, then when the truck is junked, a Loss Expense can be taken for the Scrap Value, in this case, $1,000.

• PROBLEM 12–10

The Hamlin Car Rental Agency purchased a fleet of 5 rental cars for a total price of $100,000. It is estimated that after using these cars for a period of 4 years, there would be no Residual or Scrap Value. Since these business cars depreciate the most rapidly during their first year of use, it has been decided to use the Double-Declining-Balance Method to depreciate these cars. Set up a Depreciation schedule for these cars and explain the schedule.

SOLUTION:

The first step is to divide the number of years of expected life of the Asset into 100 (the 100 standing for 100%). Thus, 100 divided by four gives 25 (or 25%). The law allows the accountant to double his figure. There is no good reason for this except that this is a legal way of allowing more Depreciation during the first year of use. (Thus, doubling 25% we get 50%.) (25% × 2 = 50.) Each year the balance (previous balance) or (Declining Balance) is used as the basis and multiplied by 50% to get the next year's Depreciation as follows in the upcoming table:

Table 6
Hamlin Car Rental Agency
Depreciation Schedule for Fleet of Five Cars
Purchased January 2, 2000

Double-Declining-Balance Method of Depreciation

Year	Previously Determined Percentage		Previous Balance	Yearly Depreciation	Accumulated Depreciation	Book Value
						$100,000
2000	50%	×	$100,000	$50,000	$50,000	50,000
2001	50%	×	50,000	25,000	75,000	25,000
2002	50%	×	25,000	12,500	87,500	12,500
2003	50%	×	12,500	6,250	93,750	6,250
2004	50%	×	6,250	3,125	96,875	3,125

At the beginning of the year 2000, the 5 business cars are purchased for $100,000. These must be business cars, since personal cars cannot legally be depreciated.

The percentage to be used in the Double-Declining-Balance method for 4 years of Depreciation is 50% ($100,000 Purchase Price divided by 4 years = 25) (25 × 2 = 50).

In the Double-Declining-Balance method, the first year the 50% is multiplied by the original cost (in this case, $100,000), giving a first-year's Depreciation of $50,000. Since the Accumulated Depreciation Account had no previous balance, this first-year's Depreciation of $50,000 also becomes the balance of the Accumulated Depreciation account ($50,000). For the Book Value at the end of the first year (in this case, the year 2000), the $50,000 balance in the Accumulated Depreciation Account is subtracted from the previous balance in the Book Value column (in this case the original purchase price of $100,000) to get $50,000.

During the second year of use, in this case the year 2001, we multiply the 50% by the book value of the previous year (in this case $50,000) to get the yearly Depreciation for the second year ($25,000) ($50,000 × 50% = $25,000). Then the $25,000 Depreciation for the second year is added to the previous balance in the Accumulated Depreciation column ($50,000) to get $75,000 for the balance in the Accumulated Depreciation column at the end of the second year (the year 2001) ($25,000 + $50,000 = $75,000). In order to determine the Book Value at the end of the second year, we subtract the second year's Depreciation of $25,000 from the previous book value balance of $50,000 to get $25,000—the new Book Value at the end of the second year of use.

During the third year of use, in this case the year 2002, we multiply the 50% by the book value of the previous year (in this case $25,000) to get the yearly Depreciation for the third year ($12,500) $25,000 × 50% = $12,500). Then the $12,500 Depreciation for the third year is added to the previous balance in the Accumulated Depreciation column ($75,000) to get $87,500 for the balance in the Accumulated Depreciation column at the end of the third year (the year 2002) ($12,500 + $75,000 = $87,500). In order to determine the Book Value at the end of the third year, we subtract the third year's Depreciation of $12,500 from the previous Book Value balance of $25,000 to get $12,500—the new Book Value at the end of the third year of use.

During the fourth year of use, in this case the year 2003, we multiply the 50% by the Book Value of the previous year (in this case $12,500) to get the yearly Depreciation for the fourth year ($6,500) ($12,500 × 50% = $6,500). Then the $6,250 for the fourth year is added to the previous balance in the Accumulated Depreciation column ($87,500) to get $93,750 for the balance in the Accumulated Depreciation column at the end of the fourth year (the year 2003) ($6,250 + $87,500 = $93,750). In order to determine the Book Value at the end of the fourth year, we subtract the fourth year's Depreciation of $6,250 from the previous Book Value balance of $12,500 to get $6,250—the new Book Value at the end of the fourth year of use.

Deducting 50% of the previous year's Depreciation each year will never get the Depreciation down to zero. The table goes on for a fifth year; and, certainly, if the rental cars are still usable the fifth year, it would be legal to depreciate them $6,250 as the table shows. However, if the cars are no longer serviceable, the Book Value figure could be debited as a loss in the year the cars are junked.

• PROBLEM 12-11

The Smith Car Rental Company purchased a fleet of cars for $210,000 and decided to depreciate them over a period of five years, using the Double-Declining-Balance Method, with an estimated Residual Value at the end of five years of $16,230. The Double-Declining-Balance Method was chosen since this legally gives the largest Depreciation in the early years and cars do their greatest amount of Depreciating in early years. Make a Depreciation table and explain it.

SOLUTION:

Table 7
Smith Car Rental Company
Depreciation Schedule for a Fleet of Cars
Purchased January 2, 2000

Double-Declining-Balance Method of Depreciation

Year	Previously Determined Percentage		Previous Balance	Yearly Depreciation	Accumulated Depreciation	Book Value
						$210,000
2000	40%	×	$210,000	$84,000	$84,000	126,000
2001	40%	×	126,000	50,400	134,400	75,600
2002	40%	×	75,600	30,240	164,640	45,360
2003	40%	×	45,360	18,144	182,784	27,216
2004	40%	×	27,216	10,886	193,670	16,230

The Depreciation Percentage (in this case 40%) is computed as follows: divide the 5 years of estimated life of the cars into 100% to get 20%. Since the law allows us to double this, we get 40% (20% × 2 = 40%). The original Purchase Price of $210,000 is used as the Book Value the first year. In this Double-Declining-Balance method, we do not deduct the Residual Value, since the method never gets the book value down to zero. Thus, the Book Value at the end of the 5th year, in this case is the real Residual Value.

In the first year that the fleet of cars is used, in this case the year 2000, 40% of the original cost of $210,000 is computed to be $84,000 ($210,000 × 40% = $84,000). This figure is placed in the Yearly Depreciation column. Since there was no previous figure in the Accumulated Depreciation column, this figure of $84,000 is also put down in that column. Then $84,000 is deducted from the cost of $210,000 to arrive at the Book Value at the end of the first year of $126,000.

In the second year that the fleet of cars is used, in this case the year 2001, 40% of the previous Book Value of $126,000 is computed to be $50,400 (40% × $126,000 = $50,400). This is the Depreciation for the second year, and the figure is placed in the Yearly Depreciation column. Then the $50,400 Depreciation for the second year is added to the previous balance in the Accumulated Depreciation column (in this case $84,000) to arrive at $134,400, the accumulated Depreciation at the end of the second year. Then the $134,400 is deducted from the original price of $210,000 to arrive at $75,600, the Book Value of the fleet at the end of the second year ($210,000-$134,400 = $75,600).

In the third year that the fleet of cars is used, in this case the year 2002, 40% of the previous Book Value of $75,600 is computed to be $30,240 (40% of $75,600 = $30,240). This is the Depreciation for the third year, and the figure is placed in the Yearly Depreciation column. Then the $30,240 Depreciation for the third year is added to the previous balance in the Accumulated Depreciation column (in this case $134,400) to arrive at $164,640, the accumulated Depreciation at the end of the third year. Then the $164,640 is deducted from the original price of $210,000 to arrive at $45,360, the Book Value of the fleet at the end of the third year ($210,000 − $164,640 = $45,360).

In the fourth year that the fleet of cars is used, in this case the year 2003, 40% of the previous book value of $45,360 is computed to be $18,144 (40% of $45,360 = $18,144). This is the Depreciation for the fourth year, and the figure is placed in the Yearly Depreciation column. Then the $18,144 Depreciation for the fourth year is added to the previous balance in the Accumulated Depreciation column (in this case $164,640) to arrive at $182,784, the accumulated Depreciation at the end of the fourth year. Then the $182,784 is deducted from the original price of $210,000 to arrive at $27,216, the Book Value of the fleet at the end of the fourth year ($210,000 − $182,784 = $27,216).

In the fifth year that the fleet of cars is used, in this case the year 2004, 40% of the previous Book Value of $27,216 is computed to be $10,886 (40% of $27,216 = $10,886). This is the Depreciation for the fifth year, and the figure is placed in the Yearly Depreciation column. Then the

$10,886 Depreciation for the fifth year is added to the previous balance in the Accumulated Depreciation column (in this case $182,784) to arrive at $193,670, the accumulated Depreciation at the end of the fifth year. Then the $193,670 is deducted from the original price of $210,000 to arrive at $16,230, the Book Value of the fleet at the end of the fifth year ($210,000 – $193,670 = $16,230). Since this is the end of the fifth year and it was originally estimated that the fleet would last only five years, the $16,230 Book Value at the end of the fifth year is also the Residual or Scrap Value. If the fleet is junked at the end of the fifth year, the Scrap Value of $16,230 could be debited as a Loss.

• PROBLEM 12–12

What is MACRS depreciation?

SOLUTION:

MACRS means Modified Accelerated Cost Recovery System. Cost Recovery System is a fancy use of words meaning Depreciation. Accelerated means that the user gets faster Depreciation in the first years of life of the property. The term, Modified, is used because the Income Tax law of 1986 modified or changed the previous ACRS or accelerated system that was in use for a few years prior to 1986. The MACRS rules set up a required lifetime for the property, which is usually shorter than the actual life of the property. The method is faster than the Straight-Line method, and there is no Salvage Value. For instance, a landlord having rental housing lasting between 20 and 25 years would be able to call this 15-year property and depreciate it in 15 years using the 150% Declining Balance method of Depreciation.

• PROBLEM 12–13

What is the half-year convention, and why is it used in MACRS depreciation?

SOLUTION:

The term Convention in this context means Rule. So the half-year rule means that only half of the Depreciation can be deducted in the year that the Asset is purchased and only half of the Depreciation is deducted in the year in which the Asset is sold or junked. The 1986 Income Tax law requires the half-year convention to be used if the MACRS system of Depreciation is chosen; however, this half-year convention is worked into the tax tables so that if one uses the tax Depreciation tables, this convention will be taken care of automatically. The tax Depreciation tables are published by the Internal Revenue Service.

• PROBLEM 12–14

When one of the Accelerated Depreciation methods is used, the government allows the taxpayer to switch over to the Straight-Line method of Depreciation in the year in which the Straight-Line Depreciation is higher than the Accelerated method. Why do most people switch over at this time?

SOLUTION:

The MACRS depreciation methods allow greater amounts of Depreciation during the first years of Asset life, but these diminish greatly in the later years of Asset life. About halfway through the Asset life, the yearly Depreciation figures reach a point where the Straight-Line method of Depreciation allows faster Depreciation than does the Accelerated method. So the government allows the taxpayer using the Accelerated method to switch to the Straight-Line method at this time if he or she wishes; thus, the taxpayer supposedly gets the best of both possible worlds.

• PROBLEM 12-15

On January 2, 2000, the James Computer Company purchased a computer for $4,000 and decided to depreciate using the Modified Accelerated Cost Recovery System of Depreciation. Make a Depreciation schedule for this and explain it.

SOLUTION:

Under the Modified Accelerated Cost Recovery System, the government rules determine the number of years of life of the property and the percentage of Depreciation. For instance, computers with an estimated life of 4 years, but less than 10 years, are classed as 5-year property and are to be depreciated by the 200% (Double) Declining Balance method using the half-year convention with the following Depreciation percentages:

Year 1	20%
Year 2	32%
Year 3	19.2%
Year 4	11.52% (moving to Straight-Line Depreciation)
Year 5	11.52%
Year 6	5.76%

Why are there 6 years of Depreciation listed when it is so-called "5-year property?" Because the half-year convention allows only half of the year's Depreciation the first year, and a half after the 5th year, which then goes into the 6th year. For instance, since it is 5-year property, we divide 5 into 100% to get 20%. Then, since it is the Double-Declining-Balance Method of Depreciation, we double the 20% to get 40% (20% × 2 = 40%). So you would think the first year would get 40% Depreciation, but since the half year convention is being used, we then take half of 40% to get 20% the first year (1/2 of 40% = 20%).

On January 2, 2000, the computer was purchased by the James Computer Company for $4,000. Under the Internal Revenue Service Schedule for MACRS for 5-year property, using the half-year convention, the Depreciation for the first year, in this case the year 2000, is 20%. So we multiply the 20% by the $4,000 Purchase Price to get $800 Depreciation the first year. The reason the first-year Depreciation in this case is less than the second year Depreciation is because under the half-year convention only half the proper Depreciation is allowed the first and last years of

Table 8
James Computer Company
Depreciation Schedule for Computer
Purchased January 2, 2000

Modified Accelerated Cost Recovery System of Depreciation
Using the Half-Year Convention

Year	MACRS %	Yearly Depreciation	Accumulated- Depreciation	Book Value
				$4,000
2000	20% × $4,000 =	$ 800	$ 800	3,200
2001	32% × $3,200 =	1,024	1,824	2,176
2002	19.2% × 2,176 =	417.79	2,241.79	1,758.21
2003	11.52% × 1,758.21 =	202.55	2,444.34	1,555.66
2004	11.52% × 1,555.66 =	179.21	2,623.55	1,376.45
2005	5.76% × 1,376.45 =	79.28	2,702.83	1,297.17

property life. Since the Accumulated Depreciation column had no previous balance, the $800 first-year's Depreciation is carried over to the Accumulated Depreciation column. Then the $800 balance in the Accumulated Depreciation is subtracted from the original cost of $4,000 to get the $3,200 Book Value at the end of the first year.

For the second year, in this case the year 2001, the assigned Depreciation is 32%. So we multiply the 32% by the $3,200 previous Book Value to get $1,024 Depreciation for the second year. This $1,024 Depreciation for the second year is then added to the previous balance of the Accumulated Depreciation Account ($800) to get $1,824, the balance of the Accumulated Depreciation column at the end of the second year. The $1,824 is then subtracted from the Purchase Price of $4,000 to get $2,176, the Book Value of the computer at the end of the second year.

For the third year, in this case the year 2002, the assigned Depreciation is 19.2%. So we multiply the 19.2% by the $2,176 previous Book Value to get $417.79 Depreciation for the third year. This $417.79 Depreciation for the third year is then added to the previous balance of the Accumulated Depreciation account ($1,824) to get $2,241.79, the balance of the Accumulated Depreciation column at the end of the third year. The $2,241.79 is then subtracted from the Purchase Price of $4,000 to get $1,758.21, the Book Value of the computer at the end of the third year.

For the fourth year, in this case the year 2003, the assigned Depreciation is 11.52%. So we multiply the 11.52% by the $1,758.21 previous Book Value to get $202.55 Depreciation for the fourth year. This $202.55 Depreciation for the fourth year is then added to the previous balance of the Accumulated Depreciation Account ($2,241.79) to get $2,444.34, the balance of the Accumulated Depreciation column at the end of the fourth year. The $2,444.34 is then subtracted from the Purchase Price of $4,000 to get $1,555.66, the Book Value of the computer at the end of the fourth year.

For the fifth year, in this case the year 2004, the assigned Depreciation is 11.52% The reason it is the same percentage (11.52%) as the year before is that we have now switched to the Straight-Line method of Depreciation where all the percentages are the same each year. So we multiply the 11.52% by the $1,555.66 previous book value to get $179.21 Depreciation for the fifth year. This $179.21 Depreciation for the fifth year is then added to the previous balance of the Accumulated Depreciation Account ($2,444.34) to get $2,623.55, the balance of the Accumulated Depreciation column at the end of the fifth year. The $2,623.55 is then subtracted from the Purchase Price of $4,000 to get $1,376.45, the Book Value of the computer at the end of the fifth year.

For the sixth year, in this case the year 2005, the assigned Depreciation is 5.76%. This is half the 11.52% Depreciation of the previous year. The reason for this is the half-year convention, and on this last year we get to deduct only half as much as we did in the previous year.

So we multiply the 5.76% by the $1,376.45 previous Book Value to get $79.28 Depreciation for the sixth year. This $79.28 Depreciation for the sixth year is then added to the previous balance of the Accumulated Depreciation Account ($2,623.55) to get $2,702.83, the balance of the Accumulated Depreciation column at the end of the sixth year. This $2,702.83 is then subtracted from the Purchase Price of $4,000 to get $1,297.17, the Book Value of the computer at the end of the sixth year. This $1,297.17 is also considered to be the Scrap Value.

• PROBLEM 12-16

The Promer Oil Company purchased 50 acres of Wyoming Land because their officials said oil drilling prospects appeared excellent in that location. The cost of the Land was $25,000. What entry should be made on the books of the Promer Oil Company and why?

SOLUTION:

Acquisition Cost, Undeveloped Property	25,000	
Cash		25,000

Acquisition Cost, Undeveloped Property refers to the Asset Land and other costs involved in the purchase of Land, such as title search and expenses of recording land at the court house. Cash is credited to show the cash outflow when this property was purchased.

• PROBLEM 12-17

The Promer Oil Company purchased 50 acres of Wyoming Land because their officials said oil drilling prospects appeared excellent in that location. The cost of the Land was $25,000. They purchased the Land, debiting the account Acquisition Cost, Undeveloped Property for $25,000 and crediting the account Cash for $25,000. Later they decided there was no oil in the vicinity and decided not to drill. They had to sell the Land for $20,000. What entry would Promer Oil Company make on its books at this time?

SOLUTION:

Cash	20,000	
Loss on Sale of Undeveloped Land	5,000	
Acquisition Cost, Undeveloped Property		25,000

Since they were receiving $20,000 Cash for the sale of this Land, they debited Cash for $20,000. They were giving up the Land that they had previously purchased for $25,000; so the account Acquisition Cost, Undeveloped Property was credited for $25,000. The difference of $5,000 is debited to the Expense Account entitled Loss On Sale Of Undeveloped Land. This Expense Account can legally be deducted in the Income Statement and thus lowers the total Net Income.

• PROBLEM 12-18

The Promer Oil Company purchased 100 acres of Utah Land because their officials said oil drilling prospects appeared excellent in that location. The cost of the Land was $30,000. The costs of searching the Land for the proper drilling location and actually drilling the oil well were $30,000. Intangible Development Costs such as erecting the oil well itself were $3,000. This is a total of $63,000 ($30,000 Land + $30,000 Drilling Costs + $3,000 Intangible Development Costs = $63,000).

How would this be shown on the books of the Promer Oil Company?

SOLUTION:

Land 30,000		
Drilling Costs	30,000	
Intangible Development Costs	3,000	
Cash		63,000

Land, Drilling Costs, and Intangible Development Costs could all be considered Assets; so these three Asset accounts would all be debited and Cash would be credited for the $63,000, since that much cash is being expended.

• PROBLEM 12-19

The Promer Oil Company purchased 100 acres of Utah Land because their officials said oil drilling prospects appeared excellent in that location. The cost of the Land was $30,000. The costs of searching the Land for the proper drilling location and actually drilling the oil well were $30,000. Intangible Development Costs such as erecting the oil well itself were $3,000. This is a total of $63,000. Engineers estimated that there were approximately 1,000,000 gallons of oil in the field. During the first year,10,000 gallons of oil were extracted. What entry should be made on the books for the Depletion Expense?

SOLUTION:

2000		($ in dollars)
December 31 Depletion Expense	630	
Accumulated Depletion		630

The Units of Production method of depletion is the chief method used in depleting natural resources, such as oil. The cost of the oil well has been determined to be $63,000 as follows: Land $30,000; Drilling Costs $30,000; and Intangible Development Costs $3,000—or a total of $63,000. The officials and engineers have estimated that the oil field contains approximately 1,000,000 gallons of oil.

The $63,000 costs are divided by the 1,000,000 approximate gallons of oil in the field to get $.063 depletion per gallon. During the first year, 10,000 gallons of oil were extracted from the ground; so we multiply the 10,000 gallons by the $.063 depletion per gallon to get $630 Depletion Expense allowed for the year.

• PROBLEM 12-20

The Promer Oil Company purchased 100 acres of Utah Land because their officials said oil drilling prospects appeared excellent in that location. The cost of the Land was $30,000. The costs of searching the land for the proper drilling location and actually drilling the oil well were $30,000. Intangible Development Costs such as erecting the oil well itself were $3,000. This is a total of $63,000. Engineers estimated that there were approximately 1,000,000 gallons of oil in the field. During the first year, 10,000 gallons of oil were extracted. The $63,000 costs are divided by the 1,000,000 approximate gallons of oil in the field to get $.063 depletion per gallon. During the first year, 10,000 gallons of oil were extracted from the ground; and during the second year, 60,000 gallons of oil were extracted from the ground.

What depletion entry will Promer Oil Company make on its books at the end of the second year and how will the Accumulated Depletion account look at the end of the second year?

SOLUTION:

2001		($ in dollars)
December 31 Depletion Expense	3,780	
Accumulated Depletion		3,780

At the end of the second year of oil extraction, on December 31, 2001, Depletion Expense is debited for $3,780 and Accumulated Depletion is credited for $3,780. This figure is computed by multiplying the $.063 depletion per gallon previously computed by the 60,000 gallons extracted from the ground during the year ($.063 × 60,000 gallons = $3,7801).

Accumulated Depletion		
	12/31/2000	630
	12/31/2001	3,780
		4,410

The depletion in the year 2000 was $630; the depletion in the year 2001 was $3,780; so the accumulated depletion at the end of 2001 is $4,410 ($630 + $3,780 = $4,410).

• PROBLEM 12–21

> The Promer Oil Company purchased 100 acres of Utah Land because their officials said oil drilling prospects appeared excellent in that location. The cost of the Land was $30,000. The costs of searching the land for the proper drilling location and actually drilling the oil well were $30,000. Intangible Development Costs such as erecting the oil well itself were $3,000. This is a total of $63,000. These costs are all being depleted.
>
> The Company decides to build several temporary buildings at the oil well site. This is done at the cost of $4,000. Should these be depleted or depreciated, and how?

SOLUTION:

Since the buildings are tangible property, they should be depreciated rather than depleted. This should be done over a period of years of the approximate life of the buildings or of the approximate life of the oil field, whichever is lower. It is estimated that the buildings will last about 10 years and the life of the oil field will be about 8 years. So the buildings are depreciated by the Straight-Line Method of Depreciation over 8 years as follows:

$4,000 divided by 8 years = $500 yearly Depreciation.

2001	($ in dollars)	
December 31 Depreciation Expense—Buildings	500	
Accumulated Depreciation—Buildings		500

The Expense Account, Depreciation Expense—Buildings is debited for $500 because, during the year 2001, the company got the use of the buildings. Accumulated Depreciation—Buildings is credited for $500. It is a Contra-Asset Account and shows the estimated Depreciation on the buildings for the first year of their use. The Asset account, Buildings, is not credited until the buildings are either sold or razed.

• PROBLEM 12–22

The Promer Oil Company purchased 100 acres of Utah Land because their officials said oil drilling prospects appeared excellent in that location. The cost of the Land was $30,000. The costs of searching the land for the proper drilling location and actually drilling the oil well were $30,000. Intangible Development Costs such as erecting the oil well itself were $3,000. The company decides to build several temporary buildings at the oil well site. This is done at the cost of $4,000. These are depreciated by the Straight-Line Method over the approximate 8-year life of the oil field, since this is shorter than the approximate 10-year life of the buildings. The oil field was used in the years 2000 and 2001. The buildings were constructed on January 1, 2001; so have been used only one year as of the date December 31, 2001. How will these items appear on the Balance Sheet of the Promer Oil Company on December 31, 2001?

SOLUTION:

Promer Oil Company
Balance Sheet
December 31, 2001

Assets

Land, Drilling Costs, and Intangible Development Costs	63,000	
Less: Accumulated Depletion	-4,410	58,590
Buildings	4,000	
Less: Accumulated Depreciation—Buildings	- 500	3,500

At the end of the calendar year, 2001, the $4,410 Accumulated Depreciation balance is subtracted from the original cost of the Land, Drilling Costs, and Intangible Development Costs, to get a Book Value of $58,590, which is added in with the Assets. The buildings, built on January 1, 2001, cost $4,000, and during the year 2001 depreciated by the Straight-Line Method a total of $500. So the $500 Accumulated Depreciation for the year 2001 is subtracted from the cost of the buildings, $4,000, to get a Book Value of $3,500, which is added in with the other Assets.

• PROBLEM 12-23

On January 2, 2000, Henry Sawyer purchased 3,000 acres of timber land at $1,000 per acre. Realtors estimated that the land without the timber would sell for only $300 per acre and they also estimated that the 3,000 acres contained approximately 4,000,000 board feet of timber. During the year 2000, the cutting crews logged 500,000 board feet of timber. What will be Sawyer's Depletion Expense for the year 2000 and what will be his book entry?

SOLUTION:

1. Multiply the 3,000 acres by $1,000 cost per acre to get $3,000,000 Total Cost of the property

   (3,000 acres × $1,000 cost per acre = $3,000,000).

2. Multiply the 3,000 acres by $300 cost per acre without timber, to get $900,000 Total Cost of land without timber

   (3,000 acres × $300 = $900,000).

3. Subtract the $900,000 cost of land without timber from the $3,000,000 cost of land with timber to get $2,100,000 cost of the timber alone.

   ($3,000,000 – $900,000 = $2,100,000 cost of timber alone)

4. Divide the $2,100,000 cost of the timber alone by the 4,000,000 estimated board feet of timber on the land to get $.525 depletion per board foot

   ($2,100,000 ÷ 4,000,000 = $.525 depletion per board foot).

5. Multiply the $.525 depletion per board foot by the 500,000 board feet logged during the year 2000 to get $262,500, the first year's depletion.

2000	($ in dollars)
December 31 Depletion Expense	262,500
Accumulated Depletion	262,500

Like Oil Well Depletion, Timber Depletion is based on the Units of Production method of depreciation. However, the land itself cannot be depreciated or depleted; therefore, it is first necessary to separate the cost of the timber from the cost of the land.

In the first step of the solution, the 3,000 acres of land is multiplied by the $1,000 cost per acre to get the $3,000,000 Total Cost of the land with the timber on it.

In the second step of the solution, the 3,000 acres of land is multiplied by the $300 cost per acre without the timber. Of course, this $300 per acre figure is merely the estimate of the realtors, but it is a necessary step in separating the cost of the land itself from the cost of the timber itself.

In the third step of the solution, we subtract the $900,000 cost of the land without the timber from the $3,000,000 cost of land with the timber to get $2,100,000 cost of the timber alone.

In the fourth step of the solution, we divide the $2,100,000 cost of the timber alone by the 4,000,000 estimated board feet of timber on the land to get $.525 depletion per board foot. Of course this 4,000,000 estimated board feet of timber on the land is just a guess by the realtors; however, the realtors are considered professionals at this type of estimation.

In the fifth step of the solution, we multiply the $.525 depletion per board foot by the 500,000 board feet logged during the first year of operations, the year 2000, to get $262,500 depletion for that year. Although the figure $.525 is an educated professional guess, the 500,000 board feet is the actual figure logged for the year.

• PROBLEM 12-24

The Horton Construction Company buys a Warehouse and the Land surrounding it for $30,000. Realtors estimate that the Building itself is worth $15,000 and the Land is worth $10,000. However, Horton Construction Company must pay $30,000 for the whole thing. How should this be recorded on the books of the Horton Construction Company and how should the Goodwill be amortized over a period of 15 years?

SOLUTION:

2000		($ in dollars)	
January 2	Land	10,000	
	Building	15,000	
	Goodwill	5,000	
	Cash		30,000

The Land and Building are purchased on January 2, 2000. The Land Account is debited for the $10,000 Appraisal Value set by the realtor. The Building is debited for the $15,000 Appraisal Value set by the realtor. Since $30,000 cash is paid by Horton Construction Company, the account Cash is credited for that amount. The difference between the Appraised Values and the cash paid is $5,000, and this is debited to the Intangible Asset account, Goodwill.

Recently, the Financial Accounting Standards Board has begun allowing businesses to amortize Goodwill over a period of 15 years. Amortization is a gradual writing off of Intangible Assets over their estimated life, and it is similar to Depreciation, though Depreciation is recorded on Plant and Equipment type Assets. We decide to amortize Goodwill over 15 years; so divide the $5,000 Goodwill by 15 to get $333 yearly Amortization of Goodwill.

The entry at the end of the year 2000 to amortize Goodwill for that year would be:

2000		($ in dollars)	
December 31	Amortization Expense	333	
	Goodwill		333

It is noted that in Amortization entries the Amortization Expense is debited, but there is no Accumulated Amortization Account to be credited; so the Intangible Asset, Goodwill, is credited in this case.

• PROBLEM 12-25

The Horton Construction Company buys a Warehouse and the Land surrounding it for $30,000. Realtors estimate that the Building itself is worth $15,000 and the Land is worth $10,000. However, Horton Construction Company must pay $30,000 for the whole thing. The purchase of the Land and Building is recorded on the books by debiting Land for $10,000, debiting Building for $15,000, debiting Goodwill for $5,000, and crediting Cash for $30,000. The Goodwill is an Intangible Asset and is the difference between the cash paid and the Appraised Value of Land and Building. This goodwill is written off at the end of each year for 15 years by debiting Amortization Expense and crediting Goodwill for $333. How does the Goodwill account look at the end of the 15th year?

SOLUTION:

Goodwill

1/2/2000	5,000	12/31/2000	333.33
		12/31/2001	333.33
		12/31/2002	333.34
		12/31/2003	333.33
		12/31/2004	333.33
		12/31/2005	333.34
		12/31/2006	333.33
		12/31/2007	333.33
		12/31/2008	333.34
		12/31/2009	333.33
		12/31/2010	333.33
		12/31/2011	333.34
		12/31/2012	333.33
		12/31/2013	333.33
		12/31/2014	333.34
			5000.00

CHAPTER 13

INTANGIBLE ASSETS

> **Basic Attacks and Strategies for Solving Problems in this Chapter. See pages 397 to 438 for step-by-step solutions to problems.**

Intangible Assets are those which cannot be touched, while Tangible Assets can be touched. Tangible Assets include: Buildings, Land, Equipment, Inventory, and Furniture. Intangible Assets are such things as Trademarks or Trade-Names, Copyrights, Patents, Computer Software, Goodwill, Badwill, Franchises, Permits, Organizational Costs, Bond Premiums, and Discounts.

Intangible Assets are important because they cost businesses money and have to be accounted for. The government, and some accounting associations, do not always allow Intangible Assets to be regarded as a loss. They often have to be expensed gradually over a period of years as determined by either the government or accounting associations. This gradual process is termed **Amortization**. Amortization is little understood by the general public.

The first problems in Chapter 13 discuss trademarks or trade names (e.g.: Rexall Drugs, Coca Cola, Royal Crown Cola). When these names are approved by the U.S. Patent Office, they belong to the business indefinitely as long as they are reapplied for every 20 years. Accounting associations recommend, however, that trade names be amortized over a period not to exceed 40 years.

Copyrights are exclusive rights to written materials and are set up by the Library of Congress in Washington. These rights allow the exclusive use of such things as architectural plans, music scores, books, and magazine articles. They last for the author's lifetime plus 50 years and cannot be renewed. Patents are exclusive rights to new inventions and last 17 years with the possibility of renewal. They are registered at the United States Patent Office in Washington, D.C. The U.S. Constitution gives the federal government exclusive control over patents, to encourage invention.

It is often difficult to distinguish between an Expense and an Intangible Asset. For instance, Changeover Expense in the auto industry might be classified by some as an Intangible Asset. However, the accounting profession advises that Changeover Expenses be "expensed" or "written off" in the year incurred. This is also true for Research and Development costs which should not be debited to an Intangible Asset account and amortized. Rather, they should be expensed immediately according to the accounting profession's Financial Accounting Standards Board.

Even though a patent, copyright, or trade name is protected by the government, the owner who thinks he or she is being infringed upon by competitors must still take the case to court. In the case of legal fees and court costs for a successful infringement suit, the costs, if any, should be debited to an Intangible Asset account and amortized over the period of years benefited. In the case of legal fees and court costs for an *unsuccessful* infringement suit, the costs should be expensed immediately.

The costs of patents are easily determinable when purchasing a patent from an inventor because there is a definite purchase price which can be debited to the patent account. These can then be amortized over the remainder of the legal life of the patent or the number of years benefited, whichever is less. If the patent is developed within the company, the in-house costs can also be capitalized (debited to an Asset Account such as patents), then amortized over a period of 40 years or less.

Computer software that costs money to develop and that is to be used within the company should be expensed immediately. Computer software that costs money to develop and that is to be sold or leased, should be capitalized (debited to an Asset Account such as "Computer Software") then amortized over the beneficial life of the software.

Goodwill is an Intangible Asset that should be entered in the books only if the purchasing company buys another firm at a price higher than the firm's Assets. The difference is Goodwill which should be written off over the years that it can benefit the company. Goodwill generated internally should not be placed on the books at all. The government will not allow an Income Tax deduction for amortizing internally (generated Goodwill). Additionally, the accounting profession does not recommend debiting Goodwill if it is internally generated primarily because the amount would be too subjective.

Negative goodwill, sometimes called "Badwill," is developed by a lucky purchase, where the Assets purchased are greater than the money paid. The difference is Badwill. It has a credit balance and is a Deferred Credit Account located in the Liabilities section of the Balance Sheet. This account should be gradually amortized to an Amortization Income account. In order to do away with the account Badwill in the first place, the Assets purchased are often registered as a lower figure on the purchaser's books.

Franchise is a another Intangible Asset in which legal permission is granted by a larger business in order to help a smaller business. This is usually done through business advice, use of name, and use of merchandise. If the smaller business has to pay for this, it can debit an Intangible Asset Account, Franchise. This can be amortized over a period of years.

The startup costs of a new corporation can be debited to the Intangible Asset, Organization Costs, and these can be amortized over a period of between five years (government minimum) and 40 years (accounting association maximum).

Step-by-Step Solutions to Problems in this Chapter, "Intangible Assets"

• PROBLEM 13-1

The Luscious Chocolate Company is thinking of going out of business. Its competitor, the Brown Candy Company, likes the name, "Luscious," and offers the Luscious Chocolate Company $3,000 for its name. This is agreeable, and the name is purchased by the Brown Candy Company for $3,000.

What entry should be made on the books of the Brown Candy Company at this time?

SOLUTION:

2000		($ in dollars)
January 2	Tradename	3,000
	Cash	3,000

The tradename, "Luscious," is an Intangible Asset, and it should be recorded on the books of the Brown Candy Company because the Brown Candy Company had to make an outlay of $3,000 for the name. Evidently the Brown Candy Company thought this payment was worthwhile and would eventually help the Brown Candy Company's business. The account, Tradename, would be listed among the Intangible Assets on the Brown Candy Company Balance Sheet.

• PROBLEM 13–2

The Luscious Chocolate Company is thinking of going out of business. Its competitor, the Brown Candy Company, likes the name, "Luscious," and offers the Luscious Chocolate Company $3,000 for its name. This is agreeable, and the name is purchased by the Brown Candy Company for $3,000. An entry is made on the Brown Candy Company books debiting Tradename for $3,000 and crediting Cash for $3,000, on January 2, 2000.

What would the entry be on December 31, 2000, to amortize this Intangible Asset?

SOLUTION:

2000		($ in dollars)
December 31	Amortization Expense	75
	Tradename	75

A Trademark or Tradename, as long as reapplication to the U.S. Patent Office is made every 20 years, can be used indefinitely by the company owning it. However, accounting practice requires that it be written off over a maximum period of 40 years, or over its useful life if less than 40 years. Assume that Brown Candy Company decides to amortize this Intangible Asset over 40 years. They divide the $3,000 cost by 40 years to get $75 Amortization or write-off per year. Thus, they debit Amortization Expense for $75, cutting down their Net Income by that amount, and credit the Intangible Account, Tradename, by that amount. Therefore, at the end of 40 years, the Tradename account will be down to zero.

The officers of the Brown Candy Company think that the benefits of using Luscious on their candy will only last five years. If they then divide the $3,000 cost of the Intangible Asset by five years to get $600. The Amortization entry would therefore be as follows:

2000		($ in dollars)	
December 31	Amortization Expense	600	
	Tradename		600

This latter choice of debiting the Amortization Expense Account by $600 would greatly (and legally) cut down their Net Profit and their Income Tax.

• PROBLEM 13-3

The Joshua Soft Drink Company has developed a new name for its new soft drink. It is to be called Joshua Cola. This name was chosen after a costly national campaign to find the right name. The national campaign cost $50,000.

What entry will the Joshua Soft Drink Company make on its books to record this cost?

SOLUTION:

2000		($ in dollars)	
January 2	Tradename	50,000	
	Cash		50,000

Usually a Tradename developed within the company has small expenses that could be expensed immediately in the year of development. But since these expenses were so great—$50,000—they should be capitalized and written off over either 40 years, or the period of time that the company would probably benefit by using the Tradename.

• PROBLEM 13-4

The Joshua Soft Drink Company has developed a new name for its new soft drink. It is to be called Joshua Cola. This name was chosen after a costly national campaign to find the right name. The national campaign cost $50,000. The company debited the account, Tradename, for $50,000.

What Amortization entry will be made at the end of the first year of use?

SOLUTION:

2000		($ in dollars)
December 31 Amortization Expense	1,250	
Tradename		1,250

The Joshua Soft Drink Company has decided to write off the Tradename over the maximum time allowed by the Financial Accounting Standards Board (40 years). They divide the $50,000 cost of the campaign by 40 years to get $1,250. They then debit Amortization Expense for the $1,250, thus cutting the Net Income by that amount, and credit the Intangible Asset Account, Tradename, by $1,250. At that rate they will have completely written off the Tradename account in 40 years.

On the other hand, if they think the name Joshua Cola will not benefit them for that period of time, they could write it off for between 5 and 40 years. Let us say they think the benefits will last only 5 years. Then their entry would be as follows:

2000		($ in dollars)
December 31 Amortization Expense	10,000	
Tradename		10,000

They divide the $50,000 cost of the campaign by 5 years of benefit to get $10,000 Amortization each year. They then debit Amortization Expense for $10,000, thus cutting the Net Income by that amount, and credit the Intangible Asset Account, Tradename, by $10,000. At that rate they will have completely written off the Tradename account in 5 years.

• PROBLEM 13-5

Arthur Rutherford wrote many songs, both ancient and modern, during his lifetime, the most famous of which was "Old Pete." He copyrighted each of these songs through the Library of Congress which gave him exclusive use of these songs and exclusive right to allow others to publish these songs or to sell these songs during his lifetime and 50 years thereafter. He died at the age of 76 in 1990 and left these songs to his son, Ned. The Star Book Corporation has wished for a long time to publish all of Rutherford's songs in one book and sell them to the public. They finally prevailed upon Ned Rutherford to sell the copyright for a sum of $500.

What entry should be made on the books of the Star Book Corporation at the time the copyright was purchased?

SOLUTION:

2000		($ in dollars)
January 2	Copyright to Arthur Rutherford's Songs	500
	Cash	500

The Star Book Corporation received the copyright, so the Intangible Asset Account entitled Copyright to Arthur Rutherford's Songs was debited for $500. They paid cash, so **Cash** was credited for that amount.

• PROBLEM 13–6

Arthur Rutherford wrote many songs, both ancient and modern, during his lifetime, the most famous of which was "Old Pete." He copyrighted each of these songs through the Library of Congress which gave him exclusive use of these songs and exclusive right to allow others to publish these songs or to sell these songs during his lifetime and fifty years thereafter. He died at the age of 76 in 1990 and left these songs to his son, Ned. The Star Book Corporation has wished for a long time to publish all of Rutherford's songs in one book and sell them to the public. They finally prevailed upon Ned Rutherford to sell the copyright for a sum of $500, on January 2, 2000. At that time the Star Book Corporation debited the account, Copyright to Arthur Rutherford's Songs, $500, and credited Cash $500.

What Amortization entry will be made at the end of the year 2000 on the Star Book Corporation's accounts?

SOLUTION:

2000	($ in dollars)
December 31 Amortization Expense	12.50
Copyright to Arthur	
Rutherford's Songs	12.50

United States laws dealing with copyrights are somewhat different from United States laws regarding patents, though they are both intangible Assets. The Constitution gives the federal government control of patents to encourage invention. This national control also carries over to copyrights, though there are different rules. For instance, the United States Patent Office controls and issues patents for inventions, while the Library of Congress issues copyrights. Also, patents last for 17 years and can be renewed, whereas copyrights last for 50 years after the author's death and cannot be renewed.

Patents cover inventions, while copyrights cover original writings such as books, articles, architectural plans, musical scores, paintings, and sculptures. In the case of either patents or copyrights, infringers can be sued by the person or firm holding the patent or copyright.

In this case the Star Book Corporation purchased the exclusive right to publish and sell all of Arthur Rutherford's songs for the duration of the copyright. The copyright law allows copyright holders the exclusive right to their works for their life plus fifty years. Since Arthur Rutherford died in 1990 and the copyright was not purchased until the year 2000, 10 years after his death, the copyright privilege had only 40 more years left (50 years after death less 10 years already elapsed = 40 more years).

Over what period shall the Star Book Corporation amortize this $500 purchase?

Since the exclusive right to the copyright will last for the Star Book Corporation only 40 more years, and since the Financial Accounting Standards Board recommends that copyrights be amortized over a period of not more than 40 years, then the term of 40 years seems to be the proper Amortization time. Divide 40 years into the $500 purchase price to derive $12.50 per year Amortization. Thus, the account, Amortization Expense, is debited for $12.50 and the Intangible Asset Account, Copyright to Arthur Rutherford's Songs, is credited for $12.50. If this entry is made at the end of each year for 40 years, the account Copyright to Arthur Rutherford's Songs will be written off entirely to expense.

However, the Amortization period need not be this long. It could be written off in as few as five years if it is believed that the benefits will only last this long. If this is the case, we would divide five years into the $500 cost of the Copyright to get $100 yearly Amortization, and the entry would be as follows:

2000	($ in dollars)	
December 31 Amortization Expense	100	
Copyright to Arthur		
Rutherford's Songs		100

If this entry were made at the end of each year for a period of five years, the total $500 balance of the Copyright account would have gradually been written off to expense.

The officers of the Star Book Corporation may decide upon an intermediate date, such as, 20 years. Divide the 20 years into the $500 cost of the Copyright to get a yearly Amortization of $25, and the entry would be as follows:

2000	($ in dollars)
December 31 Amortization Expense	25
Copyright to Arthur Rutherford's Songs	25

If this entry were made at the end of each year for a period of 20 years, the total $500 balance of the Copyright account would have gradually been written off to expense.

• PROBLEM 13-7

The Warren Auto Firm is spending $50,000 in revamping its production-line machinery in a changeover from the 1999 model to the year 2000 model.

How will this be recorded on the books of the Warren Auto Firm?

SOLUTION:

2000	($ in dollars)
January 2 Changeover Expense	50,000
Cash	50,000

Some accountants would claim that these Changeover Costs should be debited to an Intangible Asset and amortized, but the majority of the accounting profession would advise expensing the Changeover Costs in the year the changeover was made. Debit the Expense Account, Changeover Expense, and credit Cash. This expense cuts down the reported Net Income in the year the changeover was made. Since it is a yearly changeover, the expense will need to be incurred every year, and it should therefore be deducted as an expense on the company's Income Statement each year.

• PROBLEM 13-8

The Smith Manufacturing Company receives a 5-year note from its subsidiary, the Burton Manufacturing Company, for $50,000, which the Smith Manufacturing Company has loaned it.

How should this be recorded on the books of the Smith Manufacturing Company?

SOLUTION:

2000			($ in dollars)
January 2	Notes Receivable (Long-Term)	50,000	
	Cash		50,000

Although it would appear that this is an Intangible Asset, it is not. It is placed in the Balance Sheet with the Plant Assets and is not amortized (as Intangible Assets would be). If, at a later date, the Smith Manufacturing Company realizes that part or all of the loan will never be repaid, it will at that time write it off by debiting the Expense Account entitled Loss.

• PROBLEM 13-9

The Tandem Hosiery Company has several chemists employed full time to develop new hosiery for both men and women. Sometimes they work for long periods of time with no apparent results. Other times, they come out with a new type of stocking which produces a product which has made the company great amounts of money. Each month the company must buy new chemicals for the laboratory, new machinery, and must also pay the salaries of the chemists in the Research and Development department.

How should the entry for the chemists' supplies, machinery, and salaries be recorded on the books of the Tandem Hosiery Company?

SOLUTION:

2000		($ in dollars)
January 31 Research and Development Expense	2,600	
Cash		2,600

The Financial Accounting Standards Board states that Research and Development Expenses should be debited to expense accounts in the year that the expenses were incurred, so it is proper to debit all costs of the Research and Development Department of the Tandem Hosiery Company to Research and Development Expense and to write them off immediately. In earlier years some accountants had thought it best to debit an Intangible Asset Account and to amortize this account, but this is no longer true.

• PROBLEM 13–10

The March Manufacturing Company several years ago bought a patent on a cereal-making machine. In touring the plant of the Staver Cereal Company, it was noticed that a similar machine to that patented by the March Manufacturing Company was being used, and that this machine had not been purchased from the March Manufacturing Company. After intensive discussion, the disagreement could not be peacefully settled, so it was taken to court where the March Manufacturing Company sued the Staver Cereal Company for patent infringement.

The March Manufacturing Company won the suit and the Staver Cereal Company promised to quit using the machine and not use anything connected with the patent until the patents rights had run out. However, $5,000 in extra legal fees were still to be paid by the March Manufacturing Company.

How will this $5,000 payment be recorded on the March Manufacturing Company books?

SOLUTION:

2000		($ in dollars)
January 2	Patents	5,000
	Cash	5,000

According to regulations of the Financial Accounting Standards Board, extra costs of a successful patent infringement suit should be debited to the Intangible Asset Account, Patents, and amortized. In this case, Patents was debited for the $5,000 extra costs and Cash was credited.

• PROBLEM 13–11

The March Manufacturing Company several years ago bought a patent on a cereal-making machine. In touring the plant of the Staver Cereal Company, it was noticed that a similar machine to that patented by the March Manufacturing Company was being used, and that this machine had not been purchased from the March Manufacturing Company. After intensive discussion, the disagreement could not be peacefully settled, so it was taken to court where the March Manufacturing Company sued the Staver Cereal Company for patent infringement.

The March Manufacturing Company won the suit and the Staver Cereal Company promised to quit using the machine and not use anything connected with the patent until the patent rights had run out. However, $5,000 in extra legal fees were still to be paid by the March Manufacturing Company. When these were paid, the March Manufacturing Company debited the Intangible Asset Account, Patents, for $5,000 and credited Cash for $5,000.

How will the Patent account be amortized?

SOLUTION:

2000		($ in dollars)
December 31	Amortization Expense	1,000
	Patents	1,000

According to accounting rules and customs, patents are amortized over periods not exceeding 40 years and not less than 5 years, with the most appropriate time period the amount of time that the Asset will be useful to the business. Since a successful patent infringement suit will probably be useful to the business for only a minimum length of time, it is best to amortize this Asset over the minimum allowable period of years—in this case, 5 years.

The extra Legal Expenses debited to Patents were $5,000, thus divide the $5,000 by the 5 minimum years to get $1,000 Depreciation each year. The $1,000 Amortization Expense each year will cut down the Net Income on the books by that amount and will lower the March Manufacturing Company's Income Tax. Also, the Patent account will be completely amortized, as far as these Legal Expenses are concerned, in the minimum period of five years.

• PROBLEM 13–12

The Hassan Novelty Company years ago purchased a patent on a Santa Claus toy. Last year it was discovered that the Greater Toy Company had been manufacturing and selling a somewhat similar Santa Claus toy. The Hassan Novelty Company negotiated with the Greater Toy Company, showing them proof that they had purchased this patent, but to no avail. Finally, the Hassan Novelty Company sued the Greater Toy Company for patent infringement in court.

The Hassan Novelty Company lost the suit. The jury concluded that the Santa Claus toys were not exactly similar and that Santa Claus comes in all shapes and sizes.

The Hassan Novelty Company was forced to pay Legal Expenses for both sets of lawyers and to pay the Court Costs, all of which totaled $7,000.

What entry should the Hassan Novelty Company make on its books?

SOLUTION:

2000		($ in dollars)	
January 2	Legal Expenses	7,000	
	Cash		7,000

Accounting rules allow a company to expense all costs in an unsuccessful patent infringement suit. Therefore, in the year in which the company had to pay the costs, the entire payment could be debited to the account, Legal Expenses, and deducted from Revenue in computing Net Income for that year.

• PROBLEM 13–13

Swenson Candy Company had been selling various types of candy bars for years. A new competitor, the Lyndon Sweets Corporation, had just invented a new Lyndon Candy Bar that was taking the country by storm, and was being purchased by every child with a sweet tooth. Lyndon was reaching retirement age and had no heirs, so he approached his competitor, the Swenson Candy Company, and mentioned that he had the recipe for the Lyndon Candy Bar patented but was willing to sell the patent for $10,000. Eventually the Swenson Candy Company did buy the patent for this amount.

How should the Swenson Candy Company record this on their books and why?

SOLUTION:

2001		($ in dollars)	
January 2	Patents	10,000	
	Cash		10,000

The federal government will not allow the purchaser of a patent to write it off completely in the year purchased. Therefore, the firm must debit the Intangible Asset, Patent, and credit Cash. The only legal way this purchased patent can be expensed is gradually over the life of the patent, with a minimum of 5 years and a maximum of 40 years.

• PROBLEM 13-14

Swenson Candy Company had been selling various types of candy bars for years. A new competitor, the Lyndon Sweets Corporation, had just invented a new Lyndon Candy Bar that was taking the country by storm, and was being purchased by every child with a sweet tooth. Lyndon was reaching retirement age and had no heirs, so he approached his competitor, the Swenson Candy Company, and mentioned that he had the recipe for the Lyndon Candy Bar patented but was willing to sell the patent for $10,000. Eventually the Swenson Candy Company did buy the patent for this amount, debiting the intangible account, Patents, for $10,000 and crediting Cash for $10,000.

What entry would the Swenson Candy Company make at the end of the first year of patent use to amortize the patent?

SOLUTION:

2001	($ in dollars)
December 31 Amortization Expense	2,000
Patent	2,000

Let us say the Swenson Candy Company was not sure just how long the purchase of this patent would benefit them, so they decided to write off the patent cost to expense over the shortest period possible—5 years. We thus divide the $10,000 purchase price of the patent by the 5-year period to get $2,000 yearly Amortization. This $2,000 debited at the end of each year to Amortization Expense will legally cut down the Net Income and thus decrease the Income Tax. At the end of five years it will also close out the intangible asset account, Patent.

• PROBLEM 13-15

Swenson Candy Company had been selling various types of candy bars for years. A new competitor, the Lyndon Sweets Corporation, had just invented a new Lyndon Candy Bar that was taking the country by storm, and was being purchased by every child with a sweet tooth. Lyndon was reaching retirement age and had no heirs, so he approached his competitor, the Swenson Candy Company, and mentioned that he had the recipe for the Lyndon Candy Bar patented but was willing to sell the patent for $10,000. Eventually the Swenson Candy Company did buy the patent for this amount, debiting the intangible asset account, Patents, for $10,000 and crediting Cash for $10,000. At the end of the first year of patent use the company debited Amortization Expense for $2,000 and credited Patent for $2,000.

What other methods of Amortization could be used?

SOLUTION:

2001	($ in dollars)	
December 31 Amortization Expense	250	
Patents		250

The purchase price of the patent, $10,000, could have been spread over the maximum length of time suggested by the Financial Accounting Standards Board, that is 40 years, by dividing 40 years into the $10,000 purchase price, with the answer of $250. Thus, by debiting Amortization Expense for $250 and crediting Patents for $250 at the end of each year, it would take 40 years to write off this account. This method would probably only be undertaken if the Swenson Candy Company actually thought that the benefits derived from the purchase of the patent recipe would last 40 years.

Other methods of Amortization might be some intermediate period between the 5-year minimum and the 40-year maximum, let us say, 20 years. In this case the entry would be as follows:

2001	($ in dollars)	
December 31 Amortization Expense	500	
Patents		500

The $500 Depreciation figure is derived by dividing 20 years into the $10,000 purchase price. This is one of the many other choices.

Some business firms set up Contra-Asset accounts entitled Accumulated Amortization of Patents. If this method is used, then the entry would appear as follows:

2001	($ in dollars)
December 31 Amortization Expense	500
Accumulated Amortization—Patents	500

This method, while not used so often with Intangible Assets as with "plant and equipment" type Assets, is perfectly legal and is also approved by the accounting profession.

If the Accumulated Amortization method is used for amortizing patents, how would the Patents account look in the Balance Sheet of the Swenson Candy Company at the end of the first year of patent use?

Swenson Candy Company
Partial Balance Sheet
December 31, 2001

Intangible Assets

Patents	10,000
Less: Accumulated Amortization—Patents	– 500
	9,500

If the 20-year life of the patent is chosen, divide 20 years into the patent purchase price of $10,000, to get $500 Amortization each year. When the Contra-Asset account., Accumulated Amortization—Patents, is used, the Patent account itself is not actually changed at all at the end of each year. Therefore, at the end of the first year (in this case the year 2001), in the Balance Sheet, the Patent account remains at the original purchase price of the patent that is, $10,000. The Accumulated Amortization—Patents account has a credit balance of $500, so this $500 is subtracted in the Balance Sheet from the $10,000, giving the Patent a book value of $9,500. This amount of $9,500 is then added in with the company's other Assets to determine the Total Asset figure.

• PROBLEM 13-16

The Luxury Mousetrap Company has just developed a faster type of electric mousetrap and had it patented at the United States Patent Office. The in-house costs of developing the patent, plus the legal fees, plus the payments to the United States Patent Office, amounted to a total of $4,000.

What entry should be made on the books of the Luxury Mousetrap Company?

SOLUTION:

2002		($ in dollars)
January 2	Patents	4,000
	Cash	4,000

Both the accounting profession rules and the government laws allow quite a bit of leeway here. Since the amount is considerable, it would be possible to "capitalize" the costs of $4,000, as done above, by debiting Patents for the entire $4,000.

• PROBLEM 13-17

The Luxury Mousetrap Company has just developed a faster type of electric mousetrap and had it patented at the United States Patent Office. The in-house costs of developing the patent, plus the legal fees, plus the payments to the U.S. Patent office, amounted to a total of $4,000. The Luxury Mousetrap Company debited Patents (an intangible asset) and credited Cash for $4,000. What entry would be made at the end of the first year of patent use to amortize the patent?

SOLUTION:

2002	($ in dollars)
December 31 Amortization Expense	800
Patents	800

The $800 yearly Amortization is computed by dividing the Total Costs of $4,000 by the 5-year minimum Amortization period. This entry would be made at the end of each year for 5 years until the Patents account would have been written off. Following is the way the Patent account would look in the ledger at the end of the fifth year:

Patents

1/2/2002	4,000	12/31/2002	800
		12/31/2003	800
		12/31/2004	800
		12/31/2005	800
		12/31/2006	800
			4,000

In-house development of patents can be expensed immediately if the costs are relatively small which is subjective and would depend on the size of the corporation. If the corporation were large, like General Motors, a $4,000 expenditure would be considered meager and might be written off as follows:

2002		($ in dollars)
January 2	Patent Expense	4,000
	Cash	4,000

In this case, the entire $4,000 cost would be debited to expense in the year the patent was purchased, and there would be no need for Amortization at all. The use of this method is strengthened by the Financial Accounting Standards Board which recommends that all Research and Development Costs be expensed immediately, and an in-house development of an item to be patented seems to fit these requirements.

• PROBLEM 13–18

The Long Computer Software Company developed new computer software programs costing $3,000,000. They plan to use these programs exclusively within the company.

How should this be handled on the books?

SOLUTION:

2000			($ in dollars)
January 2	Software Development Expense	3,000,000	
	Cash		3,000,000

Since the Long Computer Software Company plans not to sell or lease this software, but to use it only within the company, it is perfectly legal and within the accounting rules to expense it in the year developed.

• PROBLEM 13–19

The Long Computer Software Company developed new computer software programs costing $3,000,000. The software is the type that would be of interest to other firms and useful to them. The Long Computer Software Company plans to sell and/or lease this software.

How should this be handled on the books of the Long Computer Software Company?

SOLUTION:

2000			($ in dollars)
January 2	Computer Software	3,000,000	
	Cash		3,000,000

"Computer Software" is an Intangible Asset that is debited for the complete cost of $3,000,000. Cash is credited, since this amount was spent for developing the computer software.

• PROBLEM 13–20

The Long Computer Software Company developed new computer software programs costing $3,000,000. The software is the type that would be of interest to other firms and useful to them. The Long Computer Software Company plans to sell this software. During the year 2000 the software sales amounted to $2,000,000, and there still is enough software for sales of $4,000,000 next year. The company has determined to use the "Percent of Revenue" approach in Amortizing this software.

What will be the entry on the books of the Long Computer Software Company to amortize this Intangible Asset at the end of the year 2000?

SOLUTION:

2000	($ in dollars)	
December 31 Amortization Expense	1,000,000	
Computer Software		1,000,000

The sales of the developed computer software during the calendar year 2000 were $2,000,000 and there is enough software for $4,000,000 sales, so the Long Computer Software Company plans a total of $6,000,000 in sales before this computer software becomes obsolete ($2,000,000 sales this year + $4,000,000 anticipated future sales = $6,000,000 total sales).

Since the cost of the computer software is $3,000,000, and since the sales during the year 2000 were $2,000,000 out of a probable $6,000,000 sales, we use the following formula:

$2,000,000/$6,000,000 × $3,000,000 = $1,000,000, or 1/3 × $3,000,000 = $1,000,000.

Thus, according to the "Percent of Revenue" approach, since we have sold 1/3 of the total anticipated sales of this computer software, we multiply the 1/3 by the Total Cost of the software, $3,000,000, to get $1,000,000 Amortization during the calendar year 2000. The Expense Account, Amortization Expense, is debited for $1,000,000. This effectively cuts down the Net Income by this amount. The Intangible Asset, Computer Software, is credited for $1,000,000. At the end of the year 2000, the

Computer Software Intangible Asset account would appear on the books of the Long Computer Software Company as follows:

Computer Software

1/2/2000	3,000,000	12/31/2000	1,000,000
	2,000,000		

The Computer Software Intangible Asset Account, on January 2, 2000, was debited for the cost of the software, 3,000,000. On December 31, 2000, the Amortization entry was made for the year and the Computer Software account was credited for $1,000,000. Thus, at the end of the year, the Computer Software account had a balance of $2,000,000.

• PROBLEM 13-21

The Long Computer Software Company developed new computer software programs costing $3,000,000. The software is the type that would be of interest to other firms and useful to them. The Long Computer Software Company plans to sell this software. During the year 2000 the software sales amounted to $2,000,000, and there still is enough software for sales of $4,000,000 next year. The company has determined to use the "Percent of Revenue" approach in the Amortization of this software, and they plan to use an allowance account. On January 2, when the software was paid for, the company debited the Intangible Asset account, Computer Software, for $3,000,000 and credited Cash for $3,000,000.

What will be the entry on the books of the Long Computer Software Company to amortize this Intangible Asset at the end of the year 2000, using the Allowance Account?

SOLUTION:

2000	($ in dollars)	
December 31 Amortization Expense	1,000,000	
Allowance for Amortization		1,000,000

The sales of the developed computer software during the calendar year 2000 were $2,000,000, and there is enough software for $4,000,000 more sales, so the Long Computer Software Company plans a total of $6,000,000 in sales before this computer software becomes obsolete ($2,000,000 sales this year + $4,000,000 anticipated future sales = $6,000,000 total sales).

Since the cost of the computer software is $3,000,000, and since the sales during the year 2000 were $2,000,000 out of a probable $6,000,000 sales, we use the following formula:

$$\$2,000,000/\$6,000,000 \times \$3,000,000 = \$1,000,000,$$

or $1/3 \times \$3,000,000 = \$1,000,000.$

Thus, according to the "Percent of Revenue" approach, since we have sold 1/3 of the total anticipated sales of this computer software, we multiply the 1/3 by the Total Cost of the software, $3,000,000, to get $1,000,000 Amortization during the calendar year 2000. The Expense Account, Amortization Expense, is debited for $1,000,000. This effectively cuts down the Net Income by this amount. The contra-asset account, Allowance for Amortization, is credited for $1,000,000. At the end of the year 2000, the Computer Software Intangible Asset Account and the Allowance for Amortization Contra Asset account would appear as follows in the ledger of the Long Computer Software Company:

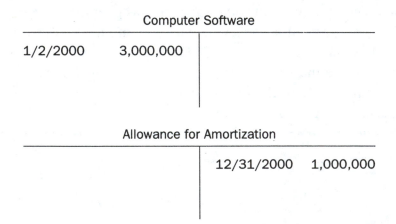

Computer Software

1/2/2000	3,000,000	

Allowance for Amortization

	12/31/2000	1,000,000

The Computer Software Intangible Asset Account was debited for $3,000,000 on January 2, 2000, the date that the computer software was paid for. A year later, on December 31, 2000, $1,000,000 was amortized and credited the Allowance for Amortization account for $1,000,000.

These accounts would appear in the Intangible Assets section of the Long Computer Software Company as follows:

The Long Computer Software Company
Partial Balance Sheet
December 31, 2000

Intangible Assets

Computer Software	3,000,000
Less: Allowance for Amortization	1,000,000
	2,000,000

In the Balance Sheet of the Long Computer Software Company the Intangible Asset Account, Computer Software, is shown with its balance of $3,000,000. Following this, the Allowance for Amortization Contra Asset account, with its balance of $1,000,000, is deducted, giving a Book Value at year's end of $2,000,000.

• PROBLEM 13–22

The Long Computer Software Company developed new computer software programs costing $3,000,000. The software is the type that would be of interest to other firms and useful to them. The Long Computer Software Company plans to sell this software. During the year 2000 the software sales amounted to $2,000,000, and there still is enough software for sales of $4,000,000 next year. The company has decided to use the "Straight Line" approach in the Amortization of this software. On January 2, when the software was paid for, the company debited the Intangible Asset Account, Computer Software, for $3,000,000 and credited Cash for $3,000,000. The company plans to sell the remainder of the software in the year 2001.

What will be the entry on the books of the Long Computer Software Company to amortize this Intangible Asset at the end of the year 2000?

SOLUTION:

2000		($ in dollars)
December 31 Amortization Expense	1,500,000	
Computer Software		1,500,000

The cost of the computer software was $3,000,000, and the Long Computer Software Company plans to sell all this software in two years—in this case, the years 2000 and 2001. Divide the $3,000,000 cost by 2 years to get $1,500,000 Amortization each year under the Straight-Line method.

($3,000,000/2 = $1,500,000).

• PROBLEM 13-23

The Long Computer Software Company developed new computer software programs costing $3,000,000. The software is the type that would be of interest to other firms and useful to them. The Long Computer Software Company plans to sell this software. During the year 2000 the software sales amounted to $2,000,000, and there is still enough software for sales of $4,000,000 next year. The company has decided to use the "Straight Line" approach in the Amortization of this software. On January 2, when the software was paid for, the company debited the Intangible Asset Account, Computer Software, for $3,000,000 and credited Cash for $3,000,000. The company plans to sell the remainder of the software in the year 2001. They are also setting up a Contra-Asset account entitled Allowance for Amortization.

What will be the entry on the books of the Long Computer Software Company to amortize this Intangible Asset at the end of the year 2000?

SOLUTION:

2000		($ in dollars)
December 31 Amortization Expense	1,500,000	
Allowance for Amortization		1,500,000

The cost of the computer software was 3,000,000, and the Long Computer Software Company plans to sell all this software in two years— in this case, the years 2000 and 2001. So we divide the $3,000,000 cost by 2 years to get $1,500,000 Amortization each year under the Straight-Line method.

• PROBLEM 13–24

The Royal Manufacturing Company purchased the Linden Manufacturing Company for $500,000. The Assets of the Linden Manufacturing Company on the day of purchase were as follows: Land, $100,000; Building, $150,000; Machinery, $75,000; and Furniture, $25,000.

How will this purchase be recorded on the books of the Royal Manufacturing Company?

SOLUTION:

2000		($ in dollars)
January 2	Building	150,000	
	Machinery	75,000	
	Furniture	25,000	
	Land	100,000	
	Goodwill	150,000	
	Cash		500,000

As seen from the information above, the Assets received from the Linden Manufacturing Company did not equal the $500,000 cash that the Royal Manufacturing Company paid to purchase the Linden Company (Building $150,000 + Machinery $75,000 + Furniture $25,000 + Land $100,000 = $350,000). Thus, the Royal Manufacturing Company received

$350,000 worth of Linden Assets for cash of $500,000. The difference in this case is debited to Goodwill in the amount of $150,000 ($500,000 − $350,000 = $150,000).

Why would Royal Manufacturing Company pay $500,000 to Linden Manufacturing Company for only $350,000 assets? Evidently the Linden Manufacturing Company is worth more than $350,000 to the Royal Manufacturing Company, or they would never have consented to this purchase. Perhaps the Linden Manufacturing Company is a "growing concern" and has a fine reputation and many loyal customers. This is shown by the Intangible Asset, Goodwill.

Since Royal Manufacturing Company paid $150,000 more to the Linden Manufacturing Company than the value of the Assets received, why doesn't the Royal Manufacturing Company debit the $150,000 to an expense account entitled Loss on purchase of assets?

The government does not allow all the loss to be expensed in the year of the purchase. Such a thing would greatly lower the Income Tax of the Royal Manufacturing Company. The government insists that at the time of purchase, the Royal Manufacturing Company debit the Intangible Asset Aaccount, Goodwill, and write off this Goodwill over the years that the Goodwill will help the Royal Manufacturing Company.

• PROBLEM 13–25

The Royal Manufacturing Company purchased the Linden Manufacturing Company for $500,000. The Assets of the Linden Manufacturing Company on the day of purchase were as follows: Land, $100,000; Building, $150,000; Machinery, $75,000; and Furniture, $25,000. The purchase was recorded on the books of the Royal Manufacturing Company by debiting Building for $150,000; debiting Machinery for $75,000; debiting Furniture for $25,000; debiting Land for $100,000; debiting Goodwill for $150,000; and crediting Cash for $500,000.

How will Goodwill be amortized on the books of the Royal Manufacturing Company at the end of the first year?

SOLUTION:

2000		($ in dollars)
December 31 Amortization Expense	10,000	
Goodwill		10,000

Accountants usually write off Goodwill over a period not to exceed 15 years. In this case it was thought that the purchase of the Linden Manufacturing Company would benefit the Royal Manufacturing Company for 15 years, so the Goodwill was decided to be written off over that period of time ($150,000 divided by 15 = $10,000). Amortization Expense was debited for $10,000 on December 31, 2000, thus cutting down the Net Income of the Royal Manufacturing Company by that amount. The Intangible Asset, Goodwill, was credited for $10,000, thus cutting down the value of that account on the books.

• PROBLEM 13–26

The Royal Manufacturing Company purchased the Linden Manufacturing Company for $500,000. The Assets of the Linden Manufacturing Company on the day of the purchase were as follows: Land, $100,000; Building, $150,000; Machinery, $75,000; and Furniture, $25,000. The purchase was recorded on the books of the Royal Manufacturing Company by debiting Building for $150,000; debiting Machinery for $75,000; debiting Furniture for $25,000; debiting Land for $100,000; debiting Goodwill for $150,000; and crediting Cash for $500,000. Goodwill was amortized at the end of the first year on the books of the Royal Manufacturing Company by debiting Amortization Expense and crediting Goodwill for $10,000.

How will the Goodwill account appear on the books of the Royal Manufacturing Company at the end of the first year?

SOLUTION:

Goodwill			
1/2/2000	150,000	12/31/2000	10,000
	140,000		

On January 2, 2000, when the Royal Manufacturing Company purchased the Linden Manufacturing Company, the value of the Total Assets received by the Royal Manufacturing Company were $150,000 less than the cash paid. This $150,000 was debited to the Intangible Asset Account, Goodwill. An adjusting entry on December 31, 2000, credited Goodwill for $10,000, which is one-fifteenth of the $150,000 value of Goodwill at the time of purchase. This $10,000 credit cuts down the balance of the Goodwill account to $140,000 at the end of the year 2000.

At the end of each year the Amortization entry will debit Amortization Expense for $10,000 and credit Goodwill for $10,000, so that at the end of the 15th year, in this case, at the end of the year 2014, the Goodwill account will have a balance of 0 ($150,000 − $150,000 = 0).

• PROBLEM 13–27

The Schutz Restaurant has been in business in Central City for 25 years. During that time it has continued to expand both in terms of size of building and in terms of sales, as well as profits generated. Customers flock to the restaurant because of its excellent food and surroundings. The Board of Directors of the Schutz Restaurant is pleased that the sales and profits are increasing every year and believes that the Goodwill generated by the restaurant has not only brought more business to the restaurant itself but has helped the town of Central City expand. The board figures that this Goodwill generated over the years for the restaurant is worth at least $100,000.

Should they debit Goodwill on their Balance Sheet for $100,000 or for some other figure?

SOLUTION:

The accountant suggests that Goodwill not be placed on the Balance Sheet of the Schutz Restaurant at all. The accountant admits that because of the restaurant's location, good food, and atmosphere that a great deal of Goodwill has been generated not only for the restaurant itself but for the entire community, because people drive from miles around to visit the restaurant, and it is even recommended by nationally known restaurant associations. In fact, people come to eat at this restaurant from all parts of the country.

However, the accountant suggests that accountants agree that internally generated Goodwill, no matter how much and how important, should not be placed on the Balance Sheet of the corporation. In the first place, it is difficult to determine. In the second place, it is against the rules of the accountants. The only time that Goodwill should be listed on the Balance Sheet of a firm as an Intangible Asset is when the firm buys Assets of another firm for a price higher than the Total Assets are worth.

• PROBLEM 13–28

The William Restaurant Corporation owns a large restaurant on the west side of Sioux City that is doing well. Every year the sales and Net Income of this restaurant increase. On the east side of town is another restaurant named James Restaurant that is gradually "going under" financially. Each year the customers are fewer and the Net Loss is greater. Elderly Mr. James wants to retire to Florida and has been looking for a buyer, without success. Finally, he approaches representatives of the William Restaurant Corporation asking them if they will buy out his business. Appraisers determine that the Assets of the James Restaurant are as follows: Land, $8,000; Building, $6,000; Kitchen Appliances, $1,000; and Furniture, $1,000. With these figures in mind, the representatives of the William Restaurant Corporation offer Mr. James $10,000 for all the Assets. Mr. James agrees.

What entry will be made on the books of the William Restaurant Corporation at the time of purchase?

SOLUTION:

2000		($ in dollars)	
January 2	Land	8,000	
	Building	6,000	
	Kitchen Appliances	1,000	
	Furniture	1,000	
	Cash		10,000
	Badwill		6,000

Accountants and accounting associations generally agree that when the Assets purchased are worth more than the money paid, that the value of the Fixed Assets be decreased enough so that they total the amount of the cash paid.

The Board of Directors of the William Restaurant Association meet and agree to lower the price of the Land from $8,000 to $6,000, thus saving $2,000 ($8,000 – $6,000 = $2,000). They agree to lower the price of the Building from $6,000 to $3,000, thus saving $3,000 ($6,000 – $3,000 = $3,000). They agree to lower the price of the Kitchen Appliances from $1,000 to $500, thus saving $500 ($1,000 – $500 = $500). They agree to lower the price of the Furniture from $1,000 to $500, thus saving another $500 ($1,000 – $500 = $500). The total of the $6,000 for the Land plus the $3,000 for the Building plus the $500 for the Kitchen Appliances plus the $500 for the Furniture adds up to the $10,000 paid for the Assets of the restaurant.

Why would Mr. James agree to sell $16,000 assets for a mere $10,000? In this case he is old, wants to quit business, and cannot find an owner. Perhaps the restaurant has given poor service and has built up "Bad Will" which the new owner will have to counter with several years of losses while trying to build up internal Goodwill.

• PROBLEM 13–29

The Short Lumber Company is being sold to the Handel Construction Company. Just prior to the sale the Short Lumber Company sold all its inventory and paid all its debts. The Balance Sheet of the Short Lumber Company appears as follows:

Short Lumber Company
Balance Sheet
December 31, 1999

Assets:		
Land	10,000	
Building	50,000	
Furniture	10,000	
Equipment	6,000	
Total Assets		76,000
Owner's Equity		
Common Stock (par value)	100,000	
Deficit	– 24,000	
Total Equity		76,000

Officials of the Handel Construction Company determine from brokers that the Market Value of the Short Lumber Company stock is now worth only $10,000, so they offer Short Lumber Company $10,000 cash for their business. (The Asset Values were those of the purchase or Cost Prices years ago, and it is determined they are no longer of any value.) The Short Lumber Company accepts the offer.

What entry will be made on the books of the Handel Construction Company?

SOLUTION:

2000			($ in dollars)
January 2	Investment in Common Stock of the Short Lumber Company	100,000	
	Land	10,000	
	Building	50,000	
	Furniture	10,000	
	Equipment	6,000	
	Cash		10,000
	Badwill		166,000

The Handel Construction Company is investing in the stock of the Short Lumber Company, Par Value of which is $100,000. So on the Handel Construction Company books we debit the Asset Account, Investment in Common Stock of the Short Lumber Company, for $100,000. The assessors at this time have estimated that the value of the Land is $10,000; the value of the Building is $50,000; the value of the Furniture is $10,000; and the value of the Equipment is $6,000. Proceed to debit Land for $10,000; Building for $50,000; Furniture for $10,000; and Equipment for $6,000.

The Handel Construction Company is paying the Short Lumber Company $10,000, credit Cash for $10,000.

The plug figure to make debits equal credits is a credit of $166,000; credit Badwill for $166,000. Negative Goodwill (or Badwill) is a deferred credit and should he placed in the Liabilities section of the Balance Sheet. It should be written off over 15 years or less.

• PROBLEM 13–30

The Short Lumber Company has been sold to the Handel Construction Company. Because of a favorable purchase for the Handel Construction Company, there is a deferred credit called Badwill which is credited on its books for $166,000.

How is this Badwill amortized?

SOLUTION:

2000		($ in dollars)
December 31 Badwill	11,066	
Amortization Income		11,066

Badwill should be amortized over 15 years or over some lesser time that the board of directors determines. In this case, the board of directors decided to amortize the Badwill over 15 years. The $11,066 figure is determined by dividing the $166,000 Badwill by the 15 years, ($166,000 divided by 15 years = $11,066).

Badwill has a credit balance of $166,000 during the year of 2000. At the end of the year, on December 31, 2000, Badwill is debited for $11,066, bringing the balance in the Badwill account down to $154,934. An account entitled Amortization Income is credited for $11,066. This will add to the Handel Construction Company's Income for the year 2000, and the Handel Construction Company will have to pay Income Tax on it. On January 2, 2000, the Handel Construction Company made a bargain purchase gaining $166,000, but this gain is spread over 15 years, so only 1/15 of the gain ($11,066) needs be reported as Income during the year 2000.

• PROBLEM 13–31

The Short Lumber Company has been sold to the Handel Construction Company. Because of a favorable purchase for the Handel Construction Company, there is a deferred credit called Badwill which is credited on its books for $166,000. On December 31, 2000, Badwill is amortized by debiting Badwill for $11,066 and crediting Amortization Income for $11,066.

How will the Badwill account appear on the books of the Handel Construction Company on December 31, 2000?

SOLUTION:

	Badwill		
12/31/2000	11,066	1/2/2000	166,000
			154,934

On January 2, 2000, the Handel Construction Company made a bargain purchase gaining $166,000. This $166,000 was debited to a deferred credit account entitled Badwill. On December 31, 2000, an adjusting entry was made amortizing Goodwill for 1/15 of the $166,000 figure, or $11,066 (1/15 × $166,000 = $11,066). Thus, Badwill was debited for $11,066, bringing the balance of the Badwill account down to $154,934. Each year the Badwill account will be amortized for another $11,066, until at the end of the 15th year, in this case December 31, 2014, the Badwill account will be reduced to zero.

• PROBLEM 13–32

The Short Lumber Company is being sold to the Handel Construction Company. Just prior to the sale the Short Lumber Company sold all its inventory and paid all its debts. The Balance Sheet of the Short Lumber Company appears as follows:

Short Lumber Company
Balance Sheet
December 31, 1999

Assets:		
Land	10,000	
Building	50,000	
Furniture	10,000	
Equipment	6,000	
Total Assets		76,000
Owner's Equity		
Common Stock (par value)	100,000	
Deficit	–24,000	
Total Equity		76,000

Officials of the Handel Construction Company determine from brokers that the Market Value of the Short Lumber Company stock is now worth only $10,000, so they offer Short Lumber Company $10,000 cash for their business. (The Asset Values were those of the purchase prices years ago, and it is determined they are no longer of any value.) The Short Lumber Company accepts the offer.

What entry or entries will be made on the books of the Short Lumber Company on the date of the sale?

SOLUTION:

2000		($ in dollars)	
January 2	Common Stock	100,000	
	Deficit		24,000
	Land		10,000
	Building		50,000
	Furniture		10,000
	Equipment		6,000
January 2	Cash	10,000	
	Business		10,000

The Short Lumber Company debits Common Stock for $100,000 to close out the Common Stock account on its books which had a credit balance of $100,000.

The Short Lumber Company credits Deficit for $24,000 to close out the deficit account which had a debit balance on its books of $24,000. The Land account is credited for $10,000 to close it out, since it previously had a debit balance of $10,000. The Building account is credited for $50,000 to close it out, since it previously had a debit balance of $50,000. The Furniture account is credited for $10,000 to close it out, since it previously had a debit balance of $10,000. The Equipment account is credited for $6,000 to close it out, since it previously had a debit balance of $6,000.

The second entry debits Cash to show the receipt of $10,000 cash for the sale of the business. Since all the other accounts have now been closed out, a new temporary account entitled Business is credited for $10,000.

A third entry could be made as follows:

2000		($ in dollars)	
January 2	Business	10,000	
	Cash		10,000

The temporary account, Business, is debited for $10,000 to close it out. Cash is credited for $10,000 to show the payment of Cash to the Common Stockholders.

• PROBLEM 13-33

The Brown Drug Store has decided to become the Rexall Drug Store for Central City, the town in which it is located. There is no other Rexall store in Central City, and the national Rexall chain has agreed to have the Brown Drug Store represent them in the area. The Brown Drug Store is to change its name to the Brown Rexall Drug Store, buy all its drugs from the Rexall chain and to make the Rexall chain a one-time payment of $5,000 for the privilege of using their name. The Brown Drug Store feels that this contract will improve its business.

What entry will the Brown Rexall Drug Store make on its books on the date that the contract is signed and the money paid?

SOLUTION:

2000		($ in dollars)
January 2	Franchise	5,000
	Cash	5,000

The Brown Rexall Drug Store is purchasing an Intangible Asset so it debits Franchise for $5,000. It is paying Cash, so it credits Cash for $5,000.

• PROBLEM 13–34

The Brown Drug Store has decided to become the Rexall Drug Store for Central City, the town in which it is located. There is no other Rexall store in Central City, and the national Rexall chain has agreed to have the Brown Drug Store represent them in the area. The Brown Drug Store is to change its name to the Brown Rexall Drug Store, buy all its drugs from the Rexall chain and to make the Rexall chain a one-time payment of $5,000 for the privilege of using their name. The Brown Drug Store feels that this contract will improve its business.

Therefore, on January 2, 2000, the date on which the contract is signed and the money paid, the Brown Rexall Drug Store debits Franchise for $5,000 since it is getting the Intangible Asset, Franchise. It credits Cash since it is paying $5,000 cash.

What entry will be made on the books of the Brown Rexall Drug Store on December 31, 2000, to amortize this Intangible Asset?

SOLUTION:

2000		($ in dollars)
December 31 Amortization Expense	500	
Franchise		500

The owner of the Brown Rexall Drug Store has decided to amortize the franchise over a period of 10 years. Since the franchise cost is $5,000, the Amortization entry will be for $500 ($5,000 divided by 10 = $500). Amortization Expense will be debited for $500, and this expense will effectively cut down the Net Income of the business for the year 2000 by that amount. The Intangible Asset, Franchise, will be credited for $500.

• PROBLEM 13-35

The Brown Drug Store has decided to become the Rexall Drug Store for Central City, the town in which it is located. There is no other Rexall store in Central City, and the national Rexall chain has agreed to have the Brown Drug Store represent them in the area. The Brown Drug Store is to change its name to the Brown Rexall Drug Store, buy all its drugs from the Rexall chain, and make the Rexall chain a one-time payment of $5,000 for the privilege of using their name. The Brown Drug Store feels that this contract will improve its business.

Therefore, on January 2, 2000, the date on which the contract is signed and the money paid, the Brown Rexall Drug Store debits Franchise for $5,000 since it is getting the Intangible Asset, Franchise. It credits Cash since it is paying $5,000 Cash.

On December 31, 2000, the Brown Rexall Drug Store makes its first adjusting entry to amortize the Intangible Asset, Franchise, by debiting Amortization Expense for $500 and crediting Franchise for $500. The owner of the Brown Rexall Drug Store has decided to amortize the franchise over a period of 10 years. Since the franchise cost $5,000, the Amortization entry was $500 ($5,000 divided by 10 = $500).

How will the Franchise account appear on the books of the Brown Rexall Drug Store at the end of the year 2000 after the Amortization entry has been made?

SOLUTION :

	Franchise		
1/2/2000	5,000	12/31/2000	500
	4,500		

On January 2, 2000, when the franchise agreement was signed and the $5,000 paid by the Brown Rexall Drug Store to the Rexall Company, the Intangible Asset, Franchise, was debited for $5,000. On December 31,

2000, after the Amortization entry was made, the account, Franchise, was credited for $500, thus leaving a balance in the Franchise account at the end of the year 2000 of $4,500 ($5,000 – $500 = $4,500).

Each year the Franchise account will be amortized another $500, so at the end of 10 years (in this case by December 31, 2009), the Franchise account will be completely written off and will have a balance of zero.

• PROBLEM 13–36

The Keller Hardware Store has decided to incorporate. Legal fees come to $500, and incorporation fees come to $100.

How should these be recorded on the books of the Keller Hardware Corporation?

SOLUTION:

2000		($ in dollars)
January 2	Organization Costs	600
	Cash	600

Organization Costs is an Intangible Asset, so this is debited for $600, the sum of the $500 legal fees and $100 incorporation fees ($500 + $100 = $600).

• PROBLEM 13-37

The Keller Hardware Store has decided to incorporate. Legal fees come to $500, and incorporation fees come to $100. So, on January 2, 2000, the date of incorporation, the Intangible Asset, Organization Costs, is debited for $600. Since Cash is paid out, the account Cash is credited for $600.

The Internal Revenue Service allows Organization Costs to be amortized over five years, so the Board of Directors of the new corporation decides to amortize these Organization Costs over the first five years of the business.

What will be the first Amortization entry at the end of the year 2000?

SOLUTION:

2000	($ in dollars)	
December 31 Amortization Expense	120	
Organization Costs		120

The board has decided to amortize the $600 Organization Costs over the first five years of existence of the business. Therefore, the amount to be amortized each year is $120 ($600 divided by 5 years = $120).

Amortization Expense is debited for $120, and this expense tends to cut the Net Income of the business down by that amount. The Intangible Asset Account, Organization Costs, is credited for $120.

• PROBLEM 13–38

The Keller Hardware Store has decided to incorporate. Legal fees come to $500, and incorporation fees come to $100. On January 2, 2000, the date of incorporation, the Intangible Asset, Organization Costs, is debited for $600. Since Cash is paid out, the account, Cash, is credited for $600.

The Internal Revenue Service allows Organization Costs to be amortized over five years, so the Board of Directors of the new corporation decides to amortize these Organization Costs over the first five years of the business. On December 31, 2000, they debit Amortization Expense for $120 (1/5 of the $600 in the Organization Costs account) and credit Organization Costs $120.

How will the Organization Costs account appear on the books of the Keller Hardware Corporation at the end of the year 2000?

SOLUTION:

Organization Costs

1/2/2000	600	12/31/2000	120
	480		

On January 2, 2000, the date of incorporation, the Intangible Asset Account, Organization Costs, was debited for $600. On December 31, 2000, at the end of the first year of the corporation's existence, Organization Costs was credited for $120, which is 1/5 of $600 cost of organizing. (The Organization Cost is to be written off over 5 years). Thus, the balance of the account at the end of the first year will be $480 ($600 – $120 = $480).

Each year the Organization Costs account will be amortized another $120, so that at the end of the fifth year (in this case, December 31, 2004), the Organization Cost account will be completely amortized and its balance will be zero.

CHAPTER 14

CURRENT LIABILITIES

> **Basic Attacks and Strategies for Solving Problems in this Chapter. See pages 441 to 485 for step-by-step solutions to problems.**

Separating **Current Liabilities** from **Long-Term Liabilities** is crucial. Current Liabilities are debts of a business that must be paid within a year, or the creditors can force the business into involuntary bankruptcy. On the other hand, Long-Term Liabilities do not have to be paid for awhile and are not as crucial. It is important therefore, that the accountants of a business are careful to list all the short-term debts in the Current Liabilities section of the balance sheet so that stockholders, bondholders, and potential lenders can adequately discern the financial condition of the business.

Some notes require that Interest be paid in advance. These notes have their face value the same as the maturity value, and they are called **Non-Interest-Bearing Notes** (also referred to as Zero Interest Notes). Instead of using the account Interest Expense, they use a Contra-Liability account called **Discount on Notes Payable**.

Assume that the corporation declares stock dividends just prior to the year's end, but has not paid these stock dividends yet. In this case, a new Owners' Equity type of account called **Stock Dividends Distributable** should be placed in the capital section of the Balance Sheet.

Utilities often require that new customers make a returnable deposit with the utility before getting their gas or electricity or water turned on. A Deposits account will therefore need to be set up.

Most states have sales taxes. When a business sells merchandise, it collects sales tax from the customers and needs to credit a Liability Account called **Sales Taxes Payable**. At the quarter's end when the business mails the sales tax to the state, it would debit Sales Tax Payable to close out this debt and credit Cash.

Most local governments collect real property taxes. At month's end the business will need to debit an account called **Property Tax Expense** and credit **Property Tax Payable**. This entry will place the proper amount as an expense for doing business during that month. Finally, when the actual amount of the property tax is mailed by the business to the local government, the account Property Tax Payable is debited to close out this debt, and Cash is credited.

At the end of the year when the business figures the approximate Income Tax it owes the government, it debits **Income Tax Expense** for this amount and credits **Income Tax Payable**. When the business sends its Income Tax check to the government, it debits Income Tax Payable to close out this account and credits Cash.

At the end of the month the business determines how much vacation pay is owed the employees, and the business debits **Vacation Pay Expense** and credits **Vacations Payable** for this amount. Finally, when the employees take their vacation the Business debits Vacations Payable to close out this account and credits Cash.

Nowadays businesses often give warranties when they sell a product, especially those products requiring servicing. At year's end the business will debit **Warranties Expense** and credit **Warranties Payable** for the amount they think they will eventually have to pay for this year's sales, as warranties. Finally, when the warranty is paid, the business will debit Warranties Payable to close out this debt and credit Cash.

It is often difficult to tell a Current Liability from a Long-Term Liability. For instance, Notes Payable could be either one, depending on the length of the note. If a note runs for a year or less, it should be classified as a Current Liability. If a note runs for over a year, it should be classified as a Long-Term Liability.

The importance here is crucial. When banks are considering lending businesses money, they look over their Balance Sheets and Income Statements for several years past. One of the most important sections of Balance Sheets to possible lenders is the Current Liability section of the Balance Sheet. These list the debts of the firm that must be paid within a year. If the firm does not have the cash to pay when the debts become due, the creditors of the firm can force the firm into involuntary bankruptcy. The firm must have cash flow. It must have the cash to pay the bills as they come due. The bills coming due are the debts listed in the Current

Liability section of the Balance Sheet. Therefore, it is terribly important that the accountants separate the Current Liabilities from the Long-Term Liabilities accurately.

Step-by-Step Solutions to Problems in this Chapter, "Current Liabilities"

• PROBLEM 14–1

The Wilson Company records purchases at gross and uses a periodic inventory system. On August 1, 2000, the Wilson Company purchases $50,000 worth of inventory.

Make the entry that would appear on the books.

SOLUTION:

2000		($ in dollars)	
August 1	Purchases	50,000	
	Accounts Payable-Smith		50,000

Merchandise is coming into the company at Cost Price of $50,000, so the Cost Expense account Purchases is debited for $50,000. At this date (August 1, 2000), the Wilson Company is not yet paying cash, so it credits Accounts Payable for $50,000, and in the subsidiary ledger (Accounts Payable subsidiary ledger) it credits Smith, the company from whom the merchandise was purchased.

• PROBLEM 14–2

The Wilson Company records purchases at gross and uses a periodic inventory system. On August 1, 2000, the Wilson Company purchases from the Smith Company $50,000 worth of inventory. Purchases is debited and Accounts Payable—Smith is credited for $50,000. On September 1, 2000, the Wilson Company gives the Smith Company a $50,000, 10-month note at 8% in payment of account.

Show the entry on the books of the Wilson Company.

SOLUTION:

2000	($ in dollars)	
September 1 Accounts Payable—Smith	50,000	
Notes Payable		50,000

On August 1, 2000, when the Wilson Company purchased the merchandise, it gave its oral promise to pay the $50,000 by crediting Accounts Payable—Smith for $50,000. On September 1, 2000, the Wilson Company receives back its oral promise to pay by debiting Accounts Payable—Smith for $50,000. It then gives the Smith Company a written promise to pay—it gives a note for $50,000—and credits the account Notes Payable on its books for $50,000.

• PROBLEM 14–3

The Wilson Company records purchases at gross and uses a periodic inventory system. On August 1, 2000, the Wilson Company purchases from the Smith Company $50,000 worth of inventory. Purchases is debited and Accounts Payable—Smith is credited for $50,000. On September 1, 2000, the Wilson Company gives the Smith Company a $50,000, 10-month note at 8% in payment of account. It debits Accounts Payable—Smith for $50,000 and credits Notes Payable for $50,000.

On December 31, 2000, what adjusting entry should be made on the Wilson Company books to show accrual of Interest?

SOLUTION:

2000	($ in dollars)	
December 31 Interest Expense	1,333	
Interest Payable		1,333

The note is for $50,000 at 8%. This is $4,000 Interest per year ($50,000 × 8% = $4,000). The note was written on September 1, 2000, and it is now December 31, 2000, or four months later (the months of September, October, November, and December). Since there are 12 months in a year, 1/3 of a year has passed (4/12 = 1/3). The Interest accrued or built up for these four months is $1,333 ($4,000 Interest per year × 1/3 of a year elapsed = $1,333).

Interest Expense is debited for $1,333. This expense can be subtracted from the Gross Income in the Income Statement to cut down the Net Income by that amount and the Income Tax also. Since the Wilson Company is not paying any cash at this time, the Current Liability Account Interest Payable is credited for the $1,333.

• PROBLEM 14-4

The Wilson Company records purchases at gross and uses a periodic inventory system. On August 1, 2000, the Wilson Company purchases from the Smith Company $50,000 worth of inventory. Purchases is debited and Accounts Payable—Smith is credited for $50,000. On September 1, 2000, the Wilson Company gives the Smith Company a $50,000, 10-month note at 8% in payment of account. It debits Accounts Payable—Smith for $50,000 and credits Notes Payable for $50,000.

On December 31, 2000, the Wilson Company makes an adjusting entry for accrued Interest on its books as follows: it debits Interest Expense and credits Interest Payable for $1,333 ($50,000 × 8% × 1/3 of a year = $1,333).

What entry will be made on the maturity date when the Wilson Company pays the Smith Company both the Principal and the Interest?

SOLUTION:

2001		($ in dollars)	
July 1	Interest Payable	1,333	
	Interest Expense	2,000	
	Cash		3,333
July 1	Notes Payable	50,000	
	Cash		50,000

On December 31, 2000, the adjusting entry credited Interest Payable for $1,333 for Interest accrued during the months of September, October,

November, and December in the year 2000. Now this account is closed out by an entry debiting Interest Payable for $1,333. Interest Expense is debited for $2,000 for the months of January, February, March, April, May, and June of the year 2001 ($50,000 × 8% × 1/2 year = $2,000).

The account Cash is credited for $3,333, which is the total Interest for 10 months ($50,000 × 8% × 10/12 of a year = $3,333).

In the second entry the Wilson Company receives back its note marked "Paid" so debits Notes Payable for $50,000. It pays the Principal of $50,000 so credits Cash for $50,000.

• PROBLEM 14–5

The Wilson Company records purchases at gross and uses a periodic inventory system. On August 1, 2000, the Wilson Company purchases from the Smith Company $50,000 worth of inventory. Purchases is debited and Accounts Payable—Smith is credited for $50,000. On September 1, 2000, the Wilson Company gives the Brown Company a $50,000, 10-month note at 8% in payment of account. It debits Accounts Payable—Smith for $50,000 and credits Notes Payable for $50,000.

On December 31, 2000, the Wilson Company makes an adjusting entry for accrued Interest on its books as follows: it debits Interest Expense and credits Interest Payable for $1,333 ($50,000 × 8% × 1/3 of a year = $1,333).

How will the Liabilities appear on the Balance Sheet of the Wilson Company on December 31, 2000?

SOLUTION:

Wilson Company
Partial Balance Sheet
December 31, 2000

Current Liabilities:

Notes Payable	50,000
Interest Payable	1,333

• PROBLEM 14–6

On November 1, 2000, the Wilson Company borrowed $40,000 from the First National Bank of Central City at 10% for one year and signed a Non-Interest-Bearing note for $44,000.

What entry will they make on their books at this time?

SOLUTION:

2000		($ in dollars)	
November 1	Cash	40,000	
	Discount on Notes Payable	4,000	
	Notes Payable		44,000

The Wilson Company receives $40,000 from the First National Bank, so the Wilson Company debits Cash on its books for $40,000. The Wilson Co. gives the bank a note, the face value of which is $44,000, so credits Notes Payable for $44,000. The difference between the $44,000 and the $40,000 is $4,000 ($44,000 – $40,000 = $4,000). This $4,000 is debited to a Contra-Liability account entitled Discount on Notes Payable.

• PROBLEM 14–7

On November 1, 2000, the Wilson Company borrowed $40,000 from the First National Bank of Central City for 10% for one year and signed a Non-Interest-Bearing note for $44,000. The Wilson Company debited Cash for $40,000, debited Discount on Notes Payable for $4,000, and credited Notes Payable for $44,000.

What entry will Wilson Company make on its books to record accrued Interest on December 31, 2000?

SOLUTION:

2000		($ in dollars)	
December 31	Interest Expense	667	
	Discount on Notes Payable		667

The Interest accrued on the Note Payable (built up on the Note Payable) is $667 for the two months of November and December. The money was borrowed on November 1, 2000, and two months have since elapsed. It is now December 31, 2000, and Interest has to be computed on the note for those two months at 10%. This amounts to $667 ($40,000 ×10% × 2/12 = $667).

Thus, Interest Expense is debited for the $667. This is an expense account and will serve to cut down the Net Income for the year 2000 for the Wilson Company by that amount. The money was being used by Wilson Company during November and December, and the expense of borrowing that money is one of the company's expenses for the year 2000. The account, Discount on Notes Payable, is credited for the $667.

• PROBLEM 14–8

On November 1, 2000, the Wilson Company borrowed $40,000 from the First National Bank of Central City for 10% for one year and signed a Non-Interest-Bearing note for $44,000. The Wilson Company debited Cash for $40,000, debited Discount on Notes Payable for $4,000, and credited Notes Payable for $44,000. On December 31, 2000, the Wilson Company debited Interest Expense for $667 and credited Discount on Notes Payable for $667.

How will the Discount on Notes Payable account appear in the ledger of the Wilson Company at December 31, 2000?

SOLUTION:

Discount on Notes Payable

11/1/2000	4,000	12/31/2000	667
	3,333		

On November 1, 2000, the Discount on Notes Payable account was debited for $4,000, the difference between the amount borrowed $40,000, and the face of the note, $44,000 ($44,000 − $40,000 = $4,000). On

December 31, 2000, the amount of the Interest Expense for November and December of 2000 ($667) was credited to Discount on Notes Payable, leaving a balance in this account at year's end of $3,333. In actuality, the $3,333 is the amount of Interest that will be incurred during the remaining 10 months of the note's life.

• PROBLEM 14–9

On November 1, 2000, the Wilson Company borrowed $40,000 from the First National Bank of Central City for 10% for one year and signed a Non-Interest-Bearing note for $44,000. The Wilson Company debited Cash for $40,000, debited Discount on Notes Payable for $4,000, and credited Notes Payable for $44,000. On December 31, 2000, the Wilson Company debited Interest Expense for $667 and credited Discount on Notes Payable for $667.

How will the Liabilities sect,ion of the Wilson Company Balance Sheet appear at December 31, 2000?

SOLUTION

Wilson Company
Balance Sheet
December 31, 2000

Current Liabilities:

Notes Payable	44,000
Less: Discount on Notes Payable	3,333
	40,667

The Notes Payable is listed at the face value of the note—$44,000. The balance of the Discount on Notes Payable account at year's end is $3,333 ($4,000 – $667 = $3,333). This brings up the Net Amount owed by Wilson Company at year's end to $40,667. Thus, if Wilson Company wished to pay the note at this time, December 31, 2000, it would owe the bank $40,667.

• PROBLEM 14–10

On November 1, 2000, the Wilson Company borrowed $40,000 from the First National Bank of Central City for 10% for one year and signed a Non-Interest-Bearing note for $44,000, the Maturity Value. Thus, the face value of the note and the maturity value of the note are the same—$44,000. The Wilson Company debited Cash for $40,000, debited Discount on Notes Payable for $4,000, and credited Notes Payable for $44,000. On December 31, 2000, the Wilson Company debited Interest Expense for $667 and credited Discount on Notes Payable for $667, the amount of accrued Interest for the months of November and December, 2000.

What entry will be made on Wilson Company's books when the note is paid off at maturity date?

SOLUTION:

2001		($ in dollars)	
November 1	Notes Payable	44,000	
	Cash		44,000
November 1	Interest Expense	3,333	
	Discount on Notes Payable		3,333

The note runs for a year and was written on November 1, 2000. The maturity date is one year later, November 1, 2001. At this time the Wilson Company receives the note marked paid, and the face value of the note is $44,000. Thus, Wilson debits Notes Payable for $44,000 and closes out this account. Wilson Company is paying the First National Bank $44,000, so it credits Cash for $44,000.

In the second entry, Wilson Company debits Interest Expense for $3,333. This is the interest expense running from January 1, 2001, until November 1, 2001, or 10 months ($40,000 × 10% × 10/12 = $3,333). This Interest Expense is for the use of the money for the first ten months of the year 2001 and is legally deductible on the books of the Wilson Company for that year. The account, Discount on Notes Payable, is credited for $3,333 and this serves to close out that account.

• PROBLEM 14-11

The Sanson Corporation board of directors has decided to construct a new Factory Building on a piece of land that they already own. The factory building will cost $100,000. The company has not been able to borrow this money on a Long-Term basis but has received a Short-Term loan from the bank for $100,000 at 6% for 6 months. At the end of each 6-month period, the company plans to pay both the Principal and Interest on the note and continue renewing the note for a period of 10 years.

What entry should be made on the books of the Sanson Corporation when the money is borrowed, and how should this note appear in the Balance Sheet at year's end?

SOLUTION:

2000		($ in dollars)
December 31 Cash	100,000	
Note Payable		100,000

$100,000 Cash is being received by the Sanson Corporation, so Cash is debited for $100,000 on December 31, 2000, the date the money was borrowed from the bank. Note Payable is credited for $100,000 since this note was given to the bank at that time.

The note should be listed under Current Liabilities on the Balance Sheet of the Sanson Corporation on December 31, 2000. Even though the corporation plans to continue renewing the note every six months for the next ten years, the bank might not, in the future, agree to this. Thus, the note must be listed as a Current Liability, even though this weakens the Balance Sheet.

• PROBLEM 14-12

The Stanton Company, on December 1, 2000, declared a $.40 per share dividend on all the 10,000 shares of Common Stock it had outstanding. In the past, it had been in the habit of paying the dividend about 6 weeks after the board declared the dividend. There was no legal requirement that the corporation pay the dividend this quickly, however.

The corporation wishes to borrow money from a local bank and wants to make the Balance Sheet at year's end look as good as legally possible. The accountant suggests that Dividends Payable in the amount of $4,000 be listed on the Balance Sheet as a Long-Term Liability rather than as a Current Liability.

Is this according to Generally Accepted Accounting Standards?

SOLUTION:

Corporations must pay declared dividends within a year of the declaration, so they must be listed on the Balance Sheet as a Current Liability.

The $4,000 dividend is computed as follows: 10,000 shares of Common Stock outstanding times $.40 declared dividend equals $4,000 (10,000 × $.40 = $4,000).

• PROBLEM 14-13

The Babson Company is having a cash-flow problem and has not paid either Common or Preferred dividends in 3 years. There are 10,000 shares of 10% $100 Par Preferred Stock outstanding. This is a Total Par Value of $1,000,000 (10,000 shares × $100 Par Value per share = $1,000,000). Since the dividend rate is 10%, the dividend to be paid on the Preferred Stock each year is $100,000. ($1,000,000 Total Par Value × 10% = $100,000 yearly preferred dividends.) The dividends have not been paid for 3 years and amount to $300,000 ($100,000 yearly preferred dividends × 3 years = $300,000).

How should these dividends in arrears be reported on the Babson Company Balance Sheet on December 31, 2000, the end of the third year in arrears?

SOLUTION:

Babson Company
Partial Balance Sheet
December 31, 2000

Stockholders' Equity Section:

Preferred Stock, $100 Par, 10,000 shares

    outstanding, 10% dividend rate $1,000,000

    (dividends 3 years in arrears)

Some businesses disclose the dividends in arrears in parentheses, as above, and other businesses disclose the dividends in arrears as a footnote at the bottom of the Balance Sheet. This is part of the Capital section, not part of the Liability section, since dividends don't become a debt to the firm until the board of directors declares them.

• PROBLEM 14–14

The Richards Company has 3,000 shares of Common Stock outstanding and has just declared a 30% stock dividend. The accountant made the following entry on the corporate books:

2000		($ in dollars)
December 31 Retained Earnings	10,800	
Common Stock Dividends		
Distributable		9,000
Paid-In Capital in Excess of Par		1,800

Three thousand shares of Common Stock are outstanding, and a 30% stock dividend was declared by the board of directors of the Richards Company. So this is a total stock dividend of 900 shares (3,000 shares outstanding × 30% = 900 share dividend). The Par Value of the stock is $10 per share, so the Total Par Value of the Common Stock dividend is $9,000 (900 share dividend × $10 Par per share = $9,000).

The Market Value of the Richards Company Common Stock on December 31, 2000 is $12 per share, so the Total Market Value of the Common Stock dividend is $10,800 (900 share dividend × $12 Market Value per share = $10,800).

In the above entry, Retained Earnings account is debited for $10,800, the total Market Value of the Common Stock dividend declared. The stockholders' equity account, Common Stock Dividends Distributable, is credited for $9,000, the Total Par Value of the Common Stock dividend. The difference between the two—$1,800—is credited to a stockholders' equity account entitled Paid-In Capital in Excess of Par ($10,800 – $9,000 = $1,800).

How should these undistributed Common Stock dividends be reported on the Richards Company Balance Sheet on December 31, 2000?

SOLUTION:

Richards Company
Partial Balance Sheet
December 31, 2000

Stockholders' Equity Section:

Common Stock, 3,000 shares outstanding,	
Par Value $10 per share	$30,000
Common Stock Dividends Distributable, 900 shares	
@ $10 per share Par	9,000

It will be noted that the $9,000 stock dividend is placed in the Stockholders' Equity Section of the Balance Sheet because the account, Common Stock Dividends Distributable, is a Stockholders' Equity account. Although the dividend has been declared (but yet unpaid) by the board of directors, it is not a Liability to the corporation because the corporation will not be paying Cash, but stock certificates.

• PROBLEM 14–15

The Northern Electric Company requires a $20 returnable fee from each potential customer before the electric lights are turned on. At present they have 150,000 customers, therefore hold $3,000,000 in returnable fees. There is a 10% turnover of customers, on the average, each year.

What entry will be made on the Books when a new customer pays his/her fee; what entry will be made on the books when a customer leaves town; and how will these fees be placed in the Balance Sheet of the Northern Electric Company at year's end?

SOLUTION:

2000		($ in dollars)
February 1	Cash	20
	Returnable Deposits	20

A new customer has arrived in town, and he advances the Northern Electric Company $20 before his lights will be turned on. The company debits Cash for $20 since it is receiving this amount of money. It credits the Liability account, Returnable Deposits, since it now owes the customer this amount of money.

2000		($ in dollars)
April 1	Returnable Deposits	20
	Cash	20

On April 1, a customer moves away from town and asks for his $20 deposit. This is given to him. The company debits the Liability Account, Returnable Deposits, since this cuts down the company's debt to the customer. The company credits cash, because $20 is leaving the company's coffers and going to the customer.

Northern Electric Company
Partial Balance Sheet
December 31, 2000

Liabilities:

Current Liabilities:

    Returnable Deposits (Current Portion)   300,000

Long-Term Liabilities:

    Returnable Deposits (Long-Term Portion)   2,700,000

Returnable Deposits are definitely a Liability to the Northern Electric Company, because the company must pay the customers their $20 when they leave town. But should these be Current Liabilities or Long-Term Liabilities?

At present there are 150,000 customers, so the total amount of money in the Returnable Deposits account is $3,000,000 (150,000 customers × $20 fee = $3,000,000).

From past experience it is determined that there is a 10% turnover of customers during the average year, so 10% of the $3,000,000 needs to be on hand to pay customers leaving town (10% × $3,000,000 = $300,000). Thus, $300,000 should be placed in the company's Balance Sheet as a Current Liability. The remaining $2,700,000 should be placed in the company's Balance Sheet as a Long-Term Liability ($3,000,000 − $300,000 = $2,700,000).

• PROBLEM 14–16

The A. J. Ludkins Department Store issues gift certificates for future purchases.

    What entry does it make when customers purchase these gift certificates?

SOLUTION:

2000		($ in dollars)
October 20	Cash	50
	Unearned Revenue, Gift Certificates	50

Let us say that on October 20, 2000, a $50 gift certificate is sold. Cash is received by the store, so Cash is debited for $50. A Liability Account entitled Unearned Revenue, Gift Certificates is credited for $50. It has been determined through past experience that most gift certificates are used within a year of their purchase, so this account is listed in the store's Balance Sheet among the Current Liabilities.

• PROBLEM 14–17

The A. J. Ludkins Department Store issues gift certificates for future purchases. When a gift certificate is purchased, Cash is debited and a Liability Account entitled Unearned Revenue, Gift Certificates is credited.

What entry is made on the books of the A. J. Ludkins Department Store when the gift certificate is used?

SOLUTION:

2000		($ in dollars)
November 30 Unearned Revenue, Gift Certificates	50	
Sales		50

On November 30 the gift certificate is presented to the store clerk in payment of merchandise being purchased. The accountant debits the Liability Account Unearned Revenue, Gift Certificates for $50, since the Liability of the store is being decreased. It credits Sales, since merchandise is leaving the store. In this way, the account Unearned Revenue, Gift Certificates will always show the amount of the outstanding gift certificates as a Liability to the store.

• PROBLEM 14-18

The Romer Department Store is located in a state with a 5% sales tax. At the end of a typical business day the Gross Sales for the day are $10,000. In addition to this a sales tax of $500 has also been collected ($10,000 sales × 5% = $500 sales tax).

What entry will be made by the accountant on the books of the Romer Department Store to record this sale?

SOLUTION:

2000		($ in dollars)
February 1 Cash	10,500	
Sales		10,000
Sales Tax Payable		500

A total of $10,500 has been collected during the day and rung on the cash register, so Cash is debited for $10,500. Of this $10,500, $10,000 is sales, so the account Sales is credited for $10,000. Sales is a Revenue account. The difference of $500 is credited to the Liability Account entitled Sales Tax Payable. This money is owed to the state government.

• PROBLEM 14-19

The Hazel Department Store is located in a state with a 5% sales tax. At the end of a typical business day the Gross Sales are rung on the cash register along with the sales tax, and these total $10,500.

What entry will be made?

SOLUTION:

2000		($ in dollars)
February 1 Cash	10,500	
Sales		10,500

Cash is debited for $10,500, since that is the amount of cash collected during the day. Sales is credited for the total amount of $10,500.

However, the $10,500 is really the total of the Sales plus the Sales Taxes Payable. It is now necessary to separate the Sales from the Sales Taxes. The $10,500 amount is really the total of both. Let us call Sales 100%. We know that sales taxes are 5% of sales, so the figure $10,500 is really 105% (100% is sales and 5% is sales tax, or 100% + 5% = 105%). We now divide the $10,500 by 105% to get $10,000 which is the amount of the sales. The next step is to subtract the sales of $10,000 from the combined total of sales plus sales taxes ($10,500) to get $500 sales tax. The next journal entry will move the sales tax portion of the $10,500 from the sales account to the Sales Tax Payable account as follows:

2000		($ in dollars)
February 1	Sales	500
	Sales Tax Payable	500

At the end of the day, the Sales account will appear as follows:

Sales			
2/1/2000	500	2/1/2000	10,500
			10,000

In the first entry, Sales is credited for $10,500, but this figure is actually the total of the sales plus the sales taxes for the day. The second entry debits sales for $500, which is actually the sales taxes for the day. Thus, the balance of $10,000 ($10,500 − $500 = $10,000) is really the total of the sales for the day.

• PROBLEM 14–20

The Hazel Department Store is located in a state with a 5% sales tax. At the end of a quarter of a year the Sales Tax Payable account has a credit balance of $45,000. So the Hazel Department store mails a check for this amount to the State Department of Treasury.

What entry should the accountant make on the books of the Hazel Department Store at this time?

SOLUTION:

2000		($ in dollars)
March 31	Sales Tax Payable	45,000
	Cash	45,000

The debit to Sales Tax Payable for $45,000 closes out this account because the Hazel Department Store no longer owes the state this money. Cash is credited because the $45,000 is being sent to the state government.

• PROBLEM 14–21

The Royal Department Store receives from the county its yearly tax notice in January and pays half of its taxes in June and half in December. On January 15, 2000, the store receives a tax bill of $12,000 for the year 2000.

What entry will the store's accountant make on the books at the end of each month, and why?

SOLUTION:

2000		($ in dollars)
January 31	Property Tax Expense	1,000
	Property Tax Payable	1,000

The Royal Department Store has decided to accrue its Property Tax Expense monthly. Since the property taxes assessed for the year are $12,000, and since there are 12 months in a year, the monthly Property Tax Expense is $1,000 ($12,000 divided by 12 = $1,000).

Thus, on January 31, 2000, the end of the first month, the account Property Tax Expense is debited for $1,000 because the store enjoys the use of the property for the month. Since no money is paid to the county during January, the Liability Account Property Tax Payable is credited for $1,000. A similar entry is made at the ends of February, March, April, and May, so that at the beginning of June, the Property Tax Payable account appears as follows:

Property Tax Payable

1/31/2000	1,000
2/29/2000	1,000
3/31/2000	1,000
4/30/2000	1,000
5/31/2000	1,000
	5,000

• PROBLEM 14-22

On June 15, 2000, the Royal Department Store makes its semi-annual tax payment by sending a check to the county for $6,000, which is half the annual fee of $12,000.

What would the entry on the books look like?

SOLUTION:

2000		($ in dollars)	
June 15	Prepaid Property Tax	1,000	
	Property Tax Payable	5,000	
	Cash		6,000

Prepaid Property Tax is a Current Asset Account, and it is debited for $1,000 because this amount is paid in advance. Property Tax Payable is a Liability Account with a credit balance of $5,000. The debiting of this account temporarily closes it out, since the Royal Department Store no longer owes the county any money. Cash is credited for $6,000 since this is the amount of money being sent to the county.

On June 30, 2000, the following adjusting entry is made on the books of the Royal Department Store:

2000		($ in dollars)	
June 30	Property Tax Expense	1,000	
	Prepaid Property Tax		1,000

As is done each month, the Property Tax Expense account is debited for $1,000 because the store enjoys the use of the property for the month.

The property tax for the first six months of the year was paid on June 15, 2000, and since the June property tax was prepaid, the account Prepaid Property Tax is credited for $1,000, closing it out.

2000		($ in dollars)
July 31	Property Tax Expense	1,000
	Property Tax Payable	1,000

As is done each month, the Property Tax Expense is debited for $1,000 because the store had the use of the property for the month. Since the Prepaid Property Tax account is now closed out, the Liability Account Property Tax Payable is credited for $1,000. This same entry is made at the ends of August, September, October, and November. By the first part of December the Property Tax Payable account will have a credit balance of $5,000 ($1,000 each for the months of July, August, September, October, and November).

On December 15, 2000 the second property tax payment of $6,000 is made by the Royal Department Store to the county, and the entry on the books is as follows:

2000		($ in dollars)
December 15	Prepaid Property Tax	1,000
	Property Tax Payable	5,000
	Cash	6,000

Prepaid Property Tax is a Current Asset Account, and it is debited for $1,000 because this amount is paid in advance. Property Tax Payable is a Liability Account with a credit balance of $5,000. The debiting of this account for $5,000 temporarily closes it out, since the Royal Department Store no longer owes the county any money. Cash is credited for $6,000 since this is the amount sent to the county.

On December 31, 2000, the following adjusting entry is made on the books of the Royal Department Store:

2000		($ in dollars)
December 31	Property Tax Expense	1,000
	Prepaid Property Tax	1,000

As is done each month, the Property Tax Expense account is debited for $1,000 because the store enjoys the use of the property for the month. The property tax for the last six months of the year was paid on December

15, 2000, and since the December property tax was prepaid, the account Prepaid Property Tax is credited for $1,000.

• PROBLEM 14–23

On December 31, 2000, the John Brown Construction Company estimates its Income Tax Liability to the federal government for the year is $23,000.

What entry will it make on its books at this time?

SOLUTION:

2000		($ in dollars)
December 31 Income Tax Expense	23,000	
Income Tax Payable		23,000

Income Tax Expense is an expense of a corporation, but not of a partnership or single proprietorship. Partnerships and single proprietorships, as such, pay no Income Taxes, but these are paid through the personal Income Taxes of the partners or of the proprietor. Assume that the John Brown Construction Company is a corporation. The Income Tax Expense is the next-to-last line in a corporation's Income Statement and is the last deduction prior to the Net Income—the last line of the Income Statement. Income Tax Payable is credited for $23,000, and it is a Current Liability Account which will be closed out a couple of months later when the corporation pays its Income Tax. Of course, the corporation could pay an estimated tax earlier than this to avoid extra Interest or penalties from the government for not paying its taxes earlier.

• PROBLEM 14–24

On December 31, 2000, the John Brown Construction Company estimates its Income Tax Liability to the federal government for the year is $23,000. It debits Income Tax Expense and credits Income Tax Payable for $23,000 on that date. On January 15, 2001, after completing its Income Tax forms in more detail, it determines that it only owes the government $22,500, so sends in the forms and a check for $22,500 on that date.

What entry will the John Brown Construction Company make on its books?

SOLUTION:

2001		($ in dollars)	
January 15	Income Tax Payable	23,000	
	Deferred Tax Liability		500
	Cash		22,500

Income Tax Payable is debited for $23,000 to close out this account. Cash is credited to show that $22,500 was sent to the government. The difference of $500 is credited to Deferred Tax Liability, a Long-Term Liability account which may or may not need to be paid in the future.

• PROBLEM 14–25

The Henry Smith Company began business on January 2, 2000. They immediately hired five employees. The employment contracts stated that the employees would get two weeks' paid vacation each year, beginning with the second year of employment.

What entry or entries, if any, would the Henry Smith Company make on its books during the year 2000, the first year of employment?

SOLUTION:

2000	($ in dollars)
December 31 Wages Expense	4,000
Vacation Wages Payable	4,000

Each employee receives $400 gross wages per week, and there are 5 employees, so this is $2,000 gross wages per week that the employer must pay (5 employees × $400 per week each = $2,000 per week). Vacation pay is 2 weeks per year, beginning the second year of employment, so vacation pay is $4,000 ($2,000 gross wages per week × 2 weeks' vacation = $4,000).

Therefore, there are no paid vacations during the year 2000, since the contract does not allow paid vacations the first year. However, the first year's work determines the vacations for the second year. Therefore accrued (built up) monies for vacations at the end of the first year amount to $4,000 (2 weeks' pay at first year's wages). Thus, on December 31, 2000, an adjusting entry is made on the books of the Henry Smith Company debiting Wages Expense for $4,000. This is an expense of the year 2000, since the employees' work in that year builds up to pay for their vacations the following year. The Liability Account entitled Vacation Wages Payable is credited for $4,000 to show that at the end of the year 2000 the company has a Liability built up during the year 2000 to pay the employees vacation pay during the year 2001.

• PROBLEM 14–26

The Henry Smith Company began business on January 2, 2000. They immediately hired five employees. The employment contracts stated that the employees would receive two weeks' paid vacation each year, beginning with the second year of employment.

Each employee receives $400 gross wages per week during the first year of employment (the year 2000), and there are 5 employees, so this is $2,000 gross wages per week that the employer must pay (5 employees × $400 per week each = $2,000 per week). Vacation pay is for 2 weeks per year, beginning the second year of employment, so vacation pay is $4,000 ($2,000 gross wages per week × 2 weeks' vacation = $4,000).

The first year's work determines the vacations for the second year, therefore accrued (built up) monies for vacations at the end of the first year amount to $4,000 (2 weeks' pay at first year's wages). Thus, on December 31, 2000, an adjusting entry is made on the books of the Henry Smith Company debiting Wages Expense for $4,000. This is an expense of the year 2000, since the employees' work in that year builds up to pay for their vacations the following year. The Liability Account entitled Vacation Wages Payable is credited for $4,000 to show that at the end of the year 2000 the company has a Liability built up during the year 2000 to pay the employees' vacation pay during the the year 2001.

At the beginning of the year 2001 the Henry Smith Company raises each employee's pay from $400 per week to $410 per week.

What entry will the company make on its books at the end of the year 2001 to show payment for vacations, assuming that each employee takes a 2-week vacation during the year 2001?

SOLUTION:

2001		($ in dollars)
December 31 Vacation Wages Payable	4,000	
Wages Expense	100	
Cash		4,100

The adjusting entry at the end of the year 2000 credited Vacation Wages Payable for $4,000 showing the accrued wages for vacations at the end of that year. Now debit Vacation Wages Payable for $4,000 to close out that account. Cash is credited because that amount is paid the employees for their two weeks' vacation at the new higher wage rates for the year 2001 (5 employees × $410 per week new wages × 2 weeks' vacation = $4,100). The difference between the old two weeks' wage of $4,000 and the new two weeks' wage of $4,100 ($100) is debited to Wages Expense and is an expense of the year 2001.

Also on December 31, 2001, another accrual entry needs to be made to accrue the vacations earned by the employees during the year 2001 but not paid to them until the next year. This entry will be as follows:

2001		($ in dollars)
December 31 Wages Expense	4,100	
Vacation Wages Payable		4,100

The figure $4,100 is the total wages for the two-week period at the new wage rate for the year 2001. This amount is debited to Wages Expense and is an expense for the year 2001 that the employees have built up during that year but that will not be used until the year 2002. Vacation Wages Payable is a Liability Account and credited for the $4,100 since it is owed to the employees who will use it next year.

• PROBLEM 14-27

The William Smith Company is beginning business. William Smith, the owner, works full time and has just employed Mary Harmon to be his office secretary at a gross wage of $500 per month, as of the first of January, 2000. She gets paid once a month.

What entry will the William Smith Company make on its books on January 31, 2000, the first payday for Mary Harmon?

SOLUTION:

2000		($ in dollars)
January 31	Wages and Salary Expense	500.00
	Withholding Taxes Payable	75.00
	FICA Taxes Payable	38.25
	United Way Payable	10.00
	Cash	376.75

Assume that the William Smith Company is located in a place where there are no state and local withholding taxes. William Smith debits Wages and Salary Expense for the full gross wages of $500, and this amount is a Deductible Expense in Smith Company's Income Statement.

William Smith looks at a government withholding table and also looks at the W-4 form that Mary Harmon filed when employed to see how many exemptions Mary reports. He then notices that since he pays monthly he should withhold $75 from Mary's pay for the Federal Withholding Tax. He thus credits the Liability Account Withholding Taxes Payable for $75.

The social security withholding is called FICA, meaning Federal Insurance Contributions Act, and this money goes to old age payments and to Medicare. At present (1991) it is 7.65% of the gross wages, so it is $38.25 ($500 gross wages × 7.65% = $38.25). Therefore, the Liability Account entitled FICA Taxes Payable is credited for $38.25. Mary Harmon has also given her employer written consent to withhold $10 from each month's paycheck for United Way, so we also credit the Liability Account, United Way Payable for $10. This leaves only $376.75 to Mary Harmon for takehome pay, so we write her a check for this amount and credit Cash $376.75 ($75.00 Federal Withholding + $38.25 FICA + $10. United Way = $123.25 Total Deductions. $500.00 Gross Pay − $123.25 Total Deductions = $376.75 Net Pay or Takehome Pay).

• PROBLEM 14–28

The William Smith Company is beginning business. William Smith, the owner, works full time and has just employed Mary Harmon to be his office secretary at a gross wage of $500 per month, as of the first of January, 2000. She gets paid once a month.

Assume that the William Smith Company is located in a place where there are no state and local withholding taxes. William Smith debits Wages and Salary Expense for the total gross pay of $500. He credits Withholding Taxes Payable for $75, a figure which he gets from a federal withholding table. He credits FICA Taxes Payable for $38.25 ($500 gross pay × 7.65% = $38.25). He also credits United Way Payable for $10 and credits Cash for the take-home pay of $376.75.

What entry will the William Smith Company need to make on its books on January 31, 2000, for employer payroll taxes, and why?

SOLUTION:

2000		($ in dollars)	
January 31	Payroll Tax Expense	70.75	
	FICA Taxes Payable		38.25
	FUTA Taxes Payable		4.00
	SUTA Taxes Payable		28.50

For the Federal Insurance Contributions Act, the employer is required to match the amount that he withheld from the employee. In this case it is $38.25 ($500 gross pay × 7.65% = $38.25). Therefore, FICA Taxes Payable is credited for $38.25. The Federal Unemployment Tax Act requires employers to withhold .8% of the employee's gross pay up to a ceiling of $7,000 at the present time. Since this is the first month of the year and the employee, Mary Harmon, has not yet earned the ceiling amount, all of her gross pay is subject to the .8% tax which is just on the employer ($500 gross pay × .8% = $4). Thus the employer credits FUTA Taxes Payable for $4. FUTA stands for Federal Unemployment Tax Act.

Most states force employers to pay 5.7% of the employee's gross pay. Assume that this state has the 5.7% rate. The employer then credits SUTA Taxes Payable for $28.50 ($500 gross pay × 5.7% = $28.50).

The total of the three taxes is $70.75 ($38.25 Federal Insurance Contributions Act + $4 Federal Unemployment Tax Act + $28.50 State Unemployment Tax Act = $70.75). Thus the account Payroll Tax Expense is debited for $70.75. This is a regular expense of the business and is deductible in the Income Statement of the William Smith Company.

• PROBLEM 14-29

The William Smith Company is beginning business. William Smith, the owner, works full time and has just employed Mary Harmon to be his office secretary at a gross wage of $500 per month, as of the first of January, 2000. She gets paid once a month.

Let us assume that the William Smith Company is located in a place where there are no state and local withholding taxes. On January 31, 2000 William Smith debits Wages and Salary Expense for Mary Harmon's gross pay of $500; credits Withholding, Taxes Payable for $75; credits FICA Taxes Payable for $38.25; credits United Way Payable for $10; and credits Cash for $376.75. For the employer tax he on the same date debits Payroll Tax Expense for $70.75; credits FICA Taxes Payable for $38.25; credits FUTA Taxes Payable for $4; and credits SUTA Taxes Payable for $28.50.

These two entries are also made on the last day of February and the last day of March, 2000.

How will the Withholding Taxes Payable account and the FICA Taxes Payable account appear on the books of the William Smith Company on March 31, 2000?

SOLUTION:

Withholding Taxes Payable		
(employee withholding)	1/31/2000	75.00
(employee withholding)	2/29/2000	75.00
(employee withholding)	3/31/2000	75.00
		225.00

FICA Taxes Payable

(employee withholding)	1/31/2000	38.25
(employer taxes)	1/31/2000	38.25
(employee withholding)	2/29/2000	38.25
(employer taxes)	2/29/2000	38.25
(employee withholding)	3/31/2000	38.25
(employer taxes)	3/31/2000	38.25
		229.50

• PROBLEM 14–30

The William Smith Company is beginning business. William Smith, the owner, works full time and has just employed Mary Harmon to be his office secretary at a gross wage of $500 per month, as of the first of January, 2000. She gets paid once a month.

Assume that the William Smith Company is located in a place where there are no state and local withholding taxes. (There still are some places left, such as Wyoming.) On January 31, 2000, William Smith debits Wages and Salary Expense for Mary Harmon's gross pay of $500; credits Withholding Taxes Payable for $75; credits FICA Taxes Payable for $38.25; credits United Way Payable for $10; and credits Cash for $376.75. For the employer tax, he, on the same date, debits Payroll Tax Expense for $70.75; credits FICA Taxes Payable for $38.25; credits FUTA Taxes Payable for $4; and credits SUTA Taxes Payable for $28.50.

These two entries are also made on the last day of February and the last day of March, 2000. Each quarter the William Smith Company is to mail in the Withholding Tax and the FUTA tax to the federal government.

How much will this be, and what entry will be made on the books of the William Company?

SOLUTION:

2000		($ in dollars)	
March 31	Withholding Taxes Payable	225.00	
	FICA Taxes Payable	229.50	
	Cash		454.50

At March 31, 2000, the Withholding Taxes Payable account has a credit balance of $225 ($75 per month times three months = $225). At March 31, 2000, the FICA Taxes Payable account has a credit balance of $229.50 ($38.25 deducted twice each month for three months = $38.25 × 6 = $229.50).

Therefore, on March 31, 2000, at the time the William Smith Company remits its taxes to the federal government, Withholding Taxes Payable account is debited for $225.00 to close out this account. Also, FICA Taxes Payable account is debited for $229.50 to close out this account. Cash is credited for the total of $454.50 which is remitted by check to the federal government ($225.00 + $229.50 = $454.50).

• PROBLEM 14–31

The William Smith Company is beginning business. William Smith, the owner, works full time and has just employed Mary Harmon to be his office secretary at a gross wage of $500 per month, as of the first of January, 2000. She gets paid once a month.

On January 31, 2000, William Smith debits Wages and Salary Expense for Mary Harmon's gross pay of $500; credits Withholding Taxes Payable for $75; credits FICA Taxes Payable for $38.25; credits United Way Payable for $10; and credits Cash for $376.75. For the employer's tax, the employer on the same day debits Payroll Tax Expense for $70.75; credits FICA Taxes Payable for $38.25; credits FUTA Taxes Payable for $4; and credits SUTA Taxes Payable for $28.50.

These same two entries are also made on the last day of February and the last day of March, 2000.

Each quarter the William Smith Company is to mail in the Withholding Tax and the FUTA tax to the federal government. They do this by debiting Withholding Taxes Payable for $225.00; debiting FICA Taxes Payable for $229.50; and crediting Cash for $454.50.

This same entry is made on the last day of the year.

What other entries need to be made on the last day of the year by employer?

SOLUTION:

2000	($ in dollars)	
December 31 FUTA Taxes Payable	48.00	
Cash		48.00
December 31 SUTA Taxes Payable	342.00	
Cash		342.00
December 31 United Way Payable	120.00	
Cash		120.00

The federal government requires employers to remit their Federal Unemployment taxes annually. In this case the monthly withholding for employee Mary Harmon was $4 ($500 monthly gross wage × .8% = $4.00). The FUTA Taxes Payable account was credited for $4 each month for all the 12 months of the year, and at year's end totaled $48 ($4 monthly × 12 months = $48.00). The William Smith Company sends the federal government a check for $48 at year's end and debits FUTA Taxes Payable for $48, thus closing out this account, and credits Cash for $48.

Each month the employer credits State Unemployment Taxes Payable for $28.50 ($500 gross pay × 5.7% = $28.50). At year's end, after 12 such entries, the State Unemployment Taxes account would have a credit balance of $342.00 ($28.50 × 12 = $342.00). So the employer debits SUTA Taxes Payable to close out this account and credits Cash on the last day of the year when he mails a check for $342.00 to the State Department of Treasury.

When Mary Harmon was employed, she signed a statement allowing her employer to withhold $10 per month from her pay for the United Way fund. At year's end the account United Way Payable has a credit balance of $120 ($10 monthly × 12 months in a year = $120). So on December 31, 2000, the employer debits the account United Way Payable for $120, thus closing out the account, and credits Cash when they send a check for $120 to the United Way.

• PROBLEM 14–32

The William Smith Company is beginning business. William Smith, the owner, works full time and has just employed Mary Harmon to be his office secretary at a gross wage of $500 per month or $6,000 per year ($500 per month × 12 months per year = $6,000), as of the first of January, 2000. She gets paid once a month.

ERISA, a government pension law passed in the 1970s, encourages businesses to set up pension plans for their employees, and if these pension plans are set up according to government standards, the businesses can deduct the Pension Expense as Business Expenses, thus lowering their Income Taxes.

In a contract with employee Mary Harmon, the William Smith Company promises to set aside pension money each year equal to 5% of her yearly income.

How will this pension be recorded on the books of the William Smith Company at the end of the first year of Mary's employment?

SOLUTION:

2000		($ in dollars)
December 31 Pension Expense	300	
Pension Payable		300

Let us assume that the William Smith Company is following the government guidelines for an approved pension plan. The firm, at the end of the year 2000, sets aside $300 to begin Mary Harmon's pension fund ($6,000 annual salary × 5% = $300). Pension Expense is debited for $300, and this expense, if the government rules are followed, can be legally deducted from Gross Income in determining Net Income in William Smith Company's income statement for the year 2000. The Liability Account, Pension Payable, is credited for the $300. Each year that Mary Harmon continues to work for the William Smith Company this Pension Payable will build up for her future. If Mary is not yet of retirement age, this will be placed under the Long-Term Liability section of William Smith Company's Balance Sheet. However, if Mary plans to retire in the next year, this Pension Payable account would have to be placed in the Current Liability section of the Balance Sheet.

• PROBLEM 14–33

The William Smith Company is beginning business. William Smith, the owner, works full time and has just employed Mary Harmon to be his office secretary at a gross wage of $500 per month or $6,000 per year ($500 per month × 12 months per year = $6,000), as of the first of January, 2000. She gets paid once a month.

William Smith is good natured. Also, he wants Mary Harmon to feel herself to be an integral part of the business, meaning the harder she works the better the business will be. To encourage Mary to feel this way, William Smith tells Mary that at the end of the year she, in addition to her salary, will receive a bonus of 10% of the firm's profits. On December 31, 2000, the Net Income of the William Smith Company is determined to be $80,000.

How much of this is bonus to Mary Harmon, and how will this be recorded on the books of the company?

SOLUTION:

2000	($ in dollars)
December 31 Bonus Expense	7,272
Bonus Payable	7,272

The Net Income before bonus is $80,000, but Mary Harmon's bonus is 10% of the Net Income after bonus, because bonus is a Legal Expense of the business. So the bonus is determined by a simple algebraic equation as follows:

B = Bonus

B = .10 ($80,000 – B)

This equation means that the Bonus equals 10% of the $80,000 Net Income before bonus less bonus.

The equation is solved as follows:

B = .10 ($80,000 – B)

The first step is to multiply the .10 by the figures within the parentheses, as follows:

10 times $80,000 is $8,000.

.10 times B is .10B.

Thus, after multiplying the figures within the parentheses by .10, we get the following equation:

B = $8,000 – .10B

The next step is to move the –.10B to the other side of the equation. When this is done, the –.10B becomes a plus .10B, as follows:

1.00 B + .10B = $8,000

The next step is to add the "B", which can also be expressed as 100%B or 1.00B to the .10B to get 1.10B.

1.10B = $8,000

The next step is to divide the $8,000 by the 1.10 to get $7,272. Thus, the equation reads as follows:

$$\frac{1.10B}{1.10} = \frac{\$8,000}{1.10}$$

B = $7,272 (Bonus = $7,272)

This can be proven as follows:

Net Income before bonus	$80,000
Less: Bonus	−7,272
Net Income after bonus	72,728

The bonus is 10% of the Net Income after bonus, figured as follows:

$72,728 × 10% = $7,272.

• PROBLEM 14–34

The William Smith Company is beginning business. William Smith, the owner, works full time and has just employed Mary Harmon to be his office secretary at a gross wage of $500 per month or $6,000 per year ($500 per month × 12 months per year = $6,000), as of the first of January, 2000. She gets paid once a month.

William Smith is good natured. Also, he wants Mary Harmon to feel herself to be an integral part of the business, meaning the harder she works the better the business will be. To encourage Mary to feel this way, William Smith tells Mary that at the end of the year she, in addition to her salary, will receive a bonus of 10% of the firm's profits.

On December 31, 2000, the Net Income of the William Smith Company is determined to be $80,000 before Bonus Expense is deducted. The bonus is determined to be $7,272 (see problem immediately before this one). On January 2, 2001, Mary receives the cash bonus.

How much does she receive and how will it be recorded on the company books?

SOLUTION:

2001		($ in dollars)	
January 2	Bonus Payable	7,272.00	
	Federal Withholding Tax Payable		1,090.80
	FICA Tax Payable		556.31
	Cash		5,624.89

The Bonus Payable Account is debited for $7,272, the amount of the bonus. Since on December 31, 2000, this account was credited for $7,272, this debit entry will serve to close out the account. The Federal Withholding Tax Payable amount will depend on a Federal Tax table. Here, for convenience, we are merely taking 15% percent of the Bonus Payment (15% × $7,272 = $1,090.80). So we credit Federal Withholding Tax Payable for $1,090.80.

The FICA tax on the bonus is 7.65% of the bonus (7.65% × $7,272 = $556.31). Credit FICA Tax Payable for $556.31. Next, credit Cash for the take-home pay of $5,624.89 ($7,272.00 bonus − $1,090.80 federal withholding tax − $556.31 FICA tax = $5,624.89 Net Pay).

• PROBLEM 14-35

Elderly Mrs. Lottabucks is walking on a snowy icy day in front of the offices of the Buck Construction Company. She slips and breaks her leg and is in terrible pain. Finally, the ambulance comes and transports her to the hospital where she runs up a huge bill. She sues the Buck Construction Company for $500,000. As of December 31, 2000, the case has not come up in court, the lawyers for the Buck Construction Company are not sure which side will win, or how much the actual indemnity will be, if any.

How should this be presented, if at all, in the books of the Buck Construction Company?

SOLUTION:

Buck Construction Company
Partial Balance Sheet
December 31, 2000

Footnote: On February 1, 2000, Mrs. Lottie Lottabucks slipped on the ice on the sidewalk in front of the Buck Construction Company office. She is suing the company for $500,000. At this time the lawyers for the company have no idea whether or not Mrs. Lottabucks can win the case or how much, if any, the company will have to pay.

Has a probable Liability occurred? We will have no idea until the court decides the case. Mrs. Lottabucks may lose and there will be no Liability to the company at all. Can the amount be reasonably estimated? No.

Therefore no Liability should be placed in the Liabilities section of the Buck Construction Company Balance Sheet. Only a footnote similar to the one above should be placed at the bottom of the Balance Sheet to notify the reader of a Contingent Liability.

• PROBLEM 14–36

Elderly Mrs. Lottie Lottabucks has been walking on a snowy icy day in front of the offices of the Buck Construction Company. She slips and breaks her leg and is in terrible pain. Finally, the ambulance comes and transports her to the hospital where she runs up a huge bill. She sues the Buck Construction Company for $500,000. The jury has decided in Mrs. Lottabucks' favor, but only for the amount of the actual hospital costs, which are $100,000. These have not been paid yet by the Buck Construction Company because they are taking the case to a higher court.

How should this be reported in the general journal at year's end?

SOLUTION:

2000	($ in dollars)
December 31 Estimated Loss	100,000
Loss Liability	100,000

In this case the court has declared that the Buck Construction Company has a definite Liability. Also, the jury has awarded Mrs. Lottabucks $100,000, so the amount of the Liability is definitely known. The only thing that makes it a Contingent Liability (maybe debt) is that the higher court could reverse the decision. Therefore, the company should debit an expense account (in this case the expense account is entitled Estimated Loss) for $100,000. This Estimated Loss account is a valid expense, and the company can deduct it on its December 31, 2000, Income Statement in computing the Net Income. Thus, it will legally cut down the company's Income Tax.

The account, Loss Liability, is credited for $100,000, and this will appear in the Current Liabilities section of the company's Balance Sheet, even though it is a Contingent Liability because there is a definite Liability and the amount is known.

• PROBLEM 14–37

The Rudolph Broom Company sells regular brooms for $10 apiece. Each broom has a warranty that if it wears out within two months of the sale, the $10 sales price will be returned to the customer.

What entry will be made on the books of the Rudolph Broom Company at the end of the year, assuming that 50,000 brooms have been sold?

SOLUTION:

2000	($ in dollars)
December 31 Cash	500,000
Sales	500,000

Let us assume that all sales are cash sales. 50,000 brooms have been sold during the year for $10 each, so the total sales in dollars for the year are $500,000 (50,000 brooms × $10 sales price per broom = $500,000).

During the year, 3,000 brooms have been returned because they wore out in the first 2 months of use, and $30,000 total was refunded to customers (3,000 brooms returned × $10 sales price per broom = $30,000).

2000		($ in dollars)
December 31 Warranty Expense	30,000	
Cash		30,000

Warranty Expense was debited for $30,000, and this is a true expense of the business, deductible on the Income Statement for the year 2000.

This is the Cash Method of Accounting for Warranty Expenses and is the only one allowed for Income Tax purposes.

• PROBLEM 14–38

The Smithson Chevrolet Company has a regular 2-year warranty with each car, promising to repair the car free of charge during that period. At the time of sale, the Smithson Chevrolet Company also offers to sell the customer an additional 2-year warranty for $500. This would cover repairing the car for the third and fourth years after the sale. Some customers buy this additional 2-year warranty and others do not. Bill Hanson, a customer, buys a car for $15,000 and also pays $500 extra for the 2-year additional warranty.

How will this be handled on the books of the Smithson Chevrolet Company?

SOLUTION:

2000		($ in dollars)
January 2 Cash	15,000	
Sale		15,000
January 2 Cash	500	
Unearned Warranty Revenue		500

As with any cash sale, Cash is debited here for $15,000, the purchase price of the car, and Sale (an Income Account) is credited for $15,000. An additional entry is made to record the additional warranty which the customer has purchased. Cash is debited for $500 to show the extra cash coming in from the sale of the extra warranty and a Liability Account entitled Unearned Warranty Revenue is credited for $500.

• PROBLEM 14–39

The Smithson Chevrolet Company has a regular 2-year warranty with each car, promising to repair the car free of charge during that period. At the time of sale, the Smithson Chevrolet Company also offers to sell the customer an additional 2-year warranty for $500. This would cover repairing the car for the third and fourth years after the sale. Some customers buy this additional 2-year warranty and others do not.

Bill Hanson, a customer, buys a car for $15,000 and also pays $500 extra for the 2-year additional warranty, on January 2, 2000. The company debits Cash for $15,000 and credits Sales for $15,000. The company also debits Cash for $500 and credits a Liability Account entitled Unearned Warranty Revenue for $500.

What entry will the Smithson Chevrolet Company make regarding this warranty in future years?

SOLUTION:

During the years 2001 and 2002 the Smithson Chevrolet Company will make no entries regarding the warranty, because during that time Bill Hanson's car is protected under the first warranty that goes along with the original sales price of the car.

However, on December 31, 2003, the Smithson Chevrolet Company will make the following entry on its books:

2003		($ in dollars)
December 31 Unearned Warranty Revenue	250	
Warranty Revenue		250

The additional Warranty Cost the customer $500 and it runs for two years. Thus, for each of the two years the earnings would be $250 ($500 divided by 2 years = $250). On December 31, 2003, the Liability Account

Unearned Warranty Revenue is debited for $250, thus cutting the balance of this account down to $250. The Income Account entitled Warranty Revenue is credited for $250. This $250 will have to be added to the earnings of the Smithson Chevrolet Company for the year 2003.

The same entry, debiting Unearned Warranty Revenue for $250 and crediting Warranty Revenue for $250, will be made at the end of the year 2004, thus closing out the Unearned Warranty Revenue Liability Account.

• PROBLEM 14–40

The Hansen Grocery decided to purchase green trading stamps and issue them to customers purchasing certain products in order to enhance its sales.

What entry or entries would be made on its books?

SOLUTION:

2000		($ in dollars)	
January 2	Trading Stamps	10,000	
	Cash		10,000

The Hansen Grocery purchases $10,000 worth of trading stamps from the Green Trading Stamp Company. This Green Trading Stamp Company has stores here and there where luxury items are sold for their trading stamps. Hansen Grocery debits the Asset Account Trading Stamps for $10,000 and credits Cash $10,000, sending the Green Trading Stamp Company a check for $10,000.

During the year the Hansen Grocery makes $500,000 worth of Cash Sales and records these as follows:

2000		($ in dollars)	
December 31	Cash	500,000	
	Sales		500,000

During the year Cash is coming in, so the account Cash is debited for $500,000. Merchandise is going out at sales price, so Sales is credited for $500,000.

During the year the trading stamps are being given out with the sales of certain products as follows:

2000	($ in dollars)
December 31 Stamp Expense	6,000
Trading Stamps	6,000

During the year $6,000 of trading stamps have been issued to customers. So, the expense account entitled Stamp Expense is debited for $6,000 because the use of these trading stamps by the Hansen Grocery is meant to enhance sales. The Asset Account Trading Stamps is credited for $6,000, because $6,000 worth of the stamps have been issued to customers.

How will the Asset Account Trading Stamps be shown on the Balance Sheet of Hansen Grocery at year's end?

Hansen Grocery
Partial Balance Sheet
December 31, 2000

Assets

Current Assets:

Cash	xxxxxxxx
Trading Stamps	4,000

Originally $10,000 worth of trading stamps were purchased from the Green Trading Stamp Company; during the year, $6,000 of these stamps were issued. The remaining $4,000 are listed in the Balance Sheet as a Current Asset at year's end.

• PROBLEM 14–41

The Green Trading Stamp Company has a gift store in one part of a large city where it has lamps and other luxuries that it sells for its own green stamps. It makes its money by selling green stamps to various service stations and stores throughout the city. The service stations and stores buy the green stamps and issue them to their customers in order to enhance their sales.

During the year 2000, the Green Trading Stamp Company sold $100,000 worth of their own trading stamps to service stations and stores.

What entry will they make on their books?

SOLUTION:

2000	($ in dollars)	
December 31 Cash	100,000	
Trading Stamps		100,000

During the year the Green Trading Stamp Company received a total of $100,000 for selling their trading stamps to businesses throughout the city, so Cash is debited for $100,000. The Asset Account entitled Trading Stamps is credited for $100,000, because the trading stamps worth $100,000 were issued to the various businesses.

• PROBLEM 14-42

The Green Trading Stamp Company has a gift store in one part of a large city where it has lamps and other luxuries that it sells for its own green stamps. It makes its money by selling green stamps to various service stations and stores throughout the city. The service stations and stores buy the green stamps and issue them to their customers in order to enhance their sales.

During the year 2000 the Green Trading Stamp Company sold $100,000 worth of their own trading stamps to service stations and stores. They debited Cash $100,000 and credited Trading Stamps $100,000. During the year they bought lamps and other knick knacks to stock their distribution store.

What entry did they make for this?

SOLUTION:

2000		($ in dollars)
January 2	Premium Articles	90,000
	Cash	90,000

When the Green Trading Stamp Company bought these knick knacks to stock their store, they debited the Asset Account Premium Articles for the $90,000 that these items cost. They credited Cash for $90,000 since Cash was going out.

During the year 2000, the customers with green stamps bought the lamps and other knick knacks at the distribution store amounting to $70,000. How would this be recorded on the books of the Green Trading Stamp Company?

2000		($ in dollars)
December 31	Trading Stamps	70,000
	Premium Articles	70,000

The customers came in bringing their trading stamps, so during the year $70,000 worth of trading stamps were received.

The lamps and other items were purchased by customers during the year, and these amounted to $70,000, so the Asset Account Premium Articles was credited for $70,000.

• PROBLEM 14-43

The Green Trading Stamp Company has a gift store in one part of a large city where it has lamps and other luxuries that it sells for its own green stamps. It makes its money by selling green stamps to various service stations and stores throughout the city. The service stations and stores buy the green stamps and issue them to their customers in order to enhance their sales.

During the year 2000, the Green Trading Stamp Company sold $100,000 worth of their own trading stamps to service stations and stores. They debited Cash $100,000 and credited Trading Stamps $100,000.

During the year they bought lamps and other luxuries to stock their distribution store, debiting the Asset Account entitled Premium Articles and crediting Cash for $90,000. Also, the customers with green stamps bought lamps and other knick knacks at the distribution store amounting to $70,000. On the books, the Green Trading Stamp Company debited the Asset Account Trading Stamps for $70,000 and credited the Asset Account, Premium Articles for $70,000.

How would the Liability for the trading stamps still outstanding at year's end be recorded?

SOLUTION:

2000		($ in dollars)
December 31 Trading Stamp Expense	25,000	
Trading Stamp Liability		25,000

From past experience it has been determined that 95% of the people possessing green stamps will redeem them at the distribution store. During the year, $100,000 worth of green stamps were sold to service stations and stores throughout the city. 95% of $100,000 is $95,000 (95% × $100,000 = $95,000), so it is assumed that eventually stamps worth $95,000 will be redeemed at the distribution store. So far, only $70,000 of stamps sold in the year 2000 have been redeemed ($95,000 − $70,000 = $25,000). Thus, it is assumed that $25,000 worth of stamps sold in the year 2000 will probably be redeemed in the year 2001. Therefore, the account Trading Stamp Expense is debited for $25,000 and Trading Stamp Liability is credited for $25,000, since the amount of $25,000 is presumed to still be owed to the trading stamp holders at the end of the year 2000.

CHAPTER 15

LONG-TERM LIABILITIES

> **Basic Attacks and Strategies for Solving Problems in this Chapter. See pages 489 to 517 for step-by-step solutions to problems.**

Current Liabilities must be paid off within a year, the amount of which is used by readers of Balance Sheets to determine the Liquidity (Short-Term financial health) of a business. Long-Term Liabilities are those Liabilities which are not due within the next year and are analyzed by readers of the Balance Sheet to determine the Long-Term health of the business. Long-Term Liabilities are usually bonds, mortgages, and Long-Term Notes Payable.

Assets are backed up by equities. The two equities are Liabilities and capital (also called Owners' Equity). Adding the capital to the Long-Term Liabilities on a business' Balance Sheet is called "capitalization." This means the Long-Term undergirding of the Assets of the business. The Long-Term Assets can be supported through a long period of time. If the capital and the Long-Term Liabilities are sound, it bodes well for the Long-Term fiscal health of the business.

Often when a business or a branch of the government (such as a city) needs money for capital improvements (such as a new school building or a swimming pool), it sells bonds to the public. These Bonds Payable become part of the Long-Term debt. Mortgages are Long-Term debt instruments that are backed by real property. Long-Term notes are also used as Long-Term debt instruments although they are less formal (less complicated) usually than are bond agreements (indentures).

To exemplify, suppose that a city is selling municipal bonds to build a swimming pool. The city does not receive all the face value of the bonds because these are Speculative bonds, called Income bonds. Additionally, the Interest Rate printed on the face of the bonds is not high enough to attract enough purchasers to bring in the total desired amount of money.

When the Interest Rate printed on the bonds happens to be higher than the effective national Interest Rate at the time, the bonds are sold at a premium.

When bonds are sold at a premium or at a discount, these bonds have to be amortized on the books of the corporation over the life of the bonds. A book entry should be made in order to amortize the bond discount at the end of the first year of its life. Some bonds pay Interest every half year. The bond type should be determined by the corporation at the time the bond indenture (agreement) is first printed and before the bonds are sold. Income bonds are the type that pay Interest to bondholders only in the years that the project makes money. Returning to the pool example, if it were to make no money in its first year, there would be no Interest paid on the bond. Continuing with this illustration, assume that in the second year of the bond's life, the swimming pool did earn $8,000 before paying bond Interest Expense. If this figure were less than the total yearly Interest owed, then the $8,000 would need to be paid out in Interest, bringing the actual Net Income of the pool for that year down to zero.

Imputed Interest is hidden Interest. One illustration of this might be the purchase of Land and Building with the corporation giving a Non-Interest-bearing Note Payable in return. In this case the hidden Interest is the difference between the appraised value of the Land and Building and the face value of the note.

Sometimes prospective bondholders or stockholders do not have the entire amount of money needed to purchase the securities at that time. This is especially true when stocks and bonds of the employing company are sold to employees. In this case, subscriptions are sold to the employees. After the employees have made perhaps several partial payments and the complete amount of cash is received by the corporation, then the subscriptions are turned in by the employees for the full stock or bond certificate.

Many times, due to poor business or poor management, nations, businesses, cities, and counties are not able to pay off bonds and notes when they come due. Often banks and other financial institutions, such as savings and loan associations, are forced to restructure their debts in order to minimize their losses. Many types of restructuring are possible, including lengthening the time to pay the debt, reducing the Interest Rate, or receiving other Assets in lieu of cash, which are often worth less than the face value of the note. In this last case, the lender suffers a loss and the borrower receives a gain which must be recorded on the books.

Step-by-Step Solutions to Problems in this Chapter, "Long-Term Liabilities"

• PROBLEM 15–1

The City Council of Central City voted to build a swimming pool for the community which was to cost $500,000. Financial consultants advised that bonds could be sold at Par with 9% Interest and that they should be Income bonds, with Interest Payable only during years when the swimming pool made money. These were to be 10-year bonds with the maturity date on December 31, 2010.

Because the bond indenture mentioned that these were Income bonds, it was difficult for the investment banker to sell the bonds, and they brought in only $490,000. Of this amount, the investment banker took $10,000 as his fee. What should be the entry on the books of Central City when these bonds were sold, and why?

SOLUTION:

2000		($ in dollars)
December 31 Cash	480,000	
Discount on Bonds Payable	10,000	
Selling Expense	10,000	
Bonds Payable		500,000

Cash is debited for only $480,000 because that is all that Central City received for its swimming pool. The face value of the bonds is $500,000, but the investment banker could sell them for only $490,000. The investment banker took another $10,000 out for himself, so the city received the difference—only $480,000 ($500,000 face value of the bonds – $10,000 discount – $10,000 Broker's Expense = $480,000). Discount on Bonds Payable is debited for $10,000. This is the difference between the face value of the bonds ($500,000) and the amount the investment banker received from selling the bonds $490,000 ($500,000 – $490,000 = $10,000). Discount on Bonds Payable is a Contra-Liability account and appears on the Balance Sheet as a subtraction from the Liability Account,

Bonds Payable. The government will not allow the city to expense the entire $10,000 as a loss in the first year, but it must amortize or write off this figure over the life of the bonds—in this case, 10 years.

Selling Expense is debited for $10,000 because this is the investment banker's fee for selling the bonds to the public.

The Liability Account, Bonds Payable, is credited for $500,000, since this is the face value of the bonds being issued to the bondholders at this time. It is also the maturity value of the bonds.

• PROBLEM 15-2

The City Council of Central City voted to build a swimming pool for the community which was to cost $500,000. Financial consultants advised that bonds could be sold at Par to raise the money to build the pool and that 9% Interest would be advisable, and that they should be Income bonds, with Interest Payable only during the years when the swimming pool made money. These would be 10-year bonds with maturity date on December 31, 2010.

Because the bond indenture agreement mentioned that these were Income bonds, it was difficult for the investment banker to sell the bonds, and they brought in only $490,000. What should be the entry on the books of Central City to amortize the bond discount at the end of the first year of the bonds' life?

SOLUTION:

2001		($ in dollars)
December 31 Bond Interest Expense	1,000	
Discount on Bonds Payable		1,000

The bond discount of $10,000 is gradually amortized (written off) at the end of each year over the 10-year life of the bonds. The $10,000 discount on Bonds Payable is divided by the 10 years of the bonds' life to get $1,000 Amortization each year ($10,000 ÷ by 10 = $1,000).

Bond Interest Expense is debited for $1,000 and is a deductible expense in the Income Statement in determining net income for the year. The account, Discount on Bonds Payable, is credited for $1,000. It previously had a debit balance of $10,000, and this credit of $1,000 brings the balance down to $9,000 at the end of the first year.

• PROBLEM 15–3

The City Council of Central City voted to build a swimming pool for the community which was to cost $500,000. Financial consultants advised that bonds could be sold at Par to raise the money to build the pool and that 9% Interest would be advisable, and that they should be Income bonds, with Interest Payable only during the years when the swimming pool made money. These would be 10-year bonds with a maturity date on December 31, 2010.

Because the bond indenture agreement mentioned that these were Income bonds, it was difficult for the investment banker to sell the bonds, and they brought in only $490,000. Since these are Income bonds and are dependent on the Income of the swimming pool, Interest, if any, is paid only once a year. At the end of the year 2001, it was determined that the swimming pool business made a loss of $3,000. What entry should be made on the books of Central City at this time to pay the Interest to the bondholders?

SOLUTION:

No Entry. Interest is paid only in the years in which the swimming pool makes a profit. Since the pool ran a loss during the year 2001, no Interest is paid to the bondholders, and no entry is made on the books of the city.

• PROBLEM 15-4

The City Council of Central City voted to build a swimming pool for the community which was to cost $500,000. Financial consultants advised that bonds could be sold at Par to raise the money to build the pool and that 9% Interest would be advisable, and that they should be Income bonds, with Interest Payable only during the years when the swimming pool made money. These would be 10-year bonds with a maturity date on December 31, 2010.

Because the bond indenture agreement mentioned that these were Income bonds, it was difficult for the investment banker to sell the bonds, and they brought in only $490,000. Since these are Income bonds and are dependent on the Income of the swimming pool, Interest, if any, is paid only once a year. At the end of the year 2001, it was determined that the swimming pool business made a loss of $3,000, so no Interest was paid at that time. At the end of the year 2002, the swimming pool made a Net Income before Bond Interest Expense of $8,000. How much Interest should the city pay on the bonds, and what entry should be made on the city's books?

SOLUTION:

2002		($ in dollars)
December 31 Bond Interest Expense	8,000	
Cash		8,000

The Total Value of the bonds outstanding on the swimming pool is $500,000, and the yearly Interest is 9%. This means that, if possible, $45,000 yearly Interest should be paid to the bondholders ($500,000 × 9% = $45,000). However, during the year 2002, the Net Income before Bond Interest Expense was only $8,000, so only $8,000 can be paid to the bondholders. This will bring the Net Income for the swimming pool for the year 2002 down to zero ($8,000 Net Income – $8,000 Bond Interest Expense = 0).

Bond Interest Expense is debited for $8,000, and Cash that is paid out is credited for $8,000.

• PROBLEM 15-5

The City Council of Central City voted to build a swimming pool for the community which was to cost $500,000. Financial consultants advised that bonds could be sold at Par to raise the money to build the pool and that 9% Interest would be advisable, and that they should be Income bonds, with Interest Payable only during the years when the swimming pool made money. These would be 10-year bonds with a maturity date on December 31, 2010.

Because the bond indenture agreement mentioned that these were Income bonds, it was difficult for the investment banker to sell the bonds, and they brought in only $490,000. At the time of the sale, the account Discount on Bonds Payable was debited for $10,000, the difference between the $490,000 brought in from the sale of the bonds and the $500,000 face value of the bonds issued. At the end of the first year, on December 31, 2001, Bond Interest Expense was debited for $1,000 and Discount on Bonds Payable was credited for $1,000.

What Amortization entry should be made at the end of the second year, on December 31, 2002, to record bond Amortization, and how will the account Discount on Bonds Payable appear on the books of Central City at that time?

SOLUTION:

2002		($ in dollars)
December 31 Bond Interest Expense	1,000	
Discount on Bonds Payable		1,000

The bond discount of $10,000 is gradually amortized (written off) at the end of each year over the 10-year life of the bonds. The $10,000 discount on Bonds Payable is divided by the 10 years of the bonds' life to get $1,000 Amortization each year ($10,000 ÷ by 10 = $1,000).

Bond Interest Expense is debited for $1,000 and is a deductible expense in the Income Statement in determining the Net Income for the year. The account Discount on Bonds Payable is credited for $1,000. It previously had a debit balance of $10,000 on December 31, 2000. One year later, on December 31, 2001, it was amortized for $1,000, then also on December 31, 2002, it was amortized for another $1,000, bringing the balance of the account down to $8,000, as follows:

Discount on Bonds Payable

12/31/2000	10,000	12/31/2001	1,000
		12/31/2002	1,000
	8,000		

• PROBLEM 15-6

The City Council of Central City voted to build a swimming pool for the community which was to cost $500,000. Financial consultants advised that bonds could be sold at Par to raise the money to build the pool and that 9% Interest would be advisable, and that they should be Income bonds, with Interest Payable only during the years when the swimming pool made money. These would be 10-year bonds with a maturity date on December 31, 2010.

Because the bond indenture agreement mentioned that these were Income bonds, it was difficult for the investment banker to sell the bonds, and they brought in only $490,000. At the time of the sale, the account Discount on Bonds Payable was debited for $10,000, the difference between the $490,000 brought in from the sale of the bonds and the $500,000 face value of the bonds issued. At the end of the first year, on December 31, 2001, Bond Interest Expense was debited for $1,000 and Discount on Bonds Payable was credited for $1,000. Each year that the swimming pool made money, this money was used to pay Interest on the bonds. The yearly Interest was supposed to be $45,000 ($500,000 face value of the bonds × 9% Interest Rate = $45,000), but in no year was the Net Income before bond Interest Expense as high as $45,000. This meant that in the years of loss, no Interest was paid, and in the years when there was Income before Bond Interest Expense, all this amount was paid out to the bondholders.

In the tenth year, the year 2010, the swimming pool earned $10,000 before Bond Interest Expense. Give the entries to record the payment of Interest, the discount Amortization, and the final payment on Principal.

SOLUTION:

2010		($ in dollars)
December 31 Bond Interest Expense	10,000	
Cash		10,000
31 Bond Interest Expense	1,000	
Discount on Bonds Payable		1,000
31 Bonds Payable	500,000	
Cash		500,000

The bond indenture (agreement) provided that in the years when the swimming pool ran at a loss, no Interest needed to be paid to the bondholders. In the year that the swimming pool showed an Income before Bond Interest Expense, this amount was to be paid to the bondholders up to $45,000 ($500,000 × 9% = $45,000). In no year did the Income of the pool before Bond Interest Expense reach $45,000.

During the year 2010 the Net Income before Bond Interest Expense was $10,000, and this entire amount was paid out to bondholders in the first entry above, debiting Bond Interest Expense for $10,000, because the city had the use of the bondholders' money, and crediting Cash, because Interest checks were mailed to the bondholders.

The second entry above amortizes the Contra-Liability account, Discount on Bonds Payable. When the bonds were sold 10 years ago, they brought in only $490,000, yet the face amount of the bonds was $500,000. This $10,000 difference was at that time debited to Discount on Bonds Payable, and the $10,000 was amortized $1,000 each year. This tenth Amortization entry of $1,000 effectively writes off this account to a balance of zero, as follows:

Discount on Bonds Payable			
12/31/2000	10,000	12/31/2001	1,000
		12/31/2002	1,000
		12/31/2003	1,000
		12/31/2004	1,000
		12/31/2005	1,000
		12/31/2006	1,000
		12/31/2007	1,000
		12/31/2008	1,000
		12/31/2009	1,000
		12/31/2010	1,000
	10,000		10,000

During the 10 years (2001–2010), the swimming pool made no Net Income because no extra money was paid out in Interest to the bondholders, and in no year did the bondholders receive their full 9% Interest. However, at the end of the tenth year, at the maturity date of December 31, 2010, the $500,000 was due, and the city had to pay off the debt to the bondholders. The entry debited Bonds Payable for $500,000, since the city received back all the bond certificates from the bondholders. Cash was credited for $500,000, since this amount was paid to the bondholders.

• PROBLEM 15-7

The Sioux Indian Tribe was granted federal permission to build a gambling casino on their land. It was going to cost $700,000 and the financial consultants advised that 10% Interest should be paid. By the time the bonds were sold, the national effective Interest Rate was somewhat lower than that figure. Also, the prospective bondholders believed the gambling casino would be a "gold mine" and wanted to buy the bonds. So the bonds were sold for $800,000, of which $100,000 was premium ($800,000 cash received − $700,000 face value of bonds = $100,000 premium). How would this entry be shown on the books of the Sioux Tribe if the investment bankers were paid $5,000 for their work?

SOLUTION:

2000		($ in dollars)
December 31 Cash	795,000	
Bond Selling Expense	5,000	
Premium on Bonds Payable		100,000
Bonds Payable		700,000

The amount of cash that the investment bankers received from the bondholders was actually $800,000, but the investment bankers took $5,000 of this for their work of selling the bonds and actually remitted only the difference of $795,000 to the Sioux Tribe ($800,000 – $5,000 = $795,000). Thus, the account Cash was debited for $795,000 on the tribe's books, and this amount was used to build the casino.

Bond Selling Expense was debited for $5,000 because the tribe received $5,000 of services from the investment bankers in selling the bonds through brokers all over the world. The Long-Term Liability Account entitled Bonds Payable was credited for $700,000, because bond certificates totaling this amount were mailed to the new bondholders everywhere. The First National Bank in Sioux Falls, South Dakota, was appointed trustee, and they kept the names and addresses of the bondholders and the dollar amounts that each bondholder held.

Finally, the Liability Account entitled Premium on Bonds Payable was credited for $100,000. This is the difference between the money the investment bankers received from the bondholders ($800,000) and the face value of the bonds ($700,000) ($800,000 – $700, 000 = $100,000).

• PROBLEM 15-8

The Sioux Indian Tribe was granted federal permission to build a gambling casino on their land in South Dakota. It was going to cost $700,000, and the financial consultants advised that 10% Interest should be paid. By the time the bonds were sold, the national effective Interest Rate was somewhat lower than that figure. Also, the prospective bondholders believed the gambling casino would be a "gold mine" and wanted to buy the bonds. So the bonds were sold for $800,000, of which $100,000 was premium ($800,000 cash received − $700,000 face value of bonds = $100,000 premium). This money was received by the tribe on December 31, 2000.

Around May 1, 2001, when the weather became warm enough, construction began on the casino, and it opened July 4, 2001. Give the Amortization entry and the Interest Payment entry at the end of the bonds' first year, on December 31, 2001.

SOLUTION:

2001		($ in dollars)
December 31 Bond Interest Expense	70,000	
Cash		70,000
2001		
December 31 Premium on Bonds Payable	10,000	
Bond Interest Expense		10,000

These are 10-year bonds, sold on December 31, 2000 and maturing 10 years later, on December 31, 2010. The yearly Interest is $70,000, because the face value of the bonds was $700,000 and the Interest Rate printed on the face of the bonds was 10% ($700,000 × 10% = $70,000).

Thus, Bond Interest Expense was debited for $70,000, because the tribe received the use of the borrowed money ($700,000) during the entire year. Cash was credited for $70,000 because the trustee sent $70,000 out as Interest checks to the bondholders worldwide on December 31, 2001.

The figure of $10,000 was amortized at the year's end. The Liability Account entitled Premium on Bonds Payable had been credited for $100,000 on December 31, 2000, and this amount is to be written off each year for the 10-year life of the bonds (1/10 × $100,000 = $10,000). So

Premium on Bonds Payable is debited for $10,000 to begin to write off this premium of $100,000, and Bond Interest Expense is credited for $10,000. This credit to Bond Interest Expense effectively cuts down the amount of this expense account. Both bond premiums and bond discounts are amortized through Bond Interest Expense.

• PROBLEM 15-9

The Sioux Indian Tribe was granted federal permission to build a gambling casino on their land in South Dakota. It was going to cost $700,000, and the financial consultants advised that 10% Interest should be paid. By the time the bonds were sold, the national effective Interest Rate was somewhat lower than that figure. Also, the prospective bondholders believed the gambling casino would be a "gold mine" and wanted to buy the bonds. So the bonds were sold for $800,000, of which $100,000 was premium ($800,000 cash received – $700,000 face value of bonds = $100,000 premium). This money was received by the tribe on December 31, 2000.

Around May 1, 2001, when the weather became warm enough, construction began on the casino, and it opened July 4, 2001. At the end of each year of the life of the bonds, an entry to amortize the bond premium and also an entry to pay the bond Interest were made on the books of the tribe.

What entries will be made on the books of the tribe on December 31, 2010, the maturity date of the bonds?

SOLUTION:

2010		($ in dollars)	
December 31	Bond Interest Expense	70,000	
	Cash		70,000
31	Premium on Bonds Payable	10,000	
	Bond Interest Expense		10,000
31	Bonds Payable	700,000	
	Cash		700,000

The yearly Interest on the bonds is $70,000, because the face value of the bonds was $700,000 and the Interest Rate printed on the face of the bonds was 10% ($700,000 × 10% = 70,000).

Bond Interest Expense was debited for $70,000, because the tribe received the use of the borrowed money ($700,000) during the entire year of 2010. Cash was credited for $70,000, because the trustee sent $70,000 out as Interest checks to the bondholders worldwide on December 31, 2010.

The figure of $10,000 was amortized at the end of the year 2010, as had been done at the ends of all the nine years preceding. The Liability Account entitled Premium on Bonds Payable had been credited for $100,000 on December 31, 2000, and this amount was to be written off each year for the 10-year life of the bonds (1/10 × $100,000 = 10,000). Premium on Bonds Payable is debited for $10,000 as the final write-off of this premium of $100,000, and Bond Interest Expense is credited for $10,000. This credit to Bond Interest Expense effectively cuts down the amount of this expense account. Both bond premiums and bond discounts are amortized through Bond Interest Expense.

After making the final Amortization entry on December 31, 2010, the Premium on Bonds Payable account is written off and has a zero balance, as follows:

Premium on Bonds Payable

12/31/2001	10,000	12/31/2000	100,000
12/31/2002	10,000		
12/31/2003	10,000		
12/31/2004	10,000		
12/31/2005	10,000		
12/31/2006	10,000		
12/31/2007	10,000		
12/31/2008	10,000		
12/31/2009	10,000		
12/31/2010	10,000		
	100,000		100,000

Let us say that the casino has done very well, and during the 10 years since it was built it has put aside enough money to pay off the bondholders. (Even if this had not been true, the bondholders are due their Principal on maturity date, and if they do not get their money, they could force the casino into bankruptcy.)

The entry to pay the Principal to the bondholders on the maturity date (in this case, December 31, 2010) debits Bonds Payable because the trustee bank receives all the bond certificates from all the bondholders in the total amount of $700,000. Cash is credited for $700,000 because the trustee bank at this time mails checks in this amount to the bondholders worldwide, and the debt is canceled.

• PROBLEM 15–10

The Marshall Manufacturing Company believes that employees will be happier if they own stock in the company, so they have decided to sell stock subscriptions to their employees. In order to make it easier for more employees to buy the stock, the subscription certificates allow the employees to make two partial payments instead of making one full payment. Each subscription certificate allows the purchaser to buy 10 shares of Marshall Manufacturing Company Common Stock at a price of $30 per share. (The market price is $40 per share at this time, so the employees are buying the stock at a lower figure than what the market says it is worth.) There is a one-month window in which company employees are allowed to buy subscriptions at this low price. During the month, 100 employees each buy a subscription. What entry does the Marshall Manufacturing Company make on its books at the month's end to show the 100 subscriptions sold?

SOLUTION:

2000		($ in dollars)
December 31 Subscriptions Receivable	30,000	
Common Stock Subscribed		10,000
Paid-In Capital in Excess of Par		20,000

Each subscription certificate allows the employee purchaser to buy 10 shares of Common Stock at a price of $30 per share (10 shares × $30 = $300). One hundred employees each buy a subscription (100 employees × $300 cost per subscription = $30,000). Thus, the Contra-Owners' Equity account entitled Subscriptions Receivable is debited for $30,000, the amount the corporation hopes eventually to receive from the employees.

(Since there is no legal Liability by the employees to pay this money, the account Subscriptions Receivable is not usually considered as an Asset to the corporation, but is a deduction in the Owners' Equity section of the Balance Sheet.)

The account Common Stock Subscribed is credited for $10,000. Common Stock Subscribed is an Owners' Equity account on the corporation Balance Sheet, and it shows the stock at Par Value. In this case, the Par Value of a share of stock is $10, and each subscription allows the holder of the subscription to buy 10 shares of stock ($10 Par Value of a share × 10 shares = $100). 100 employees have been given subscriptions ($100 × 100 employees = $10,000).

The account Paid-In Capital in Excess of Par is credited for $20,000; This is the difference between the Subscriptions Receivable, $30,000, and the Common Stock Subscribed of $10,000 ($30,000 − $10,000 = $20,000).

• PROBLEM 15-11

The Marshall Manufacturing Company believes that employees will be happier if they own stock in the company, so they have decided to sell stock subscriptions to their employees. In order to make it easier for more employees to buy the stock, the subscription certificates allow the employees to make two partial payments instead of making one full payment. Each subscription certificate allows the purchaser to buy 10 shares of Marshall Manufacturing Company Common Stock at a price of $30 per share. (The market price is $40 per share at this time, so the employees are buying the stock at a lower figure than what the market says it is worth.) There is a one-month window in which company employees are allowed to buy subscriptions at this low price. During the month, 100 employees each buy a subscription.

Marshall Manufacturing Company debits Subscriptions Receivable for $30,000, credits Common Stock Subscribed for $10,000, and credits Paid-In Capital in Excess of Par for $20,000, on December 31, 2000.

On March 1, 2001, all the 100 employees make individual payments of $150 each, or 50% of the promised payment. This is a total of $15,000 (100 employees × $150 = $15,000). What entry does the Marshall Manufacturing Company make on its books at this time?

SOLUTION:

2001		($ in dollars)
March 1	Cash	15,000
	Subscriptions Receivable	15,000

The Marshall Manufacturing Company debits Cash for $15,000, since it is receiving this amount from its employees who hold the subscriptions. It credits Subscriptions Receivable for $15,000, since the amount that the employees have promised the corporation has been cut down from $30,000 to $15,000, as follows:

Subscriptions Receivable

12/31/2000	30,000	3/1/2001	15,000
Balance	15,000		

The Marshall Manufacturing Company believes that employees will be happier if they own stock in the company, so they have decided to sell stock subscriptions to their employees. In order to make it easier for more employees to buy the stock, the subscription certificates allow the employees to make two partial payments instead of making one full payment. Each subscription certificate allows the purchaser to buy 10 shares of Marshall Manufacturing Company Common Stock at a price of $30 per share. (The market price is $40 per share at this time, so the employees are buying the stock at a lower figure than what the market says it is worth.) There is a one-month window in which company employees are allowed to buy subscriptions at this low price. During the month, 100 employees each buy a subscription.

Marshall Manufacturing Company debits Subscriptions Receivable for $30,000, credits Common Stock Subscribed for $10,000, and credits Paid-In Capital in Excess of Par for $20,000, on December 31, 2000.

On March 1, 2001, all the 100 employees make individual payments of $150 each, or 50% of the promised payment. This is a total of $15,000 (100 employees × $150 = $15,000). The company debits Cash, $15,000 and credits Subscriptions Receivable for $15,000 at that time.

On June 1, 2001, the employees are all supposed to make the second partial payment of 50%. All but one employee makes this second partial payment, so the corporation receives $14,850 (99 employees × $150 payment each = $14,850).

What entry will be made on the books of the Marshall Manufacturing Company when they receive this payment?

SOLUTION:

2001		($ in dollars)	
June 1	Cash	14,850	
	Subscriptions Receivable		14,850

Cash of $14,850 is received on June 1, so the Cash account is debited for this amount. The Contra-Owners' Equity account entitled Subscriptions Receivable is credited for $14,850 because the amount the employees need to pay the corporation is cut down by that amount. As of June 1, the Subscriptions Receivable account appears as follows:

		Subscriptions Receivable		
12/31/2000	30,000	3/1/2001	15,000
		6/1/2001	14,850
			29,850
Balance	150		

The $150 balance in the Subscriptions Receivable account is the money that the corporation did not receive from the defaulting subscriber. The corporation now decides to pay back to the defaulting subscriber-employee the $150 that this person had paid in on March 1. So the entry is as follows:

2001		($ in dollars)	
July 1	Paid-In Capital in Excess of Par	200	
	Common Stock Subscribed	100	
	Subscriptions Receivable		150
	Cash		150

The corporation now also receives the subscription certificates from the 99 fully-paying employees and gives them the Common Stock certificates as follows:

2001		($ in dollars)	
July 1	Common Stock Subscribed	9,900	
	Common Stock		9,900

In the first entry above, the Paid-In Capital in Excess of Par account is debited for $200 (in this case, twice the Par Value) because the corporation loses this amount of extra money because of the defaulting subscriber. The account Common Stock Subscribed is also debited for the Par Value of the stock that would have been given to the defaulting subscriber. Subscriptions Receivable is credited for $150 to close this account and to show that subscribers no longer owe the corporation any money, and Cash is credited for $150 because this amount is remitted to the defaulting subscriber.

In the entry just above, the account Common Stock Subscribed is debited for $9,900 as the subscription certificates are reclaimed by the corporation from the subscribers. Common Stock is credited for $9,900, since this is the Par Value of the Common Stock certificates now being issued to the subscribers who did not default. (Each subscriber who did not default gets 10 shares @ $10 Par (10 shares × $10 = $100). Ninety-nine people did not default, and each gets stock the Par Value of which is $100, as follows: $100 × 99 people = $9,900.

The accounts on the books of the Marshall Manufacturing Company after July 1, 2001 appear as follows:

Subscriptions Receivable

12/31/2000	30,000	3/1/2001	15,000
		6/1/2001	14,850
		7/1/2001	150
	30,000		30,000

When the subscriptions were first given out to the employees on December 31, 2000, the Subscriptions Receivable account was debited for $30,000, the amount the corporation hoped eventually to receive from the subscriber-employees. On March 1, 2001, 50% of this amount (or $15,000) was received, so the account Subscriptions Receivable was credited for $15,000. On June 1, 2001, $14,850 more was received from the subscriber-employees, so Subscriptions Receivable was credited for $14,850. Finally, on July 1, 2001, the defaulting subscriber was written off for $150, thus closing the account.

Common Stock Subscribed

7/1/2001	100	12/31/2000	10,000
7/1/2001	9,900		
	10,000		10,000

Common Stock Subscribed is an Owners' Equity account recorded at Par Value. On December 31, 2000, 100 subscriptions were issued to 100 employees, and each subscription was worth $100 par (10 shares each × $10 par = $100). At that time the Common Stock Subscribed account was credited for $10,000 ($100 × 100 subscribers = $10,000) to show the Par Value of the subscriptions issued.

On July 1, 2001, the subscription was reclaimed from the defaulting subscriber in the amount of $100, and that amount was debited to the Common Stock Subscribed account. Also, on July 1, 2001, all the paying subscribers turned in all their subscription certificates in the amount of $9,900 Par, so that amount was debited to the Common Stock Subscribed account, thus closing it, since Common Stock Subscribed only has a balance when subscriptions are in the hands of subscribers.

Paid-In Capital in Excess of Par			
7/1/2001	200	12/31/2000	20,000
		Balance	19,800

The account Paid-In Capital in Excess of Par shows the difference between the Par and Sales Value of the stock or the subscriptions outstanding when the stock or the subscriptions are sold for amounts in excess of Par. On December 31, 2000, subscriptions were sold for $30,000 on stock with a Par Value of only $10,000. Therefore, the account Paid-In Capital in Excess of Par was credited for the difference, in this case $20,000 ($30,000 sales price – $10,000 Par Value = $20,000 paid-in capital).

On July 1, 2001, Common Stock subscriptions with a Par Value of $100 and a Sales Value of $300 were reclaimed from the defaulting subscriber. The difference, $200 ($300 – $100 = $200), was debited to Paid-In Capital in Excess of Par, thus bringing the balance of this account to $19,800.

Common Stock		
	7/1/2001	9,900

The 99 employees who fully paid for their stock received stock certificates, the Par Value of which was $9,900. (Each fully-paying employee

+received 10 shares of stock, the par value of which is $10 per share, or 10 shares × $10 = $100. Ninety-nine people were fully paid. 99 × $100 = $9,900. Thus, the Common Stock account was credited for $9,900 on the date that the Common Stock certificates were sent out to the 99 fully paying employees.)

• PROBLEM 15-13

On January 2, 2000, the Horton Construction Company purchases Land for $25,000 and a Building for $75,000. These are figures estimated by the appraiser. The Horton Construction Company in return gives the seller a 2-year Non-Interest-Bearing note for $105,000. There was no established price for the Land and Building, and there was no ready market for the note. How shall this purchase be recorded on the books of the Horton Construction Company?

SOLUTION:

2000		($ in dollars)	
January 2	Land	25,000	
	Building	75,000	
	Prepaid Interest	5,000	
	Note Payable		105,000

Since there was no ready market for the Land or Building, we debit the Land account for the appraiser's estimate of $25,000; we debit Building for the appraiser's estimate of $75,000. Since there is no ready market for the note, we credit Note Payable for the face value of $105,000. The difference between the Total Value of the Land and Building, $100,000 ($25,000 + $75,000 = $100,000), and the face value of the note, $105,000, is $5,000 ($105,000 − $100,000 = $5,000). Since this is an Arms-Length Transaction and there is Interest in these business transactions, the Non-Interest-Bearing portion of the note would be looked on with skepticism. This $5,000 difference is really Imputed (Hidden) Interest. Therefore, the Current Asset account, Prepaid Interest, is debited for the $5,000.

• PROBLEM 15–14

On January 2, 2000, the Horton Construction Company purchased Land for $25,000 and a Building for $75,000. These are figures estimated by the appraiser. The Horton Construction Company in return gave the seller a 2-year Non-Interest-Bearing note for $105,000. There was no established price for the Land and Building, and there was no ready market for the note. On its books the Horton Construction Company debited Land for $25,000, debited Building for $75,000, debited Prepaid Interest for $5,000, and credited Note Payable for $105,000. What adjusting entry should the Horton Construction Company make on its books at the end of the first year of the note's life?

SOLUTION:

2000	($ in dollars)	
December 31 Interest Expense	2,500	
Prepaid Interest		2,500

The Imputed Interest was determined to be $5,000 ($105,000 face value of the note – $100,000 value of Land and Building = $5,000). Since the note runs for two years, the yearly Imputed Interest would be $2,500 ($5,000 interest ÷ 2 years = $2,500). We debit Interest Expense for $2,500 because we enjoyed the use of the Land and Building during the year 2000 without yet having to pay Cash for these Assets. The account Prepaid Interest is credited for $2,500 to show that the elapse of a year's time has eroded the value of this account.

• PROBLEM 15–15

On January 2, 2000, the Horton Construction Company purchased Land for $25,000 and a Building for $75,000. These are figures estimated by the appraiser. The Horton Construction Company in return gave the seller a 2-year Non-Interest-bearing note for $105,000. There was no established price for the Land and Building, and there was no ready market for the note. On its books the Horton Construction Company debited Land for $25,000, debited Building for $75,000, debited Prepaid Interest for $5,000, and credited Note Payable for $105,000. At the end of the same year, on December 31, 2000, the Horton Construction Company made an adjusting entry on its books debiting Interest Expense for $2,500 and crediting Prepaid Interest for $2,500. What entry or entries should the Horton Construction Company make on its books on December 31, 2001, the date it repays the note?

SOLUTION:

2001		($ in dollars)
December 31 Interest Expense	2,500	
Prepaid Interest		2,500
31 Note Payable	105,000	
Cash		105,000

On the date the Land and Building were purchased, the note's Imputed Interest was determined to be $5,000 ($105,000 face value of the note − $100,000 value of Land and Building = $5,000). Since the note runs for two years, the yearly Imputed Interest would be $2,500 ($5,000 Interest ÷ 2 years = $2,500). At the end of each of the two years, we debit Interest Expense for $2,500 because we derived the use of the Land and Building during the years 2000 and 2001 without yet having to pay Cash for these Assets. The account Prepaid Interest each year is then credited for $2,500 to show that the elapse of a year's time has eroded the value of this account. After the second such entry, the account's balance is zero, as follows:

	Prepaid Interest		
1/2/2000	5,000	12/31/2000	2,500
		12/31/2001	2,500
	5,000		5,000

Finally, the $105,000 note is paid off. Note Payable is debited for $105,000, because the Horton Construction Company receives its note payable back from the seller, marked "Paid," and Cash is credited for $105,000, because at this time the Horton Construction Company sends the seller a check for that amount.

• PROBLEM 15–16

On January 2, 2000, the Brown Construction Company borrowed $100,000 from the First National Bank to build a new warehouse. Because of high Interest Rates, there was little construction that year, and the Brown Construction Company had a negative Cash Flow and could not pay the 10% Interest on the note on December 31, 2000. The Brown Construction Company offered to give the First National Bank 300 shares of Brown Construction Company stock in lieu of the Interest. The Par Value of a share of stock in this company was $10 and the Market Value was $30. What entry should be made on the books of the First National Bank if they accept this offer?

SOLUTION:

2000		($ in dollars)	
December 31	Interest Receivable	10,000	
	Interest Income		10,000
31	Investment in Common Stock of		
	Brown Construction Company	9,000	
	Extraordinary Loss	1,000	
	Interest Receivable		10,000

The first entry, debiting Interest Receivable and crediting Interest Income for $10,000, is an adjusting entry which is made at the end of each year. The note is for $100,000 at 10% Interest ($100,000 × 10% = $10,000). Thus, the Interest on the note is $10,000 each year. The above entries are on the books of the bank.

Interest Receivable is debited for $10,000. It is a Current Asset account and shows that Interest of $10,000 is due from the Brown Construction Company. The Revenue account entitled Interest Income is credited for $10,000, to show that during the year 2000 the bank has earned $10,000 Interest Income on the note.

The second entry is really the restructuring entry. The Asset account entitled Investment in Common Stock of Brown Construction Company is debited for $9,000, the Fair Market Value of the Brown Construction Company stock on December 31, 2000 (300 shares @ $30 = $9,000). The Interest Receivable account (debited for $10,000 in the previous entry) is now credited for $10,000 to close it out and to show that the Brown Construction Company no longer owes the First National Bank any Interest money. The difference between the $10,000 Interest previously due and the $9,000 Fair Market Value of the stock, $1,000, is debited to an expense account entitled Extraordinary Loss ($10,000 – $9,000 = $1,000). It is an Extraordinary Loss and should be placed in a special section near the bottom of the Income Statement of the First National Bank. It is Extraordinary, because it was the result of a restructuring agreement between the bank and the Brown Construction Company. The purpose of the restructuring was to help the Brown Construction Company with their Cash Flow problem and also to minimize the loss to the First National Bank.

• PROBLEM 15–17

On January 2, 2000, the Brown Construction Company borrowed $100,000 from the First National Bank to build a new warehouse. Because of high Interest Rates, there was little construction that year, and the Brown Construction Company had a negative Cash Flow and could not pay the 10% Interest on the note on December 31, 2000. The Brown Construction Company offered to give the First National Bank 300 shares of Brown Construction Company stock in lieu of the Interest. The Par Value of a share of stock in this company was $10 and the Market Value was $30. The First National Bank accepted this offer and the stock was transferred to the First National Bank. What entry or entries should be made on the books of the Brown Construction Company on December 31, 2000?

SOLUTION:

2000		($ in dollars)	
December 31	Interest Expense	10,000	
	Interest Payable		10,000
31	Interest Payable	10,000	
	Common Stock		3,000
	Additional Paid-In Capital		6,000
	Extraordinary Gain		1,000

At the end of the year 2000, Interest Expense was debited on the books of the Brown Construction Company for $10,000. The construction company had the use of the $100,000 for the entire year at a cost of $10,000 Interest, supposedly. The Liability Account entitled Interest Payable was credited for $10,000, since the Brown Construction Company is in no position to pay Cash for the Interest. So it hereby gives its oral promise to pay the $10,000 at a later date.

The second entry debits Interest Payable for $10,000 to remove the previous Liability for the Interest, since the debt restructuring cancels the Interest Liability. Common Stock is credited for $3,000, since Common Stock is recorded at Par Value. 300 shares of the Brown Construction Company are turned over to the First National Bank, and the Par Value per share is $10 (300 shares × $10 per share Par Value = $3,000).

Extraordinary Gain, a Revenue account, is credited for $1,000. This is the difference between the amount of Interest foregone ($10,000) and the Market Value of the stock, $9,000. (300 shares × $30 per share Market Value = $9,000.) (Also, $10,000 Interest – $9,000 Market Value of stock = $1,000 gain.) This is a gain to the Brown Construction Company because the bank is cancelling its $10,000 Interest Payable in return for Common Stock of the Brown Construction Company worth only $9,000.

The Owners' Equity account entitled Additional Paid-In Capital is credited for $6,000, the difference between the Par Value of the stock ($3,000) and the Market Value of the stock ($9,000). Thus, $9,000 – $3,000 = $6,000.

• PROBLEM 15–18

On January 2, 2000, the Second National Bank of Murphy Springs loaned the Murphy Broom Corporation $15,000 to buy broom making equipment for its factory. It was a five-year note due on January 2, 2005. The Interest Rate was 8%. Over the years the Murphy Broom Corporation was able to pay the Interest at the end of each year, but at maturity date they did not have the cash to pay off the principal.

On January 2, 2000, the Second National Bank made the following entry on its books:

2000		($ in dollars)	
January 2	Notes Receivable	15,000	
	Cash		15,000

On January 2, 2000, the Murphy Broom Corporation made the following entry on its books:

2000		($ in dollars)	
January 2	Cash	15,000	
	Notes Payable		15,000

On January 2, 2000, the Second National Bank received a note from the Murphy Broom Corporation for $15,000, so it debited the

Asset account Notes Receivable for that amount. On the same date, it lent the Murphy Broom Corporation $15,000, so it debited the account Cash for that amount.

On January 2, 2000, the Murphy Broom Corporation borrowed $15,000 from the bank, so it debited Cash for $15,000. It gave a note to the bank for that amount, so it credited Notes Payable for $15,000.

At the end of the first year of the note's life, the Murphy Broom Corporation paid the Second National bank the Interest on the note. The Second National Bank made the following entry on its books:

2000	($ in dollars)	
December 31 Cash	1,200	
Interest Income		1,200

The Interest of $1,200 was computed as follows: $15,000 Principal at 8% Interest equals $1,200 (15,000 × 8% = $1,200). The Second National Bank received a check for $1,200, so it debited Cash. It was giving the Murphy Broom Corporation the use of the $15,000 during the entire year, so it credited Interest Income for $1,200.

At the end of the first year of the note's life, the Murphy Broom Corporation paid the Second National Bank the Interest on the note. The Murphy Broom Corporation made the following entry on its books:

2000	($ in dollars)	
December 31 Interest Expense	1,200	
Cash		1,200

The Interest of $1,200 was computed as follows: $15,000 Principal at 8% Interest equals $1,200 ($15,000 × 8% = $1,200). The Murphy Broom Corporation had the use of the $15,000 during the entire year, so it debited Interest Expense for $1,200. On December 31, 2000, it mailed a check for $1,200 to the Second National Bank, so it credited Cash for $1,200. This was done at the end of each year for the five years that the note ran.

Because of poor business, the Murphy Broom Corporation did not have the cash to pay the note. Murphy Broom Corporation offered the Second National Bank 5 acres of undeveloped land that it owned for the full release of its debt. The Second National Bank, in an attempt to recoup a complete loss, agreed to the deal. Appraisers estimated that the 5 acres of undeveloped land had a Fair Market Value as of

December 31, 2004, of $12,000. The Murphy Broom Corporation had originally purchased the land some years ago for a price of $9,000. What entries should be made on the books of the Second National Bank, and what entries should be made on the books of the Murphy Broom Corporation at this time, and why?

SOLUTION:

The entry on the books of the Second National Bank:

2005		($ in dollars)
December 31 Real Estate	12,000	
Extraordinary Loss	3,000	
Notes Receivable		15,000

The Second National Bank accepted title to the real estate with an appraised value of $12,000 and debited Real Estate (an Asset account) for that amount. It gave back to the Murphy Broom Corporation its $15,000 note marked "Paid," and credited Notes Receivable for $15,000. The difference of $3,000 ($15,000 face amount of the note − $12,000 appraised value of the real estate = $3,000) was debited to Extraordinary Loss. This is really a loss to the Second National Bank because the loan that should have been received was $15,000, and the Appraised Value of the real estate actually received was only $12,000. The loss is called Extraordinary Loss and is listed in a separate section toward the bottom of the Second National Bank's Income Statement as a deduction.

The entry on the books of the Murphy Broom Corporation:

2005		($ in dollars)
December 31 Notes Payable	15,000	
Real Estate		9,000
Extraordinary Gain		3,000
Gain on Real Estate		3,000

On December 31, 2005, the Murphy Broom Corporation received its note back marked "Paid." This note had a face value of $15,000, so Murphy Broom Corporation debited Notes Payable for $15,000. In turn, it signed over 5 acres of its real estate to the Second National Bank. The real estate was undeveloped and had been purchased some years ago for $9,000. In order to remove this from the books of the Murphy Broom

Corporation, they credited Real Estate for $9,000, thus closing out that account.

The gain on the real estate to the Murphy Broom Corporation was $3,000—the difference between the original purchase price of the real estate ($9,000) and the Present Value of the real estate ($12,000). ($12,000 – $9,000 = $3,000.) This is a Revenue account and is listed under Other Revenue in the Income Statement of the Murphy Broom Corporation.

Extraordinary Gain, in this case, is also $3,000. This is the difference between the amount of the note ($15,000) and the Fair Market Value of the Land ($12,000). ($15,000 – $12,000 = $3,000). This is the amount that the Murphy Broom Corporation saved by receiving back the $15,000 note and only giving land worth $12,000. It might be termed as a "once-in-a-lifetime deal" and is really Extraordinary Gain. This is placed toward the bottom of the Murphy Broom Corporation's Income Statement under the title Extraordinary Gain.

CHAPTER 16

RECOGNIZING REVENUE

> **Basic Attacks and Strategies for Solving Problems in this Chapter. See pages 520 to 568 for step-by-step solutions to problems.**

It is important for accountants to recognize when Revenue should be credited to an Income account on the books. This is extremely important because the date that the Income is recorded must be in accordance with the date that the business will be able to pay the Income Taxes it owes to federal, state, and local governments as it will be shown on the Income Statement of the firm.

Although it would seem to be simpler to record this Revenue when the cash is received, this is the cash basis of accounting which is approved by the government *only* for service-type businesses. Most businesses must keep books on the so-called **accrual basis** of accounting because they are mercantile businesses. This means that Revenue must be recorded when earned, whether or not cash is received at that time.

There are several exceptions to this rule. For instance, should Revenue be placed on the books of the company at Gross amount or at Net amount? (The difference between Gross and Net in this case is discount.) The **percentage-of-completion method** of accounting is an exception to the rule, which is legal for contracts lasting over a year. This formula is often used in the construction industry where a dam, bridge, or highway may take over a year to complete. In this type of accounting, the Revenue for the year is based on the percentage of the bridge that was constructed during that year.

The **installment method** is yet another anomalous technique that is allowed when the cash receipt is uncertain and regular payments are received over a relatively long period of time. The percentage of Gross

Profit to sales is computed and this percentage is recorded as profit each time cash is received from the debtor. Even the installment method itself has an exception, known as the **cost recovery method** wherein the first payments from the debtor are not even recorded as Gross Profit at all, until all the cost of the sale has been recovered. From that time on, all the cash received is counted as Income. One example of a business recognizing Revenue would be an airline selling tickets with frequent flyer awards. A separate Liability Account known as Awards Payable is often setup at the time of ticket sale to record as a Liability to the airline the estimated amounts that the company will eventually lose, because the frequent flyer awards are really Liabilities to the airline.

Step-by-Step Solutions to Problems in this Chapter, "Recognizing Revenue"

• PROBLEM 16-1

The Central Airlines had a policy of awarding free miles of travel to its customers that fly frequently. From past experience, it has been determined that 5% of miles flown are extra awards to frequent flyers. During the month of November 2000, the cash sales of tickets used amounted to $1,500,000. How should this be reported on the airline's books?

SOLUTION:

Choice 1

2000		($ in dollars)
November 30 Cash	1,500,000	
Sales		1,500,000

Choice 2

2000		($ in dollars)
November 30 Cash	1,500,000	
Sales		1,425,000
Awards Payable		75,000

Let us assume that this is a small airline and that cash for the tickets sold is collected in the same month in which the airplane rides were taken. The usual method of accounting would be Choice 1, debiting Cash for the $1,500,000 collected and crediting Sales for the $1,500,000 worth of rides given. Another choice could be crediting the account Services, instead of Sales.

However, many customers purchasing tickets are doing so with the expectation of building up frequent flyer awards. In fact, from past experience, it has been determined that future free flights will amount to 5% of tickets sold. Five percent of $1,500,000 tickets sold is $75,000, which is really a Liability or debt of the Central Airlines for future "free" flights. Therefore, the Liability Account entitled Awards Payable is credited for $75,000. The difference, $1,425,000 ($1,500,000 – $75,000 = $1,425,000), is then credited to Sales.

Of course, if the ticket sales are made in a different month from that in which the flights are actually taken, the following procedure could be used:

2000	($ in dollars)	
November 30 Cash	1,500,000	
Unearned Revenue		1,500,000

2000	($ in dollars)	
December 31 Unearned Revenue	1,500,000	
Sales		1,500,000

Let us say that the tickets were sold in November but were not used until December. Then in November, Cash would be debited for $1,500,000 because the cash was actually received during that month. The current Liability Account entitled Unearned Revenue would be credited for $1,500,000 because the airline owes the customers for their future flights.

In December, the customers who actually purchased their airline tickets in November now use their tickets. So, on the books of the Central Airlines, the account Unearned Revenue is debited to cancel it out, and Sales is credited to show the revenue in the month of December, the month in which the money was actually earned by giving rides to the clients. Instead of crediting Sales, an alternative would be to credit the Revenue account Services.

Let us say that the tickets were sold in November but were not used until December, and that the Central Airlines also gives frequent flyer awards. Let us also surmise that 5% of the miles flown will eventually be claimed as extra awards to frequent flyers. In the month of November the following entry would be made on the books of the Central Airlines:

2000		($ in dollars)
November 30 Cash	1,500,000	
Unearned Revenue		1,500,000

In November, Cash would be debited for $1,500,000 because the cash was actually received during that month. The current Liability Account Unearned Revenue would be credited for $1,500,000 because the airline owes the customers that amount for their future flights.

In the month of December, the following entry would be made on the books of the Central Airlines:

2000		($ in dollars)
December 31 Unearned Revenue	1,500,000	
Sales		1,425,000
Awards Payable		75,000

In December, the customers who actually purchased their airline tickets in November now use their tickets. So, on the books of the Central Airlines, the account Unearned Revenue is debited to cancel it out. However, many customers with tickets expect to build up frequent flyer awards. In fact, from past experience, it has been determined that future free flights will amount to 5% of tickets sold. Five percent of $1,500,000 of tickets sold is $75,000, which is really a Liability or debt of the Central Airlines for future "free" flights. Therefore, the Liability Account Awards Payable is credited for $75,000. The difference, $1,425,000 ($1,500,000 – $75,000 = $1,425,000), is then credited to Sales. Instead of crediting Sales, an alternative would be to credit the Revenue account Services.

• PROBLEM 16–2

The Harley Restaurant chain has decided, in addition to its chain of restaurants that it directly manages, to go into the franchise business and sign franchise agreements with other restaurants that wished to adopt its wholesale purchasing methods and its advertising schemes. The Harley Restaurant chain would be the franchisor and the individual restaurant owner would be the franchisee. The franchisee, already a going-concern restaurant, would get to adopt the name Harley Restaurant, get national advertising benefits, get help with local advertising, and would get help training workers. For this help, the franchisee would pay the franchisor a one-time-only fee. How would this one-time-only fee be recorded on the books of the franchisor— Harley Restaurant chain?

SOLUTION:

Franchisor's Books
Choice 1

2000		($ in dollars)
January 31 Cash	1,000	
Services		1,000

The easiest method would be, as above, to debit Cash for the fee received, in this case $1,000, and to credit the Revenue account Services for $1,000.

However, if the franchisor's services to the franchisee are ongoing, in reality the franchisor has not performed all the services as of January 2000. The Securities and Exchange Commission of the United States Government has suggested that some of this income be postponed to later months. An example of this follows:

Franchisor's Books
Choice 2

2000			($ in dollars)
January 31	Cash	1,000	
	Services		500
	Training Services Payable		250
	Advertising Payable		250
February 29	Training Services Payable	100	
	Advertising Payable	100	
	Services		200
March 31	Training Services Payable	150	
	Advertising Payable	150	
	Services		300

In January, the one-time-lump-sum payment of $1,000 is received by the franchisor from the franchisee, so the franchisor debits Cash for $1,000. Let us assume that at this time the franchisor allows the franchisee to use the franchisor name and to begin to purchase restaurant supplies and equipment wholesale through the franchisor company, and that the franchisor has instituted a training program for the employees and has instituted a local advertising program for the franchisee restaurant. Let us also assume that these services amount to $500. Thus, the account Services is credited for $500. It is assumed that the other $500 in Services will be given in February and March. So in the January 31 entry the current Liability Account Training Services Payable is credited for the postponed training to be given out in the next two months, and the current Liability Account Advertising Payable is credited for the postponed advertising to be given out in the next two months.

During February, let us say that the franchisor gives the franchisee restaurant $100 more of employee training services and $100 more of local advertising under the new name. On February 29, 2000, an entry would be made on the books of the franchisor debiting Training Services Payable for $100 and debiting Advertising Payable for $100 to cut down these two Liability Accounts. The Revenue account Services would be credited for $200, to show the amount of service given by the franchisor to the franchisee during the month of February.

During March, let us say that the franchisor gives the franchisee restaurant $150 more of employee training services and $150 more of local advertising under the new name. On March 31, 2000, an entry would be made on the books of the franchisor debiting Training Services Payable for $150 and debiting Advertising Payable for $150 to close out these two Liability Accounts. The revenue account Services would be credited for $300, to show the amount of service given by the franchisor to the franchisee during the month of March.

At the end of March, the Training Services Payable account would appear on the books of the franchisor as follows:

Training Services Payable			
2/29/2000	100	1/31/2000	250
3/31/2000	150		
	250		250

On January 31, 2000, when the franchisor received the cash from the franchisee, the franchisor credited Training Services Payable for the $250 in services being postponed to the following months. On February 29, 2000, the Training Services Payable account was debited for the $100 services that the franchisor had performed for the franchisee during the month of February. On March 31, 2000, the Training Services Payable account was debited for the $150 services that the franchisor had performed for the franchisee during the month of March.

At the end of March, the Advertising Payable account would appear on the books of the franchisor as follows:

Advertising Payable			
2/29/2000	100	1/31/2000	250
3/31/2000	150		
	250		250

On January 31, 2000, when the franchisor received the Cash from the franchisee, the franchisor credited Advertising Payable for the $250 in services being postponed to the following months. On February 29, 2000, the Advertising Payable account was debited for the $100 in services that the franchisor had performed for the franchisee during the month of February. On March 31, 2000, the Advertising Payable account was debited for the $150 in services that the franchisor had performed for the franchisee during the month of March.

• PROBLEM 16–3

The James Construction Company has signed a contract with Smithson County to build a small bridge across the Pascagoula River at Third Avenue Road. The contract calls for a total contract price of $100,000 to be paid at the end of each year until the bridge is completed. In other words, there will be yearly progress billings.

The contract is signed on January 2, 2000, and the James Construction Company immediately begins work. On December 31, 2000, the James Construction company has spent $30,000 for Material, Labor, and Overhead, and engineers estimate that it will take $60,000 more in costs to complete the bridge. What billings will the James Construction Company make to Smithson County as of December 31, 2000 and why?

SOLUTION:

The James Construction Company will present Smithson County a bill for $3,333.33 for the year 2000, with computations as follows:

Cost to Date:	$30,000.00
Plus: Estimated Cost to Complete	60,000.00
Estimated Total Cost	$90,000.00

The Cost to Date is 1/3 of the Estimated Total Cost ($30,000 ÷ $90,000 = 1/3). Thus, the project, at the end of the year 2000, is about 1/3 completed, at least as far as spending is concerned.

The estimated Gross Profit at the end of year 2000 is $10,000. ($100,000 contract price – $90,000 Estimated Total Cost = $10,000 estimated Gross Profit.)

Since approximately 1/3 of the costs of the bridge have already been spent, we multiply the Estimated Gross Profit of $10,000 by 1/3 to get

$3,333.33, the Gross profit for the year 2000. Thus, at this time, the James Construction Company will present Smithson County with a bill for $3,333.33.

• PROBLEM 16–4

The James Construction Company has signed a contract with Smithson County to build a small bridge across the Pascagoula River at Third Avenue Road. The contract calls for a total contract price of $100,000 to be paid at the end of each year until the bridge is completed. In other words, there will be yearly progress billings.

The contract is signed on January 2, 2000, and the James Construction Company immediately begins work. On December 31, 2000, the James Construction Company has spent $30,000 for Materials, Labor, and Overhead, and engineers estimate that it will take $60,000 more in costs to complete the bridge. Adding $30,000 and $60,000 together, we discover that $90,000 is the Estimated Total Cost as of year's end. Thus, the Cost to Date is 1/3 of the Estimated Cost to Complete, and the project at the end of the year 2000 is about 1/3 completed, at least as far as spending is concerned. The Estimated Gross Profit at the end of the year is $10,000. ($100,000 contract price − $90,000 Estimated Total Cost = $10,000 Estimated Gross Profit.)

Since approximately 1/3 of the costs of the bridge have already been spent, we multiply the Estimated Gross Profit of $10,000 by 1/3 to get $3,333.33, the Gross Profit for the year 2000. What is the billing for the year 2001?

SOLUTION:

At the end of the year 2001, the costs to date amount to $70,000 and the engineers estimate that it will take $25,000 more to complete the bridge, or a total of $95,000 Estimated Total Cost ($70,000 + $25,000 = $95,000).

The Estimated Gross Profit is now $5,000. ($100,000 contract price − $95,000 Estimated Total Cost = $5,000 Estimated Gross Profit.)

The Cost to Date is $70,000 and the Estimated Total Cost (as of December 31, 2001) is $95,000; so, approximately 14/19 of the bridge is completed. ($70,000 Cost to Date ÷ $95,000 Estimated Total Cost = 70/95. Dividing 5 into $70,000, we get $14,000; dividing 5 into $95,000, we get $19,000 or a fraction of $14,000/$19,000, which equals 14/19.)

As of December 31, 2001, the Estimated Gross Profit figure has dropped to $5,000. ($100,000 contract price − $95,000 Estimated Total Cost = $5,000 Estimated Gross Profit.) Since approximately 14/19 of the project has been completed, we multiply 14/19 by $5,000 to get $3,684.21, the amount of Gross Profit to be recognized in the first two years of the project (14/19 × $5,000 = $3,684.21).

Since $3,333.33 was billed to the county as of December 31, 2000, we should now, at the end of the year 2001, bill the county for $350.88 more. ($3,684.21 Gross Profit to be recognized in the first two years of the project − $3,333.33 recognized at the end of the year 2000 = $350.88 to be billed to the county at the end of the year 2001.)

• PROBLEM 16–5

The James Construction Company has signed a contract with Smithson County to build a small bridge across the Pascagoula River at Third Avenue Road. The contract calls for a total contract price of $100,000 to be paid at the end of each year until the bridge is completed. In other words, there will be yearly progress billings.

The contract is signed on January 2, 2000, and the James Construction Company immediately begins work. On December 31, 2000, the James Construction Company has spent $30,000 for Materials, Labor and Overhead, and engineers estimate that it will take $60,000 more in costs to complete the bridge. Adding $30,000 and $60,000 together, we discover that $90,000 is the Estimated Total Cost as of year's end. Thus, the Cost to Date is 1/3 of the Estimated Total Cost, and the project at the end of the year 2000 is about 1/3 completed, at least as far as spending is concerned. The Estimated Gross Profit at the end of the year is $10,000. ($100,000 contract price − $90,000 Estimated Total Cost = $10,000 Estimated Gross Profit.)

Since approximately 1/3 of the costs of the bridge have already been spent during the year 2000, we multiply the Estimated Gross Profit of $10,000 by 1/3 to get $3,333.33, the Gross Profit for the year 2000.

At the end of the year 2000, the Costs to Date amount to $70,000 and the engineers estimate that it will take $25,000 more to complete the bridge, or a total of $95,000 Estimated Total Cost ($70,000 + $25,000 = $95,000).

The Estimated Gross Profit is now $5,000. ($100,000 contract price – $95,000 Estimated Total Cost = $5,000 Estimated Gross Profit.)

The Cost to Date is $70,000, and the Estimated Total Cost (as of December 31, 2001) is $95,000; so, approximately 14/19 of the bridge is completed. ($70,000 Cost to Date divided by $95,000 Estimated Total Cost = 70/95. Dividing 5 into $70,000, we get $14,000; dividing 5 into $95,000, we get $19,000 or a fraction of $14,000/$19,000, which equals 14/19.)

As of December 31, 2001, the Estimated Gross Profit figure has dropped to $5,000. ($100,000 contract price – $95,000 Estimated Total Cost = $5,000 Estimated Gross Profit.) Since approximately 14/19 of the project has been completed, we multiply 14/19 by $5,000 to get $3,684.21, the amount of Gross Profit to be recognized in the first two years of the project (14/19 × $5,000 = $3,684.21).

Since $3,333.33 was billed to the county as of December 31, 2000, we should now, at the end of the year 2001, bill the county for $350.88 more. ($3,684.21 Gross Profit to be recognized in the first two years of the project – $3,333.33 recognized at the end of the year 2000 = $350.88 to be billed to the county at the end of the year 2001.)

For what should we bill the county at the end of construction in the year 2002?

SOLUTION:

During the year 2002 the bridge is completed at a Total Cost of $96,000. Since the contract price is $100,000, the Gross Profit is $4,000. ($100,000 contract price – $96,000 Total Cost = $4,000 Gross Profit.)

The Gross Profit that the James Construction Company billed the county in the year 2000 was $3,333.33, and the Gross Profit billed in 2001 was $350.88, or a total of $3,684.21. ($3,333.33 billed in 2000 + $350.88

billed in 2001 = $3,684.21 total billing for the first two years of the project.)

The actual Gross Profit was $4,000 (see above), so the billing for the final year of 2002 is $315.79. ($4,000 actual Gross Profit – $3,684.21 total billings for the first two years = $315.79 billing for the year 2002.)

• PROBLEM 16–6

The Runcie Wholesale Hardware Company sells wholesale hardware items at a 2% discount if payment is received within 10 days after the sale. They have always recorded sales at the Gross amount. On January 2, 2000, they made a $10,000 sale of merchandise to the Harlem Hardware Store. On January 8, 2000, they received a check in full payment of the purchase. What entries should be made on the books of the Runcie Wholesale Hardware Company?

SOLUTION:

2000			($ in dollars)
January 2	Accounts Receivable—Harlem Hardware	10,000	
	Sales		10,000
January 8	Cash	9,800	
	Sales Discounts	200	
	Accounts Receivable—Harlem Hardware		10,000

On January 2, 2000, the date of the sale, Runcie Wholesale Hardware Company debits Accounts Receivable—Harlem Hardware for $10,000 because it is receiving Harlem Hardware's oral promise to pay the $10,000. It credits Sales since it is delivering wholesale hardware such as sleds, nails, and hammers worth $10,000.

On January 8, 2000, the Runcie Wholesale Hardware Company receives a check for $9,800, so it debits Cash for $9,800. The terms of the sale were 2% discount if paid within 10 days after the date of the sale. In this case, the sale was January 2 and the date of payment was January 8, so that is within 10 days of the sale. The $9,800 Cash Remittance is figured as follows: $10,000 amount of sale multiplied by 2% discount is a $200 discount. We then subtract the $200 discount from the $10,000 value of sale, to get $9,800 amount of remittance ($10,000 – $200 = $9,800).

• PROBLEM 16-7

The Runcie Wholesale Hardware Company sells wholesale hardware items at a 2% discount if payment is received within 10 days after the sale. They have always recorded sales at the Gross amount. On January 2, 2000, they made a $10,000 sale of merchandise to the Harlem Hardware Store. On January 15, 2000, they received a check in full payment of the purchase. What entries should be made on the books of the Runcie Wholesale Hardware Company?

SOLUTION:

2000			($ in dollars)
January 2	Accounts Receivable—Harlem Hardware	10,000	
	Sales		10,000
January 15	Cash	10,000	
	Accounts Receivable—Harlem Hardware		10,000

On January 2, 2000, the date of the sale, Runcie Wholesale Hardware debits Accounts Receivable—Harlem Hardware for $10,000 because it is receiving Harlem Hardware's oral promise to pay the $10,000. It credits Sales since it is delivering wholesale hardware such as sleds, nails, and hammers worth $10,000.

On January 15, 2000, the Runcie Wholesale Hardware Company receives a check for $10,000. The terms of the sale were 2% discount if paid within 10 days after the date of the sale. Since January 15 is more than 10 days after the date of the sale (the sale was made on January 2, 2000, and the tenth day would be January 12, 2000—12 – 10 = 2), the full amount of the sale, $10,000, is received, so the Asset account Cash is debited for $10,000. Accounts Receivable—Harlem Hardware is credited because Harlem receives back its oral promise to pay.

• PROBLEM 16–8

The Hamm Wholesale Hardware Company sells wholesale hardware items at a 2% discount if payment is received within 10 days after the sale. They have been in the habit of recording sales at Net, because they always intend to receive payment from reliable customers within the 10-day discount period. On January 2, 2000, they made a $10,000 sale of merchandise to the Slocum Hardware Store. On January 10, 2000, they received a check in full payment of the purchase. What entries should be made on the books of the Hamm Wholesale Hardware Company?

SOLUTION:

2000		($ in dollars)	
January 2	Accounts Receivable—Slocum Hardware	9,800	
	Sales		9,800
January 10	Cash	9,800	
	Accounts Receivable—Slocum Hardware		9,800

On January 2, 2000, Hamm Wholesale Hardware Company made a sale of merchandise to the Slocum Hardware Store for $10,000 Gross. The terms were 2% discount if paid in 10 days. Since the Hamm Wholesale Hardware Company keeps records of sales at Net, rather than Gross, the company debits Accounts Receivable—Slocum Hardware for $9,800 (2% of $10,000 = $200 discount; $10,000 gross amount of sale – $200 discount = $9,800 net amount). At the same time, Hamm Wholesale Hardware Company credited Sales for $9,800 Net price.

On January 10, 2000, the Hamm Wholesale Hardware Company received a check from their customer, the Slocum Hardware Store, for the net amount of $9,800. This was within the discount period. (January 10 (date of cash receipt) less January 2 (date of sale) = 8 days; so it is within the 10-day discount period and only the net amount of $9,800 needs to be remitted.) Therefore, Hamm Wholesale Hardware Company debits Cash for $9,800, the Net amount, since it is receiving this amount of money. It credits Accounts Receivable—Slocum Hardware for $9,800, since it is giving them back their oral promise to pay.

• PROBLEM 16-9

The Hamm Wholesale Hardware Company sells wholesale hardware items at a 2% discount if payment is received within 10 days after the sale. They have been in the habit of recording sales at Net, because they always intend to receive payment from reliable customers within the 10-day discount period. On January 2, 2000, they made a $10,000 sale of merchandise to the Slocum Hardware Store. On January 20, 2000, they received a check in full payment of the purchase. What entries should be made on the books of the Hamm Wholesale Hardware Company?

SOLUTION:

2000		($ in dollars)	
January 2	Accounts Receivable—Slocum Hardware	9,800	
	Sales		9,800
January 20	Cash	10,000	
	Discounts Gained		200
	Accounts Receivable—Slocum Hardware		9,800

On January 2, 2000, Hamm Wholesale Hardware Company made a sale of merchandise to the Slocum Hardware Store for $10,000 Gross. The terms were 2% discount if paid in 10 days. Since the Hamm Wholesale Hardware Company keeps records of sales at Net, rather than Gross, the company debits Accounts Receivable—Slocum Hardware for $9,800 (2% of $10,000 = $200 discount; $10,000 gross amount of sale less $200 discount = $9,800 Net amount). At the same time, Hamm Wholesale Hardware Company credited Sales for $9,800 net price.

On January 20, 2000, the Hamm Wholesale Hardware Company received a check from their customer, the Slocum Hardware Store, for the Gross amount of $10,000, so it debited the Asset account Cash for that amount. The bill was not paid within the 10-day discount period. (January 20 (the date of payment) less 10 days = January 10; January 20 (the date of payment) less January 2 (the date of sale) = 18 days.) It was thus 18 days between date of sale and date of payment. Since this was not within the 10-day discount period, the full amount (Gross amount) of the sale was remitted by the Slocum Hardware Store to the Hamm Wholesale Hardware Company. So Hamm debits Cash for the full $10,000 received.

The Revenue account Discount Gained is credited for $200 on Hamm's books, since this is the difference between the amount of Cash received ($10,000) and the Net amount of the purchase ($9,800). ($10,000 – $9,800 = $200.) Discount Gained is a Revenue account on the books of the Hamm Wholesale Hardware Company and must be reported as Income on the Hamm Income Statement. Hamm Wholesale Hardware Company also credits Accounts Receivable—Slocum Hardware for the Net amount of $9,800 to close out that account.

• PROBLEM 16–10

The Slaughter Hardware Store purchased wholesale hardware such as nails, hammers, and sleds from Bingham Wholesale Hardware on June 15, 2001, in the amount of $2,500. Terms of the purchase were 2% if paid within 10 days and the remainder to be paid within 30 days after purchase. On June 20, 2001, Slaughter Hardware Store mails Bingham Wholesale Hardware a check for $2,450, the Net amount of the purchase. What entries should be made on the books of the Slaughter Hardware Store?

SOLUTION:

2001		($ in dollars)	
June 15	Purchases	2,500	
	Accounts Payable—Bingham Wholesale Hardware		2,500
June 20	Accounts Payable—Bingham Wholesale Hardware	2,500	
	Purchases Discount		50
	Cash		2,450

On June 15, 2001, Slaughter Hardware Store purchased from Bingham Wholesale Hardware $2,500 worth of merchandise, so it debits the Cost account Purchases for $2,500, the Gross amount. Since it is keeping books by the Gross method, it also credits Accounts Payable—Bingham Wholesale Hardware for $2,500, since it is giving them its oral promise to pay $2500, in the future.

On June 20, 2001, Slaughter Hardware Store sends a check for $2,450 to Bingham Wholesale Hardware and credits Cash on its books for $2,450. This is the Net amount of the purchase, figured as follows: 2% of $2,500 = $50 the amount of the discount. And $2,500 (the Gross amount of the purchase) less $50 (the amount of the discount) equals $2,450, the Net amount to be paid if the payment is made within 10 days of the purchase (2% × $2,500 = $50; $2,500 − $50 = $2,450).

The payment is made within 10 days of the purchase (June 20 − June 15 = 5 days). The Contra-Cost account entitled Purchases Discount is credited for the $50 discount on the books of the Slaughter Hardware Store.

• PROBLEM 16–11

The Slaughter Hardware Store purchased wholesale hardware such as nails, hammers, and sleds from Bingham Wholesale Hardware on June 15, 2001, in the amount of $2,500. Terms of purchases were 2% if paid within 10 days and the remainder to be paid within 30 days after purchase. On June 30, 2001, Slaughter Hardware Store mails Bingham Wholesale Hardware a check for $2,500, the Gross amount of the purchase. What entries should be made on the books of the Slaughter Hardware Store?

SOLUTION:

2001		($ in dollars)	
June 15	Purchases	2,500	
	Accounts Payable—Bingham Wholesale Hardware		2,500
June 30	Accounts Payable—Bingham Wholesale Hardware	2,500	
	Cash		2,500

The account Purchases was debited for $2,500 on June 15, 2001, to show that hardware merchandise worth $2,500 had been purchased on that date from Bingham Wholesale Hardware. Accounts Payable—Bingham Wholesale Hardware is credited for $2,500 because Slaughter Hardware

Store is giving Bingham its oral promise to pay the $2,500.

Fifteen days later, on June 30, 2001, the Slaughter Hardware Store mails a check to Bingham Wholesale Hardware for $2,500, the Gross amount of the sale. The payment was not made within the 10-day discount period, so the discount is not allowed and the full Gross amount of $2,500 must be paid. The Liability Account Accounts Payable—Bingham Wholesale Hardware is debited for $2,500, because Slaughter Hardware Store is receiving back its oral promise to pay.

• PROBLEM 16–12

Slaughter Hardware Store purchased wholesale hardware such as nails, hammers, and sleds from Bingham Wholesale Hardware on October 1, 2001, in the amount of $2,500. Terms of purchase were 2% if paid within 10 days and the remainder to be paid within 30 days after purchase. On October 9, 2001, Slaughter Hardware Store mails Bingham Wholesale Hardware a check for $2,450, the Net amount of the purchase. What entries should be made on the books of the Slaughter Hardware Store?

SOLUTION:

2001		($ in dollars)	
October 1	Purchases	2,450	
	Accounts Payable—Bingham Wholesale Hardware		2,450
October 9	Accounts Payable—Bingham Wholesale Hardware	2,450	
	Cash		2,450

On October 1, the Slaughter Hardware Store purchased $2,500 worth of merchandise from Bingham Wholesale Hardware. On Slaughter's books, Purchases was debited for $2,450, the Net amount of the purchase (2% of $2,500 = $50; $2,500 − $50 = $2,450).

Accounts Payable—Bingham Wholesale Hardware was credited for $2,450 because Slaughter Hardware Store is giving Bingham its oral promise to pay the amount of the purchase at a later date.

On October 9, 2001, the date Slaughter Hardware Store sends the payment check, and Slaughter debits Accounts Payable—Bingham Wholesale Hardware for $2,450 because Slaughter is receiving back its oral promise to pay the debt. It credits Cash for $2,450, since this is the amount of the check sent. The check is for the Net amount of $2,450 rather than the Gross amount of $2,500, since payment was made within the 10-day discount period.

• PROBLEM 16–13

Slaughter Hardware Store purchased wholesale hardware such as nails, hammers, and sleds from Bingham Wholesale Hardware on October 1, 2001, in the amount of $2,500. Terms of purchase were 2% if paid within 10 days and the remainder to be paid within 30 days after purchase. On October 20, 2001, Slaughter Hardware Store mails Bingham Wholesale Hardware a check for $2,500, the Gross amount of the purchase. But the Slaughter Hardware Store keeps its books at Net. What entries should be made on the books of the Slaughter Hardware Store?

SOLUTION:

2001		($ in dollars)
October 1	Purchases	2,450
	Accounts Payable—Bingham Wholesale Hardware	2,450
October 20	Accounts Payable—Bingham Wholesale Hardware	2,450
	Purchases Discounts Lost	50
	Cash	
2,500		

On October 1, 2001, the Slaughter Hardware Store bought $2,500 worth of merchandise from Bingham Wholesale Hardware. But since Slaughter Hardware Store keeps its books at Net rather than at Gross, it debited Purchases for $2,450, which is 98% of the $2,500 Gross purchase price ($2,500 × 98% = $2,450). Accounts Payable—Bingham Wholesale Hardware is credited for $2,450, since Slaughter Hardware Store is giving Bingham Wholesale Hardware its oral promise to pay that amount.

On October 20, 2001, the Slaughter Hardware Store sends Bingham Wholesale Hardware its check for $2,500, the Gross amount of the purchase. This is not within the discount period. The merchandise was purchased on October 1, and 19 days later, on October 20, the bill was paid. Therefore, Slaughter Hardware Store credits Cash for the full $2,500 Gross amount of the purchase. It also debits Accounts Payable—Bingham Wholesale Hardware for $2,450, since it is receiving back its oral promise to pay the Net amount and thus closes out this account. It also debits the expense account entitled Purchases Discounts Lost to show that it lost the potential discount by not paying within the 10-day discount period.

• PROBLEM 16–14

The Johnson Construction Company has just signed a contract with Erath County to build a bridge over the Erath River for the sum of $350,000, on January 2, 2000. During the year 2000, expenses of the Johnson Construction Company in building the bridge, for Material, Labor, and Overhead, were $50,000. During this time, the Johnson Construction Company billed Erath County for $40,000 and collected cash from Erath County of $25,000. What entries will Johnson Construction Company make on their books during the year 2000 and why?

SOLUTION:

2000		($ in dollars)
December 31 Construction in Progress	50,000	
Accounts Payable		50,000
December 31 Accounts Receivable	40,000	
Partial Billings		40,000
December 31 Cash	25,000	
Accounts Receivable		25,000

On December 31, 2000, the end of the first year of bridge construction, summary entries are made covering the business transactions during the year. In the first summary entry, the Asset account Construction in Progress is debited for $50,000, the amount of money spent to construct the bridge partially during the year 2000, including Material, Labor, and Overhead costs. Accounts Payable is credited for $50,000, because this is the amount owed to providers, including firms providing the Material, the Laborers, and Overhead.

The second summary entry has to do with billings, which amounted to $40,000 during the year 2000. Accounts Receivable was debited for $40,000 because the county owes Johnson Construction that much when billed. The Contra-Asset account entitled Partial Billings is credited for $40,000. If one subtracts the $40,000 in the Partial Billings account from the $50,000 in the Construction in Progress account, one derives the $10,000 difference which has not yet been billed.

The third summary entry has to do with cash received by the Johnson Construction Company from Erath County during the year 2000. This is in the amount of $25,000, so Cash is debited for that amount received. Also, Accounts Receivable is credited for $25,000, since the amount owed by the county to the Johnson Construction Company has been cut down by that amount.

During the year 2000, no entry is made to record Revenue earned by the Johnson Construction Company, because they are keeping records by the Completed Contract Method, so no earnings are recorded until the year in which the bridge is fully completed.

• PROBLEM 16-15

The Johnson Construction Company has just signed a contract with Erath County to build a bridge over the Erath River for the sum of $350,000, on January 2, 2000. During the year 2000, expenses of the Johnson Construction Company in building the bridge, for Material, Labor, and Overhead, were $50,000. During this time the Johnson Construction Company billed Erath County for $40,000 and collected cash from Erath County of $25,000. Three summary entries were made on December 31, 2000, to cover these business transactions.

During the second year of the bridge construction (year 2001), expenses of the Johnson Construction Company in building the bridge, for Material, Labor, and Overhead, were $93,000. During this time the Johnson Construction Company billed Erath County for $175,000 and collected cash from Erath County in the amount of $165,000. What entries will Johnson Construction Company make on their books during the year 2001 and why?

SOLUTION:

2001		($ in dollars)
December 31 Construction in Progress	93,000	
Accounts Payable		93,000
December 31 Accounts Receivable	175,000	
Partial Billings		175,000
December 31 Cash	165,000	
Accounts Receivable		165,000

On December 31, 2001, the end of the second year of bridge construction, summary entries are made covering the business transactions during the year. In the first summary entry, the Asset account Construction in Progress is debited for $93,000, the amount of money spent to construct the bridge partially during the year 2001, including Material, Labor, and Overhead costs. Accounts Payable is credited for $93,000, because this is the amount owed to providers, including firms providing the Material, the Laborers, and the Overhead.

The second summary entry has to do with billings, which amounted to $175,000 during the year 2001. Accounts Receivable was debited for $175,000. because the county owes Johnson Construction that much when billed. The Contra-Asset account entitled Partial Billings is credited for $175,000.

The third summary entry has to do with cash received by the Johnson Construction Company from Erath County during the year 2001. This is the amount of $165,000, so Cash is debited for that amount received. Also, Accounts Receivable is credited for $165,000, since the amount owed by the county to the Johnson Construction Company has been cut down by that amount.

During the year 2001, no entry is made to record Revenue earned by the Johnson Construction Company, because they are keeping records by the Completed Contract Method, so no earnings are recorded until the year in which the bridge is fully completed.

• PROBLEM 16–16

The Johnson Construction Company signed a contract with Erath County to build a bridge over the Erath River for the sum of $350,000, on January 2, 2000. During the year 2000, expenses of the Johnson Construction Company in building the bridge for Material, Labor, and Overhead were $50,000. During this time, the Johnson Construction Company billed Erath County for $40,000 and collected cash from Erath County of $25,000. Three summary entries were made on December 31, 2000, to cover these business transactions.

During the second year of the bridge construction (year 2001), expenses of the Johnson Construction Company in building the bridge, for Material, Labor, and Overhead, were $93,000. During this time, the Johnson Construction Company billed Erath County for $175,000 and collected cash from Erath County in the amount of $165,000.

During the year 2002, the bridge was completed. Expenses of the Johnson Construction Company in completing the bridge during that year were $157,000 for Material, Labor, and Overhead. During this time the Johnson Construction Company billed Erath County for $135,000 and collected cash from Erath County in the amount of $160,000. What entries will Johnson Construction Company make on their books during the year 2002 and why?

SOLUTION:

2002		($ in dollars)
December 31 Construction in Progress	157,000	
Accounts Payable		157,000
December 31 Accounts Receivable	135,000	
Partial Billings		135,000
Cash	160,000	
Accounts Receivable		160,000

On December 31, 2002, the end of the third year of bridge construction, summary entries are made covering the business transactions during the year. In the first summary entry, the Asset account Construction in Progress is debited for $157,000, the amount of money spent to finish the construction of the bridge during the year 2002, including Material, Labor, and Overhead costs. Accounts Payable is credited for $157,000, because this is the amount owed to providers, including firms providing the Material, the Laborers, and the Overhead.

The second summary entry has to do with billings, which amounted to $135,000 during the year 2002. Accounts Receivable was debited for $135,000, because the county owes the Johnson Construction Company that much when billed. The Contra-Asset account entitled Partial Billings is credited for $135,000.

The third summary entry has to do with cash received by the Johnson Construction Company from Erath County during the year 2002. This is the amount of $160,000, so Cash is debited for that amount received. Also, Accounts Receivable is credited for $160,000, since the amount owed by the county to the Johnson Construction Company has been cut down by that amount.

• PROBLEM 16-17

The Johnson Construction Company signed a contract with Erath County to build a bridge over the Erath River for the sum of $350,00,0 on January 2, 2000. During the year 2000, expenses of the Johnson Construction Company in building the bridge for Material, Labor, and Overhead were $50,000. During this time the Johnson Construction Company billed Erath County for $40,000 and collected cash from Erath County of $25,000. Three summary entries were made on December 31, 2000, to cover these business transactions.

During the second year of the bridge construction (year 2001), expenses of the Johnson Construction Company in building the bridge, for Material, Labor, and Overhead, were $93,000. During this time, the Johnson Construction Company billed Erath County for $175,000 and collected cash from Erath County in the amount of $165,000.

During the third year of the bridge construction (year 2002), the bridge was completed. Expenses of the Johnson Construction Company in completing the bridge during that year were $157,000 for Material, Labor, and Overhead.

During this time the Johnson Construction Company billed Erath County for $135,000 and collected cash from Erath County in the amount of $160,000. Johnson Construction Company made three summary entries to cover these business transactions.

What final entries will need to be made on the books of the Johnson Construction Company when the bridge is completed?

SOLUTION:

2002		($ in dollars)
December 31 Partial Billings	350,000	
Construction Revenue		350,000
December 31 Construction Expense	300,000	
Construction in Progress		300,000

The Contra-Asset account entitled Partial Billings had a credit balance of $350,000, illustrated as follows:

Partial Billings

	12/31/2000	40,000
	12/31/2001	175,000
	12/31/2002	135,000
		350,000

In order to close out this Partial Billings account, the Johnson Construction Company debited Partial Billings for $350,000. Construction Revenue was credited for $350,000, since this was the amount of Revenue originally agreed upon in the contract between the Johnson Construction Company and Erath County, but because the Completed Contract Method of accounting was used, this Income had not been recognized (put down on the books) until this third year (year 2002) in which the bridge was completed.

The Asset account Construction in Progress appears as follows:

Construction in Progress

12/31/2000	50,000	
12/31/2001	93,000	
12/31/2002	157,000	
	300,000	

In order to close out the Asset account Construction in Progress, the Johnson Construction Company debits Construction Expense for $300,000 and credits Construction in Progress for $300,000. This credit of $300,000 to Construction in Progress effectively closes out this Asset account.

This leaves the Johnson Construction Company with a Revenue account entitled Construction Revenue with a credit balance of $350,000 (the amount originally agreed upon in the contract with Erath County), and an expense account entitled Construction Expense with a debit balance of $300,000 (the total amount moved to it from the Construction in Progress account).

The difference between the Construction Revenue account with a balance of $350,000 and the Construction Expense account with a balance of $300,000 is $50,000, the Net Income to the Johnson Construction Company for building the bridge. This $50,000 Net Income will be reported to the government for Income Tax purposes in the year 2002, the year when the bridge construction was completed. No Net Income will be reported for the previous two years since the Completed Contract Method was used.

The Cash account would appear as follows:

Cash

12/31/2000	25,000
12/31/2001	165,000
12/31/2002	160,000
	350,000

In the year 2000, the Johnson Construction Company collected $25,000 cash from Erath County. In the year 2001, the Johnson Construction Company collected $165,000 cash from Erath County. And in the year 2002, the Johnson Construction Company collected $160,000 from Erath County, or a total of $350,000 ($25,000 + $165,000 + $160,000 = $350,000).

The $350,000 was the amount of payment agreed upon between the county and the construction company in the original contract, and this amount was gradually paid by the county to the construction company over the three years in which the bridge was built.

• PROBLEM 16–18

The Santer Furniture Company is considering selling some of its furniture using the installment basis of accounting. Is this acceptable?

SOLUTION:

Yes, under certain circumstances. The installment method of recognizing Income stresses **collection** rather than **sales**. If a firm is selling merchandise that takes a time to make collections and if these collections are not sure, then it is permissible to use the installment method. The seller is protected either by a chattel mortgage on the goods sold or by a conditional sales contract (providing no passage of title until payments are made). Either of these protections allows the seller to repossess the merchandise in case of default.

• PROBLEM 16–19

The Santer Furniture Company is considering selling some of its furniture using the installment basis of accounting. Before adopting this method, the Santer Furniture Company makes the following entry for its sales of merchandise:

SOLUTION:

2000		($ in dollars)	
January 2	Accounts Receivable	10,000	
	Sales		10,000
January 2	Cost of Goods Sold	6,000	
	Inventory		6,000

On January 2, 2000, the Total Sales of furniture for the day amounted to $10,000, so the Asset account Accounts Receivable was credited for $10,000 because the store was receiving the "good name" or "oral promise to pay" from the credit customers. At the same time, they credited the Revenue account Sales for $10,000 because furniture with a retail value of $10,000 was moving out of the store. This is the accrual method of accounting, because by crediting Sales on the date the furniture moved out of the store, this "recognizes" or puts down this Revenue on the books on the date of sale. This will immediately show a Revenue for the store which they will have to place as Income on their books for Income Tax purposes whether they eventually receive the cash or not. This method is satisfactory if the store has customers who regularly pay their bills, but let us suppose that some of the store's customers so not pay regularly and their merchandise (furniture) may have to be repossessed. In this case, it may be better for the store not to "recognize" the income immediately, go on the installment basis, and recognize the Income as the Cash eventually comes in.

The Sanger Furniture Company is also on the perpetual inventory basis. This means that when a sale is made at sales price, the Cost of Sales is also recorded at cost price. Notice the second entry above, where Cost of Goods Sold (a cost-expense type of account) is debited for $6,000—the cost price of the furniture sold on January 2, 2000. Also, the Asset account Inventory is credited for $6,000 to show that inventory at that cost price is leaving the store. The difference of $4,000 ($10,000 sales price – $6,000 cost price = $4,000 Gross Profit) is the Gross Profit, which is 40% of sales in this case (4,000 Gross Profit ÷ $10,000 sales = 40%).

• PROBLEM 16–20

The Santer Furniture Company decides to sell some of its furniture (to customers whose ability to pay is questionable) using the installment basis of accounting. What new accounts will it have to add to its chart of accounts?

SOLUTION:

1. **Installment Accounts Receivable**. Just as Accounts Receivable is an Asset account, so is Installment Accounts Receivable. But this account will only be used with customers whose accounts are kept on the installment basis.

2. **Installment Sales**. Just as Sales is a Revenue account, so is the account Installment Sales. But this account will only be used with customers whose accounts are kept on the installment basis.

3. **Cost of Installment Sales**. Just as Cost of Goods Sold is a Cost-expense type of account, so is Cost of Installment Sales. But this account will only be used with customers whose accounts are kept on the installment basis.

4. **Deferred Gross Profit**. This is a deferred credit, a type of Liability Account, with a credit balance. It is used in installment sales.

5. Realized Gross Profit on Installment Sales. This is a Revenue account used when books are kept on the installment basis.

• PROBLEM 16–21

The Santer Furniture Company decides to sell some of its furniture (to customers whose ability to pay is questionable) using the installment basis of accounting. How do the books look after two years?

SOLUTION:

	Year 2000		Year 2001	
Installment Sales	$100,000	100%	$125,000	100%
Cost of Installment Sales	75,000	75%	95,000	76%
Gross Profit	$ 25,000	25%	$ 30,000	24%
Cash Receipts:				
2000 year sales	$ 30,000		$ 50,000	
2001 year sales			$ 50,000	

Let us say that the installment sales of furniture by the Santer Furniture Company in the year 2000 were $100,000 and the installment sales in the year 2001 were $125,000. The sales in both cases are considered the basis for computation and are arbitrarily given 100%.

In the year 2000, the cost of installment sales was $75,000. This is 75% of installment sales ($75,000 cost of installment sales ÷ $100,000 sales = 75%). Next, the cost of installment sales of $75,000 is subtracted from sales for the year 2000 to get a Gross Profit of $25,000 ($100,000 sales – $75,000 cost of installment sales = $25,000 Gross Profit).

In the year 2001, the cost of installment sales was $95,000. This is 76% of installment sales ($95,000 cost of installment sales ÷ $125,000 sales = 76%). Next, the cost of installment sales of $95,000 is subtracted from sales for the year 2001 to get a Gross Profit of $30,000. ($125,000 sales – $95,000 cost of installment sales = $30,000 Gross Profit).

The cash receipts from collections on installment sales for the year 2000 are $30,000. The cash receipts from collections on year 2000 installment sales during the year 2001 were $50,000, and the cash receipts from collections on year 2001 installment sales during the year 2001 were also $50,000.

• PROBLEM 16–22

The Santer Furniture Company decides to sell some of its furniture (to customers whose ability to pay is questionable) using the install-ment basis of accounting. What cumulative entries should be made at the end of the first year?

SOLUTION:

As shown in the table in the previous problem, the installment sales of the Santer Furniture Company during the year 2000 were $100,000. Let us assume that these sales were all made on account. The entry would be as follows:

2000		($ in dollars)
December 31 Installment Accounts Receivable, 2000	100,000	
Installment Sales		100,000

The Santer Furniture Company is receiving an oral promise to pay $100,000 from its installment customers so it debits the Asset account Installment Accounts Receivable. (Regular customers who pay by the end of the month would be debited to Accounts Receivable, but installment customers who have signed an installment contract requiring regular monthly payments over a period of time would be debited to the account Installment Accounts Receivable.) Also, the account Installment Sales would be credited for $100,000, since customers signing the installment contracts would be carrying $100,000 worth of merchandise out of the store.

As shown in the previous problem, the cash received on installment sales during the year 2000 (the sales were made in the year 2000 and the cash was received in the year 2000) amounted to $30,000. The entry to record this is as follows:

2000		($ in dollars)
December 31 Cash	30,000	
Installment Accounts Receivable, 2000		30,000

The account Cash was debited for $30,000, because this amount was received for the Accounts Receivable year 2000 (on installment sales dur-ing the year 2000). The account Installment Accounts Receivable, 2000 is credited for $30,000, because the customers' oral promise to pay is being reduced or given back to them, since now that they have made a partial payment on their accounts, they no longer owe the Santer Furniture Company so much money.

At the end of the year 2000, the account Installment Accounts Receivable, 2000 will appear as follows on the books of the Santer Furniture Company:

Installment Accounts Receivable 2000

12/31/2000	100,000		12/31/2000	30,000
	70,000			

As can be seen from the "T" account, the Installment Accounts Receivable, 2000 account was debited on December 31, 2000, for $100,000, the amount of installment sales for the year. Also on December 31, 2000, the Installment Accounts Receivable, 2000 account was credited for $30,000, the amount of cash received for year 2000 installment sales collected in the year 2000. Thus, as of the end of the year 2000, the Installment Accounts Receivable, 2000 account has a debit balance of only $70,000 ($100,000 installment sales on account – $30,000 cash received on account = $70,000 still owed on installment sales).

The next entry has to do with cost of installment sales. During the year 2000, the Santer Furniture Company had installment sales of $100,000, the cost of which was $75,000. So to record the $75,000, the entry is as follows:

2000	($ in dollars)	
December 31 Cost of Installment Sales	75,000	
Inventory		75,000

Cost of Installment Sales is a Cost-expense type of account similar to Cost of Goods Sold, but used exclusively for recording installment sales. It is debited for $75,000, which is the cost price of the installment sales of Santer Furniture Company during the year 2000.

The Asset account Inventory is credited for $75,000, because during the year 2000, merchandise with the cost price of $75,000 was leaving the store. This deduction on the Inventory account helps the proprietor more accurately determine the cost price of the inventory still on hand. The next entry is a closing entry to close out Installment Sales and Cost of Installment Sales, as follows:

2000	($ in dollars)	
December 31 Installment Sales	100,000	
Cost of Installment Sales		75,000
Deferred Gross Profit, 2000		25,000

Installment Sales is a Revenue account which must be closed out at the end of the year since it is a temporary account. Installment Sales had a credit balance of $100,000, so to close it out, it is debited for $100,000. Cost of Installment Sales is a Cost-expense type of account which must be closed out at the end of the year since it is a temporary account. Cost of Installment Sales had a debit balance of $75,000, so to close it out, it is credited for $75,000. The difference of $25,000 ($100,000 installment sales – $75,000 cost of installment sales = $25,000 Gross Profit) is credited to a Liability Account entitled Deferred Gross Profit, 2000. This is also called a "deferred credit" account, since it appears in the Balance Sheet as a Liability, not in the Income Statement.

The next entry takes away from the Deferred Gross Profit account the profit received from cash collections during the year 2000. It appears as follows:

2000	($ in dollars)	
December 31 Deferred Gross Profit, 2000	7,500	
Realized Gross Profit on Installment Sales		7,500

In the installment method of accounting, the amount of Gross Profit collected on account during the year should be recognized (that is, recorded as Income on the books) as Income for that year. In this case, the amount is $7,500. ($30,000 cash received during the year 2000 on installment sales for the year 2000 × 25% Gross Profit Rate = $7,500 amount of Gross Profit realized on cash collections.) Therefore, the Liability Account Deferred Gross Profit is credited for $7,500 to cut down on that Liability. The Revenue account Realized Gross Profit on Installment Sales is credited for $7,500, since this is the amount of Gross Profit collected on installment sales during the year 2000.

The account Realized Gross Profit on Installment Sales is a Revenue account and is a temporary account that must be closed out into the Income Summary account at the end of the year. So the closing entry is as follows:

2000	($ in dollars)
December 31 Realized Gross Profit on Installment Sales	7,500
Income Summary	7,500

The Revenue account Realized Gross Profit on Installment Sales had a credit balance of $7,500. In order to close this out, debit Realized Gross Profit on Installment Sales for $7,500. Also, credit the temporary account Income Summary for $7,500. All temporary accounts, at year's end, are closed into Income Summary which is then closed into the Owner's Capital account in the case of a single proprietorship, or into the Retained Earnings account in the case of a corporation.

• PROBLEM 16-23

The Santer Furniture Company decides to sell some of its furniture (to customers whose ability to pay is questionable) using the installment basis of accounting. During the first year (the calendar year 2000), installment sales of $100,000 were made, of which $75,000 was Cost of Goods Sold and the other $25,000 was Gross Profit. Also during that year $30,000 cash was collected on year 2000 installment sales. Of the $30,000 cash collected, $7,500 was credited to the Revenue account entitled Realized Gross Profit on Installment Sales. What entries should be made during the second year (in this case the calendar year 2001) and why?

SOLUTION:

2001	($ in dollars)
December 31 Installment Accounts Receivable, 2001	125,000
Installment Sales	125,000

As shown in a previous table, the installment sales of the Santer Furniture Company during the year 2001 were $125,000. The Santer Furniture Company is receiving the oral promise to pay $125,000 from its installment customers so it debits the Asset account Installment Accounts Receivable, 2001, for that amount. (Sales made to regular customers who pay by the end of the month would be debited to Accounts Receivable, but sales made to installment customers who have signed installment contracts requiring regular monthly payments over a period of time would be debited to the account Installment Accounts Receivable.) Also, the account Installment Sales would be credited for $125,000, since customers signing the installment contracts would be carrying $125,000 worth of merchandise out of the store.

The cash received on installment sales of the year 2000 but collected during the year 2001 was $50,000. The cash received on installment sales of the year 2001 and also collected in the year 2001 were $50,000. The entry to show this follows:

2001	($ in dollars)
December 31 Cash	100,000
Installment Accounts Receivable, 2000	50,000
Installment Accounts Receivable, 2001	50,000

Let us say that during the calendar year of 2001, cash was received on the installment account of $100,000. So the Asset account Cash was debited for this $100,000. Of this amount of money, $50,000 was received in the year 2001 to pay on Accounts Receivable of sales incurred during the calendar year 2000. Therefore, the account Installment Accounts Receivable, 2000 is credited for $50,000 to lower that account by that amount, since customers no longer owe that amount of money. The other $50,000 was received in the year 2001 to pay on Accounts Receivable of sales incurred during the calendar year of 2001. Therefore, the account Installment Accounts Receivable, 2001 is credited for $50,000 to lower that account by that amount, since customers no longer owe that amount of money.

It will be seen that in installment accounting there is a separate Installment Accounts Receivable account for each year. Thus, the accounting for installment payments is quite a bit more complicated than would be the accounting otherwise.

In the year 2001, the Cost of Installment Sales was $95,000. This is 76% of installment sales ($95,000 cost of installment sales ÷ $125,000 sales = 76%). Next, the cost of installment sales of $95,000 is subtracted from sales for the year 2001 to get a Gross Profit of $30,000. ($125,000 sales – $95,000 Cost of Installment Sales = $30,000 Gross Profit.)

The entry at the end of the year 2001 to record the Cost of Installment Sales is as follows:

2001		($ in dollars)
December 31 Cost of Installment Sales	95,000	
Inventory		95,000

The Cost of Installment Sales is a Cost-expense type of account similar to Cost of Goods Sold, but it is used exclusively for recording installment sales. It is debited here for $95,000, which is the cost price of the installment sales of the Santer Furniture Company during the year 2001.

The Asset account Inventory is credited for $95,000, because during the year 2001, merchandise with the cost price of $95,000 was leaving the store. This deduction on the Inventory account helps the proprietor more accurately determine the cost price of the inventory still on hand.

As was mentioned previously, in installment accounting there has to be a separate Installment Accounts Receivable account for each year, since the Gross Profit Rate, on which profit is based, varies from year to year. At the end of the year 2001, the Installment Accounts Receivable will appear as follows:

Installment Accounts Receivable, 2000

12/31/2000	100,000	12/31/2000	30,000
		12/31/2001	50,000
			80,000
	20,000		

Installment Accounts Receivable, 2001

12/31/2001	125,000	12/31/2001	50,000
	75,000		

During the year 2000, $100,000 of sales were made on installment account, and the account Installment Accounts Receivable, 2000 was debited for $100,000. Also during the year 2000, the installment customers who had purchased furniture during the year 2000 repaid $30,000, bringing the Installment Accounts Receivable, 2000 account down to $70,000 ($100,000 sales on installment account – $30,000 cash paid = $70,000 still owed). During the calendar year 2001, customers who had purchased furniture on installment account during the calendar year 2000 repaid $50,000 more, bringing the balance of this account down to $20,000 ($100,000 – $30,000 – $50 ,000 = $20,000 still owed).

During the calendar year 2001, $125,000 of installment sales were made. This was debited to an account entitled Installment Accounts Receivable, 2001. Also during the year 2001, $50,000 of this amount was repaid, so the account Installment Accounts Receivable, 2001, was credited for $50,000, bringing the balance of this account down to $75,000 ($125,000 – $50,000 = $75,000).

The next entry is a closing entry to close out Installment Sales and Cost of Installment Sales, as follows:

2001	($ in dollars)	
December 31 Installment Sales	125,000	
Cost of Installment Sales		95,000
Deferred Gross Profit, 2001		30,000

Installment Sales is a Revenue account which must be closed out at the end of the year since it is a temporary account. Installment Sales had a credit balance of $125,000, so to close it out, debit it for $125,000. Cost of Installment Sales is a Cost-expense type of account which also must be closed out at the end of the year, since it is a temporary account. Cost of Installment Sales had a debit balance of $95,000, so to close it out, credit it for $95,000. The difference of $30,000 ($125,000 installment sales – $95,000 Cost of Installment Sales = $30,000 Gross Profit) is credited to a Liability Account entitled Deferred Gross Profit, 2000. This is also called a "deferred credit" account, since it appears on the Balance Sheet as a Liability, not on the Income Statement. The next entry takes away from the Deferred Gross Profit, 2000 and the Deferred Gross Profit, 2001 accounts the profit received from cash collections during the year 2001. It appears as follows:

2001	($ in dollars)	
December 31 Deferred Gross Profit, 2000	12,500	
Deferred Gross Profit, 2001	12,000	
Realized Gross Profit on Installment Sales		24,500

In the installment method of accounting, the amount of Gross Profit collected on account during the year should be recognized (that is, recorded as Income on the books) as Income for that year. In this case, the amount is $12,500. ($50,000 cash received during the year 2001 on installment sales for the year 2000 × 25% Gross Profit Rate for the year 2000 = $12,500, the amount of Gross Profit realized during 2001 on cash collections that year from merchandise sold in the year 2000.) Therefore, the account Deferred Gross Profit, 2000 is debited for $12,500 to cut down the value of that Liability Account. Also, the amount of $12,000 ($50,000 cash received during the year 2001 on installment sales for the year 2001 × 24% Gross Profit Rate for the year 2001 = $12,000, the amount of Gross Profit realized during 2001 on cash collections that year from merchandise sold in the year 2001). Therefore, the account Deferred Gross Profit, 2001 is debited for $12,000 to cut down the value of that Liability Account. The Revenue account Realized Gross Profit on Installment Sales is credited for $24,500 (the sum of the $12,500 and the $12,000), since this is the amount of Gross Profit to be recognized (placed on the books as Income) from installment sales during the calendar year of 2001.

Finally, the account Realized Gross Profit on Installment Sales must be closed out at year's end to the Income Summary account as follows:

2001	($ in dollars)	
December 31 Realized Gross Profit on Installment Sales	24,500	
Income Summary		24,500

The Revenue account Realized Gross Profit on Installment Sales has a credit balance of $24,500. In order to close this out, we now debit Realized Gross Profit on Installment Sales for $24,500. Also, we credit the temporary account Income Summary for $24,500. All temporary accounts, at year's end, are closed into Income Summary which is then closed into the Owner's Capital account in the case of a single proprietorship, into the Partners' Capital accounts in the case of a partnership, and into the Retained Earnings account in the case of a corporation.

• PROBLEM 16–24

The Slossen Furniture Store sells merchandise using the installment method of accounting. On January 2, 2000 it sold to one of its customers furniture costing $5,000 for a sales price of $6,000. The terms of the contract were that the customer should make yearly payments for 5 years with Interest on the unpaid balance of 9%. How will this be computed?

SOLUTION:

The Slossen Furniture Store is in the habit of making up a payment schedule for each customer. The first step is to look in a Present Value table for the Present Value of an Ordinary Annuity of 1 for 5 periods at 9%. A portion of this table is reproduced below:

Table for the Present Value of an Ordinary Annuity of 1

Periods	8%	9%	10%	11%	12%
5	3.99271	3.88965	3.79079	3.69590	3.60478

As can be seen from the table above, the Present Value of an ordinary annuity of 1 at 9% for 5 years is 3.88965.

The next step is to divide this Present Value of 3.88965 into the sales price of the furniture—in this case $6,000 ($6,000 ÷ 3.88965 = $1,542.56). This figure of $1,542.56 is the annual payment that should be made by the customer at the end of each year for a period of five years. The payment schedule for this customer is as follows:

Interest Payment Schedule
Name of Customer: James Lyons

Date	Cash Debit	Interest Earned Credit	Installments Receivable Credit	Installment Unpaid Balance	Realized Gross Profit
1/2/00				6,000.00	
12/31/00	1,542.56	540.00	1,002.56	4,997.44	167.11
12/31/01	1,542.56	449.77	1,092.79	3,904.65	182.11
12/31/02	1,542.56	351.42	1,191.14	2,713.51	198.52
12/31/03	1,542.56	244.22	1,298.34	1,415.17	216.39
12/31/04	1,542.56	127.37	1,415.19	0	230.87

On January 2, 2000, a customer of the Slossen Furniture Store purchased merchandise from Slossen. This customer's name is James Lyons. The cost price of the furniture is $5,000 and the sales price is $6,000, so the cost is 5/6 of sales. Another way of stating it is that the Gross Profit is 1/6 of sales (6/6 − 1/6 = 5/6).

The first line of the table shows the $6,000 purchase (or sales) price on January 2, 2000.

The second line of the table is dated December 31, 2000, and shows the first payment of $1,542.56 at the end of that year. Of that payment, $540.00 is interest ($6,000 price of furniture × 9% = $540 Interest). The next column shows the reduction of the debt, where Installments Receivable is credited for $1,002.56. ($1,542.56 cash payment − $540.00 Interest = $1,002.56 reduction of debt.) This brings the installment balance down to $4,997.44. ($6,000.00 sales price − $1,002.56 reduction of debt = $4,997.44 the amount still owed at the end of the first year.)

The Gross Profit is 1/6 of the selling price, since the Cost of Goods Sold is 5/6 of the selling price ($6,000.00 selling price − $5,000.00 Cost of Goods Sold = $1,000). Therefore, the Gross Profit realized during the year 2000 is 1/6 of the Installment Receivable Credit (decrease in debt) or $167.11. ($1,002.56 Interest Receivable Credit × 1/6 = $167.11 realized Gross Profit.)

In the year 2001, the end-of-year payment is the same as in all other years, $1,542.56. The Interest is 9% of the unpaid balance of $4,997.44, or $449.77 ($4,997.44 × 9% = $449.77) The Installment Receivable Credit (the amount of decrease in the debt) is $1,092.79, which is the payment of $1,542.56 less the Interest of $449.77 ($1,542.56 − $449.77 = $1,092.79). The realized Gross Profit at the end of the year 2001 is $182.11, which is 1/6 of the Installment Receivable Credit of $1,092.79 (1/6 × $1,092.79 = $182.11).

In the year 2002, the end-of-year payment is the same as in all other years, $1,542.56. The Interest is 9% of the unpaid balance of $3,904.65 or $351.42 ($3,904.65 × 9% = $351.42). The Installment Receivable Credit (the amount of decrease in the debt) is $1,191.14, which is the payment of $1,542.56 less the Interest of $351.42 ($1,542.56 − $351.42 = $1,191.14). The realized Gross Profit at the end of the year 2002 is $198.52, which is 1/6 of the Installment Receivable Credit of $1,191.14 (1/6 × $1,191.14 = $198.52).

In the year 2003, the end-of-year payment is the same as in all other years, $1,542.56. The Interest is 9% of the unpaid balance of $2,713.51, or $244.22 ($2,713.51 × 9% = $244.22). The Installment Receivable Credit (the amount of decrease in the debt) is $1,298.34, which is the payment of $1,542.56 less the Interest of $244.22 ($1,542.56 − $244.22 = $1,298.34). The realized Gross Profit at the end of the year 2003 is $216.39, which is 1/6 of the Installment Receivable Credit of $1,298.34 (1/6 × $1,298.34 = $216.39).

In the year 2004, the end-of-year payment is the same as in all other years, $1,542.56. The Interest is 9% of the unpaid balance of $1,415.17 or $127.37. ($1,415.17 × 9% = $127.37). The Installment Receivable Credit (the amount of decrease in the debt) is $1,415.19, which is the payment of $1,542.56 less the Interest of $127.37 ($1,542.56 − $127.37 = $1,415.19). The realized Gross Profit at the end of the year 2004 is $230.87, which is 1/6 of the Installment Receivable Credit of $1,415.19 (1/6 × $1,415.19 = $230.87).

• PROBLEM 16–25

Using the same payment schedule for James Lyons as in the previous problem, let us assume that we sell James Lyons furniture for $6,000 on January 2, 2000, and that on December 31, 2000, December 31, 2001, and December 31, 2002, he makes regular payments of $1,542.56. However, on December 31, 2003, he defaults and the Slossen Furniture Store is forced to repossess the furniture. What entry should be made on the books of the Slossen Furniture Store and why?

SOLUTION:

2003		($ in dollars)
December 31 Repossessed Merchandise	2,261.25	
Deferred Gross Profit	452.26	
Installment Accounts Receivable		2,713.51

As of the last installment payment on December 31, 2002, the accounts on the books of the Slossen Furniture Store appeared as follows:

Installment Accounts Receivable

1/2/2000	6,000.00	12/31/2000	1,002.56
		12/31/2001	1,092.79
		12/31/2002	1,191.14
			3,286.49
	2,713.51		

Deferred Gross Profit

12/31/2000	167.11	1/2/2000	1,000.00
12/31/2001	182.11		
12/31/2002	198.52		
	547.74		
			452.26

Realized Gross Profit

		12/31/2000	167.11
		12/31/2001	182.11
		12/31/2002	198.52
			547.74

On January 2, 2000, when the merchandise was sold on account, the account Installment Accounts Receivable was debited for $6,000, the amount the customer owes the furniture store. At the end of the year 2000, the Installment Accounts Receivable account was credited for $1,002.56, the amount that the debt was decreased. On December 31, 2001, Installment Accounts Receivable was credited for $1,092.79, the amount the debt was decreased. Finally, on December 31, 2002, Installment Accounts Receivable was credited for $1,191.14, the amount the debt was decreased, bringing the balance of that account down to $2,713.51

On January 2, 2000, when the $6,000 sale was made, 1/6 of this amount, $1,000, the amount of the expected Gross Profit, was credited to a Liability Account entitled Deferred Gross Profit. On December 31, 2000, $167.11 of the first payment was considered Gross Profit so it was debited to the Deferred Gross Profit account. On December 31, 2001, $182.11 of the second payment was considered Gross Profit so it was debited to the Deferred Gross Profit account. On December 31, 2002, $198.52 of the third payment was considered Gross Profit so it was debited to the Deferred Gross Profit account. All three of these entries successively cutting down this account to the balance of $547.74.

The final repossession entry on December 31, 2003, debits Deferred Gross Profit for $452.26 to close out this account. The final repossession entry on December 31, 2003 credits Installment Accounts Receivable for $2,713.51 to close out this account. The Asset account entitled Repossessed Merchandise is a plug entry for $2,261.25, derived by subtracting the debit of $452.26 from the credit of $2,713.51 ($2,713.51 – $452.26 = $2,261.25). This figure of $2,261.25 is the approximate value of the repossessed merchandise at the time of repossession. However, if that is not the true Appraised Value, the appraiser could have an entry made for the difference debiting the expense account Loss and crediting the Asset account Repossessed Merchandise. If the appraiser believes the repossessed merchandise to be of greater value, the appraiser could have an entry made for the difference debiting the Asset account Repossessed Merchandise and crediting the Revenue account Gain.

• PROBLEM 16–26

The Hampdon Furniture Company sells the Brown Company $18,000 worth of merchandise which originally cost the Hampdon Company $12,500, on January 2, 2000. During the year 2000, the Hampdon Company received a cash payment from the Brown Company of $9,000. During the year 2001, the Hampdon Company received a cash payment from the Brown Company of $6,000. During the year 2002, the Hampdon Company received a cash payment from the Brown Company of $3,000. This makes a total of $18,000 sales price. At the date of sale the Hampdon Furniture Company felt that there was no real way of knowing whether or not the Brown Company would be able to pay regularly, so they decided to use the Cost Recovery Method of accounting. This means that no Gross Profit would be recorded until the entire cost price was received from the customer.

What entries should be made on the Hampdon Furniture Company books and why?

SOLUTION:

2000		($ in dollars)	
January 2	Installment Accounts Receivable	18,000	
	Installment Sales		18,000
January 2	Cost of Sales	12,500	
	Inventory		12,500

Installment Accounts Receivable, an Asset account, was debited for $18,000 because the Hampdon Furniture Company was getting the Brown Company's oral promise to pay the $18,000 value of the furniture. Installment Sales, a Revenue account, was credited because furniture was moving out of the store and being sold, worth $18,000.

At the same time, the Cost-expense account entitled Cost of Sales was debited for the cost price of $12,500, since this is a cost or expense of the Hampdon Furniture Company. Inventory, an Asset account, is credited for $12,500, since merchandise with the cost of $12,500 is leaving the store.

At the end of the year 2000, the temporary accounts entitled Installment Sales and Cost of Sales are closed out and the Liability Account Deferred Gross Profit is credited, as follows:

2000		($ in dollars)	
December 31	Installment Sales	18,000	
	Cost of Sales		12,500
	Deferred Gross Profit		5,500

On January 2, 2000, when the merchandise was originally sold, the Revenue account Installment Sales was credited for the sales price of $18,000. Now, at year's end, the temporary account Installment Sales is closed out by debiting it for $18,000. On January 2, 2000, when the merchandise was originally sold, the Cost-expense account entitled Cost of Sales was debited for the cost price of $12,500. Now, at year's end, the temporary account Cost of Sales is credited for $12,500 to close it out. The balance of $5,500 is credited to a Liability Account entitled Deferred Gross Profit. It is not known at this time whether or not this deferred Gross Profit will be collectible at all, so any report of profit will be postponed until a future date to see if cash is forthcoming from the customer, in this case the Brown Company.

Also on December 31, 2000, the Hampdon Furniture Company receives the first cash payment from the Brown Company of $9,000. This is recorded on the books of the Hampdon Furniture Company as follows:

2000	($ in dollars)
December 31 Cash	9,000
Installment Accounts Receivable	9,000

On December 31, 2000, the accounts on the books of the Hampdon Furniture Company appear as follows:

Installment Accounts Receivable

1/2/2000	18,000	12/31/2000	9,000
	9,000		

Installment Sales

12/31/2000	18,000	1/2/2000	18,000

Cost of Sales

1/2/2000	12,500	12/31/2000	12,500

Deferred Gross Profit

		12/31/2000	5,500

The Installment Accounts Receivable Asset account was debited for $18,000 on January 2, 2000, the date of sale, to show how much the customer owed the Hampdon Furniture Company. On December 31, 2000 Hampdon received a payment of $9,000, cutting this account down to the $9,000 still owed.

On January 2, 2000, the date of sale, Installment Sales were credited for $18,000, the amount of the sale. On December 31, 2000, an adjusting entry was made debiting Installment Sales for $18,000, thus closing out this temporary account.

On January 2, 2000, the date of sale, Cost of Sales was debited for $12,500, the cost price of the inventory sold. On December 31, 2000, an adjusting entry credited Cost of Sales for $12,500, thus closing out this temporary account.

On December 31, 2000, the Liability Account entitled Deferred Gross Profit was credited for $5,500. This is the amount that the Hampdon Furniture Company will earn if all the payments are eventually received, but it is not profit yet, and under the Cost Recovery Method, the entire cost of sales must be received before any Gross Profit is recorded on the books.

2001		($ in dollars)
December 31 Cash	6,000	
Installment Accounts Receivable		6,000
December 31 Deferred Gross Profit	2,500	
Realized Gross Profit		2,500

On December 31, 2001 the Hampdon Furniture Company received the second annual payment from the Brown Company, and this payment was for $6,000. So, Cash was debited for the $6,000 received. The Asset account Installment Accounts Receivable was credited for the $6,000, bringing its balance down to $3,000 ($18,000 − $9,000 − $6,000 = $3,000). Under the Cost Recovery Method, no realized Gross Profit is put down on the books until the Cost of the Installment Sale has been recovered. The cost of the sale was $12,500. In the year 2000, $9,000 cash payment was received. Since this didn't amount to the cost of $12,500, no Gross Profit was realized in the year 2000. However, in the year 2001, $6,000 more was received, bringing the total of cash received thus far to $15,000 ($9,000 received in year 2000 + $6,000 received in year 2001 = $15,000). Since the cash received thus far ($15,000) is greater than the cost price ($12,500), the difference is realized Gross Profit ($15,000 − $12,500 = $2,500). Thus, Realized Gross Profit is credited for $2,500. This is Revenue and must be reported on the books as Income for the year 2001. The account Deferred Gross Profit is debited for $2,500 to cut down this Liability Account. At the end of the year 2000, the Deferred Gross

Profit account had been credited for $5,500, the amount of profit hoped for if all the money was forthcoming from the Brown Company. Now, at the end of the year 2001, $2,500 is debited to this account, bringing the balance down to $3,000, as follows:

Deferred Gross Profit

12/31/2001	2,500	12/31/2000	5,500
			3,000

The $3,000 balance of the Deferred Gross Profit account is the amount still hoped for if more cash collections can be obtained in the future from the Brown Company.

On December 31, 2002, the Hampdon Furniture Company receives the final payment from the Brown Company of $3,000. Two entries are made on the Hampdon books as follows:

2002		($ in dollars)
December 31 Cash	3,000	
Installment Accounts Receivable		3,000
December 31 Deferred Gross Profit	3,000	
Realized Gross Profit		3,000

Cash has just been received from the Brown Company, so on the books of the Hampdon Furniture Company they debit Cash for $3,000. The Asset account Installment Accounts Receivable is credited for $3,000 to close out that account, showing that the Brown Company no longer owes the Hampdon Company any money. The Installment Accounts Receivable will now appear as follows:

Installment Accounts Receivable

1/2/2000	18,000	12/31/2000	9,000
		12/31/2001	6,000
		12/31/2002	3,000

The above account shows that when the sale was made on January 2, 2000, the Brown Company owed the Hampdon Furniture Company

$18,000. On the credit side of the account are the three cash payments that the Hampdon Furniture Company received from the Brown Company as follows: $9,000 on December 31, 2000; $6,000 on December 31, 2001; and $3,000 on December 31, 2002. Since these three payments add up to $18,000, the debt is cancelled.

As of December 31, 2002, the Deferred Gross Profit account appears as follows:

Deferred Gross Profit

12/31/2001	2,500	12/31/2000	5,500
12/31/2002	3,000		
	5,500		

In the year 2000 at year's end, it was determined that if Brown Company finally paid all of its bill, the Gross Profit of the Hampdon Furniture Company would be $5,500 ($18,000 sales price – $12,500 cost price = $5,500 Gross Profit). Since the payment at the end of the year 2000 didn't match the cost price, no deferred Gross Profit was debited that year. The payment at the end of the year 2001 plus the payment at the end of the year 2000 brought the Total Cash Revenue of the Hampdon Furniture Company to a figure $2,500 greater than cost, so this extra amount ($2,500) was debited to Deferred Gross Profit, since the books are being kept by the Cost Recovery Method of accounting.

Finally, on December 31, 2002, the final payment of $3,000 was received from the Brown Company. All of the $3,000 was debited to Deferred Gross Profit, thus bringing its balance down to zero.

• PROBLEM 16–27

The Richmond Furniture Store has a glut of furniture that it cannot seem to sell rapidly. So it makes an agreement with the Smith Furniture Store across town to consign some of its inventory to them. The Smith Furniture Store, if it sells the merchandise, may keep a commission of 20% of the selling price. What entries should be made on the books of the Richmond Furniture Store?

SOLUTION:

It is not necessary to make an entry. However, a memorandum entry may be made as follows: January 2, 2000: Richmond Furniture Store sends $20,000 worth of merchandise to consignee Smith Furniture Store.

• PROBLEM 16-28

The Richmond Furniture Store has a glut of furniture that it cannot seem to sell rapidly. So it makes an agreement with the Smith Furniture Store across town to consign some of its inventory to them. The Smith Furniture Store, if it sells the merchandise, may keep a commission of 20% of the selling price. On January 2, 2000, the date that the furniture is transported to the Smith Furniture Store, the Richmond Furniture Store makes a memorandum entry as follows: January 2, 2000: Richmond Furniture Store sends $20,000 worth of merchandise to consignee, Smith Furniture Store. The $20,000 figure is the projected sales price.

On January 31, 2000, the Smith Furniture Store reports to the Richmond Furniture Store that it has sold $5,000 worth of the merchandise (furniture) that it had on consignment and remits $4,000 to the Richmond Furniture Store. What entry should Richmond make on their books?

SOLUTION:

2000			($ in dollars)
January 31	Cash	4,000	
	Consignment Expense	1,000	
	Inventory		5,000

The Richmond Furniture Store receives $4,000 in cash from the Smith Furniture Store so it debits Cash for $4,000 on its books. The Smith Furniture Store is allowed to keep 20% of the sales price, which in this case is $1,000 ($5,000 sales × 20% consignee commission = $1,000).

To the consignor (the Richmond Furniture Store) this is a selling expense called Consignment Expense, so Richmond debits Consignment

Expense for the $1,000. It also credits the Asset account Inventory for $5,000, because $5,000 of its inventory has been sold. This $5,000 is the sales price of the inventory.

CHAPTER 17

INCOME TAX ACCOUNTING

> **Basic Attacks and Strategies for Solving Problems in this Chapter. See pages 571 to 606 for step-by-step solutions to problems.**

Everyone is familiar with the fact that crooks keep two sets of books. But now, many businesses must keep two sets of books also, even when the businesses are running legally. Or at least they have to reconcile their books at year's end. Why is this? It's because the Income Tax laws vary from the rules of good accounting.

The rules of good accounting are set up by past and present accounting boards, the latest of which is known as FASB, the Financial Accounting Standards Board. Accountants try to follow the statements of this board so they can keep all records logically and in the same manner. But since these rules do not always conform with Income Tax rules set up by Congress and the Internal Revenue Service, accountants must be aware of these differences and keep two sets of records accordingly.

These differences are so complicated and are so often expressed in accountants' technical terms, that it is often difficult for the average non-accountant to understand them. This chapter attempts to show, in simple language and through examples, the differences between government rules and accountants' rules.

There are Permanent differences and Temporary differences. (Temporary differences are also called "Timing differences.")

The first Permanent Difference discussed has to do with the depreciation of a new truck, either by the Straight-Line Method or by MACRS (Modified Accelerated Cost Recovery System), with the so-called "half-year convention" which is also explained. Another Permanent Difference between government rules and accounting rules has to do with municipal

Bond Interest Income which is not reportable for Income Tax purposes but which is reportable for financial accounting purposes.

A third discussed Permanent Difference has to do with insurance proceeds received upon death, which are not taxable for Income Tax purposes but which are taxable for financial accounting purposes. Another discussed Permanent Difference has to do with company life insurance premiums which are not deductible as expenses for Income Tax purposes but which are deductible as expenses for financial accounting purposes.

An additional Permanent Difference has to do with Amortization of (the writing off of) Goodwill, which is deductible for financial reporting purposes but which is not usually deductible for Income Tax purposes.

Yet one other Permanent Difference has to do with depletion of oil wells which is 22% of Oil Income for Income Tax purposes but which is usually deductible by the Straight-Line Method for financial purposes.

The first Temporary or Timing Difference discussed has to do with installment sales, which can be deducted using the Gross Profit percentage by the installment method as the cash comes in, for Income Tax purposes, but which is usually recorded by the Accrual Method for financial purposes.

A second Temporary or Timing Difference discussed has to do with the Equity method of reporting Dividend Income for financial purposes versus the Cost method most often used for Income Tax purposes.

Another Temporary or Timing Difference discussed has to do with self-construction projects, where accrued Interest expense can be deducted immediately under the Income Tax Method but where Accrued interest expense is usually capitalized (Asset debited and then depreciated or Amortized over the life of the Asset) for financial reporting purposes.

Yet another Temporary or Timing Difference discussed has to do with rent received in advance, where this cash must be reported as Income immediately for Income Tax purposes, whereas it can be reported as earned, for financial reporting purposes.

One Timing Difference has to do with royalty money received in advance, where, for Income Tax purposes, the royalty money must be reported as income immediately, for financial reporting purposes the royalty money may be reported as Income over the life of the contract.

Another Temporary or Timing Difference has to do with sale and leaseback contracts. For Income Tax purposes, the firm must report the sale as Revenue immediately in the year of the sale, while for financial reporting purposes the firm reports the sale as Income only gradually over the life of the sale-and-leaseback contract.

Yet another Temporary or Timing Difference has to do with Bad Debts expense which must be reported as an expense only when the debtor goes bankrupt—for Income Tax purposes. However for financial reporting purposes, the bad debts can be estimated and expensed at year's end with an adjusting entry—this is known as the Allowance Method.

The last Temporary or Timing Difference explained in the chapter has to do with recording investments in stock of other companies at lower of Cost or Market. For Income Tax purposes, Loss in Investment Stock Value cannot be reported until the stock is actually sold at a loss. But for financial reporting purposes, any "paper" loss for the year can be reported at year's end by an adjusting entry when the Market Value at the end of the year is below the original cost or purchase price.

Step-by-Step Solutions to Problems in this Chapter, "Income Tax Accounting"

• PROBLEM 17–1

The Harrison Construction Company purchases a light-duty truck for work in its business on January 2, 2000 for $180,000. Its estimated life is 6 years, with an estimated Residual Value of $10,000 at the end of that time. For financial purposes, it has been decided to depreciate the truck by the Straight-Line Method. For Income Tax purposes it has been decided to depreciate the truck by MACRS (Modified Accelerated Cost Recovery System), using the MACRS tables which actually use the 200% Declining-Balance Method with the half-year convention. At the beginning of the sixth year, the truck is sold for $9,000 cash. Give the journal entries for the purchase of the truck, for the yearly depreciations, and for the sale of the truck under both the Tax Method and the Financial Method, and explain the reasons for these entries.

SOLUTION:

The Harrison Construction Company uses different depreciation methods for Income Tax purposes than it does for financial purposes. Federal Tax laws allow faster depreciation in the first years of the Asset's life if MACRS is used. For financial reporting purposes, the Harrison Construction Company believes it is fairer to stockholders to use the Straight-Line Method of Depreciation (although the Straight-Line Method of Depreciation is also legal for Income Tax purposes).

Even though we assume that the truck will last six years, the government MACRS rules place light-duty trucks under the 5-year depreciation rules, and the tables are set up by the government for so-called 5-year property as follows:

Tax Life of Asset in Years: 5

Year of Life	
1	20.00%
2	32.00%
3	19.20%
4	11.52%
5	11.52%
6	5.76%

Note from the Federal Tax table above that all the percent figures add up to 100%, so there is no provision in the table for Residual Value, and the entire cost is depreciated over the six years. It is a so-called 5-year life because of the use, in the tables, of the half-year convention. (A convention is an accounting rule.) This half-year convention depreciates only half as much as allowed under the 200% Declining Balance Method in both the first and last years of the asset's life, so the number of years is always one year longer than planned. (In other words, this is a so-called 5-year life, but it is depreciated over six years.) Some trucks might be purchased during the first part of the year and other trucks might be purchased during the last part of the year. To make all things even, they assume the truck was purchased half-way through the year and only allow half as much percentage as would otherwise be allowed.

For instance, under the usual method of computing percentage by the 200% Declining Balance Method of Depreciation, the accountant would divide the number of years of life (in this case 5 years) into 100%, getting

20%. Then, since it is legally the 200% Declining Balance Method, one would multiply the 20% by 2 to get 40%. Thus, one could depreciate 40% during the first year of the Asset's life. However, since this is the half-year convention, we then divide the 40% by 2 to get back to 20%, the first year depreciation by MACRS.

The light-duty truck is purchased on January 2, 2000, and the following entry would be made on the books of the Harrison Construction Company:

2000		($ in dollars)	
January 2	Truck	180,000	
	Cash		180,000

The truck is purchased, so the Long-Term Asset Truck is debited for the cost of $180,000. (Some firms might debit the account Delivery Equipment rather than Truck.) Let us say cash is paid at this time, so Cash is credited for $180,000.

On December 31, 2000, the truck has been used for one year, and the following entry is made to depreciate the truck for the first year.

2000		($ in dollars)	
December 31	Depreciation Expense	36,000	
	Accumulated Depreciation—Truck		36,000

Under MACRS rules for depreciating 5-year property, the cost of the truck ($180,000) is multiplied by 20%, the percentage allowed under MACRS for the first year of 5-year property ($180,000 × 20% = $36,000). The Harrison Construction Company is getting the use of the truck during the whole year, so Depreciation Expense is debited for $36,000. The account Truck is not credited for $36,000, because Truck is only credited when the truck is either sold or scrapped. Instead, the Contra-Asset account Accumulated Depreciation—Truck is credited for the $36,000, because this is merely an estimated figure of how much of the truck has worn out during the first year of use.

During the second year (in this case the year 2001), the government MACRS tables allow us to depreciate the truck by 32% of its original cost, as follows:

2001	($ in dollars)
December 31 Depreciation Expense	57,600
Accumulated Depreciation—Truck	57,600

The $57,600 is computed by multiplying the original cost of the truck ($180,000) by 32%, table percentage for the second year of the Asset's life ($180,000 × 32% = $57,600). The business is getting the use of the truck throughout the entire year of 2001 so it debits Depreciation Expense for $57,600. Since this is merely an estimated amount, the Contra-Asset account entitled Accumulated Depreciation—Truck is credited for $57,600. At the end of the second year of the truck's life, the Accumulated Depreciation—Truck account appears as follows:

Accumulated Depreciation—Truck

12/31/2000	36,000
12/31/2001	57,600
	93,600

As can be seen from the "T" account just above, the depreciation during the year 2000 was $36,000 and during the year 2001 the depreciation was $57,600, making a total accumulated depreciation so far of $93,600. Thus, the book value of the truck was $86,400 at the end of the second year of truck usage, December 31, 2001 ($180,000 cost of truck − $93,600 accumulated depreciation at the end of the second year of the truck's life = $86,400 book value of the truck at this time).

During the calendar year 2002, the third year of the truck's life, the government tables allow a depreciation of 19.2% of the Asset's cost, and at the end of the year 2002 the following depreciation entry is made on the books:

2002	($ in dollars)
December 31 Depreciation Expense	34,560
Accumulated Depreciation—Truck	34,560

The figure of $34,560 was computed by multiplying the original cost of the truck ($180,000) by 19.2%. the table figure for the third year of life of a so-called 5-year asset ($180,000 × 19.2% = $34,560).

During the calendar year 2003, the fourth year of the truck's life, the government tables allow a depreciation of 11.52% of the Asset's cost, and at the end of the year 2003, the following depreciation entry is made on the books:

2003	($ in dollars)
December 31 Depreciation Expense	20,736
Accumulated Depreciation—Truck	20,736

The figure of $20,736 was computed by multiplying the original cost of the truck ($180,000) by 11.52% the table figure for the fourth year of life of a so-called 5-year Asset ($180,000 × 11.52% = $20,736).

During the calendar year 2004, the fifth year of the truck's life, the government tables allow a depreciation of 11.52% of the Asset's cost, and at the end of the year 2004 the following depreciation entry is made on the books:

2004	($ in dollars)
December 31 Depreciation Expense	20,736
Accumulated Depreciation—Truck	20,736

The figure of $20,736 was computed by multiplying the original cost of the truck ($180,000) by 11.52% the table figure for the fifth year of life of a so-called 5-year asset ($180,000 × 11.52% = $20,736). The reason the depreciation for the fourth year and the fifth year of the Asset's life are the same is because the government schedule is moving from the 200% Declining Balance Method to the Straight-Line Method of computation as the Asset reaches an older age.

The truck is getting decrepit. It has been used hard for five years, and on January 2, 2005, the truck is sold for $9,000 cash. Let us see how the accounts Truck and Accumulated Depreciation—Truck appear at this time:

Truck

1/2/2000	180,000	

Accumulated Depreciation—Truck		
	12/31/2000	36,000
	12/31/2001	57,600
	12/31/2002	34,560
	12/31/2003	20,736
	12/31/2004	20,736
		169,632

The account Truck is debited for $180,000, the cost of the truck. The account Accumulated Depreciation—Truck is credited for $169,632, the total accumulated depreciation for the five years of the truck's use by the Harrison Construction Company. Thus, at this time, the book value of the truck is $10,368, computed as follows:

Cost Price of the truck was $180,000, and accumulated depreciation thus far, during the first five years of the truck's life, was $169,632. Subtract these and one gets a book value of $10,368 ($180,000 − $169,632 = $10,368). The entry for the sale of the truck is as follows:

2005		($ in dollars)
January 2	Cash	9,000
	Loss on Sale of Truck	1,368
	Accumulated Depreciation—Truck	169,632
	Truck	180,000

The account Cash is debited for $9,000, the amount of money that the Harrison Construction Company received for selling the truck. The expense account entitled Loss on Sale of Truck is debited for $1,368, computed as follows:

Book value of truck was $10,368 less cash received for truck of $9,000 ($10,368 book value of truck − $9,000 cash received for truck = $1,368 loss on sale of truck).

This account, Loss on Sale of Truck, is an expense of the business and is deductible on the Income Statement of the Harrison Construction Company, thus cutting down the reportable Net Income and the Income Tax. This Income Statement is for tax purposes, not for annual report purposes. The annual report Income Statement will show depreciation by the Straight-Line Method.

The account Accumulated Depreciation—Truck is debited for

$169,632 to close out this account. The account Truck is credited for $180,000 to close out this account now that the truck has been sold.

For financial reporting purposes to the stockholders and others, the Harrison Construction Company decided to use the Straight-Line Method as follows:

Cost of Truck	$180,000
Less: Residual Value (Est.)	– 10,000
Depreciable Value	$170,000

The $170,000 depreciable value ÷ 6 years estimated life = $28,333 yearly depreciation by the Straight-Line Method.

The truck is purchased on January 2, 2000, and the following entry would be made on the books of the Harrison Construction Company:

2000		($ in dollars)
January 2	Truck	180,000
	Cash	180,000

On December 31, 2000, the truck has been used for one year, and the following entry is made to depreciate the truck for the first year:

2000		($ in dollars)
December 31	Depreciation Expense	28,333
	Accumulated Depreciation—Truck	28,333

The cost of the truck was $180,000. The estimated Residual Value was $10,000, so the Depreciable Value is $170,000 ($180,000 – $10,000 = $170,000 Depreciable Value). The $170,000 Depreciable Value is divided by the 6 years of estimated life to obtain $28,333 yearly depreciation by the Straight-Line Method ($170,000 ÷ 6 years = $28,333).

At the end of each year for five years, this same entry is made. At the end of 5 years (in this case, on December 31, 2004) the Accumulated Depreciation—Truck account on the books of the Harrison Construction Company would appear as follows:

Accumulated Depreciation—Truck		
	12/31/2000	28,333
	12/31/2001	28,333
	12/31/2002	28,333
	12/31/2003	28,333
	12/31/2004	28,333
		141,665

The account Truck is debited for $180,00, the cost of the truck. The account Accumulated Depreciation—Truck is credited for $141,665, the total accumulated depreciation for the five years of the truck's use by the Harrison Construction Company. Thus, at this time, the book value of the truck is $38,335, computed as follows:

Cost price of the truck was $180,000, and accumulated depreciation thus far, during the first five years of the truck's life, was $141,665. Subtract these and one gets a book value of $38,335 ($180,000 − $141,665 = $38,335).

The entry for the sale of the truck is as follows:

2005			($ in dollars)
January 2	Cash	9,000	
	Loss on Sale of Truck	29,335	
	Accumulated Depreciation—Truck	141,665	
	Truck		180,000

The account Cash is debited for $9,000, the amount of money that the Harrison Construction Company received for selling the truck. The expense account entitled Loss on Sale of Truck is debited for $29,335, computed as follows:

Book value of truck was $38,335 less cash received for truck of $9,000 ($38,335 book value of truck − $9,000 received for truck = $29,335 Loss on Sale of Truck).

This account, Loss on Sale of Truck, is an expense of the business and is deductible on the Income Statement of the Harrison Construction Company. This Income Statement is part of the annual report but not used for Income Tax purposes. The Loss on Sale of Truck for Income Tax purposes (as explained earlier in this chapter) amounted to $1,368, while the Loss on Sale of Truck for financial accounting purposes amounted to

$29,335. This is a difference of $27,967 ($29,335 − $1,368 = $27,967), and this difference is due to the two different methods of depreciation.

Let us assume that the Harrison Construction Company is in the 30% tax bracket. Under the MACRS method of depreciation, the loss was $1,368 and the tax deduction would then have been $410.40 (1,368 × 30% = $410.40). Under the Straight-Line Method of Depreciation, the loss was $29,335 and the tax deduction would then have been $8,800.50 ($29,335 × 30% = $8,800.50). Under the present Income Tax law, either the MACRS Method of Depreciation or the Straight-Line Method of Depreciation may be used for Income Tax purposes.

• PROBLEM 17-2

The James Construction Company has extra cash so it purchases municipal bond in the City of Birmingham for $5,000, as follows: Explain the entries.

SOLUTION:

2002		($ in dollars)
January 2	Investment in Municipal Bond	5,000
	Cash	5,000

The Long-Term Asset account entitled Investment in Municipal Bond is debited for $5,000 because the James Construction Company acquires this investment. Cash is credited for $5,000 because money is used to pay for the bond by the James Construction Company.

Let us say this is a 5% bond that pays dividends yearly on December 31 of each year. On December 31, 2002, the James Construction Company receives its first Interest check for $250 and makes the following entry on its books:

2002		($ in dollars)
December 31	Cash	250
	Bond Interest Income	250

Cash is being received, so Cash is debited for the amount of the check in this case, for $250. The James Construction Company has given the City of Birmingham the use of its money, so it credits the Revenue account entitled Bond Interest Income for $250 ($5,000 × 5% = $250).

For tax purposes, the James Construction Company would not record this entry, because this Interest Income on municipal bonds is not taxable. (However, a separate record must be kept of Non-Taxable Income to be recorded but not added in on the corporation's Income Tax form.)

For financial accounting purposes, it is proper to credit Bond Interest Income in this case, because the Assets of the corporation (in this case unneeded cash) were invested productively to earn this Income, and the stockholders should be apprised of this fact.

• PROBLEM 17–3

The Lincoln Construction Company has $100,000 life insurance policies on each of its executives, and the premiums on these policies are paid by the construction company itself. Also, the Lincoln Construction Company is named in each policy as the beneficiary of these policies.

On June 22, 2000, Ronald Hampstead, one of the vice presidents of Lincoln Construction Company, dies, and on August 15, 2000, the Lincoln Construction Company receives a check from the Citizens Insurance Company for $100,000, the face value of the policy. How should this be entered on the books of the Lincoln Construction Company?

SOLUTION:

2000		($ in dollars)
August 15	Cash	100,000
	Life Insurance Proceeds Income	100,000

The Asset account Cash is debited for $100,000, because cash is coming into the bank account of the Lincoln Construction Company. The Revenue Life Insurance Proceeds Income is credited for $100,000, because this is Revenue to the company and the company is giving up the valued services of one of its vice presidents.

For Income Tax purposes, this entry is not placed in the Income Statement used for tax purposes, because the federal law specifically exempts life insurance proceeds payable upon death. However, for financial accounting purposes, it is proper to credit Life Insurance Proceeds Income, because the stockholders of the Lincoln Construction Company have the right to know that Income was received by the corporation because of the loss of a valued executive.

• PROBLEM 17–4

The Lincoln Construction Company has $100,000 life insurance policies on each of its five top executives with the Citizens Insurance Company. Each year the premiums on these five policies amount to $5,000. They are term policies. What entry, if any, will the Lincoln Construction Company make on its books at the end of the calendar year when these premiums are paid?

SOLUTION:

2000		($ in dollars)
December 31 Life Insurance Premium Expense	5,000	
Cash		5,000

The expense account entitled Life Insurance Premium Expense is debited for $5,000, because the Lincoln Construction Company is getting the protection, in that if it would lose the valued services of any of its officers through death, it would be remunerated with $100,000 cash. It is crediting Cash because the amount of $5,000 is being sent to the Citizens Insurance Company to pay the premium on these policies. The account Life Insurance Premium Expense is not deductible on the Income Statement used for Income Tax purposes, because the government does not allow life insurance premium expense as a taxable deduction. However, for financial accounting purposes, this expense should be shown on the Income Statement of the corporate annual report so that stockholders and other interested persons would know that $5,000 was being expended for life insurance protection of the executives.

• PROBLEM 17-5

On January 2, 2001, the Lincoln Construction Company purchased the Assets of a former competitor, the Harold Construction Company. What entry is made on the books at this time?

SOLUTION:

2001			($ in dollars)
January 2	Land	80,000	
	Buildings	200,000	
	Equipment	40,000	
	Goodwill	30,000	
	Cash		350,000

At the time of purchase, an appraiser decided the Land was worth $80,000; the Buildings were worth $200,000; and the Equipment was worth $40,000. This adds up to a total of $320,000 ($80,000 Land + $200,000 Buildings + $40,000 Equipment = $320,000).

However, a total of $350,000 was paid for the Assets of the Harold Construction Company by the Lincoln Construction Company. So the asset account Cash was credited for $350,000. The difference, in this case $30,000, was debited to the Intangible Asset account entitled Goodwill. It was decided at this time by the officers of the Lincoln Construction Company that the benefits of the purchase of the Assets of the Harold Construction Company would last at least 5 years, so the account Goodwill was to be amortized over the next five years by the Straight-Line Method. What will the first Amortization entry be on the books of the Lincoln Construction Company at the end of the year 2001 and why?

2001		($ in dollars)
December 31 Amortization Expense	6,000	
Goodwill		6,000

Amortization Expense is debited for $6,000 because the Lincoln Construction Company is deriving the benefits of having the Assets of the Harold Construction Company. The amount is $6,000, because this is 1/5 of the amount of the Goodwill—$30,000 ($30,000 ÷ 5 = $6,000.) Goodwill, an Intangible Asset account, would be credited for $6,000, thus bringing its balance at the end of the year 2001 down to $24,000. The

Asset Goodwill would then appear on the books of the Lincoln Construction Company as follows:

	Goodwill		
1/2/2001	30,000	12/31/2001	6,000
	24,000		

Each year on December 31, a similar entry will be made, debiting Amortization Expense for $6,000 and crediting Goodwill for $6,000, until at the end of the year 2005, the Goodwill account balance will be zero.

These entries are made for financial accounting purposes and the account Amortization Expense is debited, thus showing the stockholders and other interested readers of the financial statement that goodwill is being gradually written off through Amortization Expense. However, this usually cannot be done on the Income Statement for Income Tax purposes because the government laws will not usually allow the write-off of Goodwill unless there is evidence of a decline in the value of the Assets or unless the Assets purchased have a limited life. In these cases, then, it would be possible to debit Amortization Expense for Income Tax purposes.

• PROBLEM 17–6

The Harton Petroleum Corporation purchased land, dug a successful oil well, and started producing oil from this well. The costs of land purchased and drilling were debited to an Asset account entitled Oil Well and came to $100,000. Engineers estimated that the well would last for 10 years. Oil was discovered on January 2, 2000, and during the year 2000, Revenues from the oil produced by the well that year amounted to $60,000. Let us also say that the federal laws to encourage the search for oil allow 22% Depletion Expense on oil wells.

What entries should be made under financial accounting and under Income Tax accounting to Depletion Expense and why?

SOLUTION:

2000	($ in dollars)
December 31 Depletion Expense	13,200
Oil Well	13,200

The account Depletion Expense is debited for $13,200 because the Harton Petroleum Corporation is getting the use of the well and the oil in the well. The Asset account Oil Well is credited for $13,200 because there is less oil in the well at the end of the year than there was at the beginning of the year. The amount is $13,200 for Income Tax purposes because the government is trying to encourage people and corporations to drill for more oil, and the drilling is risky, so the government allows a depletion deduction of 22% of Revenue. The Revenue of the oil well for the year 2000 was $60,000. ($60,000 Revenue × 22% depletion rate = $13,200 Depletion Expense allowed by the government.)

Generally Accepted Accounting Principles do not allow the 22% rate. They state that wasted assets (such as oil, natural gas, coal, zinc, etc.) should be depleted by the Straight-Line Method of Depreciation. In this case, the oil well Assets cost $100,000, and it was estimated that the well would produce for 10 years ($100,000 cost ÷ 10 years estimated life of the well = $10,000 yearly depletion).

Thus, for financial accounting purposes the following entry would be made:

2000	($ in dollars)
December 31 Depletion Expense	10,000
Oil Well	10,000

This $10,000 Depletion Expense would be shown as an expense on the Income Statement of the Harton Petroleum Corporation in the annual report to stockholders and other interested persons, and these books would be kept according to Generally Accepted Accounting Principles. However, on the Income Statement for Income Tax purposes, the full legally allowed $13,200 would be expensed, thus cutting down the Net Income for Income Tax purposes and also cutting down the legal Income Tax that the Harton Petroleum Corporation would have to pay the government.

• PROBLEM 17-7

The Richmond Construction Company has a surplus of cash, so it has decided to invest some of this in Common Stock of the Jackson Construction Company. They decide to invest $10,000 on January 2, 2000. The Jackson Construction Company on December 15 declared a dividend, and on December 31, 2000, the Richmond Construction Company received a dividend check for $500. How will the Richmond Construction Company report these events on its books?

SOLUTION:

2000		($ in dollars)
January 2	Investment in Common Stock of Jackson Construction Co.	10,000
	Cash	10,000

The Richmond Construction Company receives Common Stock in the Jackson Construction Company so it debits the Asset account Investment in Common Stock of Jackson Construction Co. for $10,000. It pays cash of $10,000, so it credits Cash for $10,000.

2000		($ in dollars)
December 31	Cash	500
	Dividend Income	500

For financial reporting purposes on the books of the Richmond Construction Company, Cash is debited for $500, because Richmond is receiving a check for this amount. The Revenue account entitled Dividend Income is credited for $500, because the Jackson Construction Company is receiving the use of Richmond Construction Company's investment. Thus, in the Income Statement of the Richmond Construction Company, this Dividend Income of $500 would be reported for the perusal of stockholders and other interested persons.

However, the federal government has a special Dividend Deduction of 80%, called a Dividend Received Deduction on the corporate Income Tax form. Congress passed this deduction because of complaints by the public that this was "double taxation" when one corporation owned part of another corporation, that every corporation that received dividends would otherwise have to pay tax on these dividends. So Congress exempted 80%

of these dividends that one corporation receives from another corporation. In this case, then, the Richmond Construction Company would only have to report $100 as Dividend Income rather than $500 (100% of taxes – 80% Dividends Received Deduction = 20% taxable portion; $500 dividends received by the Richmond Construction Company × 20% = $100 taxable dividend).

• PROBLEM 17–8

The Harrison Furniture Company sells a living room suite to Mr. and Mrs. James Brown for $1,000, with terms $200 down and $100 per month. The cost of the living room suite to the Harrison Furniture Company was $700, giving a Gross Profit of $300 ($1,000 sales price – $700 Cost of Sales = $300 Gross Profit). And this is 30% of sales ($300 ÷ $1,000 sales = 30%.)

Sales	$1,000	100%
Cost	– 700	70%
Gross Profit	$ 300	30%

On January 2, 2000, the date of the sale, the Harrison Furniture Company receives from Mr. and Mrs. James Brown the down payment of $200 and turns over to them the living room suite. What entry or entries would be made on the books of the Harrison Furniture Company at this time and why?

SOLUTION:

2000			($ in dollars)
January 2	Cash	200	
	Accounts Receivable	800	
	Sales		1,000

For financial reporting purposes, the Harrison Furniture Company would debit Cash for $200, because that amount is being received. Accounts Receivable would be debited for $800, because that is the amount that Mr. and Mrs. James Brown owe the Harrison Furniture Company at this time. ($1,000 sales price – $200 down payment = $800 Accounts Receivable still owed.) Sales is credited for $1,000, because this is the price of the furniture that is moving out of the store. Thus, for financial reporting purposes, when the account Sales is credited, this adds $1,000 to the Revenue reported on the Income Statement of the Harrison Furniture Company in its annual report to stockholders and other interested persons.

However, the federal laws allow installment sales to be reported as Income as the cash is collected. The Gross Profit of $300 is 30% of sales, so for Income Tax purposes only 30% of the cash need be reported as Income. So for Income Tax purposes the following entry could be made:

2000		($ in dollars)	
January 2	Cash	200	
	Inventory		140
	Revenue		60

Cash is debited for $200 because that is the amount of down payment that the Harrison Furniture Company is receiving. Inventory is credited, because the Cost Price of the living room suite moving out of the store is $140. Revenue is credited for $60, which is 30% of the down payment received. Thus, under the installment method, an Income Tax is paid only on the $60 Revenue, not on the entire $1,000 Revenue.

• PROBLEM 17-9

The Swanson Furniture Company purchased controlling interest in the Stevens Furniture Company for $100,000 on January 2, 2000, buying a 2/3 interest in Stevens Furniture. On December 31, the Stevens Furniture Company reported a Net Income for the year 2000 of $15,000. On January 15, 2001, the board of directors of the Stevens Furniture Company declared a dividend of $1 per share. Since Swanson Furniture Company held 3,000 shares of Stevens Furniture Company, on January 30, 2001, the Swanson Furniture Company received a dividend check for $3,000. What entries will be made on the books of the Swanson Furniture Company and why?

SOLUTION:

2000			($ in dollars)
January 2	Investment in Common Stock of Stevens Furniture Co.	100,000	
	Cash		100,000

2000			
December 31	Investment in Common Stock of Stevens Furniture Co.	10,000	
	Income		10,000

2001			
January 30	Cash	3,000	
	Investment in Common Stock of Stevens Furniture Co.		3,000

On January 2, 2000, the Swanson Furniture Company received a stock certificate showing that it had invested in 3,000 shares of Stevens Furniture Company. This cost Swanson $100,000, so on its books Swanson debits the Asset account Investment in Common Stock of Stevens Furniture Company for $100,000. Cash of $100,000 is being paid out so Cash is credited for $100,000.

On December 31, 2000, the Stevens Furniture Company announces that it has earned a Net Income during the year 2000 of $15,000. Since Swanson owns 2/3 of the stock of Stevens, Swanson on its books debits the Asset account Investment in Common Stock of Stevens Furniture Company for $10,000 (15,000 total Income of Stevens × 2/3 portion of Stevens stock owned by Swanson = $10,000 increase in Asset). At this time Swanson also credits the Revenue account Income for $10,000, showing the portion of Stevens Income due to Swanson. On January 30, 2001, the Swanson Furniture Company receives a dividend check from Stevens Furniture Company for $3,000 so debits the Asset account Cash for $3,000. It also credits the Asset account Investment in Common Stock of Stevens Furniture Company for $3,000, because $3,000 of its investment is being turned into cash. The account Investment in Common Stock of Stevens Furniture Company will appear as follows on the books of the Swanson Furniture Company:

Investment in Common Stock of Stevens Furniture Company

1/2/2000	100,000	1/30/2001	3,000
12/31/2000	10,000		
	110,000		
	107,000		

On January 2, 2000, when Swanson Furniture Company purchased 2/3 of the stock of Stevens Furniture Company for $100,000, they debited the Asset account Investment in Common Stock of Stevens Furniture Company for $100,000. On December 31, 2000, when Stevens Furniture Company announced their Net Income for the year 2000 to be $15,000, the Swanson Furniture Company debited their Asset account Investment in Common Stock of Stevens Furniture Company for $10,000, their share of the profits ($15,000 × 2/3 = $10,000).

On January 30, 2001, Swanson Furniture Company received a dividend check from Stevens Furniture Company for $3,000, so they credited their Asset account Investment in Common Stock of Stevens Furniture Company for $3,000, since $3,000 of their investment was being returned to them in the form of cash. This brings their investment account down to a balance of $107,000 as of January 30, 2001.

The above methods of accounting are acceptable for financial account purposes, but money can be legally saved on Income Taxes by different reporting for Income Tax purposes, as follows:

2000			($ in dollars)
January 2	Investment in Common Stock of Stevens Furniture Co.	100,000	
	Cash		100,000

2001			
January 30	Cash	3,000	
	Dividend Income		3,000

The January 2, 2000, entry for purchasing the stock is the same as previously, with the Asset account Investment in Common Stock of Stevens Furniture Company being debited for the Cost Price of $100,000, and cash being credited for the amount of cash being paid out (in this case, $100,000). Under this Cost Method, no entry is made on December 31, 2000, when the Stevens Furniture Company announces the amount of its year's income. On January 30, 2001, when the Swanson Furniture Company receives the Stevens Furniture Company dividend check for $3,000, it could debit Cash for $3,000 on its books and credit Dividend Income for $3,000, although under the Dividends Received Exclusion for corporations, only 20% of this need be reported for Income Tax purposes, or $600 ($3,000 × 20% = $600).

• PROBLEM 17–10

The Swenson Dairy Farm, Incorporated, needed another large barn on its property and decided to build the barn itself. On January 2, 2000, it borrowed $10,000 from the First National Bank and used this money to buy building material and to hire labor. The $10,000 loan was for one year at the Interest Rate of 10%. Show how the Interest and the material costs were reported for Income Tax purposes, and then for financial reporting purposes.

SOLUTION:

2000		($ in dollars)
January 2	Cash	10,000
	Notes Payable	10,000

On January 2, 2000, Swenson Dairy Farm borrowed $10,000 from the First National Bank and received the cash, so it debited Cash for $10,000. It gave the bank a note, so it credited Notes Payable for $10,000.

2000		($ in dollars)
December 31	Interest Expense	1,000
	Interest Payable	1,000

On December 31, 2000, the Swenson Dairy Farm, Inc., had held the borrowed money ($10,000) for a period of a year. Therefore, they owed the bank a year's Interest, which in this case came to $1,000, because the Interest Rate is 10% ($10,000 × 10% × 1 year = $1,000).

The Swenson Dairy Farm had the use of the loan money for an entire year so its debits Interest Expense for $1,000. It did not at this time pay the bank the Interest but only owes the Interest, so the Current Liability account entitled Interest Payable is credited for $1,000. This adjusting entry is made at year's end even though the Interest is not paid, because under Income Tax accounting, the Interest accrued is deductible in the year 2000.

2000		($ in dollars)
January 2	Materials Expense	6,000
	Cash	6,000

On January 2, 2000, as soon as the $10,000 was borrowed from the bank, $6,000 of this money was used to purchase building materials for the dairy barn. Income Tax accounting allows building materials to be expensed immediately, so the expense account entitled Materials Expense is debited for the $6,000, and Cash is credited for the $6,000.

This Materials Expense of $6,000 is carried over into the expense section of the Swenson Dairy Farm Income Statement and legally cuts down on the reported Income and thus cuts down legally on Swenson's Income Tax for the year 2000 when these costs were incurred.

For financial reporting purposes, companies often debit asset accounts and depreciate them over the life of the asset. For instance, when the material is purchased for the barn, an entry could be made as follows:

2000		($ in dollars)
January 2	Barn	6,000
	Cash	6,000

As seen above, the Asset account Barn is debited for $6,000 (rather than debiting the account Materials Expense). The account Cash is credited as in the previous example, because money is going out of the firm's treasury.

Also, the Interest could be shown as follows:

2000		($ in dollars)
December 31	Barn	1,000
	Interest Payable	1,000

As can be seen above, at the end of the year, the Asset account Barn is debited for the amount of the Accrued Interest (in this case, $1,000). As in the previous example, however, the Current Liability account entitled Interest Payable is credited for $1,000, because the Interest has not yet been paid, and the Swenson Dairy Farm still owes the bank this money.

Let us assume also that the labor had not yet been accomplished on the barn, and that the Interest and materials were all the charges as of the end of the year 2000. The account Barn would then appear as follows:

	Barn	
1/2/2000	6,000	
12/31/2000	1,000	
	7,000	

Since the barn has not yet been built and is therefore not yet in use, the account Barn will not be depreciated at the end of the year 2000.

In comparing the two methods (the Income Tax Method of "expensing" immediately and the Financial Reporting Method of "capitalizing," that is, debiting the Asset account Barn), it will be seen that under the Income Tax Method two expense accounts were debited. Interest Expense was debited for $1,000 and Materials Expense was debited for $6,000. This tended to increase the total expenses of the dairy farm by $7,000, which also tended to cut down the dairy's Net Income for the year 2000 by a total of $7,000, thus cutting considerably the Income Tax expense for the Swenson Dairy Farm. On the other hand, the financial reporting method would allow neither of these expenses until the barn is actually being used and can be depreciated through the account Depreciation Expense over the estimated lifetime of the barn.

• PROBLEM 17-11

The Davidson Land Management Corporation rents out and leases out apartments and single-family dwellings. Many of the single-family dwellings are rented out for a minimum of a year, and a year's rent is receivable in advance. On October 1, 2000, the Davidson Land Management Corporation receives a check for $6,000 from Mr. and Mrs. James Smith, who are the new tenants of rental property at 304 Jones Street, Richmond, Virginia, at a monthly rent of $500 or a yearly rent of $6,000 (500 monthly rent × 12 months per year = $6,000 yearly rent). The period of rental thus runs from October 1, 2000 until September 30, 2001. How is this reported for Income Tax purposes and how is it reported for financial accounting purposes?

SOLUTION:

For Income Tax purposes, the following entry would be made by the Davidson Land Management Corporation on October 1, 2000, the date the Rental Income money was received from Mr. and Mrs. James Smith:

2000			($ in dollars)
October 1	Cash	6,000	
	Rental Income		6,000

The account Cash is, of course, debited for $6,000, the amount received, and the Revenue account entitled Rental Income is credited for $6,000, because the federal law requires all the Income to be reported in the year the Rental Income is received, even though part of the Revenue is earned in the next year. Thus, the full $6,000 is credited to the Revenue account Rental Income and reported as Income for Income Tax purposes for the year 2000.

However, for financial accounting purposes, the following entry could be made on the books of the Davidson Land Management Corporation:

2000			($ in dollars)
October 1	Cash	6,000	
	Rental Income		1,500
	Unearned Rent		4,500

Again, the account Cash is debited for $6,000, the amount of cash received on October 1, 2000. The Revenue account entitled Rental Income is credited for $1,500, the amount of Rent Revenue that the Davidson Land Management Corporation earns during the calendar year 2000. (The house was rented out during the last three months of the year 2000, October, November, and December, at the rate of $500 per month – $500 per month × 3 months = $1,500 earned by the Davidson Land Management Corporation during the calendar year 2000.) The Liability account entitled Unearned Rent is credited for the remainder (in this case $4,500), the amount that will be earned in the first nine months of the calendar year 2001 ($500 per month rent × 9 months = $4,500).

On September 30, 2001, at the end of the year's rental period, the Davidson Land Management Corporation could make the following adjusting entry on its books:

2001	($ in dollars)
September 30 Unearned Rent	4,500
Rental Income	4,500

The Liability account entitled Unearned Rent had a credit balance on the books of $4,500 because, in a way, this amount is owed the tenant by the landlord if the tenant cannot for some reason inhabit the property during the year 2001. Let us say that the tenant inhabits the property for the first nine months of 2001, as well as for the last three months of the year 2000. The Unearned Rent Liability is now cancelled with this debit to that account as of September 30, 2001. The Revenue account entitled Rental Income is credited for $4,500 to show the rent that the Davidson Land Management Corporation has actually earned during the calendar year 2001.

The financial reporting entries are really better than the Income Tax accounting entries, because the financial reporting entries allocate the $1,500 to Rental Income for the year 2000 and the $4,500 for the year 2001, the amount that the Davidson Land Management Corporation actually earned in those years. But the government does not go along with this method of reporting, and for tax purposes, the entire $6,000 must be reported in the year received, that is, 2000.

Another method of reporting this same cash payment in advance would be as follows:

2000		($ in dollars)	
October 1	Cash	6,000	
	Rental Income		6,000
December 31	Rental Income	4,500	
	Unearned Rent		4,500
2001			
September 30	Unearned Rent	4,500	
	Rental Income		4,500

This method allows the adjusting entry to come on December 31, 2000, the last day of the calendar year.

On October 1, 2000, Cash is debited for $6,000, the amount received by the Davidson Land Management Corporation on that date. The revenue account Rental Income is credited for $6,000 at that time. Then three months elapse. Only $1,500 is actually earned during those three months ($500 monthly rent × 3 months of October, November, and December, 2000 = $1,500 rent earned). In order to reduce the Rental Income account from its balance of $6,000 down to the amount earned in the calendar year 2000 ($1,500), the Rental Income account is debited on December 31, 2000 for $4,500. (Rental Income had a credit balance of $6,000, and now it is debited for $4,500, bringing its credit balance down to the $1,500 actually earned during the last three months of the calendar year 2000.) The account Rental Income would appear as follows at year's end:

Rental Income

12/31/2000	4,500	10/1/2000	6,000
			1,500

On the same date (December 31, 2000), this Rental Income account is closed out into the catch-all account Income Summary in the amount of the Rental Income account's balance of $1,500, thus bringing Rental Income, a Temporary account, down to a balance of zero at year's end, as is done with all Temporary accounts.

On September 30, 2001, an adjusting entry is made debiting the Liability account Unearned Rent for its balance of $4,500. It had a credit balance of $4,500, and this debit of $4,500 closes out the account since the landlord no longer owes any money to the tenant, since the tenant has occupied the house for a year's time (from October 1, 2000 until September 30, 2001). The Revenue account entitled Rental Income is credited for $4,500 to show the Income for the first nine months of the year 2001 (January through September).

The above explained method of accounting for prepaid rent is probably the best way, because it uses the adjusting entry at year's end, December 31, 2000. However, this method is not allowed for Income Tax purposes, because the government wants to be sure of its Income from Income Tax in the year that the Davidson Land Management Corporation actually receives its money (in this case, the calendar year 2000.)

• PROBLEM 17-12

> The Jackson Farm Management Company owns several farms on which its employees actually do the farming. In the year 2000, the Hanson Petroleum Company surveyed one of the farms and came to the conclusion that there might be oil possibilities under the farmland. The Jackson Farm Management Company and the Hanson Petroleum Company signed an agreement by which the oil company would pay the farm company $500 on September 1, 2000 for oil rights under the land, which would run for a year from September 1, 2000 until August 31, 2001. What entries should be made on the books of the Jackson Farm Management Company for income tax purposes and also for financial management purposes?

SOLUTION:

2000		($ in dollars)
September 1 Cash	500	
Royalty Revenue		500

Cash was debited because on September 1, 2000, $500 was received by the Jackson Farm Management Company for oil rights. The Revenue account entitled Royalty Revenue was credited for $500, and this entire

$500 will have to be included in Jackson Farm Management Company income for the year 2000 because the government requires this method of accounting for cash received in advance as far as Royalty Income is concerned.

On the other hand, entries for financial management purposes follow:

2000		($ in dollars)	
September 1	Cash	500	
	Unearned Revenue		500
December 31	Unearned Revenue	166.67	
	Royalty Revenue		166.67
2001			
August 31	Unearned Revenue	333.33	
	Royalty Revenue		333.33

On September 1, 2000, Cash is debited for $500, because this amount is received by the Jackson Farm Management Company from the Hanson Petroleum Company for rental of oil rights under the farmland. At the same time, the Liability account Unearned Revenue is credited for $500 to show that this money is so far unearned by the Jackson Farm Management Company. (It will be gradually earned over the next 12 months.)

On December 31, 2000, an adjusting entry is made on the books of the Jackson Farm Management Company debiting Unearned Revenue for $166.67. This is 1/3 of the total royalty of $500 (1/3 × $500 = $166.67). This takes $166.67 from the previous $500 balance in the Unearned Revenue account, bringing it down to $333.33 as follows:

	Unearned Revenue		
12/31/2000	166.67	9/1/2000	500.00
			333.33

Also, on December 31, 2000, the Income account Royalty Revenue is credited for $166.67, showing the amount of royalty earned by the Jackson Farm Management Company during the calendar year 2000. (In this case, actually the last third of the year—the time from signing the contract on

September 1, 2000, to the end of the year—December 31, 2000. This would be for the months of September, October, November, and December, 2000.)

Finally, on August 21, 2001, the end of the contract, the Liability account Unearned Revenue would be debited for $333.33 to close out this account and to show that the Jackson Farm Management Company no longer owes anything to the Hanson Petroleum Company, since the petroleum company had the underground rights for a full 12 months. Also, the Income account Royalty Revenue is credited for $333.33 to show the amount that the Jackson Farm Management Company actually earned during the calendar year of 2001.

The Financial Accounting Method is actually better because it allocates the $166.67 as Income during the calendar year 2000 and the remaining $333.33 as Income during the year 2001. However, for income tax purposes, the entire $500 must be reported in the year the cash was actually received. in this case, the calendar year 2000.

• PROBLEM 17–13

The Stockton Railroad Corporation needs to buy more railway cars but does not have the money to pay for them at this time. However, they know that if they can buy $50,000 worth of new railway cars, they can use them regularly and make enough profit in future years to pay for them and more. Instead of borrowing money at the bank and having to pay Interest, they sign an agreement with the Harvard Finance Company to sell the railroad cars to the Harvard Finance Company and the finance company will then immediately lease the cars back to the railroad. This will mean that the railroad can immediately pay off the purchase price of the railroad cars and will carry no debt on them. How would this sale and lease-back be reported for Income Tax purposes and for financial reporting purposes for the Stockton Railroad Corporation?

SOLUTION:

2000			($ in dollars)
January 2	Railroad Cars	50,000	
	Cash		50,000
January 3	Cash	50,000	
	Sales (of Railroad Cars)		50,000
December 31	Rental Expense	10,000	
	Cash		10,000

On January 2, 2000, the Stockton Railroad Corporation buys $50,000 worth of railroad cars so it debits the Asset account Railroad Cars for $50,000. It pays cash of $50,000 so it credits the Cash account.

On January 3, 2000, the Stockton Railroad Corporation needs the money to cover its $50,000 check, so immediately sells the railroad cars to the Harvard Finance Company for the same amount—$50,000. It debits Cash for $50,000, since it receives this amount of money from Harvard Finance Company. However, it must credit the Revenue account Sales and report this $50,000 as Income for the year 2000 because the federal government requires this type of reporting for Income Tax purposes.

Let us say that the terms of the lease agreement are that the Stockton Railroad Corporation pays the Harvard Finance Company $10,000 rent on the cars each year. Thus, on December 31, 2000, Stockton Railroad Corporation debits the Rental Expense account for $10,000, because during the entire year of 2000 it was getting the use of the railroad cars. Cash was credited for $10,000, because on the last day of the year 2000 the railroad company mailed a check to the Harvard Finance Company for that amount.

Actually, then, under Income Tax accounting, the Net Revenue for the year 2000 will really be $40,000 ($50,000 sales – $10,000 expense = $40,000). Then each year thereafter it will be able to deduct another $10,000 expense as it continues to pay the rent year by year.

On the other hand, for financial reporting purposes, the accounting entries on the books of the Stockton Railroad Corporation could be as follows:

2000			($ in dollars)
January 2	Railroad Cars	50,000	
	Cash		50,000
January 3	Cash	50,000	
	Railroad Cars		50,000
December 31	Railroad Cars	10,000	
	Cash		10,000

On January 2, 2000, the Stockton Railroad Corporation buys the railroad cars for $50,000 so it debits the Asset account Railroad Cars. It credits Cash because it pays $50,000 cash at that time.

On January 3, it turns around and sells the same railroad cars to the Harvard Finance Company for the same price of $50,000. So it debits Cash for $50,000, since it receives this amount of money from the finance company. It credits Railroad Cars, since the title to the railroad cars is being turned over to the new owner—in this case, the Harvard Finance Company.

On December 31, 2000, in effect the Stockton Railroad Corporation is gradually buying the railroad cars back from the finance company, so the asset account Railroad Cars is debited for $10,000. Also, Cash is credited for $10,000 to show the annual payment of the Stockton Railroad Corporation to the finance company.

• PROBLEM 17-14

On January 2, 2000, the Larsen Wholesale Hardware Company sold the James Hardware Store $10,000 worth of merchandise. On September 7, 2000, the Larsen Wholesale Hardware Company receives a check for $2,000 from the James Hardware Store in partial payment of the debt. From past experience, the Larsen Wholesale Hardware Company believes that it will lose approximately 5% of its sales on account, so on December 31, 2000, it writes off $400 ($8,000 remaining debt × 5% = $400 approximate loss; $10,000 original sales − $2,000 partial payment = $8,000). On March 1, 2001, the Larsen Wholesale Hardware Company learns to its dismay that the James Hardware Store has gone bankrupt and that probably none of the remainder of the debt will be collected, so the account is written off. How will Larsen handle this on its books for Income Tax purposes and how might it handle this on its books for financial reporting purposes?

SOLUTION:

Books of the Larsen Wholesale Hardware Company

For income tax purposes:

2000			($ in dollars)
January 2	Accounts Receivable—James Hardware	10,000	
	Sales		10,000
September 7	Cash	2,000	
	Accounts Receivable—James Hardware		2,000
2001			
March 1	Bad Debts Expense	8,000	
	Accounts Receivable—James Hardware		8,000

On January 2, 2000, Larsen Wholesale Hardware Company makes a sale of $10,000 inventory to the James Hardware Store. Larsen debits Accounts Receivable—James Hardware for $10,000, because Larsen is getting James Hardware's good name or oral promise to pay the $10,000. Larsen credits the account Sales because merchandise at sales price is moving out of the wholesale hardware company.

On September 7, 2000, Larsen receives from James Hardware a check for $2,000, so it debits Cash for that amount. It then credits Accounts Receivable—James Hardware for $2,000 to cut down on James' debt by that amount, meaning that James Hardware then owes only $8,000.

No adjusting entry is made at the end of the year 2000, because the government insists that for Income Tax purposes businesses use the so-called Direct Write-Off Method of accounting for bad debts, so bad debts can only be "expensed" when it is learned that companies with whom business is done have gone bankrupt.

On March 1, 2001, it is actually learned that James Hardware Store has gone bankrupt and that probably no more money will be forthcoming. So Larsen debits Bad Debts Expense for $8,000, the amount James Hardware still owes, and credits Accounts Receivable—James Hardware for the same amount. This serves to close out James Hardware's account on the books of the Larsen Wholesale Hardware Company. This follows the rules of the Internal Revenue Service.

The only trouble with this Direct Write-Off Method, in this case, is that the Bad Debts Expense was put down in the year 2001, instead of the year 2000 when the sale was actually made. In order to derive the true Net Income for the years 2000 and 2001, the bad debts should have been expensed in the year 2000 when the sale was made. The financial accounting method for this is shown as follows:

2000			($ in dollars)
January 2	Accounts Receivable—James Hardware	10,000	
	Sales		10,000
September 7	Cash	2,000	
	Accounts Receivable—James Hardware		2,000
December 31	Bad Debts Expense	400	
	Allowance for Doubtful Accounts		400
2001			
March 1	Allowance for Doubtful Accounts	8,000	
	Accounts Receivable—James Hardware		8,000

On January 2, 2000, the Larsen Wholesale Hardware Company sells $10,000 worth of merchandise to the James Hardware Store. On the Larsen books, Accounts Receivable—James Hardware is debited for

$10,000, because Larsen is receiving James' oral promise to pay the $10,000 at a later date. The Revenue account Sales is credited, because $10,000 of merchandise is moving out of the Larsen Wholesale Hardware Company warehouse.

On September 7, 2000, Larsen receives from James a check for $2,000, so Larsen debits Cash for that amount. It also credits Accounts Receivable—James Hardware for $2,000, which cuts down James' debt to Larsen to $8,000. ($10,000 original purchase − $2,000 partial payment = $8,000 amount still owed.)

From past experience, Larsen Wholesale Hardware Company has lost about 5% of its sales on account, so at year's end it multiplies the $8,000 still owed it by 5% to get a write-off of $400 ($8,000 still owed × 5% = $400 write-off). The Contra-Asset account Allowance for Doubtful Accounts is credited for the $400 since this is an estimate.

On March 1, 2001, it is regretfully learned that James Hardware Store has gone bankrupt and that there is little possibility of collecting the $8,000 still owed by the store. The Allowance for Doubtful Accounts is debited for $8,000, and Accounts Receivable—James Hardware is credited for $8,000. This effectively cuts down the James Hardware account to zero, since more money will probably not be collected from this bankrupt company.

• PROBLEM 17-15

The Ford Lumber Company has $50,000 unneeded cash on hand which it has placed in a checking account at a local bank. Financial counsellors have suggested to the Board of Directors of Ford Lumber that they place this unneeded cash in investments which will bring them either Interest or Dividends, in other words—make their money work for them.

They use this $50,000 to buy 10,000 shares of Hartford Telephone Company at the market price of $5 per share (10,000 shares × $5 market price per share = $50,000). This is done on March 3, 2000. On December 31, 2000 the stock of Hartford Telephone Company is selling for $4 per share, which means that it could be sold for $40,000 on that date ($50,000 original cost of the stock − $10,000 = $40,000). This is a $10,000 loss if the stock were sold on the last day of the year 2000. On May 1, 2001, the stock is sold for $43,000. What entries should the Ford Lumber Company make on its books for Income Tax purposes and for financial accounting purposes?

SOLUTION:

2000			($ in dollars)
March 3	Investment in Stock of Hartford Telephone Co.	50,000	
	Cash		50,000
2001			
May 1	Cash	43,000	
	Loss	7,000	
	Investment in Stock of Hartford Telephone Co.		50,000

On March 3, 2000, the Ford Lumber Company used its surplus cash of $50,000 to buy 10,000 shares of Common Stock of Hartford Telephone Company for $5 per share. At this time, it debited the Asset account entitled Investment in Stock of Hartford Telephone Co. for $50,000 because it was getting this Asset. It credited Cash for $50,000 because this amount of cash was leaving the account of the Ford Lumber Company.

For Income Tax purposes no entries are made at year's end. However, on May 1, 2001, the stock was sold for $43,000. So the Asset account Cash was debited for $43,000 because this amount of money was coming into the Ford Lumber Company. The expense account entitled Loss was debited for $7,000 because the Internal Revenue Service allows this loss to be recorded on the books at the time of sale of the investment ($50,000 Cost of the Stock – $43,000 Sales Price of the Stock = $7,000 loss).

It will be noted that for Income Tax purposes, the expense account Loss cannot be debited until the date on which the stock is actually sold for a loss. An estimate is not good enough here.

The following entries will be made for financial accounting purposes:

2000			($ in dollars)
March 3	Investment in Stock of Hartford Telephone Co.	50,000	
	Cash		50,000
December 31	Loss	10,000	
	Allowance for Lower of Cost or Market		10,000
2001			
May 1	Cash	43,000	
	Allowance for Lower of Cost or Market	10,000	
	Investment in Stock of Hartford Telephone Co.		50,000
	Gain		3,000

On March 3, 2000, the Ford Lumber Company used $50,000 of its extra cash to buy stock in the Hartford Telephone Company. It debited the Asset account entitled Investment in Stock of Hartford Telephone Co. for $50,000, because it was receiving this stock certificate. Cash was credited for $50,000, because this amount of cash is moving out of the bank account of the Ford Lumber Company.

At year's end, on December 31, 2000, the Hartford Telephone Company stock has dropped from $5 per share to $4 per share, which is a "paper" loss of $10,000 (10,000 shares × $5 per share = $50,000 purchase price; 10,000 shares × $4 per share Market Price at December 31, 2000 = $40,000 present Market Price.) ($50,000 Purchase Price – $40,000 Present Market Price = $10,000 "paper" or potential loss). This is only a loss on paper and is not a real loss, because the stock is not being sold at this time. It therefore cannot be reported for Income Tax purposes. However, for financial reporting purposes, we debit the expense account entitled Loss for the $10,000 that we would have lost had we sold the stock at year's end. We credit a Contra-Asset account entitled Allowance For Lower of Cost or Market for the $10,000, because at year's end the Market Price is $10,000 lower than the Cost Price.

On May 1, 2001, the Hartford Telephone stock is finally sold for $43,000. The Asset account Cash is debited for $43,000, because that amount of cash is coming into the coffers of the Ford Lumber Company. The Contra-Asset account Allowance For Lower of Cost or Market is also debited to close out that account which previously had a credit balance of $10,000. The Asset account Investment in Stock of Hartford Telephone Co. is credited for $50,000 to close out this account, since the stock certificate has to be relinquished at the time of sale. The Investment in Stock of Hartford Telephone Co. had previously had a debit balance of $50,000. This credit of $50,000 effectively closes this account out on the books of the Ford Lumber Company because Ford no longer owns this stock. The Revenue account **Gain** is credited to show the gain of $3,000 on the transaction ($10,000 loss previously recorded at the end of the year 2000 – $7,000 actual loss = $3,000 reported gain). The $10,000 reported loss is the difference between the original Purchase Price of $50,000 and the Reported Price of $40,000 ($50,000 Purchase Price – $40,000 Reported Price = $10,000 reported loss). Since this loss was reported for financial purposes on December 31, 2000 by a debit to the Loss account of $10,000, we now credit the Gain account for $3,000 which gives a Net of $7,000—the actual loss ($10,000 – $3,000 = $7,000).

CHAPTER 18

ACCOUNTING FOR PENSIONS

Basic Attacks and Strategies for Solving Problems in this Chapter. See pages 609 to 616 for step-by-step solutions to problems.

In the last several decades, pensions have become important. A pension plan is an agreement between a company and its employees for retirement benefits. These are usually based on the employee's Income and on his or her years of service. Employees prefer working for firms with a qualified pension plan. Employers are interested in pension plans because they reduce employee turnover and keep employees more loyal to the company. There are two important types of pension plans: **defined benefit plans** and **defined contribution plans**.

The **defined benefit plan** states how much money the employer will have to pay the employees each month after retirement until the employee's death. The company has the main risk because it is responsible for these payments.

The **defined contribution plan** states how much the employer will have to contribute each month or each year that the employee works for the company. This is a more secure plan for the employer because the time is defined rather than open-ended.

The rules for accountants regarding pensions are found in pronouncements of the Financial Accounting Standards Board and in the law entitled ERISA (Employee Retirement Income Security Act of 1974).

There are all types of retirement plans, some are funded and some are unfunded. A funded plan is one where the employer makes periodic payments to a trustee. The trustee invests the money in real estate or in stocks and bonds of other corporations. The Rent Income, Dividend Income, or

Interest Income is reinvested in other real estate, stocks, and bonds. The trustee then has the funds to pay the employees monthly when they retire. An unfunded plan is one where the employer makes no payments to the trustee. Upon retirement of the employee, the company pays the employee directly each month from the company's current Assets.

The funded plan is much more sound than the unfunded plan because a company may go bankrupt which would leave the employees penniless. ERISA, the Employee Retirement Income Security Act of 1974, does not allow corporations to use unfunded pension plans if they want to qualify their pension fund payments as deductible business expenses for Income Tax purposes. However, these rules do not apply to partnerships and single proprietorships, many of which, as a result, have only partially funded plans. There are contributory and non-contributory retirement plans. A contributory plan is one in which the employees, as well as the employer, put money into the plan on a regular basis. Non-contributory plans are those in which the employees are not required to contribute to the plan. Only the employer contributes in these cases.

If a pension plan meets the requirements of ERISA, there are four benefits that result. The money given over by the employer to the trustee is deductible by the employer as a business expense for Income Tax purposes. If the employee also contributes, these contributions are not taxable to the employee until he or she receives them back after retirement. Also, pension fund earnings (such as Rental Income, Dividend Income, and Interest Income) are not subject to Income Tax. Finally, employees pay no income taxes on the money the employer contributes to the pension fund until this money is actually received by the employees after retirement.

Step-by-Step Solutions to Problems in this Chapter, "Accounting for Pensions"

• PROBLEM 18-1

The Johnson Construction Company has five employees. For several years they have been clamoring for the corporation to set up a retirement pension plan for them. The accountant for the company determines that if the plan is set up properly so that it is actuarially sound, following the general requirements of the Employee Retirement Income Security Act of 1974, corporation payments into the plan can be deducted as business expenses in determining corporate Net Income for tax purposes.

After determining the soundness of the corporate finances over the past several years, the Board of Directors of the Johnson Construction Company decides on a defined contribution plan. This means that the company will guarantee to place with a trustee a certain percent of the employees' incomes regularly at the end of each year. The contribution each year will be guaranteed, not the future benefits. The Board decides that the corporation can afford 5% of the employees' incomes as a defined contribution.

During the year 2000, all 5 employees earn combined Incomes of $300,000. Five percent of this figure is $15,000 ($300,000 total incomes × 5% determined percent figure = $15,000). What entry will be made on the books of the Johnson Construction Company and why?

SOLUTION:

2000		($ in dollars)
December 31 Pension Expense	15,000	
Cash		15,000

The Board of Directors of the Johnson Construction Company appoints the Trust Department of the First National Bank to be the Pension Agent. At the end of the year 2000, the Johnson Construction Company sends a check for $15,000 to the Trust Department of the First National Bank and makes the above entry on its books—that is, on the books of the Johnson Company.

Pension Expense is debited for $15,000, and because this is a plan set up according to the guidelines of the ERISA (Employee Retirement Income Security Act of 1974), this Pension Expense is fully deductible as a corporation business expense for Income Tax purposes, legally cutting down the corporate Net Income by this amount. The Asset account Cash is credited for $15,000, because this amount of money is leaving the Johnson Construction Company and being paid to the Trust Department of the First National Bank.

• PROBLEM 18–2

The Johnson Construction Company during the year 2000 had five employees. A defined contribution plan set up according to ERISA guidelines during the year 2000 was climaxed on December 31, 2000, when the Johnson Construction Company sent a check for $15,000 to the Trust Department of the First National Bank. The bank used this money to purchase real estate and stocks and bonds for the account.

During the year 2001, the Johnson Construction Company expanded and had 10 people on the payroll during the entire year. At the end of the year 2001, the accountant determined that the total Gross Pay of all the employees for the entire year amounted to $600,000. The defined contribution plan was continued, and 5% of this amount was paid to the Trust Department of the First National Bank in the amount of $30,000 ($600,000 total salaries of all the employees × 5% determined figure = $30,000 payment figure).

What entry will be made on the books of the Johnson Construction Company at the end of the year 2001 and why?

SOLUTION:

2001		($ in dollars)
December 31 Pension Expense	30,000	
Cash		30,000

Pension Expense is debited for $30,000, and because this is a plan set up according to the guidelines of the Employee Retirement Income Security Act of 1974, this Pension Expense is fully deductible as a corporation business expense for Income Tax purposes, legally cutting down the reportable corporate Net Income by this amount. The Asset Cash is credited for $30,000, because this amount of money is leaving the Johnson Construction Company and being paid to the Trust Department of the First National Bank.

• PROBLEM 18–3

The Johnson Construction Company during the year 2000 had five employees. A defined contribution plan set up according to ERISA guidelines during the year 2000 was climaxed on December 31, 2000, when the Johnson Construction Company sent a check for $15,000 to the Trust Department of the First National Bank. The bank used this money to purchase real estate and stocks and bonds for the account.

During the year 2001, the Johnson Construction Company expanded and had 10 people on the payroll during the entire year. At the end of the year 2001, the Johnson accountant determined that the total Gross Pay of all the employees for the entire year amounted to $600,000. The defined contribution plan was continued, and the predetermined 5% of this amount was paid to the Trust Department of the First National Bank in the amount of $30,000 ($600,000 total salaries of all the employees × 5% determined figure = $30,000 payment figure).

At the end of the year 2000 the Johnson Construction Company made an entry on its books debiting Pension Expense for $15,000 and crediting Cash for $15,000. At the end of the year 2001 the Johnson Construction Company made an entry on its books debiting Pension Expense for $30,000 and crediting Cash for $30,000. On December 31, 2001, the Johnson Construction Company received a notice from the Trust Department of the First National Bank that the $15,000 originally deposited with them on December 31, 2000 and held during the year 2001 had been invested in stocks and bonds of other firms and had brought in during the year 2001 Interest and Dividends totaling $1,200. What entry or entries should be made on the books of the Johnson Construction Company?

SOLUTION:

No entry should be made on the books of the Johnson Construction Company. The Assets of the trust are building up, but they are not the property of the Johnson Construction Company. In effect, they are really the future Assets of the employees. However, it is beneficial for the accountants of the Johnson Construction Company at the end of each year to send each employee a notice giving the total amount of Pension Asset that is presently being saved for that particular employee. This will include not only the amount of the corporate contribution for that employee but also that employee's share of the Invested Income.

At the end of the year 2000, the accountant's report for the pension plan would be as follows:

Name of Employee	Annual Gross Salary	Pension Asset Amount
Harmond, James	$100,000	$5,000
Stacy, Mary	70,000	3,500
Loren, Mark	50,000	2,500
Stark, Loretta	40,000	2,000
Mander, Harry	40,000	2,000
Totals	$300,000	$15,000

After this report has been approved by the Board of Directors of the Johnson Construction Company, each employee would receive a letter from the company giving the amount of the Pension Asset that has so far been built up for them. Of course, in each case this would be the figure in the rightmost column of the table. As can be seen from the table above, the Pension Asset amount is exactly 5% of each employee's annual salary. This is true because the pension amount was not contributed by the Johnson Construction Company to the Trust Department of the First National Bank until the end of the year, so the trust department during the year 2000 had no time to invest the money or earn Income during that year.

During the year 2001, the Trust Department of the First National Bank reported that the trust investments had earned a total in Interest and Dividends of $1,200. This amount will be divided up proportionately among the 10 employees according to their respective salaries, and a report will be presented by the corporate accountant to the Board of Directors as follows:

Johnson Construction Company
Employees' Pension Report
December 31, 2001

Name of Employee	Year 2001 Wages	Year 2000 Contribution	Year 2001 Contribution	Year 2001 Share of Trust Income	Total Value Proportion of Trust Assets
Harmond, James	$100,000	$5,000	$5,000	$275.86	$10,275.86
Stacy, Mary	70,000	3,500	3,500	193.10	7,193.10
Loren, Mark	50,000	2,500	2,500	137.91	5,137.91
Stark, Loretta	40,000	2,000	2,000	110.34	4,100.34
Mander, Harry	40,000	2,000	2,000	110.34	4,110.34
Stein, Katherine	35,000	0	1,750	96.55	1,846.55
Hobart, William	30,000	0	1,500	82.76	1,582.76
Black, Roland	25,000	0	1,250	68.98	1,318.98
Poland, Harold	25,000	0	1,250	68.98	1,318.98
Swartz, Mary	20,000	0	1,000	55.18	1,055.18
Totals	$435,000	$15,000	$21,750	$1,200.00	$37,950.00

Explanation of Employees' Pension Report

The first column gives the names of the ten employees of the Johnson Construction Company. The second column gives the wages of the individual employees (Gross Wages prior to deductions), followed by the total Gross Wages of all the employees for the year 2001. The third column gives the company contribution for each individual employee for the year 2000. This figure is determined by multiplying the individual employee's annual Gross Salary by the 5% rate determined by the Board of Directors.

For instance, the first employee, James Harmond, earned $100,000 Gross Salary for the year 2000, and this is multiplied by 5% to derive the $5,000 figure (100,000 × 5% = $5,000). The fourth column gives the company contribution for each individual employee for the year 2001. It will be noted that during the year 2000 there were only five employees, the first five names on the list. During the year 2001 there was a total of ten employees. The first five employees continued during the year 2001 at the same salaries they earned during the year 2000, and five new employees were added; the last five names on the list.

The fifth column gives the share of the year 2001 Trust Income assigned to each employee. During the year 2001 the trust earned an Income from Dividends and Interest of $1,200. This income is divided among the various employees in proportion to their relative Incomes and is computed as follows: the total Gross Incomes of all the employees for the year 2001 is $435,000 (lower left-hand figure on the Employees' Pension Report). This figure of $435,000 is divided into the $1,200 Trust Income to derive .275862%, which means that the Trust Income during the year 2001 was .275862% of the total annual salaries for that year. This .275862% can also be expressed as .00275862). Thus, in order to derive the figures for the fifth column, the accountants multiplied the individual employee's Gross Salary for the year by .00275862. For instance, the first employee, James Harmond, earned $100,000, so this was multiplied by .00275862 to derive the figure $275.86, which was his share of the Trust Income for the year 2001. It will be noted that the total figure for the fifth column is $1,200, the amount of the Trust Income for the year.

Finally, the sixth column, the Total Value Proportion of the Trust Assets, is computed by adding columns 3, 4, and 5. For instance, for the first employee on the list, James Harmond, $5,000 was contributed in the year 2000, another $5,000 in the year 2001, and $275.86 from the Trust Income, making his Total Asset Value in the trust amount to $10,275.86 ($5,000 + $5,000 + $275.86 = $10,275.86). At the end of the year a letter will be sent to each employee telling him or her the total value of his or her Retirement Assets in the trust. This will be done each year for each employee of the company.

• PROBLEM 18–4

The Lander Wholesale Hardware Company has 15 employees during the year 2000. The Board of Directors of Lander decides to set up a defined benefit pension plan for its employees. This means that the employees' pension benefits will be guaranteed when they retire. The Board decides that no retroactive benefits will be given to the employees. This means that employees who have worked a number of years previous to January 1, 2000, will get no extra benefits for their work in the years before the plan was adopted.

Actuaries determine that the Service Cost (the expense to the company for the pension plan) will be $200,000 for the year 2000, $210,000 for the year 2001, and $216,000 for the year 2002. The actuarial projected benefit obligation at the beginning of the year 2001 is $200,000, and the actuarial projected benefit obligation at the beginning of the year 2002 is $420,000. (Projected benefit obligation means that this is the amount of future money owed present employees when they retire.) For convenience, let us also assume that the Discount Rate is 10% on today's money and also that the Expected Rate of Return on Plant Assets is 10%. Let us also assume that the Lander Wholesale Hardware Company makes payments to the trustee (in this case the Security Mortgage Association) at the end of each calendar year.

Using the above information, the only Pension Expense at the end of calendar year 2000 is the $200,000 service cost. This is true because there is no Interest Cost during the year 2000 since the first Interest Payment to the trustee is made at the end of the year so there has been no elapse of time. Also, the Board of Directors of the Lander Wholesale Hardware Company has determined not to burden themselves with so-called "prior service costs." Also, there is no Gain or Loss because we have assumed that both the Discount Rate and the Actual Rate of Return, as well as the Expected Rate of Return are all 10%, which we assume is the "Going Interest Rate" at the present time.

What will be the general journal entries for the Lander Wholesale Hardware Company for the first two years, and why?

SOLUTION:

2000	($ in dollars)	
December 31 Pension Expense	200,000	
Cash		200,000

Pension Expense is debited for $200,000, and this is a fully deductible business expense since the pension plan has been set up to meet the requirements of the Employee Retirement Income Security Act of 1974. This expense will serve to cut down the Net Income of the firm by $200,000, thus lowering the company's Income Tax also. Cash is credited for $200,000 because this amount of money is being turned over by the Lander Wholesale Hardware Company to the trustee, the Security Mortgage Association.

For the year 2001, the computations are somewhat more complicated, because not only "Service Costs" are to be computed, but also Interest Cost and return on Plant Assets. The Service Costs for the year 2001 are assumed to be $210,000 (previously stated). The Interest Cost is 10% of $200,000 or $20,000 ($200,000 given the trustee at the end of the year 2000 × 10% = $20,000). These Assets of $200,000 are invested in stocks and bonds of other companies and we assume they will bring in a return of 10% also, or $20,000. Therefore, the projected Pension Expense for the Lander Wholesale Hardware Company is $210,000 ($210,000 Service Cost + $20,000 projected Interest Expense − $20,000 projected Dividend and Interest Income).

So the journal entry on the books of the Lander Company would be as follows:

2001	($ in dollars)	
December 31 Pension Expense	210,000	
Cash		210,000

Pension Expense is debited because the company is following the ERISA guideline requirements and so Pension Expense is fully deductible by the Lander Wholesale Hardware Company in computing their Income Tax. Cash is credited, because the Lander Company is paying $210,000 cash to the Security Mortgage Association on this date.

CHAPTER 19

LEASES

> **Basic Attacks and Strategies for Solving Problems in this Chapter. See pages 618 to 631 for step-by-step solutions to problems.**

There are both **operational leases** and **capital leases**. An operational lease is the rental of land, buildings, or other property for a period of time. The owner of the property is termed the Lessor; the tenant is termed the Lessee. At the end of the term the Asset reverts back to the original owner—in this case the Lessor. A capital lease is what is commonly known as "rent to buy." It allows the Lessee, at the end of the contract, to buy the property under terms of the contract, usually at a "bargain price."

The Financial Accounting Standards Board has attempted to define the difference between a capital lease and an operating lease by listing four stipulations, any one of which makes the lease a capital lease. If none of these stipulations apply, the agreement is automatically an operating lease.

The FASB postulates that if any of the following conditions occur, it is a capital lease.

1) The lease transfers ownership to the Lessee.

2) There is a "bargain-purchase" option.

3) The length of the lease is equal to 75% or more of the estimated economic life of the leased property.

4) The Present Value of the lease payments is equal to 90% or more of the Fair Value of the lease property to the Lessor.

If a lease agreement does not meet any of the four stipulations listed by the Financial Accounting Standards Board, it is an operating lease.

Leased property can be depreciated or amortized. This chapter gives arguments for each answer. It addresses some advantages of leasing to the Lessee and also addresses whether the Lessee should buy or lease the Asset. This chapter also gives two advantages of leasing over selling, from the Lessor's point of view. It would seem, from all these advantages of leasing that leasing would be more popular. Today, leasing is becoming more popular because of all the advantages to both the Lessor and Lessee.

If there are so many advantages of leasing to both the Lessor and Lessee, why isn't leasing more popular? Three excellent reasons are given in the chapter to show the weaknesses of leasing arrangements.

Step-by-Step Solutions to Problems in this Chapter, "Leases"

• PROBLEM 19–1

The Rayburn Land Management Corporation leased an apartment to Mr. and Mrs. James Brown on January 2, 2000 for a period of 5 years at $25,000 per year. The cost of the apartment as of this date is $150,000 to the Lessor, the Rayburn Land Management Corporation. The Lessor agrees to pay insurance, maintenance costs, and taxes. The apartment reverts to the Rayburn Land Management Corporation at the end of the lease period. The lease does not give Mr. and Mrs. James Brown the choice of renewing the lease at the end of the five-year lease period. The Present Value of an annuity due in advance of 5 payments of $25,000 each at the present 12% Interest Rate is $100,933.625. (Present Value of 5 payments of $25,000 in advance at 12% (3.037349 + 1.000000) × $25,000 = $100,933.625.)

There is no agreement to transfer ownership from the Rayburn Land Management Corporation to Mr. and Mrs. James Brown at the end of the lease. The economic life of the apartment is estimated by assessors to be at least 10 years. Is this agreement an operating lease or a capital lease, and why?

SOLUTION:

This is an operating lease, not a capital lease. A capital lease must contain at least one of the following stipulations, according to the Financial Accounting Standards Board:

1. The lease transfers ownership to Lessee at term's end.

2. The lease contains a bargain purchase option.

3. The lease term is equal to 75% or more of the estimated economic life of the leased property.

4. The Present Value of the minimum lease payments is equal to 90% or more of the Fair Value of the leased property to the Lessor.

Looking at the first rule, the lease in this problem does not transfer ownership to the Lessee at the end of the term; therefore, the first rule does not apply in this case. The lease does not contain a bargain purchase option; therefore, the second rule does not apply in this case. (A bargain purchase option means that at the end of the lease period the Lessee is able to buy the apartment at a reasonable price. No such agreement is contained here.)

Looking at the third rule, the lease term should be 75% of the economic life of the property being leased. In the case of this apartment, the lease term is 5 years, and the estimated economic life of the apartment is 10 years, so the lease term is only 50% of the economic life of the property (5 divided by 10 = 50%).

Looking at the fourth rule, the Present Value of lease payments is 90% of the Fair Value. The cost of the apartment to the Lessor is $150,000, and the Fair Present Value of the five $25,000 yearly payments, paid in advance, is $100,933.625. Thus, the Present Value ($100,933.63) is 67.289% of the Total Cost ($150,000). ($100,933.625 divided by $150,000 = 67.289%.) For the fourth rule to be valid, the Present Value of the lease payments must be 90% of the Fair Value. But it is only 67.289%. Therefore, the fourth rule is not valid either. Thus, none of the rules apply, so this is an operating lease rather than a capital lease.

$$100,933.63 \div 150,000 = 67.289$$

• PROBLEM 19-2

What is the main difference between an operating lease and a capital lease?

SOLUTION:

An operating lease is a rental contract, and a capital lease can work out under the best of circumstances to be "rent to buy."

• PROBLEM 19-3

What is a bargain purchase option?

SOLUTION:

A bargain purchase option is a term in a capital lease where, at the end of the lease, the Lessee has an opportunity to buy the leased article at a favorable price.

• PROBLEM 19-4

What is a bargain renewal option?

SOLUTION:

A bargain renewal option is a term in a capital lease where, at the end of the lease, the Lessee has an opportunity to renew the lease at a favorable price.

• PROBLEM 19–5

> How does Estimated Residual Value of leased property differ from Residual Value of purchased property?

SOLUTION:

The Estimated Residual Value of leased property is the amount that the property is believed to be worth at the end of the lease period, while Residual Value of purchased property is the amount that the property is believed to be worth at the end of its economic life.

• PROBLEM 19–6

> Should leases be amortized or depreciated?

SOLUTION:

Most leased property is listed in the Long-term Asset section of the Balance Sheet under Plant and Equipment, because most property leased would be such things as trucks, cars, equipment, and furniture. So from this point of view one would think that leased property would be depreciated.

However, the Financial Accounting Standards Board usually refers to "Amortization" in discussing leasing, and technically it is correct, because leased property is Intangible property, and Intangible Assets are amortized.

• PROBLEM 19–7

What are some of the advantages of leasing to the Lessee?

SOLUTION:

1. The Lessee has little or no down payment. (If the Lessee were actually purchasing a business car, there would be a sizable down payment. On the other hand, if the Lessee is merely leasing a business car, there is usually merely the regular monthly rental payment to the lessor.) This means that the Lessee's cash outflow is not large. The cash can be conserved by the Lessee. This gives more cash on hand, places the business in better financial shape, and could prevent bankruptcy.

2. Little risk of the equipment being too small or outdated. If the equipment is purchased and later found to be too small for the job or too outdated, the owner might lose a great amount of money having to purchase larger or more up-to-date equipment. On the other hand, if the business person is leasing the equipment, he or she can usually turn it in for larger equipment or more up-to-date equipment, without financial loss.

3. Income Tax savings. Usually the rental payments of the Lessee are business deductions and can be placed as business rental expenses on the Income Statement, thus legally cutting down the amount of Net Income and, thus, cutting the amount of Income Tax. (Of course, some of this can be done by the purchaser through depreciation deductions too.)

4. In case of default, only the articles leased are lost, not the entire Assets of the business. Let us say that the broom factory leases a broom-making machine, and several years later defaults on its lease payments to the lessor. The most that the Lessor can do is take the machine back. On the other hand, if the broom factory buys the broom-making machine on the installment plan and later cannot make the regular payments, the entire Assets of the corporation could be at stake.

5. The lease agreement does not affect the Total Liabilities, Current Ratios, or Rate of Return on investment of the corporation. Let us say that Corporation X leased a broom-making machine for $10,000 per year. The corporation gets the use of the machine without adding to its Assets or to its Liabilities. This is true because it is merely a rental. On the other hand, if the corporation had purchased the broom-making machine on the install-

ment plan, not only would the Assets of the corporation have increased, but the Liabilities would have increased greatly with the huge debt on the machine. This might lower the Current Ratio (Current Assets divided by Current Liabilities) and might have hurt the Rate of Return on Investment (Net Income divided by Capital). If these ratios are lowered, it often means that banks will decline to lend the corporation needed money. In other words, corporations are in better financial shape often if they lease rather than purchase.

• PROBLEM 19-8

What are some of the advantages of leasing, to the Lessor?

SOLUTION:

1. A lease, from the Lessor's viewpoint, is considered to be an indirect sale. This is especially true of a capital lease. The Lessee gradually pays the Lessor most of the value of the property leased. Even though it is not legally a sale, it has the appearances of a sale, in that the property is in the hands of the Lessee and the payments are made by the Lessee to the Lessor.

2. The Lessor derives profit and Interest Income from the lease. In the contract the Lessor make the payments high enough to make him or her a profit and also to cover Interest, or the use of the money (the value of the property leased).

• PROBLEM 19-9

If there are so many advantages of leasing to both the Lessor and the Lessee, why isn't leasing more popular?

SOLUTION:

Leasing is getting more popular all the time, because of its many advantages to both the Lessor and Lessee. However, there are some disadvantages as follows:

1. Title to the property does not pass to the Lessee in an operating lease. On the contrary, title remains with the Lessor. The Lessee makes many payments and still does not own the property.

2. The Lessor loses control of the property to the Lessee who may use the property improperly and even destroy it.

3. Under a capital lease it is true that the Lessee may eventually gain title to the property at the end of the lease, but in most instances this so-called "rent to buy" is much more expensive than if the Lessee had purchased the property in the first place.

• PROBLEM 19–10

On January 2, 2000, the Jerison Broom Company leased a broom-making machine from the Harrison Machine Works for $40,000 per year.

The broom-making machine has a Sales Price of $110,000 and a Cost Price to the Lessor of $100,000, with a resultant Gross Margin of $10,000 ($110,000 – $100,000 = $10,000). This is a three-year contract. What entries will be made on the books of the Lessor, the Harrison Machine Works, during the year 2000, the first year of the contract? (Interest Rate 10%)

SOLUTION:

Books For Harrison Machine Works

2000		($ in dollars)	
January 2	Lease Receivable	110,000	
	Sales Revenue		110,000
January 2	Cost of Goods Sold	100,000	
	Machine		100,000
January 2	Cash	40,000	
	Lease Receivable		40,000
December 31	Lease Receivable	7,000	
	Interest Revenue		7,000

Let us assume that this is a capital lease and that at the end of the three-year lease period the Lessee has the right to purchase the broom-making machine through a bargain purchase agreement. On January 2, 2000, the Lessor debits the Asset account, Lease Receivable, for $110,000, the Sales Price of the broom-making machine. The account Lease Receivable is similar to account Accounts Receivable. To the Lessor in this case, the capital lease is recorded somewhat similar to a sale, with the owner receiving the promise to pay at a later date. Also, the account Sales Revenue is credited for $110,000 since the Lessor is treating this capital lease as a sale. This then records the $110,000 as Income to the Lessor in the year 2000.

On the same date, the Cost of Goods Sold account is debited for the Lessor's Cost Price of $100,000, and the Asset account Machine is credited for $100,000, since the broom-making machine is leaving the Harrison Machine Works office.

On the same date, January 2, 2000, the Harrison Machine Works receives a check from the Jerison Broom Company for $40,000, the first annual lease payment. Harrison debits Cash for $40,000, since this is the amount of money coming in. It credits the Asset account Lease Receivable to cut down the amount of money that Jerison Broom Co. supposedly owes Harrison Machine Works.

Finally, at year's end on December 31, 2000, the Harrison Machine Works records the Interest accrued during the year 2000. This is in the amount of $7,000 computed as follows: the so-called Sales Price of the machine was $110,000. The lease amount paid in advance for the year 2000 was $40,000. If one considers this as really a sale, this means that there is still $70,000 owed by the Lessee to the Lessor. ($110,000 sales price $40,000 amount already paid = $-70,000 still unpaid.) The going Interest Rate is assumed to be 10%, so 10% of $70,000 is $7,000 ($70,000 × 10% = $7,000). Therefore, the Asset account Lease Receivable is debited for $7,000 to show that, on the books at least, the Lessee (Jerison Broom Company) owes the Lessor (Harrison Machine Works) another $7,000 for the accrued Interest. Also, the Income account entitled Interest Revenue is credited for the $7,000, and this is reportable Earned (though uncollected) Income to the Harrison Machine Works that has to be reported on Harrison's Income Statement and for Income Tax purposes for the year 2000.

• PROBLEM 19-11

On January 2, 2000, the Jerison Broom Company leased a broom-making machine from the Harrison Machine Works for $40,000 per year.

The broom-making machine has a Sales Price of $110,000 and a Cost Price to the Lessor of $100,000, with a resultant Gross Margin of $10,000 ($110,000 − $100,000 = $10,000). This is a three-year contract. What entries will be made on the books of the Lessee, the Jerison Broom Company, during the year 2000, the first year of the contract? (Interest Rate 10%)

SOLUTION:

Books of the Jerison Broom Company

2000		($ in dollars)	
January 2	Leased Property	110,000	
	Lease Liability		110,000
January 2	Lease Liability	40,000	
	Cash		40 000
December 31	Interest Expense	7,000	
	Lease Liability		7,000
December 31	Depreciation Expense	36,000	
	Accumulated Depreciation		36,000

Let us assume that this is a capital lease and that at the end of the three-year lease period the Lessee has the right to purchase the broom-making machine through a bargain purchase agreement. On January 2, 2000, the lessee (Jerison Broom Company) debits the Asset account Leased Property for $110,000, the purchase price of the broom-making machine. The Asset Leased Property is debited because a capital lease is similar to a purchase in some respects. At the same time Lease Liability is credited for the $110,000 Purchase Price because the Lessee really does not own the machine and owes the Lessor the return of the machine at a later date, perhaps.

On the same date the Lessee pays the Lessor in advance $40,000, the amount of the first year's lease payment. And the account Lease Liability is debited for $40,000, since the Liability is cut down by that amount through this cash payment. Naturally, the account Cash is credited for $40,000 on the books of the Jerison Broom Company, since cash of that amount is leaving the Jerison office.

The next entry, also dated January 2, 2000, debits Interest Expense for $7,000. This $7,000 is computed as follows: the Purchase Price of the machine was $110,000, and $40,000 lease payment was paid on this machine immediately, leaving the amount still to be paid $70,000 ($110,000 – $40,000 = $70,000).

The going Interest Rate is 10%, and $70,000 is owed. So we multiply $70,000 by the rate of 10% to get the Interest of $7,000 ($70,000 × 10% = $7,000).

This $7,000 Interest is not paid at this time. But it is recorded at year's end because it is a legal expense of the Jerison Broom Company business. Therefore, Interest Expense is debited for $7,000. This is listed as one of the business expenses of the firm on its year-end Balance Sheet and thus cuts down on the Net Income of the business, also lowering its Income Tax legally. The account Lease Liability is also credited for $7,000, which increases the amount that the Jerison Broom Company owes the Harrison Machine Works by that amount, since the broom company is getting the use of the machine during the entire year 2000.

Also, at the end of the year 2000, the account Depreciation **Expense** is debited for $36,000. Straight-line Depreciation is used in this computation. The Purchase Price of the machine is $110,000, and the estimated life of the machine is 3 years. There is no Scrap Value estimated in this computation. Therefore, the depreciation for the entire year 2000 is $36,000 ($110,000 divided by 3 = $36,000). Also, the Contra-Asset account entitled Accumulated Depreciation is credited for the $36,000 figure, because this is merely an estimate.

• PROBLEM 19–12

The Jerison Broom Company leases a broom-making machine for a year. Because of problems with the machine, Jerison terminates the lease contract at the end of the year 2000, the first year. What entries should be made on the books of the Lessor, the Harrison Machine Works?

SOLUTION:

Books of The Harrison Machine Works

2000	($ in dollars)
December 31 Machine	105,000
Lease Receivable	77,000
Gain on Lease Termination	28,000

The broom-making machine is being returned to the Harrison Machine Works, and this machine should be placed on the books at the lower of its original cost or Present Market Value. Its original cost to Harrison Machine Works was $110,000 and let us assume that its Present Market Value at the end of one year of use is $105,000. Since the lower of these two figures is $105,000, we debit Machine for that figure.

The Lease Receivable Asset account on the books of the Harrison Machine Works at this time appears as follows:

Lease Receivable

1/2/2000	110,000	1/2/2000	40,000
12/31/2000	7,000		
	117,000		
	77,000		

On January 2, 2000, the date the lease agreement was signed between the Harrison Machine Works and the Jerison Broom Company, the account Lease Receivable was debited for $110,000 on the books of the Harrison Machine Works. This is the sales price of the broom-making machine and is similar to Accounts Receivable, in that at the time the contract was signed and the machine delivered to the Jerison Broom Company, it was considered a capital lease that might eventually result in a sale of the machine.

On the same date, the Lessee, the Jerison Broom Company, paid the $40,000 annual lease payment to the Harrison Machine Works, and the account Lease Receivable was credited for that figure, meaning that the amount of Jerison's debt to Harrison had decreased by that amount. (This is only a "so-called" debt, because it is a capital lease agreement and not actually a sale and the Lessee has a right to return the machine.)

On December 31, 2000, Interest Revenue is recorded for the machine for a year's use. This is computed as follows: Sales Price of the machine was $110,000, and a $40,000 annual lease payment was made, so we subtract the $40,000 from the $110,000 to get a Net amount still to be paid of $70,000. The going Interest Rate at this time is considered to be 10%. And 10% of $70,000 is $7,000. So, on December 31, 2000, the Asset account Lease Receivable is debited for this $7000 Accrued (built up) Interest, bringing the balance of the Lease Receivable account up to $77,000.

Now, the Lessee, the Jerison Broom Company, has decided to cancel the contract and has returned the broom-making machine to the Lessor, the Harrison Machine Works, so in order to remove the account Lease Receivable with a debit balance of $77,000 from its books, it credits Lease Receivable for the $77,000. The difference between the Present Market Value of the machine ($105,000) and the $77,000 Lease Receivable is $28,000, and this is credited to Gain On Lease Termination and is reported as a Revenue on the books of the Harrison Machine Works.

• PROBLEM 19-13

The Jerison Broom Company has leased a broom-making machine from the Harrison Machine Works for a year. Because of problems with the machine, Jerison terminates the lease contract at the end of the year 2000, the first year. What entries should be made on the books of the Lessee, the Jerison Broom Company, at this time?

SOLUTION:

Books of The Jerison Broom Company

2000		($ in dollars)
December 31 Lease Liability	77,000	
Accumulated Depreciation	36,000	
Leased Property		110,000
Gain on Lease Termination		3,000

The Lease Liability account on the books of the Jerison Broom Company at this time appears as follows:

Lease Liability

1/2/2000	40,000	1/2/2000	110,000
		12/31/2000	7,000
			117,000
			77,000

On January 2, 2000, the Jerison Broom Company signed a capital lease with the Harrison Machine Works. The Purchase Price of the machine at this time was considered to be $110,000, although this capital lease was not actually considered to be a purchase. Usually, however, a capital lease can develop into a purchase over a period of time. Therefore, the Lease Liability account was credited for $110,000, meaning that Jerison Broom Company, if it continued to carry out the terms of the lease, really owed Harrison Machine Works the $110,000. Also on the same date, January 2, 2000, the Jerison Broom Company paid Harrison Machine Works its first year's lease payment of $40,000. The account Lease Liability was debited for this $40,000, thus cutting down the debt by that figure.

Finally, on December 31, 2000, an adjusting entry was made on the books of the Jerison Broom Company accounting for the Interest Expense incurred during the year 2000. This Interest Expense amounted to $7,000 and is computed as follows: $110,000 was the so-called Purchase Price of the broom-making machine. A lease payment of $40,000 was made by the Jerison Broom Company on January 2, 2000, thus cutting down the debt to $70,000. ($110,000 Purchase Price − $40,000 cash payment = $70,000 debt still owed.) The going Interest Rate at this time is considered to be

10%, so 10% of the $70,000 debt is $7,000. ($70,000 debt × 10% going Rate of Interest = $7,000.) The Interest Expense is not paid by the Jerison Broom Company on the last day of the year 2000, but Jerison can debit Interest Expense anyway for the amount of Interest incurred during the year, cutting down its Net Income figure and also its Income Tax. At the same time Lease Liability is credited (increased) for the $7,000 bringing the account at year's end up to a balance of $77,000.

The final entry on December 31, 2000, the date when the Jerison Broom Company returns the broom-making machine to the Lessor, the Harrison Machine Works debits the account Lease Liability for the $77,000 balance, thus closing out this Liability account, since by returning the machine, Jerison Broom Company no longer owes Harrison any-thing—the lease agreement is cancelled.

Also, the Contra-Asset account Accumulated Depreciation, which has a credit balance of $36,000, is debited for $36,000, thus closing out this account.

The Asset account Leased Property had originally been debited for the purchase price of $110,000. Since the lease is no longer in effect, this account is cancelled by a credit of $110,000. Also, the Revenue account Gain on Lease Termination is credited for $3,000. This is a "plug entry" to make the debits equal the credits; but it does show that the Jerison Broom Company has made an overall gain of $3,000 on the lease during the year 2000, and this $3,000 entry will have to be reported on the Income Statement of Jerison for the year, increasing the Net Income by $3,000 and also increasing the Jerison Income Tax.

CHAPTER 20

CHANGES IN ACCOUNTING SYSTEMS AND ANALYSIS OF ERRORS

Basic Attacks and Strategies for Solving Problems in this Chapter. See pages 635 to 671 for step-by-step solutions to problems.

The Financial Accounting Standards Board requires companies with retirement plans to deduct expenses for the employees during the years they are working for the firm. Additionally, the companies may not wait to deduct these retirement expenses until employees have retired. This policy increases the expenses companies claim on their Income Statements, thus effectively cutting down on the Net Income shown on the books.

Banks often lose money on loans they have made and must account for these losses on their books. Companies start out depreciating their Assets over a certain number of years, then, in the middle of the depreciation period, decide to change the length of time that the asset will last. Not only do they change the length of estimated Asset life, they often change the estimated Scrap or Residual Value figures.

Accounting is not a science, it is an art. Because of depreciation, along with other reasons, Net Income cannot always be determined precisely. Depreciation of company Assets is, at best, an estimate based on past experience and these estimates can be legally challenged.

This chapter attempts to give examples in everyday language of some of these changes. A business might wish to change its depreciation computations from the **Sum-of-Years-Digits** method to the **Straight-Line** method. Firms depreciate by different methods because the Income Tax law allows this; and certain methods allow them to legally decrease their Income Tax during the early years of the life of an Asset. To start with, a business may depreciate its Assets by the Straight-Line Method for Income Tax purposes and by the Sum-Of-Years-Digits Method for financial purposes. However, the firm may want to depreciate the same way (in this case, by the Straight-Line Method) for both Income Tax and financial reporting purposes, so it would switch from the Sum-Of-Years-Digits Method to the Straight-Line Method.

It is also possible for a firm to switch from the **First-In First-Out** Method of valuing inventory to the **Last-In First-Out** Method. Firms make this switch, especially during times of high inflation, because at times, the LIFO method shows a smaller Income Tax than does the FIFO method. Also, the government allows firms to switch once from FIFO to LIFO without a governmental audit of their books.

It is also legally possible for a firm to switch from the Last-In First-Out Method to the First-In First-Out Method of valuing inventory, but this change usually initiates an audit by the Internal Revenue Service.

Step-by-Step Solutions to Problems in this Chapter, "Changes in Accounting Systems and Analysis of Errors"

• PROBLEM 20-1

The Horton Brewing Corporation has been depreciating its machinery by the Straight-Line Method for Income Tax purposes and by the Sum-of-Years-Digits Method for financial reporting purposes for the last two years, since it purchased the brewery machinery on January 2, 2000. It is now December 31, 2001, and the accountants for the brewery have determined to change their financial reporting method of depreciation from the Sum-of-Years-Digits Method to the Straight-Line Method, so that from henceforth both the Income Tax accounting and the financial reporting will be according to the Straight-Line Method of depreciation.

When the machinery was purchased on January 2, 2000, it was estimated that it would last 15 years, and the Purchase Price was $40,000. It was estimated that at the end of 15 years the machinery would have no Scrap Value and would have to be junked. So under the Sum-of-Years-Digits Method of depreciation, the numerator of the fraction would be 15, the number of estimated years of life of the machinery being depreciated. The denominator of the fraction is computed as follows: 15 + 14 + 13 + 12 + 11 + 10 + 9 + 8 + 7 + 6 + 5 + 4 + 3 + 2 + 1 = 120. So the fraction is 15/120. This fraction is multiplied by the Cost Price less the Scrap Value. In this case, the cost price of the machinery is $40,000 and the Scrap Value is 0 ($40,000 cost price − $0 scrap value = $40,000). We then multiply the fraction of 15/120 times the $40,000 to get $,5000, the depreciation for the year 2000 on the machinery for the Sum-of-Years-Digits method of depreciation.

For the second year (in this case the year 2001), we have 14 more years to depreciate, so we use the fraction 14/120 and multiply 14/120 times $40,000 to get $4,667. For the Straight-Line Method of depreciation for Income Tax purposes, we divide 15 years into $40,000 depreciable cost to get $2,667 depreciation each year.

What entries will be made on the books of the Horton Brewing Corporation at the beginning of the year 2002 to change from the Sum-of-Years-Digits Method of depreciation to the Straight-Line Method of depreciation for financial reporting purposes and why?

SOLUTION:

Depreciation Table

Year	Sum-of-Years-Digits Depreciation	Straight-Line Depreciation	Difference	Tax Effect 28%	Effect on Income (Net of Tax)
2000	$5,000	$2,667	$2,333	$653.24	$1,679.76
2001	4,667	2,667	2,000	560.00	1,440.00
TOTALS	$9,667	$5,334	$4,333	$1,213.24	$3,119.76

The above computations are for the accountants only, to help them compute the journal entries to change the depreciation method for financial reporting purposes. The left-most column shows the two years that have elapsed since the purchase of the machines—that is, the full calendar years of 2000 and 2001. The second column shows the Sum-of-Years-Digits Method of depreciation of these machines, and these computations have been explained on the previous few pages. The depreciation is $5,000 for the year 2000 and $4,667 for the year 2001.

The third column shows the Straight-Line depreciation of these machines, and these computations have been explained on the previous few pages. The Straight-Line depreciation is always the same for each year (unless Assets have continued to be purchased or unless some of the Assets have been scrapped). So it is seen that on these machines the Straight-Line depreciation for the year 2000 is $2,667, and for the year 2001 it is also $2,667.

The fourth column entitled Difference is merely a subtraction of the figures in the third column from the figures in the second column. For instance, in the calendar year 2000, the $2,667 Straight-Line depreciation is subtracted from the $5,000 Sum-of-Years-Digits depreciation to get a so-called Difference of $2,333. Also in the calendar year 2001, the $2,667 Straight-Line depreciation is subtracted from the $4,667 Sum-of-Years-Digits depreciation to get a so-called Difference of $2,000.

The fifth column entitled Tax Effect 28% is merely the product of multiplying the *difference* by 28%. For instance, for the year 2000, the *difference* of $2,333 is multiplied by the tax bracket of 28% to derive $653.24 ($2,333 difference × 28% tax bracket = $653.24). For the year 2001, the difference of $2,000 is multiplied by the tax bracket of 28% to derive $560.00 ($2,000 difference × 28% tax bracket = $560.00 tax effect).

The sixth and last column entitled Effect on Income (Net of Tax) is the remainder of subtracting column 5 from column 4. For instance, in the year 2000, column 5 ($653.24) is subtracted from column 4 ($2,333.00) to derive $1,679.76, which is the difference between the two methods after the 28% Income Tax amount has been subtracted. In the year 2001, column 5 ($560.00) is subtracted from column 4 ($2,000) to derive $1,440.00, which is the difference between the two methods after the 28% Income Tax amount has been subtracted.

The Totals are merely the figures of each of the columns added.

Now let us examine the accounting entries for the years 2000 and 2001 regarding the depreciation of these machines by both the Sum-of-Years-Digits Method and the Straight-Line Method of depreciation:

2000		($ in dollars)	
January 2	Machines	40,000	
	Cash		40,000

Sum-of-Years-Digits Method of Depreciation

2000			
December 31	Depreciation Expense	5,000	
	Accumulated Depreciation		5,000
December 31	Deferred Tax Asset	653.24	
	Income Tax Expense	1,679.76	
	Income Tax Payable		2,333
2001			
December 31	Depreciation Expense	4,667	
	Accumulated Depreciation		4,667
December 31	Deferred Tax Asset	560	
	Income Tax Expense	1,440	
	Income Tax Payable		2,000

Straight-Line Method of Depreciation

2000		($ in dollars)	
December 31	Depreciation Expense	2,667	
	Accumulated Depreciation		2,667

2001

December 31 Depreciation Expense	2,667
Accumulated Depreciation	2,667

In order to understand the general journal entries immediately above, the reader should also consult the Depreciation Table immediately prior to the above entries.

On January 2, 2000, the machines were purchased for $40,000, so the Asset account Machines was debited for that amount. Also Cash was credited for $40,000 because that amount of cash was leaving the Horton Brewing Corporation. The adjusting entry on December 31, 2000, using the Sum-of-Years-Digits Method of depreciation, is to debit Depreciation Expense for $5,000. (The $5,000 is computed by multiplying the $40,000 cost of machines by the fraction 15/120.) Depreciation Expense is debited because the Horton Brewing Corporation had the use of the machines for the entire calendar year of 2000, and these machines depreciated in value during that year of use. The Contra-Asset account Accumulated Depreciation is credited for $5,000 because this entry is merely a guess, so the Asset account Machines cannot be credited unless and until the machines are either sold or scrapped.

The second entry on December 31, 2000 debits the Asset account entitled Deferred Tax Asset for $653.24. Looking at the Depreciation Table, we see that the $653.24 is derived by multiplying the difference between the Straight-Line Method of depreciation and the Sum-of-Years-Digits Method of depreciation ($2,333) by the 28% Income Tax Rate to derive the figure $653.24 ($2,333 difference × 28% tax rate = $653.24). This figure of $653.24 is actually the amount of Income Tax that Horton Brewing Corporation saves during the year 2000 between the two methods. However, here it is really in the reverse, and the corporation is losing the $653.24 because, for Income Tax purposes, it is using the Straight-Line Method and for financial reporting purposes, it is using the Sum-of-Years-Digits Method. It is really losing the $653.24 temporarily, but it is "building up" a savings account, in a way, and that is why the Asset account Deferred Tax Asset is debited. In later years, the Sum-of-Years-Digits method of depreciation will allow a smaller write-off than will the Straight-Line Method of depreciation, and this tax savings will revert to the benefit of the Horton Brewing Corporation. Until that time arrives, the Asset account Deferred Tax Asset will remain on the books. The account Income Tax Expense is debited for $1,679.76. Looking at the Depreciation

Table for the calendar year 2000, one sees that this figure of $1,679.76 comes from the right-most column of the table entitled Effect on Income (Net of Tax). This is the remainder of the difference between the two depreciation methods, after the 28% tax is deducted, and it is debited to the Income Tax Expense account and legally deducted on the Income Statement as a true business expense of the business, legally cutting down the Net Income of the business for financial reporting purposes, but not for Income Tax purposes in this case. Finally, the Liability account entitled Income Tax Payable is credited for $2,333, which shows the Income Tax liability for financial reporting purposes, under the Sum-of-Years-Digits Method of reporting. However, this is not the actual tax Liability for Income Tax reporting purposes, because these are being kept by the Straight-Line Method of reporting. One will note that under the Straight-Line Method of reporting for the calendar year 2000, Depreciation Expense is debited for $2,667, which in this case is the amount used for the true deduction for Income Tax purposes. This $2,667 is derived by dividing the $40,000 cost of the machinery by the 15 years estimated life of the machinery ($40,000 ÷ 15 years = $2,667).

The adjusting entry on December 31, 2001, using the Sum-of-Years-Digits Method of depreciation, is to debit Depreciation Expense for $4,667. (The $4,667 is computed by multiplying the $40,000 cost of the machines by the fraction 14/120.) Depreciation Expense is debited because the Horton Brewing Corporation had the use of the machines for the entire calendar year of 2001, and these machines depreciated in value during that year of use. The Contra-Asset account Accumulated Depreciation is credited for $4,667 because this entry is merely a guess, so the Asset account Machines cannot be credited unless and until the machines are either sold or scrapped.

The second entry on December 31, 2001 debits the Asset account entitled Deferred Tax Asset for $560. Looking at the Depreciation Table, we see that the $560 is derived by multiplying the difference between the Straight-Line Method of depreciation and the Sum-of-Years-Digits Method of depreciation ($2,000) by the 28% Income Tax Rate to derive the figure $560 ($2,000 difference × 28% tax rate = $560). This figure of $560 is actually the amount of Income Tax that Horton Brewing Corporation spends extra during the year 2001 because for Income Tax purposes it is using the Straight-Line Method and for financial reporting purposes it is using the Sum-of-Years-Digits Method. It is really losing $560 temporarily, but it is "building up" a savings account, in a way, and that is why the Asset account Deferred Tax Asset is debited. In later years, the Sum-of-Years-Digits Method of depreciation will allow a smaller write-off than will the Straight-Line Method of depreciation, and this tax savings will revert to the benefit of the Horton Brewing Corporation. Until that time, the Asset account Deferred Tax Asset will remain on the books. The account Income Tax Expense is debited for $1,440. Looking at the Depreciation Table for the calendar year 2001, one sees that this figure of $1,440 comes from the right-most column of the table entitled Effect on Income (Net of Tax). This is the remainder of the difference between the two depreciation methods, after the 28% tax is deducted, and it is debited to the Income Tax Expense account and legally deducted on the Income Statement as a true business expense of the business, legally cutting down the Net Income of the business for financial reporting purposes, but not for Income Tax purposes in this case. Finally, the Liability account entitled Income Tax Payable is credited for $2,000, which shows the Income Tax Liability for financial reporting purposes, under the Sum-of-Years-Digits Method of reporting. However, this is not the actual tax Liability for Income Tax reporting purposes, because these are being kept by the Straight-Line Method of reporting. One will note that under the Straight-Line Method of reporting for the calendar year 2001, Depreciation Expense is debited for $2,667, which is in this case the amount used for the true deduction for Income Tax purposes. This $2,667 is derived by dividing the $40,000 cost of the machinery by the 15 years estimated life of the machinery ($40,000 ÷ 15 years = $2,667).

Adjusting Entry for the Year 2002

2002			($ in dollars)
January 2	Accumulated Depreciation	4,333.00	
	Deferred Tax Asset		1,213.24
	Cumulative Effect		3,119.76

In order to get a good explanation of the above entry, look at the Depreciation Table several pages before this. It will be noted in column 4 of the Depreciation Table that the total difference in depreciation between the two methods for the two calendar years of 2000 and 2001 is $4,333. Thus, the Accumulated Depreciation account with a credit balance at the end of the year 2001 of $9,667 using the Sum-of-Years-Digits Method of depreciation is $4,333, too high for the Straight-Line Method to which we are transferring. Therefore, in order to correct this account, we debit Accumulated Depreciation for the $4,333 difference to cut it down to size. It will also be noted in column 5 of the Depreciation Table that the total tax effect for the two calendar years of 2000 and 2001 is $1,213.24 higher than it should be. So, in changing from the Sum-of-Years-Digits Method of depreciation to the Straight-Line Method of depreciation, we must cut down the Asset account Deferred Tax Asset by $1,213.24 by crediting this account. Finally, the Revenue account Cumulative Effect is credited for the difference—in this case, $3,119.76.

• PROBLEM 20–2

The Dorcas Service Station for the past years has been keeping its gasoline inventory under the FIFO (First-In First-Out Method). In the last few years, gasoline prices have increased considerably because of inflation, and many businesses, to legally save money on Income Taxes, have switched from the First-In First-Out Method to the Last-In First-Out Method of recording inventory. The Last-In First-Out Method allows the sale of the higher priced, more recent gasoline, and the gasoline remaining is the earlier, lower-priced inventory. This shows a lower profit on the books and thus the corporation can legally pay a lower Income Tax.

The Dorcas Service Station decides to switch from FIFO to LIFO at December 31, 2000. The gasoline purchases for the year 2000 follow:

Dorcas Service Station
Wholesale Gasoline Purchases
For the Year 2000

1/1/2000	Beginning Inventory	80,000 gallons @ $.90 =	$72,000
3/10/2000	Purchase	60,000 gallons @ $.94 =	56,400
5/20/2000	Purchase	40,000 gallons @ $.89 =	35,600
8/15/2000	Purchase	70,000 gallons @ $.92 =	64,400
10/20/2000	Purchase	35,000 gallons @ $.93 =	32,550
	Available	285,000 gallons	$260,950
	Ending Inventory		
	12/31/2000	–50,000 gallons	
	Gallons sold	235,000 gallons	

As can be seen from the chart above, the Dorcas Service Station began the year 2000 with 80,000 gallons of gasoline on hand which it had purchased at $.90 per gallon for a total cost of $72,000. On March 10, 2000, it purchased 60,000 gallons at $.94 for a total of $56,400. On May 20, 2000, it purchased 40,000 gallons at $.89 for a total of $35,600. On August 15, 2000, it purchased 70,000 gallons at $.92 for a total of $64,400. Finally, on October 20, 2000, it purchased 35,000 gallons at $.93 for a total of $32,550.

The grand total of the beginning inventory and all the purchases during the year comes to 285,000 gallons of gasoline with a dollar value at Cost Price of $260,950.

On December 31, 2000, the Dorcas Service Station had a total inventory of 50,000 gallons of gasoline. Thus, if no gasoline had been stolen or had been lost through evaporation, the total number of gallons sold during the year 2000 would be 235,000 gallons (285,000 gallons available − 50,000 gallons in ending inventory = 235,000 gallons sold).

What is the dollar value of the Ending Inventory on December 31, 2000 using the First-In First-Out Method of inventory valuation and why?

SOLUTION:

First-In First-Out Method of Inventory Computation

35,000 gallons at $.93 =	$32,550
15,000 gallons at $.92 =	$13,800
50,000 gallons	$46,350

Under the First-In First-Out Method of inventory valuation, the originally purchased gallons are sold first. Therefore, the Ending Inventory (those gallons of gasoline not sold) will be the most-recently-purchased gallons. Looking at the chart of **Wholesale Gasoline Purchases**, we start at the bottom of the chart and work upwards until we reach the 50,000 gallons in the ending inventory.

Note that the last line of the Wholesale Gasoline Purchases chart shows 35,000 gallons @ $.93 = $32,550. Since 35,000 gallons is not as high as the 50,000 gallons needed in the ending inventory, we copy this line as the first line in the FIFO Method of Inventory Computation table.

The next step is to work up the Wholesale Gasoline Purchases chart to the next-to-last line which is 70,000 gallons @ $.92 = $64,400. The last line of the table with 35,000 gallons plus the next-to-last line of the table with 70,000 gallons add up to more than the 50,000 gallons needed for the Ending Inventory, so this is too much. We only need 50,000 gallons. So the 50,000 gallons will be taken as follows: 35,000 gallons from the last line's unit price of $.93 per gallon = $32,550, and 15,000 gallons from the next-to-last line's unit price of $.92 per gallon = $13,800. (Only 15,000 gallons need to be used of the $.92 per gallon gasoline, because we only need 50,000 gallons in total. 50,000 gallons – 35,000 gallons = 15,000 gallons.)

In looking at the First-In First-Out Method of Inventory Computation chart above, we see that the 35,000 gallons at $.93 cost us $32,550. We also see that the 15,000 gallons at $.92 cost us $13,800. Adding these two figures together we get a total Ending Inventory by the First-In First-Out method of $46,350.

• PROBLEM 20–3

The Dorcas Service Station for the past years has been keeping its gasoline inventory under the FIFO (First In First Out) Method. In the last few years, gasoline prices have increased considerably because of inflation, and many businesses, to legally save money on Income Taxes, have switched from the First-In First-Out Method to the Last-In First-Out Method of recording inventory. The Last-In First-Out Method allows the sale of the higher priced, more recently purchased gasoline, and the gasoline remaining is the earlier, lower-priced inventory. This shows a lower profit on the books and thus the corporation can legally pay a lower Income Tax.

The Dorcas Service Station decides to switch from FIFO to LIFO on December 31, 2000. The gasoline purchases for the year 2000 follow:

Dorcas Service Station
Wholesale Gasoline Purchases
For the Year 2000

1/1/2000	Beginning Inventory	80,000 gallons @ $.90 =	$ 72,000
3/10/2000	Purchase	60,000 gallons @ $.94 =	56,400
5/20/2000	Purchase	40,000 gallons @ $.89 =	35,600
8/15/2000	Purchase	70,000 gallons @ $.92 =	64,400
10/20/2000	Purchase	35,000 gallons @ $.93 =	32,550
	Available	285,000 gallons	$260,950
	Ending Inventory	–50,000 gallons	
	Gallons sold	235,000 gallons	

As can be seen from the chart above, the Dorcas Service Station began the year 2000 with 80,000 gallons of gasoline on hand, which it had purchased at $.90 per gallon for a total cost of $72,000. On March 10, 2000, it purchased 60,000 gallons at $.94 for a total of $56,400. On May 20, 2000, it purchased 40,000 gallons at $.89 for a total of $35,600. On August 15, 2000, it purchased 70,000 gallons at $.92 for a total of $64,400. Finally, on October 20, 2000, it purchased 35,000 gallons at $.93 for a total of $32,550.

The grand total of the Beginning Inventory and all the purchases during the year comes to 285,000 gallons of gasoline with a dollar value at Cost Price of $260,950.

On December 31, 2000, the Dorcas Service Station had a total inventory of 50,000 gallons of gasoline. Thus, if no gasoline had been stolen or had been lost through evaporation, the total number of gallons sold during the year 2000 would be 235,000 gallons (285,000 gallons available – 50,000 gallons in ending inventory = 235,000 gallons sold).

What is the dollar value of the Ending Inventory on December 31, 2000, using the Last-In First-Out Method of inventory valuation and why?

SOLUTION:

Last-In First-Out Method of Inventory Computation

50,000 gallons @ $.90 = $45,000

Under the Last-In First-Out Method of inventory valuation, the most recently purchased gallons are sold first. Therefore, the Ending Inventory (those gallons of gasoline not sold) will be the lower priced gallons originally purchased. Looking at the chart of Wholesale Gasoline Purchases, we start at the top of the chart and work down until we reach the 50,000 gallons in the Ending Inventory. Note that the first line of the Wholesale Gasoline Purchases chart shows 80,000 gallons @ $.90 = $72,000. Since we are only interested in the 50,000 gallons still left in the Ending Inventory, we multiply 50,000 gallons at the $.90 per gallon rate to get $45,000, the value of the Ending Inventory under the Last-In First-Out method of inventory valuation.

The Dorcas Service Station for the past years has been keeping its gasoline inventory under the FIFO (First-In First-Out) Method. In the last few years gasoline prices have increased considerably because of inflation, and many businesses, to legally save money on Income Taxes, have switched from the First-In First-Out Method to the Last-In First-Out Method of recording inventory. The Last-In First-Out Method allows the sale of the higher priced, more recently purchased gasoline, and the gasoline remaining is the earlier, lower priced inventory. This shows a lower profit on the books and thus the corporation can legally pay a lower Income Tax.

The Dorcas Service Station decides to switch from FIFO to LIFO on December 31, 2000. The gasoline purchases for the year 2000 follow:

Dorcas Service Station
Wholesale Gasoline Purchases
For the Year 2000

1/1/2000	Beginning Inventory	80,000 gallons @ $.90 =	$ 72,000
3/10/2000	Purchase	60,000 gallons @ $.94 =	56,400
5/20/2000	Purchase	40,000 gallons @ $.89 =	35,600
8/15/2000	Purchase	70,000 gallons @ $.92 =	64,400
10/20/2000	Purchase	35,000 gallons @ $.93 =	32,550
	Available	285,000 gallons	$260,950
	Ending Inventory	–50,000 gallons	
	Gallons Sold	235,000 gallons	

As can be seen from the chart above, the Dorcas Service Station began the year 2000 with 80,000 gallons of gasoline on hand which it had purchased at $.90 per gallon for a total cost of $72,000. On March 10, 2000, it purchased 60,000 gallons at $.94 for a total of $56,400. On May 20, 2000, it purchased 40,000 gallons at $.89 for a total of $35,000. On August 15, 2000, it purchased 70,000 gallons at $.92 for a total of $64,400. Finally, on October 20, 2000, it purchased 35,000 gallons at $.93 for a total of $32,550.

The grand total of the Beginning Inventory and all the purchases during the year comes to 285,000 gallons of gasoline with a dollar value at Cost Price of $260,950.

On December 31, 2000, the Dorcas Service Station had a total inventory of 50,000 gallons of gasoline. Thus, if no gasoline had been stolen or had been lost through evaporation, the total number of gallons sold during the year 2000 would be 235,000 gallons (285,000 gallons available – 50,000 gallons in Ending Inventory = 235,000 gallons sold).

First-In First-Out Method of Inventory Computation

35,000 gallons at $.93 = $32,550
15,000 gallons at $.92 = $13,800
50,000 gallons $46,350

Thus, the dollar value of the Ending Inventory for gasoline on December 31, 2000 using the FIFO Method of inventory valuation is $46,350.

Last-In First-Out Method of Inventory Computation

50,000 gallons @ $.90 = $45,000

Thus, the dollar value of the Ending Inventory for gasoline on December 31, 2000 using the LIFO Method of inventory valuation is $45,000.

What adjusting entry should be made on December 31, 2000, for the Dorcas Service Station to change from the First-In First-Out Method of inventory valuation to the Last-In First-Out Method of inventory valuation, and what are the Income Tax consequences?

SOLUTION:

2000		($ in dollars)
December 31 Merchandise Inventory (LIFO)	45,000	
Retained Earnings	1,350	
Merchandise Inventory (FIFO)		46,350

At the end of the year 2000, the Dorcas Service Station's Merchandise Inventory (gasoline) account appears as follows:

Merchandise Inventory (Gasoline)

12/31/2000	46,350	

It is now necessary for this Asset account entitled Merchandise Inventory (Gasoline) with a debit balance (FIFO) of $46,350 to be closed out and changed to a debit balance (LIFO) of $45,000. Therefore, on December 31, 2000, we debit Merchandise Inventory for $45,000, the new balance using the Last-In First-Out Method of inventory valuation. We also credit Merchandise Inventory for the $46,350 (FIFO) to close out the old First-In First-Out balance. The difference between these two figures is $1,350 ($46,350 − $45,000 = $1,350). This plug figure of $1,350 is debited to Retained Earnings. Retained Earnings usually has a credit balance, so this debit of $1,350 decreases the Retained Earnings balance by that amount. Why is this? It is because we are lowering the Asset account Merchandise Inventory from $46,350 to $45,000. It is like losing some of our merchandise; therefore, it cuts down the Retained Earnings account, literally cutting down the amount of investment that the stockholders have in the business.

How does this change from the FIFO method to the LIFO method affect Income Tax Liability of the Dorcas Service Station? Not at all in this case. Internal Revenue Service rules at present allow businesses to switch once from the First-In First-Out Method to the Last-In First-Out Method without incurring any additional Income Taxes. However, along with their Income Tax return, they do have to notify the Internal Revenue Service of this switch.

• PROBLEM 20-5

To turn matters around, let us now say that the Dorcas Service Station for the past years has been keeping its gasoline inventory under the LIFO (Last-In First-Out) Method. It now wants to change to the FIFO (First-In First-Out) Method.

The dollar value of the Ending Inventory for gasoline on December 31, 2000, using the LIFO Method, is $45,000. The dollar value of the Ending Inventory for gasoline on December 31, 2000, using the FIFO Method, is $46,350.

What adjusting entry should be made on December 31, 2000, for the Dorcas Service Station to change from the Last-In First-Out Method of inventory valuation to the First-In First-Out Method of inventory valuation. What are the Income Tax consequences, and what challenges would there be in the Income Statement and Retained Earnings Statement for Dorcas Service Station on December 31, 2000?

SOLUTION:

2000	($ in dollars)	
December 31 Merchandise Inventory (FIFO)	46,350	
Retained Earnings		1,350
Merchandise Inventory (LIFO)		45,000

The books of the Dorcas Service Station, in this case, have been kept by the LIFO Method of inventory accounting. Therefore, at the end of the year 2000, the Merchandise Inventory account would have a balance of $45,000. This is to be changed to $46,350 or the FIFO Method by the above entry. Note that the Asset account Merchandise Inventory is debited for $46,350, the new figure. Also, Merchandise Inventory is credited for $45,000, the old figure, to erase that amount from the account. The difference, $1,350, is credited to the Retained Earnings account. Retained Earnings usually has a credit balance, so when that account is credited, it adds to the value of that account. Why is the account Retained Earnings "added to" in this case? It is because the Asset account Merchandise Inventory is being increased in value from $45,000 to $46,350. Since the Asset is being increased, it also adds to the value of the firm for the stockholders.

This fact can be further illustrated by the following chart:

Dorcas Service Station
Change in Accounting for Inventory

	LIFO	FIFO	Difference	Tax 30%	Difference Net of Tax
Ending Merchandise Inventory 12/31/2000	$45,000	$46,350	$1,350	$405	$945

As seen in the table above, the Ending Merchandise Inventory under the LIFO Method is $45,000, and under the FIFO Method is $46,350. The difference between these two figures is $1,350. Since in this case we are switching from the LIFO to the FIFO Method of inventory accounting, the Merchandise Inventory is being increased by $1,350.

Let us also say that the Dorcas Service Station is in the 30% Income Tax bracket. Thirty percent of the $1,350 difference is $405, and this means that because of the change in accounting procedure, the Dorcas Service Station will have to remit $405 more in Income Tax to the federal government in this case. The difference net of tax is $945. (The $1,350 difference between the merchandise inventory kept by the LIFO Method versus Merchandise Inventory kept by the FIFO Method – $405 extra income tax = $945 difference Net of tax, or increase in Income for the Dorcas Service Station after the government has received its share.)

The changes in the Dorcas Retained Earnings Statement due to this change from LIFO to FIFO are illustrated below:

Dorcas Service Station
Retained Earnings Statement
December 31, 2000

Retained Earnings, January 1, 2000	$700,000
Add Difference Net of Tax	
(from Change in Accounting	
for Inventory Statement)	945
Beginning Balance as Adjusted	700,945
Net Income after Income Tax, year 2000	+ 200,000
Retained Earnings, December 31, 2000	$900,945

Let us say that the Retained Earnings account for the Dorcas Service Station as of January 1, 2000 had a credit balance of $700,000. The difference Net of tax from the Change in Accounting for Inventory Statement is $945 ($1,350 difference – $405 income tax = $945). In the Retained Earnings Statement the $945 difference Net of tax is added to the $700,000 Retained Earnings balance as of January 1, 2000, to derive Beginning Balance as adjusted of $700,945 ($700,000 + $945 = $700,945).

Let us also assume that the Net Income after Tax for the Dorcas Service Station for the year 2000 was $200,000. This $200,000 Net Income after Tax is added to the $700,945 beginning Balance as Adjusted to derive Retained Earnings, December 31, 2000 of $900,945.

• PROBLEM 20-6

The Hammond Broom Company purchased a broom-making machine for 51,000 on January 2, 2000. At the time of purchase, from past experience, the management of the corporation estimated that the machine would last 10 years, after which time it would have a scrap value of $1,000. The machine was used for four years (in this case, the calendar years of 2000, 2001, 2002, and 2003) to manufacture brooms in the business. On December 31, 2003, the managers estimated that the machine would only be functional for 4 more years (instead of 6 more years as originally anticipated). (10 years originally estimated – 4 years just passed = 6 more years.) Thus, instead of lasting a total of 10 years as originally estimated, it now (as of the end of the fourth year of use) appears that the machine will last only a total of 4 more years. (8 years – 4 years = 4 years.)

What entry or entries should be made at the end of the fifth, sixth, seventh, and eighth years of the machine's life, assuming that the Straight-Line Method of depreciation is used?

SOLUTION:

During the first 4 years of the machine's life it was depreciated $5,000 each year. During the remainder of the machine's life it should be depreciated $7,500 per year, computed as follows:

Machine Cost	$51,000
Less estimated Scrap Value	– 1,000
Amount to be depreciated	$50,000

Of course, the Scrap Value of $1,000 is just an educated guess, but it is based on past experience from similar machines. Another estimate is the number of years that the machine will last in production. At the time the machine was purchased (in this case, January 2, 2000), it was estimated that the machine would last 10 years. So we divide the $50,000 amount to be depreciated by 10 years of estimated life to get $5,000 yearly depreciation.

The entry at the end of the year 2000 would be as follows:

2000	($ in dollars)	
December 31 Depreciation Expense	5,000	
Accumulated Depreciation		5,000

At the end of four years, making this same depreciation entry at the ends of the years 2000, 2001, 2002, and 2003, the Accumulated Depreciation account would appear as follows:

Accumulated Depreciation

12/31/2000	5,000
12/31/2001	5,000
12/31/2002	5,000
12/31/2003	5,000
	20,000

The Asset account Machine would appear as follows:

Machine

1/2/2000 51,000	

On December 31, 2003, after four years of machine life, the book value of the machine is $31,000. (Original cost of the machine was $51,000 and from that we subtract the $20,000 depreciated over the first four years of life of the machine to get $31,000. $51,000 − $20,000 = $31,000.) From this $31,000 book value, we subtract the $1,000 scrap Value to get $30,000 still to be depreciated ($31,000 − $1,000 = $30,000). However, at this time, it has been determined that the machine will be functional probably for only four more years, so we divide the $30,000 by

4 to get $7,500, the amount to be depreciated each year from now on ($30,000 ÷ 4 = $7,500). Thus, the depreciation entry at the end of the year 2004 would be as follows:

2004		($ in dollars)
December 31 Depreciation Expense	7,500	
Accumulated Depreciation		7,500

This entry would be made at the end of the following years: 2004, 2005, 2006, and 2007. Finally, at the end of the year 2007, the Accumulated Depreciation account would appear as follows on the books of the Hammond Broom Company:

Accumulated Depreciation

12/31/2000	5,000
12/31/2001	5,000
12/31/2002	5,000
12/31/2003	5,000
12/31/2004	7,500
12/31/2005	7,500
12/31/2006	7,500
12/31/2007	7,500
	50,000

Thus, at the end of the year 2007, the Machine account will still have its Beginning Balance of $51,000, and now the Accumulated Depreciation account has a credit balance of $50,000, bringing the book value of the machine down to its Scrap Value of $1,000 ($51,000 – $50,000 = $1,000).

Note that in computing the change in the estimated years of life of the machine, (in this case on December 31, 2003, the previous depreciation figures are not changed) only the future depreciation figures are recomputed.

• PROBLEM 20-7

The Hammond Broom Company purchased a broom-making machine for $51,000 on January 2, 2000. At the time of purchase, from past experience, the management of the corporation estimated that the machine would last 10 years, after which time it would have a Scrap Value of $1,000. The machine was used for four years (in this case, the calendar years of 2000, 2001, 2002, and 2003) to manufacture brooms in the business. On December 31, 2003, the managers estimated that the machine would only be functional for 4 more years (instead of 6 more years as originally anticipated). (10 years originally estimated – the 4 years just passed = 6 more years.) Thus, instead of lasting a total of 10 years as originally estimated, it now (as of the end of the fourth year of use) appears that the machine will last only a total of 4 more years (8 years – 4 years = 4 years.

What entry or entries should be made at the end of the fifth, sixth, seventh, and eighth years of the machine's life, assuming that the Sum-of-Years-Digits Method of depreciation is used?

SOLUTION:

Using the Sum-of-Years-Digits Method of depreciation, the number of years of life of the machine are first determined. In this case, the original estimate is 10 years. So 10, 9, 8, 7, 6, 5, 4, 3, 2, and 1 are added as follows: 10 + 9 + 8 + 7 + 6 + 5 + 4 + 3 + 2 + 1 = 55. Thus, the sum of years equals 55 in this case. For the depreciation the first year (in this case, the year 2000), we multiply 10/55 by the $50,000 to be depreciated ($51,000 cost – $1,000 Scrap Value = $50,000 to be depreciated). When we multiply 10/55 by $50,000, we get $9,090.91, the first year's depreciation. (Note that the highest depreciation in this method is during the first year of the machine's life.)

For the depreciation the second year (in this case, the year 2001), we multiply 9/55 by the $50,000 to be depreciated ($51,000 cost – $1,000 scrap value = $50,000 to be depreciated). When we multiply 9/55 by $50,000, we get $8,181.82, the second year's depreciation.

For the depreciation the third year (in this case, the year 2002), we multiply 8/55 by the $50,000 to be depreciated, to get $7,272.73, the third year's depreciation.

For the depreciation the fourth year (in this case, the year 2003), we multiply 7/55 by the $50,000 to be depreciated, to get $6,363.64, the fourth year's depreciation.

For the depreciation the fifth year (in this case, the year 2004), we multiply 6/55 by the $50,000 to be depreciated, to get 5,454.55, the fifth year's depreciation.

For the depreciation the sixth year (in this case, the year 2005), we multiply 5/55 by the $50,000 to be depreciated, to get $4,545.45, the sixth year's depreciation.

For the depreciation the seventh year (in this case, the year 2006), we multiply 4/55 by the $50,000 to be depreciated, to get $3,636.36, the seventh year's depreciation.

For the depreciation the eighth year (in this case, the year 2007), we multiply 3/55 by the $50,000 to be depreciated, to get $2,727.27, the eighth year's depreciation.

For the depreciation the ninth year (in this case, the year 2008), we multiply 2/55 by the $50,000 to be depreciated, to get $1,818.18, the ninth year's depreciation.

For the depreciation the tenth year (in this case, the year 2009), we multiply 1/55 by the $50,000 to be depreciated, to get $909.09, the tenth year's depreciation.

This can readily be shown in chart form as follows:

Calendar Year	Year of Machine Life	Fraction	Amount to be Depreciated			Depreciation that Year
2000	First	10/55	×	$50,000	=	$9,090.91
2001	Second	9/55	×	$50,000	=	$8,181.82
2002	Third	8/55	×	$50,000	=	$7,272.73
2003	Fourth	7/55	×	$50,000	=	$6,363.64
2004	Fifth	6/55	×	$50,000	=	$5,454.55
2005	Sixth	5/55	×	$50,000	=	$4,545.45
2006	Seventh	4/55	×	$50,000	=	$3,636.36
2007	Eighth	3/55	×	$50,000	=	$2,727.27
2008	Ninth	2/55	×	$50,000	=	$1,818.18
2009	Tenth	1/55	×	$50,000	=	$ 909.09
						$50,000.00

Thus, the entire $50,000 amount to be depreciated is finally depreciated over the 10-year period, leaving only the $1,000 Scrap Value as the book value also ($51,000 original cost – $50,000 depreciated over the 10-year period = $1,000 Scrap Value).

However, in this problem, at the end of the fourth year (in this case, as of December 31, 2003), the management decides that the machine will probably last only four more years. As of December 31, 2003, the accounts on the books of the Hammond Broom Company would appear as follows:

Machine		
1/2/2000	51,000	

Accumulated Depreciation		
	12/31/2000	9,090.91
	12/31/2001	8,181.82
	12/31/2002	7,272.73
	12/31/2003	6,363.64
		30,909.10

It will be noted above that the broom-making machine originally cost $51,000. Also, the Accumulated Depreciation account as of December 31, 2003, has a credit balance of $30,909.10. So the book value of the machine at this time is $20,090.90 ($51,000 cost – $30,909.10 accumulated depreciation = $20,090.90). From this amount, we subtract the estimated Scrap Value of $1,000 to derive the amount still to be depreciated of $19,090.90. At this time, it has been estimated that the machine will last for four more years, so we divide the $19,090.90 amount still to be depreciated by the 4 years to get $4,772.73 depreciation each year from now on for the next four years of 2004, 2005, 2006, and 2007. It will be noted that the Straight-Line Method of depreciation (rather than the Sum-of-Years-Digits Method of depreciation) is used for the last half of the life of the machine, because the MACRS (Modified Accelerated Cost Recovery System) allows the Straight-Line Method to be used during the last half of an Asset's life.

• PROBLEM 20-8

The Hammond Broom Company purchased a broom-making machine for $51,000 on January 2, 2000. At the time of purchase, from past experience, the management of the corporation estimated that the machine would last 10 years, after which time it would have an estimated Scrap Value of $1,000. The machine was used for four years (in this case, the calendar years of 2000, 2001, 2002, and 2003) to manufacture brooms in the business. On December 31, 2003, the managers estimated that the machine would only be functional for 4 more years (instead of 6 more years as originally anticipated). (10 years originally estimated – the 4 years just passed = 6 more years.) Thus, instead of lasting a total of 10 years as originally estimated, it now (as of the end of the fourth year of use) appears that the machine will last only a total of 4 more years. (8 years – 4 years = 4 years.)

What entry or entries should be made at the end of the fifth, sixth, seventh, and eighth years of the machine's life, assuming that the Double-Declining-Balance Method of depreciation is used?

SOLUTION:

During the first four years of the machine's life, it was depreciated as follows:

In the Double-Declining Balance Method of depreciation, the Asset's estimated number of years of life is the divisor and 100% is the dividend, as follows: 100% ÷ 10 years = 10%. Next, this answer is multiplied by two, since the federal law allows doubling in this case (10% × 2 = 20%).

Next, the original cost ($51,000) is multiplied by the 20% to derive the first year's depreciation: $51,000 × 20% = $10,200.

The next step is to subtract the first year's depreciation ($10,200) from the original cost of the machine ($51,000) to get the Declining Balance at the end of the first year of the machine's use, as follows: ($51,000 cost – $10,200 first year's depreciation = $40,800, the Declining Balance at the end of the first year.

In order to compute the second year's depreciation, we multiply the $40,800 Declining Balance at the end of the first year by the 20% originally computed to get $8,160, the second year's depreciation.

The next step is to subtract the second year's depreciation ($8,160) from the $40,800 Declining Balance at the end of the first year to get $32,640, the Declining Balance at the end of the second year ($40,800 − $8,160 = $32,640).

In order to compute the third year's depreciation, we multiply the $32,640 Declining Balance at the end of the second year by the 20% originally computed to get $6,528, the third year's depreciation ($32,640 × 20% = $6,528).

The next step is to subtract the third year's depreciation ($6,528) from the $32,640 Declining Balance at the end of the second year to get $26,112, the Declining Balance at the end of the third year ($32,640 − $6,528 = $26,112).

In order to compute the fourth year's depreciation, we multiply the $26,112 Declining Balance at the end of the third year by the 20% originally computed to get $5,222.40, the fourth year's depreciation ($26,112 × 20% = $5,222.40).

The next step is to subtract the fourth year's depreciation ($5,222.40) from the $26,112 Declining Balance at the end of the third year to get $20,889.60, the Declining Balance at the end of the fourth year ($26,112 − $5,222.40 = $20,889.60).

These computations can be shown in tabular form as follows:

Broom-making Machine
First Four Years' Depreciation by Double-Declining Balance Method

Year	Declining Balance at Beginning of Year		Percent		Depreciation	Declining Balance at End of Year
2000	$51,000	×	20%	=	$10,200.00	$40,800.00
2001	$40,800	×	20%	=	$ 8,160.00	$32,640.00
2002	$32,640	×	20%	=	$ 6,528.00	$26,112.00
2003	$26,112	×	20%	=	$ 5,222.40	$20,889.60

At the end of the first four years of the machine's life, the machine is worth $20,889.60 (see lower right figure in the chart above), according to the Double-Declining-Balance Method of depreciation. The federal government's MACRS (Modified Accelerated Cost Recovery System) allows the use of the Straight-Line Method during the last half of the Asset's life, and this is more favorable to the taxpayers; most corporations using accelerated methods of depreciation do switch to the Straight-Line Method at this time.

The Double-Declining-Balance Method of depreciation did not deduct the $1,000 Scrap Value in its original computation, so the next step is to do this ($20,889.60 – $1,000 = $19,889.60). Thus, the $19,889.60 is the amount to be depreciated over the remaining life of the machine. Since it is now (as of December 31, 2003) assumed that the machine will only last four more years, we divide the $19,889.60 by 4 to derive $4,972.40, the amount to be depreciated at the ends of the years 2004, 2005, 2006, and 2007, to bring the Declining Balance down to the scrap value of $1,000.

This can be shown in chart form as follows:

Broom-making Machine
Depreciation Schedule
First Four Years' Depreciation by Double-Declining Balance Method
Second Four Years' Depreciation by Straight-Line Method

Year	Declining Balance at Beginning of Year	Percent			Depreciation	Declining Balance at End of Year
2000	$51,000	×	20%	=	$10,200.00	$40,800.00
2001	$40,800	×	20%	=	$ 8,160.00	$32,640.00
2002	$32,640	×	20%	=	$ 6,528.00	$26,112.00
2003	$26,112	×	20%	=	$ 5,222.40	$20,889.60
2004	$20,889.60				$ 4,972.40	$15,917.20
2005	$15,917.20				$ 4,972.40	$10,944.80
2006	$10,944.80				$ 4,972.40	$ 5,972.40
2007	$ 5,972.40				$ 4,972.40	$ 1,000.00

Note in the chart above that the 20% Double Declining Balance figure is used only for the first four years. For the last four years, the Straight-Line depreciation figure of $4,972.40 is used in each of the final four years. Note also that the lower right-hand figure in the table is $1,000, which is the Estimated Scrap or Residual Value.

• PROBLEM 20–9

The Hammond Broom Company purchased a broom-making machine for $51,000 on January 2, 2000. At the time of purchase, from past experience, the management of the corporation estimated that the machine would last 10 years, after which time it would have a Scrap Value of $1,000. The managers of the corporation decided that the machine should be depreciated by the Straight-Line Method, and the annual depreciation was computed to be $5,000 as follows:

Purchase Price of Machine	$51,000
Less Scrap (Residual) Value estimated	– 1,000
Amount to be depreciated	$50,000

The next step was to divide the amount to be depreciated ($50,000) by the estimated number of years of useful life for the machine (10 years) to get $5,000 annual depreciation ($50,000 ÷ 10 years = $5,000 yearly depreciation).

The broom-making machine was purchased on January 2, 2000, and depreciated $5,000 per year for each of five years. At the end of this time, on December 31, 2004, the material in the machine had greatly increased in value, and the managers of the Hammond Broom Company determined that at the end of five more years the machine's Residual Value would probably be $5,000 instead of $1,000.

What entries should be made to depreciate the machine during the first five years of its life, and what entries should be made to depreciate the machine during the last five years of its life?

SOLUTION:

During each of the first five years of the machine's life, it would be depreciated $5,000.

During each of the last five years of the machine's life, it would be depreciated $4,200.

The $5,000 yearly depreciation for the first five years of the machine's life is computed as follows:

Cost of Machine	$51,000
Less estimated Scrap Value	
(first estimation)	− 1,000
Amount to be depreciated	$50, 000
Divided by estimated number	
of years of the Asset's life	10
Yearly depreciation	$ 5, 000

$50,000 to be depreciated ÷ 10 years of life = $5,000 yearly depreciation.

At the end of 5 years, the Accumulated Depreciation—Machinery account would appear as follows:

Accumulated Depreciation—Machinery

12/31/2000	5,000
12/31/2001	5,000
12/31/2002	5,000
12/31/2003	5,000
12/31/2004	5,000
	25,000

Thus, a total of $25, 000 has been depreciated on the machine during the first five years of its life.

At the end of the fifth year of the machine's life, the managers of the company decide that the Residual Value of the machine should be $5,000 instead of $1,000. They revise their depreciation computations as follows:

Cost of Machine	$51,000
Less estimated Scrap Value	
(second estimation)	− 5,000
Amount to be depreciated	$46,000
Less amount already depreciated	
during the first 5 years of Asset's life	− 25,000
Amount still to be depreciated over	
the remainder of the Asset's life	$ 21,000
Divided by the estimated remaining	
years of the Asset's life	5
Yearly amount to be depreciated	
after December 31, 2004	$ 4,200

($21,000 ÷ by 5 = $4,200.)

At the end of 10 years, the Accumulated Depreciation—Machinery account would appear as follows:

Accumulated Depreciation—Machinery		
	12/31/2000	5,000
	12/31/2001	5,000
	12/31/2002	5,000
	12/31/2003	5,000
	12/31/2004	5,000
	12/31/2005	4,200
	12/31/2006	4,200
	12/31/2007	4,200
	12/31/2008	4,200
	12/31/2009	4,200
		46,000

Note that at the end of 10 years the Accumulated Depreciation—Machinery account has a credit balance of $46,000, meaning that is the amount depreciated over the 10-year life of the machine. Since this machine originally was purchased for $51,000, it now has a book value of $5,000. ($51,000 original cost – $46,000 total accumulated depreciation = $5,000 book value. This $5,000 book value is the same as the Estimated Residual Value, which was also determined to be $5,000 from the second estimation.)

• PROBLEM 20–10

The Hammond Broom Company purchased a broom-making machine for $51,000 on January 2, 2000. At the time of purchase, from past experience, the management of the corporation estimated that the machine would last 10 years, after which time it would have a Scrap Value of $1,000. The managers of the corporation decided that the machine should be depreciated by the Sum-of-Years-Digits Method, and the annual depreciation was computed as follows:

Purchase Price of Machine	$51,000
Less estimated Residual Value	– 1,000
Amount to be depreciated	$50,000

The Sum-of-Years-Digits Method for 10 years is computed as follows: 10 + 9 + 8 + 7 + 6 + 5 + 4 + 3 + 2 + 1 = 55. This 55 figure is used as the denominator of the fraction and the 10 is used as the numerator of the first fraction, with 9 used as the numerator of the second fraction, and 8 used as the numerator of the third fraction, and so on, as follows:

Machine Depreciation Schedule
First Five Years of Asset Life Under Sum-of-Years-Digits Method

Calendar Year	Year of Machine Life	Fraction		Amount to be Depreciated		Depreciation that Year
2000	First	10/55	×	$50,000	=	$ 9,090.91
2001	Second	9/55	×	$50,000	=	8,181.82
2002	Third	8/55	×	$50,000	=	7,272.73
2003	Fourth	7/55	×	$50,000	=	6,363.64
2004	Fifth	6/55	×	$50,000	=	5,454.55
						$36,363.65

As the above table shows, under the Sum-of-Years-Digits Method of depreciation in this case, 10/55 of the $50,000, or $9,090.91, is depreciated in the first year of the machine's use. 9/55 of the $50,000, or $8,181.82, is depreciated in the second year of the machine's use. 8/55 of the $50,000 is depreciated in the third year of the machine's use, and this amounts to $7,272.73. 7/55 of the $50,000 is depreciated in the fourth year of the machine's use, and this amounts to $6,363.64. 6/55 of the $50,000 is depreciated in the fifth year of the machine's use, and this amounts to $5,454.55. These total to $36,363.65 on December 31, 2004, the end of the fifth year of the machine's use.

At this time it is discovered that the machine is more valuable than was previously thought, and probably the Scrap Value at the end of the tenth year (Residual Value) will be $5,000 instead of $1,000. What amounts should be depreciated at the ends of each of the next five years?

SOLUTION:

The amount $1,927.27 should be depreciated at the ends of each of the next five years. This is computed as follows:

Cost of Machine	$51,000.00
Less amount depreciated under the Sum-of-Years-Digits Method during the first 5 years of the Asset's life	– 36,363.65
Net Amount	$14,636.35
Less new estimated Residual Value	– 5,000.00
Amount to be depreciated during the last 5 years of the Asset's life	$ 9,636.35
Divided by the estimated number of years of the Asset's life remaining after December 31, 2004	5
Amount to be depreciated for each of the last 5 years of Asset's life	$ 1,927.27

As can be seen above, the $36,363.65 amount already depreciated is deducted from the $51,000.00 cost of the machine to derive a Net amount of $14,636.35. From this is subtracted the $5,000.00 new estimated Residual Value to derive $9,636.35, the amount to be depreciated during the last five years of the life of the machine. This figure is then divided by the 5 years of remaining useful life of the machine to get $1,927.27, the yearly depreciation for each of the last five years of Asset's life.

Note that the last five years of Asset depreciation are kept by the Straight-Line Method because this is allowed and almost always used under MACRS (Modified Accelerated Cost Recovery System). It is also allowed by the Internal Revenue Service in Income Tax computation.

Following is a Machine Depreciation Schedule for the broom-making machine during its entire 10 years of useful life, but using a $5,000 Scrap Value instead of a $1,000 Scrap Value:

Calendar Year	Year of Machine Life	Fraction		Amount to be Depreciated		Depreciation that Year
2000	First	10/55	×	$50,000	=	$ 9,090.91
2001	Second	9/55	×	$50,000	=	8,181.82
2002	Third	8/55	×	$50,000	=	7,272.73
2003	Fourth	7/55	×	$50,000	=	6,363.64
2004	Fifth	6/55	×	$50,000	=	5,454.55
2005	Sixth					1,927.27
2006	Seventh					1,927.27
2007	Eighth					1,927.27
2008	Ninth					1,927.27
2009	Tenth					1,927.27
						$46,000.00

As can be seen from the table above, the total depreciation over the 10-year life of the machine is $46,000. If the $46,000 total depreciation is subtracted from the $51,000 original cost of the machine, the difference is the $5,000 estimated Residual Value. The $5,000 is also the book value of the machine at the end of the tenth year.

• PROBLEM 20-11

The Hammond Broom Company purchased a broom-making machine for $51,000 on January 2, 2000. At the time of purchase, from past experience, the management of the corporation estimated that the machine would last 10 years, after which time it would have an estimated Scrap Value of $1,000. After the machine had been used for five years, management determined that the machine was much more valuable than had been previously anticipated, and that the estimated Scrap Value of the machine at the end of its tenth year of use would probably be $5,000 instead of $1,000.

What depreciation should be recorded for each year of the machine's life under this revision?

SOLUTION:

During the first five years of the machine's life, it was depreciated as follows:

In the Double-Declining Balance Method of depreciation, the Asset's estimated number of years of life is the divisor and 100% is the dividend, as follows: 100% ÷ 10 years = 10%. Next, this answer is multiplied by two, since the federal law allows doubling in this case (10% × 2 = 20%).

Next, the original cost ($51,000) is multiplied by the 20% to derive the first year's depreciation ($51,000 × 20% = $10,200).

The next step is to subtract the first year's depreciation ($10,200) from the original cost of the machine ($51,000) to get the Declining Balance at the end of the first year of the machine's use, as follows: $50,000 cost − $10,200 first year's depreciation = $40,800, the Declining Balance at the end of the first year.

In order to compute the second year's depreciation we multiply the $40,800 Declining Balance at the end of the first year by the 20% originally computed to get $8,160, the second year's depreciation.

The next step is to subtract the second year's depreciation, ($8,160) from the $40,800 Declining Balance at the end of the first year, to get $32,640, the Declining Balance at the end of the second year ($40,800 − $8,160 = $32,640).

In order to compute the third year's depreciation we multiply the $32,640 Declining Balance at the end of the second year by the 20% originally computed to get $6,528, the third year's depreciation ($32,640 × 20% = $6,528).

The next step is to subtract the third year's depreciation, ($6,528) from the $32,640 Declining Balance at the end of the second year, to get $26,112, the Declining Balance at the end of the third year ($32,640 − $6,528 = $26,112).

In order to compute the fourth year's depreciation, we multiply the $26,112 Declining Balance at the end of the third year by the 20% originally computed to get $5,222.40, the fourth year's depreciation ($26,112 × 20% = $5,222.40).

The next step is to subtract the fourth year's depreciation ($5,222.40) from the $26,112 Declining Balance at the end of the third year, to get $20,889.60, the Declining Balance at the end of the fourth year ($26,112 − $5,222.40 = $20,889.60).

In order to compute the fifth year's depreciation, we multiply the $20,889.60 Declining Balance at the end of the fourth year by the 20% originally computed to get $4,177.92, the fifth year's depreciation ($20,889.60 × 20% = $4,177.92).

The next step is to subtract the fifth year's depreciation ($4,177.92) from the $20,889.60 Declining Balance at the end of the fourth year, to get $16,711.68, the Declining Balance at the end of the fifth year ($20,889.60 − $4,177.92 = $16,711.68).

At the end of the fifth year of the machine's life, management has determined that the Residual or Scrap Value of the machine at the end of the tenth year of the machine's life will be $5,000; therefore, $5,000 is subtracted from the $16,711.68 Declining Balance at the end of the fifth year, to get $11,711.68, the amount to be depreciated over the last five years of the machine's life.

The next step is to divide the $11,711.68 amount to be depreciated over the last five years of the machine's life by 5 years to get $2,342.34, the amount of yearly depreciation during these last five years. Note that for the final five years of the machine's life, in this case, we revert to the Straight-Line Method of depreciation because the federal government's Internal Revenue Service allows companies to switch to the Straight-Line Method of depreciation during the final years of an Asset's life under MACRS (Modified Accelerated Cost Recovery System) for Income Tax purposes.

These computations can be shown in tabular form as follows:

Broom-making Machine
Depreciation Schedule
First Five Years' Depreciation by Double-Declining Balance Methold
Second Five Years' Depreciation by Straight-Line Method

Year	Declining Balance at Beginning of Year	Percent	Depreciation	Declining Balance at End of Year
2000	$51,000	× 20% =	$10,200.00	$40,800.00
2001	$40,800	× 20% =	$ 8,160.00	$32,640.00
2002	$32,640	× 20% =	$ 6,528.00	$26,112.00
2003	$26,112	× 20% =	$ 5,222.40	$20,889.60
2004	$20,889.60	× 20% =	$ 4,177.92	$16,711.68
2005	$16,711.68		$ 2,342.34	$14,369.34
2006	$14,369.34		$ 2,342.33	$12,027.01
2007	$12,027.01		$ 2,342.34	$ 9,684.67
2008	$ 9,684.67		$ 2,342.33	$ 7,342.34
2009	$ 7,342.34		$ 2,342.34	$ 5,000.00

As can be seen from the lower right-hand figure in the table above, the Declining Balance at the end of the tenth year reverts to $5,000, the same figure as the Estimated Residual or Scrap Value of the machine.

• PROBLEM 20–12

On December 31, 2000, the Heath Book Company rented out part of its building to the James Hardware Store for $30,000 for the year 2001. On December 31, 2000, Heath received a check from James for $30,000 for next year's rent. The Heath Book Company made the following entry on its books:

2000		($ in dollars)
December 31 Cash	30,000	
Rent Income		30,000

No adjusting entry was made at the end of the year 2000. This was discovered a year later, on December 31, 2001. What mistake was made, and what entry is needed to correct this mistake on December 31, 2001?

SOLUTION:

The Rent Income of $30,000 was credited to the year 2000 instead of the year 2001, when it was actually earned. An adjusting entry on December 31, 2000, should have been made debiting Rent Income for $30,000 and crediting Unearned Rent for $30,000. Since this was not made, the Net Income for the Heath Book Company was $30,000 too high in the year 2000 and $30,000 too low in the year 2001, since the $30,000 Income should have been shown for the year 2001, when it was mistakenly shown for the year 2000.

To correct this mistake on December 31, 2001, the following entry should be made:

2000	($ in dollars)	
December 31 Retained Earnings	30,000	
Rent Income		30,000

The extra $30,000 Income had already been placed in the Retained Earnings account of the Heath Book Company. This correcting entry debiting Retained Earnings for $30,000 cuts down the Retained Earnings account (which usually has a credit balance) by that amount, bringing it back to where it should be. The credit to Rent Income for $30,000 puts the Income back in the year 2001 when it was actually earned.

The above entry would be made if the books for the year 2001 have not been closed. However, if the books have been closed, no entry would need to be made to correct the original error, because the error would be automatically corrected over the two-year period. That is, the Retained Earnings account would have the correct balance, although the Income in the Income Statement for the year 2000 would be $30,000 too high and the Income in the Income Statement for the year 2001 would be $30,000 too low.

• PROBLEM 20-13

On December 31, 2000, the Brown Wholesale Corporation counted inventory and found they had $60,000 in inventory so debited to the Merchandise Inventory account for that figure. Several days later, in January of the year 2001, it was discovered that the persons counting the inventory had neglected to count $20,000 inventory stashed in another warehouse. What correcting entry would need to be made in this instance and why?

SOLUTION:

2001		($ in dollars)	
January 16	Merchandise Inventory	20,000	
	Retained Earnings		20,000

The balance in the Merchandise Inventory account was $60,000 when it should have been $80,000, so the debit to Merchandise Inventory of $20,000 brings the account up to the balance it should be. When Assets increase and there are no changes in Liabilities, the Retained Earnings also increase, meaning that the owners have more investment in the business than was previously realized. Therefore, in the correcting entry, Retained Earnings is also increased by crediting it for $20,000.

• PROBLEM 20-14

On January 1, 2000, the Harrison Construction Company bought a 2-year insurance policy for $300, making the following entry on its books:

2000		($ in dollars)	
January 1	Insurance Expense	300	
	Cash		300

They made no adjusting entry at year's end. How can this mistake be corrected when found on December 31, 2001?

SOLUTION:

2001		($ in dollars)
December 31 Insurance Expense	150	
Retained Earnings		150

On December 31, 2000, the Harrison Construction Company should have made an adjusting entry debiting Prepaid Insurance for $150 and crediting Insurance Expense for $150, since only $150 of the insurance should be deducted as an expense during the year 2000, because it was a two-year policy ($300 payment ÷ 2 years = $150 Insurance Expense each year).

In the correcting entry above, we debit Insurance Expense for $150 to show the Insurance Expense deduction for the year 2001. We credit Retained Earnings for $150, because the Net Income for the year 2000 was understated by $150 (the expense deducted was $150 too high last year). By crediting Retained Earnings for $150, we add back to Retained Earnings the amount mistakenly deducted last year.

However, if the books for the year 2001 have already been closed, no correcting entry would have to be made, because the books would automatically correct themselves over the two-year period as far as the ledger was concerned. (However, the Income Statement would be $150 too low in the year 2000 and $150 too high in the year 2001.)

CHAPTER 21

CASH FLOW

> **Basic Attacks and Strategies for Solving Problems in this Chapter. See page 675 to 680 for step-by-step solutions to problems.**

The **Balance Sheet**, the **Income Statement**, the **Statement of Owner's Equity**, and the **Retained Earnings Statement** have long been the backbones of accounting. Within recent years, however, the **Statement of Cash Flows** has gained not only acceptance, but also great importance.

In the past, the accrual basis of accounting has been all-important, with the Cash Basis of accounting relegated only to small businesses that provided services.

The Cash Basis of accounting has been recently revitalized as an essential accounting method. Modern businesses treasure the Statement of Cash Flows because so many businesses are going bankrupt. The cause of bankruptcy, a business' lack of cash flow. They do not have sufficient cash to pay their immediate bills. In some instances, businesses may report a Net Income on the accrual basis but still go bankrupt. This occurs when their Assets are not immediately convertible into enough cash to pay their immediate bills. As a result their creditors force them into involuntary bankruptcy.

The Statement of Cash Flows is also important for the financial planning of future purchases of such big-ticket items as a new plant or a fleet of trucks. Either money is set aside for several years in order to purchase these high-priced Assets, or loan sources are tapped to finance these items. Companies sometimes tie up too much of their resources in Long-Term Assets such as Buildings, Plants, and Equipment. They also may tie up too much of their Assets in such Current-Asset items as Accounts Receivable and Inventory. None of these Assets can be immediately turned into needed cash.

In constructing the Statement of Cash Flows, the firm starts with the beginning and end of the year cash figures. The firm then must account for the cash activities during the year (i.e. operating activities, investing activities, and financing activities).

Operating activities are those where Cash Flows in or out in the average running of the business. This includes such items as the purchase of merchandise, the paying of Interest, the receiving of Interest Income, and the receipt of Income from sales. Investing activities include the buying and selling of Fixed Asset items in the business such as Land, Building, and Equipment. Financing activities consist of buying or selling the company's own stock or bonds, and paying Interest and Dividends. In this chapter, each item or line in the Statement of Cash Flows is analyzed. To exemplify, the account **Accumulated Depreciation** is presented, showing how **depreciation expense** figures are derived from analyzing this account and why depreciation expense is added back to the Net Income figure in computing the Net Cash provided by operating activities. **Accounts receivable** and **accounts payable** are also analyzed, along with **prepaid rent**, to show their effect on the Statement of Cash Flow.

The next section, the statement of cash flow is the **Cash Flow from Investing Activities**, and the various purchases, such as the purchase of Land, Building, and Equipment, are discussed, as is their effect on the Statement of Cash Flow.

The following section of the Statement of Cash Flow is the **Cash Flow from Financing Activities**, showing the cash inflow from the sale of bonds and the cash outflow from the payment of dividends. The **Retained Earnings** account is analyzed. Start with the Beginning Balance, add the Net Income, and deduct the dividends paid out. Through this process, the Ending Balance of the Retained Earnings account for the year is obtained.

Step-by-Step Solutions to Problems in this Chapter, "Cash Flow"

• PROBLEM 21–1

At the beginning of the year 2000, the Halburton Construction Company had cash on hand of $100,000. At the end of the year their cash on hand was $126,500. The reported Net Income for the year 2000 on the accrual basis was $100,000. The Depreciation Expense amounted to $10,000. Accounts Receivable at the beginning of the year was $26,000, and at the end of the year was $29,000. Accounts Payable at the beginning of the year was $45,000, and at the end of the year was $47,000. Prepaid Rent at the beginning of the year amounted to $500, and at the end of the year was $2,000.

During the year, $30,000 land was purchased. Building purchased was $50,000. Equipment purchased was $10,000.

Bonds sold during the year amounted to $20,000. Cash dividends paid out were $11,000.

Prepare a Statement of Cash Flows including sections for Operating Activities, Investing Activities, and Financing Activities.

SOLUTION:

Accumulated Depreciation

1/1/2000	18,000
12/31/2000	10,000
12/31/2000	28,000

The Accumulated Depreciation account for the Halburton Construction Company at the beginning of the year 2000 amounted to $18,000, and at the end of the year was $28,000. The difference of $10,000 was derived by an adjusting entry at year's end as follows:

2000	($ in dollars)
December 31 Depreciation Expense	10,000
Accumulated Depreciation	10,000

Thus, depreciation for the year was $10,000. This is a business expense that was deducted in the Income Statement from gross income to derive net income. Since depreciation expense takes no cash outflow, it must be added back in the Statement of Cash Flows to determine Cash Provided by Operating Activities.

Accounts Receivable

1/1/2000	26,000	
12/31/2000	3,000	
	29,000	

As of January 1, 2000, customers owed the Halburton Construction Company $26,000. As of year's end the customers owed Halburton $29,000. This means that Accounts Receivable increased $3,000 during the year. When Accounts Receivable increase during the year, this means that the Sales on Account were (in this case) $3,000 higher than the collections. This makes an outflow of cash of $3,000 for the year because of the increase in Accounts Receivable.

Accounts Payable

	1/1/2000	45,000
	12/31/2000	2,000
		47,000

As of January 1, 2000, the Halburton Construction Company owed creditors a total of $45,000. As of year's end Halburton owed creditors $47,000. This means that the Halburton Construction Company owed $2,000 more at year's end than it did at the beginning of the year. By not paying this $2,000, Halburton conserved cash that it should have paid out in bills. This makes an inflow of cash of $2,000 for Halburton.

Prepaid Rent

1/1/2000	500	12/31/2000	500
12/31/2000	2000		
	2500		
	2000		

At January 1, 2000, the Halburton Construction Company had Prepaid Rent to the landlord of $500. During the year 2000, the Rent Expense of $500 was deducted from Prepaid Rent and Halburton prepaid another amount of $2,000, leaving a balance in the Prepaid Rent account at year's end of $2,000. Subtracting the $500 balance of Prepaid Rent at the beginning of the year from the $2,000 balance in the account at year's end, we get an increase in Prepaid Rent during the year of $1,500. Of course, this increase in Prepaid Rent was paid with cash so it is an outflow of cash of $1,500.

In order to derive Cash Provided by Operating Activities we add the Net Income (accrual basis) of $100,000, add back the Depreciation Expense of $10,000, deduct the increase in Accounts Receivable of $3,000, add the increase in Accounts Payable of $2,000, and deduct the increase in Prepaid Rent of $1,500, giving Cash Provided by Operating Activities of $107,500. ($100,000 + $10,000 − $3,000 + $2,000 − $1,500 = $107,500 Cash Provided by Operating Activities.) We have thus turned the accrual basis figure, $100,000 Net Income, into the cash basis figure $107,500 Cash Provided by Operating Activities.

The next section of the Cash Flow Statement is entitled Cash Flows from Investing Activities, and this involves mainly the purchase and sale of such Long-Term Assets as Land, Building, and Equipment. During the year a piece of Land was purchased for $30,000 cash. This totaled a cash outflow of $30,000. Also during the year a Building was purchased for $50,000. This totaled a cash outflow of $50,000. Also during the year Manufacturing Equipment of $10,000 was purchased for cash. This totaled a cash outflow of $10,000. No Long-Term Assets were sold during the year 2000. Thus, Net Cash used (expended) through investing activities during the year totaled $90,000 ($30,000 + $50,000 + $10,000 = $90,000).

The final section of the Cash Flow Statement is entitled Cash Flows from Financing Activities.

During the year 2000, the Halburton Construction Company sold at par $20,000 worth of its own bonds to help purchase some Long-Term Assets. This sale of bonds resulted in a cash inflow of $20,000.

During the year 2000, the Halburton Construction Company declared and paid its stockholders dividends of $11,000. This dividend resulted in a cash outflow of $11,000.

The Net Cash provided by Financing Activities was $9,000. ($20,000 cash received from selling bonds − $11,000 cash paid out in dividends = $9,000 increase in cash) (or cash provided) by financing activities.

Let us now take a look at the Retained Earnings Statement for Halburton Construction Company for the year 2000.

Retained Earnings			
		Beginning Balance	
		1/1/2000	500,000
		Net Income	
12/31/2000		12/31/2000	100,000
Dividend	11,000		600,000
			589,000

At the beginning of the year 2000, the Retained Earnings account of the Halburton Construction Company was $500,000. The Net Income of $100,000 for the year was added to this figure, giving a total of $600,000 on the credit side of the account. On the debit side of the Retained Earnings account is the $11000 dividends declared during the year. Subtracting the $11,000 dividends from the $600,000 credit total, we get an Ending Balance of $589,000 in the Retained Earnings account.

Halburton Construction Company
Statement of Cash Flows
For Year Ended December 31, 2000

Cash Flows from Operating Activities:

Net Income		$100,000
Adjustment to reconcile Net Income to		
Net Cash provided by operating activities:		
Depreciation Expense	10,000	
Increase in Accounts Receivable	(3,000)	
Increase in Accounts Payable	2,000	
Increase in Prepaid Rent	(1,500)	7,500
Net Cash Provided by Operating Activities		$107,500

Cash Flows from Investing Activities:

Purchase of Land	(30,000)	
Purchase of Building	(50,000)	
Purchase of Equipment	(10,000)	
Net Cash Used by Investing Activities		(90,000)

Cash Flows from Financing Activities:

Issuance of Bonds	20,000	
Payment of Cash Dividends	(11,000)	
Net Cash Provided by Financing Activities		9,000
Net Increase in Cash		26,500
Cash on Hand Balance, January 1, 2000		100,000
Cash on Hand Balance, December 31, 2000		126,500

The Statement of Cash Flows moves the reader from the accrual basis (Net Income) to the Cash Basis. This statement has become extremely important in recent years, because firms go bankrupt from the lack of immediate cash to pay immediate debts.

The Statement of Cash Flows for the Halburton Construction Company for the year 2000 begins with the Net Income (figured on the accrual basis) of $100,000. To this is added back Depreciation Expense of $10,000, because Depreciation Expense had been subtracted in the Income Statement as an expense, when actually this expense takes no cash outflow. Accounts Receivable has increased $3,000 during the year, so the $3,000 is deducted because it takes $3,000 extra cash. Accounts Payable has increased $2,000 during the year, and this has saved the firm that much cash which should have been paid to creditors, so this results in a cash inflow of $2,000. Prepaid Rent of $1,500 more was paid out during the year than was used up, so this results in a $1,500 decrease in cash. All these added algebraically result in Net Cash Provided by Operating Activities of $107,500 ($100,000 + $10,000 − $3,000 + $2,000 − $1,500 = $107,500).

Regarding the Cash Flows from Investing Activities, during the year the firm purchased Land for Cash amounting to $30,000. This resulted in a cash outflow of $30,000. During the year the firm purchased Building for Cash amounting to $50,000. This resulted in a cash outflow of $50,000. During the year the firm purchased Equipment for Cash amounting to $10,000. This resulted in a cash outflow of $10,000. The total cash outflow from investing activities therefore was $90,000 ($30,000 + $50,000 + $10,000 = $90,000).

Regarding the Cash Flows from Financing Activities, during the year the Halburton Construction Company sold its own bonds at Par, resulting in Cash Income of $20,000. Also during the year, Halburton paid out $11,000 dividends to its stockholders. This resulted in a cash outflow of

$11,000. The Net Cash Provided (incoming cash) by Financing Activities therefore amounted to $9,000 ($20,000 – $11,000 = $9,000).

In recapitulation, Net Cash Provided by Operating Activities amounted to $107,500. Net Cash Used (spent) by Investing Activities amounted to $90,000. Net Cash Provided (incoming) by Financing Activities amounted to $9,000. Adding algebraically, the Net Increase in cash was therefore $26,500 ($107,500 – $90,000 + $9,000 = $26,500).

The Cash on Hand at the beginning of the year 2000 was reported as $100,000. This is added to the Net Increase in cash of $26,500, to get Cash on Hand at year's end of $126,500 ($100,000 + $26,500 = $126,500).

On the cash basis, the actual cash on hand at year's end was $126,500, and the actual cash on hand at the beginning of the year was $100,000. This Statement of Cash Flows informs the reader how the cash was handled during the year.

CHAPTER 22

ANALYSIS OF FINANCIAL STATEMENTS

> **Basic Attacks and Strategies for Solving Problems in this Chapter. See pages 682 to 698 for step-by-step solutions to problems.**

Financial statements are placed in the quarterly and annual reports of corporations and mailed to the stockholders. These statements should be analyzed, just as a medical doctor analyzes x-rays, to determine the financial health of the corporation.

The Balance Sheet, Income Statement, and the Cash Flow Statement for the present year should be compared with similar statements from the past year to show whether the firm is doing better or worse. These ratios and percentages should then be compared to those ratios and percents of competitors to determine what can be done to compete, to find what things are going well, and where things could use improvement. This must be done promptly to avoid any problems or complications.

The first type of comparisons is known as **Liquidity Ratios**, which determines whether a company can gather together enough money to pay off current debts and avoid bankruptcy. Two liquidity ratios are the **Current Ratio** and the **Acid Test Ratio**.

Activity ratios allow compatable computation. These include **Accounts Receivable Turnover**, **Inventory Turnover**, and **Asset Turnover**.

Profitability Ratios compare Net Income from this year with past years. Types of profitability ratios include **Profit Margin on Sales**, **Rate of Return on Assets**, **Rate of Return on Stockholders' Equity**, **Earnings Per Share**, **Price-Earnings Ratio**, and **Payout Ratio**.

Computations used to determine the Long-Term health of the business include **Debt to Total Assets**, **Times Interest Earned**, and **Book Value Per Share**.

There are limits to the use of these ratios and percents. It is true they are easy to compute and seem definitive. However, they are not all as accurate as they seem. Businesses carry Assets at their Historical Cost, not at Present Value. Also, various competing businesses purchased their Assets at different times when the dollar was worth a different value in terms of purchasing power. No figures are definite—especially not depreciation which is, at best, an estimate.

It is difficult to compare one firm with its competitors because of the varying bookkeeping techniques. For instance, when paying cash, some firms debit Asset accounts whereas other firms debit expense accounts. Some firms expense post-retirement benefits as they accrue whereas other firms wait until employees have retired to expense these benefits.

Step-by-Step Solutions to Problems in this Chapter, "Analysis of Financial Statements"

• PROBLEM 22-1

The comparative Income Statements and Balance Sheets for the Bonner Wholesale Hardware Company for the years 2000 and 2001 are shown on the following pages.

Give examples of ratios, tell how they are computed, and explain how these computations help in analyzing the financial statements.

SOLUTION:

LIQUIDITY RATIOS

The Liquidity Ratios are computed to show the ability of a firm to meet its current obligations as they come due. Here, we look mainly at current Liabilities. Does the firm have enough cash on hand, or can it

Bonner Wholesale Hardware Corporation
Comparative Income Statements
For Years Ending December 31, 2000 and 2001

	2000	2001
Revenues:		
Net Sales	$800,000	$750,000
Interest Income	3,000	2,000
Other Revenue	1,000	1,000
Total Revenue	804,000	753,000
Costs & Expenses:		
Cost of Goods Sold	600,000	500,000
Depreciation	25,000	20,000
Selling & Administrative Expenses	100,000	90,000
Interest Expense	5,000	3,000
Total Costs & Expenses	730,000	613,000
Income before Taxes	74,000	140,000
Less Income Taxes (30%)	– 22,200	42,000
Net Income after Taxes	$ 51,800	$ 98,000
Number of Shares outstanding	10,000	10,000
Earnings Per Share	$5.18	$9.80

procure enough cash on hand to pay the current Liabilities as they come due? If it can, the firm can stay solvent. If it cannot, bankruptcy may ensue. Banks and other Short-Term creditors are especially interested in these ratios.

Current Ratio

The current ratio for the Bonner Wholesale Hardware Corporation is computed as follows:

$$\frac{\text{Current Assets}}{\text{Current Liabilities}}$$

The current Assets (see Balance Sheet) for the year 2000 are $515,000, and the current Liabilities for the year 2000 are $237,000. So, we divide $515,000 by $237,000 to get 2.17299578 times.

The current Assets (see Balance Sheet) for the year 2001 are $482,000, and the current Liabilities for the year 2001 are $180,000. So, we divide $482,000 by $180,000 to get 2.677777 times.

Bonner Wholesale Hardware Corporation
Comparative Balance Sheets
December 31, 2000 and December 31, 2001

	2000	2001
Assets		
Current Assets:		
Cash	$20,000	$22,000
Marketable Securities (at Cost)	70,000	70,000
Accounts Receivable	225,000	200,000
Inventories (at lower of Cost or Market)	200,000	190,000
Total Current Assets	515,000	482,000
Investments (at Cost)	150,000	150,000
Fixed Assets:		
Property, Plant, & Equipment (at Cost)	900,000	850,000
Less Accumulated Depreciation	(100,000)	(90,000)
	800,000	760,000
Goodwill	25,000	12,500
Total Assets	1,490,000	1,404,500
Liabilities & Stockholders' Equity		
Current Liabilities:		
Accounts Payable	75,000	70,000
Notes Payable	150,000	100,000
Accrued Liabilities	12,000	10,000
Total Current Liabilities	237,000	180,000
Long-Term Debt		
Bonds Payable	600,000	700,000
Long-Term Notes Payable	200,000	150,000
Total Long-Term Debt	800,000	850,000
Total Liabilities	1,037,000	1,030,000
Stockholders' Equity:		
Common Stock, $10 Par	100,000	100,000
Additional Paid-In Capital	300,000	300,000
Retained Earnings	53,000	(25,500)
Total Stockholders' Equity	453,000	374,500
Total Liabilities & Stockholders' Equity	1,490,000	1,404,500

Another way to express this ratio is as follows:

Current Ratios:

Year 2000: $\dfrac{\$515,000}{\$237,000}$ = 2.17299578 times

Year 2001: $\dfrac{\$482,000}{\$180,000}$ = 2.677777 times

Many analysts believe that a current ratio of at least 2 to 1 is adequate for the average business. This means that current Assets are twice as high as the current Liabilities, because usually in an emergency the current Assets can be turned into cash to pay the current Liabilities as they come due. It is also helpful to see whether or not the current ratio is improving from year to year. Looking at the current ratios for the Bonner Wholesale Hardware Corporation above, one sees that in both years 2000 and 2001 the ratios are higher than 2 to 1, which means that in this respect the corporation is in good shape. Also, the ratio of current Assets to current Liabilities has gone up from 2.17 to 1 in the year 2000, to 2.677 to 1 in the year 2001, which is excellent.

Acid-Test Ratio (Quick Ratio)

Sometimes a business with a satisfactory current ratio can still go bankrupt because so much of the current Assets are tied up in inventory that perhaps cannot be turned into cash rapidly enough to pay off the current creditors. In order to take this possibility into consideration, the so-called Acid-Test Ratio has been developed. Another name for this is the Quick Ratio. It is computed by dividing the Quick Assets by the Current Liabilities. Quick Assets are those current Assets that can easily be turned into cash if necessary to pay off current creditors. Quick Assets are determined by subtracting Merchandise Inventory and prepaid items from total current Assets. Since this current problem involving the Bonner Wholesale Hardware Corporation has no prepaid items (such as Prepaid Rent or Prepaid Insurance), it is only necessary here to deduct the Merchandise Inventory from the current Assets in order to get the Quick Assets. Then, the Quick Assets are divided by the current Liabilities to get the Acid-Test Ratio (Quick Ratio).

For the year 2000, the inventory is $200,000. This is subtracted from the total current Assets of $515,000 to get Quick Assets of $315,000. Next, the Quick Assets of $315,000 are divided by the current Liabilities of $237,000 to get the Acid-Test Ratio for the year 2000 of 1.329113924 to 1.

For the year 2001, the inventory is $190,000. This is subtracted from the total current Assets of $482,000 to get Quick Assets of $292,000. Next, the Quick Assets of $292,000 are divided by the current Liabilities of $180,000 to get the Acid-Test Ratio for the year 2001 of 1.6222 to 1.

Another way of expressing these acid-test ratios follows:

$$\text{Year 2000: } \frac{(\$515,000 - \$200,000)}{\$237,000} = \frac{\$315,000}{\$237,000} = 1.329113924 \text{ to } 1$$

$$\text{Year 2001: } \frac{(\$482,000 - \$190,000)}{\$180,000} = \frac{\$292,000}{\$180,000} = 1.6222 \text{ to } 1$$

Most analysts believe that an Acid-Test Ratio of 1 to 1 or higher is good, because this means that in an emergency the Quick Assets could be turned into cash to pay off current Liabilities, and thus, stave off bankruptcy. It will be noted in the computations above that in both the years 2000 and 2001 the Acid-Test Ratios have been higher than 1 to 1.

Now we should compare the Acid Test Ratios for the two years. It will be noted that in the year 2000 the ratio was 1.329 to 1 and in the year 2001 the ratio rose to 1.622 to 1. So, not only are the ratios for the two years higher than 1 to 1, but also, the ratio has improved with the ratio in the year 2001 being better than the year 2000, showing that the Bonner Wholesale Hardware Corporation is in a better financial position and better able to pay off its immediate debts in the year 2001 than it was in the year 2000.

Accounts Receivable Turnover

Accounts Receivable Turnover is computed by dividing the Net Sales by the average receivables. This shows how many times the Net Sales are greater than the average receivables, or, in other words, how many times the receivables have turned over in the form of sales during the year. In the year 2000 the Net Sales were $800,000. It is not possible to exactly determine the average receivables because we do not know the receivables at the end of the year 1999. So, we divide the Net Sales by the receivables at the end of the year 2000, which are $225,000, to get 3.56 times. This means that the net sales are 3.56 times as high as the receivables in the year 2000.

For the year 2001 the Net Sales are $750,000. The receivables at the end of the year 2000 are $225,000 and the receivables at the end of the year 2001 are $200,000, giving average receivables as $212,500

($225,000 + $200,000 = $425,000; $425,000 divided by 2 = $212,500). We then divide the Net Sales of $750,000 by the average receivable of $212,500 to get 3.53 times for the Accounts Receivable turnover for the year 2001.

Another way to show this is as follows:

Year 2000: $\dfrac{\$800,000}{\$225,000}$ = 3.56 times (Accounts Receivable turnover)

Year 2001: $\dfrac{\$750,000}{\$212,500}$ = 3.53 times (Accounts Receivable turnover)

As seen from the computations above, the Accounts Receivable turnover has dropped from 3.56 times in the year 2000 to 3.53 times in the year 2001. This does not seem to be a significant decrease in the turnover and is probably due to the drop in sales between the two years. Whether 3.56 times or 3.53 times is a good enough ratio is not discernable here and should be compared to the Turnover Ratio for the entire wholesale hardware industry.

Inventory Turnover

The Inventory Turnover is computed by dividing the Cost of Goods Sold by the Average Inventory. In the year 2000, the Cost of Goods Sold is $600,000. The Average Inventory cannot be determined because we do not have the figures for the year 1999, so we will use the inventory at the end of the year 2000 which is $200,000. $600,000 divided by $200,000 means that during the year 2000 the inventory turned over 3 times.

In the year 2001, the Cost of Goods Sold is $500,000. The Average Inventory is computed by adding the inventory at the end of the year 2000 ($200,000) to the inventory at the end of the year 2001 ($190,000) and dividing by 2 ($200,000 + $190,000 = $390,000; $390,000 divided by 2 = $195,000). We then divide the $500,000 Cost of Goods Sold for the year 2001 by the $195,000 Average Inventory to get 2.564 times.

This can be stated another way as follows:

Year 2000: $\dfrac{\$600,000}{\$200,000}$ = 3 times

Year 2001: $\dfrac{\$500,000}{\$195,000}$ = 2.564 times

It will be noted that the Inventory Turnover dropped from 3 times in the year 2000 to only 2.564 times in the year 2001. This is a dangerous red flag and should be more closely examined. Why is the inventory moving more slowly? It will be noted that the Cost of Goods Sold dropped greatly, from $600,000 in the year 2000 to only $500,000 in the year 2001. And the reason that the Cost of Goods Sold dropped was because the sales dropped. Of course, the inventory dropped too (from $200,000 in the year 2000 to only $190,000 in the year 2001), but this was only a $10,000 difference ($200,000 – $190,000 = $10,000). The difference in the Cost of Goods Sold between the two years was $100,000 ($600,000 – $500,000 = $100,000). Proportionately, the Cost of Goods Sold dropped a much greater extent than the inventory. This is a danger signal in that the inventory that the firm is carrying is probably too high in proportion to the sales that are being made. How should this be corrected? Perhaps the firm should do more advertising in order to increase the sales next year. Or the firm should not buy as much new merchandise until some of the merchandise sitting in the warehouse is sold.

Is a turnover of 2.5 to 3 times satisfactory for the Bonner Wholesale Hardware Corporation? This can only be answered by comparing Bonner's inventory turnover with that of competing firms, probably through national statistics provided by the trade association.

Asset Turnover

Another method of financial analysis of the business is the Computation of Asset turnover. This is found by dividing the Net Sales by the average total Assets, not including investments, to determine how well the Assets are being used to bring in sales. The investment figures are not used in this computation because investments are extra money invested in businesses other than this business.

For the year 2000 we take total Assets of $1,490,000 and subtract investments of $150,000 to get Assets used in the business of $1,340,000. We cannot get average Assets as such, since we do not have the figures for the year 1999. We divide the Net Sales for the year 2000 ($800,000) by the Assets used in the business during the year 2000 ($1,340,000) to get .59. This means that the Net Sales during the year are only 59% of the value of the assets used in the business to make those sales.

For the year 2001 we take the total Assets of $1,404,500 and subtract investments of $150,000 to get $1,254,500 Assets used in the business at the end of the year 2001. The Assets used in the business at the end of the year 2000 have previously been computed to be $1,340,000. The average of these two figures is $1,297,250, which is found by adding these two figures together and dividing by 2 ($1,254,500 + $1,340,000 = $2,594,500; $2,594,500 divided by 2 = $1,297,250). Now we divide the Net Sales for the year 2001 of $750,000 by the average total Assets used in the business of $1,297,250 to get .57. This means that the Net Sales during the year are only 57% of the value of the average Assets used in the business to make those sales.

This can be stated in another way as follows:

Year 2000: $\dfrac{\$800,000}{\$1,340,000} = .59$

Year 2001: $\dfrac{\$750,000}{\$1,297,250} = .57$

How should these figures be interpreted? In the year 2000, the sales were only 59% of the Assets used to make the sales. In the year 2001, the sales were only 57% of the average Assets used to make the sales. This is a slight drop, and what caused it? In the first place, there was a significant drop in sales between the years 2000 and 2001. The Assets used to make the sales also dropped but not as greatly percentage-wise. The slight drop in Asset turnover is probably not too significant, but the drop in Net Sales is certainly a red flag.

Is the 59% or 57% Asset turnover proper? This can only be determined by comparing these figures with the Asset Turnover Rate of competitors.

Profit Margin on Sales

Further analysis into the financial health of the Bonner Wholesale Hardware Corporation can be determined by computing the Profit Margin on Sales. This can be done by dividing the Net Income for the year by the Net Sales for the year.

In the year 2000, the Net Income was $51,800 and the Net Sales were $800,000. Dividing the Net Income of $51,800 by net sales of $800,000, we get a Profit Margin of .06475 or 6.475%. This means that for each dollar of sales we earn a profit of $.06475.

In the year 2001, the Net Income was $98,000 and the Net Sales were $750,000. Dividing the Net Income of $98,000 by net sales of $750,000, we get a Profit Margin of .1306666 or 13.0666%. This means that for each dollar of sales we earn a profit of $.1306666.

Another way to express these computations is as follows:

Year 2000: $\dfrac{\$51,800 \text{ Net Income}}{\$800,000 \text{ Net Sales}}$ = 6.475%

Year 2001: $\dfrac{\$98,000 \text{ Net Income}}{\$750,000 \text{ Net Sales}}$ = 13.0666%

This margin on Net Sales shows an excellent increase for the company. In the year 2000, the firm earned only a little over 6¢ on each dollar of sales, and in the year 2001 the firm earned a little over 13¢ on each dollar of sales. Why the bountiful increase? The important reason is that Net Income almost doubled. It increased from $51,800 in the year 2000 to $98,000 in the year 2001, and also, Net Sales decreased from $800,000 in the year 2000 to $750,000 in the year 2001. Of course, it is not good to have sales decrease, but in the time of a decrease in sales the Net Profit almost doubled. How could this be? It was because cost and expenses dropped so radically, especially Cost of Goods Sold.

Rate of Return on Assets

Another analysis computation is Rate of Return on Assets. This is found by dividing Net Income by average total Assets used in the business.

For the year 2000, the total Assets were $1,490,000, and from this figure we deduct $150,000 investments which are Assets not used in the business to get $1,340,000 Assets used in the business. We then divide the Net Income of $51,800 by $1,340,000 Assets used in the business to get .038656716 or 3.8656716%.

For the year 2000, the total Assets were $1,404,500, and from this figure we deduct $150,000 investments which are Assets not used in the business to get $1,254,500 Assets used in the business. We then divide the Net Income of $98,000 by the 1,254,500 Assets used in the business to get .07811877 or 7.811877%.

Another way to express these computations follows:

Year 2000: $\dfrac{\$51,800 \text{ Net Income}}{\$1,340,000 \text{ Assets used in business}}$ = 3.8656716%

$$\text{Year 2001:} \quad \frac{\$98,000 \text{ net income}}{\$1,254,500 \text{ assets used in business}} = 7.811877\%$$

This means that in the year 2000, the Assets used in the business were bringing in a Net Income of 3.866% of the value of these Assets. It also means that in the year 2001, the Assets used in the business were bringing in a Net Income of 7.812% of the value of these Assets.

The percent increased from 3.866% of the Assets in the year 2000 to 7.812% of the Assets in the year 2001, and this is good. But the percentages themselves seem somewhat too low for a good business investment. However, to be sure, these figures would have to be compared to the Rate of Return on Assets of competitors in the industry.

Rate of Return on Common Stockholders' Equity

Another important analysis computation is the Rate of Return on Common Stockholders' Equity. Stockholders, especially, are interested in the percentage of return that their investment in the company is making. This computation is determined by dividing the Net Income minus the Preferred Stock Dividends by the average Common Stockholders' Equity.

For the year 2000, the Net Income was $51,800. Since the Bonner Wholesale Hardware Corporation has no Preferred Stock outstanding, the computation is easier, and we merely divide the $51,800 Net Income by the total equity for the year 2000 of $453,000. The total equity figure for the year 1999 is not available so we use the total equity figure for the year 2000 and cannot get average equity $51,800 Net Income divided by $453,000 is 11.4348785%.

For the year 2001, the Net Income was $98,000. Since the Bonner Wholesale Hardware Corporation has no Preferred Stock outstanding, the computation is easier, and we divide the $98,000 Net Income by the average Common Stockholders' Equity. To determine the average Common Stockholder Equity, it is necessary to add the Stockholders' Equity at the end of the year 2000 ($453,000) to the total Stockholders' Equity at the end of the year 2001 ($374,500) and divide by 2 ($453,000 + $374,500 = $827,500; $827,500 divided by 2 = $413,750n which is the average Common Stockholders' Equity). We now divide the Net Income of $98,000 by the average Common Stockholders' Equity of $413,750 to get 23.6858%.

Another way of expressing this follows:

Year 2000: $\dfrac{\$51,800 \text{ Net Income}}{\$453,000 \text{ Stockholders' Equity}} = 11.43\%$

Year 2001: $\dfrac{\$98,000 \text{ Net Income}}{\$1,254,500 \text{ average Stockholders' Equity}} = 23.6858\%$

During the year 2000, the Common Stockholders earned 11.43% on their investment, and in the year 2001, the Common Stockholders earned 23.6858% on their investment. This is an excellent increase in return which should greatly please the stockholders. These Rates of Return also seem extremely high but must be compared with those returns of competitors also. Why did the Rate of Return on Common Stock Equity jump so greatly between the two years? It was mainly due to the increase in Net Income, which is good, but it is also due to the decrease in Stockholders' Equity, which is bad, and which needs more looking into.

Earnings Per Share

Stockholders and potential stockholders are interested in a corporation's Earnings Per Share—that is, the amount that a person would earn who holds only one share of the corporation's stock. This is determined by dividing the Net Income for the year by the Weighted Average of shares outstanding.

For the year 2000, the Net Income is $51,800. The Weighted Average of shares outstanding is computed for firms buying or selling their own stock during the year. However, the Bonner Wholesale Hardware Corporation had the same number of shares outstanding at the beginning of the year as they did at the end of the year (in this case 10,000 shares), so no Weighted Average needs to be computed in this case. We divide the $51,800 Net Income by the 10,000 shares outstanding to get $5.18 Earnings Per Share for the year 2000.

For the year 2001, the Net Income is $98,000. We divide this by the 10,000 shares outstanding to get $9.80 Earnings Per Share for the year 2001.

In comparing the $5.18 Earnings Per Share for the year 2000 with the $9.80 Earnings Per Share for the year 2001, we notice a large increase. Since the number of shares outstanding did not increase, this increase in Earnings Per Share is completely due to the increase in Net Income.

Price-Earnings Ratio

Investors and potential investors are interested in the Price-Earnings Ratio. This is the number of times that the Market Price of the stock is higher than the Earnings Per Share for the year. It gives investors and potential investors a benchmark whereby they can compare this stock with other stocks to determine which stocks are the best buy at the time. The ratio is determined by dividing the Market Price by the Earnings Per Share.

Let us say that as of December 31, 2000, the Market Price of Bonner Wholesale Hardware Corporation stock is $50 per share. The Earnings Per Share for the year 2000 have been determined to be $5.18. We then divide the $50 by the $5.18 to get 9.6525. This means that the Market Price is over nine times as much as the Earnings Per Share. Let us say that as of December 31, 2001, the Market Price of Bonner Wholesale Hardware Corporation stock has increased to $52 per share. The Earnings Per Share for the year 2001 have been determined to be $9.80. We then divide the $52 by the $9.80 to get 5.3. This means that the Market Price is over 5 times as much as the Earnings Per Share.

In comparing the Price-Earnings Ratio between the two years, we note that the ratio was 9.6 times in the year 2000 and that it had dropped to only 5.3 times in the year 2001. Is this drop good or bad? Many times investors noting lower Price-Earnings Ratios will believe that this denotes a good time for them to be buying the stock; so, in this respect, it is good. But why did the ratio drop? There are two reasons. In the first place, the price of the stock only increased $2 per share ($52 − $50 = $2). This is a very small increase. Between these two years the Earnings Per Share increased by $4.62 ($9.80 − $5.18 = $4.62). This is a great increase.

Another way to express this Price-Earnings Ratio is as follows:

$$\text{Year 2000:} \quad \frac{\$50 \text{ per share price}}{\$5.18 \text{ Earnings Per Share}} = 9.6525 \text{ times}$$

$$\text{Year 2001:} \quad \frac{\$52 \text{ per share price}}{\$9.80 \text{ Earnings Per Share}} = 5.3 \text{ times}$$

The main reason for the drop in the Price-Earnings Ratio in this case is the great increase in the Earnings Per Share between the two years.

Payout Ratio

Some investors are interested in buying growth stocks that perhaps pay little or no dividends. Other investors are more interested in "milk cow" types of stocks that pay higher dividends but that may not increase so much in Market Value. This second type of investor who wants high dividends is especially interested in stocks that have a High Payout Ratio.

The Payout Ratio is determined by dividing the Cash Dividends by the Net Income less Preferred Dividends. Since the Bonner Wholesale Hardware Corporation has no Preferred Stock, the Payout Eatio is computed by dividing the Cash Dividends by the Net Income.

Let us assume that Bonner Wholesale Hardware Corporation paid out $25,000 in dividends in the year 2000 and paid out $30,000 in dividends in the year 2001.

For the year 2000, we divide the Cash Dividends paid out that year ($25,000) by the Net Income for that year ($51,800), to get a 48.2625% Payout Ratio. This means that during the year 2000, over 48% of the earnings were paid out to the stockholders in dividends.

For the year 2001, we divide the Cash Dividends paid out that year ($30,000) by the Net Income for that year ($98,000), to get a 30.6122% Payout Ratio. This means that during the year 2001, over 30% of the earnings were paid out to the stockholders in dividends.

Another way of expressing this ratio follows:

$$\text{Year 2000:} \quad \frac{\$25,000 \text{ dividends paid out}}{\$51,800 \text{ Net Income}} = 48.2625\% \text{ payout ratio}$$

$$\text{Year 2001:} \quad \frac{\$30,000 \text{ dividends paid out}}{\$98,000 \text{ Net Income}} = 30.6122\% \text{ payout ratio}$$

As seen from the figure above, the Dividend Payout Ratio has greatly decreased, from over 48% in the year 2000, to over 30% in the year 2001. This might not be good news to investors wanting higher Dividend Payout Ratios, but let us examine this further and see why the Payout Ratio has decreased.

Actually, the dividends themselves have increased from $25,000 in the year 2000, to $30,000 in the year 2001. This means that the corporation has been more generous with its stockholders. The real answer is that the Net Income has increased so greatly—from only $51,800 in the year 2000 to $98,000 in the year 2001. Both the dividends and the Net Income have increased; but the Net Income has increased at a much faster clip than the dividends, and this accounts for the decrease in the Payout Ratio.

Debt to Total Assets

A Long-Term solvency computation of importance to creditors is the Debt to Total Assets computation. The creditors feel safer if the ratio of debt to total Assets is decreasing or is already low. This computation is found by dividing debt (total Liabilities) by total Assets.

In the year 2000, the total Liabilities of the Bonner Wholesale Hardware Corporation were $1,037,000 and the total Assets were $1,490,000. If we divide $1,037,000 by $1,490,000, we get 69.597%. This means that at the end of the year 2000, the Liabilities were over 69% of the Assets.

In the year 2001, the total Liabilities of the Bonner Wholesale Hardware Corporation were $1,030,000 and the total Assets were $1,404,500. If we divide $1,030,000 by $1,404,500, we get 73.3357%. This means that at the end of the year 2001, the Liabilities were over 73% of the Assets. Another way of showing these computations follows:

$$\text{Year 2000: } \frac{\$1,037,000 \text{ total Liabilities}}{\$1,490,000 \text{ total Assets}} = 69.597\% \text{ Debt to Asset Ratio}$$

$$\text{Year 2001: } \frac{\$1,030,000 \text{ total Liabilities}}{\$1,404,500 \text{ total Assets}} = 73.3357 \text{ Debt to Asset Ratio}$$

As can be seen from the above figures, the Debt to Asset Ratio has increased from over 69% in the year 2000 to over 73% in the year 2001. This is scary to creditors, because creditors want to see this ratio decrease. Why is this ratio going the wrong way? Liabilities of the corporation have actually decreased from $1,037,000 in the year 2000 to $1,030,000 in the year 2001 so the Liabilities are not the culprit. Let's look at total Assets. They have decreased even more than Liabilities, with the total Assets going down from $1,490,000 in the year 2000 to $1,404,500 in the year 2001. Thus, the Assets are decreasing much faster than the Liabilities. But why is this? Which Assets are decreasing? Looking at the Comparative Balance Sheets for the Bonner Wholesale Hardware Corporation near the first of this chapter, we see that Cash is increasing, and Marketable Securities are increasing, so they are not the culprits.

Accounts Receivable has decreased by $25,000 (from $225,000 in the year 2000 to only $200,000 in the year 2001). Also, Inventories have decreased $10,000 (from $200,000 in the year 2000 to only $190,000 in the year 2001). The Assets have decreased at a much greater clip than the Liabilities, and this accounts for the increase in the Debt to Asset Ratio.

Times Interest Earned

The Times Interest Earned computation is of great Interest to bondholders who want to make sure that the corporation has enough money to pay the Interest on each Interest Payment date. It is computed by taking the Income before taxes and Interest charges, and dividing this by the Interest charges. To do this, the easiest way is to work backwards up the Income Statement. Looking at the Comparative Income Statement for the Bonner Wholesale Hardware Corporation for the year 2000, we see that the Net Income after Taxes is $51,800. To this, add back the Income Taxes of $22,200 to get Income before Taxes of $74,000. To this, add back Interest Expense of $5,000 to derive $79,000, which can be called Income before Taxes, and Interest Charges. This figure of $79,000 is then divided by the $5,000 Interest charges to get 15.8 times. This means that the Bonner Wholesale Hardware Corporation has enough money to pay Interest on the bonds 15.8 times over.

Looking at the Comparative Income Statement for the Bonner Wholesale Hardware Corporation for the year 2001, we see that the Net Income after Taxes is $98,000. To this, add back Income Taxes of $42,000 to get Income before Taxes of $140,000. To this, add back Interest expense of $3,000 to get $143,000, which can be called Income before Taxes, and Interest Charges. This figure of $143,000 is then divided by the $3,000 Interest charges to get 47.667 times. This means that the Bonner Wholesale Hardware Corporation has enough money to pay Interest on the bonds 47.667 times over.

Another way of expressing this is as follows:

Year 2000:	$51,800	Net Income after Income Taxes
	+ 22,200	Income Taxes
	74,000	Net Income before Income Taxes
	+ 5,000	Interest Expense
	$79,000	Income before Taxes and Interest Charges

$79,000 divided by $5,000 Interest charges = 15.8 times

Year 2001: $ 98,000   Net Income after Income Taxes
            + 42,000   Income Taxes
             140,000   Net Income before Income Taxes
            + 3,000   Interest Expense
            $143,000   Income before Taxes and Interest Charges

$143,000 divided by $3,000 Interest charges = 47.667 times

As can be seen from the above computations, the protection for the bondholders has increased from 15.8 times to 47.667 times. Usually, in the computation of Times Interest Earned, 10 times protection would be good, but these figures are higher than that and seem to be increasing by leaps and bounds. Why is this?

There are two reasons. In the first place, the Income before Taxes and Interest Charges has increased greatly (from only $79,000 in the year 2000 to $143,000 in the year 2001). Also, the Interest Expense has decreased from $5,000 in the year 2000 to only $3,000 in the year 2001. Both these changes are good for the company and make the company stronger financially, therefore, they are also good for the company's bondholders.

Book Value Per Share

Investors and potential investors are interested in computing book value per share. This is the amount that an owner of one share of stock would get if the corporation broke up and liquidated immediately, sold all Assets, paid off all Liabilities, then paid the stockholders. Investors like to compare this book value per share to Market Value per share to see whether it is a good time to buy, or perhaps, to sell the stock. Book value per share is computed by dividing the Common Stockholders' Equity by the Number of Shares Outstanding.

In the year 2000, the Total Stockholders' Equity at year's end is $453,000. Since there are no Preferred Stockholders to pay off, the Common Stockholders' Equity is the same as the Total Stockholders' Equity. The number of outstanding shares at year's end is 10,000. We divide $453,000 by 10,000 shares to derive $45.30 book value per share. The Market Price of the stock as of December 31, 2000 is $50 per share. This means the underlying book value of $45.30 is not quite so high, and perhaps the stock is overpriced on the market.

In the year 2001, the Total Stockholders' Equity at year's end is

$374,500. Since there are no Preferred Stockholders to pay off, the Common Stockholders' Equity is the same as the Total Stockholders' Equity. The number of outstanding shares at year's end is 10,000. We divide $374,500 by 10,000 shares to get a book value per share of $37.45. As of December 31, 2001, the Market Price of the stock is $52 per share, whereas the underlying book value is only $37.45, so perhaps the stock is overpriced on the market.

Another "red flag" revealed by the Comparative Balance Sheets of the Bonner Wholesale Hardware Corporation is the Retained Earnings account. At the end of the year 2000, the Retained Earnings account had a credit balance of $53,000, and at the end of the year 2001 this had dropped to a deficit (debit balance) of $25,500. A closer look at the Retained Earnings account is in order. Also, reasons should be found for the decrease in Accounts Receivable and Inventories and in Property, Plant, and Equipment.

Numbers on this page refer to <u>PROBLEM NUMBERS</u>, not page numbers.

Index

Numbers on this page refer to <u>PROBLEM NUMBERS</u>, not page numbers.

Numbers on this page refer to <u>PROBLEM NUMBERS</u>, not page numbers.

Numbers on this page refer to <u>PROBLEM NUMBERS</u>, not page numbers.

Numbers on this page refer to <u>PROBLEM NUMBERS</u>, not page numbers.

Numbers on this page refer to <u>PROBLEM NUMBERS</u>, not page numbers.

Numbers on this page refer to <u>PROBLEM NUMBERS</u>, not page numbers.

Numbers on this page refer to <u>PROBLEM NUMBERS</u>, not page numbers.

Available at your local bookstore or order directly from us by sending in coupon below.

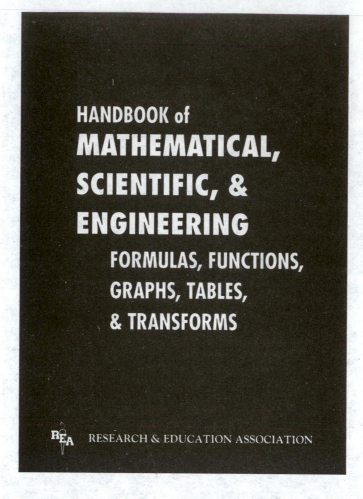

HANDBOOK of
**MATHEMATICAL,
SCIENTIFIC, &
ENGINEERING**
FORMULAS, FUNCTIONS,
GRAPHS, TABLES,
& TRANSFORMS

RESEARCH & EDUCATION ASSOCIATION

A particularly useful reference for those in math, science, engineering and other technical fields. Includes the most-often used formulas, tables, transforms, functions, and graphs which are needed as tools in solving problems. The entire field of special functions is also covered. A large amount of scientific data which is often of interest to scientists and engineers has been included.

Available at your local bookstore or order directly from us by sending in coupon below.